EDWARD KING

In thanksgiving for the life and ministry of
Canon Gilbert Houlden
*Vicar of St Peter-at-Gowts, Lincoln,
the church which had occasioned
Bishop King's trial;
and who, as the immediate successor to Canon Townroe,
one of King's biographers, 'introduced' me
to the spirit of the saintly bishop,
thereby nurturing my own faith
and vocation as a priest and pastor.*

EDWARD KING

TEACHER, PASTOR, BISHOP, SAINT

'Nothing less than a form of genius'

Michael Marshall

GRACEWING

First published in England in 2021
by
Gracewing
2 Southern Avenue
Leominster
Herefordshire HR6 0QF
United Kingdom
www.gracewing.co.uk

All rights reserved

No part of this publication may be reproduced,
stored in a retrieval system, or transmitted in any
form or by any means, electronic, mechanical,
photocopying, recording or otherwise,
without the written permission of the publisher.

© 2021, Michael Marshall

The rights of Michael Marshall
to be identified as the author of this work
have been asserted in accordance with
the Copyright, Designs and Patents Act 1988.

The publishers have no responsibility
for the persistence or accuracy of URLs for websites
referred to in this publication, and do not guarantee
that any content on such websites is, or will remain,
accurate or appropriate.

ISBN 978 085244 975 2

Typeset by Word and Page, Chester, UK

Cover design by Bernardita Peña Hurtado

Contents

List of Illustrations	vii
Acknowledgements	ix
Prologue: Bishop Hobart and the English Church	xi
Foreword	xix

Part One: The Formative Years

1. The King Family	3
2. Oxford Mentors	37
3. Ordination and the Pastoral Novice	81
4. Cuddesdon: A New Generation of Clergy	99

Part Two: Priest, Principal, Professor

5. King and Cuddesdon	129
6. The Pastoral Professor	161
7. King the European	207
8. Professor, Pastor and Preacher	233
9. The Secret of King's Influence	261

Part Three: The Lincoln Years

10. The Choice of a Bishop for Lincoln	299
11. Lincoln: The Early Years	325
12. The Bishop on Trial: The Lincoln Judgment	375
13. Calm after the Storm	417
14. King's Personal Testimony to the Lambeth Conference	451
15. The Golden Years	477
16. Epilogue	531
Select Bibliography	541
Index	547

Illustrations

Front cover. Statue of Edward King in Lincoln Cathedral
Photograph courtesy of the Revd Soon Han Choi.

Illustrations following p. 374:

1. King, with John Peake and John Day
   Photograph courtesy of Christopher Jobson.

2. King at his first ordination, May 1885
   Photograph © National Portrait Gallery (NPG x19142).

3. King in 1889
   Photograph by S. A. Walker, © National Portrait Gallery (NPG Ax38337).

4. King in old age
   Photograph by A. M. Emary, © National Portrait Gallery (NPG P1700(95)).

5. Chancel of Stone Church, Kent
   Engraving from Edward Cresy, 'Illustrations of Stone Church, Kent,' London: The Topographical Society, 1840.

6. Oriel College, Oxford, First Quadrangle
   Engraving by J. Le Kreux, after F. Mackenzie, published February 1834, for James Ingram, 'Memorials of Oxford,' vol. I, 1837.

7. Opening of Cuddesdon College
   Engraving from 'The Illustrated London News,' 24 June 1854.

8. Christ Church, Oxford, Tom Quad in the 1870s
   By kind permission of the Governing Body of Christ Church, Oxford.

9. Christ Church, Oxford, Tom Quad
   Watercolour by F. P. Barraud. By kind permission of the Governing Body of Christ Church, Oxford.

10. Christ Church, Cathedral, Oxford, *c.* 1890
    Etching by E. W. Evans, after F. P. Barraud.

11. St Mary's University Church, Oxford, interior
    Engraving by J. Le Kreux, after F. Mackenzie, published June 1833, for James Ingram, 'Memorials of Oxford,' vol. III, 1837.

12. Lincoln, Exchequer Gate *c.* 1900
    Postcard view.

13. Lincoln Cathedral, Chapter House
    Engraving by J. Tingle, after T. Allom, 1836.

14. Lincoln, The Old Palace. From the south, *c.* 1895, and from the Cathedral, 1951
    Photographs © The Francis Frith Collection (refs. 35548 and L49514).

15. St Hugh's Chapel at the Old Palace, *c.* 1890
    Photograph © The Francis Frith Collection (ref. 25652).

16. Lincoln, aerial view of the Cathedral and Minster Yard in 1933
    Photograph © Historic England (ref. EPW041645).

Acknowledgements

Any author of a book—not least a book of such ambitious proportions—is acutely aware that the finished product is nothing less than a team effort, to whom acknowledgement needs to be given.

Top of the list of that team for the purposes of these few words of acknowledgement, must rightly go to John Newton. Before John's death in 2017, he had begun to work on a large biography of King, and fragments of his extensive research were entrusted to me by John's wife Rachel, in particular, some valuable material on Bishop Sailer of Regensburg. John was a considerable scholar with a knowledge of German that enabled him to study first-hand Sailer's voluminous works, which had an enormous impact on King, who drew on them for his lectures as Professor of Pastoral Theology. Much of John's thoroughly researched material appears in Chapter 7, 'King the European.'

I am also grateful to Christopher Jobson, himself a considerable scholar of church history, for sharing with me some material from his own research, with particular reference to John Day, who was such a formative mentor and teacher for King during his time with Day at Ellesmere, before going up to Oxford.

A further debt of gratitude is owed to the Revd Dr Barry Orford, formerly priest Librarian and Archivist at Pusey House, Oxford. With his vast knowledge of the period, he undertook the tedious work of scrutinizing the manuscript in readiness for the publishers. I am especially grateful to Rowan Williams for readily agreeing to write the Foreword.

Barbara Young, widow of the Revd David Young, who was a student at Ely Theological College where I lectured on Church history in the sixties, gave me a copy of the thesis

David had produced on King's trial, and other books and writings, from which I have drawn helpful details for Chapter 12, 'The Lincoln Judgment.'

Roy Hyslop has given me invaluable practical support with his considerable computer skills, patiently and frequently rescuing me from many potential disasters.

I also want to take this opportunity to acknowledge help from the Revd Kenneth Clark, Rector of St Mary's, Stone, in Kent, the parish of King's father, who gave me ready access to the Archdeacon's personal journal—the 'Green Ledger' as it is termed. Further gratitude to the Revd Canon Dr Peter Groves; Anna Thomas; the Revd Dr Hannah Cleugh and the Bishop of Ely for access to the Minute Book of the annual meetings of the East Anglia bishops during King's episcopate; and Brian King, great grandson of King's older brother, Walker King, for his keen interest in the whole project from the outset. To all alike—and to the many others not named here, who with their various skills, connections and personal interest in King and his lasting impact in the church, have contributed to the final production of the book—my heartfelt gratitude.

Yet, none of what is in these pages would ever have seen the light of day in print, had it not been for the gracious and exceedingly generous sponsorship of the Rector, Vestry and people of the Church of the Redeemer, Sarasota, USA. It is their generosity which has enabled the book to be published in both the UK and America, where the witness and spirit of the nineteenth-century Catholic revival in the Church of England and the contemporary Catholic revival in the Episcopal Church, notably with Bishop Hobart and others, still attracts interest and a readership, as I discovered during the years I worked in the United States.

A final word of thanks to Tom Longford of Gracewing.

Prologue

Bishop Hobart and the English Church

The creative forces for change throughout history—and not least in the history of the Christian church—frequently originate and flourish from within a network of friendships and kindred spirits. In the course of time, the ideals and principles embodied and exemplified in each of the participants are forged into a single dynamic and expanding mission which ultimately extends far beyond the boundaries of the original group. It is the contention throughout this biography that such was the case with the unfolding narrative of the Oxford Movement, supremely exemplified in the hugely influential life, ministry, teaching and friendships of Bishop Edward King of Lincoln, now commemorated as a saint in the Church of England.

To no less a degree, however, we can trace a similar and lasting influence exercised by John Henry Hobart, the third Bishop of New York, who is likewise commemorated as a saint in the calendar of the Protestant Episcopal Church of America.[1] Bishop Hobart (1775–1830), through his transatlantic network of friendships and influence, not only unleased the winds of change and reform in the Episcopal Church of America, but also, through his extensive writings and correspondence—and most notably during an extended visit to Britain and Europe in 1823–5—challenged and encouraged the early fathers of the Oxford Movement several years before Keble's Assize sermon of 1833 kick-

---

[1] The author is indebted to an article by Esther de Waal, 'John Henry Hobart and the Early Oxford Movement,' *Anglican Theological Review*, LXV:3 (July 1983), p. 323.

started that movement into life. Hobart has been regarded as 'the precursor and possibly the inspirer of the Oxford Movement.'² Indeed, it has been said that under his Rectorship, the Parish of Trinity Church in New York, should be regarded as nothing less than 'the cradle of the Tractarians.'³

Although they never met or corresponded, Bishop Samuel Wilberforce of Oxford, a pivotal figure in both the Oxford Movement and the life of Edward King, paid a resounding tribute to Hobart in his monumental history of the Protestant Episcopal Church (1844). Wilberforce claimed that Hobart's appointment as Bishop of New York in 1816 constituted nothing less than 'a turning point,' and not just in the history of the Episcopal Church of America, but 'in the history of the Western Church.' Hobart was, in Wilberforce's words, 'a man who at any time would have left [on the church] an impress of his own character.'⁴

Just as the leaders of the Oxford Movement, some years later, were to oppose the encroaching secularism and liberalism in the Church of England, so Hobart, for similar reasons confessed that he 'trembled for the ark of God' in America. He saw that many of the leaders of the church were 'moralists for the most part, rather than believers.'⁵ In both England and America, deism had characterised much of the eighteenth-century church, but the 'old generation was passing away. The deists who, with Thomas Jefferson to head them, had long held undisputed sway, no longer carried every thing before them. There had been a secret upgrowth of a better race, and in the Church, as well as elsewhere, men of another temper took their places on the stage.'⁶

---

2   C. P. S. Clarke, *Bishop Hobart and the Oxford Movement*. American Congress Booklet. Milwaukee: Morehouse Pub. Co., 1933.

3   Morgan Dix (ed.), *A History of the Parish of Trinity Church in the City of New York*. New York: G. P. Putnam's Sons, 1905 (9th ed.), vol. III, p. 85.

4   Samuel Wilberforce, *A History of the Protestant Episcopal Church in America*. London: James Burns, 1844, p. 295.

5   Ibid., p. 301.

6   Ibid., p. 278.

Prologue

In his Charge to the Clergy of the Protestant Episcopalian Church in New York State, delivered at Trinity Church in 1815, Assistant Bishop Hobart (as he was then) boldly claimed, 'it is the characteristic of the Christian Church that it is not an human institution. It is a society constituted by that divine personage who purchased it by his own blood, and who still presides over and governs it as its Almighty Head.'[7]

In his own spirituality, Hobart, like Edward King, was able to hold together, in Wilberforce's words, 'evangelical truth and apostolical order: these he pressed on all the subjects closest to his own heart ... The awakening sleepers of his own communion could not understand him; and feeling only his warmth reprove their coldness, they knew not whether to reproach him as a High Churchman, or Methodist.'[8] He consistently maintained, in the teeth of much opposition, especially in his early days as bishop, that the Church's 'banner must indeed be, "Evangelical truth with apostolic order—the gospel of the Church,"'[9] in precisely the same way that King was able to hold together evangelical fervour and piety with catholic doctrine and church order.

'On laity and clergy he pressed by precept and example the supreme importance of a truly spiritual religion.' Something of a workaholic, like Wilberforce himself, Hobart 'revealed the spring of all his conduct', when, 'in answering the solicitations of affection which would have persuaded him to lessen his own labours,' he said, 'How can I do too much for that compassionate Saviour who has done so much for me?'[10]

As early as 1810, decades before the first of the *Tracts for the Times* initiated by Newman in 1833, Hobart had founded and launched the Tract Society. He realised 'the importance

---

[7] John Henry Hobart, *A Charge to the Clergy of the Protestant Episcopal Church in the State of New-York*. New York: Printed by T. & J. Swords, 1815, pp. 6–7.
[8] Wilberforce, *op. cit.*, p. 303.
[9] *Ibid.*, p. 448.
[10] *Ibid.*, p. 313.

of religious tracts for diffusing knowledge of religious truth and explaining the institutions of the church.'[11]

And yet, he observed, 'without a ministry the church cannot exist; and destitute of a learned, as well as a pious ministry, she cannot flourish.' While in England in the 1820s, Hobart 'complained that the best educated among the English clergy were well versed in other branches of learning and conscience, but ignorant of theology.'[12] In 1822, before his trip to Europe, he had presided, as one of its founders, over the opening of General Theological Seminary in New York—this was several decades before Wilberforce founded his own theological college at Cuddesdon in Oxfordshire, opened in 1854. Like Wilberforce, Hobart was a man of outstanding energies and served initially as Pastoral Professor and Dean at the Seminary, while as bishop also keeping a close eye on the fledgling foundation. Bishop Wilberforce would strive to do the same at Cuddesdon during its early years.

In the sermon he delivered at the opening of the Seminary, Hobart laid out its objectives and the principles on which it was founded. Its prime objectives were 'a learned ministry, an orthodox ministry, a pious ministry and a practical ministry, with holiness as its keynote.'[13] Above all,

> it must be a pious ministry, or all its learning, and all its orthodoxy, will be but 'as a sounding brass or a tinkling cymbal.' We may display, brethren of the clergy, the learning of Gamaliel and the eloquence of Paul; and we may even preach with the fervour and the force of the seraph; but if our tempers and our lives prove that the truths and duties which we inculcate have no efficacy on our characters and conduct, is it in nature to regard our instructions, or to profit by our exhortation?[14]

[11] Clarke, *op. cit.*, p. 3.
[12] S. C. Carpenter, *Church and People 1789–1889*. London: SPCK, 1959, vol. I, p. 69.
[13] de Waal, *op. cit.*, p. 325.
[14] John Henry Hobart, *An Introductory Address on the Occasion of the Opening*

Prologue

Both as Bishop of New York and as Dean of the Seminary, Hobart was able to gather round him, a 'band of younger men, laity as well as clergy, of a new temper—men who believed that Christ had indeed founded a spiritual kingdom, and that they had functions in it to discharge, and powers with which to fulfil them.'[15] Like King, Hobart exuded an almost magnetic and transforming influence on all with whom he met: 'Few came thus into his company without receiving some impression: all felt his influence.'[16]

By the time Hobart landed in Liverpool on 30 October 1823, he had made his diocese a living model of High Church ideals which undoubtedly influenced Wilberforce who, much later, was to change the face of the English episcopate along strikingly similar lines. He had also, through extensive correspondence and exchange of publications, built up a considerable network of friendships on this side of the Atlantic. Notable among that network were the members of the Hackney Phalanx—a fellowship of friends, lay and clerical, who shared a common commitment to High Church ideals and their application to the political and social concerns of the day.

During his stay in Britain, and in spite of ill-health, he undertook a far-reaching tour. He visited Wordsworth—King's favourite English poet—and Robert Southey in the Lakes. In Aberdeen, he met with Scottish bishops. He was entertained by Lord Shaftesbury in Westminster, and at Lambeth Palace he dined with the Archbishop of Canterbury, Charles Manners Sutton, and attended the consecration of two bishops for the Caribbean in the Palace Chapel. Archbishop Sutton not only encouraged members of the Hackney Phalanx in their work, but was also a friend of one of its leading lights, Joshua Watson, to whom Hobart

---

of the General Theological Seminary of the Protestant Episcopalian Church in the United States of America. New York: Printed by T. & J. Swords, 1822.
[15] Wilberforce, *op. cit.*, p. 303.
[16] *Ibid.*, p. 315.

would dedicate the sermon he delivered on his return to New York in October 1825.[17]

A highlight of Hobart's English tour was his visit to Oxford in March 1824, where his knowledge, his pleasing manners and his gentlemanly deportment made a lasting impression. At Oriel College, where he had been invited to dinner by the Provost, he met Newman, who wrote to his sister: 'Bishop Hobart of New York is in Oxford—I dined with him at the Provost's yesterday—he is an intelligent man and gave us a good deal of information on the affairs of the American Episcopal Church.'[18] It is inconceivable, surely, that at some point during their encounter, the importance of Tracts would not have been discussed, albeit this was some ten years before Newman and his associates employed the same strategy for disseminating the core teaching of their great 'Enterprise' in their *Tracts for the Times*.

During his sojourn In Europe, Hobart paid two trips to Continent, the first in the spring and early summer of 1824, and a second in 1824–5 which lasted for almost a year. It was during this second visit, while wintering in Rome, that he met the English High Churchman, Hugh James Rose, with whom he developed a lasting and significant friendship.[19]

> What grew from the sharing of a common enthusiasm by two men flung into each other's company over a length of time in places calculated to stimulate and challenge? It is impossible to discern the lines of influence and interaction, but it is a reminder of an area whose significance is only becoming gradually recognized as one of the great creative forces, and certainly one which no historian of these years in particular should neglect, namely the role of friendship and of the 'intimacy of

---

[17] Carpenter, Edward, *Cantuar: The Archbishops in their Office*. London: A. R. Mowbray & Co. Ltd, 1988, p. 283.
[18] *The Letters and Diaries of John Henry Newman*, ed. Ian Ker and Thomas Gornall. Oxford: Clarendon Press, 1978, vol. I, p. 173.
[19] Dix, *op. cit.*, p. 379.

Prologue

the intellect' as a creative force in the shaping of ideas and the sustaining of enthusiasm.[20]

Add to this that Newman thought highly of Rose as a close friend and we can begin to trace something of the cross-fertilization of formative ideas (as was noted at the start of this Introduction) which ultimately evolve as a powerful movement for change and reform.

On returning to New York in October 1825, Hobart delivered his great sermon or discourse entitled *The United States of America Compared with Some European Countries, Particularly England*, which he published with a dedication to Joshua Watson.[21]

Hobart was highly critical of what he had found in the Church of England. So much of what he had discerned was subsequently to form the agenda not only for Wilberforce in the reform of his diocese and the founding of Cuddesdon, but also for the whole manifesto of the emerging Oxford Movement throughout the rest of the century.

He concluded his address with an impassioned plea for the freedom of the Church of England to become the divine institution intended by its Founder:

> the establishment, the honours, and the wealth of the Church of England … weigh down her Apostolic principles; they obstruct the exercise of her legitimate powers; they subject her to worldly policy; they infect her with worldly views. Still in her doctrines, in her ministry, in her worship, 'she is all glorious within'… if the Church of England were displayed in her evangelical and apostolic character, purified and reformed from many abuses which have gradually but seriously diminished her influence, greater would be the blessings she would diffuse, more limited and less

---

[20] de Waal, *op. cit.*, p. 328.
[21] John Henry Hobart, *The United States of America Compared with Some European Countries, Particularly England: A Discourse. Delivered in Trinity Church, and in St. Paul's and St. John's Chapels in the City of New-York, October, 1825*. New York: Printed by T. & J. Swords, 1825.

inveterate the dissent from her, and more devoted the grateful attachment of her members.²²

All this was something which the Oxford reformers needed to hear, and it is clear from what Wilberforce later wrote of Hobart, that the seeds of his influence had taken root in the writings and, more importantly, in the lives of that whole generation who in turn would change the face of the Church of England, including Wilberforce and, to no lesser degree but in a less pronounced and polemical style, Edward King, Principal of Cuddesdon Theological College (Wilberforce's 'baby'), Professor of Pastoral Theology in Oxford and for twenty-five years the acclaimed and saintly Bishop of Lincoln.

The bold claims that are made for the influence of the saintly King in the pages of this biography clearly and manifestly resonate with a different, although an equally wide ranging and formative influence exercised by Hobart, albeit from a different generation and a vastly different culture. Both King and Hobart recalled the church to its true nature as a living organism rather than a human organisation, so that 'without any new plans or machinery, the Church has in her own institutions the means of meeting the wants of the times.'²³ In itself, the quiet inner confidence of such a message is still relevant in all parts of the Church and in any generation—not least in our own, and in our respective churches. Although Hobart was more of a polemicist than King, they both exercised enormous influence through a network of friendships and through holiness of life, and by their teaching and preaching ministries they changed the face of their respective churches—the underlying theme of this biography.

---

[22] *Ibid.*, pp. 38–40.
[23] *The British Critic*, XXII. London: J. G. & F. Rivington, 1837, pp. 411–12.

Foreword

It is not at first easy—at a distance of well over a century—to see why it was that Edward King made the impression he did on so many in the Church of England during and immediately after his lifetime. But that is partly because Bishop King did so much to create what we take for granted about pastoral ministry in the Church. We don't always see how unusual he was in his day. As a professor in Oxford and as principal of a theological college, he virtually invented pastoral theology as a serious subject. At a time when the average ordained priest in the Church of England was a more or less benign gentleman exercising a vaguely defined spiritual supervision of his parishioners, King was concerned to train a clergy who were pastorally, theologically and humanly competent at a different level of 'professionalism' from what had been so widely taken for granted before. Like many of those marked by the Oxford Movement, including both Newman and Manning, he recognized that the ordained ministry of the Church of England was in danger of settling into no more than a vehicle of class privilege and patriarchal condescension; it needed once again to be discovered as a ministry of Christ's Body, a ministry open to people of all backgrounds and shaped by prayer and discipline.

But King's importance does not stop there. If he invented pastoral theology, he also, by his selfless and untiring work in Lincoln, redefined the pastoral responsibility of the bishop. On his appointment, he wrote to a friend about how glad he was to be the bishop of John Wesley's diocese and about his resolve to be 'a Bishop of His Poor.' He recognized that the Victorian episcopate had still not entirely shed the legacy of the bishops of Wesley's day, and that the tragic separation of the Methodist body from the Church of England had everything to do with the perception that bishops moved in a different and remote world from other clergy, let alone the poorest among the laity. He was determined from the outset of his ministry as a bishop to turn this around. The record speaks for itself, as do the outpourings of deep affection and awed respect from the ordinary laity of the diocese. He won the trust of farm labourers, railway workers and brickmakers; he entered fully into their struggles and was glad to be their friend and advocate. He made it his task to minister personally in prisons—and was remembered for having brought to faith a young fisherman from Grimsby convicted of murder in 1887. He confirmed him, heard his Confession, and appealed in vain for his sentence to be commuted; when the appeal failed, King attended the young man to the scaffold, praying with him to the end. This direct, courageous service, an episcopal ministry without the cushions and barriers that even the best of bishops so often erected in those days, was what made him so significant a figure for so many, including many beyond the established Church. He did not stand on inherited privilege; he showed that even the Victorian Church of England could nurture truly apostolic witness. And it was the unmistakeable authenticity of that apostolic witness that made his trial for irregular ritual behaviour in 1890 so absurd and embarrassing a matter; it is not too much to say that the spectacle of the holiest and most pastorally engaged bishop in the realm being tried for making minor adjustments to the Church's liturgy made the regulation of public worship by parliament seem increasingly indefensible, and galvanized the process of rethinking and reimagining the liturgy for new generations.

It is odd that King has not had the comprehensive modern biographical study he so merits, and the present book is a wonderful rectification of that lack. It should act as a reminder to the Church in our day of the abiding need for true spiritual accountability in ministry; for bishops to model that accountability in their prayerful willingness to be tangibly alongside their people, above all those who

Foreword

believe themselves forgotten and friendless; for the Church to be a clear advocate for the vulnerable, for the humanity and dignity of workers, children, prisoners and all others at risk of different sorts of abuse or degradation. Edward King matters because he helped to restore its soul to the nineteenth-century Church of England, as did so many who were inspired or trained by him for a new kind of ministry among the needy and marginal. The centrality of that vision to any Church worth the name remains the same; we can hope that this fine study will inspire a deeper passion to see it realized for today and tomorrow.

Rowan Williams
Cardiff, November 2020

PART ONE

The Formative Years

✢ 1 ✢

The King Family

REVOLUTION, REACTION AND REFORM

The fascination of biography is to be found in tracing the many and varying factors which, in part, determine the formation of character and human personality. Unquestionably, both nature and nurture have their place, and yet so do many other factors, some more immediately obvious than others, and many of which it will be the concern of this biography to explore. In the course of a long life, such as that of Edward King (1829–1910), beginning as it does in the aftermath and with the after-shocks of the French Revolution at the beginning of the nineteenth century, spanning the lengthy reign of Queen Victoria and finally spilling over into the first decade of the twentieth century, the narrative is necessarily interwoven inextricably with the prevailing culture and the turmoil of the age as well as with the influential personalities of the time.

Change, reform, and reaction were the dominating and formative factors throughout the life of Bishop Edward King, culminating in his twenty-five years as bishop of the large and predominately rural Diocese of Lincoln. Similar factors were also reflected in the theological and ecclesiastical turmoil and upheavals which characterize the Victorian Church—that Church in which Edward King, bishop and acclaimed saint, played an elusive, largely hidden and yet highly significant and influential role.

The world into which King was born and raised was, for the majority of his fellow-countrymen, cold, hard and bitter, scarred and torn by poverty—the world of Dickens and other literary social critics like George Eliot, whose novel *Middlemarch* gives a vivid snapshot of the brutish world between 1829 and the Reform Bill of 1832. In his novel, *Sybil* (1845), Disraeli, the strong advocate of so-called 'One Nation Toryism,' wrote of 'two nations between whom there is no intercourse and no sympathy, who are ignorant of each other's habits, thoughts and feelings as if they were dwellers in different zones or inhabitants of different planets,' with a huge gap between the 'haves' and the 'have-nots,' between the privileged and the powerless.

When Queen Victoria ascended the throne on 20 June 1837, Britain was a country with the promise of rising prosperity, with the beginnings of an enlarging empire together with its attendant spoils, and with a middle-class, burgeoning and increasingly affluent from the gains of the emerging industrialism which distinguished but also scarred the Victorian era. When viewed retrospectively, it is the sheer energy at work at every level in society which is so overwhelming, and yet, and at another level, the country was in danger of tearing itself apart through engrained and largely unrelieved poverty for the many, and not least in the farming communities with which King, throughout his entire ministry, was so intimately concerned. The protests and rioting of the Chartists, with their rumoured attempts to assassinate the Queen and her Prime Minister, served only to reinforce in the ruling class, in Church and State alike, fear lest a subversive revolution akin to the anarchy and bloodshed which had characterized the French Revolution might yet be replicated in Britain.

The year of King's birth, 1829 was also the year when Robert Peel voted in favour of the Catholic Emancipation Act, albeit reluctantly, claiming that 'although emancipation was a great danger, civil strife was a greater.'[1] It was a such-like conviction which in that same year drove Peel, as Home Secretary, to found the Metropolitan Police with

The King Family

Scotland Yard as the headquarters for policing a deeply and increasingly troubled society.

Only a couple of months before King's birth, George Stephenson's 'Rocket' had won the Liverpool and Manchester railway competition. Built in Newcastle-upon-Tyne, the Rocket was the template for most steam engines and trains for the next one hundred and fifty years, heralding the age of the railways and a transport revolution. More specifically, the railways superseded the existing network of canals as the principal means for transporting the manufacturing products of the expanding industries of iron and steel, in what came to be so graphically termed 'the black country.'

All this was accompanied by a striking advancement in the various branches of science. It was to be an age of new ideas, new institutions as well as of literary ambitions, promoting and indeed broadcasting revolutionary ideas through rapid advances in printing and publishing. Books and periodicals could be more easily and more cheaply produced and marketed, as well as being available and accessible in the newly established and proliferating public lending libraries. The age of Victoria witnessed the growth of an unprecedented and far-reaching reading public, with the disturbing implication that if knowledge and information constituted power, then who should rightly have that power and how should it be used: for good, in order to encourage and build the skilled workforce required for an emerging, modern industrialized nation, or to threaten, maybe even to overthrow, a social order born of what many perceived as ill-gotten wealth.

On the title page of James Asperne's book *The Real or Constitutional House that Jack Built* (1819) is a wood-cut illustrating a very conservative rejoinder to the radical press of the day. If every picture tells a story, then this one demonstrates in dramatic picture-form the foundations on which the nation's true and lasting stability claimed to rest. Three hefty volumes, surmounted by the Crown of England, are piled on top of each other, the titles on their spines spelling out what was perceived as constituting the necessary building-blocks which make for national stability and security. At the top is 'Constitutional Principles'; this rests on 'The Laws of England,' while at the bottom, highly symbolic and the heftiest of the three, is the Bible, forming a solid foundation on which the top two volumes rest securely. In the distance can be seen, across the Channel, the ruins of the French Nation after the Revolution. At the bottom are the words, 'Order is Heaven's First Law.'[2] It was precisely the issue of law and order which was being challenged, and in turn reasserted, but with renewed strength and determination by the 'Bobbies' or 'Peelers' of Peel's newly introduced police force. More brutally, the rule of law was enforced by the army in what many speak of as the defining moment of the age, the 1819 Peterloo Massacre in Manchester. However, all perceived foundations, whether economic, social, philosophical or religious, together with their cherished unquestioned fundamentalisms were destined to be radically shaken in a seismic shift during the course of the Victorian age and the years of King's life, resulting in what are sometimes referred to as 'the quicksand years.'

All these factors, for good or ill, characterize the Victorian Age and provide the sub-text of any biography of King's life and ministry whether as a priest, professor or bishop. The Victorian label should not typecast him. English men and women of the nineteenth century provide an astonishing range of character and conviction, as richly variegated as William Langland's 'field full of folk.' Though his background was privileged and his upbringing sheltered, King's remarkable intellectual and spiritual sensitivity enabled him to respond creatively rather than react negatively to the challenging issues of the Victorian era. Furthermore, and perhaps more importantly, it was his passion for the poor which exemplifies his whole life and ministry. As the narrative of his life unfolds, during an age when wealth

The King Family

and lineage were almost totally determinative of a person's future, it is King's underlying, genuine and deeply motivated care for the poor, the uneducated and the underprivileged which is the persistent subtext of all that he believed, taught and practised. That is even more striking and worthy of study when the narrative of King's life is seen against his own cultural conditioning as the son of an archdeacon and a wealthy mother from a highly distinguished and eminent family of physicians.

A DISTINGUISHED AND PRIVILEGED ANCESTRY

It is seldom an easy or straightforward matter to locate beginnings, since what are perceived as beginnings have often originated earlier and somewhere else, at other times and in other places. Perhaps something of this explains the perennial interest in family trees, our eager curiosity to track origins in the past, which may account for, at least to some extent, prevailing characteristics in personality, makeup, and behaviour further down the line of lineage.

So, what of Edward King, in this respect? He was born, not in the Kentish countryside where he grew up, but in the heart of London, at No. 8 St James's Place, Piccadilly. It was a fashionable address, close to St James's Palace and the Royal Parks. The house still stands in its quiet enclave off St James's Street, a stone's throw from Green Park.

King's birthplace tells us something of his background. His mother, Anne, had come to London before her confinement in order to be near her father, Sir William Heberden, MD (1767–1845), who lived in a house in Pall Mall formerly belonging to his father. Like his father, Sir William was an eminent and remarkable physician, who would undoubtedly have assured the best possible care for his daughter and her new baby. Although he was safely delivered on 29 December 1829, the child was not robust. On 4 January

Edward King

1830, his father, Archdeacon Walker King, Rector of Stone in Kent, privately baptized the six-day old infant at nearby St James's Church in Piccadilly, naming him Edward.[3]

'When God forms a human life to do some appointed task, his preparatory action may be traced in the circumstances of hereditary descent, no less clearly than in other provisions, whether of Nature or of Grace.'[4] It seems almost as though in the case of Edward King, nature, nurture and grace all conspired to work together through his ancestry on both sides.

On his mother's side the new-born baby had inherited genetically from not one, but two generations of distinguished physicians. Anne's grandfather, the highly esteemed Sir William Heberden the Elder, MD (1710–1801), was a name to conjure with in the corridors of medicine where he was best known for his description of the nodular swellings resulting from osteoarthritis, still referred to as the 'Heberden nodes.' His extensive research led him to differentiate between gout, a common affliction of the day amongst the aristocracy, and arthritis, as well as accurately diagnosing angina pectoris. He was the founder of the British Rheumatology Society, at one time actually referred to as the 'Heberden Society.' William Cowper had extolled Heberden the Elder as the 'Virtuous and faithful Heberden,' while Dr Johnson styled him 'Ultimus Romanorum'—'the last of our learned physicians.' When he died, he left the house in Pall Mall to his son, William the Younger, who in turn was to become an equally eminent physician.

The younger William was elected Fellow of the Royal Society at the astonishingly early age of twenty-four. In 1806 he was appointed physician to Queen Charlotte and three years later to George III himself. As a child, his daughter Anne (Edward's mother) had been a playmate of the royal children at St James's Palace. With such genes and professional paternal care, perhaps it was not surprising that Mrs King should have enjoyed a long life together with her favourite son, Edward, until her death in 1883—a typical Victorian lady of the old school, 'full of tranquil dignity.'

However, in 1812, while Anne was still only a young girl, her own mother had died prematurely and the highly successful professional life of her father came to an abrupt end: his plans were entirely changed by his wife's death, which left him a widower with no fewer than nine children to raise and educate. He retired from his London practice and moved to Datchet, near Windsor, where he lived with his children, occupying himself with various classical studies, in which he was a considerable scholar, while his only medical practice was to remain on-call for the King at nearby Windsor Castle.

One of his sons, however, decided to follow in the footsteps of his father and grandfather by becoming a medical student at St George's Hospital in London, which occasioned the return of his father to London in 1826 to oversee his son's medical studies.

Three years later, in 1829, the year of Edward King's birth, tragedy struck again when Anne's brother at St George's, in the course of his medical studies, died from an infected dissection wound. As if that were not enough, in that same fateful year, another brother and a sister of Anne also died. (It may not be incidental to note that Edward was conceived, carried and delivered in this year of tragedy, loss and bereavement for the whole Heberden-King family.)

After the death of three children, Anne's father spent the rest of his life researching and writing on various illnesses and studying theology. He published several works of considerable scholarship, among them, *Reflections on the Gospel According to St John* (1830) and *A Literal Translation of the Apostolical Epistles and Revelation*, together with commentary (1839).

On Edward's father's side, the King family tree is a little less impressive, stemming from a mainly clerical family, of canons, a dean, and a distinguished bishop. The family of King is said to have originated in Westmoreland, and to have migrated to Yorkshire before the beginning of the seventeenth century. The landed property which they acquired in the West Riding remained in their possession for over three hundred years. Robert King was incumbent of Kirkby Malhamdale and died there in 1621. The following year his son, Thomas King, built a house in the parish which was used as the vicarage until as late as the beginning of the twentieth century.

This Thomas King had a son, Robert, a grandson called James, and a great-grandson also Thomas. James King (1715–95), who became Dean of Raphoe, had five sons, of whom the third, Walker (1751–1827), was appointed Bishop of Rochester in 1809—the first Bishop King in the family.

Bishop Walker King was a great friend of Edmund Burke, an executor of his will, and editor of his works. The close association and friendship between them cannot be over-exaggerated and must have had a lasting influence on the bishop's son, Canon Walker King, Edward's father.

Burke, by his writing, learning and oratory was a formidable Whig Member of Parliament and not least through his politically influential work, *Reflections on the Revolution in France*, in which he claimed to discern clear religious features in the motivation of all the subversive features of the revolutionaries. As the Revolution turned more radical and entered its international phase, Burke came to think of it 'as no mere exercise in extending French rule, but instead, as a crusade to destroy Christianity in Europe.'[5]

All Burke's political thought and action were grounded in his deeply held belief that religion is the foundation of a civil society, emphasizing revealed Christianity as a vehicle for social progress. For Burke, the practice of a natural religion without revelation implied retrogression to a 'savage and incoherent mode of life.'[6] The inadequacy of natural religion for both personal salvation and civil society are enduring themes in Burke's thought and writings. Issuing from this, it followed for Burke that only revealed religion and, in particular, Christianity, offered the possibility of social and political improvement.[7] Consistently for Burke therefore, morality and religion were inextricably linked, the former being unable to exist without the latter—a theme we shall revisit repeatedly in King's teaching and ministry.

Born in Ireland of a Protestant father and Catholic mother, Burke vigorously defended the Church of England, while also demonstrating a generous spirit, somewhat ahead of his time, towards Catholic concerns. He was further ahead of his time when speaking in the House of Commons in support of Catholics and Dissenters, arguing that the church was built up with the strong and stable matter of the gospel of liberty, and consequently had nothing to fear from allowing other Christian groups to worship as they wished. 'Toleration,' Burke argued, 'so far from being an attack upon Christianity, becomes the best and surest support that possibly can be given to it.'[8] If Bishop Walker King had lived until 1829, he would, under the influence of Burke, surely have voted in favour of Catholic Emancipation, passed by Parliament in that year. Furthermore, it is precisely this *largesse du cœur* and inner deep security which was to distinguish Edward King, preventing him from reacting with that defensive 'citadel mentality' to the new learning, which was to shipwreck the faith and practice of so many in the second half of the nineteenth century.

While forcefully defending the Church of England, Burke, who had spent some time in India, believed that a revealed religion was indispensable to a society's progress, but did not contend that the benefits of religion were restricted to Christianity.[9] Indeed, in a speech before the House of Commons, he specifically commended India's Hindu religion for contributing to the 'flourishing' of India.[10]

Some ornamental pieces of gold and silver, presented to Burke by an Indian Rajah after the impeachment of Warren Hastings, remained in the possession of King's descendants.

Edward King

In 1885, the Revd George Trevor (1809–88) wrote, 'One of my very earliest recollections as a little boy is leading the blind Bishop of Rochester by the hand—in the other hand, he carried a gold-headed cane as long as a footman's, given him by Burke.'[11]

Is it too fanciful to suggest that along with the gold-headed cane and other pieces of gold and silver, the King family also inherited from Burke, in the next generation, something less tangible, though of no less value? Perhaps something of a similar generosity of spirit to that which was so evident in Burke, the Whig politician, had rubbed off on his great friend, Bishop King of Rochester, and which in turn 'filtered' down to King's grandson, the future Bishop of Lincoln. Certainly, such an attitude of heart and mind was to become more strikingly evident, as we shall see, both in King's attitude towards the many Methodists and Dissenters in the Lincoln Diocese, and in his readiness to digest and learn from the writings and thoughts of Roman Catholic friends and theologians acquired in the course of his many European excursions.

Those somewhat grand associations through his family tree, with royal connections on his mother's side, and with those of his grandfather on his father's side, were rarely if ever mentioned by Edward King when he grew to manhood: name-dropping was quite alien to his nature. To use his own language, it was 'simply poor' form. If any particular class of people held his special interest and focused his concern, it was the rural poor. He had an extraordinary affinity with them, and genuinely felt at home in their company. Of more interest than any hereditary privilege or social standing in the future bishop is the double influence of ministry (from his father's side) and medicine (from his mother's side) in the formation of a character which was both pastorally and sensitively aware. King, throughout his life and long ministry strikingly exemplified an empathy and power of discernment, sometimes referred to as the 'bedside manner,' itself a notable characteristic of good physicians. Indeed, in a later age, Edward King might well have opted for the ministry of a physician rather than that of the clerical profession. To a student who was torn between ordination and taking up the study of medicine, King counselled 'Seize the opportunity and take, if possible, the full Medical Course! I know no course of study so well qualified to give you a knowledge of human character and human needs as the medical curriculum ... You will be able to do just as good a work for God as a doctor, as you ever can as a priest.'[12]

Bishop King of Rochester had a son, also called Walker (the maiden name of the bishop's mother). It was this Walker King (1797–1859) who became Rector of St Mary's at Stone, near Dartford in Kent, Canon and Archdeacon of Rochester, and father of a second, future bishop, Edward King of Lincoln. Edward, or 'Little Ted' as he soon became known in the family, was one of ten children, five boys and five girls. The eldest son, also Walker (1827–92), was two years older than Edward, preceded him to Oriel College, Oxford, as had their father before them, and was subsequently ordained into the Anglican priesthood. Canon Walker King served as a devoted and much-loved Rector of St Clement's, Leigh-on-Sea, Essex, from 1859 to 1892. Edward, who had always been regarded as having a weaker constitution, outlived him by eighteen years. Preaching at a special service in St Clement's in 'Grateful Memory of the late much-beloved Rector, Canon Walker King, MA,' Bishop Edward, as he was by then, drew a most attractive portrait of his brother as a parish priest whose life exemplified, in the words of Edward's favourite Psalm, 'the gentleness' of God—'Thy Gentleness hath made me great' (Psalm 18:35) or, as the Coverdale translation has it, 'Thy loving correction hath made me great.' Edward frequently preached on the gentleness of God, which many who knew him later in life often remarked on as being a distinctive attribute of the saintly bishop himself. Indeed, in his sermon, we can see almost a mirror image of Canon Walker's younger brother (see p. 426).

'In these days of self-advertisement and pushing,' King says of his brother, 'his spirit of gentleness and retirement possesses a rare value: always ready to listen to what other persons had to say; never over-bearing or pushing to obtain his own way. This spirit of retirement, of unobtrusive gentleness, especially in those who are placed in positions of authority, is worthy of great attention as being most precious in the sight of God.'[13] Clearly all that Edward said of his brother could, to an even greater extent, have been said of himself, and not least as of a bishop, in a position of even greater authority.

Edward's younger brother, Henry, went into the army and served in the Crimean War, surviving a life-threatening injury only to die, at the devastatingly young age of twenty-three, in a bathing accident off Malta. A memorial plaque was erected in the chancel of the church at Stone, immediately facing his father's stall, as a daily reminder of his son's tragic death.

> In affectionate memory of
> CAPTAIN HENRY KING
> Son of Archdeacon King, Rector of this parish
> Who after being by God's mercy
> preserved from death
> During the Siege of Sevastopol
> At Alma, Balaclava, and Inkerman
> In which last battle he was dangerously wounded,
> Was drowned
> While bathing at Malta, March 28th, 1857
> Aged 23 years
> And buried in the Floriana Cemetery
> 'We believe that the Lord's hand is not shortened that it could not save' — 'For His mercy endureth for ever.'
> Isai. LIX Ps. CXXXVI.

The King Family

Such a sober rehearsal of the facts cannot hide the grief of the family, nor their lively and accepting faith so clearly evident from the texts. At the time, Edward would have been twenty-seven, and in his last year as curate in Wheatley. As none of Edward's letters from 1857 have survived, we cannot estimate the intensity of his feelings at this bereavement, yet, in what was a closely knit family, he must surely have felt it keenly. We do know, however, how deeply he felt the loss of his invalid sister, Anne, to whom he was devoted. She died in 1858, just over a year after Henry and only a few weeks after Edward had taken up his new position as chaplain at Cuddesdon. Again, a memorial in the chancel of Stone church records her loss:

> In affectionate Memory of
> ANNE KING
> A beloved daughter of
> Archdeacon King, and Anne his wife,
> Born June 22nd 1831
> Died Novr. 9th 1858.
> 'Love, Joy, Peace'
> 'Long-suffering, gentleness,'
> 'Goodness, faith, meekness.'
> These are the fruits of the Spirit,
> And in these she abounded.

Anne was the closest to Edward of his four surviving sisters (the first-born had died in infancy). For twelve years before her early death, she was an invalid, and he spent much time with her. He would sit all night by her bedside, and learned Italian, which Anne already knew, so that together they might read Dante in the original. He also shared her taste in literature and her interest in flowers and plants, interests which remained with him throughout his life. Clearly, he developed an extraordinary empathy with her, an empathy that was later to be a hallmark of his pastoral ministry to the sick.

Edward King

Edward's two youngest brothers were William (1837–1920) and Charles James (1844–72). William went up to Oriel in 1855 but did not graduate, and a few years later he followed his elder brother Henry into the army as an Ensign in the 55th Regiment of Foot. But his service record, apart from recording a few personal details and the date of his commission, 17 June 1859, is completely empty.[14] By 1871 he had left the army and probably moved to Somerset, where he is later listed in directories as a JP. (The King family had connections with Somerset: Bishop Walker King had been a residentiary Canon at Wells and Edward's brother Walker was born in the county.) Though nothing appears to have survived by way of correspondence between Edward and William, they must have kept in touch, and when William's wife Isabella died young in 1880, Professor King, as Edward then was, travelled from Oxford to Curry Rivill in Somerset to conduct her funeral. The youngest brother, Charles, who did not go up to Oxford, was described as 'clerk' when he married in London in 1865. He subsequently practised as a solicitor in Australia, at Mackay in Queensland, and was involved in the development of the cane-sugar industry there. He died there of a heart condition on 30 October 1872, still only twenty-eight, and was buried in Mackay Cemetery.

King's other three sisters—Elizabeth Catherine, Mary and Sarah Frances—all married clergymen; respectively the Revd Charles Gerrard Andrews, the Revd George Frederick Wilgress and the Revd Stephen Henry Fox Nicholl.

EARLY HOME LIFE

Shortly after Edward's baptism, on 4 January 1830, Mrs King wrote from London, 'Little Ted is quite well,'[15] so that a little later, the family returned to Stone, where 'little Ted' was formally and liturgically 'received' into the Church, by

The King Family

the congregation of the parish on 17 August. St Mary the Virgin, Stone, tastefully restored since the Archdeacon's day, is a beautiful church, full of lightness and grace perched on its modest hill overlooking the Thames. It is known locally as 'the lantern of Kent' and in earlier days was a landmark helping to guide boats up the Thames estuary.

The later stages of any life can frequently be best understood by what can be gleaned from the earlier years. Certainly, in those early years of his childhood, the village life of Stone would have been largely undisturbed by the echoes of revolution still resounding from the Continent, or by the strident clamouring for political reform in Parliament, which finally exploded, though ultimately as something of a damp squib, in the Reform Act of 1832. Comparatively little of all these and similar contemporary upheavals, whether social, political or ecclesiastical, would have borne in on the home and family life of the Kings: 'Our English homes may be said to be the Castles of England,' wrote King, many years later, reflecting on his early life in Stone as the son of a country vicar, with family religion, as he termed it, the 'Keeper of the Castle.'[16] Today the parish of Stone is very built-up: encroached on by light industry, cement-making and the Bluewater Shopping Centre, it looks over to the great Queen Elizabeth II road bridge crossing the Thames. In King's time, by contrast, this was largely undisturbed countryside, providing ample fresh air and country pursuits for a growing boy whose health required just such an environment.

The deep soil of heredity, on both his father's and his mother's side, enriched both by nurture and grace, in a home life, surrounded by close family and friends, where Christian belief would have been largely unquestioned, and where the practice of daily, family prayers taken for granted—such was the environment of Edward's early and formative years, as it was of his several siblings. On arriving in the parish Archdeacon King declined to occupy the old rectory, which he found to be damp and unhealthy, and built himself an entirely new residence, Woodside or Woodside House, 'commanding fine views of the Thames and the surrounding country.' It was in this house, where the Archdeacon lived for the rest of his life and where he died in 1859, that Edward and his brothers and sisters were brought up. In 1863 Woodside House was sold and particulars of the property were printed in the local paper: it comprised 'fine drawing and dining rooms, entrance-hall, study, &c., nine bed-rooms, two dressing-rooms, and the necessary domestic offices, with lodge entrance, stabling and coach-house, kitchen garden, lawns and pleasure grounds, and about 20-acres of parklike pastures and woodland.' Subsequently known as Stone Park, King's childhood home does not survive.[17]

Woodside House, the church and the parish, provided virtually the whole setting of Edward's early life. Even his education took place at home, where both parents participated in the religious instruction of their children. Preaching in Lincoln in 1905, Edward recalled how he learned to repeat and understand the Catechism of the Church: 'I was brought up to do this every Sunday; my brother and sister and I said our Catechism to our dear mother.' In that same sermon, he urged the importance of such or similar instruction as a foundation for growth into Christian maturity: 'Any child who had learned his Catechism when he was young would find, as he grew up and came to understand things better, that he had obtained a great possession, a fair outline of his faith and duty towards God, and good lines of guidance for his social duties and conduct towards his fellow-men.'

Much of that could have been affirmed by the religion of duty and social responsibility of Thomas Arnold's school at Rugby, and by the Christianity of that broad churchmanship which predominated in the religious teaching and practice of the public schools, as well as in the Church of England in general. But it is what King went on to say in that sermon, which is strikingly significant. He insisted that an outward conformity to Christian principles of duty and mutual responsibility decidedly needed to go much further, and to embrace the inner life of the Spirit when duty is fulfilled in the two-fold commandment of love. So, King concludes: 'duty to God and duty to neighbour would be sure to have their inner meaning and best fulfilment in the love of God and love of man.' It was to affirm that inner meaning of outward religious conformity which was to become the consistent refrain of King's teaching and way of life.[18]

In those early years, when the young Edward enjoyed a privileged, warm and affectionate life in the Kent countryside, he would have learned so much about the beauty of the natural world, nurtured in the life style and culture of a largely farming community — not totally dissimilar from that of Lincolnshire where, for the last twenty-five years of his life, he was to serve as its bishop. Indeed, it was those early and formative years which in remarkable ways prepared young Edward for so much of what was to shape his long life of ministry and Christian witness.

Natural history was a frequent pursuit of the country clergy who often spent the greatest part of their lives in one parish, noting and observing the change of seasons and the migration of birds, and recording in detailed accounts the local flora as amateur naturalists.[19] So, from his earliest years, and undoubtedly strongly influenced by the rural setting of his father's parish, Edward acquired an increasing love of the natural world. Although he never had a very deep knowledge of botany, an interest originally stimulated by his sister Anne, he loved plants and flowers. 'I still love birds and flowers,' he wrote towards the end of his life, 'the marvellous creation of a bird's nest.' Alert and alive to all around him, he felt in sympathy and harmony with nature, and in some strange way in league with the animals and beasts of the field, somewhat in the reputed spirit of St Francis.[20]

Edward King

In all of this, nature and nurture worked together to prepare Edward for his future ministry as curate in a country parish; for his life in Cuddesdon, itself rooted and grounded in a country parish where the principal of the College was traditionally also the vicar of the parish; and finally, and supremely, as bishop of a large, rural and farming diocese in the fens and Wolds of Lincolnshire.

EARLY EDUCATION

Edward's older brother, Walker, was sent away to school, but Edward was not. Instead, his parents opted for home tuition, not at all unusual at that time, mainly out of consideration for his health, but also because they had doubts about public-school education after the somewhat rough treatment that Walker apparently had experienced. Whether that treatment was from bullying, or from the draconian discipline imposed by the masters, is not clear. However, Walker seems to have survived well enough.

In any event, the Archdeacon and his wife concluded that Edward was well out of it. He was no shrinking plant, but from his early years he had a refinement and sensitivity which would have been ill-suited to the ethos of some minor Eton or Rugby. Indeed, perhaps we need to go further. The religion of Arnold and Rugby-type public schools, which nurtured many of the church leaders of the nineteenth century, was very different from the spirituality in which King was nurtured and which he both taught and practised throughout his ministry and personal life. Furthermore, it could be said that one beneficial consequence of being delicate as a child was that he was spared the rigours and the narrowing influences of a boarding-school education which was to become increasingly the norm for boys of his class at the time. He completely escaped the taboo on tenderness and sensitivity for boys and young men, which was

The King Family

to have such a crippling effect on post-Victorian manhood. The open-air life of a country boy suited him far better than incarceration in a boarding school. Edward grew up to enjoy fishing, swimming, and dancing: he particularly excelled at riding, and as a young boy, if no better mount was available, he would happily ride the family's carriage horse.

It seems that it was his mother, rather than his father, the Archdeacon, who was predominantly responsible for the young Edward's Christian formation and preparation for Confirmation which, at that time, and with such a family background, would have been largely something of a formality.

In an age when clerical nepotism was still rife, the 'plum' living of Stone, together with a Canonry as Archdeacon of Rochester, would simply have fallen into his father's lap, being in the gift of Edward's grandfather, the somewhat formidable and overpowering Bishop King of Rochester. A precedent had been set early in the eighteenth century when Bishop Thomas Sprat, had gifted the parish of Stone, and an Archdeaconry, to his son, also Thomas. Bishop King had followed this precedent with the same nepotistic gift to his son, Walker King, whose successor at Stone, Frederick Murray, received the same package deal from his father, Bishop Murray of Rochester. It was Canon Murray rather than Archdeacon King who, as the longest-serving rector ever in that parish, from 1857 until 1906, did a sterling job at Stone, leaving his mark and stamp on the parish.[21]

In seeking to gain some picture of Archdeacon King, we are fortunate that he kept a detailed ledger-cum-journal from which we can catch glimpses of his day-to-day life and work, and hints and possible clues to his character and personality. He had studied at Oriel College, Oxford, and his knowledge of Greek was considerable. His journal includes references to his own scholarly pursuits, a commentary on a Greek version of the book of Genesis topping the list, together with his own translations from the original Greek of Sophocles' *Oedipus at Colonus* and *Oedipus Tyrannus*—no mean achievement. He also lists a 'History of Caryatides' written by himself, with a footnote mentioning 'one of the statues brought to England by Lord Elgin,' of the Elgin Marbles fame. The list concludes with A Gazetteer of Saints and Heresies in the 1st and 2nd centuries.

The rest of the entries in the journal nearly all relate to his responsibilities as Archdeacon of Rochester, with lists of his visitations to the many parishes of the diocese, spread over several counties, and all given in great detail. There are lists and inventories of silverware and church monuments, and a list of his sermons between 1822 and 1858, together with their chosen texts, all carefully indexed. Then there are strange little entries: Analysis of Indian Opium Trade, Description of Heresies and Schismatics, all mixed in with Regulations Regarding Church Organs. Reading between the lines, Archdeacon King was highly conscientious, with a mind for detail, though possibly somewhat lacking in flair or any other particularly striking characteristics.

One particular entry gives a little glimpse into the rather grand lifestyle enjoyed by the family during Edward's early years: 'A Grand Ball-Supper given by Mrs King on April 1st, 1834.' On an adjoining page, the Archdeacon has drawn a plan of the layout of the large dining-room, giving exact details for the necessary re-arrangement of the furniture, down to the placing of servants at strategic points for serving the guests in what was clearly to be a splendid occasion.[22]

CONFIRMATION

Arrangements appear somewhat formal on the day of Edward's Confirmation. His father called the young teenage boy into his study, examined him to see if he knew the required answers to the various questions outlined as the basis of Christian faith and practice as in the Catechism of

The King Family

the Book of Common Prayer; gave him a card certifying his readiness to be Confirmed, and told him to get on his pony and go to Foot's Cray, a short ride west back along the Thames, where Archbishop Howley, was to hold a Confirmation that day. Neither of his parents or indeed godparents are recorded as having accompanied him.

Archbishop William Howley, only son of a country vicar, educated as a classicist at Winchester and New College, Oxford, fluent in three European languages, survived into his eighties, becoming the longest serving Archbishop of Canterbury (1828–48), and also the last to wear a wig, long before the days when archbishops would take to wearing mitres. He was cautious and somewhat reactionary, strongly opposed to Catholic Emancipation, with a citadel mentality, sturdily upholding the Church as by Law Established against the onslaughts and turbulence of the day, urging in his Charge to his Clergy of Canterbury 'vigilance in a season when the Church is assailed by so many enemies.'[23]

Yet, however perfunctory the practice of Confirmation was in those days nevertheless, in the particular case of the young Edward, it would seem that Archbishop Howley's 'touch,' so to speak, had taken that day. On returning home afterwards, Edward learned that the neighbours of the village of Stone were holding a dance that evening. But when his mother said, 'I suppose, Edward, you would rather not go to the dance,' he replied that he would indeed prefer to stay quietly at home, left to his own thoughts and reflections on the past day.[24]

Although it was his mother who had been chiefly responsible for his religious education and preparation for Confirmation, it was Edward's father who in the very early stages, had given him some preliminary teaching rather than sending him away to school like his older brother. Later, however, and in place of his father, and for his further education, Edward became a daily and indeed devoted pupil of his father's curate, the Revd John Day.

Edward King

THE INFLUENCE OF JOHN DAY

In all the existing material, there are few references to Edward's father, or to his father's death, apart from two letters in which he seeks his father's advice when he was offered the post of chaplain at Cuddesdon. Might this not reasonably suggest and explain why throughout his life, and especially in the early days, King tended to resort so readily to mentors from whom he received much warmth and lasting influence and, by no means least, why he identified so eagerly with the Revd John Day, at such an early age?

John David Day deserves far more credit for young Edward's Christian formation, and possibly even more for his education, than the record of King's life has ever given. Day proved to be so very much more than simply a tutor, taking over from King's father as the teenage lad approached adolescence. Day was the first and strong link in the chain of several important mentors who profoundly influenced Edward in those early formative years.

First and foremost, Day was a pastor and teacher, two key characteristics in the ministry of King. Although undoubtedly of the Tractarian and High Church school, he was not a party man, in precisely the same way as King, whether as future principal, professor or bishop never retreated behind party barricades. About 1845, having served as curate to the Archdeacon in Stone for around ten years, Day moved to another curacy in Flintshire, taking the sixteen-year-old King with him to continue his studies.

The son of a banker in Rochester, David Hermitage Day, John Day had graduated from Brasenose College, Oxford, in 1834, during the heady early days of the Tractarian Movement. He would almost certainly have been present in the University Church the previous year to hear Keble's Assize Sermon, which, along with the influences of Newman and Pusey circulating in Oxford at that time, would have shaped him as a committed High Churchman of the Tractarian

The King Family

School. Day not only prepared Edward for study at Oxford, he also imbued him with the ideals of 'The Movement,' and with the fundamental principles of a sound and rounded education.

After a brief spell in Flintshire, Day moved to Shropshire, where he served for a short time as curate to the Vicar of St Mary's, Ellesmere, William Henry Egerton: once again, the young King was in train, along with two or three other pupils. Initially, they occupied a house together on St John's Hill in Ellesmere. In the same year, 1846, Day succeeded Egerton as vicar, and together with his little band of pupils moved into the vicarage to continue their schooling as well as to care for the parish. For the following two years or so, until he went up to Oxford in 1848, King served as a kind of lay pastoral assistant to the new vicar, singing in the choir, conducting a Bible-class for men and generally helping in the work of the parish.

Under Day, St Mary's parish was run on Tractarian lines, and during his time as vicar, he undertook a radical restoration and extension of the fabric of the church, which stands proudly today, overlooking the little town and commanding a view of the lake which gives rise to its soubriquet, the 'Cathedral of the Meres.' Day certainly set his mark on the church, as a brass memorial tablet in the chancel records: 'To the memory of John Day, Vicar of this Parish from 1846 to 1864. By his zeal and care this Church was restored. Erected by the Clergy of the Rural Deanery.' During that restoration, in 1848–9, George Gilbert Scott replaced the Norman nave (which King would have known) with a much enlarged one, and rebuilt the aisles, creating an impressive height and spaciousness which lends itself well to the more elaborate worship of the High Church tradition, which, originating with Day, continues to the present day. When Day launched an appeal for funds for the restoration, King, by then an undergraduate at Oxford, subscribed £5—no trivial gift for a student at the time and doubtless as an act of thanksgiving for all that Day had given to him.

It was there, at St Mary's, that the young Edward King, still an impressionable teenager, gained his first experience of a parish where the ideals of the Oxford Movement were routinely implemented. Undoubtedly, that experience influenced his devotional life, in that during this period with Day, he began to practise a new discipline of worship. When from time to time he returned to be with his family in Stone 'he suggested to his sisters to join him in a daily service, in the school-room, at 8 o'clock in the morning, with himself playing the Gregorian chant to which they sang the psalms of the day.'[25]

JOHN DAY AND THE WOODARD SCHOOLS

On 1 May 1847, John Peake of Hertford College, Oxford, joined Day to assist him, not just in the parish of Ellesmere, but also as tutor in Day's little school. Peake and Day proved to be a formidable team, not least in sharing their basic principles as to what constituted a rounded education of both mind and spirit. Day was not just a good parish priest, he was also a true educationalist. He profoundly believed that education should involve not just duty and the ethics of so-called 'public-school religion' along the lines of Thomas Arnold, but should also nurture a faith deeply rooted in the scriptures and the sacraments, resourcing a disciplined life of personal devotion, worship and service. In those few years together with Day and Peake, King not only caught something of the secrets of a disciplined life as a committed Churchman, which he would continue to practise faithfully when he went up to Oxford and for the rest of his life, but he was also deeply and further influenced by those same principles of education which he held to be of such great importance in train-

The King Family

ing the clergy when he was Principal of Cuddesdon, and later as Professor of Pastoral Theology at Oxford.

Day died in 1864, after years of ill-health, while still in his early fifties, but the work of his little school continued to prosper under Peake who succeeded him as Vicar of St Mary's, where he was to remain for many years. The local newspaper reported Day's funeral in glowing terms, giving substantial evidence of the outstanding impact he made in the parish. 'Every shop was closed, the blinds of private houses were drawn, and business was wholly suspended during the morning.' The sermon was preached by the Revd W. Moore, on the text: 'He being dead, yet speaketh' (Hebrews 11:4).[26] And who should have been one of the pall bearers, along with John Peake, carrying the body of his former tutor on his last journey into St Mary's Church?[27] None other than Edward King, by that time Principal of Cuddesdon, continuing to hand on, not just by word, but more powerfully by example, the principles taught by and caught from John Day during those formative and influential years when as a teenager he had been Day's pupil and protégé.

Although a little early in the narrative of King's life, it is important to look at some of the people who were present in the crowd at Day's funeral. Among the many names of the clergy and notable laity is a reference to members of the Oddfellows Society.[28] That, as we shall see later, clearly indicates that John Day, like many Evangelical and High Church clergy from a comfortable background, had been conspicuous during his ministry in his care for the poor, assisted by and working together with the Oddfellows Society, which for several centuries had existed as what was termed a 'Friendly Society' supporting the families and widows of working men in hard times (see p. 437). Along with all that King learned from Day about well-ordered worship, a disciplined life of prayer and a rounded education of both the mind and spirit, King's first mentor had also exemplified in his own ministry that care of the poor which, originally, was all part and parcel of the Tractarian package. The academic and doctrinal claims of the first generation of those same Tractarian fathers were vindicated and, indeed, authenticated by the end of the nineteenth century by priests who, with that same passion for the poor, worked so valiantly in the slum parishes of the industrial towns and cities. So, it is not over-speculative to assume that Day had been a member of the local branch of the Oddfellows Society, of which King himself, many years later as Bishop of Lincoln, was also to become a member.

But there is more: fast-forwarding to 5 August 1879, and returning to Ellesmere, where Peake was still the vicar, we see once again the same Edward King, by this time Canon King, DD, Regius Professor of Pastoral Theology at the University of Oxford, conspicuously present and in the frame, and for a very different occasion—the laying of the foundation stone of St Oswald's College, one of the great Woodard Schools, subsequently known as Ellesmere College, whose roots lay in Day's little school.

As a distinguished former pupil of Day's school, Canon King had been invited to preach at the ceremony. This was to have taken place outside, but 'owing to the continuous down pour of rain,' which persisted throughout the day, King delivered his sermon in the church, before processing to the site for the foundation stone laying.[29] He took as his text: 'Fight the good fight of faith, lay hold of eternal life' (1 Timothy 6:12). As was not uncommon at the time, a local newspaper printed a précis.

King pointed out that while 'it was true that the words might refer to contests of the arena rather than the battle field,' nevertheless they 'meant that Christians should not be surprised if their faith met with opposition; that they should, in fact, be prepared to contend earnestly for the faith, as in a contest, where there were many adversaries.' But this must be undertaken, he typically insisted, with 'no forgetfulness of the law of charity, which should ever be the true mark of Christ's disciples, nor in any bitterness of party spirit.'

In words which still ring true today, possibly in even louder decibels than when first spoken, King insisted that there existed 'a war between faith and unbelief' which could in some respects be regarded as almost a civil war, 'carried on between members of the same county, the same university, the same county, the same parish, and the same family … authority, tradition, and custom were disparaged, and each individual was left to choose for himself, more-or-less, which side he would take,—either faith or unbelief.' Among the numerous evils which Christians had to contend against, the worst 'was that of secularism in its many forms, which was gradually making headway amongst all classes in this country, more especially amongst the lower orders.'

King then continued 'eloquently' to point out the 'course which it was necessary to adopt in order to counteract the baneful effects produced.' What was that to be? 'To establish places of religion and learning especially for those classes who could not avail themselves of such an education, and it was for that very purpose that they were gathered on that momentous occasion.' For it was their desire that day, 'to plant in the soil of Old England the foundation of a building which, by God's blessing, would inculcate into the minds of the young how they might live and attain not only to the highest power and happiness in this world, but in the world to come.'

The Ellesmere Foundation was intended to provide for its pupils such a place where they 'would learn to put aside all feelings of party spirit and bitterness,' and to put within their 'reach the more valuable and fundamental doctrine of Christianity; to live for one another; to provide for them a place in which they would learn to "fight the good fight of faith"; a place in which they would be so educated as to fit them to go into the world, and, with God's help, succeed and lead them to eternal life.'[30]

After the service, the clergy and others proceeded (in the rain) to the site of the school, given by Earl Brownlow, where his wife, Countess Brownlow, laid the foundation stone. Beneath it, in a cavity in the stone below, was placed a copy of the Book of Common Prayer, representing both symbolically and actually the 'foundation' on which the school was to be built. The words of the prayer which the Earl said as the stone was laid spelled out the distinctive educational ethos, not only of Ellesmere but of all the schools bearing the name Woodard.

> In the faith of Jesus Christ we fix this stone on this foundation, in the name of the Father, and of the Son, and of the Holy Ghost; that within these walls hereon to be raised, bearing the name of St Oswald King and Martyr, the true faith and fear of God, together with brotherly love and sound learning may for ever flourish and abound. Amen.[31]

No one then or since need be in any doubt that the educational principles of Ellesmere, as indeed of every Woodard school, rested firmly on the foundation of both religion and learning according to the formularies and teaching of the Church of England by Law Established, and exercised more specifically with 'the true faith and fear of God, together with brotherly love and sound learning' inextricably bonded together. Indeed, like the founding fathers of the Tractarian Movement, Woodard was contemptuous of an Establishment in which the Church was dominated by the State. Furthermore, he was 'acutely aware of the danger of the Christian religion being divorced from everyday life, of sacred truth separated from secular knowledge.'[32]

> Nathaniel Woodard's solution to England's educational and spiritual malaise in the 1840s had been as stark as his analysis: there were parochial schools for the poor and Public Schools for the rich, but nothing for the growing class in between. To leave the State to fill the gap was unthinkable because Woodard's view of education was

The King Family

as high as his churchmanship. For him, the primary purpose of education was 'to repair the ruins of man's first disobedience': it was a means of salvation and, as such, was part of the Church's mission.[33]

Nathaniel Woodard himself was present on this occasion and spoke after the lunch which followed the foundation-stone ceremony. As was his wont, he took the opportunity, to solicit funds for the new foundation at Ellesmere: King contributed £25.

'AN ELECTRIC ARK OF PERSONAL INFLUENCE'

Woodard was not the only after-lunch speaker that afternoon. Charles Abraham, the Bishop of Wellington, who had presided at the earlier celebration of the Eucharist on behalf of the Bishop of Lichfield, spoke forcefully of the need for the Church to become more actively involved in education, 'especially of that upper part of the so-called lower classes.' Then the barrister Sir Offley Wakeman, Bart, stood to propose the health of the preacher, Canon King, who was, he said, known to many of those present 'as a warm, personal friend,' and to all of them 'as an ornament of their dear old Church of England.' (Applause.) Wakeman, a graduate of Christ Church himself, went on to say how appropriate it was that King had been invited to preach since as a Professor at Oxford he was 'already doing good work in the furtherance of religious education … But there was another and still greater reason … It was that [this] was not the first time Canon King had been to Ellesmere.'

Wakeman then made the specific connection, pointing out the significance of King's presence.

> His position [as Professor] was an example of what Ellesmere education had been in the past [originally in Day's little school], and it might be an earnest of the

future. They trusted that the boys to be educated at St. Oswald's College, would, to the best of their ability, follow in the footsteps of Canon King. If that were so they would feel that the school of which they had that day laid the foundation stone would indeed be a blessing to the Church and the nation (applause).[34]

There is more evidence from that day of King's lasting and high regard for his former tutor. Rising to thank Sir Offley for 'the flattering manner in which he had proposed the toast with regard to himself,' King began his brief speech, by saying that, 'if they would allow him, he would open up his heart a little more than he had been able to do in the church, where he had some little difficulty in keeping back what he should have liked to have said that he owed to Ellesmere' and by implication to John Day.

'There was once in that place,' he continued, 'one who would be remembered by many still there—a noble spirit who devoted himself and the whole of his resources, the whole of his time, the whole of his head and his heart, to the education of individuals.' He need hardly tell them that he was speaking of the late John Day, from whom he had learned and experienced something of the 'electric arc of personal influence,' and that if he had been able to do any little work in the world since that time, it was due, under God's blessing, to his late tutor. Indeed, the whole occasion had afforded him 'the opportunity of saying what he owed to his old master.' 'Could they not in some way,' he continued, 'do something to link the name of John David Day with the great institution which had been founded that day amongst them? Could they not inaugurate a scholarship to be called "The Day Scholarship," to be given to members of the Church of England and natives of Ellesmere?' He ended by saying he would do his 'utmost to further the proposed scholarship,' for which subscriptions had already been promised, by personally raising 'a sum, say, of £400 or £500.'[35]

There it is, spelt out loud and clear: it was John Day who had first caught the young King's interest 'in the cause of education,' a cause which he continued to support and to promote increasingly throughout his ministry, not least during his years as Bishop of Lincoln, when various educational measures came before Parliament and to the forefront of the nation's concerns. Education meant for Day what it came to mean for King in his life's work as both a pastor and a teacher: heart and head, religion and learning always inextricably bound together and addressing the whole person and not simply the intellect.

Many years later, on 12 June 1895, Bishop King, as he then was, enlarged on this theme in a sermon preached at the Commemoration Day of St Edward's School in Oxford (not a Woodard School). 'The old-fashioned Schoolmaster of the eighteenth century,' said King, 'was a useful State instrument for keeping up a gentlemanly and aristocratical standard of Education.' Mentioning the massive influence of Arnold and Rugby, King pleaded that 'when we think of our great Public Schools there seems to be a hiatus somewhere; they please our mental palate rather than our soul, and a deep sympathy and a moral yearning at the bottom of our nature is left more or less untouched by them': all this implied, though not spelt out, as being in contrast with King's own experience of learning at the feet of John Day.

Like Woodard, King saw the need to redress this balance between the education of the mind and the development of the spirit and that it was precisely with this objective that 'the great group of Woodard Schools at Lancing and Hurst, and Ardingly, Denstone, Taunton' (and here is the fascinating connection) 'and Ellesmere were begun.'[36] Woodard was adamant that his schools, like the ancient universities, should be places of both 'Religion and Learning,' where mind and spirit are developed in tandem: indeed, as he uncompromisingly stated, 'Education without religion is pure evil.' Lancing, the first of the Woodard Schools, enshrines that objective of 'Religion and Learning' in stone in its magnificent Chapel which dominates the whole of the school campus as well as the skyline of West Sussex. So it was to be with all Woodard Schools: it is their chapels which constitute the beating heart of their learning communities, and where pupils can experience transcendent worship, speaking with more durable decibels than mere verbal communication, however eloquent.

To the present day, some one-hundred-and-fifty years later, Ellesmere (formerly St Oswald's) College is still part of the Midland Division of the Woodard Corporation. In its coat of arms, granted in 1954, a raven is shown holding a ring in its beak, which, according to legend, St Oswald sent as a marriage proposal to a heathen princess. The motto, PRO PATRIA DIMICANS ('striving for one's country'), comes from the Venerable Bede's account of St Oswald.[37]

It was these and other principles of a more rounded education which King had first experienced during his time with John Day—principles which would be developed and practised when roles were reversed; when King was the teacher, and influential spiritual mentor to the clergy of future years, both as principal at Cuddesdon and later, as pastoral professor in Oxford.

FAREWELL TO JOHN DAY AND ELLESMERE

Back in 1848, when the time finally came for King to leave John Day at Ellesmere, a Book of Common Prayer was presented to him with an inscription inside which read: 'To EDWARD KING this Book of Common Prayer is presented by the Choir of Ellesmere, in token of their affectionate regard and grateful remembrance. July 19th 1848.'[38]

The chapter of Ellesmere and John Day closes that same year, with King just approaching nineteen, but 'looking older than his real age, as he was already the possessor of a

The King Family

handsome pair of whiskers.'[39] He followed in the footsteps of his brother, Walker, and set out for Oriel College, Oxford, taking with him his newly acquired High Church experience and discipline as part and parcel of Day's 'electric arc' of personal and lasting influence. Oriel College, famous—some at the time would have said infamous—as the cradle of the Oxford Movement, was where Newman's influence was still vividly present, supremely in his disciple, Charles Marriott, who was to pick up where Day had left off, and prove to be yet another major and lasting influence on the future life and ministry of Edward King.

Notes

1. Quoted in *Dictionary of National Biography*, vol. XLIV (ed. Sidney Lee). London: Smith, Elder & Co., 1895, p. 213.
2. J. Asperne, *The Real or Constitutional House that Jack Built*. London: Printed for J. Asperne, 1819, title page.
3. George W. E. Russell, *Edward King Sixtieth Bishop of Lincoln*. London: Smith, Elder & Co., 1912, p. 2.
4. *Ibid.*, p. 1.
5. Ian Harris, 'Burke and Religion,' in *The Cambridge Companion to Edmund Burke* (ed. David Dwan and Christopher J. Insole). Cambridge University Press, 2012, p. 102.
6. *Ibid.*
7. *Ibid.*, p. 103.
8. Edmund Burke, 'Speech on Relief of Protestant Dissenters,' in *The Philosophy of Edmund Burke* (ed. Louis I. Bredvoid and Ralph G. Ross). Ann Arbor: The University of Michigan Press, 1960, pp. 76–7.
9. Harris, *op. cit.*, p. 99.
10. Quoted in Harris, *op. cit.*, p. 102.
11. Russell, *op. cit.*, p. 2.
12. *Ibid.*, p. 57.
13. Edward King, 'The Gentleness of God,' in *The Love and Wisdom of God* (ed. B. W. Randolph). London: Longmans, Green & Co., 1910, p. 278.
14. The National Archives, WO 76/172, p. 46.
15. Russell, *op. cit.*, p. 2.
16. Quoted in B. W. Randolph and J. W. Townroe, *The Mind and Work of Bishop King*. London: A. R. Mowbray, 1918, p. 21.
17. *Kentish Gazette*, 22 March 1859, p. 5; 7 July 1863, p. 1; John A. Newton, *Search for a Saint: Edward King*. London: Epworth Press, 1977, p. 20;

Revd Kenneth Clark, 'The Lantern of Kent,' *A Guide to the History of St Mary, The Virgin, Stone*. London: Gavin Martin, Colournet Ltd, 2015, p. 16.

[18] Edward King, *Sermons and Addresses* (B. W. Randolph, ed.). London: Longmans, Green & Co., 1911, pp. 73–4.

[19] See Patrick H. Armstong, *The English Parson-Naturalist*. Leominster: Gracewing, 2000.

[20] Randolph and Townroe, *op. cit.*, pp. 11–12.

[21] Revd Kenneth Clark, 'The Lantern of Kent'.

[22] Original manuscript of Archdeacon King's Personal Journal ('The Dark Green Ledger'), currently in the care of St Mary's Church, Stone.

[23] Edward Carpenter, *Cantuar: The Archbishops in their Office*. London: Cassell, 1971, p. 292.

[24] Russell, *op. cit.*, p. 21.

[25] *Ibid.*, p. 3.

[26] *Border Counties Advertiser*, 13 July 1864.

[27] *Ibid.*

[28] *Ibid.*

[29] *Eddowes's Shrewsbury Journal*, 6 August 1879.

[30] *Ibid.*

[31] Sir John Otter, *Nathaniel Woodard: A Memoir of his Life*. London: John Lane, 1925, p. 265.

[32] Christopher Jobson, 'An Article to Mark the 130th Anniversary of the Laying of the Foundation Stone of Ellesmere College,' in *Mere News* (a local magazine), summer issue (no. 41), 2009.

[33] Jobson, *Ibid.*

[34] *Eddowes's Shrewsbury Journal*, 6 August 1879.

[35] *Shrewsbury Chronicle*, 8 August 1879.

[36] Edward King, 'Ideals of School Life,' in *The Love and Wisdom of God*, p. 285.

[37] Jobson, *op. cit.*

[38] Russell, *op. cit.*, p. 3n.

[39] *Ibid.*, p. 4.

✣ 2 ✣

Oxford Mentors

DISTURBING TIMES

The year King began his studies at Oriel was a tumultuous one throughout the whole of Europe. Upheavals in Paris, Berlin, Vienna, Milan, Venice, Naples, Cracow and Prague earned for 1848 the label 'Year of Revolutions.' In London, in April, there was a huge demonstration by the Chartists preparing to march on Parliament. The Establishment was taking no risks, and so serious were the riots expected to be that Lord John Russell summoned the Duke of Wellington to barricade the strategically important buildings in London, like the Bank of England and the British Museum, with 80,000 policemen specially drafted in. At the same time Queen Victoria, Prince Albert and their children, were sent off to the safety of the Isle of Wight.

Only a matter of a few weeks later, Prince Albert records how there were 'Chartist riots every night ... The organization of these people is incredible: they have secret signals and correspond from town to town by means of carrier pigeons.' (It seems that little has changed: nowadays, it is social media, rather than carrier pigeons.)

'In London,' he continued, 'there are between 10,000 and 20,000 strong, which is not much out of a population of two millions, but if they could, through their organization throw themselves in a body, upon any one point, they might be successful in a *coup de main*.'[1] ('There was no magic formula,' comments A. N. Wilson, 'which would stop the British mob getting rid of their monarchy if they were hungry enough or the politicians were sufficiently incompetent.'²)

In the same year, the *Communist Manifesto* was published with its strident call to arms:

> The Communists openly declare that their ends can only be attained by the forcible overthrow of all existing social conditions. Let the ruling classes tremble at a Communist revolution. The proletarians have nothing to lose but their chains. They have a world to win.³

The events of 1848 agitated the newspapers and the politicians, but, needless to say, there was no attempt at political revolution in the Tory stronghold of Oxford: it was undergoing fall-out from a rather different revolution—an ecclesiastical revolution, most acutely experienced and initially centred in King's own college, Oriel. Indeed, the Oxford Movement—the Catholic Revival in the Church of England—might in its origins, have been termed the 'Oriel Movement,' for that college had nurtured so many of its leaders: John Keble, Edward Pusey, Richard Hurrell Froude, Charles Marriott, and Newman himself had all been Fellows there.

However, by 1848, when King came to Oriel, Froude was dead and Newman had become a Roman Catholic, and only Charles Marriott, the Dean, together with J. W. Burgon and Richard Church were left to hold the fort. Initially, Marriott, a devoted disciple of Newman, had been sorely tempted to follow him to Rome, but in the end, he held fast, and 'throughout those anxious years he never despaired' of the English Church.⁴ Undeniably however, with the loss of Newman, the first robust generation of leaders of the Movement—the Tractarians as they came to be known—had suffered a severe body blow. When Newman left the Church of England in 1845, it only served to confirm the worst suspicions of the Evangelical and Liberal opponents of the Movement that all Tractarians were crypto-papists, and it was only a matter of time before the remaining members would follow in Newman's footsteps, as indeed several of them did.

These ecclesiastical squabbles profoundly disturbed the 'dreaming spires' and academic groves of Oxford throughout the 1840s, while, at the same time the foundations of a rather different kind were being profoundly shaken—the foundations of faith. The year 1848 also saw the publication of a disturbingly influential volume from the pen of John Stuart Mill: his *Principles of Political Economy*. The philosophy of that 'saint of rationalism' was a dominant force in the whole intellectual world of Oxford philosophy, and Mill's mode and scientific method of reasoning presented a serious challenge to the *a priori* dogmatism of much contemporary theology.

Oriel was at the centre of this philosophical, theological and ecclesiastical turmoil, where one of the Fellows, the poet Arthur Hugh Clough, 'was just then agonising himself out of Christianity'; while another, H. J. Coleridge, 'was also agonising himself out of the Church of England' and opting for Rome. 'The pulpits and Common Rooms of Oxford were not silent on the subjects which disturbed men's minds— the authority of the Church, its relations with the State, the limits of doctrine.'[5]

ORIEL COLLEGE AND OXFORD
IN THE EARLY NINETEENTH CENTURY

All this theological and intellectual turmoil needs to be seen in the wider context of the University of Oxford, itself not free from, and yet firmly resisting, the universal clamour for reform in Church and State. Throughout the previous century, Oxford had been in serious decline, not least numerically. Whereas the average annual intake in the 1630s had been five hundred or more, by the mid-eighteenth century this had slumped to a mere one-hundred-and-eighty-two. While we should not take Edward Gibbon's somewhat jaundiced assessment of the Fellows of Magdalen College in the 1750s too seriously, nevertheless in general terms it tallies closely with much that we know from other sources about the decline of the University.

> I spent fourteen months at Magdalen College; they proved the fourteen months the most idle and unprofitable of my whole life ... The schools of Oxford and Cambridge were founded in a dark age of false and barbarous science; and they are still tainted with the vices of their origin ... the government still remains in the hands of the clergy, an order of men whose manners are remote from the present world, and whose eyes are dazzled by the light of philosophy ... In the university of Oxford the greater part of the public professors have for these many years given up altogether even the pretence of teaching ... The fellows or monks of my time were decent easy men who supinely enjoyed the gifts of the founder; their days were filled by a series of uniform employments: the chapel and the hall, the coffee-house and the common room, till they retired, weary and well satisfied, to a long slumber. From the toil of reading, or thinking or writing, they had absolved their conscience ... Their conversation stagnated in a round of college business, Tory politics, personal anecdotes, and private scandal: their dull and deep potations excused the brisk intemperance of youth, and their constitutional toasts were not expressive of the most lively loyalty to the house of Hanover.

Gibbon was there referring to the High Church–Tory alliance which had blossomed from the root of the earlier Caroline Divines. They were still opposed to the so-called 'Glorious Revolution' of 1688–9, which removed the Catholic James II, and to the members of the House of Hanover who succeeded the Stuarts in 1714: throughout the eighteenth century this remained an issue for many churchmen.

Oxford Mentors

And then, almost as an aside, Gibbon commented that assent to the Thirty-Nine Articles as an enforced requirement for entry to the University, was 'signed by more than read and read by more than believe them.'[6]

A consensual view of later historians is summed up by Sir Charles Mallet: 'For a great part of the eighteenth century, Oxford was a world of drab ideals, a small society where disillusioned Jacobites and half-hearted Hanoverians contended with each other, where scholars disinclined for study, encountered teachers as indifferent as themselves, where dreamers found enthusiasm discouraged, education deadened, endowments ill-applied.'[7]

To sum up, the University of Oxford of the eighteenth century and—only marginally reformed—in the first part of the nineteenth century, was a place which saw itself as a conservative rather than an innovative institution, primarily required to provide a 'body of traditional learning on which religious orthodoxy, political and social order were thought to depend. Few imagined that a university ought to be concerned with pure research or disinterested scholarship.'[8] As a Vice-Chancellor at the end of the century put it: 'The sole purposes of our Academical Institutions' are 'maintenance of order, the Advancement of Learning, and the furtherance of Religion and morality.'[9]

R. W. Church, the future distinguished Dean of St Paul's Cathedral, in his masterpiece on the Oxford Movement, written towards the close of his life, had been a Fellow at Oriel when King came up as an undergraduate. Retrospectively, and in less abrasive terms, Church gives us an insider's snapshot of Oxford in King's day:

> Oxford stood by itself in its meadows by the rivers, having its relations with all England but, like its sister at Cambridge, living a life of its own, unlike that of any other spot in England, with its privileged powers, and exemptions from the general law, with its special mode of government and police, its usages and tastes

and traditions, and even costume, which the rest of England looked at from the outside, much interested, but much puzzled.[10]

However, there were already some within the University, and further afield clamouring for reform and for removing the strangle-hold which the established Church, the Tory party and disenchanted Jacobites had upon progress and radical change. Like most institutional reform, when it came, it came not from within the institution itself, where vested interests held powerful sway, but from outside and from a largely unsympathetic Parliament in the shape of the University Reform Acts of 1854 and 1878.

ORIEL COLLEGE AND THE 'NOETICS'

However, in the areas of teaching and scholarship things were beginning to change, and in many respects for the better, by the time young King arrived in Oxford. 'There was a rapid improvement in the quality of teaching and learning, especially in some colleges, most prominently Oriel College, which became a magnet for serious scholars in all disciplines including theology.' The period had also seen 'a series of changes to the union of Church and State which had characterized the old Tory synthesis of throne and altar. The *ancient regime* was increasingly challenged from both inside and outside the Church'[11]. By as early as 1820, Oriel 'had become perhaps the most important centre of learning in England. Competitive fellowship examinations meant that it overshadowed the other colleges in terms of its intellectual standing, setting an example that would soon be emulated by other colleges.'[12]

This had originated under the influence of the Provost, Edward Copleston, elected in 1814, who had initiated some academic reforms. Copleston, and a group of other distinguished Oriel scholars, soon came to be known as the 'Noetics,' a term in Plato's *Republic* that referred to the highest stage of intelligence.

The 'Noetic School,' as the young Samuel Wilberforce called it in 1827 when writing to R. H. Froude during his time at Oriel, would have shared the same Senior Common Room in Oriel as several of the key founding fathers of the Tractarian Movement, to whom the 'Noetics' were strongly opposed, politically and theologically. The 'School' included Richard Whately, Fellow of Oriel from 1811; Edward Hawkins, Copleston's successor as Provost from 1828 and throughout King's time as an undergraduate, and, by no means least, John Davison, Fellow of Oriel from 1800.

It was Davison, with his belief in what came to be termed 'progressive revelation,' who was to have such a great influence on the scientific thinking of Baden Powell, one of the contributors to the controversial liberal 'manifesto' *Essays and Reviews* (1860), which provoked hostility among Evangelicals and Tractarians alike: as so often, a supposed common 'enemy' serving to unite those, who at other times would be on opposing sides. This hostile union provoked bitter polemics from the highly regarded Thomas Arnold, himself a noteworthy 'Noetic,' a Fellow of Oriel from 1815, and, as headmaster of Rugby (from 1828), something of a nationally influential figure.

THE IMPACT OF THOMAS ARNOLD

Arnold was to have a profound and lasting impact, not so much during his time at Oriel but as Headmaster of Rugby, where he exercised his considerable influence on a whole generation of boys who later became prominent leaders in both Church and State. Two of his successors at Rugby—A. C. Tait and Frederick Temple—were to become Archbishops of Canterbury.

Arnold was truly a 'Broad Churchman' in the best sense. He had supported Catholic Emancipation in 1829 and in 1836 he became an early Fellow of the University of London, established, somewhat defiantly and specifically by the Whig government, as a non-denominational institution in opposition to the Anglican strongholds of Oxford, Cambridge and — to a lesser degree — the more recently founded University of Durham.

Ever since Arnold published his *Principles of Church Reform* in 1833, the same year as Keble's Assize Sermon, it had been evident to many that the clamour for reform in the nation would require radical reforms in the life of the Church. 'The Church of England as it now stands, no human power can save,' as Arnold had written to a friend.

In many ways, Arnold was ahead of his time. His analysis of the state of the Church of England called for radical change, both institutionally and theologically. In essence, he argued persuasively for the established Church to become a 'Broad Church' as the forerunner of what would later be termed Liberal Protestantism, even venturing to propose that all sects should be united by Act of Parliament with the Church of England. Not surprisingly, in this way he fell foul of both Evangelicals and Tractarians, many of them Oriel men.

Arnold refers to the Tractarians in a letter as 'exalting the Church and the Sacraments into the place of Christ, as others [Roman Catholics] have exalted Christ's mother, and others, in the same spirit [Jews], exalted circumcision.' (Despite this conviction, Arnold, as we have seen, was always in favour of Catholic Emancipation.)[13]

So, the battle lines were drawn between the 'liberals,' as they were to be termed, and the 'traditionalists' who, in reaction against the rising tide of Erastianism, militant liberalism and the encroaching secularism, looked back to a supposed golden age of faith — the faith of the Fathers once and for all delivered to the saints. In rebuttal, Newman, in his *Apologia*

Oxford Mentors

pro Vita Sua, repeatedly regards liberalism, specifically of the Arnold variety, as the great enemy and Arnold himself as the prime exemplar of that detested ideology. In one famous line, Newman, like many who claim to have a monopoly of the title 'Christian,' went so far as to ask rhetorically whether Arnold could even be considered a Christian.[14]

ORIEL COLLEGE AND THE OXFORD MOVEMENT

So, within the same hallowed walls of the same Oriel College, and in those same early decades of the nineteenth century, history rightly takes note of another, very different 'school' of thought from that of Arnold and the 'Noetics,' in the formation of the Oxford Movement, or Tractarian Movement, with its *Tracts for the Times* (somewhat akin to today's 'blogs,' only much longer and distinctly more learned), written and distributed throughout the country. If we are to begin to understand the measure and upheaval which this so-called Oxford Movement occasioned, and the vicious and politicized battles of the later Anglo-Catholic movement, in which King was to become embroiled, we need to recapture something of the intense and introspective Oxford scene of its genesis.

Oxford, 'that sweet city with her dreaming spires' (in Matthew Arnold's phrase) was essentially a small town.

> The 1831 census reported it as containing only 20,649 persons in total, of whom not many more than a thousand or so can have been undergraduates together with about seven hundred 'dons' of one kind or another (not many of them engaged in teaching). Oxford University was in 1830 one of England's only two universities. (London University, which effectively began with its 'godless institution in Gower Street' was not statutorily recognized as a university until 1836). Furthermore, no student could matriculate and receive

formal acceptance for a course of study leading to a degree, without first subscribing to the Thirty-Nine Articles of Religion of the Church of England. Then again, nearly all the dons were clergymen, of whom all but the heads of houses, masters of colleges and 'halls,' as well as some professors would have been required to be outwardly celibate, while the majority of the undergraduates who were there to work rather than to play, would have been initially intending to become clergymen.[15]

Richard Church, who was a Fellow at Oriel during the upheavals attending the Oxford Movement, pulls no punches as to how petty and ingrown much of the life of Oxford was in the years when King lived there, first as an undergraduate and later as a Professor and Canon of Christ Church. He writes:

> Oxford was a place where everyone knew his neighbour, and measured him, and was more or less friendly or repellent; where the customs of life brought men together every day and all day, in converse or discussion; and where every fresh statement or every new step taken furnished endless material for speculation or debate in common rooms or the afternoon walk. And for this reason, too, feelings were apt to be more keen and intense and personal than in the larger scenes of life; the man who was disliked or distrusted was so close to his neighbours that he was more irritating than if he had been obscured by a crowd; the man who attracted confidence and kindled enthusiasm, whose voice was continually in men's ears, and whose private conversation and life was something ever new in its sympathy and charm, created in those about him not mere admiration, but passionate friendship, or unreserved discipleship. And these feelings passed from individuals into parties ... Men struck blows and loved and hated in those days in Oxford as they hardly did on the wider stage of London politics or general religious controversy.

Oxford Mentors

At the time of writing this, Church had spent several years 'on the wider stage of London' as Dean of St Paul's, in stark contrast to the introspective culture of his Oxford days, when theological conflicts 'for a time turned Oxford into a kind of image of what Florence was in the days of Savonarola, with its nicknames, Puseyites, and Neomaniacs, and High and Dry.'[16]

It is only against such a claustrophobic, cultural background that the great storm which the Oxford Movement occasioned begins to make any sense to the quite different and much more secularized Oxford and Church of our own day.

The increasingly articulate cries for the reform of the Church, like those of Thomas Arnold and the 'Noetics,' were beginning to appear to be only too reasonable to many thinking people, not least at a time when the cry for 'reform,' in Church and State alike was gathering populist momentum. But in the case of the Church of England, the burning question was by whom should such reforms be undertaken and what form should they take? What would reform mean for the Church of England as by Law Established, and for whom the monarch of the day was constitutionally the supreme governor?

At a time when the Convocations of the Church did not meet to formulate any legislation that could lead to internal reform, and when there were no such bodies as Synods to undertake any strategic reorganization, it is little wonder that Parliament stepped in. In the 1832 Reform Act, Parliament had sought, among other things, to abolish so-called 'rotten boroughs,' so it was not such a far cry for the same constitutional body to deal with the massively over-large number of dioceses in the Church of Ireland, which is precisely what they proceeded to do the following year in the Irish Church Temporalities Act, which at the stroke abolished ten of the twenty-two Irish bishoprics and removed parish clergy who had no parishioners.

From the perspective of the likes of Pusey and Keble, such a parliamentary initiative was an outrage, leading them to assert that papal supremacy, overturned at the Reformation, was increasingly heading for replacement by Parliamentary and State supremacy. For many, not least Arnold and those of a similar mindset, it might not appear totally unreasonable for reform in the state Church, established by law, to be spearheaded by Parliament, in which two archbishops and nineteen diocesan bishops had seats and a vote in the House of Lords, while all MPs in the House of Commons had not only to be baptized members of the Established Church, but also subscribers to the Thirty-Nine Articles of Religion as set out in the Book of Common Prayer of 1662.

On 14 July 1833, while the Irish Church Bill was still under discussion, but before it had passed into law, John Keble preached against it in a famous sermon in the University Church. As Newman later recorded in his *Apologia pro Vita Sua*, 'Mr Keble preached the Assize Sermon in the University Pulpit. It was published under the title of *National Apostasy*. I have ever considered and kept the day as the start of the religious movement of 1833.'

'Touch not mine anointed and do my prophets no harm' was the clarion call of John Keble's text as, uncharacteristically for a man of such eirenic character, he launched into a measured attack on Parliament, which had not only seized the initiative in exercising what it saw as its right to reform the State in 1832 but was now planning to reform the Church as well. Newman remonstrated that if 'a nation which had for centuries acknowledged, as an essential part of its theory of government, that, as a Christian nation, she is also a part of Christ's Church, and bound, in all her legislation and policy, by the fundamental laws of the Church,' then, when 'a Government and people, so constituted, threw off the restraint which in many respects such a principle would impose upon them, nay, disavowed the principle itself,' it must be confronted as a 'direct disavowal of the sovereignty of God.'[17]

In a letter from Cuddesdon in 1868, King somewhat forcefully, and also somewhat out of character, was to echo succinctly the core of Keble's message, when he unequivocally affirms that 'the Church holds its powers from our Blessed Lord, not from the Queen or Parliament, and no man can take them away.'[18]

THE TRACTARIANS

But, by the time that King came up to Oriel in 1848, the 'Newmania' of the previous years was waning. Only three years earlier Newman had been received into the Church of Rome, while Keble, only three years after the Assize Sermon, left Oxford for the quieter life in the country parish of Hursley. Yet ecclesiastical and party strife was still all too evident, and not least at Oriel where the young King would need to find some sure footing if he were to maintain the inner life and discipline he had adopted during his time with John Day and in a very different environment.

Even at this early stage in his life, it might have been increasingly clear to him that the answer to all the current controversies and warring rivalries lay not in any one of the parties represented by the various religious and prominent personalities of the time, but rather in the pursuit of a personal 'holiness of life' which transcended all who might claim exclusive orthodoxy as the property of any one branch of the Christian Church.

In many respects, it was the quest for that holiness of life which had been at the centre of John and Charles Wesley's way of life during their time at Oxford, emerging as it ultimately did in the Methodist revival. It is perhaps not insignificant, therefore, that during his years as Bishop of Lincoln King went out of his way to befriend the Methodists who were such a strong force numerically and spiritually in Lincolnshire, the Wesley boys' home county, where their father had been the Rector of Epworth. Furthermore, the Evangelical revival within the Church of England at the end of the eighteenth century, notably with Charles Simeon in Cambridge, had ushered in a Christ-centred and spiritually disciplined way of life with a strong social conscience typified in the likes of William Wilberforce and the Clapham Sect, who mobilized their political and financial resources to bring about the abolition of slavery and other social reforms. It is also worth noting that the second generation of that earlier Evangelical awakening in people like Bishop Samuel Wilberforce and his brother Robert, together with Newman, who initially was also of the more Evangelical persuasion and in pursuit of that same holiness of life, or 'perfection' as Wesley termed it, moved on to become part of the whole Catholic revival in the Church of England. It is as though both the Evangelical awakening of the eighteenth century as well as the Catholic revival of the nineteenth, are but two branches of the same tree, radically drawing from the same sap of holiness of life—a renewed life of the Spirit—both alike working to bring about impressive social reforms, together with a genuine care and compassion for the poor and underprivileged. Only later, as entrenched 'parties,' did they become aggressively opposed to one another, with both alike degenerating into various forms of fundamentalism—the former in respect of scriptural inerrancy and the latter in respect of ritual formalism and an ingrained traditionalism.

ORIEL MENTORS

It was this call to holiness of life which was authentically affirmed for King in his encounter with three major personalities, all alike resident at Oriel during his undergraduate years. Although the glory of the early days of the Tractarian

Oxford Mentors

Movement had clearly gone, yet there were three Fellows who embodied, both in their teaching and in their way of life, the core principles of the Movement and who, in differing ways, would have been formative in the development of the young Edward. They were J. W. Burgon, later to become Dean of Chichester; Richard Church, later Dean of St Paul's; and the eccentric, scholarly and holy Charles Marriott.

John William Burgon (1813–88) was King's tutor—*in loco parentis*, as it was termed in those days. He was a somewhat rigid churchman of the 'High and Dry' school of the previous century, and although he readily embraced the witness of the Tractarians, in later life, as Vicar of the University Church from 1863, and subsequently as Dean of Chichester, he hardened his stance and sought his identity in what he was opposed to, rather than in what he affirmed. With his considerable scholarship he defended the Mosaic authorship of Genesis and biblical inerrancy in general. 'Either, with the best and wisest of all ages, you must believe *the whole* of Holy Scripture; or, with the narrow-minded infidel, you must *dis*believe the whole. There is no middle course open to you.'[19]

He dismissed the work of the scholars Westcott and Hort, and in particular the part they played in producing the Revised Standard Version of the Bible, as well as, and even more vehemently, all the interpretation of scripture by the authors of *Essays and Reviews*. Burgon was equally adamant in his opposition to the proposals later in the century for a new Lectionary for the Church of England. Not surprisingly, he openly opposed the nomination of the liberal Dean Stanley of Westminster to be the Select Preacher in the University of Oxford, and opposed in Convocation any toleration in respect of ritual and liturgy, as the Tractarian Movement evolved towards the end of his life.

Although he would undoubtedly have admired the disciplined and celibate life of his tutor, King most certainly did not have that rigidity and reactionary spirit which is always so unattractive. Throughout his own life King continued to struggle with all the new learning and the radically critical biblical scholarship coming out of Europe. Yet it is clear from the content of his Quiet Day addresses prior to the Lambeth Conference of 1897, and elsewhere, that he found a way of reading scripture which transcended, while continuing to take cognisance of the scholarship of men like Westcott and Hort, who in 1881 published their celebrated critical edition of the Greek New Testament.

Indeed, it was scholarship together with the balanced piety of Richard Church which would also have undergirded King's emerging vocation, marking out both the middle course (so despised by Burgon) in matters of biblical criticism, as well as the 'middle way' of Andrewes and the Caroline Divines. The Preface to the Book of Common Prayer of 1662 is explicit from the outset about this often despised 'Middle Way'—'It hath been the Wisdom of the Church of *England*, ever since the first compiling of her Publick Liturgy, to keep the mean between the two extremes, of too much stiffness in refusing, and of too much easiness in admitting any variation from it.'

Richard Church's balanced and visionary account of the Oxford Movement was published posthumously in 1891. He died in December 1890, having lived just long enough to see the concluding decision in King's favour in the Lincoln Judgment the previous month. As one of the triumvirate of King's mentors at Oriel, Church remained fondly in King's memory, and throughout his years as Bishop of Lincoln, he always kept a photograph of Church on his study desk.[20]

Church shared with the great Tractarians of the earlier period a primary concern for the core doctrines of Catholicism and the Church of the Fathers, but sat lightly, as indeed did Newman, Keble and Pusey, to the niceties of worship and to the more elaborate liturgical expressions of the later Anglo-Catholic movement. It is important, even at this early stage in King's development, to note that this Tractarian influence never left him. He explicitly pointed out in his Quiet Day addresses of 1897, that an over-emphasis on ritualism is always in danger of obscuring the substance within the outward forms, with the accompanying tendency to degenerate into a hollow shell of formalism—'Unless we make the externals of religion more and more subservient to promote the reality and power of it ... the mere external enjoyment of ritual is, in truth, only a modern form of Epicureanism—in fact materialism.'[21]

Much of this tension will be highlighted when we come to the trial of Bishop King in the Lincoln Judgment of 1890.

From the perspective of what one might call 'the London set'—the world of Dean Stanley, Disraeli and London's gentlemen's clubs—King would never have been regarded as being in the mainstream of Church politics. Yet it was his evident holiness and authenticity of life which had the greater and more lasting influence, far beyond that of other distinguished, more learned and better-known names of that period. But then, such is the way in which, throughout history and the whole narrative of change and transformation, it is the many who are generally speaking influenced by the few, as the few are influenced by the one. Such is the dynamism and secret of King's amazing and lasting impact upon the wider Church—a life of unbounding and formative influence, yet which at the outset was paradoxically hidden and, most certainly and elusively self-effacing. In many ways, it is precisely that energy and dynamic influence which, among other features, this biography is seeking to unravel.

CHARLES MARRIOTT

Of King's three mentors at Oriel, it was Charles Marriott, who more than any other single person had the deepest and most lasting influence on King. Eccentric, a profound scholar, a devoted disciple of Newman, but above all holy, Marriott was the son of the Revd John Marriott, sometime Student of Christ Church and later Rector of Church Lawford, in Warwickshire. Charles's mother died when he was only ten, and an aunt took over his upbringing. Four years later his father died and the orphaned Charles was sent for a few weeks as a day boy to Rugby School, but was soon transferred, as a private pupil, to the care of Andrew Burn, his father's former curate. Burn had a profound influence on his young pupil, not unlike that of John Day on the teenage King. In a personal memoir, his brother John recalls that 'In the last days of his life, Charles always looked up to Mr Burn as having been a second Father to him.'[22]

There is a further striking resemblance here between the young Charles Marriott and the young Edward King. Marriott, like King, was not robust in health, and so was not sent away to a public school. 'His health was always delicate, and I think it is very doubtful whether he could have borne the roughness and exposure incident to a more public education,' his brother records.[23] Again, like King, he was not only taught by his father's curate but, when the latter left the parish, Marriott went with him to Kynnersley in Shropshire, where Burn was first curate and then rector of the parish: as we have seen, King made a similar journey to Shropshire to continue under the tutelage of John Day. Marriott and King, therefore, had a good deal in common before ever they met at Oriel—Tractarian piety, similar health problems, and a comparable pattern of education. Both men, moreover, were to exemplify the typical Tractarian concern for the needs of the poor, both spiritual and material.

Indeed, Marriott devoted much time and energy to raising money to found a 'College for poor Scholars at Oxford,' and only his early death in 1858 prevented the completion of this project. Furthermore, he canvassed a fair-trade scheme, which would give more equitable terms to smaller Oxford traders in their purchase of supplies. These ventures may well be thought of as merely well-intentioned but impractical idealism, yet Marriott's own simple lifestyle and generous private charity are evidence of his genuine commitment to those in need. His labours among the sick when Oxford was stricken with a smallpox epidemic were outstanding, and exemplified that holiness of heart and life which would have made a powerful impression on King, who in his later ministry did precisely the same (at the risk of his own life) for the victims of cholera.

Marriott also had a lively sense of humour, which would have resonated with King, and, according to his brother, even in his prolonged final illness his cheerfulness never left him.

Marriott's influence on undergraduates generally is amply attested to by his contemporaries. In 1841, Newman had described him as 'a grave, sober, and deeply religious person … having more influence with younger men than anyone perhaps of his standing.' Dean Church makes clear that, even before he became a senior member of the University, Marriott's influence was remarkable. 'As an undergraduate and a young bachelor, he had attained, without seeking it, a position of almost unexampled authority in the junior University world that was hardly reached by any one for many years at least after him.'[24]

> His health was weak, and a chronic tenderness of throat and chest made him take precautions which sometimes seemed whimsical; and his well-known figure in a black cloak, with a black veil over his college cap, and a black comforter around his neck, which at one time in Oxford acquired his name, sometimes startled little boys and sleepy college porters when he came on them suddenly at night.

Clearly, Marriott was, in many ways, the classic eccentric don.

> His breakfast parties in his own room were things to have seen—a crowd of undergraduates, finding their way with difficulty amid lanes and piles of books,

amid a scarcity of chairs and room, and the host, perfectly unconscious of anything grotesque, sitting silent during the whole meal, but perfectly happy, at the head of the table.

Yet it is abundantly clear that it was his holiness of life which impressed his contemporaries, dons and undergraduates alike. Dean Church gives over one whole chapter to him in his classic account of the Oxford Movement, remarking not only on Marriott's eccentricities in appearance—'shy, outlandish in dress'—but without reservation claiming Marriott to be 'unmistakably, a saint.'

> There was no claimant on his purse or his interest who was too strange for his sympathy—raw freshmen, bores of every kind, broken-down tradesmen, old women, distressed foreigners, converted Jews, all the odd and helpless wanderers from beaten ways, were to be heard at Marriott's rooms.[25]

Throughout his life King frequently mentioned Marriott's holiness and goodness, perhaps most impressively in his addresses to the bishops at the 1897 Lambeth Conference,[26] where he reminisces about the debt he owed to Marriott, not only as a scholar but also as an exemplary Christian, pastor and mentor: 'If I have any good in me, I owe it to Charles Marriott. He was the most Gospel-like man I have ever met.'[27]

Marriott was also one of the finest patristic scholars in Oxford, deeply immersed in editing the Library of the Fathers, the series initiated by Newman and Pusey. Yet no matter how busy Marriott might be with his scholarly labours, he was always reluctant to turn away anyone who called on him for help or advice.

'The man of saintly life,' as Dean Burgon once dubbed him, soon came to recognize the new undergraduate's quality, and exclaimed enthusiastically, 'King is a royal fellow.'[28] King took equally readily to Marriott, who in 1841 had returned to Oriel after three years absence as the first Principal of the recently founded theological college at Chichester. Marriott's pastoral sympathy and impressive spirituality left an indelible mark on King, who almost half a century after encountering Marriott at Oriel, could write: 'Our aim, then, is to be Christ-like Christians. This endeavour to set the life of Christ before ourselves as a practical guide of life, as a pattern for the formation of our own character, was first definitely brought home to me by the example of Charles Marriott.'[29]

King saw in him a genuine Tractarian sanctity, rooted in ascesis and a 'discipline unto holiness.'

Yet for Marriott, ascesis did not imply gloom, as it tended to do for Newman, Pusey and Liddon. To say that cheerfulness kept breaking in would be a superficial view of Marriott's spirituality. Rather there was within him a spring of joy welling up continually, as fresh as it was inexhaustible. So with Edward King, in whose speaking and writings joy was never far away, and whose letters in particular sparkle with humour. Joy, second only to love as a 'fruit of the Spirit,' both of which King had in abundance, distinguished him from the introspective Pusey, and also from Newman.

Von Hügel claims incisively that it is precisely 'spiritual joy' which distinguishes the saint from the saintly—the canonized from the beatified, if you like—commenting on how he 'used to wonder,' in his frequent conversations with Newman, 'how one so good and who had made so many sacrifices to God, could be so depressing,' even asserting that 'Newman could indeed be beatified,—saintly though undoubtedly he was, though not canonized as a "saint."'[30]

Another lesson King learned from Marriott was the importance of forming a personal, pastoral relationship with undergraduates and those preparing for ordination—that 'genius for friendship' which was to become so characteristic of King' ministry. King would have seen in Marriott a striking testimony to the truth that there is no unvarying law by which profound learning must turn a man into a remote and ineffectual don. Richard Church describes him as 'naturally a man of metaphysical mind, given almost from a child to abstract and indeed abstruse thought,' who nevertheless remained 'a man with many friends of different sorts and ways, and of boundless though undemonstrative sympathy.'[31]—all of which was so demonstrably evident in King's own life and ministry.

Church further adamantly claimed that Marriott 'was by disposition, averse to anything like party, and the rough and sharp proceedings which party action sometimes seems to make natural. He might easily under different conditions have become a divine of the type of F. D. Maurice.'[32]

If we are ever to begin to understand King's amazing appeal, especially in later life, to those of very differing theological and ecclesiastical persuasions, it is precisely this 'aversion to anything like party,' with its attendant exclusive claims to orthodoxy, which rendered that attractive and winsome characteristic to his ministry. Indeed, it is the inability to 'box' or 'label' King with any particular party which gives him that freedom of spirit to respond to, rather than to react against, the challenges of new scholarship, be it biblical criticism or new scientific and philosophical learning. King seems never to fall into the trap of reactionary paranoia, or of seeking to retreat into some kind of intellectual citadel of dogmatic certainty.

Such transparent openness and holiness of life is always conspicuous and contagious, touching and transforming the lives of others, albeit unselfconsciously, with an influence which survives the test of time. 'The soul,' writes the Franciscan, Richard Rohr, 'needs living models to grow and, quite precisely, we need exemplars with the expansive energies of love. In Scholastic philosophy, we called them, "exemplary causes." People who are eager to love, change us at the deeper levels; they alone seem able to open the field of both mind and heart at the same time.'[33] We see such 'exemplary causes' in both Marriott and King, who as teachers and pastors were able to open 'the field of both heart and mind.'

For the last word in communicating the Gospel is not so much from the preacher's pulpit as from the everyday lives of ordinary people who by their actions and lifestyle authenticate the truth of the Christian faith. History consistently attests: 'The Gospel is primarily communicated by highly symbolic human lives that operate as "Prime Attractors" through actions visibly done in love; by a non-violent, humble and liberated lifestyle.'[34] Clearly Marriott was for many such a 'prime attractor,' who by his pastoral sympathy and deep spirituality made a profound and lasting impression on King.

During King's first year at Oriel, Marriott published a little book called *Hints on Private Devotion* which 'contains a sober grave devotion of mind, elevated by a sense of the unseen world, and a hidden music praising God all about us.' So, suggests Owen Chadwick, 'perhaps King's debt lay in such a type of quality of devotion.'[35] Clearly King's outstanding pastoral care and love overflowed from such an inner life of prayer, constantly aware of God's imminent as well as transcendent presence at all times and in all places.

In a long unqualified tribute, Richard Church concludes that Marriott's great contribution to the Oxford Movement 'was his solid, simple goodness, his immovable hope, his confidence that things would come right,'[36] even after the debacle of 1845 with the loss of Newman. His 'deep, unpretending matter-of-course godliness and goodness' truly and lastingly conquered Edward King, not only during his undergraduate days but throughout the rest of his life and ministry.

BROTHERHOOD OF THE HOLY TRINITY

Whatever the young Edward King had learned from John Day about personal piety and spiritual discipline before coming up to Oxford was further endorsed and developed by a significant organization founded in Oxford in the 1840s. Called the Brotherhood of the Holy Trinity, it was a kind of union of like-minded spirits, bound together in a community of prayer and committed to a Rule of Life. Such groupings, brotherhoods or fellowships of prayer had existed for some time since the Holy Club of the Wesleys in the eighteenth century, whose membership sought to pursue a rule of life including study, prayer and almsgiving.

The Brotherhood of the Holy Trinity is part of the forgotten history of the Tractarian Movement. Only finally dissolved in 1932, in its early days it numbered among a small membership some significant names: Henry Parry Liddon, a one-time colleague and life-time friend of King; Richard Meux Benson, founder of the Society of St John the Evangelist, fondly known as the Cowley Fathers; William John Butler, later to become Dean of Lincoln at the outset of King's episcopacy there; Charles Lowder, the ritualist and saintly East-End Anglo-Catholic priest, and, more particularly for our purposes, Edward King, freshly up at Oxford from Ellesmere.

The Brotherhood owed its origins to an earlier and somewhat different society, the Brotherhood of St Mary. This had been founded on 18 December 1844 at Trinity College, in the rooms of Edward Augustus Freeman (a future Regius Professor of Modern History in the University), with the explicit intention of studying art and architecture on what was defined as 'true and Catholic principles.'[37] The little Brotherhood is significant in so far as it belongs to that general renewal and revival of interest in medieval art and architecture which was one of several expressions of the emerging Romantic movement with its nostalgia for everything medieval. Much of this harping back to an earlier, supposedly 'golden age' of beauty and form, was replicated during the century in the architecture of the Gothic revival. The whole Romantic movement in art, literature, poetry and architecture (and less obviously in the spirituality of the Oxford Movement) was motivated by a reaction against the mechanization of the industrial revolution, and was to find expression later in the century in the Arts and Crafts Movement of William Morris and Edward Burne-Jones, perhaps most typically and gloriously exemplified in the windows and architecture of that magnificent 'Cathedral of the Arts and Crafts Movement,' as John Betjeman dubbed Holy Trinity, Sloane Street, in Chelsea.

However, in 1845, when eight new members joined, the aims, direction and ethos of the Brotherhood were changed, turning an artistic theological society into one with a more devotional character. Frederick Meyrick, a founding member of the newly reconstituted brotherhood (who, incidentally, had also fallen under the spell of Marriott), tells us what lay behind this change of direction, how 'having exhausted our subjects, or getting tired of them, we determined to bring the society to a close; but it occurred to some of us that the nucleus thus formed might be useful to another purpose.'

'Many young men,' he continued, 'came up to the University from pious homes and well taught at their schools, who found themselves solitary and lonely in their various colleges, and ran the risk of being absorbed into the idle or noisy set to be found in each college. It was thought that these men might be gathered up, and that they might find in a body of sympathizing elders a strength to resist the various temptations to which they were exposed. The members, therefore, of the [original] society who were especially interested in architecture withdrew, and the others set out on their new quest.'[38]

It was at this point, in 1845, that Pusey, as the champion of everything Tractarian after the departure of Newman to Rome, was requested to draw up the outline of a Rule for this newly re-constituted, devotional society, renamed the Brotherhood of the Holy Trinity, taking the form of a semi-monastic religious society whose members were united by a common rule of life. Pusey was the obvious man for this task, since coincidentally he 'was at this time engaged in the institution and establishment of sisterhoods, and he grasped at this application, which he thought might be utilized for the institution of brotherhoods also.'[39]

Having joined the Brotherhood in his early days at Oriel, King remained a member until after becoming a bishop—his name appears in the roll of the Brethren up to 1888—so clearly membership was important and significant for him, on several fronts.

In the first place the Rule represents the core spirituality of Catholic Anglicanism, setting theological study within the wider context of a disciplined inner life, nurtured by personal prayer, scripture and the sacraments and issuing in simplicity of life, service in the community (especially caring for the needs of the poor), and the tithing of income 'for God's service.' The Rule explicitly impressed the need to 'rise an hour before the time of Morning Chapel, with a view to devoting the interval to private prayers.' As for Sacramental Confession, that perennial bone of contention for critics of the Catholic revival in Anglicanism, the Rule as devised by Pusey was totally in accordance with the teaching of the Book of Common Prayer and the Anglican tradition generally, by advising its use, and the opening of one's 'grief to a priest,' only 'if the conscience be troubled.'[40]

Yet, King's membership of the Brotherhood is important for more far-reaching reasons. It is that nurturing through personal prayer and the inner life of the Spirit, early in the morning before formal worship, which was to characterize his own distinctive spirituality and the spirituality he was to encourage later throughout his entire ministry, both at Cuddesdon, for his ordinands, as well as for all who came to him for spiritual direction. For King, it is the inner life of the spirit for which the outward expressions of form and ritual are there to serve, and nourish. These will vary at different times and with different temperaments, requiring

Oxford Mentors

flexibility rather than an imposed and over-systematized rigidity: there is nothing forced, cloned or imposed in King's understanding or practice of Christian formation.

In his undergraduate diaries, and while a Student at Christ Church, H. P. Liddon, who was the same age as King, makes frequent mention of the Brotherhood and tells us that he was admitted as a member on 23 November 1848—during King's first term at Oriel.[41] So, was it Liddon who urged the new and godly undergraduate of Oriel, to whom he was to have a life-long devotion, to join with him and become a member? We cannot be certain. What is certain, however, is that Liddon and King, though very different, were later to become not only colleagues on the staff at Cuddesdon, but also life-long friends.

From the outset Liddon had been somewhat outspoken about various details in the Rule which Pusey devised. Initially, the zealous Pusey proposed that the young men should walk around 'with their eyes turned to the ground to avoid temptations and as mark of humility'—'custody of the eyes,' as the practice was fondly termed. Meyrick objected that 'such a practice was not natural for young men, nor good for them.' But Pusey had even gone even further, proposing that as a mark of membership 'we should all wear round our loins a girdle of flannel or other material as token of self-restraint.'[42] On being told of this suggestion by Meyrick, William Basil Jones, a future Bishop of St David's, retorted 'demurely': 'you will no doubt call yourselves the Worshipful Company of Girdlers.'[43] (As for keeping one's eyes on the ground, that might be seemly for an Oxford Quad, but it would hardly have been practicable for the likes of Lowder as a parish priest in the East End of London.)

Neither of these 'over the top' suggestions were adopted, but, on Pusey's recommendation, the members did accept 'the name of the Brotherhood of the Holy Trinity and some simple suggestions which might help us towards a good life, such as that we should rise early, use prayer, public and private, be moderate in food and drink, and avoid speaking evil of others.'[44]

Predictably, this was far too vague and not strict enough for the likes of Liddon and Benson. Later, as Vice-Principal at Cuddesdon, Liddon taught and imposed on others, as well as practising himself, a far more regimented way of life. Indeed, it was this very need for control and enforced spiritual practices which brought about Liddon's removal from Cuddesdon at the same time as King was appointed chaplain, and subsequently Principal.

In some respects, like the Holy Club of the Wesleys, the Brotherhood of the Holy Trinity encouraged holiness of life, an 'inner holiness,' or, to use Wesley's phrase, 'inward Christianity as opposed to outward and conventional religion.' Wesley saw religion as 'a constant ruling habit of soul; a renewal of our minds in the image of God, a recovery of the divine likeness.'[45] The Holy Club, formed in 1729, while John Wesley was a Fellow of Lincoln College, encouraged dons as well as students to live under some kind of a General Rule (initially drawn up by Wesley), which in several respects, such as 'early rising for personal prayer and frequent Communion,' bears similarities to the Rule of the Brotherhood of the Holy Trinity. In short, 'the underlying ideals of the Oxford Methodists at least in Wesley's eyes were intended to reflect a total imitation of Christ,'[46] — or, to use a consistent and recurring phrase of King's, to become more 'Christ-like Christians.'

In a sermon entitled 'The Circumcision of the Heart,' which Wesley preached in Oxford in 1733, he set out his ideal of 'Christian perfection,' seen as the goal and end to which all the disciplines of a Christian lifestyle and discipleship should point and lead.[47]

In the Oxford of the Wesleys and the Oxford of King, such a disciplined life and commitment would be held in ridicule: 'enthusiasm' in matters religious was taboo. Predictably, the Holy Club acquired a variety of nicknames, mostly derisory, especially from Christ Church and Merton men: names such as 'Enthusiasts,' 'Sacramentarians' (because of Wesley's practice of frequent communion), 'The Reforming Club' and the 'Godly Club.' There is always the danger in such clubs, brotherhoods or communities of fostering a rather forced, elitist and self-conscious ascetic—indeed, an 'earnestness,' to use another taboo word at that time—of which King could never be accused. He, unlike Liddon and certainly Pusey, never lost that freedom of the spirit, that 'playfulness' and joy, while still pursuing an interior discipline of life.

Undoubtedly, it was a suspicion of lurking 'earnestness' that prompted the somewhat stiff remarks of Provost Hawkins of Oriel, at the end of King's first term, during the formal interview known as Collections: 'I observe, Mr King, that you have never missed a single chapel, morning or evening, during the whole term. I must warn you, Mr King, that even too regular attendance at chapel may degenerate into formalism.'[48]

Edward Hawkins, who, in Newman's opinion, could be 'dry and unbending,' was known for casting around for a word of warning and rebuke for every undergraduate, even the most exemplary. Yet there may have been more to this incident than the professional astringency of Oriel's Provost. Was Hawkins still smarting from the recollection of the Tractarian spell which Newman, Froude and Robert Wilberforce, all of whom eventually went over to Rome, had previously cast over a whole generation of Oriel men? From Hawkins' perspective, could it be that a similar unfortunate chapter would be replicated if King were to fall under the spell of the hugely influential Tractarian, Charles Marriott?

Whatever the reason behind the Provost's somewhat acerbic remark, there is no sign that it had the slightest effect on King's pattern of devotion. If Hawkins thought of him as a sanctimonious introvert, he was very wide of the mark, for King was a keen sportsman, a lover of the open air, and certainly no pale *dévot*.

Edward King

King had always been keen on dancing, riding, fishing and swimming long before going up to Oriel, nevertheless, during his couple of years when, as a teenager he had worked with John Day, he would have learned and observed the disciplines of the church as outlined and ordered by the Book of Common Prayer, such as being absent from meals in Hall on the days assigned in the Prayer Book for abstinence and fasting—a practice, along with others, he continued to observe during his time at Oriel. His attendance at chapel, required though seldom enforced except on special days, was exemplary. A contemporary college friend confirms this, recording how he used to have many a pleasant afternoon's walk with Edward King,

> but he would never consent to go with you unless you promised to be back for Chapel-time, which was 4.30pm. I myself spent a good deal of my afternoon recreation-time on the river and was also a member of the College Cricket Club; but I cannot remember King ever joining in either of those pursuits. He may indeed have done so, but his strict rule about afternoon Chapel would have made boating difficult, and cricket quite impossible, as our cricket-ground at that time was on Bullingdon Common, some way out of Oxford over Magdalen Bridge.[49]

While maintaining this pattern of disciplined piety, King retained his countryman's enthusiasm for walking, riding and swimming. His obituary in the *Oriel Record* recalls that, 'As an undergraduate he was known as a good rider and as fond of fencing. A contemporary speaks of him as having a slight stoop, rather noticeable in a young man, which he retained through life, and as being exceptionally refined in manner and of a somewhat retiring disposition.'[50] The refined manner and retiring disposition may have been partly due to his education at home in the sheltered atmosphere of a devout clerical family, but there is no doubt that they were also innate.

Oxford Mentors

There is also recorded an occasion when King walked out of a college 'wine' at the singing of a bawdy song.[51] (The Rule of the Brotherhood specifically encouraged its members to 'shun all unedifying and frivolous conversation.') To mention such an event and to leave it at that would inevitably lead to portraying the young Edward as a somewhat stuffy and even intense young man, self-consciously 'witnessing to his faith.' Thankfully, we also have on record something by way of balance from a contemporary in another college: 'The first time I ever met Edward King was, oddly enough, in passing through the lock at Iffley. Someone in our boat knew him and saluted him by name,' while yet another contemporary, who entered Oriel just as King was leaving, said: 'I can only remember being greatly impressed by the singularly high-estimation in which his character was held by all sorts and conditions of men.'[52] Such respect from one's peers is never easily attained. Quietly, but firmly to refuse to go with the crowd or to stand out against trends of any kind—whether ethical or otherwise—requires a deep inner strength and security, particularly when done in such a manner as to gain respect rather than ridicule from others whose convictions or practice is otherwise.

The need to witness to one's faith and convictions in simple ways and simple things, without an attitude of self-conscious superiority, as in that event at the 'wine,' foreshadowed the advice he gave to a student at Culham Teacher Training College (founded, like Cuddesdon, by Bishop Wilberforce). In a letter, he urges the student to 'simply get out of the way of bad conversation: go away from it: it is poison and contemptible. Don't stand it but leave the fellows.'[53] That kind of punctilious observance of religious duty can, in no time at all, label a man as a pious prig, especially in a student community. Undergraduates, now as then, are not slow to affix such labels and much worse on anyone who refuses to conform to prevailing culturally accepted norms—the tyranny of conformity.

While there is a goodness and moral rectitude which can be so very unattractive, at the same time, there is another goodness which is winsome and magnetically attractive, with a spontaneity and unselfconscious response to life, which releases in others the highest qualities and most creative instincts. So, with King: paradoxically, it was as though his disciplined life was itself the secret of an inner freedom of spirit which expressed itself with humour, joy and even frivolity.

Later, this aspect of his character was to be of particular importance in so far as he never allowed Cuddesdon, during his there time as Principal, to become a hothouse of clericalism and self-conscious piety. Such characteristics distinguished him from the over-serious and somewhat lugubrious Pusey, or Liddon, who, while Vice-Principal at Cuddesdon, seemed unduly bent on requiring the young ordinands to use the Sacrament of Confession. It was King's rounded humanity which was so very self-authenticating and which throughout his life endeared him to all he encountered, even the gloomy Burgon, who wrote of King, 'He is such a one as the best and holiest were when they were young.'[54]

Yet in all of this, King was certainly not unaware or insensitive: on the contrary, he was sympathetic and extraordinarily alert to the prevailing new doubts and fears and agonies of mind experienced by many of his contemporaries. But he did not share them. His faith, so far as we can tell, was a deep, clear, still pool, the faith of a novice contemplative who has learned a quality of reflection and prayer which go far deeper than merely deductive intellectual exploration, not perhaps so much during these early years, but certainly as the years moved along.

Unlike many churchmen of the time, King does not appear to have kept a diary, apart from a travel-journal in 1852. Nor do we have many significant letters from this period, so inevitably it is one of the least well-documented of his life. From his Oriel days there is a notebook in which he wrote summaries of sermons heard in Oxford, mainly for his tutor's critical eye. It is a rather impersonal little volume, but one from which Professor Chadwick has deftly picked out an entry of some personal interest. One of his tutors, King records, commented: 'Fair. Your sentences are very long and straggling.'[55] It was a lesson which he must have taken to heart, for in later years no one could talk more simply and directly, either in public or in conversation.

However, the directness and simplicity of King's more mature style is already foreshadowed in the one letter which remains from his days at Oriel. Written on 17 July 1851, it was addressed to Richard Davies Williams, son of the Archdeacon of Llandaff. At the time Williams was fighting a battle against ill-health, a battle he finally lost later that same year, on 25 October. King's homely common-sense, his tact and delicacy, his personal warmth, and his highly developed art of thinking and feeling himself in another's mind or 'shoes,' all shine through clearly in this early letter.

> My dear Williams,
> It seems a long while since I heard from you, but perhaps it is my own fault for not writing.
>
> I hope you have been getting quite strong again and intend coming up to Oxford next Term; but I want to tell you what we have done ... Now it occurred to us all that, as you coming up is altogether hypothetical, and as, if you come, it would not be worthwhile to take rooms by yourself, by far the best plan will be to *live with us* and just trot into College of a night. Just think this over quietly. You see we shall all be reading for our Degree, and I really think it would be an advantage to all the parties to be together. You will say, 'Yes, it is very nice, but I should not like to live on my friends.' But, my dear, you shall not have this excuse, for you shall take a share of our expenses, as far as tea, candles, etc., etc.
>
> I really think that it might be a good thing for you, for it would be perfectly quiet and yet we could take

care of you, which after six months at home you will require. It will be *quiet* for we have agreed to preserve our *individuality*, and the rooms are some way apart. By this plan you could come up when you like and go down without any bother of rooms. I need not say that, if you would consent to live in *my* room, I should be delighted, but this is being too selfish; however, you *ought* to know that you are most welcome. Turn it over, and ask Mrs Williams if a warm, cheerful, family circle is not better for you than a *solitary, damp, cold, dreary, hovel* by yourself. Just do—please.

Ever, my dear Williams, your most sincere friend,
EDWARD KING[56]

STUDYING FOR MINISTRY

Out of consideration for his indifferent health and in order not to overtax his strength, and not for any want of academic ability, King had been advised not to read for an honours degree. Instead, he opted for an ordinary or Pass Degree, which he took on 13 November 1851. Throughout his ministry, he was always rather self-consciously aware that he had not taken an honours degree and tended to apologize for this—quite unnecessarily it could be said. For, while King was never primarily an academic, and certainly held no pretensions to scholarship, nevertheless both the breadth and depth of his life's reading would compare favourably with most bishops today. He would always put people before books, and pastoral care before academic achievement: the book he had planned to write during his time as Pastoral Professor remained unwritten. Yet throughout his life and ministry he was very disciplined about his reading and study and persistently commended a similar discipline to his students and as bishop to his clergy.

At Oriel his teachers included D. P. Chase and C. P. Chretien, and it was under their influence that he acquired a lifelong devotion to the works of Plato, Aristotle and Bishop Joseph Butler. The General Course he followed included Classics, Mathematics, Logic, Rhetoric and Biblical Studies. The Lecture Book in Oriel College archives gives details of his studies, term by term. During his three years (1848–51) he read the works of Herodotus, Euripides, Horace and Virgil and other classical authors. In Mathematics, he studied Euclid and Algebra. His Biblical Studies embraced the Old Testament and the Greek texts of St Luke and Acts. Two major works which were to influence his thought and practice, were Aristotle's *Ethics* and Bishop Butler's *Analogy of Religion*. It was a varied, if somewhat eclectic curriculum but certainly not one that could be indicted for narrow specialization.[57]

Many years later, in 1898, King wrote: 'Bishop Butler has been one of my lifelong and most valued companions.'[58] To the end of his life, he used Aristotle's *Ethics* and Plato's *Republic* as textbooks on which he grounded much of his social and moral teaching, combining this with a curiously strong sense of the ethical values of the *Satires* and *Epistles* of Horace.

Throughout his life, it was typical of King to immerse himself in a few seminal authors of the first rank and deepen his knowledge and appreciation of their thought. Dante, whom he read in the original, was already one of his select band; Keble, Wordsworth and Bishop Sailer would be added in due course. The man who would later advise his students to plan their reading as if they were going to live another forty years, maintained his own reading steadily and consistently throughout a long and busy life. The tutor and pastor who counselled ordinands never to drop a friendship, was likewise consistently loyal to the minds that had shaped his own. While he never attained profound learning or extensive scholarship, his reading was both deep and discriminating, though—and this is important—not so much for its own sake, as for the sake of broadening his understanding of humanity and informing his work as a pastor and 'lover of souls.' Commenting on this, Owen Chadwick writes, 'never in his life, was he tempted to put an excessive value on examinations as a test of education. He became a much more educated man, in the broad sense, than many with better records in examinations.'[59]

However, in making the case for a broadened education, it should not be assumed that King was one of those who would plead experience in the so-called 'university of life' as a substitute for sustained and serious study after undergraduate days are concluded. On the contrary, he consistently advised his ordinands to be sure to keep up their reading after ordination, not least of contemporary novels, as he himself did. At the same time, he never ceased to read, seriously and extensively, in the fields of theology, history and spirituality. The Doctorate of Divinity, automatically conferred in those days after he was made a bishop, was admittedly honorary, but not in the least incongruous, for by 1885 it can be claimed, with no little justification, that he had become a well-read divine. It may be that having had, *per force*, to lower his academic sights at Oxford, it was precisely that which motivated him with an even greater determination to press on steadily with his reading after going down.

More than twenty years after leaving Oriel, we find King writing to a former Cuddesdon student still in his first curacy, about the place of study in the life and ministry of a priest:

> My own plan, with myself has been never to consider myself likely to do anything in an intellectual way, but I regard reading as a duty to enable one to carry out one's vocation in dealing with the souls of men. In this way it has helped me, and it may you, to go quietly, regularly, laboriously on with intellectual work, regarding it as a means to an end, and hoping rather that God would bless one's well-intentioned, well-regulated efforts

Oxford Mentors

rather than expecting any great result in itself, and keep the labour of reading always by one, and to view it under the shadow of the Cross to read by the lamp of sacrifice; and that not impulsively, but in a spirit of quiet self-devotion.[60]

He would doubtless have readily concurred with some words (whether he knew them or not) of Bernard of Clairvaux, about the relationship between study and ministry which connect very relevantly to King's own teaching and practice:

> There are those who seek knowledge for the sake of knowledge; that is curiosity. There are those who seek knowledge to be known by others; that is vanity. There are those who seek knowledge in order to serve; that is love.

TRAVEL

During King's time as Professor of Pastoral Theology, he gave a lecture at the end of the summer term of 1877 in which he offered some very sound advice—advice which he had clearly applied to himself after leaving Oxford and before seeking ordination.

> Avoid, if possible, rushing straight from University into Holy Orders. Seek rather to learn as much as you can of human nature, by mixing with men and women, studying their characters and learning their needs. Travel, if you can; and, if need be, work at any honourable calling to support yourselves, until you have learned how to reach the hearts of men and women.[61]

And that was precisely what King did: travel first and then take a job for a while, and all for the same end, to 'learn about human nature,' and 'to learn how to reach the hearts of men and women'—the fundamental tools of any pastoral ministry worthy of the name, and one of King's recurring and characteristic themes.

Edward King

During the Victorian era, travel—and for those who could afford it, what was sometimes still called the 'grand tour' (an eighteenth-century invention)—was frequently seen as rounding off a person's education. So, on 3 February 1852, King set out for the Holy Land. Here again, it was not a question of travel for its own sake, but rather to experience that part of the world which had been supremely and uniquely the cradle of the Christian event, as well as to learn about human nature on a broader front.

It appears to have been the first time he had set foot out of England, and he felt his time away from home and friends poignantly. Fortunately, he kept a journal of his travels. At the outset, while crossing the Channel from Folkestone to Boulogne, he was rapidly initiated into the misery of sea sickness. So, we read:

> Feb 4th: We went on board the boat at 8.45am. It was raining and blowing. There were fifteen horses on board, which, as we expected, added greatly to the rolling of the boat; and soon my vain hopes in the powers of saffron—which, according to Mr Day's advice, I had procured in a bag—began to vanish. At first, I stood and talked loud and quick, but soon sat down on a camp-stool and underwent all the horrors of anticipation for about an hour, when the stern reality was no longer to be denied, and I suffered most miserably.[62]

Homesickness was added to sea sickness, and to both also loneliness, for he appears to have travelled alone, at least for most of the time. On 6 February, while staying in a hotel in Lyons, he made the following entry:

> The feelings with which one leaves one's home to wander on the continent for any length of time cannot be understood but by those who have experienced them, and by those they will never be forgotten.[63]

Certainly King himself never forgot. Re-reading this entry nearly half a century later, he wrote, 'Quite true, February

3rd, 1897, i.e. after having been preserved with such exceeding mercy and goodness for forty-five years, how thankful and trustful one ought to be.' Three years later he added another poignant comment against the same entry: 'Yes, this is true more and more, now I am seventy: February 3, 1900. *Deo Gratias.*' The final entry, written in a tremulous hand, was made only a month before he died: 'Yes, again, this is true more and more, now I am eighty. February 3rd, 1910. Verily, his mercy endureth for ever. *Deo gratias.*'[64]

Randolph and Townroe, in their very personal memoir of King, remark aptly on this point: 'These entries show what a profound impression this tour to the Holy Land made upon him; and in his old age, writing to a friend who was contemplating a similar pilgrimage, he says, "It is fifty-five years since I was in the Holy Land, and my visit is still a source of comfort and pleasure to me."'[65]

They might well have added that these references to the providential care of God through all the vicissitudes of the years may point back to a deepened experience of the power and love of God which came to him on his pilgrimage at that time, and therefore why the 3rd of February, the day he started his journey, had such a special and lasting significance, always remembered with thanksgiving until the very end of his life. On that first 3rd of February in 1852 he was still young and very probably alone, leaving England for the first time and was to be away for five months. The strangeness of the experience, the solitude, and the hazards of the journey, may well have combined to produce in a sensitive and devout mind a strengthened trust in the God who not only granted journeying mercies at that point, but would continue them throughout that other journey of a long life and indeed, to the journey's end.

Is it reading too much into this, to attribute to that day—3 February 1852—something of a spiritual awakening, a 'warming of the heart,' in the words of John Wesley, to verbalize a similarly momentous and frequently recalled moment? There is no record of any kind of Damascus road conversion experience in King's life, although the intimate relationship which he clearly enjoyed with God and exuded to others certainly begs some kind of questioning along such lines. To hazard such an insight into that clearly cherished day might be an important factor in seeking to account for the outstanding spiritual gifts with which King was so evidently blessed and which made such an impact on the lives of so many, lay persons and clergy alike.

RETURN HOME

Continuing on his journey, King crossed the Mediterranean, landed at Beirut, and then travelled on horseback southwards along the coast by way of Tyre, Sidon, Acre into Palestine. There he stayed in Jerusalem for some days, while making outings to the Jordan and the Dead Sea. The party returned along the Plain of Esdraelon, through Nazareth and Galilee, and on to Damascus, where King's journal ends abruptly. By June he was back in England, ready to begin a new phase of his life.

While he valued the whole experience, he did not overvalue it, and later commented that the great theological lesson which his visit to the Holy Land and the holy places had brought home to him was precisely that 'our Blessed Lord is not here *as* [i.e. in the same manner or way] He once was. He has been here, He has trod on this earth, His human eyes have looked at all this; but He Himself is now to be sought for in the spiritual world. He is still "very Man and very God" but "He is not here, He is risen."'[66]

King's pilgrimage to the Holy Land was to prove the first of many travels: throughout his life he was an inveterate traveller, for pleasure as well as for furthering his education.

On returning to England, King, at heart still very much a country boy, showed no signs of regret at leaving Oxford, or any lingering nostalgia for the place. The college had given his faith what was to be the first of many 'trials,' because as a Catholic Anglican in the nineteenth century, in those early days at Oriel and throughout the whole of his life, King would inevitably be caught in the cross-fire of religious party strife.

> Catholics of the Roman obedience could not stomach his Anglicanism. His fellow Anglicans who were either Evangelicals or Broad-Church Liberals detested his Catholicism as a betrayal of the Reformation. The question was not *whether* King would maintain his Tractarian position in the face of opposition, but *how*. Would he hold on to his faith, but only at the price of becoming intense, shrill, fanatical? Would he turn into a rigid party man? If he maintained his High Anglican churchmanship, would he also be capable of growth and development, so as to embrace a new age within his catholicity? Or would he get inside the *laager* of Boer wagons with Pusey, Liddon and Burgon, and die in the last ditch?[67]

Only time would tell.

He was not to return to live in Oxford for over two decades, and when he did it was not as a young student, but as a mature and highly esteemed professor, eager to share his experience, his study and the lessons of life, learned from both his travels and books, with any and as many as might wish to seek him out and travel with him on that inner 'journey of faith.'

Notes

[1] A. N. Wilson, *Prince Albert: The Man who Saved the Monarchy*. London: Atlantic Books, 2019, pp. 180ff.

[2] *Ibid.*

[3] Karl Marx and Friedrich Engels, *Manifesto of the Communist Party* [1848]. Moscow: Progress Publishers, 1986, p. 70.

Edward King

4 R. W. Church, *The Oxford Movement: Twelve Years, 1833–1845* (ed. Geoffrey Best) (*Classics of British Historical Literature*). The University of Chicago Press, 1970. p. 66.
5 Owen Chadwick, *Edward King: Bishop of Lincoln 1885–1910*. Friends of Lincoln Minister, Pamphlets, Second Series, no. 4, 1968, p. 3.
6 Edward Gibbon, *Autobiography* (The World's Classics). Oxford University Press, 1907, pp. 36–45.
7 Charles Edward Mallet, *A History of the University of Oxford*, 3 vols. London: Methuen & Co. Ltd, 1927, vol. III, p. 2.
8 L. S. Sutherland and L. G. Mitchell (eds), *The History of the University of Oxford, Volume V, The Eighteenth Century*. Oxford: Clarendon Press, 1986, p. 3.
9 *Ibid.*, p. 467.
10 Church, *op. cit.*, p. 113.
11 Mark D. Chapman, 'Liberal Anglicanism,' in *The Oxford History of Anglicanism* (ed. Rowan Strong). Oxford University Press, 2017, vol. III, p. 214.
12 *Ibid.*, p. 215.
13 Arthur Penrhyn Stanley, *The Life and Correspondence of Thomas Arnold, D.D., Late Head-Master of Rugby School, and Regius Professor of Modern History in the University of Oxford*, 2 vols. London: J. Murray, 1877, vol. II, p. 65.
14 John Henry Newman, *Apologia pro Vita Sua*. London: Longman, Green, Longman, Roberts & Green, 1864, p. 98.
15 Church, *op. cit.*, p. xiii (editor's introduction).
16 *Ibid.*, p. 114.
17 William Palmer, *Narrative of Events connected with the Publication of Tracts for the Times: with an Introduction and Supplement extending to the Present Time*. London: Rivingtons, 1883, p. 5.
18 *Spiritual Letters of Edward King, D.D.* (ed. B. W. Randolph). London: A. R. Mowbray & Co. Ltd, 1910, Letter XII.
19 John William Burgon, *Inspiration and Interpretation: Seven Sermons*. Oxford and London: J. H. and James Parker, 1861, p. 46 (Sermon II). For Burgon see also *Encyclopaedia Britannica*, eleventh edition. Cambridge University Press, 1910–11, vol. IV, p. 818.
20 Randolph and Townroe, *The Mind and Work of Bishop King*, p. 136.
21 Third Address at the 'Quiet Day' for the Lambeth Conference of 1897. For King's full development of this theme see Chapter 14.
22 Pusey House Library, Marriott Papers, manuscript 'Memoirs of Charles Marriott by his Brother John,' p. 5.
23 *Ibid.*, p. 4.
24 Church, *op. cit.*, chapter 5.
25 *Ibid.*
26 *Ibid.*; see also Chapter 14 of this book.
27 George W. E. Russell, *Edward King Sixtieth Bishop of Lincoln*, p. 5.

28 *Ibid.*
29 Edward King, *The Love and Wisdom of God*, p. 320.
30 Baron Friedrich von Hügel, *Essays and Addresses on the Philosophy of Religion* (1921), quoted in *The Commemoration of Saint and Heroes of the Faith in the Anglican Communion*. London: SPCK, 1957, p. 65.
31 Church, *op. cit.*, p. 59.
32 *Ibid.*
33 Richard Rohr, *A Spring Within Us. A Year of Daily Meditations* London: SPCK, 2018, p. 242.
34 Rohr, 'Daily Meditations on Line' (internet site), 25 November 2018.
35 Chadwick, *op. cit.*, p. 4.
36 Church, *op. cit.*, chapter 5.
37 W. R. W. Stephens, *The Life and Letters of Edward A. Freeman*, 2 vols. London: Macmillan & Co., 1895, vol. I. p. 58.
38 Frederick Meyrick, *Memories of Life at Oxford and Experiences in Italy, Turkey, Germany, Spain and Elsewhere*. London: John Murray, 1905, pp. 173–4.
39 *Ibid.*, p. 174.
40 Pusey House Library, Brotherhood of the Holy Trinity Minute Books, vol. I, p. 5.
41 *Ibid.*, Liddon papers, Box 12.
42 Meyrick, *op. cit.*, p. 174.
43 *Ibid.*
44 *Ibid.*
45 Henry D. Rack, *Reasonable Enthusiast: John Wesley and the Rise of Methodism*, London: Epworth Press, 1989, p. 88.
46 *Ibid.*
47 *Ibid.*, p. 92.
48 Russell, *op. cit.*, p. 5.
49 *Ibid.*, p. 6.
50 Obituary of Edward King in *Oriel Record*, March 1910, p. 80.
51 Randolph and Townroe, *op. cit.*, p. 24.
52 Russell, *op. cit.*, p. 6.
53 King, *Spiritual Letters*, Letter VI.
54 Bodleian Library, Wilberforce Papers, J. W. Burgon to Samuel Wilberforce, 6 March 1854.
55 Lincolnshire Archives, Misc. dep. 46.5.
56 Russell, *op. cit.*, pp. 7–8.
57 Oriel College Library, Lecture Book CC4A, 1848–51.
58 Russell, *op. cit.*, p. 7.
59 Chadwick, *op. cit.*, p. 3.
60 King, *Spiritual Letters*, Letter XXIV.
61 Russell, *op. cit.*, p. 57.

Edward King

62 Randolph and Townroe, *op. cit.*, pp. 26–7.
63 *Ibid.*, p. 24.
64 *Ibid.*, p. 25.
65 *Ibid.*
66 *Ibid.*, pp. 25–6.
67 John A. Newton, *Search for a Saint: Edward King*, p. 25.

✠ 3 ✠

Ordination and the Pastoral Novice

THE PROSPECT OF ORDINATION

Edward King had returned to England from Palestine in June 1852, after nearly five months away from home, family and friends. He then worked for eighteen months or so as a private tutor to the Marquess of Lothian's younger brothers, but his thoughts were increasingly focused on the prospect of ordination. On 24 September 1852, he wrote to his Oriel friend, Garnons Williams, already ordained and also, like King, the son of an archdeacon, giving an account of his travels abroad and sharing his hopes for ordination:

> I hope you have heard from others of my absence from England, or you will think worse of me than I deserve. Indeed, since I last wrote to you, I have seen a good deal. I ran away from the cold weather last winter in the first week of February and wandered on till I found myself on the shores of the Dead Sea! I think I might interest you with things I heard and saw, but in a letter it is impossible to select one or two out of so many new ideas—but first let me ask how you are, and all your family? I trust all well. I think I heard or saw that you were ordained ... when I shall be ordained I do not quite know, but not before next Trinity Sunday.[1]

In the early nineteenth century, the decision to seek ordination would in most cases not be perceived as something extraordinary, requiring some kind of specific divine revelation, or even a particular sense of 'being called.' People often spoke of 'going into the church' in much the same way as they would of entering any of the other professions. 'It has always to be remembered that the clerical profession was a profession which many adopted as the best and most natural available, without seeing the need for the divine call thought essential by later Evangelicals and Anglo-Catholics.'[2]

We have no first-hand account of King experiencing any kind of call to the ordained ministry. In his case, what is certain, is that the decision to seek Holy Orders was neither perfunctory, nor simply because his older brother had become a priest, or because the pursuit of the clerical profession would have been a matter of going with the cultural flow of the day, or simply a case of following in his father's footsteps, as many did in those days. Of course, we cannot dismiss the example of his father and his brother; his experience of parochial work with the Revd John Day; and the influence of Charles Marriott at Oriel: all these no doubt played their part. It may also be that his travels to the Middle East gave him space in which to reflect on the future course of his life, and for his sense of vocation to mature. By the spring of 1854, King was ready and resolutely committed to going forward for ordination.

In March, J. W. Burgon, who knew King as an undergraduate, wrote to Bishop Samuel Wilberforce of Oxford, strongly recommending him for a curacy in the diocese. Though he mistakes King's Christian name, Burgon gives an accurate picture of the young man whom Wilberforce would eventually appoint, not only to a curacy at Wheatley, but subsequently to the principalship of his newly founded theological college at Cuddesdon:

> My dear Lord,
> This is not to give you trouble, but (I hope) to give you pleasure. *The most pious young man I ever knew in my life* [high praise indeed from the somewhat acerbic Burgon], is a member of this College: Edmund [sic] King. His father is a Canon of Rochester—Rector of Stone, in

Ordination and the Pastoral Novice

Kent. He completed his curriculum about two years ago—and, being in delicate health, had disappeared from among us. He called upon me an hour ago—and told me with joy that Dr Watson allows him to apply for Holy Orders immediately. He will be a candidate on Trinity Sunday.

I can only judge of others by myself. I should like to have a Diocese *full* of such curates. I think it only right, at all events, to *tell* you of him: and to add that he is very desirous of coming into your Diocese. Will you find work for him as a curate *somewhere*? The only necessary conditions are (1) a dry locality; and (2) not *quite* so many a thousand souls [sic].

I will only say of Edward King—*sit anima mea cum anima illius*. He is such a one as the best and holiest were when they were young. Pray secure him for this diocese! *To save you trouble*—(for no other reason)—I enclose a letter which will bring him to you—supposing that you might like to have two minutes talk with him. I bade him make no engagement of any kind for ten days.[3]

'A GENTLEMAN AND A CHRISTIAN'

Burgon's strong recommendation, followed up by King's interview with Wilberforce bore fruit, as is clear from the Bishop's letter of 24 March 1854 to the Vicar of Wheatley, Edward Elton, assuring him that he had found the right man to be his curate: 'His name is King, a gentleman and a Christian. If you will apply to Rev. J. W. Burgon of Oriel about him *at once* you will do well.'[4] Elton was soon to discover that the double designation—'a gentleman and a Christian'—was no conventional label, but the simple truth. Once Elton had accepted King as his curate, Wilberforce lost no time in ordaining him deacon in Cuddesdon parish church on Trinity Sunday, 11 June 1854. Only a few years later, King would be officiating in that same church as Vicar of Cuddesdon, and Principal of the College, but for the moment his duties lay in the quite different setting of the country parish of Wheatley.

THE PARISH OF WHEATLEY

The village of Wheatley was about as far removed as could be imagined from the idyllic rural parishes of Stone or Ellesmere, with their stable and well-established church life, both of which had been so formative in King's early years. Wheatley in Oxfordshire, some five miles east of Oxford, was a rough place, as Lord Elton, in his charming memoir, *Edward King and Our Times*, makes clear. As the grandson of King's vicar, Lord Elton was able to tap into the stream of family reminiscences and to draw on his grandfather's memories to fill out the picture of the parish at this period:

> Wheatley in those days was a rough and lawless place, an 'open' village, owned by no landlord, so that when a landowner in some neighbouring village ejected a disreputable or disrespectful tenant, he was apt to take refuge in Wheatley. 'I had not only to be an active clergyman,' wrote my grandfather, 'but perform duty also as a quasi-policeman and keep order among a turbulent population.' In later years, the place became more civilised ... but in King's day Wheatley was full of uncouth, and sometimes criminal, country poor.[5]

When King arrived in 1854, the parish church of St Mary was in as poor a state of repair as the morals of the parishioners. Edward Elton, prompted by Bishop Wilberforce, was responsible for its rebuilding in what Pevsner describes as 'a very chaste thirteenth-century style,' with George Edmund Street as the architect. The work began in 1855, and the church re-opened for worship two years later. Thus, the new curate, arrived in time to see the demolition of the old decayed church and its replacement by the new one.

Ordination and the Pastoral Novice

King also came to Wheatley at a time of great personal sorrow for the vicar, which was really the reason why he had been recruited. Earlier that same year, in February 1854, Elton's wife had died, leaving him with four young children to bring up, and he decided he needed the help and companionship of a young curate. In his later autobiography, Elton recalls:

> I had resolved for a time to have the comfort and aid of a curate, and God's providence sent me a messenger of peace and consolation in the person of Edward King, led on, through his obvious fitness, after some years' intermediate work as Chaplain and Principal of Cuddesdon College, to a Professorship of Pastoral Theology at Oxford. He had been first ordained to the parish and during four years rendered me the most constant and affectionate help, and it is one of the comforts of my life that I have him still so near me, although his work in Oxford does not allow very frequent intercourse.[6]

Elton's debt to King is clear from this extract; but if we turn to his journal, it would be hard to glean exactly how much Elton owed to the relationship. The Revd Edward Elton had been encouraged by his father to keep a nature diary almost as soon as he could write, as did many clergy in the nineteenth century. Several volumes of Elton's have survived: 'begun when the diarist was five and continued until he was eighty-three. Every day has its entry,' with the record concentrating upon birds, flowers, animals and, unfailingly the weather. 'Indeed,' comments Elton's grandson, 'if anyone should desire to study the weather in southern England day by day from 1821 to 1898, I doubt whether he could find anywhere a completer record than in my grandfather's diaries.'

For Elton recording the phenomena of nature clearly took precedence over everything else, including personal matters and even affairs of the heart. 'The account of the diarist's wedding day,' as his grandson ironically comments, while containing 'a number of comments on birds and on the alternations of sun and rain,' contains 'scarcely any reference to the wedding, save the bare statement that it took place.'

So, Elton's journal was basically and almost exclusively a nature diary, in which any references to his young curate are brief and almost wholly factual—'dined early with E. K. and all the children at Haseley': 'walked with E. K. on the common at Horsepath, now being rapidly enclosed.'[7]

There is, however, one noteworthy exception: it records 'the lift' which King was able to give to his bereaved vicar's spirits. 'Drove E. K. to Lewknor about ten miles via Tetsworth. The valleys are now so full of corn "they laugh and sing."' Commenting on this entry, Lord Elton says: 'When he wrote this my grandfather had very recently lost his first wife, and for the time being he was a sad man; and it is conceivable that on this occasion the use of these words, which at other times would have come readily enough to a naturalist familiar with the Psalms, owed something to the contagion of King's radiant spirit, and to his sympathy during that ten-mile drive.'[8]

As a countryman himself, King shared Elton's passion for the life of the fields. He was to spend virtually the whole of the first half of his life living in the countryside. There was a considerable *rapport* between the older and the younger man, yet King's sympathy would go much deeper than that. He had what might be defined as some kind of 'fine-tuning device' in his make-up, which made him extraordinarily sensitive to the moods and feelings of others. Under the influence of the Bible, Wordsworth's poems, and Keble's *Christian Year*, he had learned to discern a sacramental significance in nature, as God's creation. The King who was able to cheer Elton and make his rural ride a sheer delight did not do so, we may be sure, by mere *bonhomie*. We are dealing here with the same man who could write in old age: 'I still go on my simple way, loving flowers and birds, and the sunlight on the apples, and the sunset, and like to think

Ordination and the Pastoral Novice

more and more of the verse—"With Thee is the well of life, and in Thy light shall we see light."'[9]

In the autumn of that same year, 1854, King's own life was clouded by concern for his younger brother Henry, who had been seriously wounded serving in the Crimean War. He set out from Wheatley vicarage and journeyed to the British military hospital at Scutari on the Bosphorus, where Henry was being nursed. Though in future years Edward was to become an ardent European traveller, this journey to Turkey must have been the most gruelling he ever experienced. The horrors endured by the men wounded in the Crimea have become proverbial, alleviated only by the devoted nursing of Florence Nightingale and her helpers. At Scutari King may conceivably have first learned the profound understanding and respect for the nurses' calling which he was later to show as Patron of the Guild of St Barnabas for Nurses. Captain Henry King recovered from his wounds, but sadly he was drowned only a few years later while bathing off Malta. Edward treasured his portrait, and during his episcopate it hung in the drawing-room of the Old Palace at Lincoln.

Back at Wheatley, the young curate found full scope for his pastoral gifts, and discovered a lasting vocation to the country poor. He entered fully into their lives and sought, as he was later to do at Lincoln, to 'draw them to God.' His special charism enabled him to influence the lads and young men, and to draw them, not merely to himself in friendship, but to a more Christian way of living and to an understanding of the Faith. Dr F. E. Brightman, a distinguished scholar, especially of the Eastern Orthodox churches, and Fellow of Magdalen College, Oxford, in a discerning memoir, sees King's curacy at Wheatley as one in which 'his characteristic gifts at once found scope: his love for the poor and simple and his sympathy and influence with young men.'[10]

Edward Elton speaks in similar tones of his curate: 'Conscientious in all parochial work, his special faculty seemed to be the getting hold of young men and boys, securing their affections and through them elevating and strengthening their moral qualities. Many a one in this place has reason to thank God that such a curate came amongst them.'[11]

King was committed to their religious development, but not in any narrow or pietistic sense. He also wanted to open their minds and give them a taste of the education they never had a chance to experience: 'He interested them in botany, he superintended a night school in the winter months ... He used to go for long walks and take immense interest in teaching the children about flowers and plants and birds.'[12] Some days he would go out picking flowers or bird's nesting with the vicar's daughters, or would be dragged up the hill, when he was in low health, by the lads of the village. He would sometimes drop into the village school and ask to take one of the boys with him on a nature walk, as he did with 'Charlie,' who, even as an old man, treasured in his memories of King's days in Wheatley and that red-letter day when the young curate delivered him from school into the Oxfordshire countryside. Charlie recalled that, 'He took me up to his room, and gave me some plums before we went out'[13] — what a memorable double treat for a small boy.

With King's encouragement, 'Charlie' eventually trained as a teacher at Culham Teacher Training College and became a lifelong friend and disciple. King corresponded with him regularly from 1857 until 1909. The first nineteen of King's posthumously published *Spiritual Letters* were written to him, and are full of shrewd practical advice on study and relaxation, moral questions, and difficulties to belief. To the country boy now embarked on his college course, King writes:

> And so now you are really at college! I hardly know what to say to you. However, go on in your old way. Don't be in a hurry to change for new ways, which others would persuade you are better or more independent, or more telling in the world. Beware of smart dealing, swaggering, loud talking, showing off your knowledge,

thinking yourself a *great government man!!* Etc. All these things are simply *poor*. Pray don't be tempted by them, my dearest Charlie.¹⁴

In these letters, King refers more than once to the simplicity and quiet joys of his years at Wheatley, as an idyllic period of his life and ministry. In 1865, for example, he writes from Cuddesdon: 'I send you a card I have made for some of my young men, just to remind you of old days.'¹⁵ Six years later, again writing from Cuddesdon, he says: 'I have been obliged these last few years to spend the best of my time in reading, but if I should be free from the College, I should go on in a parish just as we used to at Wheatley. That was a simple, unworldly affectionate life, and that is what we want.'¹⁶

Nearly a quarter of a century later, in 1895, after ten years as Bishop of Lincoln, carrying all the cares of his diocese, King expatiates to Charlie on the happiness of the days at Wheatley:

> It seems only yesterday that you used to come down to my room with dear G. and J., and we used to sit and talk together. I don't know that I have ever been happier. I was thoroughly happy with you all at Wheatley. I ought to be very thankful for all God's great goodness to me. I did not think I should live so long. [He was only 65 and was to live another 15 years.] I think our way of looking at things was the right one. We saw where true happiness was to be found. I long to promote the same kind of spirit in our country parishes.
>
> Thank you so much for your prayers. I am sure it is that which has kept me on. I should have broken down long ago but for that. I must stop now. I forget that we are not sitting over the fire at Wheatley. It was very nice, wasn't it? I hope you are able to keep the same spirit of simplicity and love round about you. Good-bye, my dear C._____. Don't forget me in your prayers. With my love and blessing to you all.¹⁷

The life of the countryside, unaffected friendship with ordinary people, the absence of pomp and circumstance ('a simple, unworldly affectionate life'), and the whole 'spirit of simplicity and love' — these were the joys of his Wheatley curacy which King never ceased to recall with gratitude. At the age of seventy-five, he was still writing to Charlie: 'In heart I feel just the same as when we were all at Wheatley together, with dear J. and G. and you and H. I often look back to those days with the greatest thankfulness and pleasure; we were all very happy … Your letter pleased me very much, because there was a spirit of content and happiness which I was most glad to see, and the love for your flowers brought back the memory of our old walks. I still love flowers and birds as much as ever.'[18]

He loved Wheatley and his friends there. In the same letter of 1905, he mentions another correspondent who sends him the local village news: 'I hear of Wheatley sometimes from James White.' James had served in King's household during his time as Principal of Cuddesdon College and when he returned to Oxford in 1873 to take up his Professorship, James went with him. In 1883, James moved to another post, but King kept in touch by letter for the rest of his life. James cherished the letters throughout his own long life, and in October 1939, presented them to the college. They are far removed from the courteous but distant notes which a leading ecclesiastic — how strange that title sounds when applied to King — might have been expected to write to a former servant. There is no formality about them; they are warm, personal and intensely human. News and reminiscence jostle with pastoral and spiritual advice, carefully framed to suit the life-situation of a young, single man in domestic service. The letter written from Christ Church on 24 August 1883, is entirely typical:

> My Dear James,
> Thank you for your nice letter. It was a great pleasure to me. I should have written yesterday, but you know how the bell keeps ringing all day, and people coming, and so I could not get the time.

Ordination and the Pastoral Novice

I am very glad you have got a good place, and I quite hope you will get on. I am glad they mean to take you with them as it looks as if they liked having you, and besides, you will see new places. Only take care you do not get mixed up with any bad companions or acquaintances. You will say, 'Ah! the old Dr is always afraid I will go to smash.' Well, dear James, it is a good thing to have someone to remind you of those sort of dangers, because in the world people only blow you up if you break a glass, or upset the soup, but there are worse things than that of which they never speak. I am not really afraid for you, only when so many young men smash, it makes any one anxious who really cares about a person ... It is very hot here now, and the harvest looks very good. I always used to enjoy the harvest time when I was at Cuddesdon. The fields all look so nice, and the people seem so busy, and I think it is healthy for them too being out all day in the air.

I hope you will come and see me if you come this way. I was very sorry to part with you, though I used to say that I was not a good Master for you. I quite hope you will really do best where you are. You will if you take care and keep up your Religion. Don't think it is a fine thing to give it up but stick to it all your life. Get to Church when you can. Whenever you like to write, I shall always be glad to hear from you, for if I was not a good Master, I don't think I was a bad Friend.

God bless you, dear James, and take care of you

I am always

  Yours affectionately

   Edward King

'If I was not a good Master, I don't think I was a bad friend': when King reproached himself for being a bad master, he did not mean that he was inconsiderate. That fault was not in his nature. He was referring rather to that aspect of his lifestyle of which he thought his new butler, the quiet and painstaking, William Tibbetts, would disapprove: 'I expect he thinks me very untidy.'

White's reply has not survived, but his cherished preservation of King's letters suggests that he judged any untidiness on his master's part as being greatly outweighed by his friendship. King treated everyone who served him in precisely this way. He was often the 'master,' responsible for other people's lives and work: as country curate, college principal, Oxford professor and diocesan bishop. At every stage, those who served him were conscious not of his 'mastery,' but of his friendship.

'I was very sorry to part with you,' King had written to White, and he evidently felt much the same nearly a quarter of a century later when Tibbetts (who replaced White in 1883) also left him, presumably for other work. A native of Oxfordshire and a bachelor, Tibbetts was fifty-three at the time of 1901 census. Before joining King, he had been Dr Heurtley's butler at Christ Church. He must have been a pivotal figure in the bishop's household and had he stayed until King's death would have received £500 under King's original will of 1902—a very considerable bequest. However, by October 1907, when King added a third codicil, Tibbetts had been replaced by William Norton, promoted from footman. King's disappointment at losing Tibbetts is seemingly reflected in the new codicil which reduces his bequest to £100, 'in consideration of the services he has rendered me in the past.' The new butler, Norton, received a legacy of £200.

Charlie and James White were typical of the country lads King influenced during his time at Wheatley and Cuddesdon. They responded to his genuine care for them. Scott Holland, a lifelong friend of King, testifies of him: 'He loved the poor with a peculiar reverence and delight. He was their man. He knew them through and through. He felt as they felt. He could get to the heart of the very rough lads who were the bane of Wheatley and Cuddesdon.'[19]

Holland is right. King's love for the poor was rooted in a profound imaginative sympathy, but it was never sentimental. It was love with its eyes open, and 'faith expressing itself through works,' as the author of the Epistle of James urges. King looked with an astringent realism at the full human nature and total needs of his villagers. He was concerned not only with their education and spiritual nurture, but with their need for adequate drains and sanitation.

In 1854, the year of King's arrival in Wheatley, there was yet another serious country-wide cholera epidemic. The prevailing wisdom about outbreaks of cholera and other contagious diseases like typhus, confidently and mistakenly asserted that the source of these infections was airborne bacteria. In Britain, only Dr John Snow of London eventually worked out the correct cause of these recurring and fatal epidemics.

Snow was well known as an early advocate of anaesthesia and he used chloroform for the births of two of Queen Victoria's children, 'but his truly pioneering theory of waterborne [not airborne] disease was not accepted by his colleagues until long after his untimely death at the early age of forty-five.' By one of those ironies of history, Snow died of a stroke on the hottest day hitherto recorded — 16 June 1858 — when 'the atmospheric impurity' and 'noxious morbific power' of the sewage-filled Thames forced Parliament to vacate the Palace of Westminster: 1858 was subsequently and notoriously known as the 'Year of the Great Stink.'[20]

In a letter to *The Times* in June 1856, headed 'Cholera and the Water Supply,' Dr Snow described his inquiries during the 1854 cholera outbreak, 'into the water supplies of two of London's water companies, the Southwark and Vauxhall Company and the Lambeth Company.' The former supplied impure water, he wrote, the latter pure: 'the ratio of deaths from cholera of recipients of water from the two companies was six to one,' and he referred to a report of his findings which had been published in 1854 in the *Medical Times*.

It is unlikely that Elton or King would have seen the report in the *Medical Times*, but more than probable they read Snow's letter in *The Times* which concluded by stating unequivocally that, in his opinion, 'many other diseases, besides cholera, can be shown to be aggravated by water containing sewage.'[21]

Was it that letter, with other local evidence, which prompted King and Elton to set to work to tackle the problem of the filthy stream flowing alongside the main street of Wheatley, which had always done duty as both water supply and sewer? In any event, vicar and curate bent their efforts to get it covered over to serve as a main drain, and eventually succeeded, though only after setting up a Local Board of Health to force through this improvement in the face of general opposition from the villagers.

With the parish wedded to old insanitary ways, it is hardly surprising that during King's curacy Wheatley should have been visited with a typhus epidemic. King persuaded Elton to let him visit all the most serious sufferers, earnestly pleading that the vicar had a family to consider, whereas his curate had none.

That quality of pastoral care is never lost on a parish, and King's words from the pulpit must have come with added force when backed by such caring. We have evidence how memorably his sermons could strike home to the most unlikely of hearers. In 1900, more than forty years after King had left Wheatley, R. W. Carew Hunt, a country clergyman, was walking along the road to High Wycombe and struck up a conversation with a passing tramp—'an odd-looking creature, half tinker, half pedlar, a true wayfaring man,' as Carew Hunt records.

> We walked along for some distance, talking about many things. Presently I said to my companion, 'I suppose you don't often go to church nowadays?' 'Bless me, sir,' he replied, 'it's years since I have been inside a church. I don't know as there is anything would get me in there except one.' 'What's that?' I said. 'Well,' he replied, 'if I could only 'ear a chap named King preach, I'd go. I heard 'im years ago at a village called Wheatley, and I

> shall never forget 'im. He was curate then, or summ'at. I wonder if he be still alive. I should dearly like to hear 'im again. I'd go many a long mile to hear 'im.'
> 'Your curate is a Bishop now,' I said. 'Lord, is he? But I would like to see 'im again. I remember that there sermon, though it's years ago since I heard 'im.'[22]

It is a pity Carew Hunt did not ask the tramp to share his recollection of that sermon. But it is a telling account and underscores the testimony of many others, that King could communicate memorably with simple people. Moreover, if a casual visitor could be so impressed by hearing the young King, it seems fairly sure that his own parishioners would have been able to echo the tramp's words, as their curate left Wheatley to become chaplain at Cuddesdon College: 'I shall never forget 'im.'

If his people did not forget their curate, neither did he forget them. H. F. B. Mackay records two items of memorabilia which King treasured in his days at Lincoln:

> near his big chair in the big window of the Palace at Lincoln in which the old Bishop used to sit and look down across the terraces of his garden, there always stood two objects; one was an ostrich egg, the great treasure of the blacksmith at Wheatley, which he had given to King as a parting present; the other was a box, a perfectly square, plain, wooden box, the parting present of the carpenter—the very box that was 'the same on every side.'[23]

'The same on every side'—that was evidently the quality the carpenter had discerned in the parish's young curate. He was the same person in his dealings with everyone, of whatever background or social status: courteous, open, considerate, honest. He was so himself: he was one person, 'the same on every side.'

For the final word on King's time at Wheatley, we need to 'fast-forward' to the time of the Lincoln Judgment, to the turbulent year of 1889, when King was awaiting the trial for his alleged illegal ritualist practices. His former vicar, Edward Elton, was still alive and chose to write a firmly supportive letter to *The Standard*, reflecting on the years when King had served under him as his curate and pastoral colleague. In it, he pays King a strongly worded tribute for his outstanding work in 'a rough and difficult parish, which had been greatly neglected.'

> It may almost go without saying that he was everything to me. Constant in labour, fervent in spirit, and cheerful in dark days …
>
> I soon discovered how pre-eminently he was a man of prayer; how deeply versed in Holy Scripture, and saintly in life; how yearning to do work for God among the depraved and ignorant people of the place. Thirty years have passed since those days, but he is not in the least forgotten in my old parish. There are several persons living now, in whose conversion to God he was instrumental, and to whom he proved, in the truest sense, a messenger of peace.[24]

If any should suppose that such a tribute to King's lasting and outstanding influence in the springtime of his ministry is over-exaggerated, then they need to read on and to see how those same remarkable characteristics and gifts matured during the summertime of his ministry at Cuddesdon and Oxford, only to reap a rich harvest in the fruits of that same pastoral ministry, in the golden, autumnal years of his life as Bishop of Lincoln.

Notes

[1] George W. E. Russell, *Edward King Sixtieth Bishop of Lincoln*, p. 9.
[2] Henry D. Rack, *Reasonable Enthusiast*, p. 17.
[3] Bodleian Library, Wilberforce Papers, Burgon to Wilberforce, 6 March 1854.
[4] Russell, *op. cit.*, p. 10.
[5] Lord Elton, *Edward King and Our Times*, London: Geoffrey Bles Ltd, 1958, pp. 32–3.

6 *Ibid.*, p. 32.
7 *Ibid.*, p. 30.
8 *Ibid.*, p. 31.
9 King, *Spiritual Letters of Edward King, D.D.*, p. 182.
10 F. E. Brightman, article on King in *A Dictionary of English Church History* (ed. S. L. Ollard and G. Crosse). London and Oxford: A. R. Mowbray & Co. Ltd, 1912, p. 307.
11 Elton, *op. cit.*, p. 32.
12 *Ibid.*, p. 34.
13 Randolph and Townroe, *The Mind and Work of Edward King*, p. 28.
14 King, *Spiritual Letters*, Letter VI.
15 *Ibid.*, Letter IX.
16 *Ibid.*, Letter XV.
17 *Ibid.*, Letter XVI.
18 *Ibid.*, Letter XVII.
19 Henry Scott Holland, *A Bundle of Memories*. London: Wells Gardner, Darton & Co. Ltd, 1915, p. 52.
20 Rosemary Ashton, *One Hot Summer: Dickens, Darwin, Disraeli and the Great Stink of 1858*. London and New Haven: Yale University Press, 2017, p. 15.
21 Dr John Snow, 'Cholera and the Water Supply,' letter to *The Times*, 26 June 1856.
22 Russell, *op. cit.*, pp. 12–13.
23 H. F. B. Mackay, *Saints and Leaders*. London: Philip Allan & Co. Ltd, 1928, pp. 208ff.
24 Russell, *op. cit.*, pp. 160–1.

✢ 4 ✢

Cuddesdon:
'A New Generation of Clergy'

NEW REQUIREMENTS NEEDED FOR CLERGY TRAINING

The year 1854 is a significant year for two seemingly contradictory reasons. Parliament passed the Act which changed the constitution and government of the University of Oxford and its associated colleges, whereby admission, hitherto restricted to members of the Church of England, was opened to Dissenters. Not unrelated to the passing of that Act, and in the same year, Samuel Wilberforce, the Bishop of Oxford, founded Cuddesdon College to provide for priestly formation and clergy training what the ancient universities were no longer equipped to do.

Until then it was almost taken for granted that an Oxford or Cambridge graduate, competent in classics, would automatically have received the necessary academic qualifications to fit him to take Holy Orders in the Church of England. There are many anecdotes illustrating the outlook of pre-nineteenth-century Anglican bishops, who would assume and, at that time, not entirely unreasonably or irresponsibly, that a university education was an adequate preparation for ordination.

After all, like Edward King himself, many undergraduates, and not least those who felt called to ordination, would have come to Oxford from families where daily Christian devotion and the duties of Christian morality would be taken for granted. Furthermore, until later in the nineteenth century, no man could take a degree at Oxford or Cambridge without professing himself to be a practising member (indeed, a communicant member), of the Church of England, and he would be expected to attend services in chapel, where the head of College, along with a large number of the Fellows and dons, would almost invariably have been in Holy Orders.

None of this necessarily calls for surprise or condemnation, and not least when we realize that most of the bishops and leaders of the Church in the nineteenth century, many of whom were outstanding in various ways, were nevertheless 'trained' by and were products of this ancient system.

Nevertheless, it was becoming increasingly evident in the Victorian Church of England, especially during the years of reform, that the ancient universities, the traditional nurseries of its clergy, were not competent to train clergy for the task of ministry which a radically changing world required. In 1835, over three hundred peers, Members of Parliament and a number of clergy had addressed a petition to the archbishops and bishops in which they affirmed that, 'The preparatory studies, pursued in those seats of learning, are of a character too general and vague to have any sufficient bearing on the future usefulness of the Christian minister.'[1]

Early pioneers of further training and ministerial formation were bishops in more remote dioceses like Sodor and Man, whose Bishop—Thomas Wilson—founded an early 'theological college.' His example was soon followed by Bishop Law of Chester in 1816 (St Bees Theological College), and by Bishop Burgess of St David's in 1822 (St David's College, Lampeter). Interestingly, these were designed mainly for non-graduates, principally because, in the days before easy travel and social mobility, there would be a scarcity of university graduates in such distant places as the fells and valleys of Cumbria or Wales. There soon followed, however, a series of colleges catering for graduates, who, though university-trained, had received little or no preparation for ordained ministry: Chichester (1839), the earliest, with Charles Marriott, King's mentor, as its first Principal; Wells (1840); St Aidan's, Birkenhead (1846); and Queen's College, Birmingham (1851).

In these early attempts at a more specific training for ordination, it fell largely to the bishops in their respective dioceses to train and prepare their men for ordination. Knowingly or unknowingly, they were reflecting the ancient method of priestly and Christian formation, whereby the bishop would be surrounded by his ordinands, in some cases actually living together in close proximity, while supervising their training for ordination. Clearly, it was something of this idea which endeared itself to Wilberforce as he planned not only the location of his college at Cuddesdon, just across the road from the Bishop of Oxford's Palace at that time, but also with the further specific requirement that it would be directly under the supervision of the bishop, a requirement firmly embedded in the wording of its Founding Charter.

In practical terms it was becoming increasingly clear that training for priestly ministry would require more than a degree in classics with a few theological extras thrown in. Cuddesdon seemed to point further to something more radical in the training of the clergy, by providing not only a college for theological education but to set all study in the context of community life, committed to regular worship and training in personal prayer, as a regulated, professional preparation for ordination. The communication of information, albeit theological or ecclesiastical, does not necessarily result in transformation of lives: put another way, in the words of Justin Martyr (c. AD 100–65), 'Knowledge is not safe, without a true life.'

In Oxford, the newly created Chair of Pastoral Theology together with the Chair of Ecclesiastical History, were early attempts to address the need for a more specific theological training of the clergy, but this did not go far enough. A changing world and a changing Church demanded from its ministers and spiritual leaders a new professionalism, equipped and competent to meet the rapidly emerging and sometimes aggressive secularism. Furthermore, a new generation of clergy was increasingly required for mission in the burgeoning cities of the industrial revolution which changed so radically the demographics of society.

In passing, it might be of interest to see a similar shift required in the training for ministry in the emerging technological revolution of our own day, with its new demands and opportunities for communication. However, the unchanging constant in any emerging and developing systems of ministerial formation must surely be safeguarded by the overriding need for the clergy to be schooled for a ministry rooted and grounded in prayer, as well as being equipped to teach prayer and offering spiritual formation for those committed to their care. In 1935, William Temple wrote to Eric Abbott, the recently appointed Warden of the theological college in Lincoln—the Bishop's Hostel, as it was known: 'You will use it as a basis for what we need more than all else,—to teach the clergy to be teachers of prayer.'[2]

The Anglo-Catholics were not alone in seeking a more professional training for the clergy. It was also the Evangelicals, such as Charles Simeon, in the aftermath of the Evangelical revival of the late eighteenth century who rose to the challenge. For some time, Evangelicals within the Church of England had been raising the standard and the ideal required of a pastor, after the example of the 'earnest' Methodists, to the point where they had come to earn the epithet of being 'methodistical.'

> The evangelicals were demanding that the Christian minister should know his commission to be of God; that he was called to a labour which separated him from the standards of the world; that in the preaching of the Word and the ministry of the Sacraments he acted as the instrument of God's eternal purpose; that

he should accept his awful responsibility for the cure of souls and know that he must render account for them in the day of judgement.[3]

The 'earnestness' of the Evangelicals soon came to be adopted and reinforced by the call from theological training in the Tractarian Movement for what came to be termed the 'clerical tone.' The diminishing race of 'squire parsons' immortalized in the polemical writings of the period—Anthony Trollope's *Barchester Towers* (1857) and George Eliot's *Scenes from Clerical Life* (1858)—brought scorn, not wholly deserved, on the so-called 'port-wine faction.' There was an emerging demand for 'unspiritual priests to obey the call to a prayerful life' and for 'worldly-wise priests to obey the call to otherworldliness,' for 'manifestly natural lives to show supernatural qualities,'[4] surely an unchanging requirement even in the perennially and rapidly changing Church of today. The watchword of the time, and not least in 1854, the year Cuddesdon was founded, was 'earnest.'

SAMUEL WILBERFORCE: THE REFORMING BISHOP

It was in such a Church, in such a world and at such a time that Bishop Wilberforce was to be so conspicuous, not only for founding both Cuddesdon Theological College and Culham Teacher Training College, but also for being central and pivotal in the whole King narrative. And it was Wilberforce, King's ordaining bishop, who set him out on a ministerial path which in the ordinary course of events he could never have expected.

Wilberforce had been consecrated Bishop of Oxford at the early age of forty. Bishops, then as now, were customarily consecrated on an Apostle's day, so it is perhaps not insignificant that Wilberforce's consecration took place on St Andrews's day, 30 November 1845, St Andrew being the Patron Saint of mission. History has largely undervalued

Wilberforce, who by his visionary founding of those two colleges sought to equip clergy and teachers alike for effective mission, and to witness personally, through their profession and lifestyle, to a living and informed faith, relevant to the changing culture of the age. He realized that church schools without Christian teachers, and churches without spiritually as well as theologically equipped clergy, could not be effective in the rapidly changing world of his day.

Son of William Wilberforce, the great Evangelical and slave-emancipator, the young bishop was possessed of boundless energy, even by the standards of the age, a considerable intellect, and an outgoing and engaging personality and charm: there is undoubtedly a sense in which he was naturally 'born to the purple.' His ability to confront the claims of Darwin in his famous debate with T. H. Huxley, should neither be scorned nor written off, and, but for his unfortunate remark at the conclusion of his speech, when hubris overtook intellectual diplomacy, history (as well as those present) might have remembered Wilberforce's contribution to the debate more favourably.[5]

Wilberforce had gone up to Oxford, as a commoner at Oriel College, for Michaelmas Term, 1823. At that time Oriel had only seventy-six undergraduates, of whom twenty-one were 'gentlemen commoners.' Among the Fellows at the time was the initial 'ginger group' of the Tractarians, forerunners of the whole Oxford Movement: Keble, Newman and Pusey.

Although Wilberforce admired and, indeed, practised much of what the Tractarians taught and believed—influenced as he undoubtedly was by his time at Oriel, along with his brothers and his brother-in-law, Manning—yet 'he never lost his reverence for the evangelicals who had taught him a personal trust in a loving Saviour,'[6] issuing in works and action for the common good, so characteristic of his late father. However, like his future protégé King, he was not a party man. Indeed, as he wrote to his mother,

Cuddesdon: 'A New Generation of Clergy'

who had accused him of falling in with the Tractarians—'I belong to no school. In many things I do not agree with the few Oxford Tracts I have read. But I do agree as far as I can with all these great lights whom God has from time to time given to his Church; with Hooker and Bramhall and Taylor, with Beveridge and Stillingfleet, and with the primitive Church of the first three centuries.'[7] Yet, by insisting that the Church of England must be comprehensive and seek to hold the middle ground, he was frequently accused of compromise, and attracted the sobriquets 'Soapy Sam'—Disraeli had described his manner as 'unctuous, oleaginous, saponaceous'—and 'Dr Trimmer,' the last coined by Francis C. Burnand, a former Cuddesdon student who became editor of *Punch*. In Burnand's autobiography, Wilberforce ('Dr Trimmer') appears as the Bishop of Bulford and Cuddesdon itself as St Bede's College.[8] Yet, Wilberforce, unlike both his brothers and Manning (and F. C. Burnand), never went over to Rome and had little time for the Romanizing of the later Ritualists of the second generation of Tractarian clergy.

During his years as Bishop of Oxford, and then briefly, before his untimely death in 1873, as Bishop of Winchester, Wilberforce can be seen, certainly with the benefit of hindsight, to have initiated a renewed form of episcopal ministry and diocesan pastoral care which undoubtedly influenced Edward King in his reforms of the role of a bishop, in both church and society. The age of the railway, with its web-like network expanding throughout the nineteenth century connecting town and countryside alike, enabled Wilberforce in Oxfordshire to know and visit his far-flung parishes as no Western bishop had ever been able to do since the earliest days of smaller dioceses.

Wilberforce, like King many years later, saw great potential and opportunity in the bishop's ministry of the Sacrament of Confirmation, as not only affording opportunities for the bishop to become a familiar face at the grass roots level of the diocese, in and around the parishes, but also, for the occasion of Confirmation, to build spiritual renewal into the diocese as a whole. In this way, Wilberforce 'personalized' the ministry of Confirmation in ways which in future years up to our own day, all the bishops dutifully do. Like King, it was through visiting parishes and ministering Confirmation that Wilberforce made his greatest impact at the parish level, with both laity and parochial clergy.

He galvanized the ecclesiastical infra-structures of his diocese so that decisions and business at the centre radiated through his archdeacon and his rural deans to his parochial clergy. 'His Archdeacon, Archdeacon Randall and his Rural Deans were an admirable machinery,' writes his biographer, 'but if that machinery was not absolutely of his own creating, it was he who put it together and brought it into working order.'[9]

He formed a Bishop's Council, with meetings held at the Palace in Cuddesdon, where he saw to it that 'the life and spirit of these meetings circulated afterwards through the rural-decanal chapters,' and through them down to parish level.[10]

The measure of his energy can be traced on two fronts. First, in the amazing number of churches built, renewed and restored during his episcopate. During the twenty-five years before Wilberforce became bishop, only twenty-two new churches were built in the three counties of his diocese (Oxford, Berkshire and Buckinghamshire); four were rebuilt and eight restored or enlarged. In the twenty-four years of Wilberforce's time at Oxford, no less than one-hundred-and-six new churches were built, fifteen rebuilt and two-hundred-and-fifty restored.

In January 1846, just a month after his consecration, he put together an 'Agenda—Things which the Diocese Needed,' and second on this list was 'Diocesan Training College for Clergy to be established at Cuddesdon.' That he was able to achieve this within ten years or so of coming into office was an outstanding achievement.[11]

Cuddesdon: 'A New Generation of Clergy'

So, although Wilberforce's considerable intelligence, vast resources of energy and an astonishing facility with speech enabled him to play a major role nationally, in the House of Lords and in Convocation—quite unlike King—he did not neglect either the clergy or the parishes of his diocese, nor the increasing and efficient diocesan administration— this also quite unlike King, who always neglected diocesan administration for the overriding and primary claims of pastoral care.

Frequently accused of worldliness because of his easy access to the Prime Ministers of the day, and his friendship with the Queen and Prince Albert, Wilberforce strove to resist the temptations which tend to accompany public office by a ruthless annual self-examination on the anniversary of his consecration. On the fourth anniversary, 30 November 1849, he observed:

> The great danger of the Church of England [is] secularity. I set to strive against this: (*a*) In myself, in my own soul ... (*b*) In my household and family ... (*c*) In trying by degrees to raise my clergy, by (1) example; (2) intercourse; (3) if God should ever give me the means, *a Diocesan College, invaluable here* (I visitor). Secularity, for many reasons, the weakness of our Church.[12]

THE FOUNDING OF CUDDESDON

The college where King was to spend the next fifteen years after leaving Wheatley, was from start to finish the brainchild of Bishop Wilberforce. Although several persons in the diocese, and further afield, viewed his proposal to build it so close to the Bishop's Palace—indeed, the original intention was to build it within the Palace grounds—as unwise, nevertheless the diocese subscribed generously to the bishop's great project. By February 1853, £3,000 had been raised. It was to be purpose-built for a residential community of staff and students, and the design was entrusted to the young George Edmund Street, still only twenty-nine years of age, who was later to become famous as the architect of the new Royal Courts of Justice in The Strand. For Street, the classical style which had prevailed in the eighteenth century in both ecclesiastical and domestic architecture was perceived as being 'barbarous and bad.' For him, it had to be 'Gothic Revival,' a style harking back to the imagined romantic period of medievalism.

The foundation stone for the new college was laid by Wilberforce on 7 April 1853, when a procession of choristers and some hundred clergy, battling against heavy rain and bitter winds, made their way 'slowly and sadly' (Wilberforce's own words) from the Palace to the site. Despite the inclement weather, Wilberforce insisted on addressing the somewhat bedraggled gathering. Outlining his vision and the purposes for which the college was to be built, he was adamant that it must be in close physical proximity to the Palace, and under the personal oversight of the bishop: 'the present mode of preparing for ordination is unsatisfactory and such preparation ought rather to be carried on under the close superintendence of the Bishop of the diocese.' And again: 'Institutions of this kind, under the direct management of the Bishop, will keep young men together in discipline, will give them parochial experience, and tend to form habits of life for the future ... Far be it from me,'—doubtless with one eye over his shoulder in the direction of nearby Oxford and the representatives of the University in the crowd—'to say anything in disparagement of our universities, yet they do not meet the case. They may be all very well for those who wish to arrive at abstruse theological learning, but we want something which shall more directly prepare men, who have gone through a general education, for the practical duties of a clergyman.'

After referring to the 'good work' done by similar institutions at Wells, Durham and Chichester, he spoke of the work with which the Church of the day was confronted in order 'to meet a growing intelligence in the masses,' for 'in proportion as the people advance, so will their teachers need the greater preparation.'

Concluding his address, he urged the assembled gathering 'to pray that God, by His grace, will finish what he has begun; that he will keep this College ever free from party and sectarian disputes, so that we may rear therein clergymen with the spirit of Richard Hooker and the temper of Lancelot Andrewes.'[13]

It is worthy of note that under the terms of the Trust Deed, the college was to be 'a school for the theological training of candidates for Holy Orders in the Church of England and Ireland, and for no other purpose whatsoever,' and with the further explicit requirement that it should 'be under the sole management and control of the said Samuel, Lord Bishop of Oxford, and his successors for the time being.'[14]

Building work proceeded slowly. A formal opening had been planned for Easter 1854, but delays, in part due to a builders' strike, meant that the first phase of the work was not completed until August 1854. Nevertheless, and notwithstanding the hiccups of the previous months, the formal opening went ahead as scheduled on 15 June 1854, when once again, as on the occasion of laying the foundation stone, there was heavy rain which fortuitously eased off when the formal ceremony began.

On this occasion there was a huge and impressive turnout. A choir one hundred strong, made up of choirboys from several Oxford parishes, students from Culham (Wilberforce's college for training teachers, founded scarcely a year previously), and members of the Oxford Plainsong Society, gathered in the schoolhouse for a lunch provided by the bishop. (Wilberforce had always maintained that music was important in acts of worship and was the first bishop to introduce singing at his Confirmations.) At about 1.30pm the choir proceeded to the parish church, taking their place in the transepts, while the chancel was occupied by seven bishops—Oxford, Blomfield of London (somewhat surprisingly), Bangor, Chichester, Worcester, St David's and Bishop Selwyn, who had landed a month before from New Zealand. The nave was filled by 250 clergy in surplices and two in black preaching gowns. For the laity it was almost completely standing room only. Selwyn preached an eloquent sermon on the text from Isaiah (60:22): 'A little one shall become a thousand.'[15]

After the service, the procession filed back to the College, and the bishops climbed up to the little chapel to dedicate it, while the concourse outside sang the *Veni Creator* and two psalms, presumably to a Plainsong setting.

Then, standing on a platform beside the main doorway, Wilberforce addressed the gathering. He had three main themes: the first, predictably, the necessity of having the college 'close to the residence of the Bishop of the diocese, where day by day, he might see and pray with and help those who were shortly to come under his hand for ordination ... as in the earlier times of the Church.' Secondly, to reject, once and for all, any suggestion of rivalry or 'opposition between two of the Church's works, as that mighty University [Oxford] and this institution,' in their ability to give to the clergy 'an opportunity of study and prayer, and the benefit of seclusion and quiet before being sent out to the work to which they are devoted.' For then, he asserted, 'those most interested in the welfare of the University' would 'regard this work [Cuddesdon College] with no narrow prejudice, but rather look upon it as calculated to aid, in the course of God's providence, the great work of evangelizing the world through the medium of Christianizing education.'[16]

And then, turning to the bishops, he rejoiced that they had come, because by their very attendance they would 'imprint by more than words upon those who have entered upon this work that, what we are doing here is for the Church of

Cuddesdon: 'A New Generation of Clergy'

our fathers; for no section of it, for nothing narrower than that true Church of England as God in His providence has planted in this island, to help us to send forth to the work of the ministry men trained to increasing activity; men trained to becoming habits and taught what it is to give their days to prayer and meditation; men fitted by practical knowledge derived from ministration in neighbouring parishes to act with usefulness in their own.'

His address concluded with a burst of typical rhetoric, asking for the prayers of all those present, so that 'the dew of God's Spirit may fall upon this place ... that God's Word may be our guide, His truth our light, His strength our guard ... that we may be enabled to send out from these walls men humble, thoughtful, careful, patient, and simple lovers of Christ's truth, lovers of souls,' then, picking up on Selwyn's earlier sermon, that God 'will make this one to become many, and our little one as a thousand.'[17]

To conclude the proceedings, the other bishops spoke in turn: Chichester giving evidence of the value of his recently founded college; Worcester, testifying that his best young clergy were those trained at the new colleges in Chichester or Wells, and Bishop Selwyn endorsing the necessity of such institutions for preparing men for work in the mission field overseas.

At the end of the day, Wilberforce was clearly satisfied with the apparent success of the proceedings, commenting in a thankful letter to his brother, Robert: 'The opening of my College went off excellently. Indeed, I do not see how it could have been better ... Now we want pupils, and all will, please God, go well.'[18]

A NEW CHALLENGE

It is clear, at least retrospectively, that everything in Wilberforce's mind pointed to Edward King, whom he had ordained, as the obvious candidate to become the second chaplain at Cuddesdon in 1858.

King had been notably happy, content and fulfilled in his ministry as the curate at Wheatley. He had been in the parish for four years, when he received a summons that was destined to change the whole pattern of his life and future ministry. Initially, the call came from the Revd Alfred Pott, Vicar of the nearby parish of Cuddesdon and first Principal of the new College. King seems to have had some inkling of what was impending, but he was still taken aback when Pott disclosed to him that Wilberforce was set on appointing him as chaplain.

The young curate's state of mind is evident from the letter he wrote to his father on 31 March 1858, the day after his interview with Pott:

> The cloud which I predicted when you were here rose yesterday morning above the horizon of imagination and is now plainly in view. Pott sent for me yesterday, he being ill, and as I expected, it was to talk about the College. The Bishop has been at Cuddesdon, and is determined on a firm change of *tone* and *persons* ... He has not asked me himself, but he has more than once told Pott to bring it about, and the Bishop will ask as soon as he returns.[19]

Wilberforce, who took the closest personal interest in his new foundation, wanted the best possible staff for its formative period and was determined to recruit King. The latter, however, was acutely conscious of his comparative lack of academic qualifications, and his indifferent health. But the overriding factor was his unwillingness to leave Wheatley.

From the letter to his father, it is clear that there were other factors which inclined him towards refusing the offer even at the risk disappointing the bishop:

> Against it there is: 1. My present work; 2. The extreme difficulty of the undertaking. I can see plainly the great judgement it requires. The extremes [in churchmanship]

Cuddesdon: 'A New Generation of Clergy'

will be up in arms, the old work will be called spoilt, and the new man not up to his work, etc., etc.; but this is all human. There is on the other side: 1. The Bishop's positive wish (if expressed, as I expect). 2. My present work is at a certain point, and not without dangers to myself on the score of popularity and personal gratification. 3. I cannot but feel that my impaired health would not warrant my playing the short game; I ought at least to fit myself for an average life of work. Three or four years at the College might supply the lack of knowledge which will be especially required by me if, as we have said, my line is to be to take a large, rather than a small, living and to guide a curate.

Pott told the Bishop that I did not wish to move, but he still persisted. Of course, I should not for a moment entertain the idea if it was merely to fill the place of the old chaplain; but the case alters if they want to do a hard work, and ask you openly to come and do it, *viz.* change the tone.[20]

In his reply, King's father, concerned about his son's health, urged him to decline. But, after a meeting between Wilberforce and King which long remained vivid in King's memory, the bishop prevailed. Years later he recalled it for an old and intimate friend—King himself standing by the stile which led into the wood between Wheatley and Cuddesdon, while the bishop, on horseback, talked persuasively to him about leaving his curacy and going to Cuddesdon as chaplain. After King had protested and rather begged (it would appear) to be allowed to stay on in his parish, Wilberforce at last, 'kicked his horse and rode off, saying, "Well, I think you ought to go."'[21]

Subsequent to that meeting and after further consideration, King finally, if reluctantly, accepted the challenge. He moved into his rooms in Cuddesdon in November 1858, and was soon at home there. His new colleague, H. P. Liddon, the Vice-Principal, wrote to a former student: 'You know that King of Wheatley has finally taken up his abode here and I hope that the new Principal [H. H. Swinny, who was about to succeed Pott] will not lead to his going. He is a great help to the whole place: a shrewd man and *such* a downright Christian,'[22]—no small compliment from a man like Liddon.

Cuddesdon, like its predecessors in other dioceses, provided a course of study related to the work of the ordained ministry, embracing biblical studies, theology, church history, pastoralia and spirituality. Yet it also had a number of distinctive features. Just across the road from the episcopal palace and directly under the bishop's watchful eye, it was on the edge of Oxford, and yet quite distinct from the University, which informed critics saw as increasingly secularized. Writing to a friend, Keble lamented:

> What sad accounts I hear of the Germanization and secularization of Oxford. I should think it would be very soon necessary for people who wish their sons to have a fair chance of being Christians to send them to some other place; and for Bishops to resort ordinarily to the Theological Colleges ... Oxford I fear is too far gone (in the Germanizing way)—unless Cuddesdon proves able to stop the decay: certainly, there seems a great blessing on that place.[23]

Nor was it only High Churchmen like Keble who perceived the signs of secularization. Matthew Arnold, writing to his wife about Oxford in 1854, the year Cuddesdon opened, observed wryly: 'The place, in losing Newman and his followers, has lost its religious movement, which after all kept it from stagnating, and has not yet, so far as I can see, got anything better.'[24]

There is also evidence that the men themselves who came up to Oxford with the intention of seeking ordination, did not think very highly of the preparation they received. R. W. Dixon, the future Tractarian church historian, entered Pembroke College in 1852, and readily confessed, 'I did not find it in a good state. The Master did nothing in tuition except a Sunday Lecture in Greek Testament. There was very little discipline, no social intercourse between the fellows and the undergraduates, and Collections were merely a nominal ceremony.'[25]

THE DISTINCTIVE CHARACTER OF WILBERFORCE'S CUDDESDON

In the mind of Wilberforce, Cuddesdon was to be the episcopal remedy for this malaise in the right place, at the right time. It not only provided a course of study carefully geared to ordination, it also linked all its academic work to pastoral practice and the clergyman's inner life of devotion. Furthermore, at the pastoral level, Cuddesdon was unique in giving the principal the additional role of vicar of the parish whom the bishop, as patron, appointed. His students, therefore, not only heard his lectures on pastoral theology; they observed him in day-to-day pastoral practice, leading worship in a country church, which they also attended, catechizing the children, visiting the sick, and fulfilling the whole round of duties of a country parson. In that way, Cuddesdon was, until recently, unique.

Another vital element in Cuddesdon's favour for the training of its ordinands was the quality of its communal life—living, studying, eating and praying together as a community under the same roof. The earlier colleges at Wells and Chichester, did not initially offer a collegiate way of life; students lived in lodgings, meeting and engaging with each other only at lectures and chapel. Cuddesdon offered an altogether fresh approach, where the idea of a common life was developed, sustained by an ordered pattern of corporate prayer and personal devotion. Formation, whether priestly or otherwise, is nurtured best in the corporate life of family or community, in which the members help to make and remake each other for better or worse. Disembodied information, in whatever form it is delivered, lacks that quality and breadth of a rounded education in the course of which formation, and indeed transformation and maturity, are realized.

Given the deficiencies of the universities in providing ordination training, it had not been uncommon for an ordinand, after graduation, to live for a time in the home of a parish priest, who would guide his reading and give him some practical experience of pastoral work, along the lines of an 'apprenticeship'—indeed, King's time with John Day at Ellesmere had been something along those lines. The outstanding exemplar of this pattern of training was provided by C. J. Vaughan (1816–97), sometime Fellow of Trinity College, Cambridge, who over thirty years as Vicar of Doncaster trained some four hundred young graduates for the ministry in a kind of apprenticeship—'Vaughan's doves,' as they were known. They received a good grounding in pastoralia, but, as they lived in separate lodgings, had little or no experience of the common life.

It was this experience of the common life as part of a community committed to prayer as well as to study, which marked out Cuddesdon as being of singular importance in the Church's understanding of what was needed for priestly formation for many years to come.

EXTERNAL OPPOSITION AND CONTROVERSY

When King joined the staff of Cuddesdon in 1858, he was conscious of being part of this new experiment in clergy training. He himself had trained in the old way in the parish, understudying his vicar and reading as and when he could. Many clergymen still thought the old way was best, and looked with undisguised suspicion, if not contempt, on what they saw as the new-fangled theological colleges. Did they not smack of the Roman seminary? Were they not in danger of becoming artificial hothouses, taking men

Cuddesdon: 'A New Generation of Clergy'

away from the realities of parish life and breeding in them an all too cloistered piety? Again, were they not likely to encourage a narrow party spirit, alien to the comprehensiveness of the Church of England? Cuddesdon, as a High Church foundation was especially open to this latter charge. As chaplain, King soon found himself embroiled in controversy—a foretaste of the dissension which, despite his eirenic spirit, was to accompany him at recurring intervals throughout his whole ministry.

INTERNAL CONTROVERSY

The controversy which overshadowed those early years, however, arose not merely from external criticism, but also from within the College itself, and from its relationship with its episcopal founder. From the outset, it had been Wilberforce's intention to have a hands-on, day-to-day relationship with his foundation, but it soon became clear that, as a reforming bishop, he also wanted that same hands-on, day-to-day relationship with the scattered parishes of his largely rural diocese. Add to that his administrative zeal focused on the root-and-branch reorganization of the diocese, to say nothing of the many calls on his time in London at the House of Lords, and countless associated commitments, and it soon became clear that his erstwhile laudable intentions, would have to be radically revised. Something had to give, and it did.

From the day of his consecration, Wilberforce's determination to improve the quality of the parish clergy was a central plank in his reforming zeal, and Cuddesdon was to be one of the prime means to this end. Unfortunately, from the start, the College and its reputation was beset by 'party and sectarian disputes,' precisely the sort of thing Wilberforce had prayed for Cuddesdon to be free from in his speech at the opening ceremony. The disputes centred on the churchmanship, or more precisely the reputed churchmanship of the College. Both students and staff, as well as the bishop, differed as to the level of churchmanship which was acceptable, and also as to the 'tone' (Wilberforce's word), which should characterize the community life there.

The first intake of students, accustomed to the freedom of their University days, did not easily or readily adjust to the stricter ethos of a theological seminary. In the harsh winter of 1855 they spent their afternoons ice-skating, and shocked the local villagers by 'wearing fez caps, coloured ties, and smoking short clay pipes'—although smoking was strictly forbidden in the College itself. This 'worldly' behaviour had led King, then still a curate at Wheatley, and Edward Sturges, curate at nearby Haseley, to make known to the Principal the consequent disquiet of their parishioners, who expected better things of those preparing for ordination.[26]

The bishop himself frowned on any suggestion that the students might be allowed to take part in organized games. He rejected out of hand (9 March 1855), a request for a fives court (an integral feature at several public schools), and 'discountenanced' a proposal for a cricket ground. It seems clear that he wanted to mark a sharp distinction between the leisurely life of the University and the disciplined ethos of his seminary. In his 'suggestions' for the pattern of life at Cuddesdon, he stressed the need to learn 'Habits of self-denial' and the 'Great importance of conduct in the eyes of others—The Village and University Men.'[27]

HENRY PARRY LIDDON AND CUDDESDON

More specifically, there was the question of Henry Liddon, appointed Vice-Principal at the age of twenty-four. From the outset, Liddon exercised a great influence over the students, notably more so than Pott, the first Principal, who lived out of College and was more preoccupied with his associated

Cuddesdon: 'A New Generation of Clergy'

duties as vicar of the parish. Liddon himself lived a life of strict and disciplined devotion, and imparted his views of priestly character and formation to the men.[28] He insisted that the rubric of the Book of Common Prayer obliged Anglican clergymen, either publicly or in private, to say the Daily Offices of Morning and Evening Prayer. Under his influence, Compline was introduced on three evenings a week: other minor monastic Offices (Prime, Terce, Sext, None) were also included in the College Office Book which Liddon had devised—*Hours of Prayer for Daily Use throughout the Year* (1856). He encouraged regular biblical meditation, and provided for his students' guidance in 'Rules for Meditating.' He was also a spiritual guide and confidant to the men, his afternoon walks with individual students proving deeply influential for those who responded to his approach.

Added to this, were strains and stresses, which soon began to appear in the life of the college. Wilberforce's intention to maintain close supervision was thwarted by his frequent absences on diocesan and national duties. Internal differences opened up between the Bishop and the Principal on the one side, and the Vice-Principal and Chaplain (initially, Albert Barff) on the other. As founder, Wilberforce had to bear the brunt of the attacks made on the college, as an allegedly extreme High Church, if not Romanizing, institution. That the college had developed a demonstrably 'Catholic' style of worship and devotion, was due largely to Liddon. Wilberforce had had scruples about appointing him, knowing him to be a devoted disciple of Pusey, whom Wilberforce regarded—quite incorrectly and unjustifiably—as being a far too zealous High Church party man, with Romanizing tendencies. Wilberforce insisted that Liddon should stop consulting Pusey for spiritual guidance, and go instead to the more moderate churchman, John Keble.

Despite this, what Wilberforce had feared might happen, through Liddon's influence on his ordinands, showed distinct signs of taking hold. During his five years as Vice-Principal (1854–9), the college acquired a strong High Church ethos. Liddon strongly recommending the use of the Sacrament of Confession for particular students. Furthermore, the College Office Book he had compiled was criticized by the 'Commission of Inquiry' instituted by the bishop following the growing number of outspoken attacks on the college. While acknowledging that the book's prayers and hymns were 'highly valuable,' the Inquiry regretted that it had 'been cast in a form which bears an unfortunate resemblance to the Breviary of the Church of Rome.'[29] The former Cuddesdon student F. C. Burnand described Liddon (under the pseudonym Mr D'Oyley Glyde) as 'the very picture of a wily Italian priest.'[30]

Evangelical churchmen joined in the fray and soon began to sharpen their knives for attacks on the college and its episcopal founder. As early as 1855, when the college held its first Annual Festival, there were rumblings of disquiet among the visiting clergy. The ceremonial for the Eucharist was put in the hands of a student, F. G. Lee, who had distinct Romanizing tendencies, and much of the liturgical proceedings shocked the visitors. By 1858, attacks on Cuddesdon had begun to appear in print. The *Quarterly Review* for January 1858 carried an anonymous article entitled 'Church Extension,' explicitly criticizing Cuddesdon. It was this article which later served as the basis for what Wilberforce termed 'an inflammatory public appeal' against the college, launched by the redoubtable controversialist Charles Portales Golightly. A devoted clergyman who once served as Newman's curate, Golightly made it his personal mission to combat all innovation in the Church of England's worship and teaching, and it was he, who, on 8 March 1841, had brought together the four leading Oxford tutors who had written a public letter to Newman condemning *Tract XC*.[31]

Before Wilberforce could reply to the *Quarterly Review* article, Golightly circulated a letter addressed to the laity and clergy of the Oxford Diocese, detailing the charges

Cuddesdon: 'A New Generation of Clergy'

against Cuddesdon contained in the article. He had already made his views known to the bishop in a letter of September 1857, in which he claimed that 'the senior members of the University, the nobility and gentry of the diocese, had a feeling of mistrust and alienation toward the Bishop on account of the system pursued at the College.' Golightly went on to stigmatize Vice-Principal Liddon as a well-known disciple of Dr Pusey, and therefore of dubious loyalty to the Church of England. These claims evidently touched a raw nerve in Wilberforce, who replied robustly to Golightly:

> You are quite right in saying that I quite abhor Romish doctrine, but you are mistaken in thinking that I like Romish rites and ceremonies. Everything Romish stinks in my nostrils. I cannot allow the truth of your remark about Cuddesdon College. Men had come there with strong Romish leanings, and have left it cured, but I do not believe anyone had there acquired any Romish tastes. There are, it is true, little things that I should wish otherwise, but men must work by instruments of the greatest possible excellence in fundamentals; and it would, in my judgment, be clearly wrong to cast them away for non-essentials. I think my Vice-Principal is eminently endowed with the power of leading men to earnest, devoted piety; with such a man I do not think I ought to interfere except as to anything substantially important. I have a strong conviction that Cuddesdon College is doing GOD'S work for men's souls mightily.[32]

The *Quarterly Review* article and Golightly's circular letter had placed the controversy over Cuddesdon squarely in the public domain, motivating Wilberforce to appoint his three archdeacons as a 'Commission of Inquiry' into the facts. He also sent out a questionnaire to all the parochial clergy to whom the college had supplied a curate, asking:

> 1. Have you observed in any Curate employed by you, who had been trained at our College, any tendency to teaching or practices other than those of the Church of England? 2. If you have observed any such tendency,

should you say that it had been fostered or repressed at Cuddesdon?[33]

Their report rebutted Golightly's charges as false, and their judgment was supported by the replies received from thirty-nine incumbents. With only two exceptions, these men of varying schools of churchmanship expressed unqualified approval of their curates. The two who gave qualified approval said that, although they had experienced some differences of view with their curates, these differences had no relation to Roman Catholic teaching or ritual.

In all this controversy, Bishop Wilberforce was in a difficult personal position. Not only was he vulnerable as the founder of a High Church college, but his own ecclesiastical position laid him open to criticism. He had been raised in the Evangelical tradition of his father and had never repudiated his Evangelical upbringing. At the same time, his thought and practice had developed in a more High-Church direction, though never espousing the Tractarian agenda or becoming a party man. In a frank and uncompromising letter to a friend, written on 31 January 1842, Wilberforce leaves no doubt as to his views:

> I never was ... in any degree a tractarian. It is far too cramped, and crotchetty, and narrow, and dogmatic a circle for you ever to have been enticed into it. I have always been (before they were warm on the subject) a staunch Churchman ... In truth, from the very first they have been essentially non-Anglican ... their hatred of the Reformation, their leaning to a visible centre of unity for the Church, the essence of Popery, their unnationality, for they have no notion of a national life; their cramped and formal dogmatism; their fearful doctrine of sin after baptism, and many other things of the same cast, revolted me long since.[34]

There was yet further embarrassment for Wilberforce in all this. By 1857, his two brothers, Robert and Henry, together with his brother-in-law, Henry Manning, had all joined

Cuddesdon: 'A New Generation of Clergy'

the Church of Rome, and in some eyes the bishop himself incurred a measure of guilt, if only by association. He was understandably doubly sensitive, therefore, to any suggestion that he was moving in the same direction.

Yet while Wilberforce vigorously rebutted outside criticisms of his college, he gradually began to have his own misgivings about the way its life was developing. Demands on time meant that Wilberforce himself was unable to continue that close supervision he had given at the beginning and increasingly the staff assumed independent control, with Vice-Principal Liddon exerting a strong High-Church influence over the students and the general ethos. On his appointment, Liddon had given Wilberforce an undertaking that he would not recommend private Confession indiscriminately to his students. Yet his pronounced High Churchmanship continued to make itself felt in that, as in other ways.

STAFF CHANGES

The pressure of the outside attacks on the college, and the attendant publicity, contributed to changes in the original staff. Albert Barff, the chaplain, had left in 1858, and later that year Pott continued to press Wilberforce to accept his resignation on the grounds of ill-health. He suffered from severe spinal troubles and that, together with the internal tensions and the controversy further afield, led him to feel that the care of the college needed to be in the hands of someone more robust and fitter in health. Wilberforce finally accepted Pott's resignation—which was formally announced to the students on 2 November 1858—on the understanding that it would not take effect until the following Easter to give the bishop time to find a successor. By this time, the student body had sunk alarmingly to only nine ordinands, itself a clear indication of the decline in morale. In that same year

Edward King

two former Cuddesdon students, J. A. Maude and F. C. Burnand, converted to Roman Catholicism, further damaging the college's reputation in the eyes of many Anglicans. From every point of view, it was in need of regeneration: and it was in this regeneration that King was destined to play a strategic role, initially as chaplain, but of a far greater and lasting significance, as Principal.

Notes

1. F. W. B. Bullock, *The History of Ridley Hall Cambridge*, 2 vols. Cambridge University Press, 1941/1953, vol. I, p. 23.
2. Martin Thornton, *English Spirituality*. London: SPCK, 1963, p. 3.
3. Owen Chadwick, *The Founding of Cuddesdon*. Oxford University Press, 1954, p. 4.
4. *Ibid.*, p. 5.
5. A. N. Wilson, *Charles Darwin: Victorian Mythmaker*. London: John Murray, 2017, pp. 258ff.
6. Chadwick, *op. cit.*, p. 15.
7. Quoted *ibid.*, p. 10.
8. F. C. Burnand, *My Time, and What I've Done with It. An Autobiography*. London; MacMillian & Co., 1874 (2nd ed.).
9. A. R. Ashwell and G. R. Wilberforce, *The Life of the Right Reverend Samuel Wilberforce, D.D.*, 3 vols. London: John Murray, 1880-2, vol. II, pp. 2ff.
10. *Ibid.*, p. 3.
11. Chadwick, *op. cit.*, p. 12.
12. Reginald Wilberforce, *Life of Samuel Wilberforce*. London: Kegan Paul, Trench & Co., 1888, p. 50.
13. Chadwick, *op. cit.*, pp. 16–17.
14. *Ibid.*, p. 18.
15. *Ibid.*, p. 21.
16. *Ibid.*, p. 22.
17. *Ibid.*, p. 23.
18. *Ibid.*
19. George W. E. Russell, *Edward King Sixtieth Bishop of Lincoln*, p. 15.
20. *Ibid.*, p. 16.
21. *Ibid.*
22. Chadwick, *op. cit.*, p. 79.
23. *Ibid.*, pp. 7ff.

Cuddesdon: 'A New Generation of Clergy'

24. *The Works of Matthew Arnold*, 15 vols. London: Macmillan & Co., 1904, vol. XIII (Letters), p. 51.
25. Douglas Macleane, *A History of Pembroke College, Oxford*. Oxford, Clarendon Press (for the Oxford Historical Society), 1897, p. 460n.
26. Chadwick, *op. cit.*, p. 28.
27. *Ibid.*
28. See Liddon's 'The Priest in his Inner Life,' in the *Ecclesiastic and Theologian*, October 1856 and January 1857.
29. *Cuddesdon College 1854–1929: A Record and Memorial*. Oxford: at the University Press, 1930, pp. 96–7.
30. Burnand, *op. cit.*, p. 413.
31. The four were: Henry Wilson (St John's); T. T. Churton (Brasenose); A. C. Tait (Balliol), later Archbishop Tait of the Public Worship Regulation Act; and J. Griffiths (Wadham). See M. A. Crowther, *Church Embattled: Religious Controversy in Mid-Victorian England*. Newton Abbot: David and Charles, 1970, p. 111.
32. R. G. Wilberforce, *Leaders of the Church, 1800–1900* (ed. George W. E. Russell). London: A. R. Mowbray & Co. Ltd, 1905, p. 106.
33. *Ibid.*, pp. 108–9.
34. S. Wilberforce and John Wilson Croker, 31 January 1842, in *The Croker Papers*, London: John Murray, 1884, vol. II, p. 411.

PART TWO

Priest, Principal, Professor

✣ 5 ✣

King and Cuddesdon

KING'S EARLY YEARS AT CUDDESDON

It was in 1858, the 'Year of the Great Stink,' that Wilberforce, after the turmoil of the first four years, took decisive steps to strategically reform his college at Cuddesdon. His first and most pressing task was to find a replacement for Pott, who was resigning his Principalship for health reasons. Throughout those early years, Wilberforce had always implicitly trusted Pott, with whom he enjoyed a good working relationship and was reluctant to lose. But having accepted Pott's resignation in November 1858, he was faced with the prospect of finding a successor by Easter 1859, when Pott's resignation took effect, and he lost no time in going out in search of one.

The first name on his list was none other than J. W. Burgon, Fellow of Oriel College, who, after his interview with Wilberforce, was strongly inclined to accept. But subsequently, and somewhat characteristically, he declined it on the grounds that he could not possibly work with Liddon: 'I have convinced myself that it would be about as reasonable to expect that a chronometer could keep time while half the mechanism is defective, as that the institution should work well, while Liddon is there.'[1] However, it is doubtful whether the contentious Burgon would ever have been the right man to bring peace and a new direction to the institution, with or without Liddon. 'He was brusque and opinionated. He enjoyed controversy, and his language in controversy sometimes went to lengths of acerbity that were grotesque.'[2]

Edward King

While he admired Liddon, Wilberforce was not unsympathetic to Burgon's opinion. In a revealing letter to a friend, he details his misgivings about the life of the college under Liddon's regime:

> Our men are too *peculiar*—some, at least, of our best men. I shall never consider that we have succeeded until a Cuddesdon man can be known from a non-Cuddesdon man only by his loving more, working more, and praying more. I consider it a heavy affliction that they should wear neckcloths of peculiar construction, coats of peculiar cut, whiskers of peculiar dimensions—that they should walk with a peculiar step, carry their heads at a peculiar angle to the body, and read in a peculiar tone. I consider all this as a heavy affliction. First, because it implies to me a want of vigour, virility and self-expressing vitality of the religious life in the young men. It shows they come out too much cut only by a machine and not enough imbued with living influences. Secondly, because it greatly limits their usefulness and ours by the natural prejudice which it excites. Then these are things in the actual life I wish changed. The tendencies to crowd the walls with pictures of the *Mater Dolorosa* etc., their chimneypieces with crosses, their studies with saints, all offend me and all do incalculable injury to the College in the eye of chance visitors. The habit of some of the men of kneeling in a sort of rapt prayer on the steps of the communion-table, when they cannot be *alone* there, when visitors are coming in and going out and talking around them: such prayers should be 'in the closet' with the 'door shut'—and setting apart their grave dangers, as I apprehend them to be to the young men, they really force on visitors the feeling of the strict resemblance to what they see in Belgium, etc., and never in Church of England churches.[3]

Part of the 'peculiar work' was to change the tone and ethos which Liddon's powerful personality had stamped on the life of the college. It is the measure of Wilberforce's deep respect for King, still not turned thirty, that the bishop turned to the new chaplain for a frank opinion as to what was amiss at Cuddesdon. King, somewhat diffidently, replied in a twelve-page letter setting out his views on the matter.

No doubt he already knew something of the college and its recent difficulties from his time at nearby Wheatley. Now, he could give the bishop his impressions with the fresh eyes of a newcomer on the staff. He discerned that there was, indeed, 'something wrong' with the college's life, and reluctantly but candidly, felt compelled to point the finger at Liddon, with whom personally he was on good terms, both as a friend and colleague: 'Most unwillingly do I write these words. I think the cause of the wrong will be found in the dear Vice-Principal. I know he is the soul of the College. *(a)* I do not mean that it is absolutely necessary that he should go—it should be the *very, very* last alteration made. *(b)* I do mean that, in my judgement at least, if he remains, he must *decidedly* change, or suffer a change to be made by another.' Perhaps one of the most telling points of King's criticism was his regret over Liddon's attempt to 'fit the Cuddesdon shoe on every foot.'[4]

Liddon's mistake, which King had put his finger on, stemmed from a misguided zeal for principles, overriding the unique makeup of persons; when religious conviction degenerates into a rigid and enforced ideology; when the spirit is forcefully surrendered to the apparently attractive, neat, efficient and prevailing system—in a word, wherever compassion and love are missing. Liddon, the great articulate preacher and compelling churchman, nevertheless lacked that personal touch which any good leader needs in order to secure the willing loyalty of his followers or those in his care, and which was such an attractive attribute of King's own personality.

On receiving King's diagnosis, Wilberforce found his own fears confirmed, and in 1859, with genuine regret, he insisted that Liddon resign his post.

Edward King

Within a year, Liddon had left to become Vice-Principal of St Edmund's Hall in Oxford. A letter to his sister is highly significant, as representing precisely that 'fortress mentality,' verging on paranoia, which pulls up the drawbridge between faith and a spirit of genuine enquiry and questioning, and between communities of faith and communities and disciplines of learning—that dangerous dualistic worldview in which ultimately both parties loose.

'I think it could be possible to turn St Edmund Hall into a little Christian Fortress in the midst of Rationalism and Indifferentism which lay modern Oxford waste.'[5] Perhaps from the outset the formation of such 'a little Christian Fortress' had been the underlying, albeit unconscious, objective of Liddon's ministry at Cuddesdon. If such were the case and the college had gone on to adopt a 'fortress mentality,' its life-span would have been severely truncated and its great influence on the wider Church neutered by the challenges to faith in subsequent years.

On leaving Cuddesdon his pupils presented him with a parting gift of seventy-three volumes of theology.

A REPLACEMENT FOR LIDDON

Providentially, in Wilberforce's mind, it was all too apparent that there in the wings, was exactly the right man who would bring peace and the new direction the college so urgently needed—Edward King, the new chaplain. Wilberforce had but one reservation about King's suitability for the job—his somewhat limited intellectual background, being, as he put it to Burgon, 'neither a Hebraist nor a patristic theologian.'

Burgon, who had always held King in high regard, succeeded in calming the bishop's reservations about King's apparent 'limited intellectual powers': 'King is the right man,' he wrote, in typically stentorian tones, underscoring his words to drive home his conviction. 'You do not want

Hebrew, my dear Lord. You want to make men *read their Bibles and understand their Prayer Books;* know *how to prepare children for confirmation* and *imbibe the pastoral spirit.* You want to make *exemplary parish priests*—good *preachers*—good *teachers*—good *visitors of the poor.*'⁶

So, Burgon persuaded Wilberforce to make the offer. King spent a week thinking and praying over it. How could he, King asserted with typical humility in a letter to the bishop, 'with every misgiving' in regard to himself, step into Liddon's shoes? 'I am most unwilling to take the place of one I love and admire *so* much.'⁷

While the bishop persisted in pressing him to take up the post of Vice-Principal, King had declined Liddon's own, somewhat disruptive suggestion that he should leave Cuddesdon and take over the notable Tractarian parish of St Saviour's in Leeds. Characteristically, King felt that he could not desert the college when morale was at such a low ebb, and that by staying on, he would be able to provide some continuity when the posts of Principal and Vice-Principal had been filled. In reply to Liddon's suggestion, he wrote:

> To be short, I do not think I ought to leave this place yet. I hope by God's blessing that I may do a little of that peculiar work here which is too insignificant to attract a stranger, but of which you know the value. This is the end of what I could say.⁸

Having been turned down by King, Wilberforce turned to the recently established theological college at Chichester, and 'pinched' the Revd W. H. Davey, who having served as Vice-Principal there for seven years was ready, it could be argued, for a move.

SWINNY SUCCEEDS POTT

At the same time as appointing Davey as Vice-Principal, Wilberforce still needed a replacement for Pott. While it might be said that Wilberforce's judgment had faltered with his appointment of Liddon, his usual impeccable instinct for selecting the right man reasserted itself when his chose Henry Hutchinson Swinny, sometime Fellow of Magdalene College, Cambridge, to be the second Principal of Cuddesdon.

Swinny was noteworthy as being theologically 'moderate,' and this, together with being a man of evident and transparent goodness, commended him as strongly to Wilberforce as it rendered him unacceptable to Liddon, who typically commented, 'Moderate opinions are not a fair and tolerable representation of the Revelation of God.'[9] Notwithstanding, Swinny and Davey together, with King as chaplain, made a very good and workable trio, not least because King provided continuity during the years of stormy waters and continuing conflict which lay ahead.

For the new appointees, the future of Cuddesdon did not omen well. When Swinny arrived for his first term in May 1859 there were only seven students in residence, with two more drifting in during the course of the summer term. The prosaic and solid new Vice-Principal had agreed to remain only for an experimental period, retaining his Sussex benefice in the Chichester Diocese as a precautionary backstop in case everything fell apart at Cuddesdon, as the prophets of doom were expecting.

However, the trio of the reliable and 'solid' Davey— described by a student as 'the tough one of the whole lot'— together with Swinny and King, proved more than equal to the task of rebuilding both the reputation and the spirit of Cuddesdon.

Swinny's time as Principal lasted a little over three years. Not a fit man when he took up the post, he suffered from severe heart disease from which he prematurely died in December 1862, aged only forty-eight. As with King, it was through his physical weakness that Swinny's inner strength and gifts of the spirit were most evident. Even the 'prosaic and solid' Davey had been aware of Swinny's deep 'spiritual-

King and Cuddesdon

ity' and the 'winning gentleness of a life spent so manifestly in the continuous realization of the power of the Divine Presence,' while Wilberforce claimed that there was in Swinny, 'a nobleness of spirit which no one who approached him could fail to appreciate: it really seemed as if a low thought could not harbour in his mind.'[10]

It was inevitable that Swinny, a middle-of-the-road Anglican, would bring about a change of tone at Cuddesdon, and, from Wilberforce's perspective, it was a change for the better. The days of Liddon's strict and rigid routine were over as the life of the college relaxed under its new regime. For the first time, games begin to appear in times of leisure and relaxation with a cricket team and students riding horses for exercise. To this day, students at Cuddesdon still enjoy a game of croquet — a very Anglican sport, if ever there was one — introduced in 1862 by Mrs Swinny, who presented hoops and mallets for the men to play in the afternoons on the bishop's lawn.

It would have been all too easy for Swinny to establish his new regime by openly contrasting it with the days of Liddon. Understandably, there were still those in the college who regretted Liddon's departure, with his clearly defined teaching and more pronounced spiritual discipline. One such avid disciple was Arthur Stanton, who later served as curate and subsequently Vicar of St Alban's, Holborn, a famous Anglo-Catholic 'shrine.' During his time as a student at Oxford, before coming to Cuddesdon, Stanton had associated himself with the disciplined and religious life of the High Churchmen of the University and had used Liddon as his confessor.

Arriving at Cuddesdon in July 1862, for just two terms of residence before his ordination at Advent later that year, and already wedded to fairly elaborate ritual, Stanton might understandably have been somewhat disappointed by the new Principal, with his 'middle-of-the road churchmanship' and more relaxed manner. (Like King, Swinny was not a card-carrying member of the Anglo-Catholic faction, with its emphasis on daily communion and the more enforced and habitual use of the confessional, which had characterized the teaching and practice of Liddon.) But for this zealous young man, it was Swinny's compelling holiness and manner of life, transcending any hardened party lines, which won over Stanton, and many others. Writing to his mother soon after his arrival at Cuddesdon, Stanton concedes:

> As you want to know the aim of the College, I send you our Principal's address; it does not breathe much Hard Discipline, etc. I wish it did more, but I like the reverent Evangelical tone of it very much.[11]

That is not only a tribute to Swinny, but also a remarkable tribute to the authenticity of that spirituality and inner life of the spirit which transcends and sits lightly to outward forms in churchmanship and ritual, seen in lives universally recognized as truly human and yet distinctively holy. Even Liddon acknowledges this when writing to Stanton in the summer of 1862:

> I am very glad indeed to get tidings of you at Cuddesdon and to find that, on the whole, it does not disappoint you. The Principal, I feel sure, will be a blessing to you as he is to all who are brought into close contact with him. And, if the system of the College does not yield all that you could imagine or wish, you will feel that it does at least afford very many opportunities for growth in holiness—opportunities of which it is a great duty to make the most while you have them. It depends upon a man himself whether such a place is to be a blessing to him or no. All the real work—all that will last—must be wrought alone—on your knees—and with God. Compared with the great question of growth in habits of private prayer—whether mental or vocal—the little external matters are not of great consequence.[12]

Can we discern here something of a softening and a growing maturity in Liddon, who was originally very anxious for the college and the change in 'tone' signalled by the arrival of the new Principal? There is evidence that on at least one occasion, later in life, Liddon had come to see that there may have been valid grounds for the attacks made on the college and on the direction in which his youthful influence had been in danger of leading it. In a diary entry made shortly after leaving Cuddesdon, he expresses the need to 'let go' a little and 'let God' work more in this as well as in other matters.

> I wish I could get to trusting the future of the College and my own connection with it more entirely to our Blessed Lord: the over-anxiety about getting new men is a regular worldly spirit, from which may God in his compassion deliver me.[13]

What is abundantly clear in all of this, is Swinny's own *largesse du cœur* and generosity of spirit, springing, as it needs must, from both a deep, inner security and a freedom from party spirit. Swinny appears to have gone out of his way to retain Liddon's affection for the college and continuing interest in its future welfare. Barely a couple of weeks after becoming Principal, he wrote the first in a long series of persistent invitations to Liddon to revisit Cuddesdon. He even addresses Liddon as 'Vice-Principal,' because, as he had discerned and says in his letter, 'the men here,' especially those who were students during Liddon's last days as Vice-Principal, still 'comfort themselves with thinking that they may still address you, as in former times … When shall you come over to see us? Always *most* welcome. The visit pleasanter to us than to yourself, I fear. Yet we do wish to see you.'[14] Eventually, in 1862, he succeeded in persuading Liddon to conduct a retreat for the college.

However, Swinny himself did not lack critics. Before he even arrived, *The Union*, a High Church periodical, was attacking him for wanting to mould the college 'after the type of the ancient Church of Laodicea'—neither hot nor cold (Rev. 3:15)—adding that if this proved to be the case, then, 'the sooner it is shut up the better; or turned into a home for decayed needle-women; or made a storehouse for apostate priests.'[15] Party strife in politics can be bad enough, but often pales into insignificance compared with party strife in religion, even in an age like our own, which might superficially appear to be indifferent to religious diversity, either in practice or belief.

In fact, the prophets of doom were to be proved quite wrong. As Burgon pointed out to Liddon, men often grow into a job, and this would appear to be exactly what Swinny did. It is clear from the direct evidence, both of Wilberforce as well as on Swinny's own admission, that during his brief time in charge the process of change at Cuddesdon in relation to its newly appointed Principal proved to be a two-way street.

At first Swinny was somewhat uneasy about the existing regime, with its frequent services and emphasis on the place of meditation and times set aside for personal or private prayer. Slowly however, he came to be convinced of their value, and to understand the need for time to be made in the daily curriculum for meditation. In the summer of 1861, he wrote to King:

> I preached on Wednesday on Meditation. I grow more and more in the conviction of its importance. We all try to do too much and don't give time enough to earnest quiet thought. I know the case is my own. Somehow even prayer, and Divine service with God's congregation, lose much of their reality without this deliberate bringing of the Unseen into sight, and basking in the Light and Warmth of it for a little season.[16]

Swinny's term as Principal may have been brief, but must be deemed a success. By the time of his death in December 1862, the college was not only full, but the internal tensions and divisions were largely healed, with many like Stanton, who had initially been suspicious of him, reflecting on the blessings he had brought to it.

King and Cuddesdon

In a letter to his sister written in November 1862, only a couple of weeks before leaving Cuddesdon, Stanton tells her how desperately ill Swinny is, before continuing:

> The blessing of having so good and spiritually minded a man among us here will of course make his removal, if such should be God's will, a great loss to us ... I am very glad I have known him, although but for so small a time; yet long enough I think to stamp his remarkable character upon one's memory.[17]

Swinny's death ('removal') occurred on the last day of term, 22 December, when, having shaken hands with the last man who was going down, he sank back into a chair and died. He was laid to rest on 27 December, under a yew tree near the north door of Cuddesdon village church, his grave as understated as his life.

The brevity of Swinny's time in charge should be seen in inverse proportion to his lasting influence and the secure foundation which he established and on which his successor could build. When Swinny spoke at the College Festival in 1861, he attributed the more confident and happy spirit as stemming from 'the common life of the students—the constant, loving, scarcely felt control of men of kindred spirits, an influence which could not be found elsewhere.'[18] It was precisely the establishment of that 'common life' and a community spirit, and all with a lightness of touch, which was to prove the distinctive characteristic of King's spell as Principal during the next ten years.

KING FOR PRINCIPAL

In the January of 1863, following Swinny's death, Wilberforce once again asked King to step up to the plate, but this time as Swinny's successor in the key position as Principal. Once more, typically, and genuinely believing that he was not up to the task, King declined. But on this occasion

Edward King

Wilberforce steadfastly refused to take 'no' for an answer. He saw clearly that in the light of the more balanced tone and spirituality established by Swinny, King, who had worked happily and loyally under him as chaplain, was precisely the right person to take the work of the college forward with a sense of confident continuity.

Wilberforce gave expression to this when, praising Swinny's 'nobleness of spirit ... true and tender sympathy ... rare singleness of purpose ... increasing saintliness,' he went on to state explicitly his conviction that King was, 'one likeminded with Swinny ... one who had worked with him in life; and who, taking up the mantle of the former prophet, set at once, and in the same strength, to continue and complete his work.'[19] And that was precisely what King achieved during his Principalship.

In many ways, Swinny and King represent the same emphasis on the inner life of the spirit in relation to its external expressions liturgically in the worshipping life of the church. A letter from Swinny to King in the summer of 1861 begins the process of placing Cuddesdon's tradition of churchmanship where it truly belonged in relation to the evolution and development of the Tractarian revival, while avoiding the excesses and extremes of ritualism, or the over-regulated system which Liddon had promoted. The struggle to hold that tension is the subtext to the whole King narrative, from his earliest days at Wheatley as curate, to his apogee as Bishop of Lincoln.

While King freely acknowledged that he was delighted to have learned from Liddon that the officers of the College should be ready to be 'audacious' (Liddon's word) in exercising their personal influence, nevertheless King's practice throughout his time as Principal was to prove distinctively different from Liddon's. 'King had discovered a momentous truth: that the right method of training ordinands was not to drive them by exhortation along preconceived tram-lines: it was to live a worshiping life in community and let the Holy Spirit do the rest.'[20]

King and Cuddesdon

THE SYSTEM AND THE SPIRIT

Although they were to pursue quite different ways in ministry, King never lost contact with Liddon, with whom he enjoyed a warm and life-long friendship. In token of this, King invited Liddon, by then the renowned Canon and preacher at St Paul's Cathedral, to give the address at the Annual Festival in 1873, which coincided with King's last day as Principal. A theological college, said Liddon, needs both a system but also a spirit. It needs the former since it must show men how to live by rule, must set forth the truth that life is given to us to 'be disposed of and laid out from first to last under the eye of Christ our Lord.' It must train them in how to arrange and order their time, so that they learn 'not to run uncertainly.' They need to reflect in their own souls 'something of that Eternal Order which is the law of the Divine Mind and Life.'

But tellingly, Liddon, in that same lengthy address, went further, insisting that the system alone is but a shell, a husk, an artificial creation. There must also be spirit, and by that he meant a moral and religious atmosphere, or, as we might say, a corporately owned and prevailing culture. The latter, Liddon contended, is far more difficult to nurture than the former, it being 'much less easy to develop a traditional temper of thought and feeling in an institution, than to lay down rules for its management.' But who is to create this spirit? To be able to breathe it into the members of any institution, is, said Liddon, 'the most rare and precious of the gifts of government; it belongs to what we term, in ordinary human language, moral genius' — in other words, the gift is of God.[21]

Who, indeed? Who over the previous decade had been quietly instilling precisely that spirit of which Liddon spoke so passionately? The answer, of course, was King, who in addition to being partially responsible for framing the system as chaplain under the two previous Principals, had gone on to infuse the system he inherited with exactly the spirit that such an institution requires if it is to develop as a living organism rather than just a prescribed one.

During those ten years of King's leadership, 'The whole place was alive with him. His look, his voice, his gaiety, his beauty, his charm, his holiness, filled it and possessed it. There was an air about it, a tone in it, a quality, a delicacy, a depth, which were his creation.'[22]

Even after his first two years or so there was a new confidence and a feeling that the troubles of the early years were largely things of the past. As early as 1865, in one of his letters to Charlie, the young lad from his Wheatley days (then a student at Wilberforce's Teacher Training College at Culham), King speaks of this new confidence: 'All goes on here well (thank God); the college is full and all work well.'[23]

LIMITATIONS

Although King's time as Cuddesdon's Principal is generally held to have been a resounding success, at the time of his appointment there were some who called into question his fitness for the post. The workload was a heavy one, and for some aspects of it King was not especially well equipped. As Principal, he would be required to be a teacher and lecturer, a pastor to the students as well as pastor to the parish.

Administrative skills had never been, and would never be, King's strong suit. His tardiness in answering letters earned him considerable criticism throughout his whole ministry. Modelling himself on Marriott in this respect, King put people and their needs first, and he would always do this, however pressing other seemingly more important matters might appear to be. The door of Cuddesdon vicarage, where King was joined by his mother after the death of his father in 1859, was always open, as the door to Marriott's rooms at Oriel had always been during King's time there. With such a lifestyle, efficiency must inevitably take second place to availability. The college had no bursar during his time and it fell to him as Principal to take on that role, although he had absolutely no qualifications. At a luncheon in his honour at Cuddesdon in June 1873, he reflected on his inadequacy as an acting bursar, claiming, much to the amusement of those present, that the Guardian Angel of the college must have kept the accounts during his last ten years, since any such achievement was quite beyond his powers.

On taking up his appointment, King felt similarly ill-equipped for the considerable load of teaching and lecturing in theology required of him. His lifelong gift for simplicity of language lacked the scholarly and powerful eloquence of a Liddon, a Butler or a Wilberforce: in preaching, teaching and conversation, King was often restrained, even to the point of appearing inarticulate.

He never made any pretence about his scholarship, or lack of it, and realized that he needed to read hard and widely if he were ever going to be an able lecturer, even during his Cuddesdon days, let alone later as an Oxford Professor. Wisely he 'bought in,' or outsourced as we might say, some of the lecturing and teaching. For lectures in Moral Theology, he invited one of Bishop Wilberforce's chaplains, J. R. Woodford, who himself, when Bishop of Ely, was to found Ely Theological College, modelled very much on the ethos of King's Cuddesdon. Others, including Robert Milman, who frequently came over from his nearby parish to lecture on the Early Fathers of the Church, and Oxford University lecturers like Dr William Bright, supplemented the Principal's own limited resources of scholarship and that of the other resident staff. The fact that King had not read for honours at Oxford consistently put him on the back foot in academic circles, always conscious of the need to catch up and to deepen and extend his reading to better equip him as a lecturer and professional teacher.

Edward King

STUDY AND READING

King was to keep up a strict regime of study and reading from his Cuddesdon days to the end of his life. He had always had a great love for and knowledge of the scriptures: 'his mind was steeped in the Bible; he believed fully in its inspiration; it was its inner meaning that he was continually dwelling upon ... He made it, if possible, his daily duty to weigh well the Scriptures.'[24] He also drew on the works of Plato and Aristotle (especially the *Ethics*), and Dante. Theologically, he was deeply indebted to the works of Hooker and Bishop Butler. Although he would never have regarded himself as an academic theologian in the professional sense, one of his early students at Cuddesdon, James Swallow, who later became chaplain there (1874–6), remembered his lectures on Christian Doctrine as 'a veritable *theologie affective*, in which the dry bones of dogmas were clothed with the sensitive flesh of living, loving devotion, and lit up with the glow of poetic contemplation, often under the guidance of Dante.'[25] In other words, King had interiorized his theology through prayerful, spirit-filled reflection, employing both heart as well as mind.

As a disciplined and keen reader, though not a natural scholar, King would always prefer to ponder books—preferably big books as he said to his students—returning to them frequently rather than perusing many smaller books superficially. 'My own plan with myself,' he wrote, 'has been never to consider myself likely to do anything in an intellectual way, but I regard reading as a duty to enable one to carry out one's vocation in dealing with the souls of men. In this way it has helped me to go quietly, regularly, laboriously on with intellectual work, regarding it as a means to an end.'[26]

In that spirit and to that end he urged his students to read Augustine, Chrysostom and Gregory the Great, Thomas Aquinas and Peter Lombard, and Richard of St Victor, along with Fénelon and Lacordaire, Andrewes and Jeremy Taylor,

Calvin and Wesley and Newman—a mixed bag, but a far broader theological syllabus than many ordinands would be familiar with in our own day, let alone any bishop in the twenty-first century.

His own discipline of reading widely served as a motivating example to his students. King always urged them to read poetry, particularly Wordsworth and Dante. One Christmas at Lincoln, a friend sent him some volumes of Wordsworth's poems as a gift, and in his letter of thanks King explained what it was about Wordsworth's poetry that appealed to him:

> It is a most beautiful and usable Wordsworth, and I am particularly glad to have it, as he seems to suit me. His love of all nature, and his constant use of it are a link to higher things which I greatly love; and his philosophical reflections, which some might think heavy, and others not purely metaphysical enough, just suit my capacities, so his poetry rests and refreshes me with new strength of head and heart, of thought and love.[27]

In addition to recommending poetry, he also advised his students to read contemporary novels, as he did himself—poetry to release the mind from the prison house of prosaic literalism by the employment of the imagination, and novels in order to gain a wide knowledge and understanding of humanity, with all its paradoxes and contradictions. The good pastor needs to know, as it was claimed in scripture, that Christ himself 'did not need man's testimony about man, for he knew what was in a man' (John 2:25). The good pastor or spiritual guide needs never to be shocked by human sin and failure.

For King it was always a question of heart and mind being in tandem, which is a rare quality in those of a more academic or scholarly bent. As St Paul contended, 'I will pray with the heart and I will pray with the mind also' (1 Corinthians 14:15). Indeed, the theologian in the Orthodox Churches of the East is not so much the one with a great intellect, but is defined simply as, 'the one who prays.' According to that definition and in that sense, King should surely be regarded as no mean theologian, resourced not only from study and reading but also from his inner life of contemplative prayer, and that quality of affective prayer of the heart, which in the words of Bishop Theophan, 'draws the head into the heart.'

It had taken Swinny some time to discover for himself the important place that meditation, in addition to the daily Offices of Morning and Evening Prayer together with Compline, should hold in the daily routine of the college. King allotted time in the timetable for silent meditation, not only for the students, but also as holding a place of special importance in his own personal discipline. Some of this King would have learned from his great friend Father Benson of the Cowley Fathers, and later, more explicitly, from Bishop Sailer of Regensburg, whose personality and writings hugely influenced him after becoming Professor of Pastoral Theology at Oxford.

As has been mentioned, the Principal of Cuddesdon was, uniquely, also a working parish priest, and it is significant that all of King's letters written during his years as Principal were not headed as coming from the college, but from 'Cuddesdon Vicarage, Wheatley.' In his role as vicar, he had additionally to attend to all those duties normally required of a parish priest: visiting the sick, burying the dead, catechizing the children, taking the normal round of parochial duties and services. It was that rare kind of pastoral training which comes close to mirroring the hands-on training of apprenticeships. It is also somewhat akin to the training of medical students who learn their medical skills by experience and by working together with and under a consultant in teaching hospitals. The pastor's touch, like the bedside manner of the doctor is caught, just as much as it is taught.

King's students would have worshipped regularly in the parish church on Sundays and at major festivals where they would observe King preaching to his rural parishioners and teaching the children—when sophisticated theological aphorisms would have been out-of-place. Writing to a priest and former student in 1871, King described his work teaching the parish children:

> We have had for nearly twelve months a children's service, at three, every Sunday afternoon. We sing a musical Litany and then catechise them. We are doing the Acts of the Apostles, and this and a few hymns and prayers takes about fifty minutes. The children are in the best part of the church, and we have the regular choir, so it is their own service, but several parents come and seem to like it. I like it myself very much. I enjoy talking to the children. If you think you could have one, I will send you one of our little Litany books.[28]

So, the students would see the vicar teaching the children the Acts of the Apostles on Sunday afternoons as the same person who, as their Principal, would be lecturing during the week to budding, future parish priests on Hooker and the Early Fathers of the Church. For King, the end and the objective of reading, study and personal devotion is the same, namely, to equip the clergy in a ministry of Christian formation and the cure of souls—in other words, ascetical theology. For the next century that was the vision of all theological colleges in the Cuddesdon tradition. Dean Eric Abbott, when he was Warden of Lincoln Theological College, assured his students, in similar manner to that of King, that 'if they took moral and ascetical theology seriously, and continued their own spiritual struggle, then he could promise that their ministry would always be sought and used.'[29]

King's faithfulness as the parish priest of Cuddesdon is tellingly told in a memoir by Fred Wilgress, his nephew and future domestic chaplain at Lincoln. 'In spite of the great claims of the College, he never allowed the parish to suffer. He was continually looking after the spiritual welfare of his flock. He was at the beck and call of anyone in sickness or in trouble. During an outbreak of small-pox he diligently visited, and when no one dared to put the dead into their coffins, he did it himself,'[30] much as he had done in similar circumstances at Wheatley and again, no doubt, following the example of Charles Marriott from Oriel days.

THE GROWING DEMANDS OF THE EMERGING MISSIONARY SOCIETIES

It was during King's time as Principal that the needs of the newly formed Missionary Societies became increasingly evident. Although Wilberforce had never intended Cuddesdon to be a training college for overseas missionaries, he did share the vision of a worldwide mission for the Church. He frequently invited one or more missionary bishops or leaders to attend the Cuddesdon Festival. Referring to the Cuddesdon experiment, Bishop Selwyn had asked rhetorically 'Who can tell the future development of this one spark of fire?'

> A word of living power spoken here may kindle a flame which will burn even to New Zealand. From this altar live coals may be borne to kindle our old cathedrals: and to quicken the zeal of our parochial ministry: and thence to spread the light and life of the Gospel to the most distant colony, and to the utmost bounds of the Gentile world. It is a seed sown in singleness of heart: it is the least of all seeds, but it will grow into a great tree: it is a little one—but it will become a thousand.[31]

The 1860 Festival saw the launch of the Cuddesdon Missionary Exhibition Fund, the objectives of which were 'To assist in a work cognate to that of the College by promoting the specific training of young men as missionaries for our colonial and other foreign work' and 'To excite and keep up among its members an interest in missionary work.'[32]

Under King's leadership, the attitude at Cuddesdon was beginning to reflect the changing attitude throughout the Church of England. Indeed, King himself even pondered from time to time whether or not he should leave Cuddesdon to work in the colonies: writing to a former pupil in 1865, he joked, 'I shouldn't wonder if I were to shake my fist at all you idle fellows lying snugly in England.'[33]

Even during King's time those sparks of which Selwyn had spoken began to catch hold of the imagination of Cuddesdon — when Robert Milman, the visiting lecturer, went to work in Calcutta; and again in 1870, when the former Vice-Principal, Allan Webb, became Bishop of Bloemfontein. Much later, the then Vice-Principal, E. F. Willis, stimulated by an address from the visiting Bishop of Bombay (Louis Mylne), drew up the Cuddesdon *Manual of Intercessions for Missions*; and in 1880, strongly backed by King, the Oxford Mission to Calcutta was founded, initiating a firm and lasting connection between Cuddesdon and Calcutta. It was not long before a large map of the world appeared in the lecture room onto which flags were pinned naming former students working in far-flung parts of the Anglican Communion, a development which had slowly been taking shape ever since Archbishop Longley convened the first Lambeth Conference of Bishops in 1867.

KING AS SPIRITUAL GUIDE AND MENTOR

But it was, supremely, as spiritual guide and mentor that King was best able in those years at Cuddesdon to develop his unique gift for moulding the common life of the community there, as well as directing the souls and forwarding the vocation of individual members of the college. 'Thy Gentleness hath made me great' (Psalm 18:35) was one of King's favourite texts, although there was nothing weak or sentimental about such gentleness. In practice, true gentleness of spirit is better exercised as restrained, even disciplined strength, rightly directed, never to put someone down, but to encourage, build and raise up. In this and in other respects King is often seen as an Anglican version of St Francis de Sales, who wrote, 'Nothing is so strong as gentleness—nothing so loving and gentle as strength.'[34]

Yet King was above all a realist when it came to human nature and would readily prick the bubble of humbug, or any self-delusion of spiritual grandeur so often assumed by religious and pious folk, with friendly wit or otherwise. An early student at Cuddesdon recalled, 'His dealings with individuals were full of sympathy, and were never allowed to interfere with a man's own personal convictions. Sympathetic teaching was left to do its own work according to the conscience of the individual. Many a rebuke, a piece of unwelcome advice, was given in a way that would give no pain to a sensitive nature. To one student on Good Friday, who had eaten extraordinarily little during the days of Holy Week, he gave the following advice, "Dearest man, eat breakfast and come down to the level of Yours, E. K."'[35]

There was nothing forced in all this, as in the admonition of John Keble not 'to wind ourselves too high, For mortal man beneath the sky.'[36] Under King, Cuddesdon never fell into the trap of becoming a hothouse, breeding a forced and self-conscious piety. King's own spirituality knew nothing of the ardent Spanish mystics like St John of the Cross or St Teresa of Avila, and is much more in line with that of George Herbert, Bishop Thomas Ken and the Caroline Divines, and, of course, with the spirit of John Keble, a copy of whose *Christian Year* was always close at hand throughout the whole of King's ministry.

Perhaps it was King's upbringing in the countryside in a farming community which kept him connected with the earth and its seasons, and which in turn was reflected in his unwillingness to enforce hasty prescriptions for development in the spiritual life or in the work of the pastoral ministry: the patience of the farmer who necessarily waits upon the mystery of growth (Mark 4:27). King clearly saw 'hiddenness in growth' in the natural world not only as an analogy, but also as a model equally applicable to the hiddenness, indeed the mystery, of spiritual growth: 'I do value highly a natural growth in holiness, a humble, grateful acceptance of the circumstances God has provided for each of us, and I dread the unnatural, forced, cramped ecclesiastical holiness, which is so much more quickly produced, but is so human and poor.' King feared artificiality, 'self-manufacturing': 'go gradually, and as far as possible, naturally, taking the circumstances God gives you, and trying to serve Him in them.'[37]

The age of King, of course, is that of the Romantic Movement, born of the work of the Lake poets, Wordsworth and Coleridge, whose love of nature, in reaction against the urban and increasingly industrialized life of the city, is immortalized in their poetry.

> The idea that the contented life was the earth-connected life, even that goodness was embeddedness, had its roots in the 1790s, perhaps drawing on what Wordsworth and Coleridge had read of Rousseau ... Co-presence with the natural world, a closeness that was inaccessible in what Coleridge always described as the 'dim' light of the city—the persistent coal smog of eighteenth-century London—was somehow a release into a form of wellbeing which normal, political, commercial, professional or even educational life would not only fail to approach but would actually disrupt and destroy. It is a powerful connection to make love of nature as the route both to a love of truth and to a love of man.[38]

King would have loudly applauded these sentiments, to which he would undoubtedly have added—'a love of God.'

He was never really at home or felt connected with the political, commercial, or professional life of London or Oxford. He was much more at home with the rural life of

Kent and the Lakes (which he experienced as a boy), then later with the farming community life of Wheatley and Cuddesdon, and, during his years as bishop, with the farming communities of the Lincolnshire fens and Wolds.

He had always loved the natural world and being in close touch with the fauna and flora, the beauty of flowers and trees enlivening his knowledge and that love of botany which he shared with his infirm sister Anne. Far from diminishing later in public and academic life, it continued with him to end of his days, in his travels in Europe and in his rural diocese of Lincoln. Rather than simply absorbing academic theology, he saw the interwovenness of the whole of life from a theological perspective.

When we speak, as many did at the time and consistently since, of King's lasting influence, especially on the small community of ordinands at Cuddesdon, we do not imply that he turned out cloned Cuddesdon men as pale imitations of himself or his own spirituality or personality. There was nothing of a personality cult about his unquestionable influence. On the contrary, in true community life in the spirit, people become closer to their true selves, while paradoxically and at the same time, closer to each other: such was the 'Cuddesdon experience' and training under King.

The two extremes of recent history in the West have been collectivism on the one hand and individualism on the other. A true spirit of community cherishes the uniqueness of each individual, while, at the same time, each finds his own true identity by being held in relationship to the wider community.

King often accused himself of being lazy and of not having achieved what others better than he might have done as Principal. Yet he displayed a maturity beyond his years and an inner security which enabled him to relax in the best sense, and by so doing setting others free to find their true inner rest and unique self, free from obsessive or driven busyness. 'We aid and influence people simply by being who

King and Cuddesdon

we are. Human integrity probably influences and moves people from potency to action more than anything else. An elder's deep and studied passion carries so much more power than superficial and loudly stated principles. Our peace is needed more than our anger.'[39]

In his sermon preached on King's last day at Cuddesdon, Liddon refers specifically, and with his customary exquisite sensitivity and language, to King's unique gift and genius for providing and fostering such a spirit of community and brotherhood which, in turn, had engendered the power to influence and transform lives.

> It is far too delicate and ethereal a power to submit to analysis, or to be bound down by conditions of time and place ... It pours itself around others, when and how they know not; it saturates them; it impregnates them with its own fervour and impetuosity.; it insensibly furnishes them with new points of view, new moods of feeling, new estimates of life; they learn like the converted Franks, to adore what they had burned, and to burn what they had adored, before they know it ...
>
> In a college such as this, as you know from its history during the last ten years, all depends, humanly speaking, on the presence of such a gift as this in its chief officer. It is this which explains the indescribable attraction and power of the place—it is this which irradiates all else; which redeems everything here from the suspicion of triviality or wearisomeness; which gilds all the habits, all the associations, all the localities—the very roads, hedges, and trees around, I had almost said—with a spiritual and moral beauty, at least in the eyes of those who amid these scenes, have first learnt what life, and work, and death, really mean.[40]

Yes, indeed. Although expressed in language which to us seems all too florid, the reality of the experience of Cuddesdon under King had clearly transcended the expectations of its founder. King had inherited the 'system' of which Liddon spoke, but had gone further—a second and third mile—to breath into it a moral and spiritual beauty, that same beauty which is also an attribute of God, along with truth and goodness: indeed, a beauty which could not be defined or even described, but only experienced in the common life of a prayerful and worshipping community.

King's Principalship had been a time when the seeds sown by his two predecessors had come into full flowering. By 1873, when he left to take up the Professorship in Oxford, Cuddesdon had securely established its place and was widely accepted throughout the Church of England. Indeed, theological colleges, as places for training Anglican ordinands, had come to be accepted as the norm and eventually as required for ordination.

KING'S LEGACY

By the time he left Cuddesdon, what he had achieved there began to change the whole mindset of the Church of England regarding residential training for ordination. At the Cuddesdon Festival in June 1865, the preacher was the Archbishop of York, William Thomson. Writing about it in his diary, Bishop Wilberforce records, with no small measure of delight, how Thomson in his sermon admitted that he had made a complete U-turn, and 'his mind had undergone a great change with regard to the usefulness of founding such an institution' as Cuddesdon. 'That feeling, however, had long passed away both from his mind, and also, he believed, from that of Oxford. Cuddesdon,' the Archbishop confidently affirmed, 'was now established beyond all cavil as a real working-place, and as a true handmaid to the University.'[41]

Thomson, it seems, was not alone in having changed his attitude to theological training. In the decade following King's departure, no fewer than seven theological colleges were opened, modelled to a greater or lesser extent on Cuddesdon, one of them, St Stephen's House in Oxford, as early as 1876, with King himself as one of the founders. In fact, by the end of his life it would come to be universally recognized that candidates for Holy Orders would be required to undergo residential training in a theological college. On 6 July 1909, just a year before King's death, the Upper House of the Convocation of Canterbury resolved that after January 1917, 'candidates for Holy Orders be required (in addition to a university degree) to have received at least one year's practical and devotional training at a recognized theological college, or under some other authorized supervision.'[42]

King had spent fifteen of his happiest years in Cuddesdon, when, in February 1873, Gladstone offered him the Chair of Pastoral Theology in Oxford. By this time he had established something not far short of a revolution in the strategic place of theological colleges for training those preparing for ordination. He had travelled abroad and visited the more important seminaries in France, and picked up useful hints about priestly formation. However, he had no intention of replicating or imposing the European model of training seminarians on the students at Cuddesdon. Theology for King was never simply a matter of digesting theological doctrine. As he repeatedly and consistently taught, in order to bring people to Christ, the pastor must himself first live a life close to Christ, requiring the sanctification of character through a life of prayer lived out within a community of the Spirit.

In a sermon he preached as Bishop of Lincoln at the first Festival of Lincoln Theological College in November 1888, King spoke at some length about the lifestyle and curriculum required for theological and ministerial formation, reflecting very much the curriculum at Cuddesdon in his own day. His words are as relevant today as they were when they were first spoken, reflecting a similar professionalism for training in similar disciplines such as education and medicine.

> In the day of technical or departmental education, the demand made upon the clergy is, not unreasonably, 'ministerial efficiency.' They should be fitted for their own work in order that they may be 'workmen who need not to be ashamed.' This implies, no doubt, many things, but the centre of it all, without which the rest is practically useless, is 'personal holiness.' If we are to undertake a spiritual charge, the cure of souls, we must be spiritual men, men of sincere, unaffected, inward piety, men of prayer ... men, that is, who know the privileges of having access to the Father in the power of the Spirit through the mediation of the Son ...
>
> We must know what prayer and worship mean ourselves before we can hope to direct and lead the worship of the people. We must do it *with* them, 'in spirit and in truth,' and not merely tell them what they ought to do ...
>
> I have confined myself, brethren, on this your first gathering, to this one requisite for the ministry — holiness. Whatever else may be required of learning, and wisdom, and toil, *this* is essential, for 'without holiness no man can see the Lord,' and, indeed, it is the promotion of this practical holiness which the great Apostle considers to be the end of the knowledge, which, as an Apostle, he claimed, for he speaks of the full knowledge of the truth which leads to practical piety — a life of holiness.[43]

Although his break with Cuddesdon came when Gladstone invited him to become a Professor in Oxford, there was also a continuity, a continuing inner thread in King's ministry, in that he went from Cuddesdon to Oxford, and developed further the experience of ten years as Principal by fusing together the teaching of theology with the practice of the cure of souls in a ministry which bound together theology and spirituality, mind and heart, in a powerful dynamism. This was to influence a whole generation of Oxford men, with a lasting 'ripple effect' throughout the Church of England. King's was a more lasting and formative influence than had ever been achieved either by the Tractarian scholars earlier in the century or, later in the century, by ritualists and liturgical enthusiasts.

In some ways, after ten remarkable years of his leadership, the 'Cuddesdon experiment' had become the victim of its own success. As the college broadened its outreach beyond the vision of the early days, it was reaching the limits of its residential capacity, at that time some twenty students. Moreover, King had grown increasingly aware of the need for some kind of continuing fellowship of former students, and the concomitant requirement for additional accommodation for those returning for rest and quiet and spiritual refreshment. When Stanton came down for the Festival of 1863, he was persuaded to stay for three days, 'in order to breathe the fresh air of the hills.'[44]

With a full college, and frequent requests for extra beds, King even pondered whether he should turn the large vicarage, into some kind of house of rest or retreat for former students. But this did not prove to be practical as long as his mother, who resided there with him, was still alive. More accommodation was needed for students; a larger chapel was required and a larger common room or lecture room.

In 1869 King had asked Wilberforce, before he was translated to Winchester later that year:

> Do you think we ought to build so as to avail ourselves of the opportunities which now are offered? I don't know enough of that sort of thing to decide. I merely want to let you know my dearest Lord, the state of things that you may watch this thing and not let my weakness hinder the work which seems to be increasing.[45]

Events, however, determined that the resolution of these matters would fall to King's successors. Furthermore, Wilberforce's move to Winchester only added to the delay in implementing any such schemes, and it was left to King's successor to pick up on some of the earlier suggestions for extending the original buildings. The laying of the foundation stone for a new and larger chapel took place in 1874, the year after he left.

King's ministry at Cuddesdon had marked the turning point in the life of the college, and subsequently in the Church of England, and on a scale that could hardly have been thought possible that momentous day, when Wilberforce had met the young King by the stile outside Wheatley, and invited him to help with the pioneering work of his brainchild up on the hill at Cuddesdon. Yet even as late as 1870, by which time his ministry had come to be warmly recognized by all who had dealings with Cuddesdon, King himself did not feel himself up to realizing the fuller potential of the college. In a letter to Wilberforce dated 11 November 1870, and marked 'Secret,' he writes, 'I do feel this place wants a greater person. I am cramping the influence of the College. I am not strong enough to do a quarter that might be done, so if it should please God to release me from such a responsible work, I would be grateful.'[46]

The release, which it appears he then sought, did not come until a few years later, and then in a form which he could not have possibly foreseen, and, indeed, for which he could reasonably have felt even more inadequate.

On St Matthias's Day, 24 February, in 1873, King announced at Compline that he would be leaving Cuddesdon to take up the Chair of Moral and Pastoral Theology in Oxford. He stayed on for the Annual Festival, which, as had become customary, was held on the Tuesday after Trinity Sunday: in 1873 this fell on 10 June.

For the preacher on the occasion of his last Festival as Principal, King invited Liddon. In a typically lengthy sermon, later printed under the title *The Moral Groundwork of Clerical Training*, Liddon alluded to what was on the minds and in the hearts of everyone present.

> Today is a day of many congratulations, natural and legitimate. Never before the present year has this college,

in the person of its officers, received such emphatic recognition from high quarters of the services which it has been permitted to render to the Church. That recognition, many of you will feel, however grateful in itself, is purchased at a very heavy cost.[47]

To mark King's leaving, a Testimonial Fund was raised by Cuddesdon men, past and present, some of which was used to commission a portrait of their departing Principal from one of the country's leading portrait painters, George Richmond. It was presented to King's mother, and after her death, King gave it to the college. More of the fund was put to furnishing King's study in Christ Church, and to purchase thirty-four volumes of theology each one inscribed in gold letters on red leather, 'Edward King, ten years Principal of Cuddesdon College.'

Only a few weeks later, on 19 July, Wilberforce was thrown by his horse while out riding and killed. Thus 1873 marks the end not only of King's influence as Principal, but also the end of the founding epoch in the history of Cuddesdon College.

Notes

[1] Bodleian Library, Wilberforce Papers, Burgon to Wilberforce, 9 December 1858.
[2] Owen Chadwick, *The Founding of Cuddesdon*, p. 83.
[3] Pusey House, Liddon Papers, MSS ii. 368.
[4] Bodleian Library, Wilberforce Papers, King to Wilberforce, 27 November 1858.
[5] Chadwick, *op. cit.*, p. 99.
[6] Bodleian Library, Wilberforce Papers, Burgon to Wilberforce, 11 February 1859.
[7] *Ibid.*, King to Wilberforce, 12 February 1859.
[8] Keble College MSS, King to Liddon, 24 October 1859.
[9] Chadwick, *op. cit.*, p. 88.
[10] *Ibid.*, p. 101.
[11] *Ibid.*, p. 107.
[12] *Ibid.*, p. 108.
[13] Pusey House, Liddon MSS, Diaries, entry for 18 October 1856.
[14] Keble College MSS, Swinny to Liddon, 20 May 1859.

15. Chadwick, *op. cit.*, p. 100. For these attacks see *The Union*, 18 March and 8 April 1859.
16. Lincoln Cathedral Archives, Swinny to King, undated.
17. George W. E. Russell, *Arthur Stanton: A Memoir*. London: Longmans, Green & Co., 1917, p. 35 (Stanton to his sister, November 1862).
18. *Cuddesdon College 1854–1904: A Record and Memorial*, pp. 51–2.
19. *Ibid.*, pp. 119–20.
20. Chadwick, *op. cit.*, p. 114.
21. H. P. Liddon, *Clerical Life and Work: A Collection of Sermons with an Essay*. London: Longmans, Green & Co., 1894, Sermon II (delivered at the Cuddesdon Festival, 1873), pp. 73ff.
22. Henry Scott Holland, *A Bundle of Memories*, pp. 51, 55.
23. *Spiritual Letters of Edward King, D.D.*, Letter IX.
24. G. F. Wilgress, *Edward King, Bishop of Lincoln 1885–1910*. [Lincoln]: Bishop of Lincoln's Appeal Fund, [?1930], p. 20.
25. Randolph and Townroe, *The Mind and Work of Bishop King*, p. 46.
26. King, *Spiritual Letters*, Letter XXIV.
27. *Ibid.*, Letter XC.
28. King, *op. cit.*, Letter XV.
29. Martin Thornton, *English Spirituality*, p. 3.
30. Wilgress, *op. cit.* p. 9.
31. Chadwick, *op. cit.*, p. 123.
32. *Ibid.*, p. 124.
33. *Ibid.*
34. *The Spiritual Maxims of St Francis de Sales* (ed. C. F. Kelley). London: Longmans, Green & Co., 1954, p. 124.
35. Wilgress, *op. cit.*, p. 8.
36. John Keble, 'Morning' (verse 13), first published in *The Christian Year*, 1827, pp. 13–15.
37. King, *op. cit.*, Letter XXI, pp. 35, 36.
38. Adam Nicholson, *The Making of Poetry: Coleridge, the Wordsworths and Their Year of Marvels*. London: William Collins, 2019, p. 15.
39. Richard Rohr, *A Spring within Us*, p. 161.
40. Liddon, *op. cit.*, pp. 87, 88.
41. Ashwell and Wilberforce, *The Life of the Right Reverend Samuel Wilberforce*, vol. III, pp. 164–5.
42. S. L. Ollard and G. Crosse (eds), *A Dictionary of English Church History* (1912), p. 591.
43. Edward King, *The Love and Wisdom of God*, pp. 271ff.
44. Chadwick, *op. cit.*, p. 125.
45. Bodleian Library, Wilberforce Papers, King to Wilberforce, 15 January 1869.
46. *Ibid.*, King to Wilberforce, 11 November 1870.
47. Randolph and Townroe, *op. cit.*, p. 44: Liddon, *op. cit.*, Sermon II.

✥ 6 ✥

The Pastoral Professor

GLADSTONE'S CHOICE

In 1868, Gladstone achieved a triumphant election victory and began his first term as Prime Minister, which lasted until 1874. In that latter year he wrote to Queen Victoria: 'For centuries there has not been a time of so much practical and hearty work, so much earnest preaching, so much instruction and consolation given, so much affectionate care for the poor and for the young.'[1] It is not clear as to what his somewhat over-optimistic remarks were referring. Could it be that he was merely indulging in some self-congratulatory comments on account of the three Tractarian appointments he had made to Oxford Professorships during that first term as Prime Minister?

First there had been the appointment of H. P. Liddon, whom Gladstone had recommended for the Chair of Ireland Professor of Exegesis after Liddon astutely refused the Wardenship of the new Keble College, for which many had thought him the obvious candidate. Soon afterwards Gladstone appointed another able scholar from among the early Tractarians, J. B. Mozley, to be Regius Professor of Divinity.

In his biography of Pusey, Liddon picks up the story of Gladstone's professorial appointments:

> At about the same time Mr. Gladstone made another not less notable addition to the power of the Church in Oxford, by nominating the Rev. Edward King, who had been for ten years Principal of the Theological

Edward King

College at Cuddesdon, to the Chair of Pastoral Theology, vacant by the death of Dr. Ogilvie. To the varied and brilliant abilities of the already remarkable body of Theological Professors, Dr. King contributed, besides other high qualifications for his office, a gift of sympathy so extraordinary that it has been well described as 'nothing less than a form of genius.' As a result of this singular power, he was already in touch with a large number of clergy in every part of the country; and soon after his arrival at Oxford he obtained an influence over the younger members of the University second only, if not equal to, that of the most distinguished of his colleagues.[2]

The Chair of Pastoral Theology, carrying with it (as it still does) a Canonry at Christ Church, had been founded during the premiership of Robert Peel in 1842. After the death of its first occupant, Charles Ogilvie, in February 1873, Gladstone (with the Queen's 'sanction') promptly offered the vacant Chair to King, as if he had known for some time who he wanted to succeed Ogilvie. Gladstone would undoubtedly have learned of King's outstanding record at Cuddesdon from his son, Stephen Gladstone, who had studied for Holy Orders there under King.

'Allow me to assure you,' Gladstone wrote, 'that in submitting your name to Her Majesty ... I have been moved by no other consideration than that of what I believe to be your gifts and merits, and the promise they afford of a tranquil, but powerful and deep, religious influence on young men within the precincts of the university.'[3]

In the context of the recent re-orderings of the ancient universities, Gladstone acted with considerable foresight. As a keen High Churchman himself, as well as having been previously returned as one of the two Members of Parliament representing Oxford, he knew precisely what he was doing in making such an offer. A measure had been passed in Parliament which had begun the long process of prising apart the firm hold which the Church of England had traditionally held on the ancient universities. This was perceived by many as further evidence of growing hostility towards the Established Church. Even with the emergence of the theological colleges, there were still those who regarded an Oxford degree as quite sufficient preparation for a young man of godly character seeking ordination.

What Gladstone had discerned was even more clearly and forcefully endorsed in the perceptive mind of Bishop Wilberforce. So perhaps the timing was exactly right for King's next strategic relocation in his life and ministry.

On 23 February 1873, the day after Gladstone had written to King, Wilberforce, who almost certainly would have had a hand in this whole process, wrote from Winchester, clearly concerned that King might yet again turn down an offer of preferment: 'Gladstone allows me to write to you on the offer which is going by this post to you. No one perhaps can so thoroughly as I can feel the responsibility of advising you at this crisis, because no one perhaps knows so well what has been the priceless worth of your work at Cuddesdon ... I am most anxious that you should accept this offer.'

From what Wilberforce goes on to say, it is clear that Gladstone had been strongly pressed to make a different appointment, one more in line with the emerging and more liberal churchmanship of what Wilberforce in his letter termed, 'the neologian party.'

> I very earnestly hope that you will not hesitate [to accept Gladstone's offer.] I know that it must be a great wrench for you to leave Cuddesdon; and I know that your extreme modesty will make you think that you are not fitted to fill with full effect this great Chair. But on that point others are really better able to judge than you are, and I have not a shadow of doubt that, in that wider sphere which Oxford will open to you, the good you have been able to do from Cuddesdon will be multiplied many-fold to the Church ... I see in this the Hand of God. May you take the office and may HE bless you in it.[4]

On this occasion, however, it appears that King did not hesitate in accepting: 'I can only say that I accept your kindness with my humble but very sincere gratitude. I am sorry that I will not bring any honours to the Chair from previous University distinction. I must trust simply to be guided and supported by the merciful God who has put up with me so long and brought me so far. I will in His strength do my best.'[5]

Gladstone replied two days later: 'I am very sensible of your honourable frankness; but I receive the announcement of your acceptance with pleasure and your appointment will now at once go forward.'[6]

For the students at Cuddesdon, however, who had got wind that something was in the air by way of 'some very important letter that had come that morning,' the announcement of their beloved Principal's departure on that bitterly cold day in February 1873, was received with no pleasure whatever, but, on the contrary, with grief and foreboding.

'The Principal had gone into Oxford,' a former student recalled. 'Nothing was known till the evening, when at Compline in the College Chapel, he said that the last Sunday he had been preaching about the Crown of Thorns, and now he was called upon to wear it—that he was called to leave Cuddesdon and go to Oxford.'[7]

Another former student recalled that 'a never-to-be-forgotten scene in the old chapel after Compline, when Dr King briefly stated that he had felt it his duty to accept the offer of a University Professorship. Strong men, well-known athletes, might be seen sobbing like children. To them, the Principal made Cuddesdon.'[8] Yet, as Liddon was quick to console them, 'If men pass, principles, truths, means of grace remain.'[9]

The Pastoral Professor

OPPOSITION TO KING'S APPOINTMENT

Although during the next twelve years Gladstone's hopes were to be exceeded beyond anything that he or others could ever have hoped for in an ever-extending influence over the young men of the University and beyond, there were several at the outset who were highly critical of the appointment and even attempted to block it. King was well known as a High Churchman at that time when High Churchmen did not lack critics. In the autumn of 1872, King had made a much-discussed and controversial speech at the Church Congress in Leeds, openly flying his High Church colours.

One of the earliest critics of the appointment was Archbishop Tait, who twice wrote to Gladstone remonstrating against it. On 24 February Tait wrote, 'I shall be very sorry if the appointment you mention takes place, for I fear it will greatly shake public confidence in the theological school at Oxford.'[10]

Others joined in the fray, such as William Edward Jelf, a priest and High Churchman 'of the Old School.' In a violent attack upon the ritualistic party, Jelf, an able scholar with a First in Classics from Oxford, pleaded that it was 'impossible not to feel the greatest distrust of the newly appointed Pastoral Professor at Oxford. A man of no university distinction, his only recommendation seems to have been the success which he has had at Cuddesdon, mainly by his personal influence, in training priestlings, under the auspices of two Bishops of Oxford.'

As though intellectual inadequacy was not sufficient to disqualify King for the post, Jelf went on to attack his expressed support for Pusey's *Declaration on Confession*, as well as his Leeds speech, when King was reported as having exhorted 'his hearers not to shrink from the discipline which the Church offered them in Confession and Absolution.' — 'What will Pastoral Theology become in his hands?' asked Jelf rhetorically.[11]

What indeed? For, without the advantage of hindsight, and given King's reputation as a High Churchman, some of the accusations would have been regarded as being not entirely without substance. Tait's opposition, and that of others, went much further, however, and not solely on the grounds of churchmanship. King had left Oriel with only a Pass Degree and he was certainly not regarded as a scholar, least of all by himself. To have been Principal, however outstanding, of a small, recently established theological college was one thing, but to be a Regius Professor in Oxford would inevitably prove to be far more intellectually demanding.

In the House of Commons, the announcement of King's appointment was greeted with surprise and mild derision when an MP asked Gladstone to state King's academic qualifications for the post. Gladstone defended his choice with characteristic dexterity, marking off the pastoral professorship as requiring what he foresaw as 'a more personal charge than the other Professors of Divinity, and the gentleman appointed ... should be possessed of strong sympathies and of the power of exercising a healthy and beneficial influence over character.' Those qualifications, he believed, from his experience of 'some duration,' Mr King possessed 'not only in an ordinary, but in an eminent degree.'[12]

On the other hand, many welcomed the appointment, notably the Revd J. W. Burgon, one of King's former mentors at Oriel: 'I had no idea till I reached Oxford yesterday evening, what good fortune had befallen us. I am really more glad than I can tell you of your appointment.'[13]

The Revd E. C. Woollcombe of Balliol was equally fulsome:

> You, with only a very few others, have been labouring long and well in this field already; you will, I am sure, gladly afresh devote yourself to what has been, I suppose, the work of your life; and to those of us who desire above all things that the work of the Church of England may be strengthened, it is a matter of deepest

> thankfulness that in the midst of the trials of our time your labours should be transferred to Oxford.[14]

'Transferred to Oxford' though he was, King certainly did not escape the 'trials' of the times: on the contrary, after the comparative quiet of rural Cuddesdon, he entered the first of what would prove to be many chapters of trials and deeply unsettling controversies. Not the least of these was that persistent charge of High Churchmanship which was to stick to him for the rest of his life, however unjustifiably. King was never a 'Romanizer,' theologically, culturally or spiritually: he was far too inwardly secure, socially and spiritually, to come anywhere near to following Newman and others in their conversion to the Roman Catholic Church.

In spite of the dissenting voices and, indeed, his own personal misgivings, only a few weeks later, in April 1873, King, accompanied by his mother, arrived in Oxford, to be formally installed in his Canonry at Christ Church, where the Cathedral also serves as the college chapel. The knowledge of his assumed ritualistic leanings preceded him, and King used to relate how, on his arrival, 'the dear things' (i.e. the undergraduates) had 'hung up a surplice on the lamp-post' outside his new home in Tom Quad.[15]

Happily, from the outset, King and his mother had friendly neighbours. Pusey was in one corner of Tom Quad and Liddon on the other side of the gateway. Canon Bright, the Professor of Ecclesiastical History and one of King's visiting lecturers at Cuddesdon, lived in a house opposite, scarcely a hundred yards from King's own lodgings. In time they were joined by younger men like Francis Paget and Henry Scott Holland. Paget arrived as a Senior Student at Christ Church in 1873 at the same time as King moved into Tom Quad, and he remained a life-long close friend, admirer and disciple, as did Scott Holland. As King's protégés, they both achieved great prominence and were influential in the unfolding Catholic revival in the

Church of England—Scott Holland as a Canon of St Paul's Cathedral, where he helped to spearhead the application of his theology in social action, flowering a little later in the Christian Socialist Movement. Paget was in the 'apostolic line of succession,' succeeding King as Regius Professor in 1885, and following yet further in King's footsteps when he too was raised to the episcopate as Bishop of Oxford. With others less well known, whose lives were influenced and transformed by King's teaching and example, both Scott Holland and Paget continued to model, remodel and apply everything they had first learned and caught first-hand from King during their formative years.

DEATH OF WILBERFORCE

As a matter of form and custom, the degrees of BD and DD were conferred on King by Decree of Convocation on 14 June 1873. Scarcely had he established himself in his new home than, together with the whole Church of England, he was horror-struck by the news of Wilberforce's fatal riding accident on 19 July.

Lord Granville, who was present, has left a first-hand account of the accident in the letter he wrote to Wilberforce's son, Robert. The bishop was 'galloping very fast up the long hill, apparently careless as to the ground, talking incessantly on political, religious and social topics. Going down the steep decline, we broke into a gentle canter over a smooth stretch of turf.'

'I was riding on his left,' said Granville, 'slightly in advance. I heard a thud on the ground and, turning round, I saw him lying motionless. It appeared that the horse, probably a little tired, had put his foot in a gutter of the turf and stumbled without coming down. Your father,' he concluded, 'must have turned a complete summersault'[16] and shortly afterwards was pronounced dead.

The Pastoral Professor

To this day a large, granite Memorial Cross on what is now the National Trust's Abinger Roughs in Surrey marks the exact spot of the accident. It is one of those little ironies of history, that Wilberforce was thrown from his horse only a short distance from Abinger Hall where in the 1870s Charles Darwin was frequently the guest of the owner, Thomas Henry Farrer, who by keeping a 'Worm Journal' helped Darwin in some of his research and who, together with Darwin, would have walked through the very same woodlands in which Wilberforce was to meet his untimely end.

Throughout the formative years of King's ministry, there had been the closest and most affectionate relationship and deepest of friendships between him and Wilberforce. To Ernest Wilberforce, the bishop's second surviving son and domestic chaplain, King wrote expressing his 'most sincere and affectionate sympathy,' adding, 'You know how much I owe to your dear, great Father, and how sincere my Love is for him'; and, on another occasion, again to Ernest Wilberforce, 'I cannot say what I owe to your dear, great Father. Tho' he was so far above me, I felt I could sincerely love him, and few if any pleasures of my life have been greater than his kindness to me.'[17] In his last year as Bishop of Lincoln, King was to write to Wilberforce's daughter-in-law: 'The old Bishop, and all round him, had a large place in my earlier life.' It is not an overstatement to claim that without Samuel Wilberforce, we might never have had Edward King, priest, principal, professor and bishop.

KING'S ACADEMIC LIMITATIONS

The old misgivings about King's supposed academic limitations had never been far absent both from his mind and the minds of others. Years later, on the day of King's consecration as Bishop of Lincoln, Archbishop Benson, who had always been a great friend and something of an admirer, made an interesting note in his diary: 'It is strange that a great many years ago, when I was at Wellington, I remember Dean Wellesley's showing me some most strong letters to the Queen and Ministers against King's being made Professor at Oxford—on the ground of intellectual inadequacy. The Dean gave me plenty of indication of the untruth of the allegation. I recommended him to persevere with the recommendation of King. The attacking party were not likely to be so strong against what was purely to their advantage, and they must have had their own reasons for expecting his influence for the Church and Christianity to be great. And, so it has proved.'[18]

King had never been naturally 'academic,' and he certainly never assumed a 'donnish' posture. On taking up his new responsibilities in the October term of 1873, he would have been acutely aware of the contrast between giving lectures in the academic atmosphere of the University and the vastly different ethos of Cuddesdon, and he later confessed 'I was in a dreadful fright at having to face learned Oxford.'[19]

It took some time, therefore, for the many who already recognized him as patently a good and holy man, also to discover his formidable gifts of wisdom and insight, as well as his informed opinions on many of the intellectual questions current in the university of his day.

> Intellectually [claimed Brightman] he has sometimes been depreciated, perhaps because he never achieved any notable academic distinctions. But those who knew him will perhaps think that he was among the most intellectual persons they have ever known; only, as was perhaps the case with St. Anselm, to whom he has been compared, his intelligence was so much a part of his character, so wholly himself, that it might easily escape notice in the simplicity and charm of his personality. He had a singularly alert mind and was interested in everything: no one ever saw him bored, and 'he never touched a topic without displaying an original view';

and he was keenly alive to the intellectual difficulties of his day. He knew and could talk French, German, and Italian: and in a mixed company he could talk in at least three languages at once—no small accomplishment; while his English was admirable. And he read widely to the end.[20]

Dr Edward Talbot, a future Bishop of Winchester, who was already at Oxford when the appointment was made, many years later reflected on King's time as Regius Professor:

> We knew that he would do the work in some ways most admirably, for to all Cuddesdon men, and to many others by repute, the Principal's Pastoralia lectures were something by themselves. But we hardly knew how he would fit into the academical surroundings. He had been so identified with his quiet and beautiful surroundings at Cuddesdon that, joyful as we were to welcome him, we wondered how it would go.
>
> He himself with his quick, delicate tact and perception, felt acutely how great a change it was; and what a venture of faith for a man without academical distinction and experience; how difficult and even formidable a place a university is to enter in advanced middle life; how he would be in contact with new problems, or old problems in a new atmosphere ... He always keenly felt the difference between himself and academical folk, and the want of familiarity with academical studies and ways of thought. He would express this in his own whimsical way by speaking to us dons as 'You great people'; shall I say that this was three parts modesty and sincerity, and one part irony—so good for us too, and absolutely without sting.
>
> His weapons were not quite academical ones. But the old characteristic influence came out in Oxford, intensive and personal still, but now upon a broader field and with larger reach ... His professorial lectures (I never heard them)—but perhaps they were not altogether such as the word 'professorial' would naturally suggest. But they were worked for carefully.[21]

Talbot was not the only academic to perceive the distinctive nature of King's work as a lecturer. Whatever intellectual shortcomings King may have had as a professor, were more than abundantly compensated for by his person, his presence and his presentation, as W. H. Hutton, the future historian, readily attests. Writing shortly after King's death, he reflected on the impact his lectures had made on him thirty years previously, when he heard King give them in Oxford in 1880.

> It is a memory which to hundreds of those who share it is one of the most precious things in our lives. We remember those crowded lectures, so fresh and unconventional yet so full of meaning and value, so lastingly impressive; I expect that for many like me he was the only professor all of whose courses were attended, and that for pure pleasure and profit.[22]

Any contemporary criticism of King's 'limited' academic abilities, should be set against today's Bench of Anglican Bishops, when 'For the first time in living memory there are no former theological academics' among them—'they lack theological weight.'[23] King, by comparison, would be regarded as having more than average theological competence and exceptionally well read.

King's study contained between three and four thousand books, some of them he had inherited from his father, the Archdeacon, who had bequeathed his Greek, Latin and Hebrew books to his two ordained sons, Walker and Edward—Edward also inherited from his father 'the unbound vellum copy of Mr Burke's History of England,' which had presumably belonged to his grandfather, the Bishop. Two bookcases were filled with French and German theological texts, except for a corner where space was reserved for books by or on Dante. The great tomes of the Fathers; Dr Pusey's books; Dr Liddon's volumes of sermons, marked and marked again; Bishop Butler, in Gladstone's famous edition; a large and curious assortment of bishops'

The Pastoral Professor

Charges and Pastorals—he was an inveterate reader of these at home and abroad; volumes of Bishop Magee, greatly treasured, 'the most reasonable of all reasoners,' as he said in the sermon he preached at Peterborough after Magee's funeral; a large assortment of French, German and Italian theology—volumes often just bought and read and marked for a certain purpose and then laid aside. There were also a great number of books dealing with Higher Criticism—a line of study he regarded with anxious interest but little real sympathy, of which, nevertheless, he felt the need to be appraised. Charles Marriott had taught him that there was no need to ignore or to fear the recent biblical criticism, for as Marriott frequently taught, 'the utmost criticism can do, is to prepare a correct text for the reading of the spiritual eye'[24]—a maxim King frequently quoted.

In short, the faith King taught all his life was communicated by the life he lived: as the saying goes, 'to live the life, is to know of the doctrine.' 'He was a teacher of the Faith that was in him, not an echo of other men's thoughts—a disciple, but a "disciple" [as Marriott had been to Newman] with an independent mind.'[25]

KING'S INTELLECTUAL RESOURCES AS PROFESSOR

King had no pretensions to being an academic philosopher or to have thought through systematically the relation of his faith to rational knowledge. In a sermon preached at the University in 1879, clearly directed more to students than to the dons, he tackles head-on the relation of faith to reason in what amounts almost to a personal witness, concerning the foundations of his own faith:

> Do not be alarmed because you cannot give to another a simple proof of your belief. Such belief is not the mere product of reason or authority; it comes with the right use of reason and right obedience, it fits in with the

> highest exercise of reason, and the fullest harmonies of creation: but it is so intertwined with all our being, our reason, our moral sense, our affections, our will, that any proof, which addresses itself only to the reason, leaves upon us a sense of incompleteness and dissatisfaction. I am not thinking of objections to The Faith, but of books on the side of Theism, of apologies for belief: I thank God, I lay them down one after another with a feeling of incomplete satisfaction. They may remove the difficulties which have presented themselves to my reason, but my belief rests upon something more than that.[26]

'Something more' — yes, indeed, 'something more' than mere reason: all that was in line with the writings of Bishop Joseph Butler (1692–1752) of whom King had always been a keen disciple and from whom he frequently quoted. Butler, in his *Analogy of Religion* (1736) and throughout his teaching had always acknowledged that reason alone was not enough, and that 'something more' was required, namely, 'reason joining with the affections which God has impressed upon the heart.'[27]

On moving from the pulpit to the lecture room, King was never ashamed to resort to the best minds of his day in order to give to his students at his lectures an appropriate intellectual grounding for their studies in what was loosely termed pastoral theology. Fortunately, the parameters for the syllabus of pastoral theology were still largely undefined, leaving King a measure of freedom to tackle his new work in his own inimitable way. His official duties were primarily concerned with the candidates for Holy Orders, but it was clear from the outset that his influence would extend to a much wider circle. In his lectures he dealt not so much with disputed points of doctrine as with the deepest facts of moral and spiritual experience. Much of this did not come from books, but rather from long experience in personal contact with souls and spiritual formation. Indeed, it had always been King's keen insight into human nature which gave that 'something extra' to what otherwise might well have been the dry bones of 'the cure of souls,' as it was often termed in those days. In summary, King's teaching married heart and head, devotion and dogma in a wholly personal way which went right to the heart of whatever matter he was seeking to communicate, to the hearts as well as to the minds of his students.

It is fortunate that we still have a detailed outline of the content of the lectures he gave in 1874. Largely, though not exclusively, they would have been addressed to those considering ordination. These lecture notes have survived in the notebook of one of his ordinands, Canon Frewer of Brede, in Sussex. Edited for publication in 1932 by Eric Graham, at the time Principal of Cuddesdon College and later Bishop of Newcastle, they provide valuable and vivid evidence of King's conception of ministry and pastoral care.

In general terms, the formal lectures for which King was responsible fall into three parts: Ethics, Pastoralia and Preaching. To all three, King brought his own distinctive insights, while drawing readily on a wide range of other resources. His teaching on preaching, as we shall see later, marks a sharp break both in style and content from the preaching of the first of the great Latitudinarian, Broad Church preachers, Archbishop Tillotson, whose sermons from the previous century were still widely read: the watchwords in such preaching, as in the public-school religion of Arnold, were morality, effort and duty, with the person of Jesus Christ as the supreme model and example. Contrary to this, both during his time at Cuddesdon, and in his homiletic lectures at Oxford, King sets the preaching of the Gospel in the context of Christian formation through Word and Sacrament rather than as an exhortation to duty and moral responsibility.

Likewise, in his pastoralia lectures he gives a theological foundation for the practice of pastoral care and spiritual direction, emphasizing the role of the pastor as primarily a

Edward King

physician of the soul. Although King made frequent references to Richard Baxter's *The Reformed Pastor*, here again, as with his lectures on preaching, there is less of an exhortatory, didactic tone and more of a call to the inner life of the spirit manifested with sympathy, compassion and even something of the bedside manner. Baxter had listed seven pastoral functions: conversion of the unconverted; advice to enquirers; building up the already converted; oversight of families in the congregation; visiting the sick; reproof of the impenitent; exercise of discipline. Baxter's whole approach to pastoral care is summed up in a phrase of a twentieth-century Barthian theologian, Eduard Thurneysen: 'Communication to the individual of the message proclaimed in general to the congregation in the sermon,'[28] (which in today's world might well earn the retort—'Don't preach at me').

For many of his pastoralia lectures King drew deeply from a very different source, from the European mind and prodigious writings of Bishop Johann Michael Sailer of Regensburg (1751–1832), who, like King, was also a Professor of Pastoral Theology. Both King and Sailer were conspicuous in bringing to their work as professors in a University context a radically different approach to our understanding of both theology and pastoral care—a difference which the Church today would do well to revisit.

Bishop Talbot, recalling in particular King's pastoralia lectures during his time at Oxford, wrote:

> I remember how he talked of the big work on Pastoral Theology, by Sailer, Bishop of Ratisbon [i.e. Regensburg], at which he had worked hard, and his [Sailer's] was a pastoral chair; and in that line of teaching, he [King] was inimitable, so human, so sagacious, so penetrating, so devout. The spell was felt at once. His class rolled up to unprecedented figures, and hundreds of young candidates for Holy Orders went out from Oxford carrying with them not only such and such convictions which he had helped to form in his interpretation of Hooker, but even more with his thoughts and hints

The Pastoral Professor

about dealing with their flocks of which they must have felt the touch most in the least controversial and most practical parts of their work. It was the old influence of the Cuddesdon Parochialia deepened and widened.[29]

Unquestionably, it would have been in those same pastoralia lectures that King would have been most at home, drawing on his time and experience at Cuddesdon as both Vicar and Principal.

'One felt all the time,' wrote one graduate who had stayed on to read for Holy Orders, 'that one was in the presence of a master, but at the same time of one whose conception of the Pastoral Office was the outcome not merely of wide reading, but of profound conviction based on personal experience.'[30]

For his pastoralia lectures he drew on a huge range of writers from a broad range of traditions; from the Early Fathers and the Schoolmen, to St Gregory's classic treatment in his *Pastoral Care*; from St Bernard of Clairvaux and St Augustine's *Confessions* and his *De Doctrina Christiana Book IV*, especially for homiletics; St Chrysostom, St Basil and St Bonaventura. In his teaching on scripture and the Book of Common Prayer he drew on a cross section of Anglican Divines: Hooker, Andrewes, Jeremy Taylor, Bishop Bull, all laced with frequent quotations from the great Tractarians, whose disciple he openly confessed himself to be: Newman, Pusey, Keble, Marriott, Liddon, Mason Neale. Yet, at the same time he found fruitful matter for training in pastoral understanding in the works of Juvenal, Suetonius and Aristotle.

Although, as we shall see, there is a practical and 'hands-on' approach throughout all of King's teaching about pastoral care, it is all directed towards the inner life of the spirit, in what was effectively a course in spirituality and Christian formation—equally applicable whether or not leading to ordination. Of first importance and central to his teaching ministry is the prominence given to training in personal prayer. Large sections are devoted to guidance for the prayerful conducting of public worship and the administration of the sacraments, but, King insists, this must be underpinned and daily renewed in times set aside for personal prayer, nurtured by the inner life of the spirit, as he had previously taught and practised at Cuddesdon.

The published notes contain little reference to the influence of Sailer's three volumes on pastoral theology, to which King had frequent recourse, but it was the genius of these two men that through an applied theology of pastoral care derived from a life time's experience, a whole generation of clergy were given a new vitality and skill to equip them in their future ministry.

'The lively presentation, the wealth of source material—these were important; but even more, King's lectures drew men because they mediated his profound sympathy with all sorts and conditions of men. It is the same sympathy we find in his letters and sermons, and in all his pastoral dealings. The width of his sympathy determines the breadth of his reading, so that we can say of the *Pastoral Lectures* ... all human life is there.'[31] King's later distinguished successor as Professor of Pastoral and Moral Theology, Kenneth Kirk, who also went on to become a bishop, claims in his classic study of moral theology that 'The aim of moral theology is ... to accumulate from every available source whatever information will be of use to the priest for his task of shepherding individual souls.'[32]

What has happened to the teaching of pastoral theology in today's Church? Where and how would such a concept be used, let alone taught? In the last century, Thomas C. Oden commented specifically on the absence in modern pastoral counselling literature of any interest in the classical models of pastoral care:

> Recent pastoral counselling has incurred a fixated dependency and indebtedness to modern psychology and to modern consciousness generally that has prevented it from even looking at pre-modern wisdoms

The Pastoral Professor

of most kinds including classical pastoral care ...We have bet all our chips on the assumption that modern consciousness will lead us into vaster freedom, while our specific freedom to be attentive to the Christian pastoral tradition has been plundered, polemicized and despoiled.[33]

George W. E. Russell, an Oxford student of King's and author of his first full-dress biography, who never went on to be ordained, gives an insightful description of King's lectures and of the impact they had on the many students who fell under the professor's spell:

> In his hands Pastoral Theology, which had meant a dry system of perfunctory lectures, became a living, and effective power. Of course, his official duties were primarily concerned with the candidates for Holy Orders; but his influence extended to a much wider circle. Men who, with no thought of seeking the priesthood, were yet in earnest about religion, found themselves drawn by an irresistible attraction to the private lectures which he gave at his house at Christ Church. Those lectures dealt, not with disputed points of doctrine, but with the deepest (and often the most secret) facts of moral and spiritual experience. His power of sympathy amounted to genius and gave him an almost supernatural insight into human hearts. He combined the keenest spirituality with a sanctified common sense which good people sometimes lack. He spoke to us of our past lives, of our future prospects, of our present temptations, of our besetting sins, with an intimate penetration engendered by long experience in personal contact with souls. He told us truths about ourselves which were part of our consciousness, but which we believed to have been hidden from all except ourselves.[34]

'While at Oxford as an undergraduate (1874–1877),' wrote a student who was subsequently ordained, 'I attended three courses of Dr King's lectures at Christ Church. At the last lecture of his, which I was privileged to attend, at the end of the summer term, 1877, he gave his students what I then thought, and still think, very sound advice, which ran somewhat as follows—"Avoid, if possible, rushing straight from the University into Holy Orders. Seek rather to learn as much as you can of human nature, by mixing with men and women, studying their characters, and learning their needs. Travel, if you can; and, if need be, work at any honourable calling to support yourselves, until you have learned to reach the hearts of men and women."'[35]

The heart for King was not only and always the heart of the matter, whatever that matter might be, but rather, and more poignantly, it was the hearts of pupils and friends alike which King as teacher, mentor and friend aimed to reach and to motivate towards to an ever-closer relationship with, and participation in, the life of the spirit.

From the start King gave his lectures in his own home where men would crowd into the study and the adjoining dining-room, while King himself, wearing a cassock but no gown, would stand in the doorway between the two rooms, and hold forth, with his own inimitable informality. Each year he would lecture on Hooker, on the Ordinal and on pastoral theology, but, of course, following on from his vast experience of teaching pastoralia at Cuddesdon, it was in lecturing on pastoral theology that he was most at home, mainly, though not exclusively, with those who were intending to go on to ordination.

ETHICS

The full title of King's Chair in Oxford was Regius Professor of Pastoral and Moral Theology, so the third part of the curriculum, with its obligation to deliver lectures on ethics, was something of a challenge for him. To lecture on the topic to the students at Cuddesdon was one thing, but to do it in the context of the prevailing philosophical climate of Oxford quite another, and a daunting one at that.

When he was appointed, King began reading widely with a view to writing a big book on moral theology in a response to the philosophy coming out of Germany and the writings and philosophical claims of David Hume and John Stuart Mill. (Of course, King was never to be a writer of technical scholarship. Like the great saint, the Abbé Huvelin, he much preferred to 'write in souls'; to draw out, perfect, and unfold, 'that common humanity which is in every man,' and to do it by the light of Christ.)

One of his leading characteristics had always been what one who knew him intimately called his 'ethical outlook.' All his reading was done with this perspective in view. The books in his library bear witness to this: he marked any passage or phrase which bore on the development or enrichment of character. In this way, he developed his natural insight into character by what he read.

When he first went back to Oxford, he re-read his Aristotle and took the *Ethics* as his basis, using them not as an end but a beginning. 'To go from the Bible to Aristotle,' he says, 'is to go *back* and to go *down*, and to narrow your hold on, and your sympathy with, men. The old taunt, "Oh! Can't you write a better ethic? Why as Christians do you keep going back to Aristotle?" is answered. We *do* see the deficiencies in Aristotle. We are *not* satisfied with him. We *can*, and we *do*, supply the deficiencies—in *Revelation*.'[36] King always longed for someone to bring out a good book on Christian ethics.

'Read the poets ethically—e.g., Aeschylus, Dante, Homer, Shakespeare, Milton, Tennyson. Read good sermons, such as Newman's. Read thoughtfully: analyse them.' He especially urged his students to 'read good novels. You will thus travel into circumstances, and conditions, and situations of life.' He advised them to broaden their reading, so as to enrich their own humanity. 'This knowledge of man must exist in order to apply the other knowledge. You may also learn much by a knowledge of yourself, but you must get a hold of human nature *somehow*.'[37]

THE INFLUENCE OF T. H. GREEN

The Oxford of King's professorial years would have been right at the centre of the theological and intellectual turmoil which was to characterize the second half of the nineteenth century, when the foundations of the Christian faith were severely shaken. Writing to J. B. Mozley, the newly appointed Professor of Divinity, Dr Pusey, holed up in his rooms in Christ Church on a cold February day in 1871, commented, in characteristic lugubrious tones,

> How strangely different are the times, in which you return among us, from those in which you left us. Now the fight is not for fundamentals even, but as to the existence of a personal God, the living of the soul after death, or whether we have any souls at all, whether there is, or can be any positive truth, except as to Physics, ... But we have a grand battle; I, for whatever time remains to me; you, during, I hope, many years of vigour. It is an encouragement that the battle is so desperate. All or nothing: as when the Gospel first broke in upon heathen philosophies, and the fishermen had the victory.[38]

King, although never doubting the need to uphold the truth of the Gospel, would have resonated with much of what Pusey was referring to, and yet far less anxiously. There is one side to King which was conservative in the quicksand years when 'the faith, once delivered to the saints,' as Puseyites would have referred to the deposit of faith, was being challenged on every front. 'Be careful,' he told ordinands in 1869, 'not to change the old truths for the sake of winning a harvest of present popularity.'[39] But there is another side to King which perceived that the high summer of the Tractarians and the Oxford Movement was in the past with the departure of Newman and many of his followers to Rome. It was time to move on and face new and different challenges with a spirit of genuine enquiry; to respond to, rather than react against the intellectual and social problems of the emerging new age, as well as to the more in-house questions of doctrine or scriptural criticism which had high-jacked the agenda of the Oxford Common Rooms in previous years.

Edward Talbot remembered a conservation he had had with King at about the time of his own ordination while they were out for a walk together at Cuddesdon. Talbot had spoken about the difficulties which beset faith: 'Well, you see,' said King, 'it's like this: I say to others, "The ice is thin, but I think we can get across. I mean to try myself; won't you come along?"'[40]

During his time as a professor, King became increasingly aware of the urgent need to face the cultural, political and ethical challenges of the Enlightenment and the age of Reason, with its much-vaunted claims for the supremacy of the intellect, and the empiricism in the current claims of philosophy. At the same time, neither in his teaching nor in his own spiritual journey, did he ever resort to a theological antiquarianism, which so many of his more 'Catholic' colleagues tended to settle for and cling to. He saw the need for an organic development of a theological awareness which 'evolved' and changed along similar lines to that of biological evolution; the pilgrimage, and explorative journey of faith, which, like creation itself, is experienced and realized more as an unfolding process rather than as a static, mechanistic once-for-all finished product.

Newman, as early as 1846, shortly after going over to Rome and some fourteen years before the publication of Darwin's *Origin of Species*, produced his *Essay on the Development of Christian Doctrine*. The theory of development had been brooding in Newman's mind for some years as, by his own admission, 'an hypothesis to account for a difficulty'—namely, the difference between the teachings of the primitive Church and the nineteenth-century Church. The difference was analogous, in Newman's thinking, to the difference between a boy and a grown man, as being only the difference of form rather than the constant, inner substance of character.

> If Christianity be an universal religion, suited not to one locality or period, but to all times and places, it cannot but vary in its relations and dealings towards the world around it, that is, it will develop. Principles require a very various application according to persons and circumstances, and must be thrown into new shapes according to the form of society which they are there to influence.[41]

Newman uses several analogies in support of his hypothesis, most forcefully, perhaps, that of the stream and the river.

> It is indeed sometimes said that the stream is clearest near the spring. Whatever use may fairly be made of this image, it does not apply to the history of a philosophy or sect, which, on the contrary, is more equable, and purer, and stronger, when its bed has become deep, and broad and full ... In time it enters upon strange territory; points of controversy alter their bearing; parties rise and fall about it; dangers and hopes appear in new relations, and old principles reappear under new forms; it changes with them in order to remain the same. In a higher world it is otherwise; but here below to live is to change, and to be perfect is to have changed often.[42]

The dialectic of Hegelianism, as well as the contemplative non dualistic-mind, seeks to hold together the seeming contradiction, such as that of both the 'rock' as well as the 'river' of scripture: the rock-like faith 'once delivered to the saints,' without the 'living water' that issues from out of the cleft rock, literally petrifies into a hardened, rock-like, reactionary ideology: similarly, the institutional 'Temple,' without the dynamic of the river that flows from under it, in Ezekiel. The result in such cases, is a fortress-minded ideology, imprisoned in a dogmatic antiquarianism, persistently and defensively harking back to an earlier, supposedly golden age of faith. That was never King. He had been able to hold this tension in his response to *Essays and Reviews* (1860), during his time at Cuddesdon, and later, as a bishop, during the attacks on Charles Gore at the newly founded Pusey House for his contribution to the controversial essays in *Lux Mundi* (1889). Other contributors included such admirers and disciples, and indeed, life-long friends of King as Edward Talbot, Scott Holland, R. C. Moberly and Francis Paget.

The stated purpose of the book was 'to put the Catholic faith into its right relation to modern intellectual and moral problems.' At the time of its publication, it was Charles Gore who got the most 'stick' for a few pages in his essay on 'The Holy Spirit and Inspiration.' Throughout history, most of those who have brought the dynamic of the Holy Spirit into their theological equations have paid a heavy price from established orthodoxy. Such was the case with Gore who broke with Pusey and the more conservative Tractarians, but never with King, who on becoming Bishop of Lincoln, appointed him as one of his examining chaplains.

King, like Newman, though drawing from a very different source, and with admittedly far less intellectual acumen, nevertheless felt the need to explore and respond to, rather than react against those who see faith and its expressions in doctrine as an evolving and dynamic process. Many years later, King referred obliquely to this challenge in his Quiet Day addresses to the bishops attending the 1897 Lambeth Conference. There is an intriguing and illuminating passage in one of these addresses which refers back to the 'seventies and 'eighties when he was lecturing in Oxford. In the course of the address, King refers to the struggles and intellectual turmoil of those earlier years, when 'some of us' had 'borne the heat and burden of the day,' by sharing in and helping the 'mental sufferings' and the undermining of faith 'of our fellow-men. With some of us this has been very *real*, and very *fundamental*, it has involved us in the honest consideration of the very existence of morals.'[43]

Yet even during 'the heat and burden of the day,' King's response was positive rather than combative, constantly seeking to understand. In those same Lambeth addresses, he claims that during his twelve years in Oxford there had been a philosophical turn-around. 'Then men were raised up to help us.' To whom was he referring? 'I would refer especially,' he said, 'to Professor Green of Balliol College.'[44]

Thomas Hill Green (1836–82) was elected a Fellow of Balliol in 1860, and from 1878 until his early death in 1882, was Whyte Professor of Moral Philosophy at Oxford. At the time of his appointment King was some five years into his professorship. Although unable to accept Christian dogma in its ecclesiastically packaged form, Green's main endeavour was to rethink and propagate in the English world the philosophical doctrines of Hegel, so he is often known as the English Hegelian. He protested against the narrow reductionism of a positivist science, and in so doing, reaffirmed the moral and spiritual nature of man; little wonder that that was philosophical music to King's ears, not difficult to orchestrate theologically.

Like many in the Christian Oxford of the 1870s, King was

> stirred by the idealism of T. H. Green, and the neo-Hegelian movement. His estimate of Green, strengthened in after years by his friendship with Scott Holland and Gore and [R. C.] Moberly [all contributors to *Lux Mundi*], came to amount almost to reverence. He came to believe that Green had restored to English minds the power to believe in human personality, that he had set us free from slavery to materialism. He came to see true history as the perception of the inner working of the Divine mind and life: and under this idealistic influence he was ready not only to allow that humanity was progressing, but (in the end) to contemplate Biblical criticism without being frightened of it ... He learnt from Green that

The Pastoral Professor

God is in all knowledge, that study of every kind is a drawing near of the mind to God.[45]

That was precisely the view of the contributors to *Lux Mundi*.

In this, Green stands in stark contrast to David Hume (1711–76), the prevailing influence at that time, whose empiricism, scepticism and naturalism had reigned supreme in the high summer of the eighteenth century, during which Christian theology had been forced on to the back foot and reduced to little more than a mechanistic deism.

In the nineteenth century, and during King's time at Oxford, the views of John Stuart Mill (1806–73), were very much the flavour of the month. Scott Holland describes it:

> Oxford lay abjectly imprisoned within the rigid limitations of Mill's logic. Individual Sensationalism held the field. Life was to be reduced to mechanical terms. Scientific Analysis held the key to the universe. Under this intellectual dominion we had lost all touch with the Ideals of life in Community. There was a dryness in the Oxford air, and there was little inspiration to be felt abroad. We were frightened; we saw everything passing into the tyranny of rational abstract mechanism ... Then at last, the walls began to break. A world of novel influences began to open to us. Philosophically the change in Oxford thought and temper came about mainly through the overpowering influence of T. H. Green ... He gave us back the language of self-sacrifice, and taught us how we belonged to one another in the one life of high idealism. We took life from him at its spiritual value. And then we were startled and kindled by seeing this great, intellectual teacher give himself over to civic duties, and take up personally the obligations of citizenship, and work for poor despised Oxford city. This had an immense practical effect on us.[46]

Before his untimely death in 1882, Green had published a critical *Introduction* to an edition of Hume's writings. He also wrote a large manuscript entitled *Prolegomena to Ethics*, which, edited by A. C. Bradley, a former Balliol colleague, was published posthumously in 1883. We know that King must have seized immediately on Green's work because we have his own copy of the *Prolegomena,* signed on the title page—'E. King Ch/Ch' with the date 1883. Inside the cover of King's copy are twelve sheets in his own, indecipherable handwriting, and throughout the entire book there are heavily marked passages highlighting the material King would have used in his lectures during his remaining two years as professor.

In the introduction to *Prolegomena,* Green had written that 'Moral Philosophy is a name of somewhat equivocal repute; that it commands less respect among us than was probably the case a century ago; and that anyone who professes to teach or write upon a subject to which his name is in any proper or distinctive sense applicable, is looked upon with some suspicion.'[47] (King would have undoubtedly resonated approvingly with that particular sentiment.)

Green is clearly important in that he sought to re-think and follow through the further implications of Hegel's 'Idealism.' By maintaining that reality was 'an organic whole, a world of thought relations, and not a mere aggregate; that the evidence of art,' (especially poetry, always itself, a rich seam for King and frequently commended reading for his students), together with 'morality and religion all pointed to the spiritual nature of reality; that God, the eternal consciousness, was realized in each individual person; and that, since personality alone gave meaning to the evolutionary process, the permanence and immortality of the individual was assured.'[48]

In this way, the deism of a *deus ex machina*—the god of Paley's *Evidences* of the eighteenth century, rightly dismissed as intellectually bankrupt in the light of prevailing science by the likes of the empiricists, Hume and Mill—was replaced implicitly, although not explicitly, by the God of the Incarnation and the Cosmic Christ—the God who is omnipresent in the universe, 'holding it all together' rather than as the 'god of the gaps.' Immanentism, defined as the omnipresence of God in the universe, rather than God as an 'absentee landlord,' is a necessary constituent doctrine of the Christian concept of God. Christian theology would insist that God is imminently present in the natural world (although also beyond it), leading, as it did in the nineteenth century, to the Romantic Movement of the Lake poets and the Gothic Revival—all of which had appealed to King from his youth. (There were always those ready at the time and, indeed, ever since, who are all-too swift to point out that immanentism without the paradoxical and accompanying doctrine of Divine Transcendence can so easily become indistinguishable from pantheism, rather than *panentheism,* with which Christian sacramental theology should otherwise be totally comfortable.)

Once this connection is made, it is easy to see how Green's teaching not only appealed to King, but also exercised a great influence on people like Charles Gore and Scott Holland, who were able to apply, socially, philosophically and theologically, the prophetic claims of Stewart Headlam and Christian Socialism, with their demands for a reordered society in which the 'State is seen not as an externally imposed coercive authority, but as working for the common good of all'[49]—and not least the poor.

Although many have held that Green's strength lay less in metaphysics than in social ethics, it is clear that he presented metaphysics so as to make religion and ethics inseparable, by 'creating the frame of mind which sees religion as an interpretation of the world as well as of the Church.'[50] Scott Holland was among Green's most ardent pupils—as a series of letters in his biography shows—as well as being a life-long, devoted and adoring disciple of King. From Green, Scott Holland learnt of 'the unity of the sacred and the secular' and was able to affirm the 'concept of the world as having a "spiritual" as opposed to a "materialistic" interpretation,' together with the 'frequent use of the category of "personality" for the understanding of man's place in the world and God's relation to man.'[51]

Although Green's life was cut short at the age of forty-six, he had applied his philosophy with its theological implications to energetic social action. In 1879, he sat on the Committee formed to create a Women's College at Oxford 'in which no distinction will be made between students on the ground of their belonging to different religious denominations.' This was Somerville Hall, now Somerville College.

He was also involved in local politics as a member of the Oxford Liberal Association. During the passage of the Second Reform Bill he campaigned for the franchise to be extended to all men living in boroughs, even if they did not own property, and in this way he urged even more radical and far-reaching reforms than Gladstone had envisaged.

It is important to see Green as one of the formative people in King's unfolding ministry as he strove to keep abreast of the intellectual, philosophical and ethical upheavals of his time. Green's philosophy helped to confirm King's own spiritual pilgrimage and inner life of the spirit although he did not go on, largely for reasons of age, to apply Green's work to a theology of social action. This was to come slightly later, with people like Gore, Scott Holland and even F. D. Maurice, and with the ritualist clergy out on the coal face of parish ministry in the slum parishes of industrialized urbanization. It was precisely in this way that the 'cords' of the original academic assertions of the Tractarian founding fathers were extended in 'mission' and social action, and it is in that later and broader context that Green needs to be seen as a small, yet formative influence.

BETHEL

'Term is just beginning,' King wrote to a young friend in Zanzibar in April 1876. 'Last term I started a little "Bethel"

The Pastoral Professor

in my garden; it was a washhouse, and we cleaned it out and put cocoa-nut matting and chairs and a Harmonium—very simple, but very lovely.* We had a sort of meditation every Friday evening at 8pm. We did the Seven Deadly Sins just like Cuddesdon. I enjoyed it immensely. We are having them again this Term, only at 9 o'clock, because of the boats!'[52] Moving the time back an hour is significant. King had a wider catchment in mind than just the ordinands who attended his lectures—the rowing men, who would normally be far less conspicuous at such gatherings. There is on record an account of at least one man 'caught' by King's personal ministry through Bethel—and a rowing man at that. In 1883 Scott Holland met a priest in Northamptonshire, who 'rowed in his boat at Oxford; then got wholly snared by King.'[53]

It was in that out-house, reached by passing through the professor's house and across the lawn, where perhaps the most effective and far-reaching aspect of his preaching and teaching ministry as professor was done, in those informal 'Friday addresses.' Such was his 'Bethel,' as he called it, and every Friday in term time, it was crowded by young men. No ritual here—all was absolute simplicity, as King had said, 'just like Cuddesdon.' The walls were quite bare except for a copy of Guido Reni's *Head of Christ*, which hung above a faldstool at one end of the building.

Edward Talbot recalled, 'Here on the Friday evenings came numbers of men to join in a simple service and to hear him pour out freely the fruits of his sympathy and experience, his insight into divine things and into human life, especially young life.'[54]

> The place was full before the appointed time to begin, and when 'Tom' struck nine—one can feel again, after so many years—the hush of expectation, then the opening

---

* The building in question still stands and is still called Bethel; latterly it has been used as a store but there are plans to turn it into an Education Centre and Choir Music Library.

of the door, followed by the heavy tread, and, finally, the sight of the well-known figure, as King, robed in a very ample and somewhat crumpled surplice, made his way up the room and knelt down at the faldstool; there was a pause, then a Collect, followed by a hymn (sung kneeling), accompanied by a harmonium; then a prayer, after which he would stand up and speak as he alone could speak ... What we all felt was that here was a heart beating in sympathy with my heart; it would help me if I could talk to him; and he wants me to live close to God so that I may bring others to God; for that was always his point of view. He knew that many — probably the majority — of those to whom he spoke would be looking forward to Ordination, and he would often say, 'I am speaking, dear friends, to you like this for the sake of the poor people to whom you will, please God, be going.'[55]

As the work in Oxford intensified, it began to take its toll on Dr King, as he was affectionately termed. To the on-going need for further and extensive study and reading required by any university lecturer, were added an ever-growing number of calls on his time from individuals who sought him out for personal spiritual formation and for that wise counsel for which he was becoming increasingly renowned.

On 12 May 1875, scarcely two years into King's time as professor, Dr Pusey the aging 'godfather' of the Oxford Movement, took it upon himself to send him a letter, even though King was living only a few yards away across Tom Quad: perhaps there are some things better communicated in carefully considered writing, than face-to-face.

> I hear very serious accounts of your work, not in the way of your Professorship, but because people will stick like a leech, if anyone goes near the pond where they are. Work breeds very fast ... It is only three weeks, I hear, since you were beaten down by influenza. People have noticed how ill you have been looking, and how changed you seemed during the past year ... I hear that the cause of your weakness is the ceaseless flow

of individual applications which you allow to stream in upon you—during the time of rest or exercise which you really need. I know, too, what it is to have anxious cases ... 'One hour's harass,' I said to a physician once, 'is worse than 10 hours' work.' Then your sympathizing nature makes you feel things so much, that it becomes a strain upon powers, which, economized, are of such value to the good cause here.[56]

But it was precisely that 'sympathizing nature' which had always marked King out as such a very remarkable pastor, exercizing an influence which was to bear fruit throughout the whole Church, eventually by remodelling and recovering the Church's understanding of both priestly (and not least episcopal) ministry, exercised primarily as pastors, and measured by nothing less than the One great Pastor and Shepherd of souls.

THE STORM CLOUDS OF RITUALISM

Yet in addition to the strains of overwork which Pusey had noted, there were other concerns which would have weighed heavily on King, and of far greater concern, not only amongst the High Church coterie in Oxford, but throughout the Church of England at large, and which, in later years, would have serious repercussions for King himself.

One of the consequences of Wilberforce's death was to let loose the zeal of Archbishop Tait against the Ritualists, something which Wilberforce had endeavoured consistently to restrain. In the following February, Gladstone, whose sympathies with High Churchmen were by this stage well known, ceased to be Prime Minister, and Tait seized his opportunity. On 20 April 1874, he spoke with plausible rhetoric in the House of Lords about the escalating number of 'young and inexperienced' priests exercising ritualistic practices with little if any regard for 'the just rights of parishioners,' and he asked for support for his proposed Bill which, he claimed, would substitute a proper 'summary process' in place of 'the present system of protracted litigation' in the civil courts.[57]

From the Opposition benches Gladstone poured scorn on the Bill, which he saw as being designed to make the clergy 'march, like the Guards, in the same uniform, with the same step, and to the same word of command,'[58] but he was out of office and Disraeli, his successor, proved to be even more of an opportunist than the Archbishop. 'Partly for tactical reasons, to outflank and embarrass Gladstone, Disraeli took a leading position on religious issues and cast himself as a champion of the Anglican Church.'[59]

Disraeli believed religion was essential as social cement. He was genuinely offended by the efforts of Protestant Nonconformists to dismantle the privileges of the Church of England and irritated by progressive-thinking Anglican Clergy, who in his eyes hollowed it out from within by adopting the critical thinking that was fashionable on the Continent.

It might seem strange that Disraeli would rally to the cause of the Church only a few years after its bishops had stoutly resisted allowing professing Jews to enter Parliament—a cause which many Dissenters had supported, having had their own experience of exclusion. However, Disraeli perceived that for the Jews, Nonconformist friends were a curse as much as a blessing. Throughout the 1860s, the growing influence of Nonconformity impinged on Jewish interests, notably in their demands for Sunday observance and temperance and their resistance to state-funded religious schools. By comparison, the Church of England appeared a bastion of moderation and tolerance.[60]

After several prevarications, Disraeli, the supreme political opportunist, believing that the Bill would be well received and popular, gave Tait his support. In 1874, in little less than a year after King's arrival in Oxford, it was passed into law as the Public Worship Regulation Act. It seemed that the majority of the episcopate, as well as the Government and Parliament, were of one mind in their determination to reign-back the Ritualists.

It was practice of Confession more than anything else which fuelled the increasingly aggressive denunciation of the Ritualists. A little manual entitled *The Priest in Absolution*, intended as a guide for parish priests who were obliged to hear Confessions, had been made public: predictably it aroused a storm of Protestant indignation in which Confession and those priests who practised this sacrament, were named and reviled. Lord Shaftesbury and his friends during the frenzy associated with the passage of the Public Worship Regulation Bill were anxious that it should not be limited to matters of ritual, but should deal with other controversial practices, above all Sacramental Confession. Writing on 27 March, Shaftesbury said:

> May I now presume to observe that Ritualism and all its mischievous trumperies are now matters of secondary consideration? The Confessional is carrying the day, and unless the Church can cleanse herself of the foul thing, she and all her children will sink into the dust.[61]

Typically, throughout all the storm and stress of this, King maintained something of his usual quiet, inner equanimity. He could never have suspected that only a decade or so later this controversial Act would force him onto centre stage, as the bishop, in the Lincoln Judgment of 1890.

On 2 August 1874, King wrote:

> The speeches in Parliament and Convocation have been very trying and disappointing. I suppose we shall have to go back 20 years in outward things if the Ornaments Rubric is given up by Convocation. Evidently the People are not yet won to Church Principles. I confess I was longing for rest too soon. We must turn-to again and teach in the quiet Early Tractarian way. That seems the thing to do. Not to lose heart, or get hard with

> disappointment; but to get a help in Humility, feeling that Parliament does not like us or want us; and to set to work again with individuals in the clear and healthy atmosphere of Unpopularity. We have perhaps lost of late years by gaining the masses—I mean lost in purity of intention and unworldliness. If only we can not lose heart or temper, but retain a patient energy and love, I do not fear … I don't trouble the least about Parliament. If we keep quietly on in increasing nearness to God, we shall attract and hold the People. The most spiritual and unworldly Church is the one that will attract and win the People.[62]

In a letter to Henry Scott Holland, then a Senior Student at Christ Church, King touches on the contemporary outcrop of unrest and disturbance, not only the intellectual unrest in Oxford, but also the new learning and biblical criticism, and attacks on Ritualists. Initially referring to the attacks on the practice of Confession, King writes: 'Dearest Friend, it has been rough … Yet in the end our cause must win, whether we are smashed up or not.' Typically, he goes on to reassure Scott Holland that in the end things will level out, and that he himself has managed to retain an inner solace, and 'not suffered, nor been inwardly disturbed. There is nothing that I see to shake the principles of one's inner life.'[63] It was to be that strong inner life of the spirit which was to uphold King throughout all the controversies during his ministry, and especially when the fall-out from the new Act struck at him personally.

A DOUBLE BEREAVEMENT

Towards the end of his time at Oxford, King suffered two severe personal setbacks: first from the death of Dr Pusey on 16 September 1882, and then, a little over six months later, from the death of his beloved mother on 8 April 1883.

The Pastoral Professor

On the day of Pusey's death, he wrote to the Vicar of St Barnabas, Oxford, where he frequently preached: 'The dear Dr passed away to a brighter world at 3.20 this afternoon.' In his biography of Pusey, Liddon records how King was with him at the last.

> Dr King's presence roused Pusey; he looked at him with his clear blue eye, and put out his hand, while his face lighted up with a beautiful smile ... Soon afterwards it seemed as if the end was very near; and Dr King, who had been saying prayers at his bedside, read the Commendatory Prayer.[64]

A week later, on 21 September, St Matthew's Day, Pusey's funeral was held at Christ Church, where a 'very large gathering assembled ... By the side of the coffin there walked as pall-bearers those who represented the friendships and the labours of his life,'[65] notably King and the other two Theological Professors, Dr Heurtley and Dr Bright, and Gladstone, then in his second term as Prime Minister.

> 'We are, as you know,' King wrote to a friend, a few weeks after the funeral, 'feeling a little desolate without the dear Dr, in the corner [of Tom Quad] to go to. But his end was all we could have wished. *Peace* and *Power*, I thought, were the great lessons of the last few days of his life. He has left us a noble example, and his loyal, faithful death in the Church of England, ought to strengthen any timid hearts.[66]

Even more poignant and more deeply personal was King's sorrow on the death of his mother in 1883. Edward Talbot wrote of her:

> The only thing that made the uniqueness of King feel less unique was to know Mrs King. But to see how the nature had come to him, upon which the special work of grace and discipline had wrought, only made it the more attractive. His ways with her were delightful: 'My dear mother, you know, always tells people, with so

much content, that she pays her servants just the same wages as many years ago. She does not know how they come into my study from the drawing-room on wages day and receive a nice little addition.'⁶⁷

From the outset, Edward, or 'Ted,' as she originally fondly called him, had always been especially close to his mother — closer than his elder brother, Walker — and his facial features resembled more closely hers than those of his Archdeacon father.

After the death of the Archdeacon in 1859, Anne King had gone to live with Edward in the vicarage at Cuddesdon and subsequently moved with him to Oxford, where she was his constant companion and point of reference on all matters.

A student recalled one day when he went to see King for a tutorial: King 'was not quite ready for me when I arrived: "Come and see my mother," King said, "She will do you good."'⁶⁸

'King had been, in a peculiar sense, a mother's son. It is not fanciful to suppose that his exquisite, almost feminine, refinement and delicacy had their origin in the exceptional circumstances of his early home life. He had grown up under the sacramental protection of his mother's care,' at an age when most boys would have been experiencing puberty together with the rough and tumble of school life. He had enjoyed a protected life in many respects. 'When he went up to Oxford, her love still encompassed him, and home was still the sanctuary to which he could turn for refuge from the roughness of life. His father, when dying, had commended his mother to his special charge; and, from the time when he became Principal of Cuddesdon, she had presided over his house, had been the recipient of all his confidences, and the centre of his life.'⁶⁹

Mrs King died at her son's home in Tom Quad. Of her end, King wrote movingly to Scott Holland: 'My great satisfaction is that the victory was so COMPLETE. I did not expect any fear, but there was not one word of anxiety, or care about anything; just the same trustful, bright, loving self she had always been. For the last two days she was not outwardly conscious, but she was perfectly calm. I think this is what I should have chosen before all things, if I might have chosen; and it was given unasked in greatest abundance.' He concluded, 'Pray for me, dear Friend, for a little bit, that I may be guided. I am tempted to fear the loss of her wisdom almost more than the comfort of her brightness; but I know whence it came, and it can come still.'[70]

'Her death made a great difference in his life' said Edward Talbot. 'I remember one quaint instance of it. A preacher had preached in the cathedral a sermon which he thoroughly disliked: taste and temper, form and substance. He remarked afterwards, "Now a sermon like that makes me feel how I miss my dear mother. I should have just gone into her room afterwards and said, 'Mother we've had a *beastly* sermon!' and then there would have been an end of it, i.e. all the rankle of it would have gone."'

'So, your dear, sweet mother is gone to her rest,' wrote Dr Jones, the Bishop of Cape Town, 'and to the bosom of Jesus Christ. May the light of God's face shine ever more and more upon her! She was indeed one of this earth's treasures, a jewel of God's storehouse. What a change this will make in your life … I had quite learned to love her, and I had learnt to regard her as my ideal of the Christian lady.'[71] Dr Jones continued:

> Through all the Cuddesdon, and most of the Oxford time, the most delightfully characteristic feature of his home was his mother. She had his gracious, tender ways, and it was an infinite joy to play round her with his fun. One of the prettiest sights in the world was to watch him open the little side-door into their garden out of the cathedral, and pass through with her, after the service. We used to wonder how he would ever bear her departure. But when her death came, we found he had been preparing himself for years, and that he could retain all his wonderful serenity and gentleness and confidence and courage.[72]

In many ways his mother's death marked the end of a chapter in King's life, so that as she had moved on perhaps the time had now come for King himself to move on. Here again, it was to be a matter of timing, frequently spoken of as coincidence, when to speak of providence might, with retrospect, be nearer the mark.

THE CLOSE OF A CHAPTER

As the years moved on, King's work load grew heavier and heavier: an increasingly large number of undergraduates in particular sought him out in his home and King, made as he was, would always be at the mercy of people who needed help. He was closely associated with the founding of St Stephen's House in Oxford, and with Lady Margaret Hall, despite much opposition from those, in Oxford particularly, who were deeply opposed to women's education at a university level. He also ministered to college servants, encouraging temperance, and was prominent in the White Cross League, which, along the lines of Gladstone's work, did much to save girls from being driven into prostitution.

Membership of Christ Church's Governing Body involved him in routine matters of administration, such as the election of scholars, the patronage of college livings (something he found congenial) and the management of college property—it was during his time that Bodley's controversial new reredos was installed in the Cathedral and reconstruction work carried out on the Wolsey Tower. At a more personal level he is said to have been the 'only one of the canons whom the boys of the choir school could understand and love.'[73]

The break finally came in 1885 with the offer of the See of Lincoln, and once again it was Gladstone, then coming towards the end of his second term as Prime Minister, who facilitated it. Reflecting on King's time at Oxford, Talbot is

The Pastoral Professor

overwhelmingly positive: 'We knew that Oxford would never see his like again, and we should hardly have been wrong if we had questioned whether in any other sphere he would be able to use influence as direct, as lovely, and so entirely timely as that of his Oxford professoriate.'[74]

Yet throughout the twelve years of his time in Oxford, he never became a great power or exercised a wide influence on the university *as an institution*, any more than he was to exercise a wide influence on the Church of England *as an institution* during his time as bishop, unlike other episcopal giants of the nineteenth century like Wilberforce or Blomfield, who politically, ecclesiastically and radically re-ordered the institutional Church. King's contribution, so evident from the earliest years of his ministry, was at a personal level, not only with his pupils and friends, but also with those who sought him out as a formative pastor. Pastor and prophet seldom make for good and easy bed fellows. It seems that what King might have written in any large, scholarly book, he preferred to write on the hearts of those whose lives in turn would have a continuing influence for good, as in a ripple-effect for future generations of clergy and laity alike and for many years to come.

Dr Talbot, a much younger don, whose time in Oxford overlapped with that of King, is adamant that King's influence, far from being limited to the undergraduates, was equally powerful amongst the younger dons, not so much at the intellectual level but rather as the way of truth embodied and authenticated in goodness and character:

> Of this it is a little difficult to speak. Perhaps I can speak of it best by speaking abstractly of his place in the current of the theological movement. No one indeed was less abstract, or more concrete himself than Dr King. And the knowledge that he was there among us; the living evidence given by his spirit and example of what goodness could be in one who was within our own immediate ken and touch—this was to myself,

and I am sure to others of us, a debt for which to be immeasurably thankful.

Two things stand out. He was an affectionate follower of the Tractarians, a son of the great leaders, the contemporary and close friend of the second generation, such as Dr Liddon and Dr Bright, and a profound admirer of Dean Church, with whom I have always felt that he had a certain likeness in temperament on some sides. His theology was their theology. He was *si quis alius*, a revering disciple. Yet we all felt at once a new quality in his outlook and treatment of this. He was less severe, less didactic and dominating, less preoccupied than they. With a delightful tact, he would just let us hear athwart his modesty (he would never have dreamt of being classed in comparison with them) a note of conscious, even deliberate difference. His temperament radiated sympathy, mental as well as moral and personal. He felt with men, he felt with his time, he was conscious of the movement under his feet. It did not carry him away, but there was appeal in it; he felt the appeal and responded to it. He wanted to learn as well as to guide; and I feel sure, looking back, that as he got an increasing position he felt drawn to give younger men the sympathy and help which can be given by one who, standing between generations, can feel something of the new as well as the old ...

Thus it was that both in his personality and in his teaching there was a blend of the strong austerity of the generation behind, and of the more expansive, lighter-hearted (and in many of us shallower-hearted) tone of the generation into which he lived on. Something of this was in Dr Bright, his most intimate friend; in a deeper way still, it had been anticipated in Dean Church, and was one cause of the extraordinary learning and persistent influence of one so retiring as the Dean. But (as we all know) in King it was King's. He did not suggest anyone. Selfless as he was, there was no character with a more genuine outline and idiosyncrasy.[75]

One final affirmation and confirmation of King's outstand-

The Pastoral Professor

ing influence during his years as Pastoral Professor—albeit somewhat qualified—comes from an unexpected quarter, indeed, from the same pen which, only twelve years previously, had written in such strident and even brutal terms opposing King's appointment at Oxford, namely, Archbishop Tait. Writing in his diary on 4 January 1880, he records a 'most interesting talk' he had had with a friend on the religious state of Oxford.

> It would seem, that there are numbers of young men who would easily be influenced to give themselves to the clerical life if any man of real power of influencing them, like Arnold, were to appear there as a teacher. The only person with power of influencing in this way is King, but his theological opinions do not perhaps attract the more intelligent, and ... many young men who might be led right, sink into a sort of hopeless Agnosticism or indifference from the mere want of powerful guidance.

Tait concludes by affirming that 'the right man would spring up some day, and that in a University, as shown in the case of Newman, it is wonderful how one man with great powers can affect a whole generation.'[76]

For those with eyes to see, King had done just that, not so much with 'great powers' of intellect, as with the power of the spirit and in holiness of life, turning out a whole generation of men who went on, in their various callings, to renew and re-invigorate the ministry and witness of the Church for many years to come.

It was those same unique powers to influence and touch lives which were to reach their fullest expression only five years after Tait's reflections, when Gladstone nominated King to be Bishop of Lincoln, where for the next twenty-five years the fruit of all the seminal work of the previous years was to be harvested.

Edward King

Notes

1. P. T. Marsh, *The Victorian Church in Decline: Archbishop Tait and the Church of England, 1868–1882*. London: Routledge & Kegan Paul, 1969, p. 1, Gladstone to the Queen, 22 January 1874.
2. Henry Parry Liddon, *Life of Edward Bouverie Pusey*, 4 vols. London: Longmans, Green & Co., 1893–7, vol. IV. pp. 221–2.
3. George W. E. Russell, *Edward King Sixtieth Bishop of Lincoln*, pp. 35–6.
4. Russell, *Ibid.*, pp. 36–7.
5. Gladstone Papers, British Library, Add. MS 44,437, ff. 232–3.
6. Russell, *op. cit.*, p. 37.
7. *Ibid.*, pp. 37–8.
8. *Ibid.*
9. Owen Chadwick, *The Founding of Cuddesdon*, p. 136.
10. Owen Chadwick, *Edward King, Bishop of Lincoln 1885–1910*, p. 7 (Tait to Gladstone, 24 February 1873).
11. Russell, *op. cit.*, p. 39.
12. Hansard, *Parliamentary Debates*, 3rd series, HC, vol. CCXV, col. 401 (1 April 1873).
13. Russell, *op. cit.*, p. 39.
14. *Ibid.*, p. 40.
15. Randolph and Townroe, *The Mind and Work of Bishop King*, p. 65.
16. Ashwell and Wilberforce, *The Life of the Right Reverend Samuel Wilberforce*, vol. III, pp. 424ff.
17. Russell, *op. cit.*, pp. 42–3.
18. A. C. Benson, *The Life of Edward White Benson*, 2 vols. London: Macmillan & Co. Ltd, 1899, vol. II, p. 55.
19. Russell, *op. cit.*, p. 107.
20. F. E. Brightman, article on King in *A Dictionary of English Church History* (ed. S. L. Ollard and G. Crosse), 1912, p. 308.
21. Randolph and Townroe, *op. cit.*, pp. 80ff.
22. W. H. Hutton, in *The Church Family Newspaper*, March 1910.
23. *The Times*, 15 May 2018, letter from the Revd Canon Professor Sarah Coakley.
24. Randolph and Townroe, *op. cit.*, pp. 141ff.
25. *Ibid.*, p. 143.
26. Edward King, *The Love and Wisdom of God*, p. 15.
27. Bishop Joseph Butler's *A Charge deliver'd to the Clergy* in 1751, quoted in Henry D. Rack, *Reasonable Enthusiast*, p. 21.
28. Eduard Thurneysen, *A Theology of Pastoral Care*. Richmond, Virginia: John Knox Press, 1962, p. 15.
29. Randolph and Townroe, *op. cit.*, p. 84.
30. *Ibid.*, p. 62.

31 John Newton, *Search for a Saint*, p. 62.
32 Kenneth E. Kirk, *Some Principles of Moral Theology and Their Application*. London: Longmans, Green & Co. Ltd, 1920, p. 8.
33 Thomas C. Oden, 'Freedom to Learn,' a paper presented to the International Congress on Pastoral Care and Counselling, Edinburgh, 1979.
34 Russell, *op. cit.*, pp. 54–5.
35 *Ibid.*, p. 57.
36 *Ibid.*, p. 60.
37 *Pastoral Lectures of Bishop Edward King* (ed. Eric Graham). London and Oxford: A. R. Mowbray & Co. Ltd, 1932, p. 32.
38 Liddon, *op. cit.*, vol. IV, p. 221.
39 Chadwick, *The Founding of Cuddesdon*, p. 120.
40 Randolph and Townroe, *op. cit.*, p. 89.
41 John Henry Newman, *An Essay on the Development of Christian Doctrine*. London: James Toovey, 1845, p. 96.
42 *Ibid.*, pp. 38–9.
43 See Second Lambeth Address, in King, *The Wisdom and Love of God* p. 307.
44 *Ibid.*
45 Chadwick, *Edward King*, pp. 121–2.
46 Quoted in S. C. Carpenter, *Church and People:1789–1889*. London: SPCK, 1959, vol. III, pp. 483–4.
47 Thomas Hill Green, *Prolegomena to Ethics* (ed. A. C. Bradley). Oxford: at the Clarendon Press, 1883, Introduction.
48 See W. H. Fairbrother, *The Philosophy of Thomas Hill Green*. London: Methuen & Co.,1896.
49 *Ibid.*
50 Arthur Michael Ramsey, *From Gore to Temple: The Development of Anglican Theology between Lux Mundi and the Second World War, 1889–1939* (Hale Lectures 1959). London: Longmans, Green, 1960, p. 2.
51 *Ibid.*, p. 10.
52 Russell, *op. cit.*, p. 59.
53 Newton, *op. cit.*, p. 65.
54 Randolph and Townroe, *op. cit.*, p. 85.
55 *Ibid.*, pp. 69–70.
56 Russell, *op. cit.*, p. 49.
57 See chapter XXIV in vol. II of Davidson's *Life of Archibald Campbell Tait* (ref. 61 below).
58 Hansard, *Parliamentary Debates*, 3rd series, HC, vol. CCXX, col. 1381 (9 July 1874).
59 David Cesarani, *Disraeli: The Novel Politician*. New Haven CT: Yale University Press, 2016, p. 162.
60 *Ibid.*, p. 163.

61. Randall Thomas Davidson and William Benham, *Life of Archibald Campbell Tait: Archbishop of Canterbury*, 2 vols. London: Macmillan & Co., 1891, vol. II, p. 197.
62. Russell, *op. cit.*, pp. 44–5.
63. *Ibid.*, p. 66.
64. Liddon, *op. cit.*, vol. IV, pp. 384ff.
65. *Ibid.*, pp. 386–7.
66. Russell, *op. cit.*, p. 79.
67. Randolph and Townroe, *op. cit.*, pp. 72–3.
68. *Ibid.*, pp. 62–3.
69. Russell, *op. cit.*, p. 80.
70. *Ibid.*, p. 82.
71. Randolph and Townroe, *op. cit.*, p. 73.
72. *Ibid.*, p. 74.
73. Chadwick, *Edward King*, p. 9.
74. Randolph and Townroe, *op. cit.*, p. 89.
75. *Ibid.*, pp. 85–8.
76. Davidson and Benham, *op. cit.*, vol. II, p. 524.

✢ 7 ✢

King the European

KING'S VISITS TO GERMANY

In 1876, Disraeli, without so much as consulting the Liberals, let alone debating the matter in Parliament, slipped into that year's Queen's Speech the news 'that the Prince and Princess of Wales would be visiting India,' and, furthermore, and almost incidentally, that 'from now on, the Queen would also be known as the Empress of India: Victoria R.I.'[1] Disraeli always wanted to keep his Queen happy, but this latest political sleight-of-hand went further, by helping 'to define her country's self-image ... when it thought of itself in terms of Imperial pomp.'[2]

Edward King was unusual among Victorians as being possibly the least insular of any of the bishops at that time. So many of his contemporaries tended to be 'Little Englanders' and, at their worst, somewhat akin to Dickens's Mr Pecksniff, who was quite content to refer to 'England—and whatever other countries there may happen to be.' Then there were others, avid imperialists, encouraged by Disraeli's tactics, who gloried in Britain's imperialistic aspirations, its global expansion and its overwhelming economic power. King, to the extent that he was a Victorian and a man of his age, would understandably have taken a measure of pride in such imperial achievements, and yet he was by no means an uncritical advocate of the Empire

Given the breadth of his interests and catholicity of mind and cultural outlook, it is not surprising that his imagination was more forcefully captured by something much closer to home—the cultural and religious heritage of Europe.

In the first place, he went to the Continent for the sake of his health. Although a first-class horseman who also loved walking and climbing, he had not been endowed with a robust constitution or enjoyed the best of health. As he grew older, medical advice recommended annual holidays abroad, primarily in order to take advantage of the mountain air of the Alps, and each summer would normally find him walking for a few weeks in Bavaria, France or Switzerland.

But he was also drawn to make his frequent European visits by his keen interest in the Roman Catholic Church. There is a sense in which he admired it, clearly relishing the devotion of its humblest members, the transcendence of its worship, together with the witness of its saints throughout the ages. On the other hand, he was certainly by no means uncritical of what he called 'the Roman system,' with its dogmatic stance. He found Rome's centralized, authoritarian aspect highly uncongenial, and there are no indications that he was ever tempted to abandon Canterbury for Rome. As Professor Chadwick has observed, King 'was not rigid, nor viewy, nor embattled. He was strongly Protestant, in the sense of thinking the Church of Rome to be in error.'[3]

A further factor which drew King to Europe was his considerable gift for languages. He learned Italian in order to read Dante in the original with his invalid sister. He had also become fluent in French, and when he was appointed Professor of Pastoral Theology at Oxford, he determined to learn German in order to gain direct access to the prolific contemporary theological writings in that language. On his annual holiday abroad, he would make a point of visiting the local Catholic bishop wherever he happened to be holidaying, and discuss with him his work and problems. Undoubtedly, it was his acquisition of German that gave King access to a larger and more spacious context, theologically speaking, and to those European influences which were to prove the most significant of all on his thought and practice. King's nephew, Fred Wilgress, tells us that he went to Germany,

> to learn German, in order that he might read works of German theologians. He paid a visit to Döllinger, in order to get him to recommend him books to read. He read the writings of great French divines, such as Bishop Dupanloup, of Orleans. He studied the lives of the best French priests such as Lacordaire. He visited many of the great seminaries for priests on the Continent in order to get suggestions for the improvement of the standard of English clergy.[4]

JOHANN J. I. VON DÖLLINGER (1799-1890)

Commenting on his encounter with Döllinger, as early as 24 August 1873, and before taking up his Professorship later that year, King wrote from Innsbruck to a former Cuddesdon ordinand: 'There is a great deal in the foreign clergy which we should do well to copy, but there is a good deal also which we should be very foolish to envy, and most unwise to adopt. I had a very valuable talk with Döllinger about this. He was most clear about it.'[5]

Döllinger himself was a formidable scholar. In 1873 he had just completed forty-seven years as an outstanding Professor of Ecclesiastical History and Law at Munich. However, since 1871 he was no longer in communion with the Roman Catholic Church, having emphatically rejected the First Vatican Council's dogma on papal infallibility in 1870. Döllinger had been an ardent Papalist, but as Rome became more and more reactionary in its stance against the new learning and the sciences, and more centralized in its authority in what it had decreed as an infallible Papacy when speaking *ex cathedra*, Döllinger found himself increasingly sympathetic to the Old Catholics, and was now devoting his energies in trying to bring together the union of the various Christian Churches. To that end, he took an active part in the Old Catholic Conferences in Bonn in 1874 and 1875, which King's long-standing friend and colleague, H. P. Liddon, who had known Döllinger for some time, also attended. It is not unreasonable to conjecture that it could have been Liddon who prompted King to visit Döllinger—possibly at that lunch after King's final Cuddesdon Festival, when he was planning his summer break between leaving Cuddesdon and taking up his new post in Oxford—one can image their exchange: 'Where?' Innsbruck? Then you must visit Döllinger!' Their meeting later that summer was to prove critical and formative in King's development, for it was Döllinger who introduced King to the extensive writings of Johann Michael Sailer, who, in turn was to influence King's thought, practice and teaching for the rest of his life.[6]

Almost certainly it was Döllinger's recommendation of Sailer's writings, which motivated King's second visit to Germany during the Long Vacation of 1875, determined to pursue his German language studies there in order to be able to read Sailer in the original.

KING'S SECOND VISIT TO GERMANY

That same summer the second Bonn Reunion Conference was convened and sponsored by Döllinger—an old friend of Gladstone's and 'perhaps the only man of his contemporaries whom Gladstone regarded as heroic.' 'These Conferences involved the Old Catholics of whom so much was expected and who in the eyes of many High-Churchmen including Gladstone had taken on the mantle of true Continental Catholicism.' Among those High Churchmen were notably H. P. Liddon, Christopher Wordsworth, King's immediate predecessor at Lincoln, and Edward Talbot, Gladstone's wife's nephew-by-marriage. The Conference was also attended by representatives of the Eastern Orthodox Churches, in particular, the Greeks.

'The aim of the Conferences, Gladstone believed, was in line with his own preoccupation with the nature of authority.' Gladstone, along with the self-heading Eastern Orthodox Churches, clearly saw the need to 'establish the voice of the individual Church as the legitimate traditional authority,' dispersed and localized (as indeed in the Anglican Communion), rather than centralized, as in the case of the Roman Church, in the person of the Pope. The Conferences were 'simultaneously anti-Vatican and constructive in their own right. Gladstone was asked to attend the 1875 Conference but declined; he was none the less kept in close touch with developments.'[7]

Significantly King also chose not to attend, although the agenda would have resonated with his own ecclesiology, and in spite of his close friendship with other Anglican representatives and supporters. He was never a polemicist and never identified himself with ecclesiastical politics. Instead, he chose the more homely setting of family life in Saxony. On 14 July 1875, he wrote from Dresden to his sister, Fanny:

> I am here in lodging with a German family. I have only just come in today, so I cannot tell what they will be, but they seem nice. The father and mother can't speak a word of English, and the one daughter only a very few, so I am very fortunate, as we must blunder on in German. It is rather dull at times being alone, but that is necessary to learn … I have got a nice room with a bed in one corner. I am to have breakfast and supper with the family, and go in and out when I like to talk; I suppose we shall mostly spend the evening together …
> They are capital for me, as they can't speak any English. Every now and then we came to a hopeless stop, and no amount of signs or explanations could get us out; so we had to leave that and start *afresh*. I proposed reading out loud in turns, which they seemed to like, so the

> two ladies and I read aloud one of Anderson's German tales; it did very well, and about nine I left them. One certainly learns much more than in an Hotel.[8]

This is so very characteristic of King: he was not the typical Englishman abroad, linguistically or culturally. Rather, he was anxious to learn first-hand not only the language but the more subtle tones of the prevailing culture, as well as the local educational practices in the universities. His observations on the teaching of theology in Germany, and about the German spirit and culture, are pertinent and incisive. Back in Oxford afterwards, he reflected on the secularism and unbelief which he had observed among the German people in a letter dated 5 September 1875:

> I have been in Dresden this Long Vacation, working at German. It is very interesting seeing the wonderful up-growth and power of the German nation, but the unbelief is very sad; only 3 per cent, they say, go to any sort of church in Berlin, and the unbelief is quite open. They seem to have passed through the stages of Rationalism and Pantheism, and now they have almost ceased to care about the metaphysics which we have been following, and *worshipping* in them, and they are devoting themselves to physics. That means, I fear, for many, *materialism*. Luthardt says this plainly, meaning by materialism love of money, or power, or pleasure, this seems to be the leading danger now—that people will try to be respectable, but without God; to separate morality from religion, to devote themselves to civilization and culture and forget God. The results of physical science are so directly beneficial to society that it pays in the eyes of the world, and yet one ought to know by this time, after the example of Greece and Rome, that culture may exist without morality.[9]

Whether King had a presentiment that the German religious and cultural situation in Germany was a sign and shape of things to come is hard to say, but it is hard not to believe that had he been writing in 1975 rather than in 1875, his description would not have fitted all too uncomfortably his own country, as well as much of the Western world.

THE IMPORTANT INFLUENCE OF BISHOP SAILER

By learning German and benefiting from his stay in the home of an ordinary German family, King had been able to observe with his sensitive antennae the cultural mindset of the emerging German nation better than by participating in the heady and ecclesiastical discussions of that Second Bonn Conference, and, no doubt, to gain access and further insights into the writings of Bishop Sailer.

Sailer was a towering figure, committed to the reform and renewal of the Catholic Church, whose extensive writings running to forty-two volumes in the collected edition, had been translated into many languages. Born and brought up in rural poverty in Bavaria, where his father was a village cobbler with a large family, Johann Michael had no schooling until he was ten, when he was sent away to the Jesuits in Munich. That was only possible with help from friends in the village, and for a time it was touch and go as to whether the family could afford to send him to be educated. Sailer became an outstanding scholar, but he never lost his concern for the Christian formation of the poorest folk in the villages. Edward King's social background and upbringing were quite different, but they shared a real commitment and apostolate to the poor.

In many ways Sailer's career prefigures King's own: Principal of a Theological Seminary, Professor of Pastoral Theology and Ethics at Dillingen, and subsequently, in 1829 (the year of King's birth), Bishop of Regensburg in Northern Bavaria, though only for three years until his death in 1832. Moreover, throughout Sailer's writings, there is an overriding and consistent pastoral concern, fired with a strong desire to make the Faith intelligible and appealing to the men and women of his age. He saw the Age of Reason and the Enlightenment as challenging the Christian Church to re-think its Faith and to engage in a costly programme of pastoral and theological reconstruction. Such an attitude resonated strongly with Edward King, who, as an Oxford Professor, experienced the same cold winds of secularism blowing through the University in the 1870s and 1880s, and saw them as demanding a constructive Christian response. He had, in addition, personal experience of the even more secular ethos of late nineteenth-century Germany, from having spent part of that Long Vacation of 1875 living in Dresden.

From his first acquaintance with Sailer's massive theological output, of which he was to make a life-time's study, King was clearly captivated by Sailer's spirituality and his pastoral theology. Biographers and historians of ideas are often too prone to trace 'influences,' and frequently on little more than a hunch, rather than on clearly established evidence. But that is certainly not the case here. On the contrary we possess unassailable testimony to the fact that King drew directly on Sailer's works for his own thought and practice, and not least on Sailer's writings on pastoral theology for his lectures as Professor of the subject in Oxford. There are so many overlapping interests, together with spiritual and theological insights common to both men, which would have drawn King, especially in the early years of his professorship, to both the writings and the personality of Sailer.

In the first place King would have been attracted by Sailer's engaging character and he would have warmed to Sailer's insight into human character, an insight radiating charm, hopefulness, and the joy of faith. Sailer's ecumenical sympathies, which gave him such a wide circle of Protestant friends and correspondents, would also have appealed to King, as would his commitment to the poor and his efforts to renew the worship of the Church, its teaching and its ministry.

King the European

As with King, there was a simplicity and yet a depth to Sailer's character and spirituality. His personal character is admirably captured by some words of Alexander Dru:

> He was by nature of an eirenic disposition, and it was Sailer, with his calm and his prudence, his openness of mind and unshakeable faith, who held up the ideal for the next generation. He has been called the German Francis de Sales; but if such comparisons are to be made, it would be truer to call him the German Fénelon, from whose teaching he derived so much. For in Sailer too, there is the same liberalism of outlook, the same wide sympathy, the same personal influence and a poised integrity that won the respect, even of those who did not agree with him.[10]

Dru speaks of Sailer as being read 'as much by Protestants as by Catholics' and, citing Geiselmann, as enabling Catholics to rediscover 'the mystical conception of the Church.'

Randolph and Townroe record that King kept to hand all forty-two volumes of Sailer's collected works: nor were they mere study furniture. King read and used them in his Oxford lectures and for his teaching as a bishop. We have seen the evidence for this in the comments of his close friend, Edward Talbot, previously quoted (see pp. 176–7).

In his great work on pastoral theology, Sailer consistently treats the role of the parish priest under the threefold heading of pastor, teacher and liturgist. These different aspects of the priest's calling are integrally related in Sailer's work, both theologically and practically. Likewise, much the same is so evidently and patently true of King.

Although Sailer, then as now, was scarcely known at all in Britain, nevertheless he was one of the formative figures of German Catholicism, a pioneer ecumenist, and a forerunner of the *aggiornamento* of the Second Vatican Council, of whom one recent German student writes:

> Sailer ranks as a re-founder of pastoral theology. His breakthrough to 'old truths' bound scripture and

tradition together afresh. Sailer's common Christian spirituality of serious ecumenism has not only proved to be pioneering for his own time. Many of his efforts have been realized in the objectives of the Second Vatican Council.[11]

(It is significant that at the Second Vatican Council, Pope John intervened in a debate to reinforce that same theological perception, namely that tradition and scripture were essentially yoked as what he termed a 'double source' in revelation.)

In the same vein, Hans Kung, in his study *The Church*, attributes strategic breakthroughs in ecclesiology to the works of Sailer:

> There is a world of difference between the ecclesiology of the Enlightenment which, basing itself on natural law, saw the Church from a juridical viewpoint as a *societas* having specific rights and obligations, and the later ecclesiology of Johann Michael Sailer which, under the influence of revivalist movements, mysticism and romanticism, concentrated above all on the religious and also the ethical side of the church.[12]

It is those three ingredients—revivalist movements (in particular the Wesleyan revival which was very alive in King's future diocese), mysticism and romanticism—which best position King's theology, spirituality and ecclesiology as the narrative of his life and ministry unfolds.

Alexander Dru reinforces this judgment: 'It was Sailer who led the way out of the wilderness of the old world and, starting from the renewal of personal religion, prepared the way for a full understanding of the Church.' Dru, continues, quoting Geiselmann: 'It is ... to Sailer that we owe the fact that the theology of the nineteenth century rediscovered the mystical conception of the Church as opposed to the legal conception derived from the controversial theology of the post-reformation period.'[13]

Here again, it is precisely those ingredients of 'personal religion' and the 'mystical conception of the Church' as the

Body of Christ, as an organism and not just as an organization or 'system' which feature so pre-eminently in King's theology and spirituality.

In the words of the *Biographical Dictionary of Christian Theologians*, Sailer's theology offers

> an alternative to the post-Tridentine emphasis on the hierarchical character of Enlightenment thought. His view of the Church accentuated the importance of each individual's spiritual experience. Moreover, he accentuated the role of the imagination and the affections in the spiritual life, moral decision making, religious pedagogy and preaching. In contrast to the scholastic methods found in the post-Tridentine period, Sailer marshalled his theological arguments drawing heavily from the Scriptures and the Church Fathers.[14]

Precisely the theological method as well as the spirituality of the founding Tractarian fathers.

Similarly, Gisbert Kranz stresses Sailer's contribution to patristics, spirituality and liturgy, as essentially being all of a piece. 'He laid the foundation for the rebirth of patristic studies in Catholic Germany; rediscovered the medieval mystics; published selections from them and a translation of the *Imitation of Christ.*' Kranz goes on to claim that in Sailer's books of 1788,[15] 'he became a forerunner of the Liturgical Movement.'[16]

From all this, as well as from Sailer's own writings, and from what many others have subsequently written about him, it becomes clear that it was supremely Sailer, the European bishop, monumental scholar and pastoral theologian from whom Edward King drew so much. Tragically, much of what King gained (and passed on) from his European contacts and especially from Sailer—not least Sailer's emphasis on the place of mysticism, ecclesiology and ascetical theology—was lost and submerged by the subsequent euphoria of the Liturgical Movement of the twentieth century. This overemphasized the place of corporate worship, somewhat in isolation from the other elements of the Christian life, especially personal communion with God, which King consistently encouraged his students to strive for in his teaching of ascetical theology. As scripture and tradition belong together, so also, liturgical, corporate worship and personal piety need to infuse each other for a balanced spirituality and rounded humanity which issues quite naturally in unselfconscious service in the wider community.

A BALANCED AND ROUNDED HUMANITY

In that letter written to his sister from Dresden in 1875, King develops his thoughts on the 'distortion' and lack of balance in the teaching of theology he had observed during a brief visit to Leipzig, and which had given him the opportunity to meet theologians from the University of Halle:

> I had a very interesting week at Leipzig, and saw most of the chief Theological Professors, Delitzsch, Luthardt, and Tholuck at Halle, about 20 miles off. They are very simple, and work very hard at their books, but not very much more, I think. I think in England we have a wider-reaching, and better-balanced, work than the Germans have; they have confined themselves almost to the cultivation of the intellect. I don't think it will hold the *whole* man; he needs cultivation of Heart, Feelings, Affections, etc as well.[17]

Undoubtedly, Sailer would wholeheartedly have agreed with such a sentiment. In his own pithy way, Sailer had written: 'Many people do not find their God, because they seek Him only with their heads.'[18] He had taught his students, 'that true piety must come from the heart, and put into their hands the writings of Fénelon, Teresa of Avila, John of the Cross, Francis de Sales and others.'[19]

Both King and Sailer alike emphasized the need for a proper balance between the work of the mind and the work of the spirit, not only in theology, but also in education and Christian formation generally. Sailer insisted that in true education there must be training in both mind and spirit—'a life of the spirit, not simply a life of the mind.'[20] It is not difficult to see how strongly King would have resonated with such insights and sentiments for here was a Catholic thinker who, in the words of one of Sailer's German interpreters, 'made stiffened limbs flexible … caused stagnant waters to flow, and who warmed with new life what had become frozen by the icy breath of rationalism, while he went back to the primary sources of Christian culture, to the Bible, the Council Fathers, the mystics and the Liturgy.'[21]

But there were further challenges which both King and Sailer would have faced in their lectures as professors of pastoral theology. On 12 December 1829 Sailer wrote a letter to his friend Eduard von Schenk, the Bavarian Minister of the Interior. By this time Sailer was an old man, but his life-long zeal for the spiritual renewal of the Catholic Church in Germany was quite unabated, and the letter opened with a lament that theological study, 'not only at Munich University but generally at most of the Catholic centres of theological learning of our Fatherland,' had failed to rise to the challenge offered by 'the scientific formation and activity of our time,' which was both an opportunity and a challenge.[22]

In opposition to the prevailing tendencies of the Enlightenment, Sailer pursued apologetics not just from a robust intellect, but rather by striving for the inner life of the spirit, for a living, practical Christianity, for a faith that manifested itself in holiness of life and in charitable works, and for the maintenance and practice of Christian mysticism, especially for the training of a pious and intelligent clergy. All of which could be said of King both as professor in Oxford and later as bishop in Lincoln.

'With Sailer, German piety, both Protestant and Catholic, learned again to pray. This is the peculiar characteristic of his activity.' Again, as with King, it was said of Sailer—'Do not expect from him any religious polemics; he abhorred them; what he really cherished was the idea of a sort of cooperation of the various Christian bodies against the negation of infidelity. Sailer made a breach in Rationalism, by opposing to it a piety in which both Christian bodies could unite.'[23]

A BROADER EDUCATION FOR THE CLERGY

The curriculum and syllabus for which the Oxford Professor of Pastoral Theology was responsible was, as previously mentioned, in three parts: Ethics, Pastoralia and Preaching. We have also seen that he found in T. H. Green a strong ally, albeit a somewhat unexpected one, in making out a case for the objectivity of ethics in the light of the prevailing philosophy of the day with its utilitarian emphasis. Similarly, although to a much greater extent, he found in Sailer's three volumes on pastoral theology a rich seam which he was to quarry, teach and apply in Oxford and until the end of his ministry. Sailer, in his essays on the formation of the Christian clergy, not only insists that they must have 'a life of the Spirit, not simply the life of the mind,' but also that they must be well-educated men, who cultivated the life of the mind and are at home in the realm of Letters, Science, Art and Society. Clergy thus equipped, will have 'a special skill to work in the world ... against the spirit of the world.' Sailer dealt with this same theme in a powerful sermon he preached for one of his former students at Reisbach, on 13 September 1801.

Father Schwäbl was celebrating his first Mass since ordination, and Sailer took as his theme, 'The Young Clergyman of the Nineteenth Century.' He sets out the challenge of the new age to the Church's ministers, arguing that:

> The clergyman of the nineteenth century must know more, must be willing to do more, must be able to suffer more than a clergyman in other ages had to know,

do, and suffer. He must know more, since reflection, research, writing, living, questions and answers in respect of Christianity, have in our days become more general than they once were; since general press freedom and popular freedom of travel, bring opinions for and against the Gospel more quickly into circulation than formerly was the case: [*a fortiori* our own age of technology and the social media]. Since also, what was hitherto undoubted and uncontested, is now brought publicly into doubt and conflict; since everyone claims to express his views, and is threatened with change, since men's heads are taken up with a new movement, since opinions are in open conflict, since the language of unbelief is bolder, since errors are more deceptive, since attacks on the faith of the people are more subtle, since the controversies of the learned have become intelligible to the unlearned, the priest must know more, or at least want to know more, than his predecessors.[24]

Yet, Sailer is clear that the priest must, above all, be a Spirit-filled man, steeped in prayer, and committed to Christ and his people.

The note that Sailer sounded in 1801 at the induction of that young priest, can also be heard in the sermon which King preached as late as 1907, at the dedication of the new chapel for the Bishop's Hostel in Lincoln. He too wants to see faith and knowledge integrated in the ministerial life; he too warns of the contemporary danger of making idols out of knowledge, power and money:

> While I would encourage the instruction of candidates for Holy Orders in as many branches of knowledge as possible, our paramount duty at the present time seems to me to be the maintenance of the true end and object of knowledge. Money, and what money will bring, is the practical object of at least a large part of the knowledge of the present day. The increased knowledge of natural science ought to lead us to deeper love and reverence for the power and tenderness of God. The awful power and exactness with which the laws of

nature work ought to lead us to a more holy fear in our relation to the moral government of the world; but modern knowledge, the knowledge which is in such demand at the present day, is in great danger of being divorced from the knowledge and love of God ... Men are in danger now of becoming entangled in the veil of a knowledge divorced from faith. They do well to acquire knowledge, but they ought to remember to look beyond and above.[25]

PASTORALIA LECTURES

Once King had broken through the language barrier, he found strong resonances with Sailer's approach to spirituality, doctrine and pastoral care. In his widely read book on Prayer, Sailer had emphasized the place of experience, imagination and the affections, while both men alike taught and practised that same blend of heart and head, together with a concern for doctrine and pastoral warmth, of devotion and shrewd common sense.

Take first Sailer's guidance for the pastor visiting the sick. He heads this section of his book with Christ's words, 'I was sick, and you visited me,' which gives the dominical warrant for ministering to the sick, and encourages the pastor to see in the sick person Christ himself. He then speaks of the pastor as a mediator of Christ's presence to the sick person, while stressing that 'It is not the pastor as a human being who unites the sick person to God in Christ; rather, it is God in Christ who, through the pastor, awakens and strengthens eternal life in the one who is sick.'

Then comes the robust Christian common sense: 'The experienced friend of the sick, just because he does not fear death, does not therefore despise good advice, necessary prudence and means of protection.' Sailer then gives practical advice to the priest in the sick room:

—Try to see that the air in the sick room is fresh
—Avoid breathing the infected breath of the sick person, in nose and mouth ...
—As soon as he gets home (the pastor) changes his linen, and washes face, mouth and hands with vinegar and clean water.
—Don't get over-heated hurrying on a sick call—so making the body more receptive to 'noxious vapours'
—Have breakfast before making an early morning sick visit.[26]

It is interesting to compare this advice with that King gave to his students in his Pastoral theology lectures in 1874:

> *Cases of infection.* Go everywhere, and fearlessly, but observing these simple rules: (1) A golden rule. Don't go tired or fasting. (You may break through your Friday or your Lenten abstinence for this). Go after eating. Go when you are strong. (2) Don't stand between the sick bed and the fireplace because of the draught. (3) Don't hang over the bed or hold the sick man's hand. If he holds out his hand, tell him kindly that he must keep it covered up.[27]

The pastor mistakes his calling, says Sailer, if he displays a great deal of book-learning 'instead of speaking to the sick person a word that strikes home to the heart.' He fails again if he either rouses false hopes of recovery or takes away all hope of life. He is wrong too if he preaches at the sick person, or speaks in a loud or strident tone, 'where he should let fall, in soft, gentle tones, a word here and there of comfort and instruction.'[28]

As well as giving considerable attention to the priest's pastoral ministry to the dying, Sailer devotes a long section to the needs of a prisoner who has been condemned to death and is awaiting execution. In volume eighteen of his writings, he sets out a theology of grace which is able to change the worst of sinners into a disciple of Christ, assuring the pastor: 'There is no crime so great which God cannot forgive, and which the Spirit of Christ cannot cancel.' One is reminded of Charles Wesley's claim that, 'The vilest offender may turn and find grace'; and, indeed, Sailer's words breathe an Evangelical Arminianism which the Wesleys, so beloved of King, would readily have owned: 'God wants to make all sinners holy, Christ has died for all, the Spirit of God knocks at every heart.'

This was exactly the situation that confronted King in 1887. A young fisherman was incarcerated in Lincoln gaol awaiting execution for killing his wife and Bishop King, as he was by then, visited him and told the story of the Prodigal Son. The young man, who had no previous religious background, was profoundly converted in the death cell. King confirmed him and gave him his first, and what inevitably was his last, communion. Clearly King had read and absorbed Sailer's words, and acted them out when he went all the way to the scaffold to be with that young fisherman, precisely as Sailer had written:

> In the last three hours before the execution, the pastor will no longer leave the condemned man on his own, but will strengthen him with prayers before he treads the heavy road to death, and then also, with brief expressions, all leading him to God in Christ and to a blessed eternity, will accompany him, first to the court house, where sentence of death on him will be formally pronounced before the people, and afterwards to the scaffold.[29]

Not unlike King, though for somewhat different reasons, Sailer was consistently regarded with suspicion by the Catholic hierarchy of his time, yet remained on terms of personal friendship with distinguished Catholics and Protestants. Like King, he was revered by his many pupils, among whom was Crown Prince Louis, later King of Bavaria. In 1818 Sailer had declined the offer of the Prussian Government to have him appointed Archbishop of Cologne. The following year the Bavarian Government, largely through the influence of Prince Louis, nominated him as Bishop of

Augsburg. However, since he was still regarded with suspicion in Rome, the nomination was rejected. It was not until 1829 that Sailer was finally made Bishop of Regensburg, where he died, just three years later, aged eighty—the same age as King when he died in 1910.

THE PORTRAIT

If it is true that every picture tells a story, then the story of Sailer's lasting influence on King is strongly endorsed by a gift he received in 1899 from the Guild of St Barnabas for Nurses. In 1888 King had accepted an invitation to become the Guild's Patron, and in addition to an annual Christmas letter he frequently gave devotional addresses to the nurses. These were later collected and published by E. F. Russell, Chaplain to the Guild, under the title *Counsels to Nurses* (1911). Both in his addresses and his Christmas letters, King makes frequent references to the teaching of Sailer and unashamedly admits the great debt which he owed to the former Bishop of Regensburg. In 1891 he devoted much of his annual letter to Sailer:

> I am very glad to see this year that our good chaplain has introduced you to the mind and heart of Bishop Sailer, the 'German Fénelon' as he so well calls him. Bishop Sailer was a man with a real heart and mind: he lived at a time when many minds and hearts were troubled with unbelief, and with the social and personal miseries which go with it; and he tried in all ways he could to relieve the suffering in the minds and hearts of men.
>
> He was a sort of genius. He not only had some knowledge, but his mind saw the relation of things—how one thing touches another, around, below, and above: and so his mind has that kind of freshness, and strength, and gentleness, and simplicity and depth, which follow from being in touch with the circle of the One Truth.[30]

In the same letter, King quotes Sailer specifically on ministry to the sick, with a spiritual and theological foundation to encourage his nurses, and so to rescue their ministry from sentimentality or a cold professionalism. In ministering to the sick, as in Matthew's Gospel,[31] we are ministering to Christ himself in the sick person who is being served. (The same would hold true as in Christ's parable of feeding the hungry, clothing the naked or visiting those in prison.)

> So Bishop Sailer says, 'A sick person is a suffering human being,' that is a member of the great family of man; a suffering Christian, that is a member of the Body of Christ in pain …
>
> Desire then, as the good Bishop says, 'to perceive the voice of heavenly truth which is in you. Learn to live, to suffer, and to die, in the Spirit of Jesus; then you will be able, with His Spirit, to bless, refresh, and strengthen other people in their living, suffering, dying; then you will one day hear from the lips of Christ these words: "I was sick, and ye visited Me; for inasmuch as ye have done it unto these My brethren, ye have done it unto Me."'[32]

In his 1892 Christmas letter King draws yet again on Sailer to emphasize the work of nurses as being a distinctive vocation.

> I am glad to see that your good chaplain has more than fulfilled my hope that you might know something more of the mind of Sailer, the good Bishop of Regensburg. Let me remind you of three characteristics of his writings—*simplicity, depth, repetition*; and of three of his favourite words—*light, life, and love*; and repeat his words quoted in the January Paper for 1892, p. 8: 'That mankind fallen from God may receive again a mind, heart, and spirit for God, and become one, and remain one with Him for ever.' This is the task, and final aim, of the whole Christian Church.
>
> This is the work upon which you are engaged, showing people by your self-sacrificing love that God is love, and so bringing them to believe again in Him,

in spite of the misery and sufferings with which man's sin has filled the world: and through this dark cloud of suffering the love of your life makes the light of God's love shine.[33]

As King had shared his devotion to Sailer with the nurses, so in turn, the nurses, conscious of this, presented him with a large, original portrait of his great theological and spiritual hero. King thanked them in his Christmas letter for 1899:

> Your great kindness had taken me quite by surprise, and I do not know how I can express my great pleasure and gratitude to you all.
>
> I never thought I should possess a real picture of dear Bishop Sailer, though I once went all the way to Regensburg to see his statue, and the place where he lived.
>
> I shall indeed value your kind gift exceedingly, and I hope that its presence in my room may help me to preserve, better than I have done, that spirit of inward piety crusted over, or crushed by the routine of hard work.
>
> Light, life, and love were among the good bishop's favourite words, and they are words which, when taken together and referred to their one common source, give us confidence in the brightness and tenderness and power of life whatever our outward circumstances may be.[34]

Some words from the Guild's chaplain show how much King valued this gift: 'It gave him very great pleasure, and he had an easel made for it, that it might stand always in front of him as he wrote. Here it remained for the rest of his life. Three days before he died, he bequeathed this interesting picture to the Guild.'[35]

Edward King

THE ENLIGHTENMENT: CHALLENGE AND OPPORTUNITY

While both King and Sailer were steeped in the prevailing European culture of their day, they were far from uncritical of it, not that either regarded the Enlightenment as entirely inimical to Christianity. On the contrary, the very word and concept of 'enlightenment' — like that earlier word 'renaissance' — should be central to the Christian vocabulary, instead of allowing either of them to be high-jacked by those who would claim them exclusively for an agenda rigidly opposed to the persistent evidences of faith and Revelation.

Its concerns for freedom of thought and speech, its commitment to human rights, its challenge to privilege and reaction to reform: all these have positive value in our day, as in theirs. Yet there is a shadow side to that whole era which embraces a hubris, an arrogance, a sense of the God-almightiness of human beings, which are deeply un-Christian. It is that spirit which would re-write the *Te Deum* to run, 'We praise thee, O Man, we acknowledge thee to be the Lord,' or, in Swinburne's words, 'Glory to Man in the highest, for Man is the master of things!'

Both Sailer and King read and appreciated the rich literature of the European culture, so, as King wrote:

> If you read Goethe you are not rising onward and upward. If you read Schiller, you rise at least in the love of the Fatherland. If you read Dante you rise higher unto the realms of spiritual truth, but when you read the Psalms of David there are two truths of which we are most happily and most constantly reminded: the Personality of God, and our own personality ...There is a kind of peculiar purity in it. We must always be going on, *rising through* and *up*. We may enjoy the beauties of these poets; we may admire, but we must not lie down and rest in them, except in so far as they lead us up higher.[36]

Then again, both men were pioneer ecumenists, deeply committed to the unity of Christ's people. King's efforts at understanding differing traditions embraced Roman Catholics on the one side and Free Church people on the other. Sailer's wealth of Protestant friends and correspondents made him suspect in the Vatican's eyes. Both men saw the ecumenical vocation not as a matter of ecclesiastical joinery, but rather as a call to all Christians to draw closer to Christ, in truth and holiness, and so closer to one another—a constant theme in King.

Above all, it is in the depth of their spirituality that Sailer and King have most to contribute to both the Church of their day as well as to the Church in our day. Both alike point beyond outward forms and systems, whether in liturgy or systematic theology, to the inner life and freedom of the indwelling Spirit. Both are somewhat impatient of order for its own sake, preferring as King once described the spirit of Cuddesdon in his day, as being something of 'a Christian higgledy piggledy.'[37] King writes:

> We must be continually ... growing in spiritual understanding, and interpretation of the things around us in this world, reading through the outer veil and seeing the inner meaning. We may enjoy the good things which God has given us, if we are living with the peculiar separateness which the saints of God should live in. We shall be gaining a greater independence of the things of sense.[38]

These are the words of one who struggles to speak of the experience common to the mystics and contemplatives of the church. Sailer and King would both alike have claimed to 'enjoy the good things' of the world, but would also have encouraged their students to go further and to quarry out their inner meaning and deeper significance. In this lies the lasting contribution they both made to the ongoing renewal of the Church in their own age, and to the renewal of the life of the Church in our own day, drawing on a wide spectrum of European culture as well as the theology, spirituality and teaching of both the Catholic and Reformed traditions.

Edward King

Notes

1. A. N. Wilson, *The Victorians*. London: Hutchinson, 2002, p. 391.
2. *Ibid.*
3. Owen Chadwick, *Edward King, Bishop of Lincoln 1885–1910*, p. 7.
4. G. F. Wilgress, *Edward King Bishop of Lincoln 1885–1910*, p. 10. It is unlikely that King's trip was to learn German from scratch: his father's library had contained French, German and Italian books, which he bequeathed to his wife (Edward's mother) who lived with Edward from 1859 until her death in 1883.
5. *Spiritual Letters of Edward King, D.D.*, no. XXII.
6. See George W. E. Russell, *Edward King Sixtieth Bishop of Lincoln*, p. 120.
7. H. C. G. Matthew, *Gladstone 1809–1898*. Oxford University Press, 1997, p. 264.
8. Russell, *op. cit.*, pp. 50–1.
9. *Ibid.*, pp. 53–4.
10. Alexander Dru, *The Church in the Nineteenth Century: Germany 1800–1918*. London: Burns & Oates, 1963, pp. 41–2.
11. J. M. Sailer, *Heilendes Wort: Kleine Krankenbibel* [*Healing Word: The Small Bible of the Sick*] (ed. Alfons Benning. Kevelaer). Butzon & Bercker, 1983, p. 10.
12. Hans Kung, *The Church*. New York: Sheed and Ward, 1968, p. 11.
13. Dru, *op. cit.*, p. 42.
14. Patrick W. Carey and Joseph T. Lienhard (eds), *Biographical Dictionary of Christian Theologians*. Peabody Mass: Hendrickson Publishers, 2002, p. 445.
15. See J. M. Sailer, *Geist und Kraft der Katholischen Liturgie*, [*The Spirit and Strength of the Catholic Liturgy*], and *Kirchengebete, aus dem Missale ubersetzt*, [*Church Prayers Translated from the Missal*].
16. Gisbert Kranz, *Europas christliche Literatur:1500–1960*. Aschaffenburg: Paul Pattloch Verlag, 1961, p. 192 [J. Newton trans.].
17. Russell, *op. cit.*, p. 50–1.
18. J. M. Sailer, *Sämmtliche Werke* (ed. Joseph Widmer), 40 vols. Sulzbach: J. E. v. Seidal, 1830–41, vol. XXVIII, p. 68.
19. Kranz, *op. cit.*, p. 191.
20. Sailer, *Werke*, vol. XIX, pp. 5–6.
21. Kranz, *op. cit.*, p. 191.
22. J. M. Sailer, *Briefe*, herausgegeben v. H. Schiel, Regensburg, 1952, pp. 534–5. (*Trans.* J Newton)
23. Georges Goyau, *L'Allemagne religieuse. Le Catholicisme (1800–1848)*. Paris: Perrin et Cie, 1905, vol. I, p. 294.
24. J. M. Sailer, *Sämmtliche Werke*, vol. XX, pp. 301–2.
25. Edward King, *Sermons and Addresses*, pp. 116–17.

King the European

26 Sailer, *Sämmtliche Werke*, vol. XVIII, pp. 5–9.
27 Graham (ed.), *Pastoral Lectures of Bishop Edward King*, p. 58.
28 Sailer, *op. cit.*, pp. 22–3.
29 *Ibid.*, pp. 58–63.
30 Edward King, *Counsels to Nurses ... Addresses and Letters to the Guild of S. Barnabas for Nurses* (ed. E. F. Russell). London: A. R. Mowbray & Co. Ltd, 1911, pp. 49–50.
31 Matthew 25:31–46.
32 King, *Counsels to Nurses*, pp. 51–2.
33 *Ibid.*, pp. 54–5.
34 *Ibid.*, p. 87.
35 *Ibid.*, p. ix (note on Bishop Sailer by E. F. Russell).
36 Edward King, *Duty and Conscience: Addresses Given in Parochial Retreats at St Mary Magdalen's Paddington, Lent 1883 and 1884*, p. 103.
37 *Spiritual Letters*, Letter LXXI.
38 King, *Duty and Conscience*, p. 103.

✣ 8 ✣

Professor, Pastor and Preacher

THE PREACHER AS PASTORAL THEOLOGIAN

'As a normal rule, no man can be a good preacher unless he is, in the first instance, a faithful pastor, just as no man can be a faithful pastor unless he is, in the first instance, a man of prayer.'[1] In short, for anyone aspiring to be an effective preacher, 'preaching, pastoring and prayer' are a package deal and essentially all-of-a piece in the life of any priest, whether in King's day or our own. In this respect, it is evident that King, whether as principal, professor or bishop, checked all three boxes. In King's case the proclamation and preaching of the Gospel flowed fulsomely from his spirituality and prayer life as a pastor, rooted and grounded in that pastoral theology of which he was a foundational pioneer and passionate advocate.

KING'S TEACHING ON PREACHING

Charles Simeon, the prominent leader of the 'Anglican Evangelical Revival' in the eighteenth and nineteenth centuries and renowned preacher at Holy Trinity Church, Cambridge, who had influenced the students of his day with his powerful sermons, saw the importance of a skilled training of the clergy in their preaching ministry. 'Instruction relative to the composition of sermons is of great importance, not only to ministers, but, eventually to the community at large. And it were much to be wished that more regard were paid to this in the education of those who are intended for the ministry.'[2]

Since, as is often said, there is no better way to teach oneself than by the teaching of others, King, both at Cuddesdon, and during his years in Oxford as Professor, when 'Preaching' was specifically included in the syllabus, consistently gave a high priority in his lectures to the teaching of what nowadays would be termed 'homiletics.'

Reflecting on the importance which he attached to the place of preaching, a former Cuddesdon student wrote: 'We were first awed by the consideration of the responsibilities of the preacher, and later inspired with the longing to put into practice the directions which made it possible for us to speak for God to souls.' He continues, 'the student-preacher of a written sermon, twice a week, after Evensong before the College, had the right to dine at the Vicarage and receive a detailed criticism after dinner' from the Principal. 'The extempore preacher, once a week, had a short stroll in the garden, or an interview in the study after Matins.'[3]

This informal practice from Cuddesdon days was necessarily restructured in more formal lectures when King moved to Oxford as Professor. It is fortunate that we have very full notes and outlines of those lectures, in which, page after page, King spells out the theology, theory and practice of preaching in ways that still deserve attention from would-be preachers, as well as from those who still faithfully persist in teaching the art of preaching in today's Church.[4]

From the start King contends there was a tendency by the Reformation churches and those under the later Puritan influence, as well as by the Dissenters of his own day, 'to exaggerate the importance of preaching in disparagement of the sacraments and sacramental grace.' At the same time the opposite tendency, to disparage and undervalue preaching, prevailed among keen churchmen and 'sacramentalists': 'in the ... exaltation of the priestly office men have been apt to become careless about their sermons.' Here, as in so many other places, King pleads for balance. 'These two opposite tendencies met in the time of Hooker,' and yet, Hooker as no mean sacramentalist, nevertheless chose to emphasize equally the place and importance of preaching. He quotes from Hooker: 'We should be greatly wrong, if we did not esteem Preaching as the blessed ordinance of God, sermons as keys to the Kingdom of Heaven, as wings to the soul, as spurs to the good affections of man, unto the sound and healthy as food, as physic unto diseased minds.'[5]

King begins by asking, 'What is this Christian teaching,' in sermons? It is 'an authoritative delivery of a message from God to man for the salvation of souls.' 'What sort of knowledge is required' for that ministry? 'A knowledge of God's revealed will.' And 'what is this revelation?' For the knowledge of God's revelation, the preacher requires knowledge both from the Bible as well as the 'knowledge' that comes from a deep understanding of human nature, echoing Karl Barth, who, when asked how he prepared his Sunday sermon, replied: 'I take the bible in one hand and the newspaper in the other hand.'

For the right kind of 'knowledge' of God's revelation derived from the Bible, King insisted that it was necessary to read the scriptures (especially the Old Testament) from the perspective of the Jesus of the New Testament, allowing the written words to point the reader to the living Word, made explicit in the person of Christ, as in the story of the road to Emmaus (Luke 24:36), and furthermore, as Christ himself directs when addressing the Pharisees, 'You search the Scriptures, because you think that in them you have eternal life; and it is they that bear witness about me, yet you refuse to come to me that you may have life' (John 5:39–40, ESV).[6]

As for the need of 'knowledge' of human nature, King, here as elsewhere, is consistently forthright: 'Unless you understand human nature you will not be a good preacher, though you may be a great theologian. This knowledge of human nature must exist in order to apply the other knowledge. You may also learn much by a knowledge of yourself, but you must get hold of human nature *somehow.*'

Before going on to deal with practical points about construction, style and delivery, King expounds on a 'few personal, moral qualifications' which make for authentic and effective preaching. 'If you would point the way of life to your people, you must first walk in it yourselves, so that *holiness of life* is to be cultivated.' This should be done together with *'purity of intention'* and a certain *'disinterestedness.'* 'If they think you are a party man, they are on their guard, but if you are known as being disinterested, they will receive you.'

In all this, *'prayer* will save us from hardness ... You may be full of zeal, yet all this is nothing compared with the gift of love. Without it, you will never be a preacher.'

SERMON CONSTRUCTION

When it comes to the practical matters of constructing sermons, their preparation, style and delivery, King's advice is remarkably 'hands-on,' practical and direct, drawing, as he does, on his own considerable experience of preaching in varied settings and before very different audiences.

In the first place he insisted that the parts of a sermon should be clearly demarcated and always in proportion. 'A sermon should be like a church building,' he used to say. 'There is the "porch" or introduction, which should be short; say what you are going to preach about. Then there is the "nave," the main theme of the sermon divided into two or three bays,' with the use of illustrations on the side. Finally, 'there is the "chancel," which represents the conclusion' bringing us closer to the holy place. 'Get the three main parts into right proportions,' he would add. His other illustration, like so many employed in his own sermons and letters, is so simple and yet no less telling and memorable. He would say that 'an envelope, opened out and bent backwards made a particularly good ground for a sermon. The central part of the envelope was for the main theme; the two sides, when it was split open, served as space for jotting down the illustrations; the top and bottom ends for the beginning and the conclusion respectively.'[7]

The introduction needs to 'attract their attention, to secure their goodwill, making them anxious to hear what you are going to say; interested in you and trusting you.' The main body of the sermon needs to have a clear objective, and for this the preacher must have a clear subject in mind — a 'secure unity of ideas; evolution of thought from one central idea, and consistency of expression and language and metaphor. The sermon will grow up from its idea, as a tree from a seed.' The conclusion must not be a 'mere recapitulation of the first part in the imperative mode,' nor should it 'introduce new thoughts.'

Never say, 'in conclusion and then go on for a further twenty minutes. Pack it up for the people to carry away. The sermon shouldn't just run into the sand, but rather flow bravely down into the sea.' The conclusion must be carefully crafted to carry the people on further from the point where you started.

As to the length of sermons, which were often inordinately long by today's standards, King urges 'Say what you have to say and finish!' And to drive the point home he quotes his old friend Richard Whately: 'Preach not because you have to say something, but because you have something to say.'

STYLE AND DELIVERY

As to earnestness, 'it must be unselfconscious, resulting only from the pressure of the truth. Don't lay on earnestness.' Likewise, with gesticulation: this should be as 'in ordinary life' where 'people must keep a check on themselves.' On delivery, 'there is one golden rule—be natural. Any manner will do, but no mannerisms. In copying any great preacher, copy his principles, not his peculiarities.'

He used also to dwell on Bishop Dupanloup's description of preaching. It is speaking *to* (*parler à*) the people, not merely speaking *before* (*devant*) them. 'You may fire off a great sermon *before* people, but it won't touch them unless you speak *to* them.' Furthermore, King emphasized the importance not only of speaking to the congregation but of looking at them, 'insisting on the duty of the preacher to look at the congregation,' as was his own invariable and telling practice. 'I always do look at the congregation,' he told his students at Cuddesdon, 'and the dear things think my eye is upon them and have no idea that I can't see one of them.' In the early centuries of the church, the preacher would sit to preach in the *cathedra* or teacher's chair and not stand in a pulpit, ten feet above any contradiction, talking down to the congregation in more senses than one, and therefore literally, as well as figuratively, preaching 'over their heads.' St Augustine insisted on having eye-to-eye contact with his congregation so that he could visually interact with them to see from their faces whether they were bored, or hadn't understood something he had said, so that he would then repeat himself in order to drive his point home more emphatically

AN EFFECTIVE SERMON?

'That sermon is a good sermon,' King used to say, 'not when people come out of church, saying, "What a wonderful sermon, what a wonderful preacher," but when they go quietly away and want to be alone.'[8] For King, 'The requirements of a good sermon are—Church Doctrine, Catholic phraseology, Study of Scripture and the whole tied together by love.'[9]

King himself knew, and had read, as well as urging his students to read, Augustine's great work on preaching,[10] where the saint insists on three words as being the purpose and ingredients of an effective sermon—*Doceat, Delectet, Moveat*—'teach, interest, and persuade.' Augustine, in his early years as professor of rhetoric in Milan, had borrowed this threefold direction for preaching from Cicero's *Orator* quoting that, 'To teach is a necessity, to please is a sweetness, to persuade is a victory.'

On the question of the place of Bible study and reading, King sets the bar for his students much higher than most clergy in our own day could possibly aspire to. First, they must read it 'Critically, Hebrew, Greek and Latin'—in other words using the tools of the ancient languages to get at the fuller meaning of the text. King had not much use for so-called Higher Criticism. He was later, on 31 December 1883, to write to a friend giving advice on Bible reading: 'What little I know about it, I should say that a *mixed* [method is best]. The critical often keeps one awake, opens one's eyes. Only remember, dear Charles Marriott says:— "The utmost that criticism can do is to prepare and correct text for the reading of the spiritual eye." Still, I think it often opens one's eyes. I mean, without a commentary one does not crack the nut.'[11]

For King, reading scripture after ingesting all the commentaries did not stop there, precisely because, as he put it, it did not 'crack the nut.' The commentaries open the eyes of the mind but, in order to 'read, mark, learn and inwardly digest' scripture, as the Collect from the Book of Common Prayer exhorts,[12] King's own practice was to go further and to read with that 'spiritual eye' or with 'the eyes of the heart' as Augustine had taught, in what is known in the traditional practice of reading scripture, as *lectio divina*. It is interesting that King uses the same analogy as Augustine on that self-same question of how to read scripture in order to penetrate to its deeper meaning—'cracking the nut.' In

Augustine's analogy, the commentaries only provide the outer meaning, like the outer shell of a nut. When the nut is cracked open, it reveals the 'sweet, inner kernel' or the deeper spiritual meaning of the text received through the eyes and ears of the heart, directly informed by the same Holy Spirit who first inspired the written text and who also indwells the heart of the believer. In such a method of Bible study, biblical criticism has a part to play in 'opening eyes' and keeping one 'awake,' as King says, and enlightening the mind but should never be the last word. For that reason, King was never threatened or unduly disturbed by the biblical criticism of the day, which had become so divisive, both at home and on the Continent: his was not a reactionary spirit, but rather both radical and traditional. It is not incidental that King expounds and unpacks at considerable length this approach to biblical criticism in his Quiet Day addresses at the 1897 Lambeth Conference.[13]

THE POWER OF KING'S PREACHING

If 'practise what you preach,' is an appropriate injunction for any preacher, then King exemplified in the practice of his own preaching the self-same teaching he had given to his students. For them, the memory of his lectures on preaching or homiletics would be especially cherished, together with the opportunities to hear King himself putting his teaching into practice, as and when he was called upon to preach in the Cathedral or the University Church, or at other churches in Oxford, such as St Barnabas or St Philip and St James, where he was a frequent preacher during his time as Professor.

Although many of his contemporaries speak movingly of King's ministry in the pulpit, in his customary self-deprecating way he used laughingly to say 'that he had only four or five sermons, and that his chief perplexity was to find fresh collars and cuffs for them.'[14] On another occasion,

Professor, Pastor and Preacher

and again with similar characteristic humility, he said that 'he did not often compose fresh sermons, but that he had one lantern and put in fresh slides.' And then speaking of a great preacher who had recently died, he added, 'Why was he taken, and we, the dross of the earth, left?'[15]

It was not true, of course, that he had only a handful of sermons, as his posthumously published works clearly testify. He had scores, if not hundreds of sermons and addresses. Yet it is also a fact that his preaching focused on certain major themes, to which he repeatedly returned. We know this not only from the published texts, but also from those who heard him. As with John Henry Newman, we have numerous eye-and-ear witness accounts of his preaching and the impact it made on his hearers.

King did not have Newman's power of subtle reasoning, any more than he possessed Liddon's gift of commanding oratory. Yet he had his own distinctive style, which won him a hearing with many who would have found Newman beyond them and Liddon far too overpowering. In preaching, as in writing, the style is the man. King's was quiet, modest, disarmingly simple. For some too simple: Canon A. M. Cook, a Sub-Dean of Lincoln, who knew King well, recalled the reaction of some who fancied themselves great sermon-tasters. The Revd Gilbert Walker, 'scholar, native of Lincolnshire, a country parson in King's Diocese and a great admirer' of his bishop, was staying with his father in Spilsby, where on the Sunday evening King was due to preach at the local parish church. Walker asked his father whether he would be coming to hear him, 'and was snubbed with a grumbled refusal, on the grounds that his sermons were an insult to intelligence.' However, as Canon Cook swiftly makes clear, 'there were few who thought like that. King's sermons were simple, but "the common people heard him gladly."'[16]

If the great American preacher Phillips Brooks, from whom King frequently quotes in his lectures, is right when he claimed that preaching is essentially 'truth conveyed through personality' (when the words are 'enfleshed' in a person), then surely it follows that sermons are most effective when heard first-hand, coming directly from the mouth of the preacher. 'It is always a very different thing to *read* a sermon [as the Victorians delighted to do] than to *hear* one. This is especially true in the case of Edward King. His gracious and inspiring presence, his appealing voice, his intensely sympathetic intonation, cannot be produced on the printed page, so that much, very much, is consequently lost. Those who knew him best will agree that it seemed comparatively to matter very little what he said; it was his presence and his way of saying what he had to say which seemed all-important; the magnetic attraction of his presence was in itself more than half the sermon.'[17]

Newman had always held the conviction that personal influence was an essential element in the communication of the Gospel or Christian truth, whether in teaching, but especially in preaching. In his *Lectures and Essays on University Subjects*, he maintained that 'Nothing that is anonymous will preach; nothing that is dead and gone; nothing even which is of yesterday, however religious in itself and useful.' He emphasizes that the preacher, 'comes to his audience with a name and a history, and excites a personal interest, and persuades by what he is, as well as by what he delivers.'[18]

This same understanding of the importance of the personal element in preaching is emphasized by King in 1908, when addressing the Lay Readers of the Lincoln Diocese in words and with phrases which would strongly suggest the influence, either directly or indirectly, of Newman.

> What I am anxious always for myself to have, and what I desire for you, is a *personal* sense of this message in myself, and the desire to deliver it to others. It has been truly said [presumably here referring to Newman], 'nothing *anonymous* will persuade,' i.e. that the faith and conduct of the preacher give life and power to

his message. Thus preaching is different from mere teaching. You may teach mathematics or geography without being fully convinced. But in delivering the Gospel message, if it is to be a living life-giving message, there must be in the preacher a sense of message and the desire to deliver it.[19]

Possidius, the contemporary and first biographer of St Augustine, claimed that while everyone who read Augustine's theological works would do so with great profit, 'I think that those who were able to profit still more' were those who 'could hear him speak in Church,'[20] that is to say to hear and experience Augustine in person as preacher and teacher.

The same could be said of King as a pastoral theologian: his teaching and preaching are the distillation of the Revelation through scripture, sacrament, worship, tradition and experience, with the latter drawing everything together in an incarnational theology which not only informed his pupils and congregations, but could also be reasonably expected to lead to a transformation of lives. King's sermons therefore not only address the brain with information, but also speak to the whole person in ways which engaged and challenged his hearers. He not only spoke out of his mind or intellect, but also from his whole person in what we often call 'body language.'

Unamuno, the Spanish philosopher and poet, believed that the reconciliation of intellectual requirements with the necessities of the heart and the will is the basic challenge for personhood since the Enlightenment: the effective communicator, whether teacher or preacher, should strive for a synthesis of heart and mind, body and spirit: 'There are people who appear to think only with the brain, or with whatever may be the specific thinking organ, while others think with all the body and all the soul, with the blood, with the marrow of the bones, with the belly, with the life.'[21] Of course such an enlightened attitude may not sit well with an intellectual elite, with its emphasis on articulate scholarship in a university environment, such as King laboured in as a professor, and that must surely go a long way to explain his self-deprecation of his intellectual abilities. Yet King had something much more to give, not just in his preaching and teaching, but in his whole ministry, which has been the constant theme of this biography.

'A sermon can attract and inform, but unless it moves, stirs the listener into a deeper longing for God, it cannot be distinguished from a lecture.'[22] It was precisely in this ability to 'move' congregations—that third requirement of Augustine as taught by King in his homiletic lectures—which distinguishes preaching that merely 'tickles the ears' from preaching, such as King's, which issues in the transformation of lives: 'there has been no resonance or dislocation in the conscience of the hearer.'[23] Lancelot Andrewes, preaching to the clergy in Whitehall on Ash Wednesday in 1619, insisted that the clergy were charged to preach to people 'not, what for the present they would hear, but what in another day, they would wish they had heard.'[24]

King consistently taught that only the preacher who knows from pastoral experience and his everyday dealings with those in his care can hope to connect from the pulpit with his congregation. 'It is not the depth, nor the wit, nor the eloquence of the preacher that pierces us,' insisted the great seventeenth-century preacher and poet, John Donne, 'but his *nearnesse.*'[25] 'People are affected by a preacher whose humanity seems *near* to their own. A shared sense of human experience is the heart of the resonance that the preacher seeks to create in order to communicate words that might help to reimagine the world.'[26] It was precisely that '*nearnesse*' which distinguished King's preaching—informed and enriched from years of pastoral experience—from that of the majority of his contemporaries.

But there was and is a further characteristic required for the making of an effective preacher, in addition to experience as a faithful pastor. The pastoral preacher must be steeped in prayer and, to use King's own words, 'constantly striving for holiness': it is that further requirement which gave his teaching and preaching alike its authority and authenticity. 'What brings "awe" and strong regard from the congregation,' according to the poet-preacher and pastor, George Herbert, 'is when one's beliefs and one's life seem to translate each other.' Mark Oakley opens this up even more poetically: 'The 'colours' of the preacher's human experience,' he says, 'and the life being lived, are moulded with the richness of the gospel and form a window through which the sun can stream.'[27]

King's posthumously published sermons contain several different categories of addresses from which we can discern his amazing ability to adapt to differing situations and different sorts of congregations.

KING'S UNIVERSITY SERMONS

King was always himself, whether in the pulpit of a country parish, or in the pulpit of the University Church in Oxford as Canon of Christ Church, or in his lectures on preaching as Professor of Pastoral theology. 'It was the same when he preached before the university. There was no rhetoric, no striving after effect, no parade of learning, no attempt to be startling, or novel, or paradoxical ... There was the clear statement of theological truth, so gently worded that even the most fiercely controverted questions were touched without offence or jar.'[28]

In the same year that King took up his professorial chair, Francis Paget, then an undergraduate at Christ Church heard him preach in the Cathedral. (He was only forty-three at the time, but young Paget describes him as 'an elderly canon.') Paget was so greatly struck by the quality of the sermon, that after the service he wrote to his sister from his lodgings in St Aldate's:

> One is so ready to praise even moderately good sermons, that one has no words left to extol such preaching as his according or nearly according to its deserts. He speaks without either notes or hesitation ... I think that a Liberal High Churchman is the very best thing that the world, or even Oxford, can show; and to see an elderly canon, perfect in every detail of culture, standing up to say such things as King said this morning, is a most happy confirmation of one's faith in humanity, present and future.[29]

While King could never have held a candle to that earlier occupant of the University Church pulpit—that spell-binding wordsmith, John Henry Newman—yet, in similar ways he had a strong following from many hundreds of undergraduates who fell under his spell. Neither Newman nor King, ever sought a personality cult: both men, in their pastoral care and from the pulpit, were conspicuous in pointing beyond themselves to the person of Christ. 'Newman did not try to draw men to him,' says Dean Church, 'he was no proselytiser' ... such 'was an invasion of the privileges of the heart.'[30]

King's preaching, again like Newman's, unashamedly invites his hearers to the inner, spiritual journey of faith by participation in, and communion with God in Christ in an intimate and personal relationship.

On the first Sunday of Lent Term in January 1883, by which time King was well into his stride as Professor, he preached the University Sermon, entitled 'Love and Obedience.' In it he demonstrates the limitations of striving to live 'a merely moral life' of duty and obedience, while 'falling short of the higher condition of love,' experienced through prayer and personal communion with the God of love.

> While we seek to regain a life of true *obedience*, we must not forget the primary condition of *love* ... The step from obedience to love implies the step from the impersonal Law to the personal Lawgiver ... Prayer is a test of belief in a personal God. We can obey, but we cannot

pray to a law; we must rise above the moral law to the one Lawgiver and the personal God, and to Him we can speak ... He can, and will, heal our infirmities and forgive all our sin. The conditions all may understand, and, by his grace, fulfil, *obedience* and *love*. They are fitted to your whole being, and intended to control it, your whole mind, your whole heart, your whole will. Do not think to substitute one for the other; neither morality without piety, nor piety without morality, can satisfy the conditions given you through Jesus Christ, our Lord.[31]

Even more powerfully and earnestly, in a sermon entitled 'The Promise to Jacob,' delivered in October 1881, at the beginning of the new academic year, King spells out the nature of that intimate and personal relationship with a personal God:

> Religion is not merely keeping a moral law...This is true religion; this the intended end of our free personality; not merely that we keep the moral law, but that we worship the one true and living God ... It is the consolation of a personal presence that is offered, and this consolation, we know, may be ours with a clearness not revealed to Jacob; he saw the ladder set up from earth to heaven, and angels ascending and descending, as evidence of the reality of the communion between himself and God; we know the real union between man and God through Him, who is both God and man ... The Son of God has promised to be with us always till the end of the world; and, further, He withdrew His presence that another Comforter, as true a Person as Himself, might be our companion with a closeness that no earthly companionship can equal ... The Bible calls it walking before the face of God, walking with God. Christianity in its essential working, is not a religion of detachment, but of attachment; a religion not of fear, but of love. It is the assurance of the companionship of a Friend always able and willing to guide, check, and support us in all dangers ... a Friend whose constant companionship ought to lift

up our fallen countenance, and give us, even now, on the journey of life, a brightness that should witness to those who meet us of the reality of the companionship we enjoy—all this is no mere language of theoretical theology, or excited devotional feeling, but may be the sure experience of your daily lives. A singular sense of security, a peculiar independence of place and time, a secret satisfaction, a quiet courage, an inward peace, an increasing hope, a purer, truer, and more extending love—these are some of the well-known proofs of the reality of our personal relation with God, and of His companionship with us.[32]

It is significant that both of those University sermons were delivered during the latter part of his time as Professor when he felt confident enough to preach freely from the heart and his own personal experience as a pastor. However, at least on one occasion, probably earlier in his time at Oxford, King felt constrained to preach a 'learned sermon,' buttressed by quotations from other writers and preachers. That was not his natural style, and there is evidence recorded by his friend, Edward Talbot, that it fell flat:

I never remember, however, any but one time when he seemed a little out of his element; and that was when one could feel that, from a sense of duty, he had put a strong constraint upon his natural instincts. He was preaching in the university pulpit; there had been some controversy about Confession. It was a subject on which he could have spoken out of a full experience with a characteristic blending of sympathy and firmness; but he evidently thought it his duty to preach a learned sermon; and to his modesty it seemed best to do this by appeal to great names and the Fathers of the Church rather than say much of his own, so he gave us quite a chain of patristic and other quotations; and it was 'dull,' not least perhaps to those to whom the word dull was the last epithet which they would ever have thought themselves likely to use of any utterance from that tender, humorous, pungent, winning spirit.[33]

Professor, Pastor and Preacher

Was this the sermon, 'brimming ... with patristic learning,' which the young A. E. Housman heard King preach in 1878, during Talbot's time as Warden of Keble College, when Housman was an undergraduate at St John's? In a letter to his father, Housman descanted quite critically on King's performance.

> On the Sunday before last [3 February], Canon King of Christ Church preached at St Mary's on 'binding and loosing'—a counterblast to Dean Stanley in the *Nineteenth Century*. The sermon was unconscionably long, & considerably over our heads, brimming as it did with patristic learning, until, at the end of an hour & a quarter, he concluded with an apology to his younger brethren for having bored them.

However, Housman goes on to say:

> I felt it quite worth sitting still for an hour & a quarter to watch such an interesting personality. He is tall, but stoops; & haggard in the face without grey hair; & his sermon was most masterly here & there. The exquisitely deprecating way & affected timidity with which he put forth his strongest points, & the mournful & apologetic modulation of his voice where he was pulling Dean Stanley to pieces, were really almost worthy of Disraeli, & not altogether unlike, were it not for the deadly earnest, which was rather detrimental to the oratorical effect.[34]

This is a fascinating account of King's preaching, not least because it comes from someone who would not necessarily have had much sympathy with King's approach. It is all the more powerful therefore, in that it shows the attraction of King, even when the content of the sermon was uncharacteristically tedious. Housman had all the self-assurance of an Oxford undergraduate, and his comments are shrewd. Nevertheless, they raise doubts about his perception. No one else is on record as accusing King of theatricality in the pulpit. What Housman could hardly have been expected to know when he demurred at what he calls 'the exquisitely deprecating way & affected timidity with which [King] put forth his strongest points,' was that King always felt at an academic disadvantage when preaching to a learned congregation. Moreover, he genuinely disliked controversy, though he never shrank from it if he felt that the truth was at stake.

BETHEL ADDRESSES

However, it was in that converted washhouse in the garden behind King's home at Christ Church, in what he called his 'Bethel,' that King was able to be much more himself in his Friday-evening addresses during Term time, which were attended by a very large number of undergraduates—in fact, an increasing number as time went on, so that the building eventually had to be enlarged to take allcomers. In that intimate, more informal and congenial setting, King was able to open his heart, uninhibited by the formality of the pulpit, where something more structured and measured would be required. In 'Bethel' the talks were more along the lines of informal retreat addresses, of which King became an exponent without equal.

It is in the reports of those addresses that we catch a glimpse of the width of King's appeal, for the men who came to listen were, it seems, 'not a pietistic remnant, pale young curates in the making. They were a good cross-section of the young manhood of Oxford and included plenty of rowing men. In fact the hearties as well as the aesthetes, the tough and the tender, the clever and the simple, all came to King. When he left Oxford for Lincoln, over three hundred BAs and undergraduates joined together to present him with his episcopal ring, in thanks for all the spiritual help he had given them, especially through his "Bethel" addresses.'[35]

Professor, Pastor and Preacher

OCCASIONAL SERMONS

In later years, and especially during his time as Bishop of Lincoln, he was frequently called upon to preach a one-off sermon on particular occasions, or for particular organizations or groups. From those which were subsequently published, it would seem that he enjoyed these occasions and prepared for them with great care. Often, they were addresses to Guilds or Fraternities which King delighted in as binding together with a sense of community those working in the same profession, like the nurses of the Guild of St Barnabas, or Members of the Institution of Mechanical Engineers, or the Lincoln Church Railway Guild, for whose members, along with all railway workers, King had a particular affection.

In all these occasional sermons it is fascinating to see how he puts into practice what he had taught in his homiletic classes, by connecting at the outset with the particular interests or concerns of his audience, and so winning their attention and trust by sharing a real and personal knowledge about their work or profession, a knowledge sometimes gained from his pastoral links with them, or simply by doing his homework beforehand. Having first won their interest, confidence and attention, he goes on to bring together either some teaching from the Gospels, some theological insight or some practical way of bringing work or particular common interests together with faith and Christian discipleship: here again, King is drawing on his vast pastoral experience and knowledge of humanity which he always saw as the first priority for good preaching. It was precisely because his powers in the pulpit were so versatile that his sermons crafted for particular occasions were so well received. 'He could speak to the mechanical engineers in Lincoln Cathedral so that one of his hearers afterwards said that he seemed more than any preacher he had heard to enter into the mechanician's point of view.'[36]

In a sermon preached at one of the special services for railwaymen in Lincoln Cathedral, he described the hazards and demands peculiar to a railwayman's life. After the service, which had been held for the orphans and widows of railwaymen, a veteran railway worker was heard to comment, 'He might almost have been a railwayman himself.'[37]

His sermon at the opening of the dining-hall and library at Keble College in 1878, was deemed 'a striking reminder of how completely he understood what is meant by education and educational methods,'[38] while his sermon at the 400th anniversary of the foundation of Brasenose College in June 1909—the last he ever preached in Oxford—shows, despite his age, clear evidence of robust homework by way of preparation and little or no trace of any abatement in his powers of communication through the medium of preaching. And here again, as he had consistently taught his students, effective teachers or preachers alike need to keep up their reading on a broad front throughout life: his paper for the Grantham Clerical Reading Society (1897) demonstrates the extent to which he was truly a student to the end of his life.

In addition to these occasional sermons, a series of Easter Sermons was also published. As Bishop, it was King's practice to preach on Easter Sunday at the popular and well-attended Evening Service held in the nave of Lincoln Cathedral, which Dean Butler had initiated in 1885. In his Oxford lectures on preaching, he consistently emphasized the need not only to believe and to know the historic *fact* of Christ's resurrection, but also, as St Paul testifies, to know personally and from experience the ever-present risen Christ and 'the power of his resurrection' (Philippians 3:10).

In one of those Sunday evening sermons at Lincoln entitled, 'The Risen Christ—The Source of New Life,' King said:

> In his Epistle to the Philippians, [Paul is] still praying that he might know Christ 'and the power of His Resurrection.' It was not enough for the great Apostle to accept the mere fact; it was the results of the fact, the

> full power of the Resurrection which the Apostle was still striving to know—'To know Him and the power of His Resurrection.' So, brethren, it should be with us, we should not be satisfied with a mere intellectual assent to the evidences which convince our minds of the fact of the Resurrection, but year by year, as the great Festival comes round, we should ask ourselves if we are growing in grace, and in the knowledge of our Lord and Saviour Jesus Christ, and of the power of His Resurrection, and of the results which follow from it.[39]

This need for a 'knowledge' different from the knowledge of the intellect is a consistent theme for King, not just in his teaching, but especially in his preaching, where we find little room for apologetics and the reasoning of the intellect. For King the pulpit was not the place for that. For him, the promise of a new, risen and abundant life, in the here and now, by the gift of the Holy Spirit was an ever-present reality in his own experience.

In a later sermon, also delivered in the Cathedral on an Easter Sunday, he spells this out with particular emphasis:

> Surely speaking to a Christian congregation on the evening of Easter Day it is not necessary to defend, by physical or metaphysical arguments, the fact that Christ is risen. Such arguments there are, when they are wanted; but Christianity is no mere system of thought based upon reflection, it is a life rooted in faith, and faith is more than an intellectual conviction. The springs of life are deeper than all reasoning and are to be found in the power to act and love, in those primal instincts and unconquerable emotions which cannot be reduced to formulae.[40]

CONFIRMATION SERMONS AND PREACHING IN RURAL PARISHES

Perhaps King was at his best, and delighted most of all, in the Confirmations he conducted in the scattered villages of his large diocese, 'when the ploughboys with their scrubbed faces and pomaded hair came to receive his blessing. His addresses on these occasions were simple, direct and searching,'[41] as those who heard his Confirmation addresses readily attested.

> He always used the simplest words and illustrations. Who can ever forget his Confirmation addresses — their simplicity, yet their depth, their unwearying insistence on the duty of Prayer, Bible-reading, and Holy Communion, the boldness of his illustrations, and his almost reckless repetition till the dullest of his hearers could not fail to apprehend his meaning.[42]

His illustrations would be taken from nature and the familiar world of agriculture and farming. They were not forced but spontaneous, simple without being simplistic.

Another characteristic feature of his Confirmation addresses, is the extreme simplicity with which he spoke of 'the Saviour's life':

> It is a great help and a great comfort to think of the Saviour being born in a stable, and put in a manger for His cradle, just to show us that He does not want a fine house, and smart clothes and rich people — He does not want them necessarily to come to, but that He will come to poor people, in a simple house, He plainly shows by being born in a stable ... He worked as a carpenter day after day, quite quietly, till He was thirty years of age, and within three years of His death. That is a great comfort to us. If you have to work in a little shop, in a little family, in a little way; if you feel you will never make a big fortune, it is very nice and comfortable to think, 'Nor did the Saviour, and therefore He will be with me, and I may be with Him' ... He never was in a big way of business, was never made anything of in this world. Now I say that should be a great comfort to you, and that it should preserve you from losing your self-respect, because there may be other people who are richer than you. It is the heart that God looks at; it is the life He values — not the person, nor the money.[43]

From his published Confirmation addresses, it seems his usual practice was to give two addresses: a shorter one before the laying on of hands, and one afterwards. At some point during the second address he would include some words for the older friends, godparents and families of the Confirmands. 'And now dear elder friends, perhaps you have been thinking, "I wish I had attended to all of this." Well, I thank you for coming here today, and I believe that you are trying to do what is right, and I say go on in those ways and your example will be a great help to these young people.'[44]

When he preached in rural parish churches, as he so frequently did, he would draw his illustrations from the life of country people, which he knew at first hand. 'If I were cutting a hedge,' he might begin, and at once his hearers' attention would be riveted on his accurate description of a typical farming task. There was nothing second-hand or patronizing about what he had to say. He spoke person-to-person. He knew what he was talking about and was forthright in extracting a genuine Gospel message from his understanding of the life of his people. The note was personal without being sentimental.

IN CONCLUSION

In seeking to assess King's preaching ministry it is almost a case of recapitulating from where we started:

> Any man can preach, and preach effectively, who reads his Bible and says his prayers and loves his people; and no man can preach effectively who does not read his Bible and say his prayers and love his people. He may be fluent and he may be clever, but though he speak with the tongues of men and of angels, and though he should know all mysteries and all knowledge, unless he reads his Bible and says his prayers and loves his people, his preaching will be merely wind.[45]

It will be clear by now that King, both as a preacher himself and as one who taught others the importance of preaching, habitually read, knew and loved the scriptures; that he was fervent in prayer, and that people from all walks of life loved him. Put another way, in King the message and the messenger were one, so that his person commended the message he was seeking to communicate. That was because, as has been said, 'his message was his own experience of the faith and religion of Jesus Christ. It was always thus. It was always perfectly clear, distinct, accurate; but it was the truth as it had been brought home to him in the experiences [that same recurring word again] of his long life and his dealings with souls.'[46]

The most powerful and transforming 'energy' in effective preaching has nothing to do with hysteria: rather, the love of God inspiring a speaker will, in turn, kindle love in a congregation, drawing them with something of a magnetic power through and beyond the speaker to the source of that same transforming power of love.

It was his presence and even his facial features which so often struck those who sat at King's feet. 'There was the face, deeply furrowed but still of almost faultless beauty; the hair, sprinkled with grey, but thick and curly to the last; the head prematurely bowed; the searching gaze, the exquisitely modulated voice'[47] — these and other less obvious characteristics added together, rendered King's preaching a memorable, yet challenging and even a life-changing event. 'Yes,' a busy woman once said, 'Yes, as soon as I saw him in the pulpit, I felt I wanted to be good, and I knew I could be.'[48]

'There is no need to speak of his spiritual power. Every sermon is an illustration of it, the note of deep spirituality runs through them. The love of God, the love of man, the need of humility and gentleness, the power of sacramental grace, the reality of the unseen world and of the life everlasting—all this was the atmosphere in which he habitually lived,'[49] and from which his teaching and preaching were derived. 'He was a teacher of the faith that was in him, not an echo of other men's thoughts,' which is why his sermons contain so very few quotations from others or from books, although he does not hesitate to refer with gratitude to those who have been his inspiration and his mentors. 'He had no desire to restate the faith for the modern world,' leaving that to others better equipped to do so, like Gore and F. D. Maurice. He did have, however, 'an intense and almost passionate desire to state Christian ethics in the language of the day, in words easy to be understood by the simplest people—and he often went to great lengths in doing so.'[50] It was this lively faith that,

> gave such steadiness and strength, and, at the same time, such delight and appeal to his sermons. You always knew the Faith—almost the very words in which he would express it. You never knew, and never could know beforehand, the new and manifold ways in which he would appeal for the expression of that Faith in human life. The Faith was one; the life was manifold; and it was the Faith that made possible and certain the life, lifestyle and conduct.[51]

That belief begets behaviour, certainly held true for King.

Yet it is not for the quality of his preaching that King is clearly remembered, or for which he should claim our attention today. 'In the ministerial life, it is not so much the doing of the duties that is important, as the kind of man who is doing the duties; it is not so much the sort of sermon that is being preached, as the sort of man that is behind the sermon.'[52]

While we are fortunate in having texts of some of King's sermons, it is important also to remember the comments of those who heard him deliver them. B. W. Randolph's comments in his preface to *The Love and Wisdom of God*, reminding us that much is lost in reading rather than hearing (quoted on p. 242), are also a challenge to the now widespread practice of putting up sermon texts on websites.

Edward King

King would surely have endorsed the view that a sermon should be a living communication between preacher and congregation essentially in the context of worship, not as a mini-essay for reading.

Notes

1 Charles Smythe, *The Art of Preaching: A Practical Survey of Preaching in the Church of England, 747–1939*. London: SPCK, 1940, p. 5.
2 Charles Simeon, *Horae Homileticae*, 21 vols. London: Samuel Holdsworth and Ball, 1832–6. vol. I (1832), Preface, p. v.
3 Randolph and Townroe, *The Mind and Work of Bishop King*, pp. 46–7.
4 From now onwards, unless otherwise indicated, all quotations from King's lectures, are taken from *Pastoral Lectures of Bishop Edward King*, pp. 23ff.
5 Richard Hooker, *Of the Lawes of Ecclesiastical Politie*, Book V (1597).
6 King resorted to both these texts when addressing the issue of the authority of scripture in his Quiet Day addresses prior to the Lambeth Conference in 1897, see Chapter 14.
7 Randolph and Townroe, *op. cit.*, p. 68.
8 *Ibid.*, pp. 66ff.
9 *Ibid.*, p. 52.
10 Augustine, *De Doctrina Christiana*, Bk IV, 4.6.
11 *Spiritual Letters of Edward King, D.D.*, Letter LXXXII.
12 Collect for the Second Sunday in Advent.
13 See Chapter 14.
14 Randolph and Townroe, *op. cit.*, p. 122.
15 *Ibid.*, p. 223.
16 Canon A. M. Cook, Sub-Dean of Lincoln, 'Bishop Edward King: His Memory is Still Green in Lincoln,' in *The Church Times*, 4 March 1960.
17 Edward King, *The Wisdom and Love of God*, p. vi (B. W. Rudolph's introduction).
18 John Henry Newman, *Lectures and Essays on University Subjects*. London: Longman, Green, Longman, and Roberts, 1859, p. 218.
19 Edward King, *Sermons and Addresses*, pp. 136ff.
20 Possidius, *Vita Augustini*, 31:244.
21 Miguel de Unamuno, *The Tragic Sense of Life*. London: Collins, 1962, p. 33.
22 Mark Oakley, *My Sour-Sweet Days: George Herbert and the Journey of the Soul*. SPCK, 2019, p. 36.
23 *Ibid.*
24 *Ibid.*

25 Evelyn M. Simpson and George R. Potter (eds), *The Sermons of John Donne*. Berkeley, CA: University of California Press, 1953–62, vol. III, p. 5.
26 Oakley, *op. cit.*, p. 34.
27 *Ibid.*, p. 36.
28 George W. E. Russell, *Edward King Sixtieth Bishop of Lincoln*, p. 55.
29 S. Paget and J. C. M. Crum, *Francis Paget*. London: Macmillan & Co., 1912, p. 30.
30 Richard W. Church, *The Oxford Movement: Twelve Years, 1833–1845*, p. 129.
31 Edward King, 'Love and Obedience' (Sermon IV), in *Love and Wisdom of God*, pp. 61ff.
32 King, 'Promise of Jacob,' in *Love and Wisdom of God*, pp. 45ff.
33 Randolph and Townroe, *op. cit.*, pp. 82–3.
34 *The Letters of A. E. Housman*. (ed. Archie Burnett). Oxford: Clarendon Press, 2007, vol. I, pp. 27–8.
35 John Newton, *Search for a Saint*, p. 65.
36 King, *The Wisdom and Love of God*, p. vii (Introduction).
37 Newton, *op. cit.*, p. 85.
38 King, *The Wisdom and Love of God*, p. vii (Introduction).
39 Edward King, *Easter Sermons Preached in Lincoln Cathedral* (ed. B. W. Randolph). London: A. R. Mowbray, 1914, Sermon I, pp. 7–8.
40 King, *The Love and Wisdom of God*, pp. 196–7.
41 Newton, *op. cit.*, p. 85.
42 Randolph and Townroe, *op. cit.*, p. 154.
43 King, *Sermons and Addresses*, pp. 192ff.
44 *Ibid.*, p. 167.
45 Smythe, *op. cit.*, p. 3.
46 Randolph and Townroe, *op. cit.*, p. 235.
47 Russell, *op. cit.*, p. 55.
48 Randolph and Townroe, *op. cit.*, p. 143.
49 King, *The Wisdom and Love of God*, p. vii (Introduction)
50 Randolph and Townroe, *op. cit.*, p. 143.
51 *Ibid.*
52 John Paterson Smyth, *The Preacher and his Sermon*. London: Hodder and Stoughton, 1922. p. 8.

✢ 9 ✢

The Secret of King's Influence

'NOTHING LESS THAN A FORM OF GENIUS'

King's remarkable and lasting influence amongst a wide range of friends, ordinands, students and clergy, which Liddon called 'nothing less than a form of genius,' is unquestionable. 'Here was a man,' says Canon Townroe in the opening chapter of his biography of King, 'who, during the fifty-six years of his ordained life, exercised from first to last a strangely powerful influence on those with whom he came in contact; and his influence was always of the best and highest kind. It never seemed to fail ... Wherever he went spiritual power went with him and radiated out from him to a remarkable degree.'[1]

However, such a ready and positive affirmation inevitably raises a question to which there is no ready and straightforward answer: to what can that 'strangely powerful influence'—which so many testified to during his lifetime and endured, perhaps even more strikingly, for many years after his death—be attributed?

His influence during his lifetime on the Church was not derived from anything he had written or from scholarship, like that of Dr Pusey, Dean Church, and other Tractarian Fathers. 'He had no strictly academic distinctions, but he had intellectual power of a high order, and he had wisdom. So, he was a force to be reckoned with among the senior members of the University.'[2]

Then again, King was never especially well known as an

outstanding preacher, although he had his own inimitable style, very much bound up with his own person and presence in the pulpit, embodying and exemplifying a message which certainly touched hearts and changed lives.

In attempting therefore to detect the source of King's amazing and lasting influence on the Church of England, it will be necessary to look to more hidden and less obvious aspects of his ministry, as spiritual guide and confessor as well as to the nature of his intimate friendships, much of which is to be found in his *Spiritual Letters*.

AS A SPIRITUAL GUIDE

In the first place there is his particular skill and influence as a spiritual guide, counsellor or 'Soul Friend,' as a master of what is termed 'ascetical theology,' to which we must initially turn. (John Wesley would often insist that everyone needed 'a candid friend,' who would tell him or her the truth about themselves, however painfully searching that might be.) King was just such a 'friend' to so many who sought his help and advice.

There is ample evidence that during his time in Oxford there were many—too many, said Pusey—who sought him out for spiritual counselling. And King, being the man he was, always felt compelled (like his mentor, Marriott) to be 'available' and accessible for prayerful 'soul talk,' with anybody and everybody who might wish to speak with him.

From Pusey's perspective, the 'good cause' in Oxford at that time was supremely to defend 'the Faith' with the tools of scholarship, as in the earlier *Tracts for the Times*, by more actively engaging in the current controversies raging in the college Common Rooms. That was never King's way. His influence and 'genius' were exercised in more subtle and hidden ways, which in the longer term proved no less effective, through friendship or, more formally, in a one-to-one relationship as a spiritual guide.

The Liberal politician, George W. E. Russell, a student in Oxford during King's time as Professor though never an ordinand, undoubtedly fell under King's spell, and powerfully testifies in his biography of King, to that 'influence' and his 'genius' as a spiritual guide:

> His power of sympathy amounted to genius and gave him an almost supernatural insight into human hearts. He combined the keenest spirituality with a sanctified common sense, which good people sometimes lack. He spoke to us of our past lives, of our future prospects, of our present temptations, of our besetting sins, with an intimate penetration, engendered by long experience in personal contact with souls. He told us truths about ourselves which were part of our consciousness, but which we believed to have been hidden from all except ourselves.[3]

That spirituality combined with a 'sanctified common sense' is perfectly exemplified in some advice which King gave to one of his ordinands in 1873. The man had scruples about going on a shooting expedition during the vacation: King readily advises him to go ahead and shoot.

> I am not saying all this out of false kindness ... but because I do value so highly a natural growth in holiness, a humble grateful acceptance of the circumstances God has provided for each of us, and I dread the unnatural, forced, cramped ecclesiastical holiness, which is so much more quickly produced, but is so human and so poor.[4]

This more 'bespoke' rather than 'off-the-peg' approach is evident in King's teaching about Confession, as well as in his own personal use of the confessional, which became such a vexed issue during the days of the Catholic revival in the Church of England. Although he became a noted and much sought-after confessor at Oxford and later at Lincoln, that was never a role he himself sought: he was simply drawn to the practice of it as pastoral need required.

Edward King

AS A CONFESSOR

Increasingly, over the years, King was much in demand to conduct retreats, and then as now, an opportunity would usually be given for the attendees to spend a little time, one-to-one, with the priest leading the retreat. Frequently, though not always, the interview would lead to the use of the Sacrament of Penance when retreatants would have the opportunity to make their Confession. When King became Principal of Cuddesdon in 1863 he had never been to Confession himself, which was not unusual at that time, even for High Church Anglicans. However, when one of his students asked King to hear his Confession, the request brought the whole matter to a head: 'Wait a while,' King told the student, 'I must make my own first.'[5] Shortly afterwards he rode into Oxford to see Dr Pusey to make his Confession, which marked the beginning of his lifelong practice of regular, though not over-frequent use of the Sacrament.

He was never an undiscriminating advocate of the confessional, although he openly and, indeed, courageously defended its healing power as a means of Grace. His mature judgment was that, 'it would not be amiss if some of the people who use Confession very frequently would go less often; while he wished that many who never went to Confession, would do so now and then.'[6]

His practice as a confessor, as in so many other respects, combined strength with tenderness, though, as some of his letters of spiritual counsel show, he could be stern when confronted by pride or stubborn folly. Yet the prevailing tone generally was one of gentleness and hope. 'No one was more tender and gentle with his penitents (and he heard many confessions), no one more sensitive to the sorrows of others. Yet he was a man of unconquerable hopefulness.'[7] Above all, he was a great encourager, and would often urge 'You must not let temptation take the heart out of you. You must go bravely and quietly on.'[8] After pronouncing formal

The Secret of King's Influence

absolution he would always offer up extemporary prayer with wonderful insight and directly and personally applied to the needs and difficulties of the particular penitent.

From his time as Principal, King taught the 'Doctrine of the Keys' with frank and simple courage, never as of obligation, as in the Church of Rome, but within its Anglican limitations. As a curate at Cuddesdon points out:

> King did not think it wise to be always preaching about Confession (as was rather a tendency then in some churches), but he liked to preach a definite sermon about it every Lent and every Advent. The conclusion of one such sermon was: 'But, dear people, you will be saying—"this is Roman Catholic." No, it isn't; there is a difference, and I will tell you what it is. The Roman Catholic Church says you must go to Confession once a year. The English Church says you may go whenever you like.'[9]

Similarly, writing to a priest who had sought his advice on the matter of the confessional, he takes the opportunity to spell out his own position more fully:

> Confession to a priest is not necessary, God will pardon on true repentance; therefore confession of our sins to God, with true sorrow and purpose of amendment, and prayer for pardon through Christ, will bring pardon. The necessity of confession to a priest was not enforced till the Council of Lateran (1215 A.D.) ... Our Prayer Book says, as you know, in the exhortation to Holy Communion, that if a person cannot find peace in this way, then their duty is to go to the priest for confession. We should, I think, teach the people this, and trust to the Holy Spirit to guide them when to come. In the case of sickness, as you know, we are to move the sick person to make a special confession if there is any weighty matter. Here again, if we all did this, I think a great number would be able to see what they ought to do, without any great difficulty.[10]

In this, as so often with King, his teaching and practice,

both in spiritual counselling and on the vexed matter of Confession, is radically different from that of the Church of Rome: it is all very modest and Anglican, utterly faithful to the Prayer Book. That was also typical of his attitude to other matters, such as the liturgy, worship and ritual, always deeply pastoral and thoroughly loyal to the formularies of the Church of England.

INTIMACY AND FRIENDSHIP

Yet the question remains: what precisely was the nature and 'chemistry' of that 'genius' and the transforming influence which King so undoubtedly exercised on the lives of so many through his deep and lasting friendships, mainly with men and notably with young men? It is evident from his *Spiritual Letters*, and from many contemporary accounts, that intimate, predominantly male friendships are central to a whole web of relationships, in both his personal and professional life.

The Dominican Timothy Radcliff suggests that there is something infinitely gratuitous and disinterested about true friendship: 'We fall in love,' he writes, 'but we make friends ... friendships are made, deliberately sustained and cultivated ... Befriending is a creative act. It breaks down barriers and pierces prejudices.'[11]

That was true of King: 'The longer one lives the more one values true friends! I like to think of this world as the place for making friends, and the next for enjoying them.'[12]

It might even be argued, as Radcliff does, that in some respects, friendship is superior to other relationships, because it can only continue to exist in any meaningful way while there is a bonding of love, yet if you cease to love your family they still remain as your family, albeit only in name. Radcliff concludes: 'It is possible for family members not to love one another. But it is not so with friends. If one member of a family does not love another, the relationship of kinship still remains. But unless there is love between friends, does the essential principle of friendship exist?'[13]

However, such an affirmation and validation of true friendship for many, and not least in our own inquisitive culture, might still beg the further question: what exactly was the nature of that love, which was clearly such a powerful agent in the pastoral as well as the personal, intimate friendships which characterized King's life and ministry? For many, then as now, intimate friendships, especially between two persons of the same gender, when exercised as part of any professional caring ministry, let alone a priestly ministry, could give rise to a suspicion of the homoerotic. That is precisely the conclusion which Geoffrey Faber reached in his book *Oxford Apostles* published in 1933. In a chapter entitled 'Secret Forces,' he pursues this line of argument, suggesting that among several of the men in the early days of the Oxford Movement there was a strong degree of homoerotic attraction, even naming Newman and Froude.

In 1958, Lord Elton, the grandson of King's vicar at Wheatley, wrote a short study entitled *Edward King and Our Times*, in which he tells of how, as a very small boy, he had once met Edward King. Elton confesses to a fascination with the recorded influence and saintliness of King, which he explores and seeks to unravel with both sensitivity and considerable insight. He contends that the mid-twentieth-century critic, 'for whom,' as he says, 'the very idea of sainthood, of heroic virtue deriving from religious faith, is an affront,' may 'even be prepared to assert that King's aura of radiant love was homosexual in origin.'

Such a suggestion might, Elton says, 'seem too grotesque and shocking' to many of his readers (though possibly less so in our own more explicit age). Nevertheless, his intention in writing the book was to 'investigate a saint in the setting, not of a stained-glass window, but of the contemporary world with all its malice and neuroses,'[14] and, one might add, with its particular hang-ups, confusions and persistent eagerness to categorize and label. As Archbishop Robert Runcie perceptively asserted, during the Homosexual Debate in General Synod, 'Once we were encouraged by Freud to define people in terms of their sexual feelings, the danger was there of tyrannically imposing the categories *heterosexual, homosexual* on a range of relationships and feelings that cannot be categorized in such a banal and crude way.'[15] With that caution in mind, the exploration of King's sexuality and its relationship to his personality and spirituality is a worthwhile undertaking, not least in our own day, and for precisely the reasons expressed by Runcie.

Elton points out three features of King's life and ministry which today would certainly lead many to categorize his influence, love and friendship as being rooted, implicitly if not explicitly, in a homosexual orientation.

In the first place, Elton asks: 'Until King went to Lincoln, it may be said, was not his work almost exclusively among young men?' Of course, and for the obvious reason that in the Oxford of King's day, his work with students and ordinands alike would, *per force*, have been exclusively among men, and predominantly younger men, given that there were no female undergraduates at that time, let alone ordinands, in what was an exclusively male-dominated University and Church.

Elton raises another issue, which again is not totally absent from the thinking of an age like our own: the perennial suspicion which hangs over those who never marry, and even more so of those who claim to have chosen not to marry, or as King put it, had never felt 'the call' to the married state. Not only did he never marry, but it seems he never showed any inclination for it, even after leaving Oxford when he would have been free to do so. In a letter from Lincoln in 1887 responding to a priest who had asked for his views on the married state *vis-à-vis* celibacy, King replied: 'I am single myself, but simply because I never felt

The Secret of King's Influence

called to anything else.'[16] Yet there is never even a remote suggestion in his letters, his sermons or elsewhere that he ever down-graded the married state in favour of celibacy. After all, his own brother, Walker, a faithful and greatly revered parish priest, was married.

Moreover, just how very highly King regarded the married state is clear from the letter he wrote in his early Oxford days, to a former student now a priest, who wanted King to conduct his marriage ceremony. In reply, King wrote:

> Dearest friend, Christian marriage is to me one of the greatest mysteries with which we have to do, and most sincerely do I wish you *both* all the mysterious fulness of the blessing of the many mysteries into which you enter; and for your own character, dear friend, I think it will be just what you want to save you, I trust, from that wretched selfish hardness into which I am conscious in my single life to have fallen ... I can conceive of no earthly happiness greater than to be given by God the whole of the earthly, nay, more than earthly, the whole of the human love of another. This is one of God's greatest gifts, one of the closest symbols of what He is, and of the union between Himself and us. May you richly enjoy this great gift, and may it enlarge the power of your love, and help you to turn with yet a larger heart to *His*, and *Him*. May God bless you a thousand times ... and help you with a new and renewed power to tell the people that He is Love.[17]

One further issue Elton touches on, which resonates with our post-Freudian age, is King's close and deeply loving relationship with his mother. Edward Talbot's observations on their relationship, made from the standpoint of someone who knew them both well at Oxford, has already been quoted (see pp. 197–8). Other contemporaries claim that King bore a strong resemblance to his mother in manner and even features. It is abundantly clear from such comments, as well as from King's own letters written after his mother's death, that the young, somewhat delicate

Edward King

'Ted' held a special and unique place of love and affection in his mother's heart.

Then again, although this is nowhere documented, it seems that there had been faint rumblings, even during his lifetime, which after his death had influenced the form of the striking bronze statue which stands as his memorial in the south transept of Lincoln Cathedral. Newton in his biography, picks up on this: 'Oral tradition has it that the original intention was to have King confirming a young boy, since confirming the young was a part of his work he loved best. There was apparently some misgiving about the presence of the boy, and in the event the statue portrays King in his vestments and with his hand raised in blessing but, sadly, with no child to bless.'[18] If there is any truth in that, then the inuendo would not need spelling out, although, it might well say more about the protesters than about King himself.

CAUTIONS

When reviewing these various 'pointers,' for they are neither more nor less than that, we need to strike a note of caution, not least when viewed from the perspective of the twenty-first century, with its fears and its fascinations, and (as some might say) its obsession for labelling and categorizing.

The first danger in undertaking research into this and other aspects of King's character and behaviour dating from an earlier age, is the perennial trap of making anachronistic judgments limited and even prejudiced by the culturally conditioned perspective of a later age. King's letters, couched as they are in such endearing, affectionate and intimate language, as indeed many letters written between male friends frequently were in the nineteenth century, can be wildly misinterpreted, if read from the cultural perspective of our own time. Nor should we assume that the vantage point of a later age is necessarily superior simply with the course of

The Secret of King's Influence

time—a stance which C. S. Lewis poignantly termed 'chronological snobbery.'

As Archbishop Runcie further reminded the General Synod during that debate on homosexuality:

> It was about 1897 when the word homosexual was first used as a noun by the psychiatrist Havelock Ellis, and he apologized for such bad usage. Until then people spoke of homosexual acts and not homosexual persons, and that was one of the reasons why students and others in the 19th century could write letters to one another with expressions of affection few would dare to do today.[19]

John Newton gives a striking analogy which drives home this same point:

> Terms of endearment between men, and what seems to us highly emotional language [as in many of King's letters], were much more common among upper and middle-class Englishmen in the nineteenth century than they are today. It may be as easy for us to misinterpret some of the Victorian evidence as it is for an English visitor to Nairobi to put two and two together and make five when he sees two young African men walking down the main street hand in hand. Far from being a sign of endemic homosexuality, it is merely a normal, completely accepted gesture of friendship and respect.[20]

So, perhaps, as Runcie again pointedly remarked:

> It is not the demonstrative gestures of friendship among our ancestors, but rather the absence of such gestures in our own society that calls for special explanation.[21]

However, there is another danger of a contrary posthumous investigation into the nature of King's compelling gift of love and friendship: the temptation to spiritualize and categorize the nature and various expressions of intimacy and love by rigidly applying the Greek differentiation between so-called platonic friendship (*philia*) and erotic love (*eros*) and to settle for playing safe by advocating exclusively that 'cooler' or, as some might say, more 'spiritual' brand of which religion so often prefers to speak, namely, charity (*agape*).

To the Hebrew mind and in the Hebrew language there are no such lines of demarcation between different kinds of love: the Hebrew language has only one word for love—*ahabh*—whether it be love of God, neighbour, whatever or whoever. The Jesuit, Philip Sheldrake, writes:

> If we can recover the unity between *agape* and *eros* we may be able to re-sacralise the erotic ... The relationship between the different forms of love should not be seen as opposition or choice. In the end, *eros* just as much as *agape* is expressive of the same drive towards union with the One ... Christianity's tendency to steer clear of the erotic has often set the spiritual over against human culture and experience.[22]

When seen in that way, the inclusion of the *Song of Songs* in the Canon of the Old Testament, does not come as quite such a shock, or seem so out of place. The text of the *Song of Songs* does not need to make any apologies for blatantly being, at one level, an erotic love poem. Furthermore, what we perceive as King's gift of friendship whether with friends or with God, can be seen as being fired from a deep yearning for union and essentially, as being all of a piece. 'Our openness to God,' writes Rabbi Jonathan Sacks, 'shapes and is shaped by our openness to other people. Love of God is, or should be, interwoven with our love for human beings. That surely is the meaning of the book known as *Shir HaShirim*, The Song of Songs, a poem of love for God cast in the metaphor of a dialogue between two human lovers.'[23]

All that might help to explain why throughout history, preachers from widely differing traditions, from the Cistercian St Bernard in the twelfth century to that Protestant prince of preachers, Charles Spurgeon in the nineteenth, have preached numerous sermons on that erotic love poem and not simply as an analogy, but rather as a model, indicative not only of that mystical union between Christ and his

The Secret of King's Influence

Church, but also the intimate union between God in Christ and the Christian disciple: truly it is all of a piece, as it was so conspicuously for King. 'The Song is a mixture of the sensual and the spiritual,'[24] both alike drawing us, to quote from King's favourite poet Dante, to that same 'love that moves the sun and other stars.'

Elton has a shot at something along similar lines. He suggests that King, far from either supressing elements of *eros*, or by separating out various categories of love as in Greek thought, practised for himself, as well as imparted to others, a process by which fleshly desire is 'not so much repressed as transmuted by the miracle of grace, so that the *eros* and the *epithumia* (lust) of the unregenerate, natural man are assumed into the *agape* of the saint, become part of it and minister to its power, much as the base substance of coal is transmuted into the beauty and heat of flame.'[25] Another very different source, and from a very different perspective, uses a similar analogy to make the same point: 'Good art compresses the coal of Truth into a diamond.'[26]

Following on from this, it would seem that it is not the powerful existence of what the Greek mind speaks of as erotic, so much as the direction and the end to which the unquestionable power of eros and our sexual drive is directed, as well as to what it is harnessed, which gives a strong lead in this whole enquiry into the nature of King's intimate friendships. Augustine gives a helpful analogy drawn from his own struggles with directing his erotic sexuality to appropriate ends: 'Cleanse your love' he exclaims, but not by sanitizing it or filtering out 'erotic' elements, but rather by diverting 'into the garden the water that was running down the drain,'[27] for the nurturing of flowers and the fruit of good works.

Augustine, with whose writings King was well acquainted and which he constantly recommended to his students, struggled for many years with his own powerful, sexual drives. The breakthrough for him came when he no longer separated out what he calls the 'higher things' from the 'lower things' in a dualistic world view or an idealized view of Christian spirituality. 'I no longer desired a better world, because I was thinking of creation as a whole; and in the light of this more balanced discernment, I had come to see that higher things are better than the lower, but that the sum total of all creation is better than the higher things alone.'

THE ENGLISH SCHOOL OF SPIRITUALITY

That 'more balanced discernment' of which Augustine speaks could hardly be bettered as a subtitle for what Martin Thornton calls the 'English School of Spirituality': 'sane, wise, ancient, modern, sound and simple; with roots in the New Testament and the Fathers.'[28] The guiding lights across the centuries in that distinctive tradition are St Anselm of Canterbury, Julian of Norwich, Margery Kempe of Lynn, the poet-priest George Herbert, John Donne, Nicholas Ferrar of Little Gidding, and others among whom (as hopefully will become more evident), we should include Bishop Edward King.

John Newton lists the characteristics of this English school as being 'unitive and concerned with wholeness. Its exponents are eager not to put asunder what God has joined together; head and heart, doctrine and devotion, worship and daily life, dogma and pastoral warmth and love of souls.'[29] Philip Seddon, an author from a very different tradition reiterates the need for joining together what so many throughout the centuries have doggedly kept apart, and all in the name of the sanitized spiritual.

> People have erected a middle wall of partition between two forms of love: the love of God (the New Testament word, *agape*) and passionate human yearning (*eros* — a word never found in the New Testament). I want to argue that these divorced partners need reuniting.[30]

In the more affirmative school of English Spirituality, as well as in the person and teaching of King, these two were not only reunited but also redirected in much the same way as Augustine suggests, seeking to hold together sacramentally both the sacred and the secular, the holy and the homely, in a 'unitive wholeness' (to quote Newton), or as what Augustine termed 'the lower' together with 'the higher.' In that way, the 'lower' (*eros*) is raised, fully incorporated and transposed into a 'higher' key as the 'sum total of all creation,' rather than separating out the supposedly 'higher things,' or purely spiritual things.

In some remarks at the Cuddesdon Festival in 1900, King clearly felt free to speak from the heart of that 'higher life' which he had learned and experienced during his time there:

> It was at Cuddesdon, that I learned to realize more than ever I did before the possibility of the reality of the love of God and the love of man. Somehow the cloud of conventionality which hangs over us so constantly seemed to be lifted off, and we saw something more into the hearts and lives of others.[31]

In the last sermon he preached at Christ Church before leaving Oxford for Lincoln in 1885, he spells out and applies this same Augustinian formula with telling clarity: 'By God's great goodness we Christians can look up higher than our own nature, for we have seen His nature descend, not to destroy, but to take up humanity into the Godhead.'[32]

In that way, as Aquinas insisted, grace serves to perfect what is natural rather than destroying, sublimating or supressing it, in some misguided quest for a wrongly perceived and idealized perfectionism in the pursuit of a supposedly more refined 'spirituality.' In the classic aphorism of von Hügel, 'Grace is not the cuckoo which drives all other birds out of the nest,' or, put another way, it does not drive out what many wrongly perceive as the ugly duckling of *eros* in order to make exclusive room for a supposedly 'higher' and more 'spiritual' breed.

In all of this, we must surely sense that we are now approaching 'King territory,' with the landscape, or, as Gerard Manley Hopkins might say, the 'inscape' of King's spiritualty and inner life, most conspicuously evident in and expressed through his intimate and formative friendships.

A SPIRITUALITY OF FRIENDSHIP

Archbishop Anselm, whom Thornton regards as being the founder of the English School of Spirituality, 'developed a spirituality of friendship as an aspect of the pursuit of God both in letters written before leaving Bec for Canterbury, and in his beautiful *Prayer for Friends.*'[33]

'The beginning of the twelfth century was marked by the proliferation of new orders of monks and canons whose fervour and enthusiasm [for friendship] went far beyond the respectable, if slightly tepid, monasticism common in older Benedictine houses. This new fire could not help but encourage and spread the devotion to spiritual friendship.'[34] In the writings of William of Saint-Thierry, St Anselm and particularly Aelred in *The Mirror of Charity* and *On Spiritual Friendship*, human relationships of love and friendship are held and bound together within an intimate and loving relationship with God, conceived and experienced as friendship.

Aelred, draws all this together in his bold affirmation 'God is Friendship,' as did St Richard of Chichester, also of that same English School who, in his well-known prayer, addresses God as 'Friend and Brother,' picking up on Christ's own insistence that he would no longer call those who followed him 'servants,' but 'friends' (John 15:15).

In the writings of Aelred and others of this school, there is no reticence about human friendship being perceived as an appropriate analogy for an intimate relationship with God. Both St Bernard and William of Saint-Thierry wrote vividly on spiritual friendship, notably in their many sermons based on the erotic poetry of the *Song of Songs*. They applied that same 'erotic' love between the Beloved and the Lover, not only to the 'mystical union between Christ and his Church,' in the words of St Paul, but also to that indwelling and union between the Christian disciple and a personal God who can be known and loved as a friend. Here is King:

> Personal devotedness to a Personal God is one of the chief marks of a true religion. The Bible calls it walking before the face of God, walking with God. Christianity in its essential working, is not a religion of detachment, but of attachment; a religion not of fear, but of love.[35]

And then, as though that were not sufficient, he spells out the nature of that relationship with a 'Personal God,' hammered home, gently but powerfully with some vintage King rhetoric, and authenticated by coming so clearly from experience:

> It is the assurance of the companionship of a Friend always able and willing to guide, check, and support us in all dangers; a Friend whose rod and staff will still be with us, guiding, protecting, even through the valley of the shadow of death; a Friend whose constant companionship ought to lift up our fallen countenance, and give us, even now, on the journey of life, a brightness that should witness to those who meet us of the reality of the companionship we enjoy — all this is no mere language of theoretical theology, or excited devotional feeling, but may be the sure experience of your daily lives.[36]

Clearly it was the experience of King's own daily life which in a large measure accounts for his attractive influence on all those he met. For King, as for Aelred, there was

> no conflict between love of our friends and the love of God, since all love is one, albeit differently expressed and has its source in God. The love of neighbour is no derogation of our love of God, but rather is necessary for us if we are truly to love him. It is this identification

of spiritual friendship with the perfect love of God which allowed Aelred to suggest the phrase, 'God is friendship.'[37]

By insisting on the positive moral value of friendship, Aelred 'avoided the problem of defining its moral limits,' and neither was he 'troubled by the twentieth century's pervasive consciousness of sexual drives,' or by feeling 'obliged to discuss sexual pathology in a treatise on spiritual friendship.'[38]

Biographers of Aelred readily point out that the close and very emotional friendships which he was later free to enjoy as abbot, prove that a negative reaction to his own youthful crush on a male member of the Court in Scotland before he entered the monastery, 'did not inhibit his emotional freedom in later life. It is also interesting to remember that Walter Daniel [his contemporary biographer] specifically noted that Aelred, unlike some other abbots, was not scandalized by demonstrations of affection such as holding hands, by the monks.' In other words, Aelred seems to have had not only 'confidence in his own ability to deal with the sexual component of his friendships, but to have trusted his monks to be able to do the same. Nor is there any evidence that Aelred's confidence was misjudged.'[39]

Perhaps at this point we are getting somewhere near to unravelling the secret of that 'genius' of which Liddon spoke and which Scott Holland, from experience of his long-standing close friendship with King, endorses with his customary, and admittedly euphoric eloquence:

> Throughout, one was conscious of this rounded normality There was nothing in him one-sided, or excessive, or unbalanced ... Everything hung together. Everything befitted ... His natural manhood always found itself, in whatever he did: and showed itself complete and distinctive. And Grace had so intimately mingled with his nature that it was all of one piece. Grace itself had become natural. Who could say which was which? Was it all Grace? Was it all nature? Was it not all both?

The Secret of King's Influence

> Anyhow, the whole man moved altogether, in every word and act. There were no separate compartments; and no disturbing reserves … so that the impact that he made upon one was absolutely simple and undivided. The central spirit tingled in every pressure of the hand, in every turn of the voice, in every gleam of the eye. You had the whole of him, whenever you touched him. That was one of the delights of his companionship.[40]

So yes, indeed, 'the whole man moved together,' so that 'you had the whole of him'; 'everything hung together.' Is that perhaps what the adjective 'holy' or 'whole' is striving to communicate when speaking of those whom the church delights to recognize as saints? It is to that same wholeness and integration of King's person to which Owen Chadwick, from his extensive research, also testifies, saying that King made people feel that the Christian life 'was supernatural, yes; otherworldly, yes; but not strange, or unnatural, or forced, or inhuman, or narrow. This was what man was born for. It was normality itself. It was balanced, sane, unwarped. It was man as he ought to be.'[41]

Perhaps it was something of that balanced and unwarped and proportionate sense which the carpenter sought to embody in the beautifully proportioned wooden box he presented to King when he left Wheatley. King kept this little present in his study throughout his life and always delighted in showing it to visitors, quoting, as he did so, the words of the donor: 'I knew you would like it, sir, because it is the same on each side.'[42] It was an exact square, perfectly proportioned, re-imaging, presumably, through his craft what the man had perceived and experienced in the person of King during his curacy in Wheatley.

As his life and ministry developed, King achieved this balance, this synthesis, this wholeness or, as what others who knew him well came to recognize, that 'radiant and attractive holiness,' to which Scott Holland so powerfully testified.

In words, rather than wood, Owen Chadwick re-affirms what that carpenter had observed of King's person: 'One of the secrets of his later power, was the naturalness of his faith. Faith was nothing strange in the world. The love of God was never fanatical or irrational.' King always conveyed, 'a perfect harmony between nature and grace.'[43]

We also have further evidence of this unitive wholeness from the lips of King himself when, in 1885, after his consecration as Bishop of Lincoln in the Chapter House of St Paul's Cathedral, he addressed a gathering of former Cuddesdon students in his characteristically understated, subtle and highly sensitive way:

> [At Cuddesdon], we wished to offer up our life and be happy, blessed in ourselves, and with the privilege of giving that blessedness to others ... [Cuddesdon] drew us nearer to God and to one another; giving us the peculiar freedom and elasticity which made us so loose and free (though not wild) in head and heart ... Our hearts were surrendered to be disentangled and disciplined, to find their rest when given up to God ... We were brought to love God, and one another in God, in a real and special way, not understood by people unless they themselves knew what it is to be thus free ... All grows really clear by taking God for our rest and end, with a sense of the reality of love and need of discipline. It gives a wonderful power of expansion as the love of God and man is proved as a rule of life.[44]

Such remarks are, of course, open to misinterpretation: that freedom and elasticity which made them loose and free in head and heart clearly was not understood by many then, any more than it ever has been, or, as King said, 'by people, unless they themselves knew what it is to be thus free'; and all that giving 'a wonderful power of expansion as the love of God and man is proved' (perhaps validated) 'in a rule of life' — a whole new and integrated way of life.

There is certainly nothing supressed in all of that, yet it speaks also of the need for hearts to be disentangled

The Secret of King's Influence

and disciplined, not as an end in itself but rather in order to achieve greater freedom. In spiritual direction there is generally the suggestion of a suitable rule of life as it was termed and still is. It would seem that such was the kind of rule of life by which King himself lived and which he commended to others, and all in a quest for holy freedom resulting from discipline and self-restraint, best summarized in that enigmatic and paradoxical aphorism of Augustine which King mentioned in his *Pastoral Lectures*, 'Love God and do as you like.'

FREEDOM AND DISCIPLINE

Before concluding with such affirming optimism, it is important not to overlook the place of discipline and self-restraint in King's teaching and in his own intimate and influential friendships. In all intimate relationships, there must always be a place for boundaries which respect the personal integrity of the other.

> As with God's relationships with us, human intimacy involves holding in proper balance an appropriate dissolution of personal boundaries and yet the continued respect for personal space. It is an unfortunate fact, of which we are being made increasingly aware these days, that the sexual crossing of boundaries has often been violent and abusive. At the heart of most cases of sexual abuse, including rape, lies the desire to gain power over another human being. Sexual violation of boundaries seems to be used to meet a number of needs that have little to do with real sexual desires, let alone with love. True human desire, just like God's desire for us, is respectfully attuned both to the self and to the partner. Each person may be lost in the other but individual boundaries are not abused or invaded. Each person allows them to be crossed in a way that enhances each partner rather than destroys his or her identity.[45]

Although King was optimistic about human nature, in a way so characteristic of the English School of Spirituality, he was not naïve: for all his warmth and loving pastoral affection, as one who knew him well testified, 'you felt that he had himself well in hand, that he had disciplined that strong affectionate heart and that burning zeal, and this discipline showed itself in self-restraint and gentleness.'[46]

King was unmarried, and it 'must have been a great temptation for so naturally affectionate a man to seek relief from loneliness in the society and friendship of the young. He knew, however, that for their sakes his feelings had to be disciplined in order to leave him free to love *all* with the love of Christ.'[47] What this cost him emerges in the advice he gave to a tutor at a missionary college, who was experiencing difficulty in 'getting through' to students of differing cultures in order to achieve any sense of collegiate community even vaguely resembling the community at Cuddesdon under King.

> It will want *heaps* of *talk*—MOUNTAINS of talk—with individuals, and you will have to be worn out and out, and done for, and broken-hearted, and miserable, and not understood, and deceived, before you begin to get the right sort of relationship which is absolutely necessary for the students' sake *now* ... and get them to see that you are heart and soul in earnest to bring them one and all, not to yourself but to the mind of Christ.[48]

And again, he says:

> Only by breaking your poor heart in pieces over and over again can you hope to make them begin to think of believing that there is such a thing as love! Don't mind, be miserable, but don't stop loving them ... I can only say you will never regret *all* the misery you go through.[49]

Something of those letters, written in 1880 and 1882, reveals the measure and cost of such love and care for others, as well as the self-discipline required by any seeking to influence for good those in their care. B. W. Randolph, a student of King's at Oxford, and later Principal of Ely Theological College, witnessed at first-hand the importance of that same self-discipline in King's pastoral ministry in Oxford: 'Above all he had a deep and disciplined affection for young men, and especially for the young men with whom he had to do at the Theological College ... This power of disciplined affection was one of the highest qualifications for his work.'[50]

Yet, this strong self-discipline in King should not be mistaken for self-flagellation, a practice which would have been totally out of character with him. There is clear evidence, however, that the practice of self-flagellation, the scourge or the 'discipline' as it was known, was used by some of the Tractarians associated with Gladstone. 'The idea of its use for what was intended as a punishment for sin probably came to Gladstone in a Tractarian context. Newman certainly used a scourge and described it in his novel, *Loss and Gain*, as "an iron discipline or scourge, studded with nails." Pusey asked Gladstone's closest friend, James Hope, to bring him a "discipline" from the Continent, and hoped that Keble, his confessor, would advise him to use it.'[51]

King's self-discipline, which he advocated for his ordinands as well as practised himself, was, always for the sake of those whom pastors and priests are called to serve. In his *Pastoral Lectures* he specifically warned his students to be alert and to practise vigilance in this matter: 'Let him that thinketh he standeth take heed.' He urges the need for moral purity and self-control, but always and notably for the sake of security and peace and freedom. Those who are ordained will have to offer spiritual guidance to others and must 'see the way' themselves. Supremely, 'because we must follow Christ. At least let us be pure for the sake of others. He could be in public places and elsewhere. Alone with women of infamous character because holy, guileless, undefiled, separate ... "For their sakes I sanctify myself." We want priests who can go without scandal into Sodom, and draw men out.'[52]

In those same *Pastoral Lectures*, he spells out the need to be alert to self-deception, speaking of 'little acts of affection' as being 'often the preludes to sin. Love we must, but so as to be in heaven together.' And again, 'Lust is the very essence of selfishness.'[53]

It is clear that for King such discipline was always a means to a greater end and not an end in itself, and neither was it the quest for perfectionism in any form. This is vividly exemplified in one of his many spiritual letters of guidance and advice, in which he makes it clear that the discipline which he is commending is really a 'pruning,' as in Christ's own teaching, and all for the sake of a more abundant fruitfulness, a more extended love and not less.[54] King's letter is a reply to an ordinand who enjoyed a very close friendship with 'H', with whom he lived. However, in order for H to carry out his father's wishes, there would have to be a parting of the ways, and the ordinand would need to return home to Wantage, without his friend, feeling, as King says, 'a little silently sad.' The ordinand, possibly a former student, must have known King well enough to have the confidence to confide in him on such an intimate matter and, furthermore, to feel that King, with his customary sympathy and compassion, would understand something of his pain and sadness. King's reply shows that he most certainly did:

> I should have written last night, because I felt you must be a little silently sad. But, dearest child, it will be all right. The more we can throw our wills in with the great Will of God ... the stronger our lives become; so it is much better that H. should carry out his father's wish, and that you should give up, rather than break off, and begin on you own independent wills. And then, do let me reassure you that the heart is of such immense capacity if we only give it up to God to discipline, that these woundings are rather *prunings* for greater beauty and richer fruit. Had you gone with your good friend it might have narrowed the circle of your love, and you would not have had the sense of freedom to love all

who may be waiting to be won by you to Him through your real love of them. *Now* there is a sense of solitude, of sadness, but believe me, that will be more, *infinitely more*, than filled by that which is to come. These acts of divine discipline are simply invitations to trust our hearts to *Him*.'

King is here encouraging and pastoring what might be termed a 'special friendship,' while helping to set it within the call of pastoral ministry which calls for discipline within the 'greater circle of love,' as he puts it, given by God to those who are called to bring others to a knowledge of God's greater love. In doing this 'you will be helping another soul to realize what he believes but does not quite feel, the *unity of all in Christ*, and all the while your greater love for God will give you new capacities and power to love more and more.'[55]

Clearly, this is King speaking from the heart of experience, not from some textbook on pastoral theology, and it powerfully witnesses to how he had found for himself, through God's discipline and 'pruning' that 'yet more excellent way' to that 'greater love for God' with 'new capacities and power to love, more and more.'

A PORTRAIT

In striving to hold together these two apparently contradictory opposites, freedom and discipline, as in other similar contradictory features of human personality, it requires an artist with the subtle tones of a palette and sensitive brushstrokes to capture what words can never quite achieve. In 1873, at the end of King's time at Cuddesdon, George Richmond had been commissioned to paint the portrait which the sitter later presented to the college. For Owen Chadwick, Richmond's picture is 'superlative':

> You cannot look at the portrait of King and miss the gentleness. But you cannot suppose it to be the

> gentleness of weakness, the gentleness of insignificance. The gentleness was that of a controlled strength. Yet somehow the control was neither forced nor evident. There is a saintliness which seems to spring from rigorous self-discipline. King's character did not suggest to his men that kind of quality. About the self-discipline there could be no doubt. But what was evident was the humanity, the breadth, the naturalness.[56]

Dr Talbot was similarly positive:

> the painter had rightly caught and interpreted a quality of the face, of the man, and of his inward experiences. His was the freedom which comes through and after discipline, that of a man severe with himself behind his gentleness to others; yes, and with an unflinching sincerity in him which could not help bracing those with whom he had to do.[57]

King's strong chin, to which he frequently alluded himself, was well caught by the artist. But some were disappointed, as Talbot allowed, feeling that the artist had missed 'the gracious winning countenance' and that the result was 'grave' and 'even severe.' King's friend F. E. Brightman was one of them (see p. 479).

A FAR-REACHING AND LASTING INFLUENCE

By way of conclusion, it would appear to be increasingly evident in any exploration into the nature of the remarkable and singular character of King's acclaimed 'genius,' that there are no adequate categories, psychological, genetic, physical, spiritual or indeed otherwise, which can satisfactorily frame, let alone contain the paradoxical and contradictory features of those to whom history accords such a superlative attribute. The 'geniuses' of this world, and those who are 'larger than life' in whatever field, push the boundaries of exploration on every front to the point of exhausting our prosaic vocabularies, stretching us to a point beyond our comfortable or customary reach: it would seem that such is also the case with those we choose to call saints. In a sense they deflect us from looking at them analytically: rather they invite and intrigue us to look beyond themselves to where they themselves are looking as they press forward (like athletes), striving to realize their full human potential. While it is important and helpful to examine from the various perspectives of psychology, sociology, or any other of the sciences, the various elements that constitute and motivate the lives of such outstanding people, nevertheless, we must necessarily do this with a measure of scepticism and in the knowledge that the aggregate of the parts can never convey or fully comprehend the whole: so it is in the case of King.

'It is God alone who is the perfect man,' (or 'man as he ought to be'), asserts the Greek Orthodox writer, Philip Sherrard. 'Only God is completely and utterly human. In so far as man fails to realize the divine in himself, to that extent he falls short of being completely human. He remains less than human. His human nature is truncated, just as the divine nature is truncated and less than divine if it is not humanized in Christ.'[58]

It was King's life and presence, even more than his teaching and pastoral ministry, which was the most compelling evidence of that claim that 'the divine has been humanized' once and for all in the person of Christ who came to show us God's way of being fully human. The invitation is open for our humanity, in the here-and-now, and not only in the afterlife, to be experienced, and at least partially realized, in what the Orthodox Churches of the East refer to as *theosis* or *divinization*. Indeed, there are some who would ask 'whether the primary clue to understanding the basic intuitions' of the founding fathers of the Oxford Movement is to be found 'in seeing it as a sudden epiphany within the Christian West, of the prayer, the vision, and the theology of the Greek Fathers. In a remarkable way, since their direct contacts with Eastern Orthodoxy were minimal, they succeeded in penetrating into its ethos. The doctrine of *theosis* is the key to understanding their whole vision of Christian faith and life. Without understanding that, we shall grasp little of the inspiration behind [the Oxford Movement],'[59] or indeed, one might add, behind the inner life of King, which was to have such a far-ranging influence on the Church in succeeding generations.

Cranmer gave faint hints to that same process of divine in-dwelling in the more restrained words of the 'Prayer of Humble Access' in the Book of Common Prayer, when communicants pray that 'we may evermore dwell in Him, and He in us.'

Is it something of this same mutual in-dwelling to which King, in one of his letters to Charlie, the young lad from Wheatley, obliquely referred? 'The fact is,' he says, 'there are two sorts of conversion: from a life of thoughtless sin to godliness,' and a further ongoing process of conversion 'in a life of godliness to a closer walk with God.' Significantly, King continues: 'The first, thank God, you know nothing of, nor do I' in so far as they had both been brought up as Christians in Christian families. 'But,' he continues, 'the second we both practise, and need to practise every day.'[60]

Such, it seems was the nature of that intimate relationship of friendship and companionship which King both taught and exemplified, and which the English School of Spirituality quietly affirms.

There would appear to be something of this in what Scott Holland's customary colourful prose is struggling to express:

> It was light that he carried with him—light that shone through him—light that flowed from him. The room was lit into which he entered. It was as if we had fallen under a streak of sunlight, that flickered, and danced, and laughed, and turned all to colour and gold.[61]

This, and the personal testimonies of the many who fell under King's spell, lead us to realise that the apparently

The Secret of King's Influence

straightforward, black-and-white question with which we began this whole enquiry, has turned out to be not quite so straightforward, after all. 'King's influence was a personal influence over individuals, and therefore hidden in a way which the biographer can hardly touch.'[62] It took a shepherd on the Lincolnshire Wolds to spot this something of the 'beyondness' (for want of a better word) in King, which more analytical minds could well miss. On meeting and talking with him, during one of King's many visits to the villages and parishes of his diocese, the shepherd is reputed to have said with a broad Lincolnshire accent: 'Eh! then yours is a yon-side religion, I see, sir.'[63]

One further caveat: it is abundantly clear that King's undoubted formative influence had nothing to do with a wish to control, and least of all to clone. Nothing could have been further from his distinctive way of teaching or mentoring. Talbot records how, when he was preparing to go to Keble College as its first Warden, he talked with King about his ideas for the new work and about the kind of influence that he, as Warden, would be able to exert over the students. King cautioned him against the temptation to clone: 'He gave me the wise counsel, "Don't try to Talbotize your men."'[64]

'Friend and fellow traveller' better describes the role of the spiritual guide, than 'spiritual director,' and is much more in keeping with the tone of the pastoral oversight of the School of English Spirituality with its preferred nomenclature of 'Spiritual Guide' or 'Soul Friend.' That was precisely what Alastair Campbell suggests in his *Rediscovering Pastoral Care*:

> Teachers must be *companions* on the same journey that we ourselves are making. Their authority derives from their ability to be fellow travellers, friends and comrades on this journey ... Teaching thus defined, is in essence a transaction between persons; teaching in the form of *exploration* endeavours to evoke a questioning and searching response in the learner. This is done by

> communicating something of the teacher's own struggle to understand, his own need to be a learner as well as a teacher.⁶⁵

That was precisely how King perceived his role both as a teacher and spiritual guide, and from which his self-authenticating authority derived its lasting and formative influence. Characteristically, when he was Bishop of Lincoln, he intervened during a debate in Convocation concerning the quality of teaching in theological colleges, and with his customary humility, though with no less honesty, said how much he had learned from and owed to his students—'to those whom I was supposed to be teaching.'⁶⁶ At that time, such an attitude and conviction might have marked King out as something of an odd-ball in a culture in which a teacher or pastor's authority rested on the largely unquestioned dictum—'Teacher or Father knows best.'

With King, such a radically reversed attitude to education and formation, sprang from a very different and more optimistic and affirmative view of human nature: he consistently sought to draw out from his students, or from those who sought his spiritual guidance, what was already latent in them, rather than imposing or inserting pre-packaged information. 'We truly educate,' said King, preaching at the opening of the dining-hall and library at Keble College on 25 April 1878, 'when we educe, draw out, unfold, perfect that common humanity which is in every man, wherever and whatever he may be.'⁶⁷

In precisely this way, King's influence as a teacher and pastor was in stark contrast to that of Liddon, who also, yet in a markedly different way, greatly influenced his students and those who came to him for spiritual guidance. 'Liddon perceived with trembling clarity, the deformities of human nature when seen in God's light. King perceived with a trembling sense of mystery, the image of God in human nature,'⁶⁸ albeit 'smudged,' as Manley Hopkins would have said, yet never totally overwritten or overridden, but simply awaiting the discriminating and sensitive 'retouching' of an experienced 'artist' of the spiritual life: such was King's genius and artistry.

The need for a 'light touch' in pastoral care and ministry was beautifully and memorably illustrated in a speech he gave in Christ Church Hall in support of Oxford House, Bethnal Green, on his first appearance back in Oxford after his consecration. The furniture in his house at Christ Church had been packed away in preparation for his departure, and all he had was 'a Bible, a Tertullian and a match-box. So he took his text from the box—"Rub lightly,"' and made those words the key-note of his address.[69]

'It was a marvellous speech,' commented Father J. G. Adderley, the founder of Oxford House, who was present. 'We were to rub the East-Enders—that is, we were to be definite, firm, sane, judicious; but we were to do it "lightly," with love and sympathy. We were not to use too much of the ecclesiastical "must"; but "just take them and give them a little push—no more." The speech literally took us all by storm.'[70]

This tells us something of the measure of King's transforming influence, which sought neither to control, to clone or to override, but rather to nurture and enable a trustful outpouring and confiding which is only possible in a non-threatening and secure relationship. In a lengthy letter, the Revd James Swallow, a student at Cuddesdon during King's time, attempted a description of the impact of his ministry there:

> Until now we had never understood ourselves. At last the tangle was unravelled by one as familiar, it seemed, with every twist and turn as if he himself had lived it out along with us. Doctrine, sermon, meditation each went home with direct personal application, until it was plain that our only course was to submit our lives and difficulties, our temptations and our sins, our hopes and fears to one who seemed to know them all without

needing to be told, and so benefit by the guidance for the future from one who had shown himself clairvoyant of the past.[71]

No matter to what we may attribute the secret of King's enduring and formative influence, it is to its longevity and amazing extent that, by way of conclusion, we should now turn.

The impact of the 'Great Cause,' as Pusey chose to call it, in its first generation, with the likes of Newman, Keble and Pusey and the *Tracts for the Times*, was largely confined to academic circles within the universities. The *Tracts* were distributed to parishes but their influence was limited and mainly restricted to critics—as ammunition for attacking the whole Movement—or to those, chiefly the clergy, already sympathetic to the cause.

If the movement or 'Cause' was ever to take hold in the Church at a parish and diocesan level, then any influence for change needed to begin with the training of the clergy: such is still equally true for today's Church. The fact, therefore, that King was not first and foremost either an academic or a well-known preacher, and certainly not a polemicist or a rigid party man, but primarily a pastor and teacher, who over twenty years had trained, taught and influenced many hundreds of future clergy is of huge significance.

Talbot testifies to the lasting effect of King's ministry, being transmitted through the lives and work of the many ordinands who had sat at King's feet and who later in their own ministry handed on what they had first received from their pastoral Professor:

> Hundreds of the young candidates for Holy Orders went out from Oxford carrying with them not only such and such convictions which he had helped to form in his interpretation of Hooker, but even more with thoughts and hints about dealing with their flocks of which they must have felt the touch most, in the least controversial and most practical parts of their work.

The Secret of King's Influence

It was the old influence of the Cuddesdon lectures on pastoralia, deepened and widened.[72]

It was the impact of King's teaching and example on the clergy of the next generation, above all else, which brought about a lasting change in the spiritual and pastoral direction of the Church of England and even further afield in the emerging Anglican Communion. (The liturgical changes came slightly later and from other sources.)

Randolph, the editor of King's *Spiritual Letters*, published sermons and addresses, who had himself been Principal of Ely Theological College, comments on King's 'altogether unique influence over the students,' during his Cuddesdon years, 'setting a standard in regard to the devotional life and ideals of Theological Colleges, which have profoundly influenced the English Church.'[73]

Add to that, the number of friends and former students who continued King's work of training the clergy in the proliferating theological colleges, many, like Ely and Lincoln, modelled on King's Cuddesdon. To them should be added the number of students King had trained or influenced, who went on to become bishops, modelling their episcopal ministry on King's own. The list of names of those, ordained and lay, who later held high office is immensely impressive: to name but a few—the scholarly liturgist F. E. Brightman, who was eloquent concerning the debt he owed to King from his Oxford days; the historian, W. H. Hutton; George W. E. Russell, author, parliamentarian and King's first biographer; Francis Paget, his immediate successor as Professor of Pastoral Theology and later Bishop of Oxford; A. F. Winnington-Ingram, Bishop of London; and the above mentioned B. W. Randolph; these are just some of the many in whose lives King made a striking and lasting radical difference, and who in turn went on to make a similar difference in Church and State alike.

In the light of this record, is it so outrageous to claim that it was Edward King, as pastor, teacher and bishop, more than any other one person associated with the Catholic Revival in the Church of England, who more radically and spiritually changed the character and face of what is now usually termed the Anglican Church? For throughout history and with the benefit of hindsight, it would seem that such is the way in which change, renewal and regeneration is repeatedly brought about in institutions and organizations: not so much by a plethora of new programmes, or by reorganizing structurally the furniture and fittings, but rather by engendering in a 'web' of relationships, formed often around one person in whom that change and transformation inwardly and quietly has already taken hold. Furthermore, and generally speaking, it does not begin at the 'top' or by drawing crowds and large numbers. Rather, the model is frequently turned on its head, whereby the many are influenced by the few, as the few, in turn, are influenced at the outset by the one. And again, the 'one,' at least initially, is often a somewhat hidden or even underrated figure, only recognized later, or even after their death.

It is something of this dynamic for change which we come close to in any exploration in depth into the powerful and lasting influence for change with Edward King. After all, this same dynamic for change and renewal held good for the spread of Christianity with all odds against it, spreading from the few to the many in the earliest days of the Church, and such has been repeatedly the dynamic for change, lasting renewal and regeneration ever since.

Notes

1. Randolph and Townroe, *The Mind and Work of Bishop King*, p. 3.
2. *Pastoral Lectures of Bishop Edward King* (ed. Graham), p. xiv.
3. George W. E. Russell, *Edward King Sixtieth Bishop of Lincoln*, p. 55.
4. King, *Spiritual Letters of Edward King, D.D.*, Letter XXII.
5. Randolph and Townroe, *op. cit.*, p. 53.
6. *Ibid.*, p. 54.

The Secret of King's Influence

7. *Ibid.*, pp. 6–7.
8. *Ibid.*, p. 53.
9. Russell, *op. cit.*, p. 27.
10. King, *Spiritual Letters*, Letter XLV.
11. Timothy Radcliffe, *Alive in God: A Christian Imagination*. Bloomsbury Continuum, 2019, p. 165.
12. King, *Spiritual Letters* p. 182.
13. Radcliffe, *op. cit.*, p. 168.
14. Lord Elton, *Edward King and Our Times*, p. 53.
15. Robert A. K. Runcie, *Seasons of the Spirit: The Archbishop of Canterbury at Home and Abroad* (ed. James B. Simpson). Grand Rapids MI: William B. Eerdmans Publishing Co., 1983, p. 50.
16. King, *Spiritual Letters*, Letter LXIX.
17. *Ibid.*, Letter XXVIII.
18. John Newton, *Search for a Saint*, p. 46.
19. Runcie, *op. cit.*, p. 50.
20. Newton, *op. cit.*, p. 46.
21. Runcie, *op. cit.*, p. 51.
22. Philip Sheldrake, *Befriending Our Desires*. London: Darton, Longman & Todd, 1994, p. 28.
23. Rabbi Jonathan Sacks, *Covenant and Conversation: Genesis: The Book of Beginnings*. Maggid Books and The Orthodox Union, 2009, p. 133.
24. Charlie Cleverly, *The Song of Songs: Exploration the Divine Romance*. Hodder & Stoughton Ltd, 2015, p. 16.
25. Elton, *op. cit.*, p. 54.
26. Cleverly, *op. cit.*, p. 16, quoting from Erich Auerbach (trans. Willard Trask), *Mimesis: The Representation of Reality in Western Literature*.
27. *St. Augustine on the Psalms* (translated and annotated by Dame Scholastica Hebgin and Dame Felicitas Corrigan). Westminster Md: Newman Press, 1961, p. 69 (Second Discourse on Psalm 31).
28. Martin Thornton, *English Spirituality*, p. 14.
29. Newton, *op. cit.*, p. 106.
30. Philip Seddon, *Redeeming Eros: Reading the Song of Songs*. Cambridge: Grove Books Ltd, 2010, p. 3.
31. *Cuddesdon College 1854–1929: A Record and a Memorial*, p. 52.
32. King, *The Love and Wisdom of God*, p. 138.
33. Aelred of Rievaulx, *On Spiritual Friendship* (ed. M. Basil Pennington, OCSO). Cistercian Fathers Series, Cistercian Publications Consortium Press, 1974, p. 37.
34. *Ibid.*
35. King, *The Love and Wisdom of God*, p. 46.
36. *Ibid.*
37. Aelred of Rievaulx, *op. cit.*, pp. 20–1.

38. *Ibid.*, p. 21.
39. *Ibid.*, pp. 21–2.
40. Scott Holland, *A Bundle of Memories*, pp. 49–50.
41. Owen Chadwick, *The Founding of Cuddesdon*, p. 112.
42. Randolph and Townroe, *op. cit.*, p. 139.
43. Owen Chadwick, *Edward King, Bishop of Lincoln, 1885–1910*, pp. 3–4.
44. Randolph and Townroe, *op. cit.*, p. 59.
45. Sheldrake, *op. cit.*, p. 72.
46. Randolph and Townroe, *op. cit.*, p. 14.
47. Barry A. Orford, 'Edward King 1829–1910,' in *CR Quarterly*, Number 328, 25 March 1985.
48. King, *Spiritual Letters*, Letter LXXI.
49. *Ibid.*, Letter LXXIII.
50. C. J. Smith, *Berkeley William Randolph: A Memoir*. London: A. R. Mowbray & Co., 1925, p. 58.
51. H. C. G. Matthew, *Gladstone 1809–1898*, p. 93.
52. *Pastoral Lectures of Bishop Edward King*, pp. 20–1.
53. *Ibid.*
54. John 15:2.
55. King, *Spiritual Letters*, Letter XX.
56. Chadwick, *The Founding of Cuddesdon*, p. 112.
57. Randolph and Townroe, *op. cit.*, p. 87.
58. Philip Sherrard, *The Rape of Man and Nature*. Ipswich: Golgonooza Press, 1987, p. 27.
59. Geoffrey Rowell (ed.), *Tradition Renewed. The Oxford Movement Conference Papers*. London: Darton, Longman & Todd Ltd, 1986, p. 227.
60. King, *Spiritual Letters*, Letter IX.
61. Scott Holland, *op. cit.*, p. 48.
62. Chadwick, *Bishop King*, p. 26.
63. Randolph and Townroe, *op. cit.*, p. 175.
64. *Ibid.*, p. 90.
65. Alastair V. Campbell, *Rediscovering Pastoral Care*. London: Darton, Longman & Todd, Ltd, 1986, p. 5.
66. Chadwick, *The Founding of Cuddesdon*, p. 113.
67. King, *The Wisdom and Love of God*, p. 156.
68. Chadwick, *The Founding of Cuddesdon*, p. 113.
69. Russell, *op. cit.*, p. 110: Randolph and Townroe, *op. cit.*, p. 89.
70. Russell, *op. cit.*
71. Randolph and Townroe, *op. cit.*, pp. 45ff.
72. *Ibid.*, p. 84.
73. King, *Spiritual Letters*, p. vi.

PART THREE

The Lincoln Years

✧ 10 ✧

The Choice of a Bishop for Lincoln

GLADSTONE'S CHOICE

If right timing is of the essence in the workings of Providence, then the nomination of King for the See of Lincoln was no exception, as had been the case with his appointment to the Pastoral Professorship twelve years earlier. On both occasions it fell to Gladstone to make the nomination. Not only was Gladstone highly conscientious in these matters, but he also brought to the task, as a distinguished High Churchman, a considerable ability as a lay theologian. In his retirement he produced the authoritative edition of the works of Bishop Joseph Butler, who was much revered and frequently quoted by King. Gladstone's skill and experience as a prime mover of bishops on the ecclesiastical chessboard of his day should not be underestimated.

The Tractarians did not receive any Crown patronage until 1854, when the only Tractarian bishop, W. K. Hamilton, came quietly and discreetly to the See of Salisbury because the Queen did not know of his Tractarian allegiances. So, it is almost as though Gladstone, during his terms of office as Prime Minister, had decided to make up for lost time on the Tractarian front with episcopal appointments and to redress the balance: George Moberly, Bishop of Salisbury (1869); Wilberforce, the Tractarian chief on the Bench of Bishops, to Winchester (1869); Woodford, Bishop of Ely (1873); Wilkinson, Bishop of Truro (1883); and his last and crowning Tractarian appointment, King to Lincoln (1885).

Edward King

As Gladstone had always held a high opinion of King, it was fortuitous that he was still in office when the See of Lincoln became vacant early in 1885, and as Prime Minister it was his duty to recommend names for a successor to the Queen.

The early 'eighties occasioned a major reshuffle of the Bench of Bishops (due to old age, ill-health or death) and the creation of two new diocesan bishoprics—Newcastle (1882) and Southwell (1884). Archbishop Tait had died in 1882 to be succeeded at Canterbury by Benson, thereby vacating the See of Truro. Bishop Ollivant of Llandaff also died in 1882, and Bishop Robert Bickersteth of Ripon in 1884. Bishop Jackson, a previous Bishop of Lincoln before being translated to London, also died in 1885. This in turn, facilitated Bishop Frederick Temple's translation to London, so vacating the Diocese of Exeter. In January 1885 Bishop Wordsworth of Lincoln, an 'eminent scholar and poet, not less saintly in his life than remarkable for his acquirements,'[1] but in failing health, resigned the See which he had held since 1869. There were many who felt confident, and who speculated, that the time had come for the Professor of Pastoral Theology at Oxford to be preferred to one of the several vacant bishoprics, and perhaps most conspicuously to that of Lincoln. At the same time, among others in the higher echelons of the Establishment, King would not have been regarded as an obvious candidate to replace the greatly revered and esteemed Wordsworth.

Faced, as Gladstone was, with so many episcopal appointments, he was determined, despite being attracted in his later years towards the High Church movement, to give the differing traditions of the Established Church a broad representation on the Bench of Bishops and in the Lords, as he clearly took pains to demonstrate in his nominations to the three vacant bishoprics of Exeter, Lincoln and London. For a High Church appointment, the obvious name, championed by many, and initially by Gladstone himself, was Canon Liddon at St Paul's.

The Choice of a Bishop for Lincoln

PROBLEMS OF CHURCHMANSHIP

However, there were several obstacles in the way of Liddon's preferment. He was well known as a firm friend and protégé of Pusey (and later his devoted biographer). After Pusey's death, Liddon was generally acknowledged as a leading figure amongst second generation Tractarians, with reservations about the Ritualists and outspoken opinions both as a writer and preacher. He was widely considered to be one of the greatest preachers of his day in the English Church, and yet equally branded as a staunch party man. There had been earlier attempts to promote Liddon to the episcopate, but Tait thought him far too rigid, while Queen Victoria regarded him as a divisive extremist. 'All her life, Victoria looked for what she called "tolerant" clergy, which tended to mean, those who agreed, or pretended to agree, with her own set of eclectic prejudices. As a child, she was unaware of what she would later deplore—the High versus Low squabbles of the National Church.'[2] and 'she tended to be impatient with the clergy, fearing that they would be too High Church, too Low Church, too bigoted, or, as preachers, too boring.'[3] She had always favoured Broad Church men, her ideal clergyman being none other than 'The Excellent Dr Stanley,' as he was termed, the Dean of Westminster, undoubtedly the broadest of the broad.

Archbishop Benson, who knew of King's great pastoral gifts, and also continued to harbour fond memories of Lincoln from his days as the Cathedral Chancellor, was keen to suggest the name of an alternative High Church man, namely King, for one of the three vacancies—not necessarily Lincoln, because, as Gladstone remarked, King 'is a very living power in Oxford. His kindling power would be a little lost on Wiltshire Downs or Lincolnshire Wolds.'[4]

Gladstone was prepared to risk tension with the Queen by persisting with Liddon as his first choice for Lincoln. On 22 January he met with the Archbishop in 10 Downing Street and agreed to submit three names to the Queen: Frederick Temple, a liberal, for London; the more Evangelical Edward Bickersteth (son of Bishop Robert Bickersteth) for Exeter; and Liddon for Lincoln. Before taking it any further, however, it was agreed that Dean Church of St Paul's should sound out Liddon. Accordingly, the two men met and had an hour-and-a-half's earnest discussion.

> Liddon's mind was in a turmoil, and he described the feeling afterwards as a great heartache. But he would not say yes. His reasons to the contrary did not seem strong. He just could not decide that it would be right to let his name go forward to the Queen. He was miserable for the rest of the day.[5]

The following day, Gladstone drafted a short note to the Queen submitting three names: Bickersteth, King and Temple for the dioceses of Exeter, Lincoln and London respectively. In an accompanying memorandum, Gladstone expressed (in the third person) his strong and unreserved support for King:

> Dr King, as to opinion, would be reputed a divine of the High Church. At the time when he received his important Professorship from Your Majesty, he had by a wise and loving spirit, attracted confidence and attachment from many, Bishops and others, within a wider circle than that of any special party. No occupant of a Theological Chair in Oxford has, as Mr Gladstone believes, ever done more than Dr King for the maintenance of practical and earnest religion among the younger members of the University, and few indeed have done so much. Dr King is also an accomplished modern scholar, with a noteworthy gift of languages; and a person who would in all respects bring honour to the Bench, and be a worthy successor to Dr Wordsworth, who has undoubtedly attracted as a diocesan Bishop, much veneration and affection. Mr Gladstone refrains from troubling Your Majesty, unless so commanded, with further particulars.[6]

The Choice of a Bishop for Lincoln

Although a little surprised at seeing King's name on the list, the Queen was relieved it was not Liddon's, as she had been led to expect. Immediately she sought the opinion of Randall Davidson, the Dean of Windsor, her trusted friend and advisor in such matters. Davidson had a high regard for King, and wrote to the Queen, via her secretary, Sir Henry Ponsonby, giving her advice which was forthright and strongly in support of King, who, as he said, would make a decidedly better bishop than Liddon. High Churchmen needed a representative on the Bench of Bishops, and King was nearly as prominent and popular among them as Liddon, with the added advantage that he was able to get on with all sorts and conditions of men.

Davidson perceptively claimed,

> He has a strangely winning power and has at Oxford succeeded beyond any other theological teacher, in gaining the confidence of young men of all sorts of opinions. His own views are very decidedly High Church, but he has never thrown himself actively into the *public* controversies on these subjects, and he is so bright and cheery that he has done much to counteract the rather severe and gloomy views both about the present and future which have characterised some of the other teachers who share his Church opinions: he is a remarkable man in every way.[7]

The deal was sealed: Davidson, the episcopal 'king-maker' went in person to Downing Street to express the Queen's pleasure, and his own, with the proposed nominations. However, with his customary wisdom and perception, he made a telling comment about matching the dioceses with the churchmanship of the candidates. The Diocese of Lincoln, the homeland of the Wesleys, was predominantly Low-Church, with many Nonconformists and a stronghold of Methodism. Exeter Diocese was generally considered more of the High Church persuasion. Might it not be better to send King, the High Churchman, to Exeter and the more Evangelical Bickersteth, to Lincoln? Davidson's suggestion did not prevail and on 27 January the Queen approved Gladstone's choices. 'Thank goodness,' wrote Gladstone's secretary, possibly echoing the Prime Minister's own feelings, 'there is for the moment an end of episcopal appointments, which with Mr Gladstone's excess of conscientiousness, give more trouble than almost anything else.'[8]

Gladstone moved swiftly, and on the following day, 28 January, wrote to King offering him, 'with the sanction of her Majesty,' the See of Lincoln. 'My request to you is to allow yourself to be nominated for it by the Crown. The expectations of the Diocese, after the Episcopate of Bishop Wordsworth, will be high, and I can make no better provision to save disappointment than by the proposal which I now submit to you.'[9]

King consented, although, from the wording of his reply to Gladstone on 30 January it is clear that he did not find the decision easy. 'The great offer which you have made me I dare not refuse it because, as far as I can tell, it comes to me as God's Will, and if I shrink from trying to do that I have no principle in life left.'

He might well have wished to remain at Oxford, where he was happy in his work, had many friends and was committed to his students; or, at least, have hesitated to accept, aware that a bishop's life would make considerable demands on him in terms of travel and administration. Then there was his state of health, to which he draws attention in the next paragraph of his letter of acceptance. 'I must add that my friends have raised a question about my health; and the Bishop of Oxford was good enough to say that he would write to you. I will say nothing, for I have lived already so much longer than I expected that I am quite ready, God helping me, to spend what remains as and where He pleases.'[10]

While it is difficult to assess exactly how much King welcomed the prospect of becoming a bishop, it does seem that after twelve years as a professor in Oxford he might well have thought that perhaps the time had come to pull up the pilgrim's tent pegs and move on.

In the first place there was the loss of his mother who had died two years earlier. Writing to a friend whose own mother had died, King says his own bereavement was experienced as 'a terrible loss and blank,' both in his home and in his heart. 'Life can never be quite the same.'[11]

Similarly, in a letter to Dr Heurtley, who during King's time in Oxford had known Mrs King well: 'You will believe me that I go to this new work with mingled feelings. I cannot help feeling the loss of my dear mother again very specially. We came in here together, and I feel that I go out alone; and I shall go to people who will never have known her.'[12]

A QUITE DIFFERENT KIND OF BISHOP

After a series of very different yet outstanding episcopal appointments to Lincoln during the nineteenth century, King brought just the particular qualities that were needed in the diocese at that time. Of the episcopal vacancies in the 'eighties, Lincoln was perhaps the one most suited to King, with his own background and particular gifts, albeit very different from those of his predecessor, Christopher Wordsworth.

Wordsworth, like his father, who had been Master of Trinity College, Cambridge, was a scholar of considerable standing, as well as a poet and hymn writer, some of whose hymns are still loved and sung today. Totally unlike King, his output of scholarly writings was monumental, ranging from a Commentary on the whole Bible, and his own translation and edition of the Greek New Testament, to memoirs of his uncle, the poet William Wordsworth. In 1836, at the age of twenty-nine, he became Public Orator at Cambridge and in the same year was appointed Headmaster of Harrow.

Edward King

It was only much later, in 1869, after twenty-five years as a Canon of Westminster Abbey, and nineteen years as a parish priest in the depths of rural Berkshire, that Disraeli nominated him for the See of Lincoln. In many ways, Wordsworth represents something of the dynastic element in the Church, not uncommon at that time—his brother Charles was Bishop of St Andrews and his son John became Bishop of Salisbury. For King, Wordsworth was no easy act to follow.

In the ordinary run of things, King would almost certainly never have been regarded as a suitable candidate for episcopal nomination in the nineteenth-century Church, where bishops were often drawn from the ranks of former headmasters or Fellows of Oxford or Cambridge Colleges, and certainly not if Disraeli had still been Prime Minister. Furthermore, King did not belong to the great episcopal 'dynasties' like Bickersteth: neither was he ever part of the 'London set' of Dean Stanley and the Royal Family, like Wilberforce or Davidson.

Not surprisingly, King's style of episcopacy would prove to be something of a break with that of his nineteenth-century predecessors, who in different ways were well known beyond the boundaries of the diocese for their participation in government, in national life and in the House of Lords. Jackson, Wordsworth's immediate predecessor, after only a short time at Lincoln, left to become Bishop of London, albeit somewhat surprisingly, instead of Bishop Kaye who had already distinguished himself as something of an ecclesiastical statesman and had preceded Jackson at Lincoln.

Comparisons are odious, as the saying goes, and yet understandably at the outset of King's appointment there would have been no shortage of critics to question how he could possibly hold a candle to any of his distinguished predecessors. Indeed, a cynic at the time might have been forgiven for saying that this was yet another instance of 'not what you know, but who you know'—in this case, Gladstone and for a second time, at that. Fast forward twenty-five

The Choice of a Bishop for Lincoln

years, however, and such negative appraisals had been reversed, marking King out as being the most distinguished and saintly bishop of modern times.

In any event, as soon as the appointment was announced, Gladstone, as well as King, received many letters of delight and congratulation. The great church and constitutional historian William Stubbs, Bishop of Chester, certainly no easy touch, wrote a commendatory note to the Prime Minister, assuring him: 'I am so glad to hear about Dr King's promotion that I cannot help writing to congratulate you on making the best appointment that has been made since St Anselm' — an accolade indeed from one with such a sweeping overview of history. Although such a claim might be thought to be greatly exaggerated, Stubbs was certainly not given to generous overstatements, and there were many other notables who shared his enthusiastic approval: Benson, the Archbishop of Canterbury, Dean Church of St Paul's, and other episcopal heavyweights such as Bishop Browne of Winchester and Bishop Woodford of Ely, as well as numerous well-informed ecclesiastical commentators. On hearing the news during his last days, Bishop Wordsworth simply said, 'Deo Gratias.' Later, Gladstone told King, he had heard 'nothing but praises of the nomination to Lincoln.'[13] In a reference that would have cheered King's heart, Dean Church assured him that his great heroes, now deceased — Charles Marriott, John Keble and Dr Pusey — would have rejoiced at the appointment.[14]

It so happened that King's friend and disciple, Scott Holland, was a close friend of Gladstone's daughter, Mary Drew, who rather prematurely let the episcopal 'cat out of the bag' by breaking the news of her father's nomination for Lincoln. 'Bless you for the Surprise and Delight of King!' Scott Holland typically and euphorically exclaimed. 'A St Francis de Sales at Lincoln! A joy like an old Spring, if you can fancy Spring grown old ... He will move as a benediction.'[15] Subsequently, and characteristically well over-the-top, he wrote rhapsodically to King: 'It shall be a Bishopric of Love—the Love of God behind, and above, and about you! The Love of the Blessed Spirit, alive with good cheer within! The Love of the Poor shining out from you, until they kneel under its lovely benediction.'[16]

King did not know that Liddon had been sounded out as to his willingness to accept the See if offered, so Liddon certainly would have felt a pang when on 31 January he received an affectionately worded letter from King telling him of the appointment, which was due to be made public the next day. That letter is yet another example of King's gift for sympathy and sensitivity, ensuring that Liddon would first hear the news from him directly and personally, not least because of their long friendship, dating back to the brief time they had worked together at Cuddesdon, and to the many years they were close neighbours in Oxford. 'Your note,' said Liddon, in a generous reply, 'is the first news I have had about Lincoln: thank you so much for thinking of me at such a moment.'[17] However, Liddon records in his diary how he did not sleep that night.

When the news broke, High Churchmen throughout England received it with sheer delight. For many, like Dean Church, Francis Paget (whom King himself later recommended to Gladstone as being uniquely suitable to succeed him as Pastoral Professor) and Butler of Wantage, shortly to be preferred as the new Dean of Lincoln, King's appointment was regarded as a strategic and notable Tractarian breakthrough into the leadership of the Church and the Bench of Bishops.

Then there were King's former students from Cuddesdon, his many Oxford friends, prominent Tractarians and associates, who all reached for their pens to express their delight. Some letters, especially from former Cuddesdon students, appear to a more taciturn culture like our own, as excessive in their wording, even sycophantic: 'My dear,' or 'Dearest Principal' and ending 'your grateful and affectionate son in

The Choice of a Bishop for Lincoln

Christ.' Another wrote 'How soon, alas! One almost grudges your leaving Oxford, except that one has faith that God has work elsewhere. In our selfishness, we felt the same about Cuddesdon. Dear, dear Principal, how much we owe you!'[18]

Yet, it is noteworthy that letters also poured in from a much broader constituency. Charles Gore, who was to be a very different kind of bishop, and yet a close friend of King, wrote to one of his friends, 'King is ideal for Lincoln, but oh! The blank it will be here. It is not to be thought of: Oxford will not be the same place at all. Ugh! It is grim.'[19]

There were many others, not at all from the same churchmanship 'stable,' like Dean Liddell of Christ Church (father of Alice Liddell of *Alice in Wonderland* fame), a noted theological liberal, who wrote just as warmly and fulsomely. It was hugely significant that Liddell, as Dean of Christ Church, should go further and express the general wish of his undergraduates that King would preach once again in the Cathedral before leaving for Lincoln. His closing words went even further: 'And I trust that, possibly at some future time, we may often hear a voice which has touched many hearts, and which none hear without wishing to hear it again.'[20]

To these strongly worded affirmations, which might have been anticipated in the light of King's remarkable and distinctive ministry in Oxford and at nearby Cuddesdon, were added others from some very different and unexpected admirers. One wrote from the Radcliffe Infirmary in Oxford; another from 'Her Majesty's Prison in Wandsworth'; another from Messrs Carter's Nursery at the Crystal Palace, and one, a miner, 'from the bowels of the earth.'[21]

Immediately after the announcement of King's appointment, there followed demanding and painful weeks of uprooting and preparation for the move, which necessarily involved some reordering of his daily life. As well as having to deal with a mountain of correspondence, there was much to do before his formal election took place in London, at St Mary-le-Bow, on 23 April, followed, only two days later, by his consecration in St Paul's Cathedral, and, on 19 May, by his enthronement in Lincoln Cathedral.

FAREWELL TO OXFORD

The uprooting from Oxford proved, if anything, to be even more painful than the earlier break with Cuddesdon. More than three hundred graduates and undergraduates joined to present the episcopal ring, with an address which expressed their deep gratitude for 'spiritual help' and especially for King's personal ministry throughout his years as Professor, in 'Bethel,' where theology had been authenticated in lives transformed through pastoral, loving care and prayer.

The congregation of St Barnabas, where King had frequently preached, presented a gold satin cope. Sir Henry Acland sent, with a beautifully touching letter, a paperweight made of stone from Iona, 'over which St Columba may have walked.' And to cap it all, a gift of outstanding generosity was presented on behalf of King's many friends in Oxford by the Revd J. O. Johnston (afterwards to be Principal of Cuddesdon), who forwarded a cheque for £1,500 (approx. £180,000 in today's money) as an expression of their gratitude 'for the work you have done in Oxford and elsewhere, and also for the many kindnesses and the great help that they have received at your hands.'[22] In acknowledging this gift, King wrote: 'I may accept it, as given in gratitude for the Truth which it has been my great privilege to teach. That Oxford may hold that Truth with increasing clearness, and enjoy the Unity, and Love, and Rest, which that Truth alone can give, is the sincere prayer of your grateful and affectionate, Friend in Christ.'[23] (King donated all the money to St Stephen's House, Oxford, of which he was a founder.)

The most poignant and heart-wrenching occasion was undoubtedly on the last Friday of the Lent Term, when he delivered his farewell address to his undergraduate friends who came together for the last time at 'Bethel.' 'Twelve years ago,' he said, 'I began these little addresses, first in my own study to half a dozen men, whose number quickly increased; then in a small room here, where I am standing; then that was not large enough, and we extended it to take in that further room.'[24] King apologized for the brevity of his address as being 'rough' because he feared that otherwise he might breakdown, so charged was the whole occasion. Throughout that final address it was a 'striving for *Personal Communion* with God' which is urged firmly and persistently as being at the heart of Christian discipleship, expressed in lively faith and obedience. It is that 'personal communion with God' which was consistently and increasingly the heart-beat of King's ministry and life and which marked him in the years that followed as a teaching and pastoral bishop.

CONFIRMATION OF KING'S ELECTION

On 20 March the formal election by the Dean and Chapter of Lincoln took place in the Cathedral Chapter House. Afterwards the Dean, Dr Blakesley, wrote to King:

> I cannot deny myself the pleasure of informing you by my handwriting of that which you will learn officially very soon, that you were elected as the successor of Bishop Wordsworth, this afternoon. It was a great satisfaction to me that the weather and my bodily condition were such that I was able to preside in person over the proceedings of the Chapter. There was a very large attendance of Prebendaries in the Chapter, and the effect was very striking. May you long fill the See, and never regret having left the shades of Oxford.[25]

At this point King could not have known of the storms and conflicts which lay ahead, even if he had some premonition, yet there can be little doubt that he never truly regretted taking up the tasks and challenges which awaited him in Lincoln. Generally speaking, the people of Lincolnshire were not of the High Church tradition and there were already signs, even before his arrival, that many viewed his appointment with suspicion. The Archdeacon, John Kaye, had conspicuously absented himself from the formalities of King's election in London and refused to appear in the procession at King's enthronement. So, although the misgivings about King's appointment may not have been so vocal as those who had written or spoken about it with such great euphoria, nevertheless, from his first days rumblings of opposition were evident in the clerical constituency of the diocese. Owen Chadwick goes as far as to claim that 'no good man could have started as bishop with worse publicity and with more of a handicap to overcome.'[26]

Only a matter of days after the appointment was announced, voices of opposition were heard, such as *The Record* of 6 February which spoke of it as 'a great misfortune.'[27] In late March, prior to the formal confirmation of King's election as bishop, the council of the Church Association chose to rise up in militant opposition. A memorial was presented to Queen Victoria complaining of her choice of King. They claimed that his views and teachings on the Lord's Supper, and especially on Sacramental Confession, should have automatically disqualified him from this preferment. The Queen was requested to ask for further enquiries and to put formal confirmation on hold until their objections had been fully investigated to the satisfaction of Her Majesty.

However, the confirmation went ahead as planned, although King and others would have been seriously apprehensive as to whether the proceedings would take place peacefully. The storm clouds of opposition were gathering and undoubtedly King would have been well aware of them.

For the formal confirmation of his election, King, attended by his chaplain, presented himself at St Mary-le-Bow, Cheapside on Thursday, 23 April at 11 o'clock, when the

The Choice of a Bishop for Lincoln

Archbishop of Canterbury's Vicar-General, Dr James Parker Deane, QC, held a Court and formally confirmed King's election to the See of Lincoln. Writing to a friend immediately after, King refers to what the Church Association, had 'been putting together'[28] before his confirmation, with their plans to overturn it. Formed in 1865 by ultra-Protestant Evangelicals, the Church Association—the 'Church Ass' to its opponents—was a body designed to combat ritualism, and to use every legitimate means, including litigation, to suppress it. Bishop Magee of Peterborough used to refer to it as the 'Persecution Company Limited.'

The members had been incensed and dismayed by King's appointment, and although choosing to stay their hand in 1885, it seems that more far-reaching plans were already afoot and that they were biding their time for a more opportune occasion to attack King. Four years later they struck, in what became known as the Lincoln Judgment. So, 'this happy, holy, serene, popular and harmless man now entered a world of unforeseen entanglements, which slowly gripped him, until for a time they almost destroyed his happiness.'[29]

KING'S CONSECRATION

Bishops are traditionally consecrated on an Apostle's day, marking them out as successors of the Apostles, so on St Mark's Day, 25 April 1885, in St Paul's Cathedral, before 'a mighty congregation,'[30] with King's friend Archbishop Benson presiding, together with nine consecrating bishops, and presented by the Bishops of Ely and Oxford, Edward King was consecrated bishop in the Church of God.

At his own request, the preacher was Liddon, whose sermons 'filled Ludgate Hill with as great a crowd of people on Sunday as was found on a weekday afternoon.'[31] In 1880 Liddon had dedicated a volume of his sermons, *Church Troubles*, to King. Powerful and persuasive as a preacher though Liddon undoubtedly was, tact and sensitivity could sometimes elude him. The other bishop consecrated that day was Edward Bickersteth for the Diocese of Exeter. Many of his supporters in the congregation who shared his Evangelical churchmanship would have felt uncomfortable, if not alienated by Liddon, who chose to preach 'one of the uncompromising high church sermons in the century,'[32] which was afterwards published under the title *A Father in Christ*.

For his text Liddon chose words of St Paul: 'For though you have countless guides in Christ, you do not have many fathers. For I became your father in Christ Jesus through the gospel' (1 Corinthians 4:15). A more apt text could not have been found, for it was primarily as a father in God, friend, teacher and pastor that King's long episcopate was to prove conspicuously distinctive and different from those of many of his contemporaries, and, indeed, from our practice and understanding of episcopacy in the Church today. (It is for that reason, among others, that King still has something to say to the Church by way of challenge, encouragement and example.)

After a lengthy discourse on the nature of the episcopal office, Liddon paid a warm tribute to King's predecessor, Bishop Wordsworth, who had recently died:

> He is to be succeeded, in the See of St Hugh by one whose nomination has thrilled the hearts of his brother churchmen with the deepest thankfulness and joy. Never, probably, in our time, has the great grace of sympathy, controlled and directed by a clear sense of the nature and sacredness of revealed truth, achieved so much among so many young men as has been achieved, first at the Theological College at Cuddesdon, and then from the Pastoral Chair at Oxford, in the case of my dear and honoured friend. He is surrounded at this solemn moment by hundreds, who know and feel that to his care and patience, to his skill and courage, to his faith and spiritual insight, they owe all that is most precious in life, and most certain to uphold them in the hour of death;

> and their sympathies and prayers are shared by many others who are absent from us in body, but present with us in spirit. Certainly, if past experience is any guarantee of what is to come, if there be such a thing as continuity of spiritual character and purpose, then we may hope to witness an episcopate which ... will rank hereafter with those which in point of moral beauty stand highest on the roll of the later English Church—with Andrewes, with Ken, with Wilson, with Hamilton.[33]

But it was the earlier part of the sermon which would not have been well received by Bickersteth's supporters. Benson, reflecting with characteristic detail on the service in St Paul's, wrote in his diary that 'Canon Liddon preached a Manifesto concerning the power and authority of the Episcopate, and condemning vehemently all "Modernisms," not only the Courts but more specifically and provocatively, the Public Worship Regulation Act.'

Yet, as Chadwick comments, 'To preach such a sermon before so mixed a congregation was from one point of view a courageous act of prophecy, and yet from another point of view a failure of tact,'[34] which could only have served to reaffirm Davidson's view that Liddon was not suited to be a bishop. Indeed, Benson wrote in his diary later in the day how a sense had come over him that King's bishopric held 'perils.'[35]

The Public Worship Regulation Act of 1874, which the Church Association was all too ready to invoke, had already led to the persecution and, indeed, the imprisoning of clergymen for High Church practices. Only a few years hence, it would be invoked against King himself. In that same diary entry, with the same characteristic eye for detail, Benson also commented that 'fewer persons than usual, in proportion, communicated. This is owing to the growth of "Fasting Communion" as a necessity and not as a pious practice.' This 'has taken root among the followers of the holy and influential Canon King.'[36]

In the afternoon, following the long service of consecration in the morning, nearly a hundred-and-fifty clergy, former students of King at Cuddesdon, gathered in the Chapter House of St Paul's and presented gifts to the new bishop. The Bishop of Newcastle, who was to have made the presentation, had been obliged to return immediately after the service, and in his stead the Revd F. J. Ponsonby of St Mary Magdalene, Munster Square, and the Revd T. B. Dover, Vicar of St Agnes, Kennington, presented the gifts — a chalice and paten in silver gilt, together with stoles, chalice-veils, altar-linens, and an altar book, for use in his private chapel.

Responding to the address and expressing his gratitude, the new bishop apologized that he could not offer 'a polished or formal response' for the generosity and the gracious words accompanying the gifts, owing to the 'burden which the long service' had laid upon him.

'At Cuddesdon,' he continued, 'you know, we never thought of being bishops. We didn't care for position or rank. Two things we did care for — the possession of the full counsel of God, and liberty to teach it in every way.' As King went on to reflect briefly with his former students, he sought to recapture something of the life-changing *experience* which the Cuddesdon years had retained in his heart, and similarly in theirs. It had been the community life which had given such 'a wonderful power of expansion, as the love of God and man proved, as a rule of life ... So we were brought to love God, and one another in God in a real and special way, not understood by people unless they themselves knew what it was to be thus free.' That was the formula for King's incredible influence which was to give such power to his ministry as a bishop over the next twenty-five years.

He also reflected about the time when he left Cuddesdon to be Professor of Pastoral theology, and how overwhelmed he had been by the challenge of Oxford as a place of learning, with its intellectual challenges to faith. But 'God has given me not to be shaken from faith. It has been an advantage to learn and sift things. It has made faith stronger: I am very thankful for it ... For we are not the discoverers, but witnesses to the truth.'

Before finishing, King added, with a touch of characteristic humour and humility: 'It is quite delightful to look forward to being a big curate in the diocese of Lincoln, and getting back to parish work again—ministering more simply and directly to the needs of the poor.'

Referring to the gifts which he had just received, he said in conclusion: 'I ask you to believe that I thank God for this fresh evidence of the sincerity of your love ... and I trust through your prayers not to be unfaithful to the spirit and intention in which you have given these special vessels for the service of God.'[37]

ENHRONEMENT

'The county of Lincolnshire is, my dear, flat: flat, certainly, but not without an effectiveness of its own. But Lincoln Hill is certainly most grand. And Lincoln Cathedral (with its long ridge super-cathedrically long, and its three towers, which are proportioned to one another and the ridge in a very perfect way, regarding it merely in block) is most grandest.'[38] Thus E. W. Benson wrote to his wife in March 1869, when he was acting as chaplain to Bishop Wordsworth on the occasion of the latter's enthronement as Bishop of Lincoln.

'Grandest,' indeed, standing magisterially on the top of the hill, the great Cathedral at Lincoln dominates the skyline, overshadowing the city below. Few can doubt that architecturally it is one of the foremost cathedrals in the whole of Europe. On Wednesday, 19 May 1885, Edward King, the sixtieth Bishop of Lincoln, arrived at the West Door as 'the Chapter came down the Nave to meet him, headed by the [Sub-] Dean,' in just the same way as Benson described the arrival of Bishop Wordsworth for his enthronement sixteen years before.[39] 'More than ordinary interest was attached to the ceremony,' noted the local newspaper. 'His Lordship was vested in his superb episcopal habit.'[40]

Prior to the service in the Cathedral, the Mayor and Corporation of the City presented an address to the Bishop, welcoming him on behalf of the citizens of Lincoln. In his reply, King thanked the members of the Corporation, and the City Magistrates who had accompanied them, for their warm welcome to the city and the county, making it quite clear that, in coming as their new bishop, he wished to live and work among them, not only for the sake of the diocese, but also for the welfare of the city in general.

The service of enthronement which followed in the packed Cathedral, was attended by far greater numbers than had been the case for King's predecessor. From the West Door, King moved in solemn procession through the nave as the choir sang the *Te Deum* (in the setting by Young in G). On reaching the Angel Choir, as it is known in Lincoln, with its large and impressive Bishop's throne on the south-east side, King first knelt in silent, private prayer before the altar in accordance with the ancient rubric which speaks of the bishop prostrating himself before the altar, before proceeding to the throne.

Immediately after the enthronement King celebrated the Eucharist for the first time in his Cathedral. It had not been traditional for the Eucharist to be celebrated at enthronements: Bishop Wordsworth initiated the practice, followed by King and every Bishop of Lincoln since. Evidently the influence of the Tractarian and High Church movements was beginning to take hold, even in cathedrals.

After the Creed, King delivered his address, not from the pulpit, but from the chancel steps. By modern standards, it was over-long, though by the standards of the time might have been regarded as shorter than expected for such an occasion. Yet, as was to prove so characteristic in the years which followed, always it was the personality behind the

The Choice of a Bishop for Lincoln

words, which gave the words the power and authenticity of effective 'gospel' communication. In many ways it was an improvisation on all the well-tested themes of his earlier ministry—the Gospel of reconciliation.

The objective and structure of King's sermon come through clearly and simply, even in a précis. Words and phrases that soon became familiar throughout the diocese made their first appearance here:

> It is the great work of God to bring man back again to himself, and into loving communion with his fellow men. This is the work at which our Saviour tells us his Father worked hitherto, and he worked.
>
> It is our great privilege, yours and mine, to share in this work of reconciliation, so that in God, man may find that fullness of rest which apart from him, he cannot find—rest of mind in knowing the truth, rest of the heart in coming nearer to the personal God in knowledge and love.
>
> This is the objective of the Christian ministry, and one chief object of my unworthy presence before you here today. It is to continue for you in this ancient diocese the work of reconciliation. And you my dear brothers in Christ are to share with me the burden of the cure of souls in this great diocese.
>
> This you know is the characteristic of our common ministry. It is to keep the flock in union with Christ. It is to go after the wanderers as they wander, and seek them out, and not to cease seeking until we find, and finding not to complain nor accuse, but to lift up and to carry and to bring back joyfully, rejoicing, knowing that the angels in heaven rejoice when one sinner turns back to God to repent.

And then a word to the laity:

> And to you, my dear brethren of the laity, let me beg of you not to think that this work of reconciliation is ours only of the clergy, but let it be that we all remember that the Body is one, though the members may have different work to do. The end of your life, brothers and sisters

> in Christ of the laity, if it is to be in harmony with the great work of God, must be the same as ours—to bring back all that are wandering nearer and nearer to God. Join with us ... Let the clergy and laity work in this great work which Heaven is so interested in above all other works—bringing man back to God. ... We must all be earnest in prayer. Let me ask your prayers for the clergy and for this Diocese, and let me beg of you to pray for me that I may have wisdom from God to guide those committed to my care ... And may my enthronement in your midst today, which your presence and kindness have made so magnificent, be a symbol not of mere worldly splendour nor of mere ecclesiastical authority, but rather the enthronement of that peace which, by the grace of God, should reign and rule in the heart of every member of Christ.[41]

The content of such a sermon would have little or no place in today's Church, not because of what it said—albeit so eloquently and with such sincerity—but because of what was not said: no mention of relations with Christians of other churches, let alone of other faiths, as would be *de rigueur* in our day. No mention of the place of the Church in wider society, although King had met earlier with the civic leaders when he had words of encouragement and co-operation for them. His sermon was essentially the Church talking to the Church, emphasizing the priority of reconciliation with a call and summons to personal spiritual renewal for clergy and laity alike.

But here is another example of how we must not read back into history the perspectives of contemporary culture. One might even say that bishops who still have an opportunity to speak to larger and more diverse constituencies do not talk enough about God and the Gospel, preferring rather to rush to the practical applications of faith in everyday life, often appearing to bypass the foundations on which Christian faith and practice are based. Application, however attractively communicated by the messenger, presupposes

The Choice of a Bishop for Lincoln

rudimentary information. Yet the power of King's enthronement sermon, as in all his preaching, lay in the fact that the messenger clearly embodied the message.

Commenting on this, King's first sermon in the diocese, a priest who was present wrote of the great impact it had made:

> Sentence after sentence, fresh and crisp and clear-cut and appealing, spoken in quietness and simplicity and without any apparent effort, came home to everyone in the congregation. There was the simple and fearless expression of his own mind and experience, intensely personal and yet without the slightest trace of self-assertion ... It was all perfectly and entirely natural — his gratitude, his trust, his joy and aspiration, his refreshment, his plans for the future, his hope that many of his hearers who lived at a distance would share his hospitality and the refreshment of the cathedral, his sense of divergent thoughts which might exist but which must never make separations, his trust and reliance on their prayers. Everyone was drawn to him.'[42]

In the afternoon, an Address of Welcome, signed by four-hundred-and-seventy-nine clergy of the diocese, was presented to King by the Suffragan Bishop of Nottingham, Edward Trollope (who remained suffragan to Lincoln after the Nottingham diocese was transferred to Southwell), supported by the two Proctors of Convocation.

After thanking the clergy for their kindly worded address, King spoke wisely and sincerely of his predecessor Bishop Wordsworth, as he was frequently to do in the early years: 'the example and teaching of him whom not only this diocese, but all true English Churchmen everywhere, revere and love, my great predecessor, in whose well-marked footsteps it will be my great desire to tread.'

Then, there were some unexpected words from their new bishop, a man of the Tractarian tradition which valued reserve and under-statement and tended to keep references to personal experience and the inner life to a minimum — in stark contrast to our own age in which nothing is too intimate or personal to be paraded in public.

'I am not very old yet in years,' he said, 'but I have known enough of bodily and mental suffering, both in myself and in others, to be separated, I trust, for ever from the allurements and ambitions of the world. My only reason for coming among you is to do God's will and to help others to find out the will of God as it is made known to us in Christ and by Christ in His church.'

And then the old familiar core of gospel ministry as practised throughout the years of his previous ministry, and which was to be reiterated both in words and actions throughout the next twenty-five years: all that, so 'that in Christ we may all draw nearer to God and to each other.' In his concluding words to the clergy, aware that many of them would find his churchmanship and teaching unpalatable, King said: 'Let me beg of you to give me forbearance and patience in your judgement of my words and actions, even when we agree; and, when we differ, at least to give me credit for disinterested sincerity.'[43]

There are few things more calculated to win over others of differing opinions and outlook than to share with them one's own vulnerability, as King did on that formative and important initial encounter with the diocesan clergy, whose confidence and trust he would need in order to be an effective bishop.

Notes

1. Liddon's description quoted in Russell, George W. E., *Edward King Sixtieth Bishop of Lincoln*, p. 104.
2. A. N. Wilson, *Victoria*. London: Atlantic Books, 2014, p. 5.
3. *Ibid.*, p. 407.
4. Gladstone Papers, British Library, Add. MS 44,109, fo. 113.
5. Owen Chadwick, *Edward King, Bishop of Lincoln, 1885–1910*, p. 13.
6. G. K. A. Bell, *Randall Davidson Archbishop of Canterbury*. Oxford University Press, 1938, p. 174.

7   *Ibid.*, p. 175.
8   Chadwick, *op. cit.*, p. 13.
9   Russell, *op. cit.*, p. 86.
10 British Library, Add. MS 44,489, fos 153–4.
11 Edward King, *Spiritual Letters*, Letter XCIV.
12 Randolph and Townroe, *The Mind and Work of Bishop King*, p. 97.
13 Russell, *op. cit.*, p. 87.
14 *Ibid.*, p. 88.
15 John Newton, *Search for a Saint*, p. 74.
16 Russell, *op. cit.*, p. 90.
17 *Ibid.*, p. 87.
18 *Ibid.*, p. 93.
19 G. L. Prestige, *The Life of Charles Gore: A Great Englishman*. London: William Heinemann Ltd, 1935, p. 76.
20 Russell, *op. cit.*, pp. 92–3.
21 *Ibid.*, pp. 90–4.
22 *Ibid.*, p. 99.
23 *Ibid.*
24 *Ibid.*, p. 100.
25 *Ibid.*, p. 102.
26 Chadwick, *op. cit.*, p. 17.
27 *Ibid.*, p. 14.
28 Russell, *op. cit.*, p. 103.
29 Chadwick, *op. cit.*, p. 14.
30 A. C. Benson, *The Life of Edward White Benson*, vol. II, p. 55.
31 Randolph and Townroe, *op. cit.*, p. 101.
32 Chadwick, *op. cit.*, p. 15.
33 H. P. Liddon, *Clerical Life and Work*, pp. 308–9.
34 Chadwick, *op. cit.*, p. 15.
35 Trinity College, Cambridge, E. W. Benson's diary, entry for 25 April 1885.
36 Benson, *op. cit.*, vol. II, p. 55.
37 Russell, *op. cit.*, pp. 107–9.
38 Benson, *op. cit.*, vol. I, p. 262.
39 *Ibid.*
40 *The Lincolnshire Chronicle*, 22 May 1885, p. 8.
41 *Ibid.*
42 Randolph and Townroe, *op. cit.*, p. 106.
43 *Ibid.*, pp. 108–9.

✢ 11 ✢

Lincoln: The Early Years

UPROOTING AND TRANSPLANTING

'I go to this new work with mingled feelings,'[1] King had written to Dr Heurtley, his close friend and Lady Margaret Professor of Divinity, and not surprisingly. At that time the Lincoln Diocese was the largest in the Church of England, with far-flung parishes and villages, and a far cry from the intimate, if at times claustrophobic, academic and collegiate life of Oxford. Contrasting the life of an Oxford professor with that of a bishop in Lincolnshire, one who knew King well in the early days of his episcopate refers to 'the smaller world'—the Lincolnshire world—that was to be King's first care. 'It was,' he writes, 'so different from the surroundings of the past twenty years, so much simpler in a way, and yet with its own complex problems and manifold interests.'[2]

King was only in his fifty-sixth year when he went to Lincoln but looked a good deal older—as he had done when he went up to Oxford as an undergraduate. He walked with a stoop, his head bowed, but that was a physical habit, for he was still vigorous and active with remarkable reserves of energy. It had been recorded that, 'when first [at his enthronement] they saw his spare form and bent shoulders, there were those of his flock who "reckoned" that our new Bishop, "poor 'owd man, didn't look like being long for this world."'[3] Probably neither King himself, nor many of those who met him on his arrival, would have supposed that his episcopate would stretch into the next century. At that time men and women did not covet keeping up contradictory appearances of youth, as the celebrity culture of the twenty-first century so avidly does. On the contrary, as is still the case in Eastern cultures, the old were revered for their experience and wisdom. To bishops, or indeed to any of the professions in the nineteenth century, the idea of universal, mandatory retirement at seventy would have appeared absurd, especially while good health and energy prevailed.

A long-standing friend, George W. E. Russell, whose biography of King (a rather undiscerning hagiography), was published just two years after his death, gives a vivid portrait of the newly consecrated bishop as he would have appeared on his arrival in the diocese. 'His hair was still abundant and only slightly grey, and from under his strongly marked eyebrows there looked out a pair of the keenest eyes that ever probed a character or read a situation. The features were of delicate refinement; but the mouth closed firmly, and the chin was well developed' — his 'well developed' chin was a feature to which King himself often referred.

> The voice was almost ladylike in its gentleness, and the whole face was, from time to time, suffused by a smile which lit it up, as a ray of sunshine lights a quiet landscape. That smile was the outward token of the inner life. He held that, in Liddon's phrase, 'light-heartedness is at once the right and duty of a redeemed Christian whose conscience is in fairly good order,' and he lived from hour to hour in the realized Peace of God.[4]

From the outset, King was determined to be the Bishop for his Diocese, devoting all his time and energy in and around his distant rural parishes. That may not have been so much from virtue as from his nature and the way he had worked and lived all his life within small communities, sheltered since a boy from much of the cut and thrust of politics, and the emerging industrial strife of city life.

King's life was never London-centred, as were the lives of most bishops, many of whom had a London home in addition to their official residence in the diocese. That was never going to be characteristic of King's lifestyle as a bishop. He strove to attend as faithfully as possible the meetings of Convocation, but the evidence seems to suggest that he seldom spoke and certainly that he made no attempt to contribute to debates in the House of Lords. It seems he even shunned large public meetings or Church Congresses, at which his attendance might have been expected, because he was reluctant to accept any invitations which, as he would say, took him away from his diocese: the shepherd's prime concern must always be the flock.

Nevertheless, he would need a place to lay his head in London, however infrequently. To that end, on 7 February 1887, his name was entered into the Candidates' Book (No:7953), for election as a member of the Athenaeum in Pall Mall—at that time, very much 'the Bishops' Club.' His proposers were two great friends, the Bishops of Lichfield and Winchester, respectively George Selwyn and Harold Browne.

THE OLD PALACE: A NEW HOME

From the outset, King was concerned about the wisdom of living in the bishop's very large official residence at Riseholme, some three miles from the city, where his three predecessors, Bishops Kaye, Jackson and Wordsworth, had lived (and where, incidentally, King's critic, Archdeacon Kaye, was the firmly entrenched rector of the parish). As early as February 1885, the *Lincolnshire Chronicle*, had published a letter asking whether the new bishop 'might consider the expediency of transferring the episcopal residence from Riseholme to Lincoln.' Two months later, the paper reported:

> Dr King, the Bishop-Elect of Lincoln, has, it is said, expressed his intention of selling, if possible, the Episcopal Palace of Riseholme, and building a suitable residence for himself and his successors on the site of

> the Old Palace under the shadow of the Cathedral. For the present the new Bishop will reside in the city of Lincoln.⁵

Though this is essentially what eventually happened, the paper had 'jumped the gun' for King had not yet made up his mind.

Two months before arriving in Lincoln he had written of his concerns on just this point:

> Just now, my immediate difficulty is where to live — Riseholme, with my widowed sister and all the children, or Lincoln alone. The second seems right if I can, if the Ecclesiastical Commissioners will let me sell Riseholme; but in my heart I cling to my sister and the children. However, by God's help, I hope to give myself first to the Diocese, and, if I can, live at Lincoln.⁶

King's widowed sister was Mary Wilgress, whose husband, the Revd Frederick George Wilgress, Rector of Cudmore in Buckinghamshire and a former Lecturer in Hebrew at Cuddesdon, had died in 1878, leaving Mary to bring up seven children all aged under twelve.⁷ The eldest son, Fred, was later ordained and became one of his uncle's chaplains.

As Riseholme had been acquired by the Ecclesiastical Commissioners only as recently as 1841, no historical associations would be violated if King were to move his residence back into the city. (For John Kaye, the first Bishop to live at Riseholme, the existing house had been enlarged on a grand scale by William Railton, the architect of Nelson's Column in Trafalgar Square.)

Independently of King's own reservations, the question of the bishop's residence had been raised by Canon Edmund Venables, a member of the Lincoln Chapter, in a private letter to Gladstone:

> I question much whether it will be wise for the new bishop to attempt to keep up Riseholme. It is an enormously expensive place, three miles away from the Cathedral and lacking a station. Happily, the Old

Lincoln: The Early Years

Palace, where Bishop Wordsworth was most anxious to live, still belongs to the See, and a good house could be built there, with the proceeds of the sale of Riseholme. I feel sure our new bishop will want to identify himself with the Cathedral, which he cannot well do three miles away. Besides, it removes complications (which have been very real and not a little trying during the late episcopate) for the bishop to be extra-parochial, which he would be at the Old Palace, consecrated by the memories of St Hugh and Grosseteste.[8]

Gladstone, something of a micro-manager with an obsession for recording little details, added a note to Venables' letter: 'Will take the liberty of sending to Dr King the extract about Riseholme.' On receiving Gladstone's 'clip' from Venables' letter, King replied to Gladstone's secretary: 'Will you kindly thank Mr Gladstone. At present I feel unable to decide. My inclination is to carry on at Riseholme, if I can afford it, as I think it would be pleasanter for the country clergy to come and rest quietly there, rather than in a town.'[9] On the other hand, he was also aware of possible financial disincentives for the less well-off rural clergy wanting to visit their bishop: 'It wasn't every poor parson who had half-a-crown for a cab out to Riseholme.'[10]

In the end convenience of location prevailed and King settled for what was to all intents an entirely new house built on part of the Old Palace site, and paid for from the sale of Riseholme, which had been allowed under an Order in Council of 12 August 1885. The Old Palace at Lincoln, where the medieval bishops had lived, was situated below and a little to the south of the Cathedral, with fine views over the City. It was in a ruinous state, and had been used as a quarry for stone to repair the Cathedral in the eighteenth century.[11] The site selected for King's new residence lay slightly west of the medieval ruins. Designed by the architect Ewan Christian, it was in the Tudor style and incorporated, on its west side, an existing, probably eighteenth-century house. Christian included large bay-windows along the south front from where the Bishop could enjoy the prospect over the city. This building, known as the Old Palace in King's time, is now called Edward King House.

The private chapel, though linked to King's new residence, was created in a separate building to the east, which had been the solar range of the great hall of the medieval palace, and by a different architect. Archbishop Benson, visiting Lincoln to consecrate the extension of St Peter-at-Gowts on 3 December 1887, saw the new chapel while work on it was still in progress and wrote in his diary:

> The new chapel at the Palace is rather striking. It ought to be, considering that it is the destruction of the old pantry and buttery, and that the ancient bishop's solar, an almost unique one for glory, now forms the clerestory of the chapel. But anything can be forgiven to this bishop, so sweet and so manly.[12]

The architect here was George Frederick Bodley, whom King would probably have known from his time at Oxford, where Bodley had designed a new reredos for the Cathedral. The furnishings and decoration were undertaken by members of the English Church Union, with the assistance and financial generosity of Viscount Halifax. King finally consecrated the chapel, which was dedicated to St Hugh, on 3 October 1888. Its creation by Bodley was 'surely intended to emphasize the pre-Reformation identity of [the bishop's] office,' comments the author of a major study of the architect's work: 'by its legible incorporation of medieval fabric into a modern interior, the chapel embodies with haunting intensity the High Church understanding of Anglicanism.'[13] To make that point clear, at the chapel's consecration, King's former Christ Church neighbour, Professor William Bright, delivered a short address on the continuity of the English Church.[14] Once completed, the chapel was in regular use for the recitation of the Daily Offices: it was where, together with his household, King prayed, and where the Eucharist, which had always been central to his spirituality, was daily celebrated.

Lincoln: The Early Years

SETTLING IN

King's new home was not ready for him to occupy until 1887—and it was a further year before the chapel was finished. While the work was in progress he had lived at Hilton House, a rented property in Union Road, to the west of the Castle, where he daily celebrated the Eucharist on a little portable altar which had formerly belonged to Pusey.[15]

Close to the Cathedral, which he came to love, King's new home afforded him a centre and focus for his personal ministry and pastorate, a workplace, and a venue for his warm and extended hospitality. It became an invaluable asset and tool in his pastoral ministry; a place where the bishop was readily accessible to his clergy and his flock. Not for nothing were the words *Pascite gregrem* ('Tend the flock') inscribed above the entrance.

A priest who knew him well describes what a visit to see his bishop felt like when he was received warmly in the bishop's study. 'It really was a home room; it was always a happiness to find the bishop there as he rose from his chair to meet you. It all fitted in, so to speak—the purple cassock, the pectoral cross, the friendly look, the bright word of welcome, the warm grasp of the hand. There might have been nothing else that mattered but you and what you had come for; and really for the time there was not.' It was a home, and not a business or committee room.[16]

So, working from home, as King chose to do, contrasts sharply with the practice of many bishops today who tend to work out of diocesan offices, and this at a time when many in secular employment are choosing to revert to home working, aided as we are by the flexibility of location enabled by modern technology.

'Bishops should have one wife and be given to hospitality,' urged St Paul: King lacked the former but excelled at the latter. Since his earliest days, growing up in his father's large house at Stone, he would have been accustomed to having a household of indoor servants—the census of 1841 lists six. Bishops' establishments were certainly no less well staffed: in 1861 Bishop Wigram of Rochester employed twelve indoor servants at the Palace in Danbury.[17] King's own requirements at Lincoln were a little more modest: at the time of both the 1891 and 1901 censuses the domestic staff at the Old Palace numbered eight, including two footmen. Aided by his staff, King became well known for his generous and extensive hospitality, which in those days would have been paid for out of his own pocket.

Yet, despite the difficulties facing him at the outset, it seems he got off to a good start—if the words of a fellow bishop carry any weight. A little over six months after arriving in Lincoln, King received a letter from the Bishop of Rochester, Anthony Thorold, 'an Evangelical of the Evangelicals' and a 'cadet of a great and notable Lincolnshire family.' In it, Thorold pays an extraordinary and delightful tribute to the new bishop:

> May I venture to say with what deep and grateful interest I read of your doings in my native county? My feeling, when I heard of your succeeding to the great Eastern See, was that the Master had for you the blessed and hard task of lifting up before the hearts of the clergy a new ideal of duty and holiness. As God conquers us by love, we must conquer each other. The welcome that the Lincolnshire folk are giving you seems to show that you have won in six months what some do not win in as many years.[18]

THE HIGH CHURCH BISHOP

From the outset, King became known as the bishop with a mitre—indeed, he is reputed to have been the first bishop to wear a mitre since the Reformation. (Throughout the eighteenth-century bishops, like judges, had worn wigs, a practice which lasted until the middle of the nineteenth century. One of King's predecessors, the episcopal statesman, John Kaye, was the last Bishop of Lincoln to wear a wig.) 'Hitherto, bishops had mitres on their spoons, their [coat-of-arms], their writing paper, their carriage doors, their coffins. But never since the Reformation had a bishop of the Church of England worn a mitre upon his head.'[19] A mitred bishop would signify a return to the prince bishops of the Middle Ages, and in the nineteenth century the only acceptable place for a mitred bishop was, and perhaps still is in certain quarters, on a chess-board.

How we dress can be a statement both of intent and identity, and a change of dress can signal a change of image and identity. Such perhaps was the decline in the wearing of gaiters after bishops and archdeacons ceased travelling round their dioceses on horseback. (Geoffrey Fisher was conspicuous for being the last Archbishop of Canterbury to prefer gaiters and Court dress for formal occasions: his successor, Archbishop Ramsey, opted instead for the more modest cassock which he wore consistently at formal dinners, royal occasions, garden parties and parish occasions alike, as have archbishops and bishops ever since.)

King usually wore his cope and mitre when officiating at services in his diocese, though never without the full concurrence of the incumbent of the parish. There were some, very few, who did not welcome this revival of the ancient insignia of a bishop's office.[20] Most bishops at the time, would have worn in church what they wore in the House of Lords, namely, Convocation robes and choir dress of rochet with white lawn sleeves and red or black chimere. The early Tractarians were very modest about their attire in church, usually wearing cassock, surplice and hood, even for the celebration of Holy Communion—'What is a cope?' Pusey was once reputed to have asked. King's practice from the outset was to wear whatever liturgical dress a particular parish was accustomed to and most comfortable with, this being what one twentieth-century bishop used to speak of as 'good episcopal table manners,' deferring to the wishes of your host. By and large, King was sensitive in that way, only wearing his mitre when and where he knew it would be welcome and not cause offence.

However, from the first day in his Cathedral, King chose to wear cope and mitre, which most certainly would not have gone unnoticed, nor necessarily have met with universal approval, at least at the outset of his episcopate. An even greater *occasion de choc* occurred the following year on Trinity Sunday, 20 June, King's second Trinity-tide Ordination service in the Cathedral, when he ordained twelve deacons and eight priests. The *Lincoln Diocesan Magazine* observed without comment that 'the Bishop wore a cope and a jewelled mitre lately presented to the See of Lincoln.'[21] There was nothing understated about that mitre, which still exists as one of the Cathedral's proud possessions, though seldom if ever worn.

With true episcopal courtesy, whenever he went to notably High Churches he would try to conform to their liturgical and even ritualistic customs, although he himself had not been especially schooled in all the intricacies of Anglo-Catholic ritual. In a letter to James Dawson, a very High Church young curate at Roath, who had asked King if he might act as his chaplain at some forthcoming solemn occasion, King writes: 'By all means be my Chaplain on the 22nd, and save me from scandalizing all the little acolytes by not bowing and bending as they would wish!'[22]

In this regard, as perhaps in others, there was in King 'an absence of worldly wisdom. He had lived a sheltered life, had no idea of the pressures of public life, and did not well understand the need for compromise. He was at once notorious as a high church bishop, and in the prevailing atmosphere might perhaps have taken care not to look too high church.' But, concludes Chadwick 'that was not his way.'[23]

Lincoln: The Early Years

Not long after arriving in Lincoln, King made a pastoral visit to Wrawby, in the north of the county, and on that occasion he wore the full 'fig'—the Bishop was 'vested in white rochet, white stole, cope and mitre,' reported the local paper.[24] (This was probably out of courtesy to the Rector, Canon West, because when, on the day after, King celebrated the Eucharist, he wore what the same paper calls 'the vestments customary at this church.') A local photographer, Thomas Smith from nearby Brigg, was permitted to take a photograph of King with the clergy who had gathered for his visit. It had been a hot August day, and King appears in the picture 'looking dusky and glum, surrounded by clergymen looking high church.'[25] The photographer subsequently sold the negative to a shop in The Strand which regularly displayed 'celebrities' in its window: King was clearly something of a *coup*. The Church Association, always on the lookout for this sort of thing, obtained the negative and a pamphlet entitled *A Sketch of the Life of Bishop King* subsequently appeared under the name of J. Hanchard with the photograph of King as the frontispiece, and below it 'a versicle about Priestcraft stalking through the land.'

> By his continued connection with the English Church Union, [the pamphlet read] we have the link which connects him with the Ultra-Ritualistic faction. From the approbation his Lordship has bestowed upon persistent lawbreakers, we cannot feel any confidence that he will exercise his authority to stem the tide of unreasoning sacerdotalism. By the work he maintained at Cuddesdon; by his apparently sincere regard for Romish playthings; by the display of gaudy gem-gaws at his enthronement; and by his self-conscious vanity in sitting to be 'taken' for the admiration of 'the faithful' without even having sacrificed his whiskers to the Catholic razor, he is unquestionably assisting in 'digging the grave of the Establishment.'

To add further insult to injury, the pamphlet was circulated to all the parishes of the Lincoln Diocese. King, writing in his *Lincoln Diocesan Magazine* with a light touch of humour probably not fully appreciated by many of his clergy in those early days, sought to brush it off, modestly describing himself as having been 'a little bespattered with printer's ink' and thereby having 'lost something of the gloss of novelty.'[26] Such an occasion, together with such adverse publicity in those early years, would eventually add fuel to the fire which, only a matter of three or four years later, would blaze up into the huge controversy and trial of the Lincoln Judgment.

There were also some other rumblings in the diocese which did not help King during his episcopal novitiate. After leaving Oxford and the 'warmth' of his personal life there, it is understandable that King, unmarried and living without family, tended to seek out close friends, and in particular clerical friends of the same outlook and churchmanship. This led to complaints that he had begun surrounding himself with High Church clergy. In those early days, he had living with him as his chaplain B. W. Randolph, who was a devotee, close friend and disciple. In his later years, he had his quiet, shy nephew, Fred Wilgress, as his chaplain. Furthermore, there was the question of his choice of examining chaplains, and again, at least in the early days, he had tended to appoint notable High Churchmen like Charles Gore, a founding member of the Mirfield Community, and William Bright, who was to be a frequent contributor to the *Lincoln Diocesan Magazine*, which King had started in 1886 and the first of its kind in the Church of England—the first issue was entitled *Diocesan Gazette*. It was an excellent initiative, but did leave King open to accusations that he used it to propagate his own, High Church views.

THE BISHOP, THE CATHEDRAL AND THE NEW DEAN

At the time of King's appointment to Lincoln, the Dean was the Revd Dr Joseph Williams Blakesley, who died only a few

Lincoln: The Early Years

weeks later, in April 1885. 'He belonged,' according to his obituary in the *Lincolnshire Chronicle*,

> to the old-fashioned type of scholarly divines which is now fast disappearing ... Since his appointment as Dean of Lincoln in 1872 he has ... been very little before the public in any way. He has been content to lead a life of studious retirement, unembittered by controversy, and sweetened by the intercourse of old and valued friends. He was a well-known member of the Athenaeum Club, in whose welfare he took a keen interest ... His life was not an eventful one, but it was useful, dignified, and exemplary, and it illustrates some of the best features of English society in a generation now fast giving place to its successors.[27]

Who was to be that successor, not only for the new and emerging generation but also for the new episcopate? The *Lincolnshire Chronicle* was hot on the case, circulating all kinds of rumours. The edition of 15 May picked up an item from the periodical *Truth* that 'the "fat" Deanery of Lincoln has been offered to Canon Rowsell, which appointment would be universally approved; but he is not disposed to quite his stall at Westminster.' The following week the paper reprinted an item from the *World*:

> It was positively stated at Oxford last week that Mr Wordsworth, one of the Divinity professors and Canon of Rochester had been appointed Dean of Lincoln. He is son, and was chaplain, to the late Bishop. In London clerical circles, however, Archdeacon Farrar has been favourite all along for this extremely desirable 'little bit of preferment.'

Both rumours proved to be unfounded.[28]

The appointment of deans, like that of bishops and certain other Royal Peculiar appointments (as they were and still are termed), also lay with the Prime Minister, who made recommendations to the Queen, although, since deans did not sit in the House of Lords, their appointments tended to be far less politically contentious. Initially, Gladstone wanted to offer 'the fat Deanery,' of Lincoln to his son-in-law, Edward Charles Wickham, a man of a quite different churchmanship from King, but was dissuaded from doing so by his political advisers, who thought 'it would be a bad mark to his tottering Government.'[29]

A second possibility was Professor Westcott, the Cambridge biblical scholar, who refused it. Gladstone's third choice, an Oxford Professor, Edwin Palmer, also turned him down. Always so painstakingly conscientious with such appointments, Gladstone's preference had been for a scholar, such as Blakesley had been, but fourth time around he looked for a man with parish and liturgical experience, who would work together with a team of canons, opening up the Cathedral to become, in practice, as well as title, the mother church of the diocese.

In the event, the new Dean was William John Butler, who during his comparatively short time in the post not only filled the bill, but also became a particularly congenial colleague, working in tandem with King in ways that Blakesley would never have done. From the outset, Butler and King were to mark a break with the old order which had preferred academic clergy for the posts of Dean and Bishop. Neither was primarily an academic, rather they were practitioners of pastoral ministry, exercised liturgically through Word and Sacrament.

Butler had been a distinguished Vicar of Wantage and a notable and fervent adherent to the theological and ecclesiastical principles of the Oxford Movement. Furthermore, he had known King for many years, and on hearing of his episcopal appointment in February 1885, wrote expressing unrestrained delight:

> Yes, it is very wonderful [he wrote, reminiscing back over the years of their long friendship], I think of you—first, walking with dear old Harvey and me along the road to our little hamlet of Charlton; then at Wheatley, working

among the very rough lads of that somewhat old-world place; then at Cuddesdon, after the great explosion of 1858; and then, under the Grace of God, widening and developing, from strength to strength, till you became what you are. And now you go on to be a chief ruler in the Church of Christ ... It will be something to have at length what I have ever longed for—a Bishop in whose Chapel the Blessed Sacrament will be daily celebrated. How bishops can live without that, I cannot conceive. Oh, what a task lies before you! Earnestly I pray that, as the day, so your strength may be.[30]

Butler's words must have rejoiced King's heart, though he would certainly not have seen himself as 'a chief ruler in the Church of Christ' so much as a humbler, chief shepherd and pastor of Christ's flock committed to his care. What, of course, neither of them then knew was that within only a few weeks Butler himself would be appointed Dean of Lincoln, and installed in the Cathedral on 15 July, less than two months after King's enthronement in May. In the coming years, these two High Churchmen were to form a remarkably creative partnership, both in the city and in the diocese at large. As soon as King heard the news of Butler's appointment, he wrote, on 14 June, to thank the Prime Minister.

My dear Mr Gladstone,
I am unwilling to trouble you with a letter, even tho' it needs no answer, but I feel that I ought, on behalf of the Diocese, to offer you my grateful thanks for sending us such a Dean. I think Canon Butler will be a great help in Diocesan work, and so make the Cathedral and Chapter a real part of the Diocese.

He continued with words that show, even at this very early stage in his episcopate, how sensitively he had already grasped the plight of his many clergy, underpaid and somewhat isolated in small villages throughout his large diocese.

The clergy suffer so much from isolation, and need some irradiating, vivifying, unifying power to enable them to realise the greatness and the oneness of their work, which often seems to them so separate and so small that they lose heart. Canon Butler will, I am sure, with God's help, help us to make Lincoln a living centre.

He concludes with telling words which expressed his own prospective aspirations for his future work as bishop in the diocese.

> You will, I know, be glad to hear that everybody has been most kind to me, and, when I get more among the people, I think I shall love them, very much, and I hope, by God's help, enable them to see a little more what they are, and what they might be.[31]

Do we dismiss such words and aspirations from a bishop as being merely sentimental, long out-dated and unrealistic in today's Church and world? Of course, so much has changed in the Church and indeed in society in our day, nevertheless the charge given by Christ to Peter to feed his sheep and his lambs with the love of the chief Shepherd, mediated through both the office and person of the bishop, is surely still the unchanging and abiding mandate for all chief pastors in every age. Administrative efficiency and strongly envisioned leadership in any organization are highly desirable, but the Church of God is, or should be, so very much more than a mere organization: it is intended to be a living organism, the Body of Christ in which the headship and leadership need to be conspicuously perceived and experienced primarily as pastoral, empowered by the Holy Spirit of love and expressed in loving service to the members of the Body, clergy and people alike.

Gladstone's appointment of two such like-minded churchmen as Bishop and Dean of Lincoln was to prove extraordinarily beneficial to the City, the Cathedral and the Diocese. Cathedral statutes vary enormously, and deans tend to be jealous of their rights, powers and privileges, not least in respect of their relationship with their bishop, with whom frequently they disagree, and Lincoln has had a fair share of bishops and deans at odds with each other. In popular and local tradition, the Cathedral's two splendid 'Rose Windows,' facing each other across the transepts, are known as the 'Bishop's Eye' and the 'Dean's Eye,' the implication being that although closely associated in the worship of the building, bishop and dean may by no means always see eye-to-eye. Whatever may have been true of some of their predecessors or, indeed, successors, King and Butler genuinely did agree, and their unity of purpose was effective for good and widely recognized.

A number of factors contributed to their harmonious relationship. They were already friends and fellow High Churchmen. They shared a deep concern for strengthening the life and ministry of the parish clergy. King had long been involved in clergy training, while Butler, as Vicar of Wantage, had an outstanding record in training curates, including several who became future distinguished leaders in the High Church movement.

Both were committed to furthering the ministry of women in the Church, whether in the form of the emerging religious communities and sisterhoods, or in lay associations. King was Patron of the Guild of St Barnabas for Anglican nurses. At the same time, Butler was the founder of the St Mary's Sisterhood, as part of his ministry at Wantage. The Sisterhood, of which he remained Warden until his death in 1894, became the Community of St Mary the Virgin (CSMV), which developed into one of the largest and most active of Anglican religious communities at the beginning of the twentieth century. As Dean of Lincoln, therefore, Butler continued to travel to Wantage and the other centres where CSMV had established its branches, giving active oversight and support to the sisters, without in any sense stinting himself in devotion to his decanal duties.

On arrival, Butler immediately set to work on bringing the Cathedral into the modern world, much to the delight of his bishop. King frequently attended the Daily Offices of Morning and Evening Prayer, as had been his custom in Oxford, where his residence at Christ Church was next door to the Cathedral.

Just as Butler had rejoiced at King's institution of a daily Eucharist in his chapel at the Old Palace, so he himself enriched the worshipping life of the Cathedral. He had found on arrival that there was only one Communion Service on Sundays and no worship after five o'clock on the Lord's Day. Shortly afterwards, he began a lively Sunday-evening popular service at six-thirty—a bright musical service in the nave, which proved extremely popular for ordinary working people, and furthermore, he invited King to preach at the very first of these. The November issue of 1886 of the *Lincoln Diocesan Magazine* confidently reported:

> The Evening Service which was started by the Dean some time since in the Nave has proved a great success. On each occasion the Nave has been well-filled. We hope other cathedrals will follow this good example of what a cathedral should be, wherever it is a centre of spiritual life and worship.[32]

Butler found that the ornaments and the sanctuary decorations had been sadly neglected. 'There was but one altar frontal which did duty all the year round. The altar table itself was a poor thing, furnished merely with two brass candlesticks containing candles which were never lighted.'[33] He replaced the altar with a more dignified one, with a set of frontals for the various liturgical seasons, and encouraged gifts for the new altar: vases, candlesticks and a handsome cross, the latter given by the students at the nearby Bishop's Hostel, the diocesan theological college founded by Bishop Wordsworth.

Butler valued dignity and beauty in worship but, like King, he was no great ritualist. His commitment was to 'the Church system as laid down in the Book of Common Prayer.' His biographer records that 'he understood and valued ritual indeed, but only when he conceived it to be intelligible and useful.'[34] That was very much King's position, and Butler was predictably outraged when the Church Association later engineered King's trial on charges of ritual excess.

The felicitous partnership between them is commemorated by the doors which King gave for the restored arcade of the Chapter House. His gift is recorded above the doors: 'Aptavit valvas Edwardus episcopus istas cui pateat patris caelica porta domus' ('May these doors, fitted by Bishop Edward, serve as a door to the Heavenly Father's house'); in the tympanum are the words 'Edwardus Episcopus,' the date MDCCCXC (1890), and the arms of the See of Lincoln impaling King's own arms.

In other ways too, Bishop and Dean had much in common, both in character and churchmanship. They both delighted in an annual holiday on the Continent and would take the opportunity to make the acquaintance of the local Roman Catholic clergy. They also shared a desire to build cordial relations between their cathedral and the city and people of Lincoln. Both were southerners, but were at pains to get to know the Lincolnshire people, though it has to be said that Butler found them much less to his liking than King. When Butler moved north from Wantage, he took a particular pleasure in renewing acquaintance with some of the men he had known in his youth at Westminster School and Cambridge. Otherwise, as his biographer candidly admits, 'he never quite "took to" Lincolnshire. Perhaps few people brought up in the south and coming here late in life, ever do.'[35]

Dean Butler died in 1894 (one month short of his seventy-fifth birthday) and was succeeded by E. C. Wickham, whom Gladstone had originally wished to appoint back in 1885. Wickham was very different from Butler, not least in his churchmanship, a scholar to his fingertips, and an advanced biblical critic. However, he continued and, indeed, extended the reforms which Butler had introduced while maintaining a continuing friendship with King.

Edward King

THE LINCOLN DIOCESE

For twenty-five years, from start to finish, King was essentially a diocesan bishop, in the sense that he devoted all his time and energy to his diocese, only seldom accepting invitations to speak, preach or officiate outside the diocese. It would be an unfair generalization to say that what King recovered and represented in the character and practice of his episcopate has been largely lost in recent years with other, very different models of episcopacy gaining ground. Although administratively much more efficient, these nevertheless lack an overarching practice of pastoral care and personal accessibility, and not least for the clergy for whom the bishop traditionally and conspicuously should be, above all else, the *pastor pastorum*. There have never been more bishops in the Church of England than there are today, suffragan and area bishops as well as diocesans, aided by far larger numbers of supportive staff and middle management than in King's day, and at a time when dioceses are smaller, with fewer clergy and fewer people in the pews. Furthermore, today's bishops enjoy the benefits of easier travel and the extraordinary developments in the technology of communication.

King, with a geographically huge and sprawling diocese to care for, had just one suffragan bishop to help him in his early years: later he had often to call on retired colonial bishops for help, especially when he was ill (see p. 486). It was fortuitous, therefore, that in 1905 there was an unexpected vacancy in the benefice of Grantham which, under an Act of Henry VIII, was one of the towns permitted to have a suffragan bishop. King seized the opportunity to recover Grantham as an established Suffragan See (which it remains to this day, along with the more recently created Suffragan See of Grimsby), and to the astonishment of the whole diocese appointed a well-known Low Churchman, Welbore McCarthy, to be his suffragan at Grantham. This wise move served to counter the rumblings of the Low Church clergy who complained that King had surrounded himself predominantly with High Churchmen.

At the outset he had rejected the offer of a coach and coachman, preferring to travel by train, as Bishop Samuel Wilberforce had done, making use of the extensive railway network throughout his large diocese. This greatly facilitated his intensive programme of Confirmations and parish visitations, when he travelled round his many parishes encouraging the people, and especially the clergy, many of whom were demoralized, poorly paid and under-educated. 'Accessibility' had always been the motto of his life, and continued to be throughout his episcopate.

He would never skimp or cut short his visits to the rural parishes, nor give the impression that he had more important matters to attend to back in Lincoln. He made it a practice seldom to leave a parish hurriedly after the service; 'he would always wait and see anyone who wished to see him. He would stay to luncheon, or tea, or dinner, or supper (if he could), and appeared unwearied in his talks with Church-workers or Churchwardens, as well as with neighbours' who might have asked to meet and talk with him—anybody who wanted to have a word with their bishop. 'In this way, he got to know not only the clergy, but the laity as well,' and perhaps more importantly, they came to know and love him.[36]

It was precisely King's pastoral accessibility out-and-about in his diocese, especially in ministering his numerous Confirmations, which made such an impact during his early years at Lincoln. The *Diocesan Magazine* of June 1886 was not slow to draw the attention of its readers to 'a very kind act' which 'was performed by the Bishop of Lincoln after the Confirmation at Hough-on-the-Hill, on 4 March. One young man, a candidate from Honington, being unable through serious illness to attend, the Bishop visited Honington on his way back to Lincoln and confirmed him at his home.'[37]

That watchword of 'accessibility' also held good not only while undertaking his Confirmation rounds, but also, and to no lesser extent, in his home. (Bishop Wilberforce used to say that he would like to have seen the word 'accessible' written over every parsonage door.[38])

Yet, by giving priority to visiting and receiving his clergy, together with his customary and ready accessibility, it is not surprising that, as bishop in Lincoln, as previously when professor in Oxford, he became almost too accessible: something had to give. In King's case it was administration which had never been his strong suit. Indeed, one of his examining chaplains, Canon Bright, in a letter to Liddon about the 'growlings' in the diocese at the organization, or rather lack of it, remarked that the bishop 'has not the same standard of order and method as common folks have.'[39]

Although Canon Venables at Lincoln was a great admirer, he was not unaware of King's weakness in respect of management and administration. Writing to Gladstone to commend the Prime Minister's choice of King, he added:

> One thing I hear on many sides, to his disadvantage, is that he is not a man of business and *never answers letters*. But it is never too late to mend, and I hope that the necessities of the case may convert him into a punctual correspondent. If not some of his best qualities will be neutralised.[40]

History would suggest that the two gifts of administration and the personal touch of pastoral care seldom go hand-in-hand. It is striking how in our day the giants of technology are frequently 'dwarfs' when it comes to social skills and the personal touch. King certainly had the latter in 'spades,' though apparently at the expense of the former.

King used letters as tools in his pastoral ministry of spiritual and personal counselling, as in his published *Spiritual Letters*, and even more so in his letters to the Guild of Nurses. Written in his illegible hand, many are painstakingly long by any standards—the claim that he 'never answers letters' was hardly justified, except perhaps in relation to 'official correspondence' and administrative matters. 'He did not ostensibly try to organize the Diocese, but tried to inspire life into it, and he left it to others to utilize their powers of organization to the full.' In the words of King himself, recalled by Wilgress, 'Organization does not produce life, although life may produce organization; the secret of the power is life.'[41]

Whatever King's weakness on the administrative side of things, it would seem—certainly with the benefit of hindsight—that it was almost as though Lincoln had beckoned him. It was, and indeed still is, a largely rural diocese—like those other two East Anglian dioceses, Ely and Norwich—and King was, if not exactly country-born, at least country-bred, in rural Kent. The country appealed to him and he often reflected on his early days as a curate at Wheatley.

He was constantly out and about in the diocese, and the more he could visit the small country parishes, the happier he was. He delighted in anything which took him out amongst the country people in the somewhat isolated villages of the fens and Lincolnshire Wolds. He particularly revelled in Harvest Festivals, for, as he would say, it was precisely such occasions which gave him an opportunity of speaking to many who were not always in church at other times. His special tastes and habits perfectly fitted his new environment. 'All the sights and sounds of Nature were dear to him. As a boy, he had loved birds-nesting, bird-stuffing, and egg-collecting, and to the end of his life the habits of birds were full of interest to him. It was the same with flowers. Whenever he arrived in a fresh place, one of his first enquiries was about the local *flora*, and he would eagerly purchase any book bearing on the subject. To the head of a Ladies' School, he wrote, "I am glad that the R.S.P.C.A. is taking on. The love of wildflowers helps in the same direction of gentleness and tender care. I was glad to see the Books of Wildflowers which your pupils had collected."'[42]

Though he had given up riding, he nevertheless retained a keen interest in horses:

> The sportsman's heart still beats under the purple cassock, and he loved to see a meet of hounds. The fox-hunters were not slow to reciprocate his regard. A clergyman of the Diocese said to the Master of one of the Lincolnshire packs: 'Is it true that you have only two pictures on your writing table—one your favourite hound, and the other the Bishop?' 'Yes,' replied the M.F.H., 'and why not? They are the two on whom I place the most reliance.'[43]

BISHOP IN AN AGRICULTURAL DIOCESE

Not everyone, then or now, would be as blind to the divisions and class distinctions as King appears to have been. 'Whatever else our new Bishop is,' said the laity, at least according to King's first biographer, 'he is a gentleman.'

> In the great houses of the diocese—Grimsthorpe and Brocklesby and Belton, and the like—the Bishop was as instantly and as completely at home as in the parsonages and the clergy-houses and the labourers' cottages. He had conspicuously that special mark of the gentlemanlike nature—that no surroundings could make the slightest difference to his demeanour. He was a gentleman, neither more nor less, and he knew it; and neither in Courts nor in hovels could he seem other than what he was.[44]

He was, as we might say of someone today, 'comfortable in his own skin,' which in turn, enabled everyone he met to feel comfortable in theirs.

From his earliest memories, the countryside and the world of agriculture, with its landed-gentry as well as its labourers, was King's natural habitat. As the bishop in Lincolnshire, with its rich, black soil favouring agriculture rather than industry, he seized the opportunity to use his ingrained gifts as a pastor in ways which changed the face of episcopacy from statesman and administrator to that of essentially being the chief pastor of his flock, especially in the scattered villages of the Lincolnshire fenland.

From the start, King had a clear picture in his mind of what kind of bishop he needed to be. In his Charge to the Clergy in 1889, he spoke of how throughout the history of the diocese there had 'been days when warrior-bishops' did good service to the Church, or bishops who were essentially statesmen, like Kaye, one of his predecessors, or scholars, or men of literary and social influence. But he went on to reflect upon what kind of bishop was appropriate at that point in time for an agricultural diocese. 'I am thinking of our own people,' he concluded, 'thanking God with all my heart that He has allowed me to work in an agricultural diocese.'[45]

Certainly, in dealing with farmers, his long experience of country parishes stood him in good stead: he knew first-hand the hazards and problems which frequently beset them in their day-to-day life and work. During the Cattle Plague of 1865–6, a farmer at Cuddesdon had twenty-four of his cows struck down with the disease at one time. Such experiences had taught the former country parson to sympathize with those varied woes of drought and flood, high rents and low prices, of which more academic and urban bishops would have had little, if any, first-hand knowledge. In fact, it is clear that King was perhaps 'at his best in confirming the plough boys and carters, and there were countless stories about his insight into their difficulties':[46] he could address them in their own language and the context of their hard-working daily lives.

Yet, as the twenty-five years of his episcopate were to prove, it was certainly not 'an easy time' to be a bishop of a rural diocese. 'In the Midlands and East Anglia the agricultural troubles of the previous fifteen years left a heritage of acrimony between labourer and churches, from which some country parishes never quite recovered.'[47] It would not have been long before King would have had brought home to him just how very much the countryside had changed from the relatively stable rural society of the first half of the century. As a generalization, until the middle of the nineteenth century, the life of the country village with its squire, its farmers and farm labourers, and village parson, had been a comparatively stable community.

> In 1860 the idea of a village church was still embodied in some country parishes. The squire was in his pew, his friend the parson in his stall, respectable farmers in pews, and on benches the labourers in smock frocks, delicately embroidered at front and back, their wives often in scarlet flannel shawls.[48]

However, when King came to his predominantly agricultural diocese much of that had changed or was changing. Village life had declined as many left for the industrial cities, and memories were still sore from the earlier battles between the National Agricultural Labourer's Union and the squire farmers and landowners, with whom the local parson was often perceived as having sided.

In country parishes, the parson was dependent, often to an uncomfortable extent, on the patronage of the squire, frequently finding himself caught between the privileged and age-old 'rock' of his quasi-feudal patron, and the 'hard place' of his oppressed and impoverished parishioners. Even in villages where the parson might privately be convinced, as many were, that the demands of the labourers were justified, the chances are he could not afford to risk saying so publicly. If he openly showed support for the labouring class, he might earn temporary popularity among local tenants, but incur the displeasure of his patron, the squire, upon whom he was often heavily dependent for resources, to help with such things as the upkeep of the church, the running of the church school and the alleviation of poverty: that was the way things had been for centuries. Inevitably in such cases, parishes became divided in bitterness and clergymen caught up in those situations would realize that they could best help by not taking sides.

Meanwhile the unions persisted in representing the clergy as part of the landowning system which held the labourer in subjection. From their point of view parsons were enslaved to their patrons, and such perceptions were slow to die: by the end of the 'eighties 'men still talked of the "hostility" between country labourer and village parson,'[49] so that, although patchy, such would have been the tensions and undercurrents of village life in many parishes of King's diocese.

Furthermore, by the 'eighties, many of the institutions which had served and thrived in traditional village life were in decline, as the young moved away to the towns where the opportunities for work were better and the wages higher.

> The agriculture of the country slid down towards ruin and with it everything that depended on agriculture for support—the revenue of colleges at the university, the rents of the squire, the glebe of the parson, the tithe of the ecclesiastical commissioners ... Some land in Lincolnshire or Essex went out of cultivation.[50]

The result was the slow but continuing decline of the Anglican squire, which was bad alike for the parish, the rural church, and the impoverished parson, whose lot became increasingly hard and demoralizing. In times of agricultural depression his income fell, and if his squire moved out, he was left 'the one resident to whom the poor could go for help. The demand of charity upon his purse grew as his purse grew shorter.'[51] To continue in post for years while every year the numbers of worshippers declined not surprisingly lowered the spirits of many already hard-pressed country clergy. A priest coming from a town parish could discover that he had settled in a deteriorating countryside, among slow-moving minds, and with insufficient income.

In spite of 'the long process of decline,' which 'continued until the coming of the bus and of electric power,' 'the country churches were not empty on a Sunday. But they were less full. The clergy at least, believed that they were less full,' all of which further added to the demoralization of clergymen throughout the farming communities of other predominantly agricultural dioceses. But the picture is by no means uniform. 'Samples taken in the visitation returns of Lincolnshire parishes between 1886 and 1907, show a surprising steadiness of church and chapel life in the country.'[52] To what extent the more favourable statistics are attributable to King's particular care and concern for his clergy, it is impossible to say.

From the day his appointment was announced, King had repeatedly spoken of his conviction that he had been called to be bishop 'to God's poor,' and not just to the peasants and hard-pressed farm labourers, but also to and for his clergy: and he remained committed to that for the rest of his life. During a sermon at a special service in St Edmund's, Lombard Street in London, to raise money for the Poor Clergy Relief Corporation, he spoke with passion about the financial plight of the country clergy:

> In old times the first great source of the Church's wealth was, no doubt, the bequest of land ... But we have lived to see a change. The value of land, at least for the present, has, to a very large extent, and beyond all expectations, decreased. The agricultural condition of our country is one of our country's greatest anxieties, and the original and chief source of the Church's wealth has failed ... The present needs of our clergy, owing to the unexpected fall in their incomes, are very great. There are more than 21,000 English clergy, and a very large proportion of these have only the small remuneration of £100 or £200 a year while on actual duty, with no provision for sickness or pension for old age.
>
> One of the greatest and most serious causes of distress is the inability of many of the clergy to educate their

children... When sickness comes into the family... what can be done? If sickness comes upon the clergyman himself, where is the money to provide for his duty? ... And if death comes, what then? What is the poor widow to do? She must leave her home. They may not be in debt, but they cannot have saved, and there are no pensions.

And then, in conclusion, he widened his brief: 'It is not merely for the relief of personal distress that I am asking your consideration and your help today. It is for the maintenance of our clergy, for the support of the ambassadors of Christ, to provide the means for bringing the blessings of the Gospel to the poor.'[53] Such was and always had been the overarching theme of King's whole proclamation and ministry.

The problems associated with financial poverty and deprivation among the rural clergy, were not confined to the Diocese of Lincoln. For some time they had been a pastoral concern of other bishops with predominantly rural and agricultural dioceses. Throughout his years at Lincoln, King met annually with the bishops of the neighbouring dioceses—Ely, Norwich, Peterborough and St Albans—to discuss shared problems and common pastoral concerns. These meetings generally took place over two days in the first week of November, and the minutes show the discussions repeatedly centred around shared pastoral problems, and not least the poverty and deprivation—financial and intellectual—of the rural clergy, something very close to King's heart.[54] From 1889 until his death, he never missed a meeting—though in 1908 he was only able to be present on the second day.

A BISHOP OF THE POOR

Back in 1885, in a letter to his friend Randolph dated 21 February, King says of his recently announced appointment:

> This is my great delight, and my hope, that [God] means it [his appointment] as a proof of His love, and that He means me to be a Bishop of His Poor! If I can keep that before me, I shall be happy.⁵⁵

This was a theme often repeated in the weeks that followed: it can be seen in another letter, also written in February, this time to Dr Heurtley:

> I have, as you know, no great gifts, but, by God's goodness, I have a great and real love of His poor; and, if it should please Him to let me be the bishop of His poor and enable me to help them to see more what they are to Him, and what He is to them, I think I shall be happy.⁵⁶

Such was the predominant aim of King's episcopate. It was the people in the villages to whom his thoughts naturally turned when poverty struck most severely.

Back in 1871, while still at Cuddesdon, he had written to a friend, stressing his readiness to exchange academic work for a country parish. 'I have been obliged these last few years to spend the best of my time in reading, but, if I should be free from the college, I should go on in a parish just as we used to do at Wheatley.' So, in Lincolnshire, he was able to fulfil once more his vocation to serve and care for the country poor. His letter continued, 'Our dear country poor—for I feel more suited to them than to others—require to be helped one by one. They are very ignorant, have very little time, work very hard, and often with poor food; they require a great deal of loving, watchful sympathy. If it please God, I should rejoice to give myself, wholly to spiritual work.'⁵⁷

Several years later, during his time at Christ Church, he had written: '*I* should not choose the University to work in if I had my choice. I would rather be with the simplest agricultural poor, but it is not so arranged.'⁵⁸ In 1885 it was 'so arranged,' and King welcomed what he saw as a providential opportunity for his particular style, and embraced it with open arms.

Lincoln: The Early Years

If a such a letter were read without any knowledge of the writer's character, and certainly if it were read today in the culture and context of the Welfare State, these sentiments would doubtless appear disingenuous and unconvincing. Could a senior cleric, highly privileged by any standards, writing as an Oxford Professor and a Canon of Christ Church Cathedral, lavishly housed and highly paid, as King undoubtedly was, really be sincere in claiming that he would prefer to be working among 'the simplest agricultural poor'? But if not sincere, then it calls into question the integrity of King's whole ministry, for his commitment to caring for the poor is consistently repeated not only in words but in countless actions of pastoral care and compassion from the earliest days of his ministry: it was as if Lincoln gave him the opening he sought, though in ways he could not have imagined or foreseen.

The 'Bishop's care for the agricultural poor did not end with their souls, or even their bodies. Though a stout Tory, he had supported the extension of the Suffrage to the Agricultural Labourers, saying—"They must be taught to be Citizens of the Kingdom of Heaven by being made Citizens of the Kingdom of England."'[59] He felt strongly it was his duty to help with their intellectual development, as he had done with Charlie, the young labourer in Wheatley whom he nurtured to become a devoted teacher in a profession which would normally have been barred to anyone from such an uneducated and working-class background.

Yet King knew all too well what few would admit, let alone have the courage to say publicly today, that financial plenty is no substitute for spiritual poverty.

> The real want of England is to make English hearts happy with the happiness for which God made them what they are. Money, rank, political power—these are well enough, and should be given to men as God may direct, in His own time and in His own way. But the real want of England is to know the peace and

blessedness of the love of God and the love of man in the sacramental life of Christ.[60]

Care for the poor and the under privileged rooted only in ideology, to be championed as a cause, whether to the right or the left politically, so often results in an unattractive self-righteousness and even self-justification, rather than in true justice and compassion. Changing the system without a change of heart and spirit would not seem to crack the nut.

THE BISHOP AND HIS CLERGY

From the outset of his episcopate, King realized the importance of establishing a personal and caring relationship with his clergy, many of whom, had lost heart over the years. Both by his dress and general demeanour, King was able to win their trust and confidence. From his past experience of training men for ministry he knew that he must not be perceived as being 'over and above' his clergy, but rather as working alongside and among them—like 'a big curate,' to use his own phrase. He might well have known the memorable phrase of Augustine who said of himself in relation to his people: 'For you, I am a bishop: among you, I am a Christian.'

As bishop, King continued in much the same way as he had in his days as a curate and a vicar. A neighbour at Cuddesdon, on hearing of his appointment to Lincoln, wrote: 'All new clothes now! No old boots hereafter for ever.'[61] She was not the only one to be aware of King's indifference to his outward appearance. In Canon Venables' letter to Gladstone, applauding King's nomination, he alludes to his shabby appearance: 'I could have wished that he had been a smarter man, but there again, the bishops of Manchester and Exeter have shown that reform is possible, even in not very young prelates.'[62] To the chagrin of some of his friends and more senior ecclesiastical colleagues, King persisted to the end with his shabby clothes and his worn, patched boots, and not by way of affectation, but simply and solely because that was who he was. In this way, when the country clergy were invited to come to Lincoln for a conference or retreat, they would have felt drawn to attend not by an ecclesiastical superior with good intentions for their further development, but by a friend and colleague who was, in so many ways, very much one of them.

All his past experience had taught him that the renewal of the Church required, as of first importance, the spiritual renewal of the clergy, root and branch. And furthermore, as he had learned from the writings of Bishop Sailer, renewal must encompass both a renewal of the mind and a rekindling of the spirit, and not only in the training received prior to ordination. It must continue to be persistently and consistently pursued through the succeeding years of ministry, if that ministry is to bear lasting fruit, and endure the trials and challenges of a world which was increasingly slipping into indifference to faith at best, or, at worst, into the hostility of encroaching secularism and materialism. In many ways, it was both as bishops as well as professors of pastoral theology, that King and Sailer gave priority to their care of the clergy, both spiritually, theologically and intellectually.

Both were academics and teachers, and yet, if there is an art which conceals art, there is also a pastoral theology which conceals theology, and does not use the academic language of the schools. On the contrary, it speaks deliberately in the idiom and imagery of ordinary people. Sailer and King had this gift, which meant that their liturgical thought and practice were governed by pastoral and educational needs, as well as by doctrinal fidelity. They wanted liturgy and worship to glorify God; that above all. They also wanted, through liturgy and worship, to teach the faith and to feed the flock.

In his sermon preached to a great gathering of clergy in the Cathedral at the first Festival of the Lincoln Theological College in 1888, King sets out his ideal of priestly life, setting the bar very high indeed:

> We need men ... who have thought out, as far as they can, their own relation to God, and who have realized the strength of the complex proof on which it depends, men who have walked in the threefold light of their own faculties, of revelation, and of the Church, and have seen how the three agree and lead back to *one*.
>
> We need men who have disciplined their reason by endeavouring to discern and speak the exact truth, without fear of the reproof of man, and without the desire of his praise.
>
> We need men who have endeavoured to keep a conscience void of offence, not only in the sight of men, but of God ...
>
> We need men ... who are rooted and grounded in and constrained by [Christ's] love; men who will be patient with sinners and those who are ignorant, and careless, and 'out of the way'; men who will wait and watch for single souls, as the Saviour did for the woman of Samaria at the well, although she was a woman of a false theology and a broken character; men who will love and not grow cold, but who, having loved, like Jesus, will 'love to the end.'[63]

Even these few extracts from a very long address show a great ideal for the priestly life—an ideal reflecting the ideal in the Ordinal of the Book of Common Prayer, and an ideal which is as pertinent today as it ever was and always will be.

In many ways, King simply improvised on the substance of that amazing address in the many and various diocesan retreats, spiritual conferences and Quiet Days which he held for his clergy. At Cuddesdon he had begun the practice of conducting retreats, giving opportunities for the ordinands to spend two or three days in silence during which he would give short devotional addresses, while also making himself available for individual spiritual direction, with Confession or the Sacrament of Penance on offer. It was during those years that the religious community of the Cowley Fathers, the earliest of the still surviving male monastic orders in the Church of England, was founded by Father Richard Meux Benson. In 1868 they began the practice of holding retreats. Initially these were held in their Mission House in Marston Street and it was there that they invited King to conduct one of the earliest for their little, newly founded Community.[64]

It became King's practice to gather his clergy together annually for a season of thought and devotion in the Cathedral. It was not exactly, in the technical sense of the term, a retreat: rather, it took a form well-suited for his diocesan clergy, many of whom were in charge of remote country parishes, and in need of encouragement through loving and caring support.

It was that ministry of loving and caring support which King as bishop sought to extend to his clergy. William Addison in *The English Country Parson*, speaks of King as 'the country parson's true father in God,' and claims 'Edward King might almost have been Chaucer's poor parson himself, somehow become bishop.'[65] It was manifestly true; King was deeply committed to the care and welfare of his clergy—financial, spiritual and intellectual. He spoke of it frequently, characterizing the role of a bishop as that of a curate with an over large cure of souls. As time went by, he won their hearts, even of those not in sympathy with his churchmanship, simply by the integrity of his pastoral care. 'They knew that when he prayed for them, aided by the book in which he kept a photograph of each of his clergy, he did so as one who understood the feeling of their infirmities.'[66]

King was particularly careful when choosing some experienced priest to give the retreat addresses in the three days of preparation prior to ordinations in the Cathedral. He himself always gave the last address on the night before ordination, but above all he wanted the ordinands to find, in the silence of the retreat, an experience of fellowship with God. As he said, he wanted their experience of God to rest, in Paul's words, 'not on the wisdom of man, but on the power of God' (1 Corinthians 2:4).

The formal retreats consisted of three-day devotions, with special Eucharists and spiritual conferences or addresses delivered by some of the greatest masters of the spiritual life in the English Church at that time. King himself conducted the first of them, and a priest who was present has left us a vivid account of his memories and impressions:

> We had, of course, often seen the bishop and heard him preach on special occasions. Now we seemed really to know him for the first time, to feel his whole heart and soul laid open to his clergy. It is impossible adequately to summarize or describe the addresses. They were searching and uplifting. We felt the 'spiritual life around the earthly life' ... There were flashes of humour, and then piercing appeals that drew swift, hot tears ... He was the theologian setting forth the deepest teachings of the Faith; the master of ethics playing with Aristotle and the anti-pelagian treatises of St Augustine, as we might have done with the multiplication table; the spiritual guide bringing it all into relation with every sphere of our life and duty. And it was all done with such ease and naturalness; it seemed absolutely inevitable ... We could be penitent and forgiven and start again. We had seen it all. We had a bishop, a friend, a father who knew and understood.[67]

Where can we find such men and women for our bishops today? For to paraphrase the rhetoric of King's address at that Festival of Lincoln Theological College, if the Church 'needs' clergy, men and women, of that theological and spiritual calibre like King, then, *mutatis mutandis*, perhaps even more the Church today 'needs' bishops embodying those same ideals together with spiritual and theological depth in their teaching, their preaching and, above all, in their episcopal ministry and care for their clergy. It is not so much bishops, as the parish clergy at the 'coal face,' who are brought face-to-face with the challenges and indeed the hostility of the prevailing culture throughout Western Europe.

KING'S PRIMARY VISITATION TO HIS DIOCESE

King's custom was to hold triennial visitations and to deliver what is traditionally called his Charge to the clergy: it was something over which he always took enormous care. Instead of waiting the usual three years, he held his primary visitation as early as October 1886, after only eighteen months in the diocese. Written while he was on summer holiday in Buxton, it shows, as might be expected, very great thought and care. From its extensive content it is evident that the new bishop had already gained a considerable knowledge of the circumstances prevailing throughout the diocese. He had visited a large number of the parishes; consecrated several new churches, and observed the diocesan organizations and their various committees at work. 'Confirmations had brought him into touch with the young men and girls and children of the diocese, of whom he had confirmed more than five thousand.'[68] Now, some might have though a little prematurely, he was anxious to share his observations with the clergy and their churchwardens who sat listening to their bishop delivering his Charge.[69]

That first Charge consisted mainly of a forecast of the work he believed he was sent to undertake:

> What is the special work, then, which God has called me to do? If I am not too presumptuous in speaking so definitely of myself in relation to God I will say, I hope, if it be His will, that my work may be to bring home to the hearts of the people, and especially of the poor, the blessings of the Church.

He continued by developing the challenges to faith from

biblical criticism and science, apparently so undermining to the teachings of the Church and of the Bible. But he shares with his clergy, many of whom had no intellectual pretensions and little knowledge of theology, let alone of contemporary theological writings, the foundations of his own inner journey of faith which had survived the recent storms of unbelief. This, together with his care for the poor, was to be the continuing and constant theme and the ground-bass of his teaching and practice throughout his episcopate, for, as he said in that first Charge, 'It seems to me that to this point God has been bringing us during these last thirty years. The very foundations of the Faith have been assailed; but, thanks be to God, they stand for many of us firmer than before, or rather we stand firmer in our relation to them.'[70]

In later Charges, he set forth at some length the doctrines of Holy Communion, the ministry of Absolution and Healing, the unity of the Church and the Church's teaching on marriage, much as he had done as Professor of Pastoral Theology. In that way, he recovered and practised the role of a bishop as being essentially that of a teacher, as the chair or *cathedra* in a bishop's cathedral is intended to symbolize. Universities originally took the concept of a professor's chair from that of a bishop's chair in the cathedral, the cathedral itself being simply the church in which the bishop, seated in his chair, teaches his people and his clergy. Is it totally impossible to reclaim something of that, as being part of a bishop's ministry in today's Church?

In this and similar ways, whether in Quiet Days, at retreats, at Diocesan Conferences or in his more formal Triennial Charges, or in his countless and frequent visits to their parishes in city and countryside alike, the refrain was the same: namely, to show that the bishop knew, understood and loved his clergy. He understood their difficulties first-hand; he knew that sometimes the standard he set might seem too high and beyond their reach. Yet his words were essentially those of encouragement and were not intended to encourage guilt, or give a sense that they were being put down or regarded as failures in the eyes of their bishop. Success, whether numerically or by the world's standards was not the name of the game: rather faithfulness and fruitfulness constituted the benchmark for King's measure of ministry.

Retreats, Triennial Charges and diocesan conferences all had the same end in view—holiness of life for clergy and laity alike, authenticating the witness of a Church which claimed to be not only Catholic and Apostolic, but also, and essentially, holy.

> [The Saviour] is watching, He is working; it is His Father's business that He is about, making the English priesthood *holy*; not simply intelligent, not simply moral, but *holy*. The Saviour is watching, and the people are watching too. Whatever they may be themselves, they expect that if the Church is holy, the ministry will be holy too—a city set on a hill, cannot be hid.[71]

In and through all of this, it was King's understanding and compassion for his clergy which endured to the end, and which won over many who had been not a little apprehensive about his churchmanship, or, indeed, even a little suspicious of other attributes. As Abraham Lincoln said, 'The best way to defeat your enemies is to make them your friends.'

It was King's compassion for both friends and enemies which carried the day: a compassion which, as Buddhists teach, first of all strives to know friends and enemies alike, but which goes on to love them both, to serve them both, and finally, actually to enjoy them both. It might be said that it was King's unique genius for friendship which finally overcame much of the adversity and lingering hostility. Yet that only becomes evident with the benefit of hindsight after the Lincoln Trial of 1890, the ominous clouds of which had been gathering from the moment the new bishop stepped foot into his diocese.

KING AND THE NONCONFORMISTS

The most vehement rumblings of opposition in the diocese to King's explicit churchmanship, came not, as might have been expected, from Nonconformists and Methodists—it came from the Protestant Evangelicals of the Church Association.

From first to last, King had always had a great admiration for the teachings, practice and work of John Wesley. The *Lincoln Diocesan Magazine* reported that on 30 November 1886, 'Dr King gave a lecture on John Wesley at Sheffield for the Church Lecture Society. After giving a sketch of the great Lincolnshire worthy, he commended the respect which the Wesleyans pay to the religious enthusiasm of the young. He also commended Wesley for his emphasis on the doctrine of 'perfection,'[72] so clearly akin to King's repeated exhortation to holiness and a personal relationship with God not only for the clergy but for the whole people of God.

In 1909 he was warm and generous in welcoming the Wesleyan Methodist Conference to Lincoln (see p. 369), and shortly after his death the Congregational Union, which happened to be meeting in Lincoln, 'passed a special resolution of sympathy with the Church of England in its loss.'[73]

King was always quite clear in his own mind that many of the root causes of division between Nonconformity—Methodism in particular—and the Established Church lay not in theological differences, but derived from the casualties of history in the eighteenth century, and the exclusive privileges of the Church of England, which further widened the divisions of class and culture between church and chapel. In his Visitation Charge of 1895, King spoke of the need for 'a full and fair consideration of the position of our Nonconformist brethren. There is a great need of a thorough acquaintance with the history and tenets of the various bodies which exist among us.'[74]

He was all too well aware of the differences of class, social standing and education between a typical Anglican parson and a Nonconformist or Methodist minister. The Anglican parson, until the late nineteenth century, was usually a university man, almost exclusively from Oxford or Cambridge, who would have enjoyed the privileged opportunities for education of which those from differing denominational persuasions were deprived. By way of contrast, 'the ministers who looked after the rural chapels were usually from simple homes.'[75] 'Few will doubt,' said the socialist clergyman Llewelyn Davies, from the poorer Welsh Church, 'that the Church of England greatly needs the help of Divine grace to preserve it from an undue reverence for station and property.'[76]

Yet the immense wealth of the Church of England was unevenly distributed amongst its large workforce—the parish clergy. 'By 1887 there were more than 13,000 beneficed clergymen' in the Church of England. 'More than a third of these benefices had incomes of less than £200 a year,' while 'the average stipend of a curate in 1893 was £145.'[77] Admittedly, 'by the standards of rural nonconformist pastors this was comfort. But the rural parson was given a big house and expected' (with or without the benefit of inherited or family wealth) 'to keep a gentleman's style.' It was country parsons whose income depended mainly on glebe and land who suffered the most, and by King's time they were considerably and increasingly worse off than their predecessors: 'in 1837 land was a profitable, in 1897, an unprofitable, investment.'[78]

There were other factors which played into the differing demographics of church and chapel membership. Membership of the Wesley chapel was drawn mainly from the labouring classes, where the men (and they were predominantly men) would have had a voice and a place and, for some, even the opportunity to develop leadership not only in the 'classes' of their local chapel, but also in the proliferating Agricultural Unions.

Joseph Arch, the prime mover in the foundation of the National Agricultural Labourer's Union, which by the 1870s had a membership of nearly 100,000, was a labourer from Barford and a Primitive Methodist preacher. Standing on a Norfolk village green, he reputedly told a large crowd of eager followers that 'the church belongs to rich men':[79] such is how the Established Church was perceived by many, and not just in King's time.

'I am glad it is John Wesley's diocese,'[80] wrote King, replying to a letter from Canon Ottley welcoming him to Lincoln and wishing him well. In his very first visitation, he commented on the overwhelming presence of Nonconformity, which was hardly surprising in the Wesleys' own home county, where Methodism in both its Primitive and Wesleyan forms flourished—'Lincolnshire had hardly a village without its chapel.'[81]

Methodists and other Nonconformists, had always been notoriously suspicious of bishops, and not without reason, so how much more suspicious would they be of a High Church bishop such as King outwardly was, attired in cope and mitre, with their overtones of papist dress and habits. One lady remarked that although 'a dear old gentleman,' he was 'a wee bit too gay for a gospel minister'[82]—'gay' in the nineteenth-century sense of the word.

While King never trimmed his teaching, or apologized for what he regarded as the rounded Catholic content of the Anglican position, in order to curry favour with Nonconformists, yet, by the content of his teaching, always Gospel centred and drawing richly on scripture, many from very differing traditions, especially Methodists, spoke warmly of him.

> Descendants of the men whom John Wesley had converted recognized that in their new bishop they had a man of God, who lived in prayer and preached Christ Crucified. This was what they wanted, and his sermons were often punctuated by ejaculations of 'Ah!' 'Hallelujah!' and 'Praise the Lord!' in the true fashion of the Methodists.[83]

Lincoln: The Early Years

People of varying traditions soon came to appreciate and value King's simple, direct, Evangelical style. After hearing him preach, one person was reported as saying, in a strong Lincolnshire accent, 'He's nowt but an owd Methody.'[84]

Until the end of his days, King continued to work and pray for reconciliation between the Anglican Church and the Nonconformists, notably the Wesleyans and Primitive Methodists. His care and concern about the divisions within the Church and between churches, meant, as he said to a friend, that 'what he wanted to do in the diocese was to draw men to Christ, that they might be nearer to God, and nearer to each other in the unity of His Holy Church.'[85]

He was not the first Bishop of Lincoln to have attempted to win back the Nonconformists in the diocese to mother Church. His predecessor, Bishop Wordsworth had made overtures, especially to the Wesleyans, but unfortunately, he lacked both the tact and that lightness of touch which such ecumenical advances necessarily require. It is told how he once urged the Wesleyan Methodist leader, William Arthur, to bring his people back into the Church of England, throwing in, by way of an inducement: 'Would you not be glad to preach in Lincoln Cathedral?' To which Arthur replied drily, 'Well, I should be glad to preach in Lincoln Cathedral, and I should be glad to preach in a wheelbarrow.'[86] Wordsworth was genuinely keen to restore unity but essentially on Anglican terms and Anglican turf.

As the years went by, King, by his irenic attitude and sheer goodness, and his deeply held passion for the Gospel, increasingly earned the respect and admiration of many Free Church people. Never a rigid High Churchman, he managed to combine a loyal faithfulness to Anglican formularies and teachings, while welcoming with a generosity of spirit the many Nonconformists in his diocese.

His Dean, by contrast, had a strong aversion to Nonconformists—one of the few areas where they did not see eye-to-eye. King could never have written, as Butler did after taking a service at Burton:

> The church was full both times, and the singing and general tone all that one can desire. How sad it is that the same cannot be said everywhere. It might, were it not for that horrid Methodism and other forms of Dissent; yet even they would be in a great degree neutralised if the clergy did their work faithfully and kindly.[87]

On the subject of relations with Nonconformists and Methodists, Butler's line was much more that of a rigid party man while King's was more akin to that of John Keble, who wrote to a fellow clergyman in 1864: 'Dissenters should be dealt with lovingly and forbearingly, as being, alas! the wronged party in bygone times.'[88] That was very much how King perceived the breakaway of Methodists.

It is perhaps significant that in his Visitation Charge of 1895, King took the opportunity to dwell on the need for a radical reappraisal of the prevailing attitude to the 'custom of chapel going,' so deplored by Butler, who had died the previous year. Clearly King felt free to recall the diocese to 'a full and fair consideration of the position of our Nonconformist brethren. There is a great need,' he insisted, 'of a more thorough acquaintance with the history and tenets of the various bodies which exist among us.'[89] This was nothing new for King, who had long recognized, as well as being more than ready to acknowledge, that the Church of England had in a real sense only itself to blame for the separation and growth of Methodism, as he admitted in a letter written as late as 1906, reiterating his commitment to promote goodwill and brotherly love:

> I need hardly say I have never had any harsh feeling towards Nonconformists, and, I might add, especially not towards Wesleyans and Primitive Methodists, because I have always felt that it was the want of spiritual life in the Church and brotherly love which led them to separate. The more we can draw near to Christ ourselves

and fill ourselves with His Spirit, the greater power we shall have for unity. What we want is more *Christlike Christians*. May God guide and bless your efforts to draw all nearer to Him, and in Him to one another.[90]

In this, as in so many other ways, as John Newton incisively suggests, 'Catholic and Evangelical meet in King.'[91]

In the pursuit of ecumenism, King was ahead of his time. The age of ecumenism did not really get under way until after his death. The mid-twentieth century marked the beginning of various 'Schemes' seeking to join differing bodies of Christians together—an essentially institutional ecumenism. But it had run out of steam by the end of the century because it was insufficiently an ecumenism of the spirit, drawing Christians of differing traditions closer together precisely, as King insisted, by being closer, like spokes in a wheel, to the centre where, when re-centred in Christ, we would indeed all be one in Him as He is one with his Father in the unity of the Holy Spirit. King spells out this dynamic and essentially spiritual approach to Christian unity in the letter he wrote in 1909, only months before his death, to the Wesleyan Methodist Conference then meeting in Lincoln. Writing on behalf of the Cathedral clergy, he freely acknowledges that:

> Although they and the Conference were not able in all points to see eye to eye, yet it would be unjust not to recognize the great work of those who had done so much for the religious life of their land in the days of their common neglect. They were one in faith in Christ, and that He died for all—and if they took Him to be the type and example of their life, and got others to do so too, they would be more Christlike Christians. And the more they were like Him the nearer they would get to one another, and thus realize the Saviour's prayer, that they all might be one.[92]

Only then and there can we have that inner freedom and security which can welcome and, indeed, rejoice in a rich diversity within unity, rather than in a structural conformity.

The divisions of the twenty-first century are more evident as divisions within various traditions, and not so much between churches. Today's divisions are more focused around 'issues' rather than the divisions of King's day, many of which had their roots in earlier history, both social and political. So, it is not surprising that even the witness of King throughout his ministry to a 'scriptural Catholicism,' manifestly evident in the life and teaching of this good and holy man, failed to bring about a large-scale return of Nonconformists to the Church. As, here again, Newton wisely comments:

> There were no doubt many reasons for that fact, besides the basic stubborn nature of the pre-ecumenical age in which he lived. There were deep-rooted historical and social factors separating Church and Chapel, which could not be overcome at the drop of a mitre, however saintly the head that wore it. Again, it was one thing for the bishop of the diocese to give a strong lead in the direction of church unity; quite another to translate that into practice at the parish level, where the shoe really pinched. Finally, however attractive Catholic Anglicanism may be as a form of Christian faith and life—and it could hardly be more attractive than it was in Edward King—there remain elements and expressions of life in Christ which it does not comprehend, or at least did not in King's day. Spontaneity in worship, and the intimacy and freedom of the small, committed Christian fellowship, are merely two of these.[93]

There may be a better chance in our own day, not least because the Established Church, along with all the other mainstream churches, has *per force* been compelled to eat humble pie, no longer enjoying the financial and numerical superiority of previous centuries. Then again, there is a willingness today to explore and practise alternative ways of 'doing church' that King's generation could not possibly have understood, tied as they were to the Book of Common Prayer.

Lincoln: The Early Years

Notes

1. Randolph and Townroe, *The Mind and Work of Bishop King*, p. 97.
2. *Ibid.*, p. 111.
3. *The Church Times*, 24 May 1935 — from a description of the Service of Commemoration for the fiftieth Anniversary of King's enthronement.
4. George W. E. Russell, *Edward King Sixtieth Bishop of Lincoln*, p. 111.
5. *The Lincolnshire Chronicle*, 10 February and 17 April 1885, pp. 2 and 8 respectively.
6. Russell, *op. cit.*, p. 96–7.
7. *Jackson's Oxford Journal*, 19 January 1878, p. 8.
8. Gladstone Papers, British Library, Add. MS 44,489, fos 178–9.
9. *Ibid.*, f. 194.
10. John Newton, *Search for a Saint*, p. 84.
11. Sir Francis Hill, *Georgian Lincoln*. Cambridge University Press, 1966.
12. A. C. Benson, *The Life of Edward White Benson*, vol. II, p. 151.
13. Michael Hall, *George Frederick Bodley and the later Gothic Revival in Britain and America*. New Haven and London: Yale University Press, 2014, p. 336.
14. Russell, *op. cit.*, p. 141.
15. Randolph and Townroe, *op. cit.*, p. 135.
16. *Ibid.*, p. 139.
17. Nigel Scotland, *Joseph Cotton Wigram, Bishop of Rochester*. Leominster: Gracewing, 2021, p. 124.
18. Russell, *op. cit.*, p. 115.
19. Owen Chadwick, *Edward King, Bishop of Lincoln, 1885–1910*, p. 16.
20. Randolph and Townroe, *op. cit.*, p. 163.
21. Lincolnshire Archives 27/46, *Lincoln Diocesan Magazine*, July 1886.
22. Russell, *op. cit.*, p. 129.
23. Chadwick, *op. cit.*, pp. 15–16.
24. *The Lincolnshire Chronicle*, 7 August 1885, p. 7.
25. Chadwick, *op. cit.*, p. 16.
26. Lincolnshire Archives 27/46, *Lincoln Diocesan Magazine*, January 1887.
27. *The Lincolnshire Chronicle*, 24 April 1885, p. 5 (reprinted from *The Times*).
28. *Ibid.*, 15, and 22 May 1885, pp. 5 *and* 5 respectively.
29. Chadwick, *op. cit.*, p. 23.
30. Russell, *op. cit.*, p. 91.
31. Gladstone Papers, British Library, Add. MS 44,491, fos 120–1.
32. Lincolnshire Archives, 27/46, *Lincoln Diocesan Magazine*, November 1886.
33. *Life and Letters of William John Butler*. London: Macmillan & Co., 1897, p. 322.

34 *Ibid.*, pp. 375, 358.
35 *Ibid.*, p. 362.
36 Randolph and Townroe, *op. cit.*, p. 162.
37 Lincolnshire Archives 27/46, *Lincoln Diocesan Magazine*, June 1886.
38 Randolph and Townroe, *op. cit.*, p. 162.
39 Chadwick, *op. cit.*, p. 23.
40 Gladstone Papers, British Library, Add. MS 44,489, fos 177–8.
41 G. F. Wilgress, *Edward King Bishop of Lincoln 1885–1910*, p. 16.
42 Russell, *op. cit.*, pp. 111–12.
43 *Ibid.*, p. 112.
44 *Ibid.*, p. 111.
45 Chadwick, *op. cit.*, p. 21: Edward King, *Charge delivered to the Clergy and Churchwardens of the Diocese of Lincoln*. Lincoln: J. Williamson, 1889, pp. 55, 59.
46 Russell, *op. cit.*, p. 114.
47 Chadwick, *op. cit.*, p. 21.
48 Owen Chadwick, *The Victorian Church*, 2 parts. London: Adam & Charles Black, 1966, 1970, part 2, p. 151.
49 *Ibid.*, p. 157.
50 *Ibid.*, p. 160.
51 *Ibid.*
52 *Ibid.*, p. 159.
53 Edward King, *The Love and Wisdom of God*, pp. 294ff.
54 Bishop's House Ely, 'Conferences of East Anglia Bishops: Nov. 1889.' The Minute Books gives detailed accounts of the bishops' discussions throughout the whole of King's time at Lincoln.
55 Russell, *op. cit.*, p. 96.
56 Randolph and Townroe, *op. cit.*, p. 98.
57 *Spiritual Letters of Edward King, D.D.*, Letter XIX.
58 *Ibid.*, Letter XXXI.
59 Russell, *op. cit.*, p. 114.
60 Randolph and Townroe, *op. cit.*, p. 134.
61 Russell, *op. cit.*, p. 95.
62 Gladstone Papers, British Library, Add. MS 44,489, fos 177–8.
63 Edward King, *The Love and Wisdom of God*, pp. 266ff.
64 A. C. A. Hall, 'Father Benson,' in *Church Quarterly Review*, vol. lxxx, no. 159, April 1915, pp. 37–?
65 William Addison, *The English Country Parson*. London: J. M. Dent & Sons, 1948, pp. 188–9.
66 Newton, *op. cit.*, p. 85.
67 Randolph and Townroe, *op. cit.*, pp. 185–7.
68 *Ibid.*, p. 115.

69. *Ibid.*, pp. 113–17.
70. *Ibid.*, p. 117.
71. King, *The Love and Wisdom of God*, p. 275.
72. Lincolnshire Archives 27/46, *Lincoln Diocesan Magazine*, January 1887.
73. The Times, 16 March 1910.
74. Visitation Charge of 1895, p. 33.
75. Chadwick, *The Victorian Church*, part 2, p. 182
76. *Ibid.*, p. 156.
77. *Ibid.*, p. 168.
78. *Ibid.*, p. 169.
79. *Ibid.*, p. 157.
80. Russell, *op. cit.*, p. 86.
81. Chadwick, *op. cit.* p. 181.
82. Randolph and Townroe, *op. cit.*, p. 164.
83. Russell, *op. cit.*, p. 145.
84. Newton, *op. cit.*, p. 81.
85. Russell, *op. cit.*, p. 212.
86. Recorded humorously in the *Proceedings of the Second Ecumenical Methodist Conference*. New York: Hunt & Eaton,1892, pp. 125–6.
87. *Life and Letters of William John Butler*, p. 364.
88. John Keble, *Letters of Spiritual Counsel and Guidance* (ed. R. F. Wilson). Oxford and London: James Parker & Co., 1870 (2nd ed.), p. 18n.
89. Visitation Charge of 1895, pp. 31–3.
90. *Spiritual Letters of Edward King, D.D.*, Letter LXVIII.
91. Newton, *op. cit.*, p. 81.
92. *The Methodist Recorder*, 22 July 1909, p. 4.
93. Newton, *op. cit.*, pp. 81–2.

Fig. 1. Edward King (*left*) in the garden of the vicarage at Ellesmere, with the Revd John Peake (*centre*) and the Revd John Day. This photograph, taken some time between 1854 (King's ordination) and 1864 (Day's death), shows King in his late twenties or early thirties.

Fig. 2. Bishop King (seated) and some of the clergy who attended his first ordination in Lincoln Cathedral on 31 May 1885. On the left is Jacob Clements, the Sub-Dean, and next to him (wearing glasses) is the Chancellor, Dr E. T. Leeke, who preached the sermon. The clergymen in birettas on the right are two of the Bishop's four chaplains, who included Charles Gore, the figure sporting a beard.

Fig. 3. Bishop King in a photograph published in September 1889, when King was aged 59.

Fig. 4. Bishop King in old age. Photograph taken between 1905 and 1910.

Fig. 5. Stone Church, Kent, where King's father was Rector from 1822 to 1859. View of the chancel in 1833 as it was when Edward King was growing up in the parish.

Fig. 6. Oriel College, Oxford, where King was an undergraduate from 1848 to 1851. View of the First Quadrangle in 1834.

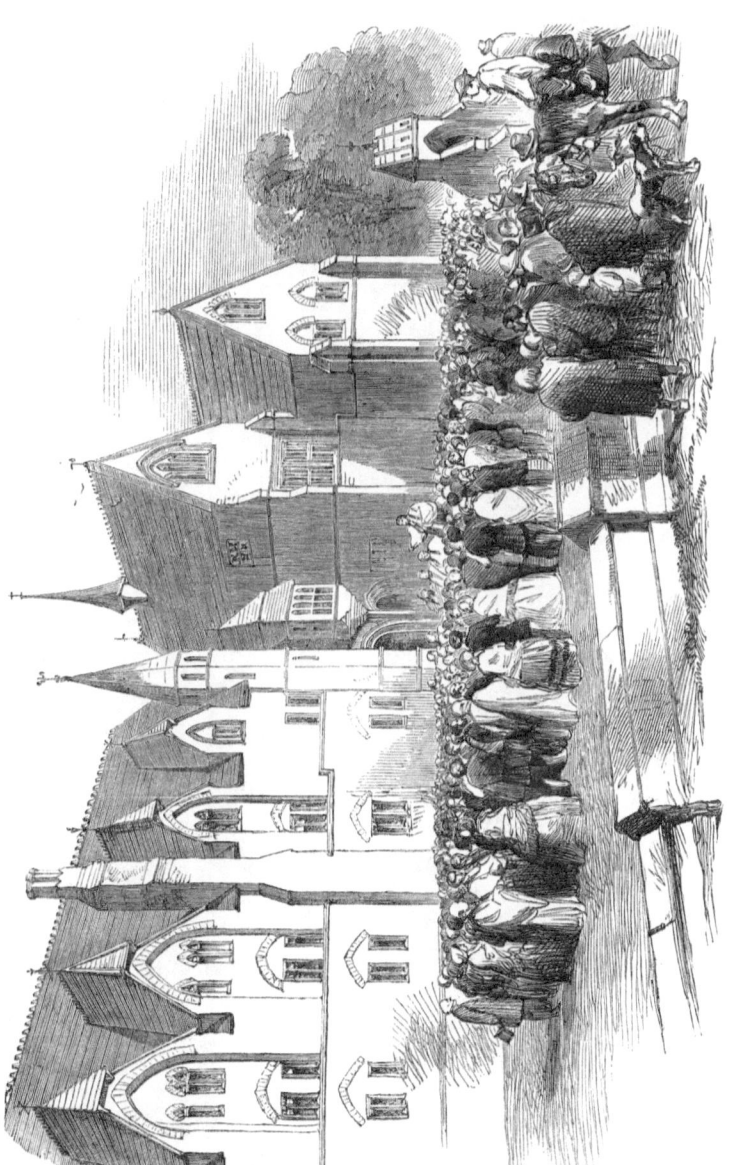

Fig. 7. Cuddesdon Theological College, Oxfordshire.
Bishop Wilberforce speaking at the opening of the College on 15 July 1854.

Fig. 8. Christ Church, Oxford, Tom Quad, where King lived from 1873 to 1885 during his time as Pastoral Professor. Photograph taken in the 1870s while building and restoration work was in progress. King was living there at the time: his lodgings were to the left of the newly opened double-arched entrance into the Cathedral from Tom Quad.

Fig. 9. Christ Church, Oxford, Tom Quad. Watercolour of the 1880s looking south-east after the completion of the building and restoration works. The newly completed Wolsey Tower is in the centre, the tower and spire of the Cathedral to the left and the Hall to the right.

Fig. 10. Christ Church, Cathedral, Oxford, where King, as Professor of Pastoral Theology, held a Canonry. The reredos, by G. F. Bodley, was installed during King's time.

Fig. 11. St Mary's University Church, Oxford, in 1833. As an undergraduate King attended services in St Mary's, and later, as Professor of Pastoral Theology, he delivered sermons from the pulpit shown here.

Fig. 12. Lincoln City in King's time. View of *c*. 1900 looking along Exchequer Gate to the Cathedral. All of the buildings seen here are still standing.

Fig. 13. The Chapter House at Lincoln Cathedral where King was formally elected Bishop by the Dean and Chapter on 20 March 1885. Following his enthronement in the Cathedral on 19 May, the Sub-Dean inducted King into the chief seat in the Chapter House and the hymn 'The Church is one Foundation' was sung.

Fig. 14. Lincoln, the Old Palace. View from the south in 1890 (*above*) and from the Cathedral in 1951 (*below*). Built in 1886-7, the Old Palace incorporates an existing building which was remodelled to match on the west, and on the east is linked to St Hugh's Chapel.

Fig. 15. St Hugh's Chapel at the Old Palace, Lincoln. Dedicated on 3 October 1888, this chapel was created for King by the architect G. F. Bodley in the ruins of the Great Hall and Solar of the medieval palace. This view of c. 1890 shows the chapel as King must have known it.

Fig. 16. Lincoln, aerial view of the Cathedral and Minster Yard looking north in 1933. St Hugh's Chapel is in the centre foreground, the Old Palace to the left, and further remains of the medieval palace to the right.

✣ 12 ✣

The Bishop on Trial: The Lincoln Judgment

A LANDMARK IN THE HISTORY OF THE CHURCH

The trial of Bishop Edward King and the judgment which issued from it proved to be a landmark in the history of the Victorian Church of England. It was also a turning point in the whole narrative of the Catholic Revival, and the bitter series of ritual disputes to which it gave rise. Edward Norman categorizes the trial as 'One of the most important, as well as one of the most extraordinary episodes in the religious history of the nineteenth century.'[1] R. W. Church, Dean of St Paul's, hailed the Judgment as, 'The most courageous thing that has come out of Lambeth for the last 200 years.'[2] Others, inevitably, given the passions roused by the ritualist controversy, took a more jaundiced view; but few serious Church people were indifferent to the result.

KING AND RITUALISM

The Lincoln Judgment of 1890 needs to be seen in the context of the Catholic Revival and the so-called Ritualists, which by the late nineteenth century had become a formidable movement and influence throughout the Church of England.

King, as we have seen, was neither a party man or a ritualist. As he said to Jacob Clements, the Sub-Dean of Lincoln

Cathedral, 'I am no Ritualist, as you know; but, where the doctrine is sound, I rejoice that our simpler (and, I believe, often better and holier) brethren may have the help which sound and sight may be to true devotion.'[3] It is difficult to label King's churchmanship satisfactorily. Perhaps the nearest we can come to it, is to speak of him as a High Church Tractarian, awakened and sensitive alike to the beauty of the natural world, the beauty of language and, in and through it all, always deeply desiring to communicate the love and wisdom of God and the doctrines and teachings of the Church, expressed in well-ordered liturgy and worship.

Theologically, King was grounded, as the Tractarians were, in scripture, the teachings of the early Church Fathers, and the Councils of the undivided Church. Together these constituted the foundation for all the *Tracts* produced at the outset of the Oxford Movement earlier in the century. His spirituality and his ecclesiology would have been much more in line with that of Keble, who himself was groomed from the earlier stable of George Herbert, Bishop Andrewes, Bishop Ken and the Caroline Divines, as Liddon pointedly demonstrated in his sermon at King's consecration in 1885.

The founding fathers of the Oxford Movement, had been much more concerned with doctrine and spirituality rather than with ritual, as indeed was King. Pusey was no ceremonialist and knew little of the theory of the subject. For many years Pusey was accustomed to celebrate the Holy Communion, standing at the north side of the altar. Only later would he wear the Eucharistic vestments in those churches where they were customarily worn.

For King, the outward forms of ritualism never constituted a 'last ditch stand.' However, on two other principles he was most certainly prepared to take a stand with what Scott Holland caricatured as the 'spirit of an old war-horse,'[4] or, as King delighted to say of himself, 'God has not given me a *chin* for nothing.'[5]

The Bishop on Trial: The Lincoln Judgment

As early as 1881 he had been one of thirty-two signatories to a memorial drawn up by Dean Church of St Paul's, and presented to Archbishop Tait in January of that year. It pleaded for 'a tolerant recognition of divergent Ritual Practice.'[6] Although King was often accused of being a Romanizer by his opponents this was untrue. Indeed, he was at times severely critical of what he termed 'the Roman system.' However, he was determined to stand for tolerance of a reasonable diversity, and a proper freedom of worship for High Church Anglicans.

From the outset of the Oxford Movement, the Tractarians consistently and vehemently reasserted the claim that the Church was not a department of State, nor merely an association for the reform of manners and morals, but nothing less than a Divine Society, founded by Jesus Christ and accountable to Him alone, as Head. They were contending for what later Nonconformists described as 'The Crown Rights of the Redeemer.' From the opening salvo of the Movement—Keble's Assize Sermon of 1833, condemning the Government's proposal to suppress ten Irish bishoprics—there had always been an inherent possibility of conflict between Church and State, which in the worst-case scenario would precipitate the disestablishment of the Church. Such were the sub-themes of the ritualist disputes and, in particular, of the trial of Bishop King.

RITUALISM

By the second half of the nineteenth century, another generation was emerging, who knew nothing first-hand of the personalities, the earlier doctrinal struggles and the hard-won sacrificial triumphs of the founding fathers of the Oxford Movement. After Dean Church attended Keble's funeral in 1866, he wrote to W. J. Copeland, who had been Newman's curate at the University Church, 'There was a meeting of old currents and new. Besides the people *I* used to think of with Keble, there was a crowd of younger men, who no doubt have as much right in him as we have, in their way—Mackonochie, Lowder, and that sort. Excellent good fellows, but who, one could not help being conscious, looked upon us as rather *dark* people, who don't grow beards, and do other proper things.'[7]

These 'younger men' were, of course, the budding Ritualists who were to come into full flower in the closing decades of the century. They were often dedicated priests, earnestly seeking to serve the poor in the slum parishes of the Industrial Revolution to whom they truly desired to communicate the glory and beauty of God. This could best be done by men, as was said of Percy Dearmer, who would 'rescue liturgiology from the pedantry of the mere man of letters' and so 'make it attractive to the whole church'[8], and not least to the poor and uneducated. That could not be achieved solely by verbal instruction, through preaching and teaching, but required the response of the senses in colourful and beautiful worship aided by vesture, posture, music and the aesthetic of form—in Dearmer's own words, 'the holiness of beauty, serving the beauty of holiness.'[9]

In their own parishes, the Ritualists emphasized the frequent celebration of the Eucharist and the Real Presence of Christ in the Sacrament of the altar, and their devotion produced not only a greater reverence in worship, but, in time, a more striking and colourful ritual. As the Movement spread from the University to the parishes, eager young clergy began introducing a markedly more Catholic element into their services. After all, a movement which began in a university, and which had been 'marketed,' exported and communicated through learned theological writings—*Tracts for the Times*—had been animated largely by scholars and Fellows of Colleges, whose whole lives were lived out in a privileged and cloistered environment. The movement needed something more if it were to catch fire in parish ministry, something which could speak to both heart and senses, and not just to the intellect. Eucharistic vestments, candles lit on the altar, the eastward-facing position of the celebrant at Holy Communion, the use of incense, bowing or genuflecting to reverence the altar or the Sacrament: these became increasingly common accompaniments of High Church worship, especially in the poorer parishes of East London, and in the industrialized cities of the North, which hitherto had been largely neglected by the ministry of the Established Church.

The best of this emerging generation of Ritualists were not sold on ceremonial for its own sake: they had a passion for the souls of their parishioners so that through prayer, scripture, sacrament and beautified worship, ordinary men and women would come to experience for themselves the love and glory of God.

To that same end, they were also concerned, through the use of the Sacrament of Confession, to lead and direct their parishioners to a deeper knowledge of God and to a conversion of life, rather than being content merely to attract more church-goers and to fill pews. The beautifying of church buildings created what many came to call 'sacred space,' aided by the Cambridge Camden Society and other similar societies, which disseminated knowledge of cathedral and old parish-church architecture—which for them had to be Gothic—in a reaction against the proliferating ugliness of the industrial cities. Increasingly, art, literature and architecture looked back to the Middle Ages as being the central point of reference in all such aspects of aesthetics. So, as the century went on, that fuse originally lit by the earlier Oxford fathers fired up an increasing number of parishes in precisely those places where more formal and less colourful worship had largely failed to draw people to experience God in transcendent worship.

Inevitably and predictably, the spread of ritualistic practices provoked a backlash among clergy and laity alike, who insisted on the fundamentally Protestant nature of their Church and who saw the Ritualists as 'Romanizers,' who, like Newman, would one day come clean, convert to Rome and seek to take their parishioners with them. The disputes kindled deeply felt passions, which can be understood only if we take seriously the virulence of anti-Catholicism in Victorian England.

The fear and hatred of Rome is difficult for our own largely secular society to grasp, where the differences between various Christian traditions of doctrine and worship would be regarded, by the majority of the population, with a measure of indifference. Perhaps the nearest contemporary analogy would be that of the most extreme Protestant sectarianism in Northern Ireland and the historically entrenched Roman Catholicism of the Republic.

Back in 1867, a Ritual Commission, chaired by the Archbishop of Canterbury, Charles Longley, had been appointed to inquire into differences of ceremonial practice in the Church of England. Its reports, published successively in 1867, 1868 and 1870, condemned eucharistic vestments, lighted candles on the altar during Communion, and the use of incense. The Commissioners also recommended that the Ornaments Rubric in the Book of Common Prayer, stating that lawful ceremonial should only be that permitted under the First (1549) Prayer Book of Edward VI, and should be left unaltered. This rubric had long been a battleground of controversy, and would remain so, despite the pious hopes of the Commissioners, who would have liked Parliament to turn their recommendations into law. But with Gladstone, a High Churchman, as Prime Minister at the time, they stood no chance.

In 1871 an important legal judgment was given in the case of a ritualist clergyman, the Revd John Purchas, Vicar of St James, Brighton. The Dean of the Arches found in favour of Purchas, but on appeal, the Judicial Committee of the Privy Council reversed this decision, and declared eucharistic

The Bishop on Trial: The Lincoln Judgment

vestments, the eastward position, the mixed chalice, and the use of wafer breads, to be illegal, and so the battles lines were finally and even more firmly drawn.

The fact that since 1833 the Judicial Committee of the Privy Council had been constituted as the Final Court of Appeal in ecclesiastical causes was anathema to the High Church party and smacked in their eyes of rank Erastianism, whereby the institutional church would become increasingly perceived as simply little more than a department of the State. After all, the members of the Judicial Committee were lay judges with no special theological training to fit them for the sensitive task of adjudicating in matters of doctrine and ritual: they did not consult the body of bishops, who were the appointed guardians and teachers of the Faith. To High Churchmen, and the second generation of the original Oxford Movement, pressing for more 'Catholic' forms of worship and ritual, it was nothing less than a travesty of Church Order that the definition of faith and the regulation of worship should be in the hands of such a secular tribunal. Nor were they overly impressed by the tinkering reform of 1873, whereby some bishops were allowed seats on the Judicial Committee, but as assessors only, not judges. Thus, many High Church incumbents felt free to ignore the Purchas Judgment, made by a tribunal they perceived as lacking all competent spiritual and theological authority.

THE ANTI-RITUALIST MOVEMENT

All the while, the anti-Ritualist movement was gathering strength. On 5 May 1873, a deputation representing 60,000 persons presented a memorial to the two archbishops at Lambeth in favour of 'the entire suppression of ceremonies and practices adjudged to be illegal.'[10] The archbishops listened to the speeches of the deputation, and after a few weeks delay, in a written statement, replied that they did 'not consider it to be the duty of the bishops to undertake judicial proceedings upon every complaint of a violation of the rubrics or upon every charge of unsound doctrine that may be laid before them.'

Their concluding remarks show a striking and indeed impressive witness to the tolerance of the Anglican tradition which relies more on 'influence gently exercised' rather than authority legally enforced. For, as they wrote:

> however much may be effected by the legitimate exercise of authority, still, in a Protestant Church like ours, it is by kindly personal influence in our several families and neighbourhoods, by sound arguments, and appeals to the loyalty of those who are in danger of falling into error, rather than by judicial acts of authoritative interference, that the tendencies of which [the protesters] had justly complained, could be met.[11]

ARCHBISHOP TAIT AND THE PUBLIC WORSHIP REGULATION ACT

At this point, Archbishop Tait, not to his liking, nor by his own devising, was propelled centre-stage, both in Parliament and in Convocation, for the better part of 1874, to devise an Act of Parliament which would deal with the whole matter of ritualism justly, firmly and finally.

Although Tait from his earliest days as Dean of Carlisle and later as Bishop of London, had been friendly to the earlier personalities and the influence of the Oxford Movement, he was, like many episcopal colleagues, strongly opposed to the emerging Anglo-Catholicism of the second half of the century. Nevertheless, he always sought to be fair-handed, especially in his dealings with the clergy, and while he had no personal sympathy with Ritualism, he had clearly perceived the measure of spiritual dynamism among those clergy, often called 'enthusiasts,' who had a passion

The Bishop on Trial: The Lincoln Judgment

for souls and who sought to bring the Gospel to the many the Established Church had hitherto failed to reach.

> I have great sympathy with earnestness, but I have no sympathy with persons who make the Church of England something quite different from that which it was made at the Reformation, and something totally different from that which the great and overwhelming majority of the people of England regard as their national Church.[12]

Moreover, the Queen, with whom Tait had a close working relationship—she had pressed for his appointment to Canterbury—was now urging him to action. 'It is clear,' she wrote to him, 'that the liberties taken and the defiance shown by the Clergy of the High Church and Ritualist party is so great that something *must be done* to check it, and prevent its continuation.'[13]

So, wise and discerning though Tait may have been on the issue of ritualists and ritualism, and in his joint response with the Archbishop of York to the speeches of that earlier deputation, he had nevertheless failed to quench the enflamed passions of the growing number of anti-ritualists. It was inevitable that, sooner rather than later, this thorny and divisive nettle of what many regarded as liturgical chaos, would have to be grasped, and it fell to Archbishop Tait to deal with the matter. He spent six months wrestling with the bishops in and out of Parliament, in order to get on the Statute Book what ultimately came to be regarded as the notorious and controversial Public Worship Regulation Act of 1874.

'How does it happen that the wisest and most respected of your Bishops, is the author of the most unpopular, ridiculous and unworkable Acts of Parliament?'[14] Such were the comments of a distinguished American churchman who visited England in 1878. Although it would be unfair to lay the blame solely at Tait's feet, nevertheless, as the drafting of the Bill proceeded, it became increasingly clear that the Archbishop was its principal author; indeed, that he had taken the whole matter to himself in his person and office as Primate of all England. As it happened several unfortunate and unforeseen events, as well as the intervention of particular personalities, delayed the Bill's hazardous passage through Parliament and at times came close to derailing it completely.

'On January 12th and 13th, 1874, the Bishops of both Provinces met at Lambeth in full force, and decided upon immediate action. A Bill was to be drafted in the first instance by the two Archbishops.'[15] Lord Shaftesbury and his anti-ritualist supporters wanted to extend its scope beyond matters of ritual to deal with other controversial practices, and on 27 March, Shaftesbury wrote the letter quoted on p. 195, denouncing the use of the Confessional. This request was again and again renewed, both in Parliament and further afield, but the Archbishop set his face against any attempt to open the discussion to include these wider topics.

All Tait's good intentions were, however, overtaken by events. Parliament was due to have met on 5 February and Convocation the following week, when the newly proposed Bill would be jointly discussed. Unexpectedly, however, on 24 January, Gladstone, a supporter of the High Church movement, dissolved Parliament and appealed to the country, only to be defeated three weeks later. Disraeli, his Tory opponent, succeeded him as Prime Minister with a large majority in the House of Commons.

Now it was a whole new ball game. How would the new Parliament, let alone the new Cabinet, with Lord Cairns, Lord Salisbury and Disraeli himself, regard the proposals of the archbishops in this first draft of their Bill? Tait knew only too well how important it was to gain the co-operation of the politicians. Accordingly, the scheme was submitted in rough outline not only to Disraeli, but also to Cairns, Salisbury, Shaftesbury, Beresford Hope, and other lay Churchmen whose opinion as to its Parliamentary possibilities and general expediency, was likely to be of value.

The Bishop on Trial: The Lincoln Judgment

This shrewd political move by Tait inflamed Convocation who had expected to have been consulted first, not for detailed discussion, but in order that the Lower House (the clergy), might be fully and formally informed of the extent to which the bishops had found themselves able to adopt the recommendations embodied in its first report.

All this had been frustrated by the unexpected dissolution of Parliament and the loss of Gladstone, a committed ally. For the next six months both Houses of Parliament, as well as the bishops and the Lower House of Convocation, juggled with various amendments to Tait's Bill, sometimes for purely political gain, sometimes for ecclesiastical party interests. Most conspicuously, it was Lord Shaftesbury, the leading Evangelical layman, who described the Archbishop's Bill on its second reading as 'so much waste paper,'[16] moving a series of amendments which would transfer decisions to a single lay judge—admittedly appointed by the archbishops—who would hear all representations under the Act, but emphatically without any intervention by the Diocesan Courts.

Tait realized that a majority in the Commons would support Shaftesbury's amendments, and that he had two options: either to speak and vote against the amendments, only to be defeated and for the Bill to be thrown out completely in favour of other more severe legislation, or to accept the new clauses with some sort of compromise arrangement.

The 'red line' for Tait, was the question of the power and authority of the local diocesan bishop to veto and override any suit against a priest for unlawful ritual practices: on that point the Archbishop refused to yield, referring in later years to the veto as being 'the very essence' of the Bill. In other words, the local bishop, knowing the priest concerned and the pastoral context of the charge against him, could retain the power of veto, so that the case would be dropped. At the time it might have been thought that, in refusing to budge on what he considered a fundamental principle, Tait was straining at the 'gnat' of his episcopal veto clause and, by compromise, swallowing the 'camel' of Shaftesbury's amendments. In fact, and certainly with hindsight, the very opposite proved to be the case: by giving the diocesan bishop pastoral discretion, Tait was providentially seeking to ensure that the bishop's primary concern as *pastor pastorum* in all matters, was pastoral and not merely juridical and managerial.

Even at this late stage of exhausting debate and bitter controversy, Shaftesbury still resisted the right of episcopal veto, insisting on an overriding appeal to the Archbishop of the Province for the final review of the local bishop's discretionary veto. On 4 August a sharp debate took place in the Lords over the insertion of this new clause, and Shaftesbury's amendment and proposed change was defeated by 44 votes to 32.

Shorn of that amendment, the Bill returned to the Commons where, contrary to Disraeli's expectation that it would be rejected, MPs reluctantly gave way and after a long and memorable debate, left the diocesan bishop's discretion unfettered. The Bill was read for the third time on 5 August and received the Royal Assent a few days later.

On Sunday evening, 9 August 1874, while resting in the archbishops' country seat at Addington, near Croydon, Tait reflected on the turbulent events of the past week, culminating in the passing of his Bill the previous Wednesday, and wrote in his personal diary:

> I and the Archbishop of York had a long talk with Disraeli. Then, at twelve, began that memorable debate, which I cannot describe. By two o'clock the Bill was safe, and I wrote in the House of Lords to the Queen—'Thank God, the Bill has passed.' I received congratulations on all sides. So ends a work which has given no rest for six months. May God grant that the peace and lasting good of His Church may follow from our labours.[17]

Although in some of its details the new Act differed from

The Bishop on Trial: The Lincoln Judgment

that first envisaged by the two archbishops with the counsel of their brethren six months previously, nevertheless the main principles for which Tait had from the first contended were still in place. The Act concerned itself purely with procedure and confined that procedure to a single and very limited class of alleged infractions of the law. It listed no new offences. Nothing which had been lawful before became unlawful under its provisions. It provided merely for the hearing of any complaint made against a priest for ritual practices to go forward, if the bishop chose not to override it by invoking his discretionary right of veto. Furthermore, it required that any complaints of irregularity had to be made by at least three *bona fide* parishioners and members of the Church of England, whereas the former Act had allowed proceedings to be instituted by anyone.

Despite Tait's genuine desire to avoid legal prosecutions for unlawful ritual practice, and his concessionary clauses giving bishops power to veto vicious complaints against hardworking clergy, four priests were subsequently convicted of ritual illegalities under the Act, and chose jail rather than submit. The first, in 1877, was the Revd Arthur Tooth, Vicar of St James's Hatcham in south-east London.

In fairness to Tait, and indeed to the Act's supporters, imprisonment had not been foreseen. This lamentable consequence arose because an Act of 1813, which substituted imprisonment for excommunication as the punishment for contempt of an ecclesiastical court, had been overlooked and was still acting as precedent.

To write off the 1874 Act as a fiasco, is to overstate the unfortunate outcome, yet, as Tait and his colleague at York had pointed out at the outset, it was inevitably bound to be so, precisely 'because it relied ultimately on force either in the form of inhibition and deprivation or through imprisonment. As ever, in a contest with determined religious conviction, force backfired on those who employed it.'[18]

Edward King

The imprisonment under the Act of Arthur Tooth (1877), and subsequently of three other men, Pelham Dale (1880), Richard Enraght (1880), and Sidney Green (1881–2), served only to bring it into discredit. As so often throughout history, it is 'the blood of the martyrs which is the seed of the church': these prosecutions caused outrage within the High Church party, as well as winning sympathy for the imprisoned priests from across a wide spectrum of churchmanship. In the long run, they only encouraged more moderate bishops to stay proceedings by exercising of their veto.

THE CHURCH ASSOCIATION

To the end of his life, Tait genuinely sought to reconcile the warring parties over the matter of ritualism and, as some people perceived the events of recent years, over the encroaching dangers of the Romanizers infiltrating both the teachings and liturgical practices of the Church of England as by Law Established. For both Ritualists and their more militant opponents, the points at issue were not only liturgical, but also doctrinal; ceremonies had clear doctrinal implications. What seemed trivial to some, touched the kernel of the Faith for others, so that after the passing of the Bill, the hardened Evangelicals of the Church Association were freshly re-invigorated to pursue prosecutions as being the only way left, as they saw it, to preserve the reformed nature of the Church of England, by seeking out High Church clergy, who in their view broke the rubrics of the Book of Common Prayer, and anything that smacked of 'Romanism.'

Back in 1867 the Association had shown its mettle by initiating proceedings against Father A. H. Mackonochie, the well-known High Church Vicar of St Alban's, Holborn, for ritualistic practices, which dragged on for many years. The Association was relentless in its pursuit of him and in 1878 instituted another prosecution under the new Public

The Bishop on Trial: The Lincoln Judgment

Worship Regulation Act, and Mackonochie was suspended for three years. Yet another round of prosecutions began in 1882, when, at Tait's request, Mackonochie resigned his living, vowing vehemently never to accept the subservience of the Church to the State. He is on record as declaring, 'Let the State send forth the Church roofless and penniless, but free, and I will say, "Thank you."' For the moment, it might have seemed that the Ritualists, by 'stooping to conquer' in the person of Mackonochie, had won the higher moral ground. However, for many militant Evangelicals, and no less for the Church Association, the real battle had only just begun. They had had King in their sights since the day in 1885 when he was named Bishop of Lincoln, and it was to Lincoln and its Bishop that they now turned their attention.

PROCEEDINGS AGAINST KING

It was as though the Church Association had only been testing the waters of litigation with Mackonochie. Now, armed with the Public Worship Regulation Act, they seized an opportunity to land a far bigger fish, and ironically, it was King's own use of the veto provided for in the Act allowing bishops to stop ritual proceedings against their clergy, which gave to the Association the opportunity to bring charges against King himself.

The storm began in a remote Lincolnshire parish with a cloud no bigger than a man's hand. In the autumn of 1886, Ernest de Lacy Read, a churchwarden at Clee-cum-Cleethorpes, brought charges of ritualism, including the wearing of vestments, against his High Church rector, J. P. Benson. King used his veto to bar the prosecution, at the same time bringing pastoral pressure to bear on young Benson to adopt simpler and more traditional practices in his Eucharistic celebrations. Read, a local solicitor, was not satisfied, and appealed King's decision to Archbishop Benson.

The Primate, a personal friend and admirer of King, refused to intervene, so Read, backed by the Church Association, decided to press forward and indict King himself. On 22 June 1888, the Association petitioned Benson to try King, as though letting go of a mere sprat of a country parson, would result in catching and finally netting a much larger and more notable episcopal mackerel.

Although King had been at Lincoln for only three years, he was already recognized as the leading High Church bishop on the Bench at the time, and renowned for his transparent goodness and holiness of life. As Liddon, pointed out to Bishop Lightfoot in June 1888, when the forthcoming storm of King's trial was becoming evident:

> That such a person as the Bishop of Lincoln should be exposed to the vexation of legal proceedings is a serious misfortune to the Church—much more serious than to the Bishop himself, who would probably regard it simply as an opportunity for growth in Christian graces. But, as a consequence of his rare and rich gift of spiritual sympathy, the number of people in all classes of society who look up to him with a strong personal respect and affection, is probably quite unrivalled in the case of any other prominent churchman of the same type, and the mere apprehension of his being attacked is already creating widespread disquietude. Anything like a condemnation would be followed by consequences which I do not venture to anticipate.[19]

Lincoln, at that time, might well have been described as a 'tale of two cities': one, the poorer part, 'below hill,' where the growing number of foundry and factory workers worked and lived in crowded streets of terraced houses, and 'up-hill,' where the wealthy lived, in their large houses under the shadow of the Cathedral.

On 5 June 1885, just a few weeks after King's enthronement, an article the *Lincolnshire Chronicle*, entitled 'Church Enlargement in the City,' reported:

The Bishop on Trial: The Lincoln Judgment

> It is proposed to enlarge the old parish church of St. Peter-at-Gowts. The Bishop of Lincoln is to speak at a meeting in the school-room on Saturday afternoon next at three o'clock. As this will be his Lordship's first public appearance below hill there is sure to be a large attendance. The parish church, which is supposed to provide church accommodation for a population of 4,000, is very small and inconvenient … If a larger and more convenient church can be built without any detriment to the Saxon, Norman, and Early English portions of the present work, a great boon will be bestowed on the parish. The church is largely attended, but very many of the seats are behind pillars, or out of sight of the pulpit. As strangers are generally placed in these places the church is little known to any except the regular congregation.[20]

It was in that church, duly extended along Tractarian and High Church lines, with an ample chancel and sanctuary with a raised, large high altar at the East end, which was fated to be the 'hotspot' for all the charges brought against King a few years later.

In a little under two years after that meeting 'below hill,' all the money for the church extension had been raised, and both King and Archbishop Benson were present for its consecration. Benson wrote in his diary on Sunday, 4 December 1887:

> Went on the 3rd to Lincoln at the request of the workingmen of the parish of St Peter-at-Gowts, whose efforts have raised half of the £2,000 which the enlargement of their church has cost. Their good Vicar, Townroe, one of the first of my *Scholae Cancellarii* has found the rest. I tried to preach to *them* only their faces preached to me. Dined and slept at the Bishop's … A large gathering at the Communion in the Cathedral which I celebrated at 8.00. The Bishop went to the consecration at St Peter-at-Gowts at 8 in white cope—if he had a mitre, he hid it. I saw him off.[21]

Neither Benson nor King could have foreseen that it was precisely what occurred on that fateful Second Sunday of Advent, 4 December 1887, and the Sunday a fortnight later, which would occasion the most momentous event of both their ministerial lives. It was on those two Advent Sundays, that King was 'observed' performing ceremonial acts, allegedly contrary to what was permitted by the Prayer Book:

> 1. Mixing water with the sacramental wine during the service and subsequently consecrating the Mixed Cup.
> 2. Standing in the 'Eastward Position' during the first part of the Communion service.
> 3. Standing during the prayer of Consecration on the West side of the table, in such manner that the congregation could not see the manual acts performed.
> 4. Causing the hymn *Agnus Dei* to be sung after the Consecration prayer.
> 5. Pouring water and wine into the paten and chalice after the service and afterwards drinking such water and wine before the congregation.
> 6. The use of lighted candles on the Communion table or on the re-table behind, during the Communion service, when not needed for the purpose of giving light.
> 7. During the Absolution and Benediction making the sign of the Cross with upraised hand facing the congregation.

THE ARCHBISHOP'S COURT

If King had been tried either by Tait or Frederick Temple, the outcome might have been quite different. At the human, personal level, Benson and King shared a number of common ties. They were the same age and both had links with Lincoln, King as the current Bishop and Benson as a former Chancellor of the Cathedral: in temperament, however, they were vastly different. King emphatically did not welcome the drama and publicity of the trial; Benson, who was something of an expert in the field of liturgical history, rather revelled in the opportunity both to exercise and exhibit it, and all with a touch of theatricality—the Primate of all England holding forth in his Court in the great library of Lambeth Palace. The Archbishop was by no means unsympathetic to High Church practice, but he was determined to act with judicious impartiality in what he knew would be a *cause célèbre*. Back in 1866, as Bishop of Truro, he had revealed his hand in the matter in his Charge to the Diocese regarding the 'efforts' of the Anglo-Catholic clergy to dignify their churches as sacred space.

> No doubt the spirit in which these efforts originated has done very much of late years to invest our houses of God with a more seemly dignity which has been found very attractive, especially to the young ... But there is an excessive ritualism of another kind ... Certain persons have taken upon themselves to alter the whole external appearance of the Lord's Supper as to make it scarcely distinguishable from the Roman Mass ... The number of those who are so committed is, I am convinced, very small.

He then continued, as though with extraordinary foresight, to express the hope,

> that good sense and good feeling of the clergy and the kindly admonitions of authority will prevail, without making it necessary to defend the Church from the innovations of a few, whether by painful legal prosecutions or by a declaratory enactment of Parliament and Convocation. If admonitions fail, then at last an enactment must explain how and under what safeguards that controlling influence, which the Church has ever contemplated as vested in its chief officers, shall be made to bear on the discretion of individual clergymen.

But now, as Archbishop of Canterbury, Benson had been pitchforked into a case of alleged unlawful practices by no lesser person than a bishop who was not only highly regarded but also a personal and admired friend. Benson was in a quandary as to whether or not to hear the case in his own Archiepiscopal Court. Even if the legal jurisdiction of the Court were to be established, the precedence about the mode of procedure was still thought by competent advisors to be doubtful. Under these circumstances, there came pressure and advice (requested and unrequested) from all sides; should the Archbishop deny the competence of his court to try the case, or should he simply veto it. Edward Talbot, then Warden of Keble College, and a leading High Churchman, was clear that the Primate should refuse to act. Writing to Randall Davidson, Dean of Windsor, in June 1888, Talbot urged:

> Isn't this little cloud which has risen out of the sea re Bishop of Lincoln threatening to become a big storm? I confess to feeling most seriously alarmed ... Surely the only course is for the Archbishop to decline to take up the case. I know that it may involve risks, first of attack by way of application for *mandamus*, then through Parliament. But even if these are possible (and the latter is most doubtful) the risks are well worth taking. He would be fighting for what on every ground of policy and principle we should desire—the right of the Church's Chief Officer to independence and discretion in the exercises of his functions.[22]

Benson thought otherwise. He believed that if he refused to act, the complainants would almost certainly apply to the Court of Queen's Bench for a writ of *mandamus*, which would compel him to hear the case. Yet there was still the question of whether the Archbishop had the legal right to hold such a court, and if so, what was the precedent for such an action? The muddy legal waters were sufficiently cleared when, in August 1888, the Judicial Committee of the Privy Council ruled that the Archbishop did indeed have a right of jurisdiction in such a case, and Benson decided to go ahead.

The Bishop on Trial: The Lincoln Judgment

In fact, there was no exact precedent for a trial of one of an Archbishop's diocesans. The closest parallel was the case of Bishop Watson of St David's, whom Archbishop Tenison in 1699, sitting with six episcopal assessors, deprived of his office for scandalous life and conduct.[23] The charges in that case, however, were moral, not liturgical, and King's blameless life was universally acknowledged.

Benson chose six bishops of the Southern Province to sit with him, not, as he made quite clear, as judges but as assessors, in this way reserving the final judgment to himself. At least two of them—Browne of Winchester and the learned Stubbs of Oxford—appear to have disagreed with Benson that he had sole jurisdiction. Indeed, Stubbs served only under protest, and could be heard, throughout the trial, muttering with his somewhat perverse and academic mannerisms, 'This is not a court; it is an Archbishop sitting in his Library.'[24] Stubbs had been a member of the 1883 Ecclesiastical Courts Commission, whose members had argued, unanimously, that if a bishop were ever to be tried, it should be by a tribunal of comprovincial bishops. Initially, that was exactly the view taken by King himself, and by his advisors and his legal counsel at the trial, Sir Walter Phillimore. They argued strongly, before even the trial got underway, that King should be tried by his peers, namely, by all the bishops of the Southern Province in Synod. It was King's protest along these lines which scuppered the arrangements for the opening of the trial.

THE PRELIMINARY HEARING

That had been due to take place on 12 February 1889, on what turned out to be a very cold day of snow and icy rain. Benson drove up to Lambeth from Canterbury to open the Court at 11.00am. That same day, King had sent a letter to every incumbent in his diocese, containing the 'Opening

Statement' he was proposing to make later that day with its plea against the composition of the Court. The letter ended with a telling word of personal explanation as to the importance of the proceedings which were about to take place.

> It is not, and it has never been, my desire to enforce any unaccustomed observance on an unwilling congregation; but my hope now is that this prosecution may, in God's providence, be so overruled as ultimately to promote the peace of the Church by leading to some authoritative declaration of tolerance for certain details of ritual observance, in regard to which I believe that they are either in direct accordance with the letter of the Prayer Book, or at the least in loyal and perfect harmony with the mind of the Church of England. Asking for your prayers that I may know and do our Divine Master's Will in all things, I am, my dear Brother, Yours sincerely,
>
> EDWARD LINCOLN[25]

Randall Davidson, the Dean of Windsor and a close adviser to Benson who had strongly advocated King's preferment in 1885, met King on the staircase at Lambeth Palace on his way to the Court. King was accompanied by his Sub-Dean, Clements, Lord Halifax, the President of the English Church Union, B. W. Randolph, and other friends and supporters. Davidson asked King if he intended to speak. 'Yes,' replied King, 'I'm going to make a statement and then leave it to my counsel. I suppose I'm right not to be in robes? Who wears robes?' 'Only the judges,' replied Davidson, 'I think you are right as you are.'[26] In fact the six episcopal assessors, looking suitably grand for the occasion wore their scarlet Convocation robes while King sat wearing a fur-lined overcoat given him by his friend, H. O. Wakeman, the Oxford historian.[27]

Davidson decided that Benson should know of King's intention to make a statement before the trial and sent Sir John Hassard, Registrar of the Province of Canterbury to tell him. 'So,' Benson recorded in his diary, 'I together with the

The Bishop on Trial: The Lincoln Judgment

Vicar-General went to the Guard Room to meet the Bishop of Lincoln with his Counsel—Phillimore—to ask whether it was a Protest. They said it was a statement ending with a kind of Protest.'[28]

In many ways this appears uncharacteristic of King, even subversive, and from a letter he wrote to Canon Perry on 6 February it is clear that he was not entirely happy with the advice he had been given. He tells Perry how he had gone up to London to meet with his counsel, Phillimore, Jeune and Kempe, and it was they 'who were again so persistent in wishing me to protest against the Archbishop's Court, and ask to be heard in Convocation by my Comprovincials.' However, not even the advice of his three defence lawyers was sufficient to convince King that his 'Protest' was the best way to proceed:

> I thought it right to go on Sunday to Oxford, where I gathered together Bright, Liddon, Bramley, Paget, Wakeman, and Gore [which may be the occasion when Wakeman gave him the fur-lined coat]; and their mind was that in the interests of the Church it would be right to protest against a Suffragan being tried by his Metropolitan, except with Comprovincials.

So, it would seem, in King's words, that 'this agreement between Lawyers and Divines (falling in, as it does to a great extent, with the Bishop of Oxford)' whom, presumably, he had also consulted, 'seemed too grave an authority for me to put aside. I have therefore determined to appear on Tuesday [12 February] *under Protest* and raise the question of the Archbishop's Court.'[29]

When Benson met him in the Guard Room, he urged King not to hold up proceedings and to make his prepared 'statement' after the Court had been opened: King and Phillimore were adamant that it should be before. Graciously, if a little reluctantly, Benson yielded. Accordingly, King rose to make his statement, before and not after what would have been the formal opening of proceedings.

> My Lord Archbishop, I appear before your Grace in deference to the Citation which I have received, and in accordance with my oath of 'due reverence and obedience' to your Grace and the See of Canterbury; but I appear under protest, desiring, with all respect, to question the jurisdiction which your Grace proposes to exercise ... There can be no doubt that, in accordance with the practice of the Primitive Church, the most proper method for the trial of a Bishop in such cases would be before the Metropolitan with the Comprovincial Bishops ... I would, therefore, humbly pray your Grace to allow me to be heard by Counsel on this point, whether your Grace's Jurisdiction would not be more properly exercised, with regard to the matters charged against me, by your Grace as Metropolitan with the Comprovincial Bishops ... of the Province.[30]

As Benson recorded in his diary, King had made it clear that he would request to be 'tried before all the Bishops of the Province, although whether as Judges or Assessors he did not explain. However, I must silence all preconceived ideas and hear the arguments with an open mind. I gave them a week at their request to extend their Protest and appointed a month hence to hear it argued.'[31] Thus the meticulously planned trial was postponed to a later date.

During that time Benson took advice from many sources and was firmly of the opinion that there was no precedent for a bishop being 'tried' with either assessors or judges drawn from all the bishops of the Province, as King was planning to request. Furthermore, as was pointed out to King, if such a change of procedure had been allowed at this late stage, Counsel for the Church Association would most likely appeal to the Queen's Bench for a prohibition and the whole matter of the Archbishop's Court could be overturned and something far less desirable would replace it.

Accordingly, the Court reconvened in May specifically to hear King make his case. When the bishops and Vicar-General, Sir James Parker Deane, had taken their places, the

The Bishop on Trial: The Lincoln Judgment

Archbishop, standing, said three Collects followed by the Lord's Prayer. King then rose to make his statement, although according to an entry in Benson's diary some weeks earlier, King's viewpoint had changed somewhat and he now much preferred 'the Court to be as it is, but thought that he ought to do something on behalf of primitive custom.' Benson's own sardonic observation was: 'That side does not seem to know that Metropolitans and Primates were introduced because Synods were so factious and unjust'[32]—an amazingly apt and surely a timeless comment.

In a long speech, on Saturday, 11 May, lasting not less than an hour-and-a-half, Benson delivered his judgment on the constitution of the Court. He convincingly established the claim that 'from the most ancient times of the Church, the Archiepiscopal jurisdiction in the case of Suffragans has existed; that in the Church of England it has been from time to time continuously exercised in various forms; [and] that nothing has occurred in the Church to modify that jurisdiction.'[33] Consequently King's claim that his case should be heard in the Synod of the Province, and judged by his fellow bishops, was overruled.

Although King's insistence that the Archbishop's Court was not the appropriate arena for his trial, and his 'Protest' had scuppered Benson's original arrangements for hearing the case, it seems to have made no difference to their friendship. Later that year, on 2 November, Benson had been invited by the Secretary of the Co-operative Association, an old friend, to come to Lincoln and speak at a working-men's demonstration. Responding, Benson insisted that King will be seen to be with him, as 'he is my very old friend.' Subsequently Benson wrote to the Dean of Windsor telling him all about his happy visit to Lincoln:

> I have just returned (midnight) from Lincoln where I have been all day at a wonderful working men's demonstration. It was a worthy sight to see dear Lincoln [King] and me sitting together in front of the working

men's platform—no one else but working men—and going off together. He is adored there.[34]

In the light of such affectionate admiration and friendship, it is hard to believe that no mention was made during the Archbishop's visit to the events of the past year, or to the forthcoming trial, finally scheduled for early in the new year.

THE TRIAL

It was now almost exactly a year since that cold, rainy day in February 1889 when, but for King's 'Protest,' the trial had originally been scheduled to begin. Now, on 4 February 1890, the full-blown hearing of the case against King opened and the proceedings meandered on for three weeks until 25 February. The venue was again the library at Lambeth Palace, with its high timbered roof, tall bookcases and darkened interior: with all the participants in place, the stage was set for the much-awaited trial of the Bishop of Lincoln to begin.

The Archbishop had taken extraordinary care to ensure that the 'ritual' of the proceedings should be as impressive as it was dignified, exactly as he had done for the Lambeth Conference in 1888. 'He had himself been to the Library before the Case was opened to see that the semi-circular table at which the bishops sat and which had been designed by him, should once again be put up exactly as he wished, on a dais at one end of the great hall—his seat in the middle was a little raised above the rest,' leaving no doubt as to who was the principal 'actor.'

Benson's son and biographer tells us that his father's 'manner as a judge was singularly impressive … Throughout the proceedings he had a grasp of the subject down to the minutest details, which was fairly astonishing. Thus, he frequently supplied to counsel names and dates which had escaped them, and pointed out possible constructions of statements and facts, which displayed a rare legal acumen.'[35] Clearly, Benson was in his element and fully in control.

The episcopal assessors were all there: Frederick Temple (London); William Stubbs (Oxford); Anthony W. Thorold (Rochester); John Wordsworth (Salisbury), and James Atlay (Hereford), taking the place of Harold Browne (Winchester), who was unable to attend on account of a bout of ill-health.

The Church Association was chiefly represented by Sir Horace Davey, QC, then aged 56, who had been Benson's pupil at Rugby. Benson wrote in his diary, 'Davey came in not knowing the difference between the First and Second Prayer Book of Edward VI, or much else of his brief. But he picked up quickly what he ought to say and said it incisively.'[36] Remarking on Davey's arguments, Benson wrote, 'It was exactly the same way that he used to construe Thucydides to me when I was school-house tutor at Rugby.'

For the Church Association, Davey was joined by Dr Thomas H. Tristram, QC, and Mr William Danckwerts. The Bishop of Lincoln was represented by Sir Walter Phillimore, Mr Francis Jeune, QC (son of a former Bishop of Peterborough), and Mr Alfred B. Kempe.

The proceedings were extensively reported, and aroused strong feelings in the press and among the general public. King had never relished controversy but was prepared to stand his ground for what he believed to be the wider good of the Church. No rabid ritualist himself, he claimed that in the service at St Peter-at-Gowts he had simply followed the pattern of worship to which the parish was accustomed.

The particular ritual customs for which he was being indicted were widely practised without harm or complaint in many English parish churches at that time. They were, as Owen Chadwick points out, 'exceedingly moderate customs, more moderate (as was observed) than were practised in London churches regularly attended by the Prime Minister and the Prince of Wales.'[37]

Throughout the trial, King had strong support from High Church Anglicans, from the English Church Union, and from his own diocese. Petitions on his behalf were widely signed, and monies raised to defray his legal expenses. At the High Church Theological College of Ely, the Logbook for 4 February 1890 records: 'Today being fixed for the resumption of the trial of the Bishop of Lincoln at Lambeth, the Holy Eucharist was offered in Chapel with the special intention of interceding that God would over-rule the trial for His greater glory and the good of His Church.'[38] Special celebrations of the Holy Eucharist were held in Newcastle Cathedral, in the palace chapel at Lichfield, and in parish churches all over the country. At one convent there was a service of intercession before the Blessed Sacrament; from another the Superior wrote to say that the Community and Associates of the convent were observing thirty days of prayer. At St Alban's, Holborn a fourteen-hour chain of intercession was formed. 'As the weeks went on, similar tokens of goodwill floated in from more distant sources—Jerusalem, New York, Iowa, Hobart, Sydney, Auckland, Singapore, Dunedin, Newfoundland, South Africa, the Highlands of Scotland, and the Catskill Mountains'[39]: the burden of all was the same—guidance of the Holy Spirit for the Archbishop and support for King.

He also enjoyed the sympathy of some who, though not themselves High Church, yet recognized that it was a distortion of the truth to present this bishop as a Romanizing zealot:

> I cannot forbear writing a few lines to express my deep and true sympathy with you under the heavy trial which you are now passing through. If you remember me at all, you will remember how much I differ from you in opinion and practice on the particular points now in dispute; but that does not prevent my sympathising most deeply with you in this time of trial. Still, we know Whose Hand directs all events, and I trust He

The Bishop on Trial: The Lincoln Judgment

> will make even these disastrous proceedings tend to His glory and the benefit of His Church and people.[40]

And perhaps an even more telling letter:

> As one of the Evangelical clergy of the Diocese, and one who has received invariable kindness at the hands of your Lordship, I write at this time to assure you of my unfeigned love to your person and sincere regard to your office. And I pray God to send to you the Light of His Holy Spirit to have a right judgement in this great and solemn subject of the Lord's Supper, and all other things, and also to rejoice in His Holy comfort. I beg an interest in your prayer to this end for myself.[41]

Undoubtedly, however, the support which would have meant most to King was a letter to *The Standard* in February 1889 from none other than his first 'boss' — the Revd Edward Elton, Vicar of Wheatley. After writing at length about King's outstanding work as his curate, when, as Elton claims, he discovered for himself 'how pre-eminently' King 'was a man of prayer; how deeply versed in Holy Scripture, and saintly in life; how yearning to do work for God among the depraved and ignorant people of the place,' he goes on to refute the false opinion expressed by his persecutors that King was 'absolutely absorbed in Ritual observance.'

> Bishop King is nothing of the kind. His heart is too full of work for God, in the ministry of souls, to be absorbed by any subordinate matter, however interesting. He dwells habitually in an atmosphere too serene to be influenced by either Party warfare or narrow prejudices. There is nothing which has more moved the indignation of his friends than the charge brought against him of disloyalty to the English Church …
>
> It has always been a guiding principle with him, to go back, not to mere Roman teaching, which he would abhor, but to the faith and practice in earlier times, the possession of which is her true and rightful heritage. Such is the man whom a promiscuous band of enemies

seek now to despoil, and whose removal from his high place they are thirsting to accomplish. God grant, for the sake of His Church, they may fail.[42]

As Elton had observed, King had always been quite clear in his own mind that ritual could run to extravagance and absurdity, but in his considered judgment, *abusus non tollit usum*. Preaching at St Barnabas, Oxford, a Tractarian parish in a poor quarter of the city, King had anticipated objections to an enriched liturgy. 'People say that it will run into extravagance, that strange things are done. Most likely it is so from the very nature of the case'; but that risk, he contended, must be taken, in order 'to bring the truth to the poor and simple-minded ... It is folly to question whether we can face large congregations, and then, being intimidated, give up because there are some who do things a little out of taste, a little out of order and time, and a little odd.' He had preached that sermon in 1872, and by the time of his trial the ritualist controversy had intensified; but his basic stance was unchanged.

However, as would inevitably be the case in our own day, there were many for whom squabbles about ritual trivia, such as 'the eastward position' of the celebrant during the Eucharist would be derisory and perceived as a colossal irrelevance to the whole human tragedy — ecclesiastical 'fiddling while Rome burns.' As Hardy protests in *Jude the Obscure*: 'They are two clergymen of different views, arguing about the Eastward position. Good God — the eastward position and all creation groaning.' Undoubtedly, there would have been many who would have echoed similar sentiments and who, like the *Guardian* at the time of the trial, would have written King off as 'a narrow, but well-meaning formalist.'[43]

Such were the similar sentiments of Maggie Benson, the Archbishop's outspoken daughter, who sat in on the trial: she thought the whole thing a liturgical storm in a teacup. As she wrote to a friend, 'I can't help being astonished at a man so absolutely saintly making such a tremendous fuss

The Bishop on Trial: The Lincoln Judgment

about such trifles, or if he doesn't think them trifles I think his views must be horribly materialistic. All the same I hope it may go in his favour—if it doesn't, I wonder what he'll do.'[44] Miss Benson might have reflected that the 'tremendous fuss' was not of King's making, but the Church Association's.

Even her father, with fewer decibels and in a lower key, had reflected in his diary in the early days of the trial:

> I do not think a single layman (who is not a fanatic high or low) cares the least about this trial or this part of it—and this is the sadness of it. It makes the laity think that the whole clergy are wrapped up in these trivial questions, and that if such is the condition and character of the Church, it is not worth saving.[45]

Yet the chances are that the Church Association may have lost the support of many of differing churchmanship (and none), when the motivation of some of the witnesses appearing for the prosecution became clear. Such was Walter Walsh, a London journalist with no personal interest whatever in the affairs of the Diocese of Lincoln, who attended those Advent Sundays services in St Peter-at-Gowts. King's counsel, Phillimore, cross-examined him on his reasons for being there.

> Phillimore: Why did you go to Lincoln?
> [W] I was asked to go by the secretary of the Church Association.
> [P] For what purpose?
> [W] To see what would take place at a church service.
> [P] When were you told about this forthcoming service at St Peter-at-Gowts on December 4th?
> [W] I got the notice only a few days before.
> [P] What were you to do there?
> [W] I was to go ... and describe what I should see ... for the benefit of the Church Association.
> [P] And your expenses?
> [W] My expenses were paid.
> [P] Have you done this sort of thing before?
> [W] It was the first time I had done that?

> [P] And since then?
> [W] I can't say at a moment's notice how often I have done it, but several times at any rate, in several parts of the country.
> [P] Were you at the celebration?
> [W] I was.
> [P] Did you communicate?
> [W] Eh ... I did not communicate.

Clearly it had been a non-communicating attendance and for no devotional reason. For what purpose then? As a paid spy, perhaps, as Phillimore proceeded to establish in his next cross-examinations.

The second of the three witnesses for the prosecution, was a Mr Joseph Clements, a commercial traveller living at Wood Green, who had accompanied Walsh to Lincoln. Phillimore made good use of his cross-examination of Clements.

> [P] Why did you go to Lincoln?
> [C] I was directed to go by the same person and paid by the same person.
> [P] You were present at the celebration?
> [C] I was.
> [P] Did you communicate?
> [C] I did not communicate.

Another case of non-communicating attendance. Finally, Ernest de Lacy Read, the instigator of the whole proceedings against King, took the stand, and Phillimore questioned him about his attendance at that service on 4 December.

> [P] Did you communicate?
> [R] No, I did not.
> [P] How did you come to be at Lincoln?
> [R] Well I went to see ... I will explain the reason.
> [P] Answer my question. Did you go to see the service?
> [R] Yes.
> [P] You went up to Lincoln to see the service.

Phillimore might well have retorted: 'I see why you went to see: you went to spy.' The point was well taken by the assessors and not lost on Benson, who in his summing up and judgment, referred explicitly to this pernicious act of spying at a religious service: 'It is not decent for religious (so-called) persons to hire witnesses to intrude on the worship of others for the purpose of Espial.'[46]

THE ARCHBISHOP'S JUDGMENT

King's hopes were to a large extent realized when, on 21 November 1890, Benson delivered his long-awaited Judgment: it was lengthy and learned, the fruit of much study in liturgical history. During the nine months or so between February and November, Benson worked on it as far as he could in London, throwing himself into the whole enterprise. Randall Davidson describes how he would go into the Archbishop's dressing-room at Lambeth Palace and find him surrounded with stacks of books, deep in liturgiology, as if he had nothing else to do; or having the Lambeth library ransacked, or making lists of references to be examined and verified in the Reading Room of the British Museum by one of his friends from earlier years, the Revd Christopher Wordsworth (son of the late Bishop of Lincoln).[47]

Benson continued to work on the Judgment during August while staying at the Rieder Furca Hotel, near the Bel Alp in Switzerland. In September he returned to England where, on 4 October, as he records in his diary, he completed the work and sent it to the printers:

> It has just struck midnight by my chimney clock and I have just finished and sent off to the printer my final proofs. It has been an immense labour. I have found the former Privy Council judgements very deficient in knowledge and with no breadth of view. But nothing will matter, if it only is itself a contribution, as I believe it ought to be, to the peace of the church. — and to a sounder, more scientific study of ritual. It has been

grievously *pénible* to write, because the topics are so infinitesimal in comparison to others which ought to be uppermost in the minds of churchmen. Still, God has given it to me to do, and what is to be done, is to be done as well as one can do it.[48]

His son Arthur gives us a glimpse of the grandeur and formality of the scene in the crowded library at Lambeth on that momentous day in November 1890 when the Judgment was delivered:

My father had a few minutes' talk with me before the proceedings, and described some of the ceremonial arrangements devised by himself, such as the laying of the Metropolitan Cross on the table beneath the judge, to be a symbol of his spiritual jurisdiction, as the mace of secular authority.[49]

The bishops sat in a semi-circle, as before, with Benson in the centre on his raised seat. They were dressed in their Convocation robes, the Vicar-General wore a scarlet doctor's gown with full-bottomed wig, lending a legal colouring to the assembly. The room was densely crowded, almost every eminent High Churchman in the land having made it his business to be present to hear the Archbishop's final deliberation.

At 10.30am precisely the Archbishop and the assessors entered the library. The Archbishop took his seat, with the Vicar-General on his right, and beyond him the Bishops of Hereford and Oxford; on his left were the Bishops of London, Rochester and Salisbury. King had chosen not to be present but awaited news of the Judgment back at the Old Palace in Lincoln. Benson opened proceedings by reciting two Collects and inviting the whole assembly to join him in the Lord's Prayer. He then delivered his written Judgment, making it quite clear that it had the full agreement of his assessors, except on one point, on which one of them had disagreed.

The charges against the bishop were all uncontested. In his Judgment, the Archbishop had striven to provide liturgical guidelines based, not on the legal precedents of the Judicial Committee of the Privy Council, but on the rubrics of the Book of Common Prayer, and the traditional practice and usage of the Church. In searching for precedent and tradition, he took for granted the continuity of the English Church across the Reformation divide, an assumption which High Church Anglicans warmly endorsed. Perhaps of greater importance and more lasting significance, Benson's findings were in effect a bold assertion of the spiritual independence for the Church, in ordering its own worship, in opposition to regulation by the State.

Overall, Benson found substantially in favour of King. On the first matter, the ceremonial mixing of water and wine, he decided that mixing, during and as part of the service, was against the law of the Church, but did not deny the use of a chalice of wine with water providing it had been mixed prior to the service. The Court allowed that such was lawful, in effect overriding an earlier decision of the Privy Council.

Then again, it was lawful to stand in the Eastward position during the first part of the Communion Service. A great deal of the time Benson had spent in research was related to this issue and his ruling once again reversed an earlier one from the Privy Council. It was, however, deemed unlawful to stand in such a position that the manual acts could not be seen by the congregation. On this matter King pleaded that he had no wish or intention to hide the acts, but the Court decided as a typical legal nicety, that 'in the mind of a minister, there ought to be a wish and intention to do what has to be done, not merely no wish or intention not to do it.' It ruled that 'the Lord Bishop has mistaken the true interpretation of the order of the Holy Communion in this particular.'[50]

Benson further decided that the singing of the *Agnus Dei* after the Consecration Prayer was lawful. As for the placing of candles, this was ruled as permissible, once again reversing an earlier ruling of the Privy Council. Finally, it found the 'ceremony' of making the sign of the cross at the blessing to be 'an innovation which must be discontinued.'

The words with which Benson concluded the delivery of his Judgment are of particular importance, for they reflect his personal attitude towards the whole matter of prosecution, and especially to the presence of 'spies' at divine service.

'Public worship,' he said, 'is one of the divine institutions, which are the heritage of the Church for the fraternal union of mankind. The Church, therefore, has the right to ask that her congregations may not be divided either by needless pursuance or by exaggerated suspicion of practices not in themselves illegal.'[51] The words 'exaggerated suspicion' were William Stubbs's sole contribution to the wording of the final judgment,[52] while Benson's distaste of 'spies' would certainly have been reinforced by Phillimore's sharp examination of the Church Association's 'delegates' and witnesses during the trial.

At the end, Benson pointedly declared, and with some emotion:

> The Court has not only felt deeply the incongruity of minute questionings and disputations in great and sacred subjects, but desires to express its sense that time and attention are diverted thereby from the Church's real contest with evil and building up of good, by those who give and by those who take offence unadvisedly in such matters.[53]

To this undoubtedly Tait, from his prolonged and tortuous experience as architect of his unfortunate Act would have responded with a very loud 'Amen.'

Back in Lincoln, at four o'clock in the afternoon, King received a telegram from Phillimore in Latin, informing him that apart from the prohibition of using the sign of the cross in blessing and absolution, and that the manual acts at the consecration of the elements must be visible to the people, *omnia alia pro te* (everything else was in King's

The Bishop on Trial: The Lincoln Judgment

favour), and therefore *in necessariis victoria*, — a 'victory in all essentials.'[54]

King readily accepted the Judgment, and wrote on 5 December, to Sub-Dean Clements of Lincoln:

> On the whole, Church-people are, I think, thankful for the Judgment. I am, myself, very thankful for the true Principles on which it has been based. If the Judgement is allowed to stand, I shall most gratefully 'turn to,' with fresh spirit, to work up our diocese to this level, and endeavour to persuade some of our friends to be guided by real Church Principles in these matters, instead of their own fancies and feelings.

For King, that meant his gentle persuasive care for his clergy on both sides of the 'divide' between the Evangelicals and the Ritualists: 'We must not pull *either* side up too sharply, as there has really been no true Church order given us.'[55]

Generally speaking, and certainly with hindsight, it would seem that the Judgment was received with gratitude as being a work of rare excellence and wisdom promoting the unity and welfare of the Church.

The Church Association, predictably, appealed against it to the Judicial Committee of the Privy Council, but their Appeal was rejected on 2 August 1892, and a telegram sent informing Benson that 'their Lordships uphold the decision of your Grace's Court on all points.'[56] The following day *The Times* declared,

> We view the decision as a legal victory for toleration, and one which may work for peace. Neither the Church Association nor the English Church Union is the Church of England.[57]

In December *The Record* added its voice,

> It is an unmixed good that Church and State should thus, as it were, be once more brought into line. The unanimity of the two courts in their decision goes far to reconcile us to its substance.[58]

King's letters make it clear that while he accepted totally, albeit somewhat reluctantly, the ruling of the Archbishop in his court, had the Appeal been upheld, he would not have accepted that a secular court could countermand the ruling of a court spiritual.

The final and determining factor in this whole vexed matter was King's own attitude and response to Benson's rulings. In the *Lincoln Diocesan Magazine* for January 1891, he published in full his statement accepting the Archbishop's Judgment, which he had previously addressed in a letter to the archdeacons and rural deans of the diocese.

> While retaining the opinion that 'a trial of a Bishop in Synod would be more in accordance with ancient precedent, and more satisfactory to the Church at large,' [his original protest at the outset of the trial] I am most thankful to have at once been able conscientiously to comply with his Grace's Judgement, and to discontinue those actions of which he disapproves.

After giving the details of the Archbishop's rulings on each matter, he continues:

> While the points that have been given in my favour are declared lawful, it is not intended that they should be obligatory. You, my Reverend Brethren, are well aware that I have never desired to enforce unaccustomed ritual upon any reluctant clergyman or congregation.
>
> At the same time, I earnestly hope that this authoritative utterance of our revered and beloved Archbishop will tend to remove the suspicion of lawlessness, and unfaithfulness to the Church of England, which has unhappily arisen in some places with regard to points of ceremonial observance. My prayer is that this Judgement may be for the greater glory of God, and for the edification of our souls in unity and peace.[59]

After the Judicial Committee had rejected the Church Association's appeal in 1892, King wrote to his chaplain in December expressing his thankfulness for the resolution of

The Bishop on Trial: The Lincoln Judgment

a much larger matter, which had always been there in the 'small print,' so to speak, throughout the whole lengthy proceedings:

> I am very thankful that we have been spared a great collision between Church and State. I do not think the country is ready for it, and it would have split the Diocese in two.[60]

IN CONCLUSION

King touches here on the whole issue of Church–State relations. The precedent Benson created by taking the whole matter out of the hands of the secular courts, and establishing the right of the Church, embodied in his office as Metropolitan, to set its own house in order, is of far more lasting significance than the settling of squabbles over the minutiae of ceremonial. The Lincoln Judgment marks another stage in the lengthy process of unpicking what had been that seamless garment of Church and State in the Reformation Settlement, which had been the burden of Keble's Assize Sermon in 1833. It raises today, even more forcefully than then, the prospect of disestablishment, with the advent of Synodical government, ordering liturgical reform and other matters which will surface increasingly in the coming years. Such divisions as exist today are drawn along rather different lines and attached to theological matters rather than ecclesiological issues or ceremonial practices, yet pursued, it has to be said, with equal, if not more tenacity and zeal.

In many ways, as was observed at the time, the Lincoln Judgment might be said to have been a blessing, albeit, like so many blessings, in disguise. In the event the Church Association's action proved counterproductive. Over time the clergy of the Lincoln Diocese were drawn together rather than divided by it, because the particular bishop the Association chose for prosecution was already revered for his saintly life across a wide spectrum of churchmanship—King was, as Benson said, 'adored' in Lincoln. 'Good men of every school were bitterly ashamed that their bishop should be prosecuted in this way and took him to their hearts and their prayers.'[61] Not everyone, of course. Some parishes were totally uninterested in the affair, and some clergymen continued to disapprove of their bishop. To nobody's surprise Archdeacon Kaye, an opponent of King's appointment from day one, refused to sign any of the addresses circulating in the diocese in support of their bishop. And there were the inevitable letters from eccentrics and extremists—one, signed 'An Irritated Parent,' addressed King as the 'Arch-hypocrite.'[62]

However, as Owen Chadwick maintains,

> more than half the Lincoln diocese, far more than half the people of Lincolnshire whether they were members of the Church of England or not, came to regard him with affection, and with the sympathy bestowed by the public upon one who for no good reason is maltreated. And half the Lincolnshire clergy looked up to him with an awe or veneration which is the lot and the embarrassment of few, and which the enchantment of his private personality alone would not have gained.[63]

But it was perhaps the overriding attitude of King himself that might be said to have finally won the day—by his readiness to accept the Archbishop's Judgment; by his willingness to observe the ruling in his own personal practice when conducting worship; and, above all, by openly demonstrating in his own conduct and bearing a refusal to show any bitterness towards those who disagreed with him, or to engage with those of a different school in any bitterness, but rather by persisting with his customary gentleness of spirit and loving attitude to everyone. In short King remained his own man, refusing to manipulate party strife or to use it for his own ends, but rather by consistently working and praying for the spiritual unity of the Church

The Bishop on Trial: The Lincoln Judgment

he loved so much, but whose Founder he loved even more. As Chadwick judiciously observes:

> In the tension of the time, a truculent Bishop of Lincoln could have split the Church of England in two. It was a mercy for the established Church that the new Bishop of Lincoln was a man without truculence.[64]

Notes

1. E. K. Norman, *Anti-Catholicism in Victorian England*. London: Allen & Unwin, 1968, p. 105.
2. G. K. A. Bell, *Randall Davidson Archbishop of Canterbury*, p. 149.
3. George W. E. Russell, *Edward King Sixtieth Bishop of Lincoln*, p. 199.
4. Randolph and Townroe, *The Mind and Work of Bishop King*, p. 8.
5. *Ibid.*
6. Berdmore Compton, *A Popular Review of the Judgement of the Archbishop of Canterbury in the Case of the Bishop of Lincoln*, 1891, p. 13. Compton was a former Vicar of All Saints, Margaret Street, London.
7. Mary C. Church (ed.), *Life and Letters of Dean Church*. London: Macmillan & Co., 1894, p. 172.
8. Nan Dearmer, *The Life of Percy Dearmer*. London: The Book Club, 1941, p. 56.
9. *Ibid.*
10. Davidson and Benham, *The Life of Archibald Campbell Tait*, vol. II, p. 115.
11. *Ibid.*, p. 116.
12. *Church Association Monthly Intelligencer*, 1 July 1869, quoted in Marsh, P. T., *The Victorian Church in Decline*, p. 116.
13. Queen Victoria to Tait, 5 January 1874, quoted in Carpenter, Edward, *Cantuar*, p. 347.
14. Davidson and Benham, *op. cit.*, vol. II, p. 186.
15. *Ibid.*, p. 189.
16. *Ibid.*, p. 208.
17. *Ibid.*, p. 234.
18. P. T. Marsh, *The Victorian Church in Decline*, p. 233.
19. A. C. Benson, *op. cit.*, vol. II, p. 323.
20. *The Lincolnshire Chronicle*, 5 June 1885, p. 8.
21. A. C. Benson, *op. cit.*, vol. II, p. 151.
22. G. K. A. Bell, *Randall Davidson Archbishop of Canterbury*, p. 12.
23. *Ibid.*, p. 132.
24. Russell, *op. cit.*, p. 177.
25. *Ibid.*, pp. 166–7.

26. Bell, *op. cit.*, p. 134.
27. John Newton, *Search for a Saint*, p. 101.
28. Benson, *op. cit.*, vol. II, p. 340.
29. Russell, *op. cit.*, p. 163.
30. *Ibid.*, pp. 165–6.
31. Benson, *op. cit.*, vol. II, p. 340.
32. *Ibid.*, p. 346.
33. *Ibid.*, p. 347.
34. *Ibid.*, p. 352.
35. *Ibid.*, p. 348.
36. *Ibid.*, p. 349.
37. Owen Chadwick, *Edward King, Bishop of Lincoln, 1885–1910*, p. 19.
38. C. J. Smith, *B. W. Randolph*, p. 37.
39. Russell, *op. cit.*, p. 157.
40. *Ibid.*, p. 158.
41. *Ibid.*
42. Russell, *op. cit.*, pp. 160–1.
43. Quoted by Chadwick, *op. cit.*, p. 18, from *Guardian* 1889, p. 355.
44. A. C. Benson, *Life and Letters of Maggie Benson*. London: John Murray, 1917, pp. 112–13.
45. A. C. Benson, *The Life of Edward White Benson*, vol. II, p. 350.
46. Russell, *op. cit.*, p. 193.
47. Benson, *The Life of Edward White Benson*, vol. II, p. 355n.
48. *Ibid.*, p. 356.
49. Russell, *op. cit.*, p. 179.
50. E. S. Roscoe, *The Bishop of Lincoln's Case: A Report of the Proceedings*. London: William Clowes & Sons Ltd, 1891, p. 145.
51. Roscoe, *op. cit.*, p. 176.
52. *Letters of William Stubbs, Bishop of Oxford, 1825–1901* (ed. W. H. Hutton). London: Archibald Constable & Co., 1904, p. 328.
53. Benson, *The Life of Edward White Benson*, vol. II, pp. 363–4.
54. Russell, *op. cit.*, p. 180.
55. *Ibid.*, p. 198.
56. Benson, *The Life of Edward White Benson*, vol. II, p. 374.
57. *Ibid.*, p. 375.
58. *Ibid.*, p. 376.
59. Russell, *op. cit.*, pp. 200–1.
60. Lincolnshire Archives, Larken Deposit, III, 59.
61. Chadwick, *op. cit.*, p. 19.
62. Russell, *op. cit.*, pp. 159–60.
63. Chadwick, *op. cit.*, p. 19.
64. *Ibid.*, p. 18.

✢ 13 ✢

Calm after the Storm

TURNING TO WITH 'A FRESH SPIRIT'

The dismissal of the Church Association's appeal against Benson's Judgment signalled the end of the upheavals of the previous two years. For King, it also signalled, as he had told Clements, an opportunity to 'turn to' the work of the diocese 'with a fresh spirit.'[1] There can be little doubt that the years between his arrival in Lincoln and Benson's Judgment had been painfully scarred by intervening events, seriously impeding his work in the diocese. So much had to be put on hold while many of the clergy held back from wholeheartedly welcoming their new bishop, awaiting the Judgment, after which 'hearts were opened to him, all over the diocese, which afore time had been closed, or, at the most, ajar.'[2]

Paradoxically, all that King endured throughout the course of the trial could be said to have benefitted his future ministry in the diocese, but in the short term there was a heavy price to pay.

He had maintained (at least outwardly) a serene demeanour both during the preliminaries and during the trial itself. Indeed, only a few days before the judgment was delivered, he was in Leeds for the dedication of a memorial to Pusey in St John's Church, when the vicar, the Revd J. Wylde, 'ventured to say there was no one to whom the coming judgment of the Archbishop of Canterbury had been less of a trouble than to the Bishop of Lincoln himself.' In his reply King said, 'that is true, but it is through the outcome of your prayers.' Then, typically, his thoughts turned to Benson himself:

> Our dear Archbishop is now in very great trouble. Not only is the judgment troubling him, but he is grievously troubled at the loss of his dear daughter. Will you remember him and Mrs. Benson in your prayers, that he may be sustained in his trouble.[3]

While King might have radiated calmness and composure, there can be little doubt that for the inner man, the opposite was the case. One of his closest friends said after his death that the trial had hung over him like 'a nightmare'[4]. King himself confirmed the stress it caused him when he wrote to a friend: 'I am thankful that the strain of the last three years has been removed, as it was becoming almost too much for my strength.'[5]

Often it is not so much during some great crisis or trauma as afterwards that the full impact kicks in: this it seems was the case with King, who during the four years or so following the trial became quite seriously ill. In the summer of 1891 he suffered from a severe attack of shingles and, not surprisingly, according to friends, looked visibly older. His handwriting is impaired in letters of that period, due to a swelling in his right hand which for a little while robbed it of power, and, as friends commented, he appeared to have lost something of his noted buoyancy. At the age of sixty-one, he was only five years into his episcopal ministry, and yet, if his biographer Russell is to be believed, it had become evident that King's pace had slowed and 'from that time forward there was a going softly all his days.'[6]

Nevertheless, as his health and strength gradually recovered, he found a new and increasing joy and satisfaction in purely pastoral work, with an ever-increasing number of Confirmations and, as *pastor pastorum*, exercising a particular care and indeed love for his clergy who, in turn, increasingly took him to their hearts. As Scott Holland had

Calm after the Storm

euphorically exclaimed at the outset 'It shall be a Bishopric of Love.'[7]

So much did he concentrate on diocesan work that he earned a rebuke from Benson for his absence from Convocation, to say nothing of his absence from the House of Lords, even for important debates directly involving the bishops. It was as though King exemplified in his person in the immediate years after the trial that universal paradox whereby unique strengths are often found, not so much despite weaknesses, but rather in and through those selfsame weaknesses.

King's 'great work in the diocese was to render the Church of England more spiritual, by deepening the spirituality of the clergy.'[8] On becoming a bishop, he had claimed that his prime concern was 'to draw men to Christ, that they might be nearer to God, and nearer to each other in the unity of His Holy Church.'[9] Achieving such an ambitious objective would clearly require a fundamental change in the usual priorities of bishops at that time, issuing in nothing less than a radical reappraisal of episcopal ministry.

CHANGING THE FACE OF EPISCOPACY

King's strong suit had always been that of pastor and teacher along the lines of his hero, Sailer, and especially in his relationship with his clergy, for whom he retained a special care, always giving readily of his time and energies to them as a priority. He knew and remembered first-hand some of the perils, problems, and indeed the corrosive poverty of the parochial clergy. 'He knew the injurious effects on character often produced by short days in a cold climate' out on the fens, with 'solitariness, dull surroundings, poverty and domestic gloom. From his death bed, he sent a message to a young architect—"Go on building houses with sunny rooms for the clergy."'[10]

A clergyman, who had taken a family Living in Lincolnshire just before King arrived, was reported as saying, 'My clerical neighbours are exhaustively divisible into three classes—those who have gone out of their minds, those who are going out of them, and those who have none to go out of.'[11] Sometimes moral aberrations would be added to intellectual failure.

The moral failings of the clergy were always a concern, as is clear from the minutes of the annual meetings of the East Anglia bishops. At the 1892 meeting, hosted by the Bishop of Ely, King asked: 'How to do our duty as pastoral fathers towards priests who have fallen into grievous sin, and as a Bishop towards the Church?' At the next meeting in 1893, with King as host and in the chair, an even more pressing issue was raised: 'The Clergy Discipline Act as it affects the fatherly relation of a Bishop to his clergy,' and more specifically, 'How to treat the Clergy suspended or deprived under the Discipline Act?' King's response has his finger-prints all over it: 'a fatherly relation must be maintained as far as possible while carrying out the requirements of the Church Discipline Act.' At the 1904 meeting, King himself pressed the question: 'How are we to regard the new arrangement for the Caution List with priests and clergy,' pleading that surely it 'does not exclude a Priest from Church work for ever?'[12]

That was, and still is, the dilemma—the double bind of holding public office in the Church as a bishop with necessary accountability to the State and wider public concern, together with the pastoral ministry exercised as a 'Father in God'—that tension between the juridical and the moral (sometimes called 'situation ethics') when applied as pastoral theology, always allowing for the possibility of repentance, redemption and renewal. We have sufficient evidence to assert with confidence that King was no soft option as a pastor, and yet from a letter he wrote to a priest—'A Moral Case'—it would seem that he preferred to err on the side

Calm after the Storm

of what many saw as being over-lenient, always striving to leave the 'back door' open for the return of the 'prodigal.'

> It is better to be over-charitable than over strict. I am sure we must run the risk of the charge brought against our Lord of being too easy with sinners.[13]

It is not easy to know how Bishop King would practise such a ministry in the climate of today's Church, with the present 'Caution List,' which seldom, if ever, allows a priest who has committed 'a grievous sin,' even one which was not a crime, to return to ministry. What is clear is that King firmly believed that no criminal, however heinous the crime, is beyond redemption, and that the Sacrament of Absolution does indeed bring God's forgiveness. As we know from his *Spiritual Letters*,[14] he believed that a penitent murderer, whom he had brought into full sacramental reconciliation while awaiting execution, could, 'by *his* prayers,' help King bring another to true repentance and restoration into the fellowship of the Church as a forgiven sinner. That letter with King's request for and reliance on the prayers of a murderer, however penitent, might raise shocked eyebrows among the hierarchy of today's Church, even more than it did in King's own day. Yet it could serve to focus our attention on just how much we actually *believe* in the forgiveness of sins and its accompanying desire for amendment of life even in the most hardened criminals, let alone run-of-the-mill sinners.

All King's previous ministry had prepared him for the ministry of a bishop, but not as understood at the time and least of all in today's Church, but rather in the more primitive understanding of the bishop as being primarily the pastor and teacher of the pastors, and a compassionate pastor at that. Such might be seen as the job description of bishops like Ambrose and Augustine in the early centuries. The Franciscan writer and teacher Richard Rohr says:

> A spiritual leader who lacks human compassion has

almost no power to change other people, because people intuitively know he or she does not represent the Whole or the Holy One. Such leaders need to rely upon rules, laws, costume and enforcement powers to effect any change in others. Such change does not go deep, nor does it last. In fact, it is not really change at all. It is mere conformity.[15]

'True spiritual leaders lead not from above and not even from below, but mostly from *within*, by walking *with* their brothers and sisters, or "with the smell of the sheep," about their person, as Pope Francis puts it.'[16]

From the start of his episcopate, King gave almost a disproportionate amount of time and attention to the theological college founded by his predecessor, Bishop Wordsworth. The Bishop's Hostel, Chancellor's School or Lincoln Theological College (as it eventually became known), was modelled along the lines of Cuddesdon. Preaching at its first Festival in November 1888, King spoke of the college in much the same way as Wilberforce had spoken of Cuddesdon as being 'our College.' Clearly he was more convinced than ever of the importance of proper residential training for the clergy, with particular emphasis on parochial ministry.

> It is the object of our College to prepare men for the Divine ministry of Christ's Church, to continue that Divine organization of the Christian ministry which the Preface to our Ordinal asserts to have been in the Church 'from the Apostles' time ... To be a theologian indeed requires many gifts and special opportunities such as possibly can rarely be found except in our Universities or in our cathedral cities, but this is not necessary for the parish priest; his business is the cure of souls. He will indeed require the knowledge of all theology to a certain degree—dogmatic theology, moral theology, and the scientific adaptation of them both to the needs of individual souls, which we call ascetic theology ... We need men who, by the power of the Holy Spirit, have comprehended something of the breadth, length,

> depth, and height of the love of Christ which passeth knowledge; men who are rooted and grounded in and constrained by this love; men who will be patient with sinners and those who are ignorant, and careless, and 'out of the way' ... men who will love and not grow cold, but who, having loved, like Jesus, will 'love to the end.'

And then, as ever with King, comes that note of strong encouragement which was always at the core of his pastoral ministry, especially for his clergy, whom he knew were often disheartened in their work. So, speaking from the heart:

> Perhaps you have found it harder than you thought; perhaps you are surprised at the indifference and the ignorance which still prevails with regard to the Church amongst our people ... perhaps you are disappointed with your brethren of the clergy around you; perhaps you are surprised and disappointed with yourselves. Brethren, do not be disheartened; these and such as these are the trials by which the priests of the Church of England are being tried; they are often not understood, not wanted, not cared for, isolated, lonely, unnoticed, unknown by the world; and all this has to be borne too often now in poverty which cannot be expressed, and it may be in actual sickness, or under the intimidation of declining health.[17]

Similar sympathy, compassion and encouragement can be found in King's Charges to the clergy, where again we see the bishop as the chief shepherd who knows the inner fears and failings of the flock committed to his care. In his first Charge of 1889, he had stepped up boldly with his customary optimistic confidence, acknowledging the good work of his predecessors but going on to say that 'something different is required now': a bishop with whom the clergy could identify as a colleague and friend.

Acutely aware that faults of life, as well as pastoral shortcomings, often result from material misery, King had turned his attention to the question of clerical incomes from his first days in the diocese. He was convinced that the law against pluralities must be modified, and that, when the income of a benefice had sunk to vanishing point, the incumbent ought to be allowed to hold another in conjunction with it. Pending a change in the law, he did his best to extend the Poor Benefices Association, subscribing very generously himself, and doing all he could to enlist the sympathy of the laity. While seeking to improve their incomes, he also strove to lighten the clergy's labours by developing the work of Lay Readers in the scattered villages and hamlets.

DEATH OF WALKER KING

King was seven years into his episcopate when he lost his older brother, Canon Walker King, Rector of St Clement's, Leigh-on-Sea, who died on 20 July 1892. It is not easy to get a handle on King's relationship with Walker, as there are no surviving letters between them. There is, however, one letter written at the time of Walker's death, in which King speaks of him with great affection and admiration. King was still recovering from the pressures of the trial and did not yet feel 'equal to going abroad,' though, he hoped 'please God, to be ready for the autumn work.'

> My dear Brother's death is a great blow to me. We were brought up together, and I had the greatest admiration and affection for him; and often have felt ashamed at the publicity of my own life compared to his life of retirement. But, indeed, he was not without his reward, for nothing could exceed the reality of the affection and devotion of his people. I never saw such sad grief. He had a wonderfully tender way of dealing with people, never crushing the natural life, but guiding and leading it up. He and his family were part of the family life of the whole Parish.[18]

It would be wrong to infer that Edward and Walker were

not especially close; both were distinguished as outstanding, loving and faithful pastors, yet Walker, a married priest with a family, clearly lacked that 'something extra' for which his younger brother was so affectionately remembered.

Walker had gone up to Oxford two years ahead of Edward and made a great impression as an oarsman, rowing for both his college, Oriel, and the University:

> In 1847 there was no proper Oxford and Cambridge boat race at Putney owing to a dispute over the conditions under which it was to be rowed. However, both the Oxford and Cambridge crews entered for the Grand Challenge Cup at Henley Regatta, King being one of the Oxford crew. Not only did Oxford beat Cambridge, but they went on to win the Grand Challenge cup. Unfortunately, because of the unusual circumstances, no blues were handed out that year.[19]

After Oriel, Walker proceeded to ordination and in 1859 was appointed Rector of St Clement's, where he remained until his death. One of his sons, Canon Robert ('Bob') Stuart King, who played football for England, was ordained by his uncle in 1889, and succeeded his father at St Clement's, remaining there until his own death in 1950. It is a remarkable record, although at the time not such an unusual one, for father and son to be rectors of the same parish for ninety years.

Walker King appears in photographs as a well-built man with a long beard, sturdier in physique than his younger brother who had always been rather delicate in health, although Edward was to outlive him by nearly twenty years. Bishop Edward often stayed in Leigh-on-Sea and 'the brothers would spend afternoons visiting parishioners in the old town and during the cholera and typhoid epidemics would sit with the sick and pray with them although many people were afraid of infection and would not go beyond the front door.'[20]

It was all of a piece and in the great Tractarian pastoral tradition of visiting the sick, those in extremis or any with special needs. Canon Robert King, following the example of his father and his uncle, 'during a typhoid epidemic went into the bedrooms of the sufferers and prayed with them when everyone had been warned not to go near.'[21] In so many ways, both Edward and Walker King were as one in their commitment to pastoral ministry and the cure of souls, their care of the poor, and in their churchmanship.

> Walker King raised the religious life of Leigh to a high level and brought to St Clements the zeal and devotion that had come to the Oxford of this time with the Tractarian movement. More than this, his pastoral interest penetrated every sphere of the life of Leigh parish, and he became its natural leader. He cared for all his people and had a sensitive social conscience in days of poverty and much suffering. It is said that he gave a large proportion of the emoluments of the benefice to worthy objects in Leigh and the relief of the needy, himself having some private means.[22]

This kinship of the two brothers was spelt out in Edward's sermon at Walker's Memorial Service in St Clement's, when the characteristics which he attributes to his brother are almost a mirror image of his own. He took as his text a favourite from the psalms: 'Thy Gentleness hath made me great' (Psalm 18:36).

> I have ventured to choose these words for my text this morning, because I feel that in many ways they represent the mind and character of him of whom for a few moments, I desire, by God's help, to speak to you … The first characteristic, perhaps, of my dear brother which would strike any one, was his *great strength and courage* … And with this strength and courage was that rarer gift which is only, I think, to be seen in perfection where courage and strength exist in a high degree—the gift of *gentleness*. Nowhere did his strength and courage show itself more truly than in the sick room and by the bedside of the suffering and the dying … Many of you must have seen this, as I have myself.

He then goes on to list three aspects of his brother's ministry, and here again they are very much a reflection of his own.

Firstly, 'fight the battle in yourselves,' he reminded the congregation. Secondly, 'stand firm and true in the defence of God's truth, remembering the lesson of gentleness implies patience and long-suffering, and waiting for God's good time and for one another'—again that lightness of touch which King always exemplified in directing and leading others in the spiritual life. Thirdly, and perhaps most tellingly, remember the gift which is 'the kindness of heart, the gift of Love. This is the mark which the Saviour Himself chose by which His disciples should be known.'[23]

KING'S THIRD TRIENNIAL CHARGE

Later that same year, in September, King issued his Third Triennial Charge, which was one of his most characteristic. While urging zeal in combatting the creeping dangers of indifference in the course of the priestly life, he shows a real understanding of the situation under which many of his clergy laboured—and especially those in the country parishes.

> What is the great difficulty which we labour under in our small and scattered parishes? Is it not isolation, the sense of loneliness, and that depression and loss of heart which arises from isolation and the sense of loneliness? And where shall we find a better remedy for all this than in the constant renewing of our Communion with our Divine Lord, in the way which He has Himself provided for us? Under the old law the priest was bound to rekindle the fire upon the altar, and to trim the lamps of the sanctuary every day. And so we need to rekindle the fire of our love and zeal, by putting ourselves in the closest relation we can with the Source of zeal and love, even with Him of whom it is written, 'The zeal of Thine House hath eaten me up.' ... He is 'the Light of the world,' and we are to shine as 'lights in the world'

by His light reflected in us. We must therefore put ourselves in His presence, and endeavour to preserve unbroken through the week the Communion into which we are thus taken.

Because many of the parishes at that time did not practise frequent, or even weekly Communion, King goes on to say:

> We need this frequency of Communion for our own souls, and for our ministerial efficiency. And do we not need it for our people? ... And we need it for the faithful few. Scattered about, even in our smallest parishes, one here and one there, are those whose hearts God has touched, who only want to be drawn out and sustained in those aspirations which we cannot see, but which we may, by our divinely given ministry assist.

Later in this same Charge, King urges the need for the regular use of the Daily Office, 'which our church has so plainly pointed out for us.' But here again, it is clear that he realized the practical difficulties of doing this especially in those scattered parishes to which he so often referred.

> The difficulties, I know, are most real and great, especially in country parishes. In some cases, I am ready to allow they are insuperable ... but still I do desire that, wherever it may be, the bell should ring out, at least once a day, to give notice of a service in church.

His follow up to that admonition is truly remarkable in its beautiful and practical application:

> There may from time to time be someone lying upon the bed of death, someone whom we have been unable to reach by our sermons or admonitions, someone who has not yet turned to God; and the sound of the bell from the House of God borne in upon the ear may, by God's grace, strike the soul with that wondrous power which belongs to sacred music; and the wanderer, even in that last hour, may think of God, and turn again and pray and be forgiven.
>
> Or there may be others, not so near the end as this, but

Calm after the Storm

still confined to the house by age or sickness, and liable to that despondency and depression which continued weakness and inability to take part in the business of life so often bring; and the sound of the bell may lead their thoughts upward and recall them to a sense of what this life really is—the school, nay, rather the infant school, for the true life beyond.[24]

JUSTICE FOR THE POOR: A LIVING WAGE

It is precisely those characteristics of pastoral ministry which he identified in his brother's ministry, that King exemplified and practised in his own, not the least being his commitment to working with and caring for 'God's poor.' On being appointed to Lincoln, King had written to a former student, E. S. L. Randolph, at the time a missionary in Zanzibar, 'now I am to go back to the cure of souls, and to be a shepherd again ... This is my great delight, that He means it as a proof of His love, and that He means me to be a Bishop of His Poor! If I can keep that before me, I shall be happy.'[25]

From the perspective of the twenty-first century, and the hard-won benefits of a Welfare State, such a sentiment, however sincere, would appear hopelessly inadequate and even condescending, bolstering the *status quo* of the 'rich man in his castle, the poor man at his gate,' in the words of King's contemporary, Mrs Alexander (1815–92). Surely, it is not sufficient simply to work amongst the poor; far better to work politically and in other ways to eradicate the scourge of poverty altogether.

We must be careful, however, not to judge King anachronistically or to read him through the lenses of a later generation and a different culture. King's passion for the poor was fired by a deep commitment to personal philanthropy, as, it would seem, was that of his brother in Leigh-on-Sea. There can be no question that throughout his time at Lincoln he was genuinely driven by sympathy and compassion, not just for the urban poor of the diocese, but also by the extensive rural poverty. Poverty for King, as for many of his contemporaries, would not have constituted a 'cause,' or be perceived in the abstract as an 'issue,' but rather as a gospel challenge to do what could be done—financially, but also in other ways—for the next poor person you met.

However, he was not alone among the Bench of Bishops in showing concern for the poor, and for the escalating poverty and the casualties of the age of imperialism and the oppression of the barons of industry and those who prospered from it. There was a newer generation of bishops, twenty or so years younger than King, who saw beyond the Victorian age of charity and philanthropy to a society, which, in the name of justice, would no longer tolerate such disparity between the overly rich and the labouring classes as depicted in the works of Dickens and Disraeli's novel *Two Nations*.

Randall Davidson, who enjoyed wealth, privilege, and prosperity as Dean of Windsor, is a prime example of that next generation of bishops and spiritual leaders. They sought to establish laws which would render such poverty obsolete, no longer so dependent upon charity and philanthropy, and also with opportunities for an education which would lift and release many from the bondage of the *status quo*.

Admittedly, it was often a case of needs-must, as protests and strikes by labourers and factory workers threatened subversive action reminiscent of the earlier Chartists.

At the same time, only a little later than King, theologians like Gore and F. D. Maurice were pushing the theological boundaries in a fresh and applied understanding of the theology of the Incarnation and the sacramental life, albeit at one stage removed and in a more academic environment. Alongside them, but at the parish level, living check-by-jowl with the poor, were the ritualist clergy who applied that theology, liturgically and pastorally in the slums of the industrial cities.

Calm after the Storm

In 1891, just when King was beginning to emerge from the trauma of his trial, the Prime Minister, Lord Salisbury, offered Davidson, at the early age of forty-two, the choice of two dioceses—Worcester or Rochester? Salisbury openly expressed the view that Davidson would almost certainly prefer the richer Diocese of Worcester. To his surprise Davidson chose Rochester, which was much more industrial with a far larger population, and at the time—after some parts of the Diocese of Winchester had been added in 1877 and before the creation of the Diocese of Southwark in 1905—included all of London south of the Thames, from Woolwich in the East to Kingston in the West. It was a region 'which had very little of the wealth of London and which was growing steadily poorer every day.'[26]

Accordingly, Davidson chose to leave behind the sheltered and privileged life of Windsor for a diocese in which the problems of poverty and social upheaval were all too clearly evident; and he chose to reside, not in some salubrious suburb, but in two houses knocked together in Kennington Park Road, easier of access for his clergy, and closer to the south London parishes, so much in need of attention.

Recording in his diary the many parish visitations he made, Davidson wrote:

> These visitations were only a part of my systematic endeavour to understand, and if possible, relieve the extreme difficulty of the work in a great poor town area like South London. Life in those parishes, and the almost insuperable obstacles to making it religiously bright and buoyant, weighed upon my thoughts by day and night.[27]

In November 1892, the year after he took up his new appointment, there was a cotton strike, followed in the late summer of 1893 by a disastrous coal strike. These and other clashes between Capital and Labour begged the question: 'Could not something be done by the various sections of the Christian Church, with a view to putting an end to, or at least diminishing, the evils of the present system of industrial warfare?'[28]

In the autumn of 1893, the editor of the *Daily Chronicle* called a Conference to be held on 14 November at Westminster Abbey (in the Jerusalem Chamber) and Davidson was one of the invitees. Others included the Bishop of Ripon, Cardinal Vaughan for the Roman Catholics, Dr Marshall Lang, Moderator of the General Assembly of the Church of Scotland, Canon Scott Holland and Charles Gore. The Chairman was King's admirer and biographer, George W. E. Russell, then Under Secretary of State for India. Prior to the meeting, a series of resolutions had been agreed, dealing especially with the 'living wage,' but when the day of the meeting came, 'for unexplained reasons,' both the Cardinal and the Moderator were conveniently absent. The Dean of Westminster (G. G. Bradley), taking the chair in the absence of Russell, and clearly apprehensive of the contemporary hot potato of the 'living wage,' 'begged the conference on no account to pass any resolutions.'[29]

Bishop Davidson (who was conspicuously and characteristically outspoken) took the Cardinal's place in introducing a resolution, which he was not allowed to press, to the effect that in the opinion of this Conference the principle of maintaining a standard of living should be recognized as an essential condition in the settlement of all labour disputes. 'He spoke up manfully,' said the *Chronicle* in its candid account of the proceedings, 'while the Bishop of Ripon, with coal fields in his Diocese, objected to all resolutions and was most doleful.'

'The general effect of the meeting,' comments Bell in Davidson's biography, 'showed the extraordinary nervousness of Church opinion at that time.' The Establishment was clearly threatened by anything that might develop into or be construed as a subversive meeting, so that, as Bell observes, Davidson was 'the only bishop whom Scott Holland, Adderley and their friends could find to say anything in public, however guarded, about a decent standard of living.'

Later that month, Benson hastily convened a Conference at Lambeth to consider 'the duty of the National Church to the aged poor.' Again, Davidson played a conspicuous part and, spurred on by what had been discussed immediately after the meeting, wrote to James Bryce, then Chancellor of the Duchy of Lancaster, suggesting that clergy should be allowed to sit on the Royal Commission recently set up to look into the Poor Laws and the whole question of old-age pensions.

> I can very easily understand that whoever appoints the Commission will greatly *simplify* his task by the omission of all clergy; but I do think he will thereby materially weaken the Commission. What I imagine is wanted, and probably intended, in such a Commission is not the representation of any class interests — or technical knowledge of Poor Laws — or of minute administrative details — but rather the mature general knowledge of the facts of English life, and especially of English life among the poor: their manner of living, in health and sickness, their family claims and responsibilities, etc, etc.
>
> Now it is, I suppose, simply indisputable that there exists no body of educated men whose knowledge on these subjects is to be compared with the knowledge necessarily possessed by the parochial clergy, whose lives have been in no small degree spent in the homes of the poor, and who have therefore an acquaintance with poor men's needs and possibilities which no other class of educated men has had the means of acquiring in the same natural and un-artificial way.[30]

Davidson's letter failed miserably to achieve its objective, largely because there was at the time, a ground swell of opinion coming from the Liberal Government and others, not least the Nonconformists, that the 'National Church' was part of the privileged class in society and that disestablishment was a more pressing issue. Such is clearly implied from the subtext of the same letter, when Davidson goes on to say:

> You know me too well I think to suppose that I am writing thus from what may be called a mere *denominational* point of view. I should say exactly the same if it were Nonconformist ministers instead of National Church Clergy, whose special knowledge it seemed to me to be in danger of being wasted. I want to see one or two clergy on such a Commission, not sitting *qua* clergy but *qua* citizens and men of education who have had absolutely unique opportunities of becoming hourly familiar with the matters which such a Commission must consider.

In October 1894, Davidson expounded at some length on the duty of the clergy with regard to the prevailing issues rising from the rash of recent strikes, in his Charge to his diocese. At the time there were many who said the clergy and the Church should not become involved in 'secular' matters or campaign on political issues, maintaining that there are some aspects of 'life and conduct' which, in Davidson's words, 'lie outside the operations of the law of Christ' — and King, coming from that slightly earlier generation, might well have sympathized with them.

It was the 'business' of the Church to refute such claims, Davidson contended, and as a disciple of Westcott he quoted from Westcott's book *The Incarnation and Common Life*, published the previous year: 'It is the office of the State to give effect to public opinion, it is the office of the Church to shape it.'[31]

> Be this our task, and men by degrees will cease to talk of social questions which affect the homes, and so the characters, of tens of thousands of English men and women and children, as lying outside the province of the clergy.

Going on to apply Westcott's distinction between the role of the Church in such matters and that of the State, Davidson added a word of caution: 'The bishop, priest, or deacon who thinks he can define in any trade, or group of trades, the limits of a "living wage" and prescribe the mode of its enforcement, must be venturesome indeed'; and yet, 'the Christian man belies his creed, who fails to recognize the law of Christ as laying an absolute obligation upon us all to accept our responsibility for the lives of others, and to see that, if we can help it, no family in Christian England shall live, perforce, in such a home as must degrade and stunt that life.'[32]

Where was King in all of this? Back in his diocese, working with and caring for the poor, rather than tackling the 'problem of poverty.' Of course, both need to work together, yet the role of prophet and pastor are seldom packaged together in the same person. To be fair, no one could rightly accuse King, either in his preaching or practice, of not 'accepting,' in Davidson's words, 'responsibility for the lives of others,' and not least in exercising such personal responsibility in relation to the poor. In many ways Davidson's time as Archbishop is a kind of 'bridge passage' spanning the High Church Tractarianism of Benson and the full-blown application of an incarnational theology expressed in the high summer of Archbishop Temple—that great prophet of Social Reform in his *Christianity and the Social Order* which gave the theological mandate for the advent of the Welfare State after the Second World War.

Theologically, King would have affirmed all the theological incarnational premises of Westcott, Maurice and Gore, or later, William Temple, in their passionate concerns for the welfare of every man, woman and child, by 'taking responsibility for the lives of others'—in the words of the commandment, 'to love your neighbour.' But he would emphasize, as he regularly did, that that commandment issues essentially from the commandment 'Whoever loves God must love their brother also' (1 John 4:21).

While adhering to the 'old ways' of the old days now long

past, King still has a word in season for today's Welfare State. In the autumn of 1909 he wrote to Charlie, his old friend from Wheatley, making a point which still resonates with its misgivings about 'concern' motivated by materialistic individualism:

> People now are trying to make themselves happy without religion, but it is a hollow, heartless kind of happiness, not worthy of the name. I believe the love of God must stand first, and then, in God, we can love one another. People want to have social security and comfort, but without religion, without the Church. We must hold fast to the old way of the love of God, and the love of one another.[33]

In the light of King's caution, it seems that we still have some way to go to realize a society of genuine equal opportunity, which realistically seeks the common good and the welfare of all. King throughout his entire ministry had not failed to become hourly familiar 'with the homes of the poor' and, furthermore, by sharing their burdens in his uniquely 'natural and non-artificial way.' Nor can it be denied that he taught a whole generation of clergy to share that same passion. But necessarily he was a man of his times, and inevitably he reflects the limitations of his culture.

Perhaps Canon Townroe, Rector of St Peter-at-Gowts, gets as near as we can to King's attitude to the political and social issues of his day:

> In politics and social questions the bishop was satisfied to enunciate great principles rather than to undertake any active work for their immediate application. He was a bishop first, not a politician or a social reformer. And yet he had a keen interest in all the questions of the day ... He was an Englishmen with a deep patriotism and loyalty, a real belief in the value of conduct and goodness in daily life, with an Englishmen's temperament and outlook, and all that this involves in religion and social life—a love of freedom, a love of justice, a fearless courage, and a quiet religious sense.

Calm after the Storm

Yet in saying this, Townroe enters an important caveat in assessing King's attitude to remedying poverty, and facing up to other issues emerging at that time.

> But how far had he realized the new England, the new questions, new criticism, new social problems? He saw them coming. He was too old to have any direct part in their working out, but he laid down quite clearly and distinctly over and over again the great lines on which he felt they must be prepared for and faced.[34]

THE ODDFELLOWS SOCIETY

At some point during his time in Lincoln, King took what would have been regarded as a rather bold step by signing-up as a member of the Oddfellows Society. He may have been consciously following in the footsteps of his old mentor John Day, who seems to have been a member — certainly members of the Society were conspicuously present at his funeral (see p. 27).

The aim of the Oddfellows was to protect workers and their families from falling into extreme poverty and destitution. Early in the eighteenth century, the old English Trade Guilds were in decline and many fraternal societies took their place to support workers with benevolence should they fall on hard times. Among them was the 'Oddfellows' — representing fellow craftsmen from an assortment of trades. It was common for the Branch (or Lodge) Surgeon to provide medical treatment for members and their families, a practice which lasted until the establishment of the NHS in 1948. Dr James Parkinson, after whom Parkinson's condition takes its name, had been a member, and he appears in a print of 1789 entitled 'Meeting Night of the Club of Odd Fellows.' In the late eighteenth century, when there had been much social unrest filtering across from France and the Revolution, the Government passed an 'Act for the more effectively preventing the ministering of unlawful oaths' (1797), aimed at societies that 'administer oaths and correspond by signs and passwords,' as the Oddfellows were suspected of doing, so that for a time the Society was deemed illegal and driven underground.

Public houses were often used as venues for regular Society business—indeed, a few retain the name *The Oddfellows' Arms* to this day. By the mid-nineteenth century the Oddfellows had become the largest and richest of the many 'Friendly Societies' spawned by the Industrial Revolution. By joining, workers could help to protect themselves and their families against the consequences of illness, injury or death. In 1912 the Oddfellows became one of the Government's approved societies to administer National Insurance.

Both the symbol and the spirit of the Oddfellows Society would have appealed to King's sense of social care, the three, interlocking links of its 'logo' representing Friendship, Love and Truth, all three of which were exemplified in the teaching, preaching, practice and life of this godly man.

THE BISHOP'S WORK IN THE VILLAGES

At New Year 1895 in a letter to Charlie, by then a teacher, married and with a family, King writes somewhat wistfully:

> I was thoroughly happy with you all at Wheatley ... I long to promote the same kind of spirit in our country parishes. The Lincolnshire people are very nice, strong-headed, deep-hearted, religious people. My happiest time is when I am confirming in the country parishes.[35]

In the years immediately following the trial, King had set to work with a new vigour in the many village churches of his diocese. It was there he felt most at home, and where he was, increasingly, most enthusiastically welcomed.

'He was content,' says Scott Holland, 'to go up and down every corner of the Diocese, and to take a whole day, on hopeless side-lines, reaching some far village in the Wolds, and laying his hands on a half-dozen beloved plough-boys, with the pomatum and all. He delighted in the far-away look to be caught in the eyes of the shepherds on the Wolds, always steadying their faces to scrutinize something seen approaching from out of the distance.'[36]

By the end of his episcopate King had obtained a unique hold upon the affection of the villages in the diocese. There is but one small caveat in that generous generalization: some of the more robust yeoman and Lincolnshire 'yellow bellies' sometimes 'looked for a man externally tougher and were not drawn by the extraordinary gentleness.'[37]

King was quintessentially a gentleman and a Victorian gentleman at that: 'Whatever else our new bishop is,' the laity were reputed to have said of him at the outset of his time at Lincoln, 'he is a gentleman,'[38] His bearing at all times was undeniably that of a gentleman, and yet, no matter the surroundings, no distinction of class or learning could make the slightest difference to his demeanour.

It is not easy to enter into the heart and mind of King in relation to class or poverty, or many of the other issues which were so divisive and contentious at the time. Writing to thank Lord Halifax for his generous contribution to the chapel in the Old Palace, King points to what he sees as the fundamental needs of a world which was losing hold of what constitutes the foundation for building a better society:

> The real want of England is to make English hearts happy with the happiness for which God made them what they are. Money, rank, political power—these are well enough, and should be given to men as God may direct, in His own time and in His own way. But the real want of England is to know the peace and blessedness of the love of God and the love of man in the sacramental life of Christ.[39]

From his perspective as bishop and pastor, it was first and foremost the proclamation of that 'love of God and the love of man in the life of Christ' which was the first priority in his life and work, faithfully offered as a small, yet no less vital contribution in fellowship and together with all who were working for the greater good of society.

KING'S MINISTRY IN THE PRISON

No account of King's ministry in Lincoln would be complete without some mention of his profoundly tender ministrations to prisoners under sentence of death. Lincoln prison, in the Castle opposite the West Front of the Cathedral, and in walking distance of the Old Palace, was still the place where condemned prisoners were hanged. During King's time at Lincoln eight men were executed there. King not only ministered to and comforted condemned prisoners, but in two cases we know of, also accompanied them to the scaffold, as Sailer had recommended.

The first occasion was in 1887, when the prison chaplain (Revd H. H. Adcock) had either asked King to help him, or consulted him about the difficulties he was experiencing in ministering to a young fisherman from Grimsby, Richard Insole, who had murdered his wife (see p. 224). Insole was entirely ignorant of the Christian faith, and King spent a fortnight teaching him about the return of the Prodigal Son. In the end he was led to make his Confession and to receive communion, the bishop remaining with him right to the scaffold.

There was a similar occasion in July 1891, when the condemned man was a 22-year-old pork butcher from Blyth called Arthur Spencer, to whom King refers simply by his initials. Unlike the young fisherman, Spencer was already confirmed. King wrote to one of his chaplains, asking for his help and especially for his prayers for the man.

> He only has until Tuesday week. He is not at all hardened. He has been confirmed and a communicant

Calm after the Storm

> often and hopes to be so on Sunday week. One cannot help feeling almost a desire to be hung or shot instead of being buried as if one was good. I am sure the poor thing understands the Gospel and all that the Gospel was meant for. It is most helpful to see a man in the power of the faith facing death in good health and young. We don't do credit to the faith by living till the body falls to pieces through old age or disease.[40]

King visited Spencer frequently in the days before his execution but did not attend him to the scaffold. On the following day, King wrote a second letter:

> Thank you indeed for thinking of *him* and me. It was most humbling. I had not the principal part to do this time; but we all hope the end was good. It is very terrible. I am very thankful that I was enabled to do the little that I did. Religion seemed to have plenty of strength, and to spare, in the midst of all those terrible surroundings. But it is very awful, and one fears that one may be presumptuous.[41]

King's hope that 'the end was good' may have been in some sense realized—the executioner was reported as saying 'He never hanged a braver man.'[42]

A third occasion was in December 1893, when King again requests prayers from one of his former chaplains, then teaching at a theological college.

> You have seen, I daresay, that we are in trouble here again. A poor dear Grimsby fisherman; it will all be over a fortnight tomorrow. Will you please remember him, H[enry] R[umbell], and ask that he may be forgiven and accepted, and for me that my sins may not hinder me from helping him. We have every hope for him, he is really most beautiful. I am just back from the gaol, so my hand shakes, but not for him; it is a great privilege if we are only equal to it.

The skipper of a fishing smack, Rumbell was in his late thirties. King visited him in prison 'some half-a-dozen times,' administered the sacrament and accompanied him to the scaffold.[43]

It is King's concluding remarks in that letter which are especially noteworthy. In a sudden flashback, he writes, as though that first occasion back in 1887 when ministering to young Richard Insole in his death cell and bringing him to faith, were but as yesterday: 'But you will remember poor Richard, and understand that I cannot help asking God to hear *his* prayer for me now, if it be His Will.'[44]

From these examples, it is abundantly clear that King was not just cognisant of Sailer's teaching on the subject of ministry to those under sentence of death, but that as well as teaching it, he also practised it himself, bringing condemned criminals to know Christ's good news of healing and salvation, even in the darkest places of human experience, for, as he is recorded as saying, 'We must not give up any soul, as hopeless.'[45]

After 1893 King is not reported as having accompanied any of the condemned to the scaffold, though doubtless he visited them, as happened in 1899, with Edward Bell, a farm hand who poisoned his wife, when King was reportedly 'frequent in his visits to the culprit.'[46]

THE RAILWAYMEN

In the late nineteenth century, guilds proliferated, and throughout his Lincoln years King strongly supported their work of bringing working men together to strengthen the social side of life inside and outside the workplace. 'It is,' he said, 'a great pleasure, and a proof of the reality of things, that those who are striving on the same road, in spite of separation and different occupations, yet find that they draw increasingly nearer to each other. This is just as it should be, and so we get Guilds and Unions.'[47]

In this spirit, he warmly encouraged the small Guild of

Calm after the Storm

Railwaymen in Lincoln, making a point of visiting them annually around Michaelmas, after returning from his summer holiday, and speaking to them about their life and their duties. He even adapted the Collect for St Michael and All Angels for use as the Guild's Prayer.

The railways featured prominently in King's ministry as Lincoln's peripatetic bishop and he came increasingly to depend on them for travelling to Confirmations in remote country parishes. He used to say that he spent much of his life in trains—in earlier times he would have been a bishop on horseback, and worn gaiters. He claimed that trains provided him with some of his quietest and most restful hours, and for that he felt that he could never sufficiently express his gratitude for all the help and kindnesses he regularly received from station porters and other railway workers, whom he came to know. Having an extraordinary memory for names and faces, he would, on arriving at a station or changing trains, regularly enquire about the health or whereabouts of a particular porter, stationmaster or train driver. He often asked the guards and inspectors about cases of sickness or trouble on the various systems by which he travelled.

In turn, the men soon came to know King as 'their' bishop. 'I saw the Bishop today in the station ... and he had a long talk with me, and told me to come to you and get prepared for Confirmation,' were the words with which one railway worker greeted his somewhat surprised vicar one morning.

Preaching on behalf of the widows and orphans of railway men in the Cathedral, King with his usual optimism waxed eloquently about the triumphs of railways and the benefits and convenience of travel which they facilitated. He claimed that the invention of the railways marked a 'great advance towards the unity and perfection of man,' on several fronts, as all travel has the potential of doing. Railways 'have made our great commercial life a quick exchange of mutual interests and a strong bond between the nations. Their rapidity and punctuality enable statesmen to communicate without delay on the highest interests of the political world.' He went even further, claiming that 'railways have a share, too, and no small share, in the education of our country. Thousands from our country villages are enabled now to visit our great cities. National and international exhibitions and agricultural shows are made possible, and thousands can go and look and learn. And our railways have enabled thousands in our crowded cities to come out and see the manifold beauty and the marvellous mystery of the works of God in nature.'

Socially, 'thousands are now enabled to enjoy days of innocent rest and refreshment which before was impossible. Scattered members of families meet at Christmas and other times. Thus, the perfection of the individual and the unity of family life and the unification of our social life as a whole are being gradually but surely promoted.'[48]

It is hard for a later age used to cars, high-speed trains and air travel, to appreciate what an incredible break-through in ease of travel the proliferation of railways meant. In that same sermon King spoke of his personal gratitude:

> I cannot let this opportunity pass without expressing my own personal obligation for the assistance, kindness, and courtesy which I am constantly receiving at the hands of the railway staff. And not only would I thank them for their kindness and courtesy and sympathy, but they have delighted me and refreshed my spirit and revived my belief in the ongoing perfection of humanity by the kindness and courtesy which I have seen them show to others, to little children, to the old and infirm, and the mother struggling in confusion with her boxes and her bairns, a kindness and courtesy shown to the poor as well as to the rich, a courtesy which, I believe, is the expression of an honest and good heart.'

On 19 September 1909, in what must have been his last words to the members of the Guild, he expressed once again his gratitude to those who worked on the railways in his diocese: 'I am so thankful to come again to speak to you in connection with the Railway Guild.' On this occasion, early into the new century and six months before his death, the tone is a little less optimistic. He spoke almost prophetically of the dangers of a materialistic age in which many are indifferent to the claims of the Christian faith, and of how outwardly respectable and even quite well-behaved people increasingly 'put worldly interests and pleasures in the place of their duty to God.'[49]

LINCOLN CITY

King used to enjoy sitting in the window of his study in the Old Palace from where he had a wonderful view of the City 'down-hill,' generally speaking the poorer parts, where he was a well-known figure through his visits to the city churches, the many Nonconformist churches, the Methodists in the Hannah Memorial Chapel in the High Street, the children in the Church Schools, and, not least, the Mayor and Corporation in the City Hall.

A couple of vignettes of King by friends who knew him well, give us a glimpse of the sort of things he enjoyed and how he was received.

> At Lincoln there are large engineering works and the foundrymen were a constant source of interest to the bishop; and they quite certainly had a place in his prayers, as he told some of them when he was living at Hilton House and where he could hear them passing under his window every morning. And besides the workmen, there were apt to be a considerable number of apprentices in the engineering works many of them sons of the clergy or of professional men. The bishop used to make a point of seeing any of these young men whom he might get to know through letters of

introduction, or in any other way. His chief plan was to ask them up, one at a time to luncheon on a Sunday and get a talk with them afterwards.[50]

Twice I went down to the Lincoln Fair with him, all among the cocoa-nuts, and the ginger-bread, and the fat women. It was a delicious experience, to note the affection that followed him about. He drew out love, as the sun draws fragrance from the flowers. He moved in an atmosphere of love.[51]

HOLIDAYS: REFRESHMENT AND RENEWAL

King often took for his text the words of the Psalmist: 'Be still then, and know that I am God,' or in the Latin of the *Vulgate*, 'Vacate et Videte.' The text is an invitation, as the Latin suggests, to take a break or vacation, and recapture the vision of God not simply with the knowledge of the mind, but rather by opening the eyes of the heart and by becoming more aware and awake to the world around as well as within.

It seems he viewed his frequent holidays or vacations along lines of a spiritual retreat, though, of course, less formal and more relaxed, which refreshed and re-animated the whole man, body, mind and spirit. Canon Wilgress, his chaplain for fifteen years, who often accompanied him, tells us that 'combined with the light-heartedness which so characterized his holidays, there was always an element of seriousness; and underlying his plan there were some real principles or objects to be kept in view and attained. There was always a threefold end to be kept in view—physical, mental, and moral.'[52]

'On one occasion,' says Wilgress, the bishop 'copied out and gave to each of his companions the words of St Anselm, which he considered summed up the true end of a holiday: "Give me rest and health of body and spirit, and at the same time leisure spent agreeably in Thee."'

Calm after the Storm

For physical refreshment 'it would be difficult to say which of the two countries—Switzerland or Italy—he liked most. Perhaps it would be truer to say that he liked each best in its own way. He immensely enjoyed the strength and grandeur of the Swiss mountains; he felt braced by the invigorating air and appreciated the strength of the Swiss character.'

According to another of his holiday companions in Switzerland, a lady friend, 'one of the great pleasures of the holiday to the bishop was the flowers; he was a keen botanist, and lover of flowers, especially of the Alpine ones, and would draw your attention to their delicacy and fragility.' The world of nature and of creation, always spoke to King of the Creator and as being 'God's first text' and, as such, reflecting something of God's image. 'At Evolena when he was looking at a patch of saxifrage growing on a rock, he quoted from Dr Moberly's book, *Sorrow, Sin and Beauty*, and said it lay in us to be beautiful, far transcending the lily.'[53]

For mental and intellectual renewal and refreshment, he

> carefully selected the books he took away with him. There would always be some book of the Bible to read; latterly he used to take a little Hebrew Psalter with Dr Kay's *Commentary*—a book which he valued very highly. He also generally took the *Paradiso*. He would then add some theological book which had recently been published, and some book on the places he was going to visit (it was the *Life of Theodoric* when he went to Ravenna), or some book on European History. Finally, he might take some book likely to give him suggestions for the forthcoming Confirmation tour.[54]

King always delighted to use his gift for foreign languages:

> He could talk French, German and Italian quite easily; and in a Catholic country he tried to glean all the information he could about the state of religion in the towns and villages. For this purpose he would call on the curé and try to elicit information from him ...

> Quite a long list might be made of the foreign bishops with whom he had such interviews. Among these in France were the Archbishop of Rheims and the Bishop of Amiens; and in Italy the Archbishops of Milan, Siena, Brescia, and Verona, and the Bishops of Como and Cremona ... If he was staying at any place where there were Old Catholics, as for example at Munich, or Zurich, or Bonn, he would try and find out the bishop or leading priests. He felt great sympathy for the Old Catholics, and at times expressed a doubt whether he had done his part by them.[55]

And finally, and by no means least, King saw the point of a holiday as being the kind of refreshment and renewal which 'should always lead on to throwing oneself with increasing zest and determination into the work awaiting one on one's return home.'

There can be no question that holidays played a significant part in King's ability to keep fresh and 'aware' for the long haul of his lengthy and demanding episcopate, and that they contributed in helping him to recover from the strain of the trial. But he was never 'driven,' as Bishop Wilberforce, one of King's episcopal mentors with all his drive and energy, clearly was. King told a companion he knew the time had come to get away when 'he was getting into that grumbling and ill-tempered state which seems to be a necessary preliminary to a holiday.'[56]

In 1897 a very special task prevented him from getting away for his customary mid-summer holiday, a task for which in some ways his whole life had been a preparation. It was the year of the fourth Lambeth Conference, and the organizers had decided that the formal opening in July should be preceded by a Quiet Day, when the assembled bishops would hear addresses from a leading cleric. The cleric invited to give them was none other than Bishop King.

Notes

1. George W. E. Russell, *Edward King Sixtieth Bishop of Lincoln*, p. 198.
2. *Ibid.*, p. 211.
3. *The Guardian*, 5 November 1890, p. 6.
4. Obituary of King in *Lincoln Diocesan Magazine*, 1910, p. 57.
5. Lincolnshire Archives, Larken Papers III, 59 (King to Bramley, 5 August 1892).
6. Russell, *op. cit.*, p. 211.
7. *Ibid.*, p. 90.
8. *Ibid.*, p. 212.
9. *Ibid.*
10. *Ibid.*
11. *Ibid.*, p. 212.
12. Bishop's House, Ely, Minutes of the Conferences of East Anglia Bishops, November 1904.
13. *Spiritual Letters of Edward King, D.D.*, Letter no. LIII.
14. *Ibid.*, Letter CXVI.
15. Richard Rohr, *A Spring Within Us*, p. 209.
16. *Ibid.*
17. From 'The Love and Wisdom of God,' sermon preached by King at the First Festival of the Theological College, Lincoln, on Tuesday, 27 November 1888, see King, *The Love and Wisdom of God*, p. 275.
18. Russell, *op. cit.*, pp. 203–4.
19. John F. Bundock, *Old Leigh: A Pictorial History*. Chichester: Phillimore & Co. Ltd, 1978.
20. Letter to Canon John Bundock, son of the author of *Old Leigh: A Pictorial History* from his aunt, Mrs I Thornton.
21. *Ibid.*
22. *Ibid.*
23. King, *The Love and Wisdom of God*, pp. 277ff.
24. Randolph and Townroe, *The Mind and Work of Bishop King*, pp. 189–95.
25. Russell, *op. cit.*, p. 96.
26. G. K. A. Bell, *Randall Davidson Archbishop of Canterbury*, p. 208.
27. *Ibid.*, p. 212.
28. *Ibid.*, p. 225.
29. *Ibid.*, 226.
30. *Ibid.*, pp. 223–4.
31. B. F. Westcott, *The Incarnation and Common Life*. London: Macmillan & Co., 1893, p. 23.
32. Bell, *op. cit.*, p. 227.
33. King, *Spiritual Letters*, Letter XIX.

34 Randolph and Townroe, *op. cit.*, pp. 252–3.
35 King, *Spiritual Letters*, Letter XVI.
36 Henry Scott Holland, *A Bundle of Memories*, p. 60.
37 Chadwick, *op. cit.*, p. 21, referring for example to *The Lincolnshire Chronicle*, 11 March 1910, p. 5.
38 Russell, *op. cit.*, p. 111.
39 Randolph and Townroe, *op. cit.*, p. 134.
40 King, *Spiritual Letters*, Letter CXIV.
41 *Ibid.*, Letter CXV.
42 *The Sheffield Independent*, 29 July 1891.
43 *The Lincolnshire Chronicle*, 22 December 1893, p. 6.
44 King, *Spiritual Letters*, Letter CXVI.
45 Randolph and Townroe, *op. cit.*, p. 254.
46 *The Lincolnshire Chronicle*, 28 July 1899, p. 8.
47 Russell, *op. cit.*, p. 268.
48 King, *The Love and Wisdom of God*, pp. 186ff.
49 King, *Sermons and Addresses*, pp. 77ff.
50 Randolph and Townroe, *op. cit.*, pp. 173–4.
51 Scott Holland, *op. cit.*, p. 61.
52 Randolph and Townroe, *op. cit.*, pp. 214–15.
53 *Ibid.*, p. 222.
54 *Ibid.*, p. 215.
55 *Ibid.*, pp. 216–17.
56 *Ibid.*, p. 218.

✧ 14 ✧

The Lambeth Conference 1897

KING INVITED TO ADDRESS
THE BISHOPS AT THE QUIET DAY

When King took up the Chair of Pastoral Theology in Oxford in 1873, it had been his intention to write a big book dealing with the subjects on which he would be lecturing the students, most of whom would be studying for ordination. Pressure of work, together with his exemplary insistence on making himself available to everybody and anybody, had left him with no time to devote to writing on the scale he had envisaged. It was the same at Lincoln, only much more so.

So, when he was invited to give the addresses at the Quiet Day preceding the 1897 Conference, it is almost as though he seized the opportunity to offer in the form of addresses, rather than in a book, the sum total of all he had learned, taught and practised throughout his previous ministry.

It is significant that large parts of his addresses are couched in the first person, admittedly the first-person plural, as though every word is from King's personal experience of his own spiritual odyssey, at times delving courageously into the many contentious theological and ecclesiological issues of the day, and all drawn from his own inner life of the spirit. There is nothing abstract, bookish or second-hand about this testimony to God's revelation of himself.

There is no record of how King came to be invited to lead the Quiet Day when the names of other, better-known bishops, from home or abroad, might more readily have come to mind.

The answer must surely lie with Archbishop Benson who had been planning the Conference down to the last detail, before his unexpected death some nine months before it took place.

DEATH OF BENSON

In October 1896, Benson with his wife were returning from a preaching tour in Ireland and took the opportunity to stay at Hawarden Castle, Gladstone's home near Chester. On Sunday, 11 October, they attended Hawarden parish church, where the Archbishop suffered a massive heart attack and died almost immediately. He was subsequently buried in Canterbury Cathedral.

Now came the question of who should succeed Benson. The matter was more pressingly urgent than usual because of the forthcoming Lambeth Conference. The Queen's favourite was Randall Davidson. A former domestic chaplain to two Archbishops (Tait and Benson), Dean of Windsor, and Bishop of Rochester, Davidson was still not yet 50 and had only recently (1895) been appointed to the See of Winchester. Nevertheless, he was an obvious candidate for Canterbury. He knew the archiepiscopal 'ropes' better than most, having been at 'the centre' for a large part of his life. But it was not to be, at least, not this time around. It was the robust and sturdy Bishop of London, Frederick Temple, who was somewhat hastily preferred to Canterbury, much to the chagrin of the Queen, who wrote to Davidson after the appointment had been made:

> You will perhaps have guessed what I wished for the Primacy? It was *yourself*, and for the following reasons: ... my opinion is that you possessed the necessary qualities for that important Post, and above all because your great intimacy with the two last, great Primates enabled you to know their views and their work. In fact *their* mantle has fallen upon you.[1]

The Lambeth Conference 1897

Since it was not to be Davidson, partly because of his relative youth, the Queen had contented herself with seeking his opinion as to who should succeed Benson. After listing four important and desirable qualifications, Davidson, when asked for a name, forcefully recommended Temple, as being, in his opinion, 'foremost beyond question, both in power and influence' although 'he is 75 years old, and his eyesight is failing.'[2]

Somewhat reluctantly, the Queen agreed to the nomination, while openly admitting, in a letter to Davidson from Balmoral, 'I do not like the choice at all, and thinking the Bishop of London's presence eminently *unsuited* to the post.'[3] Temple, characteristically and swiftly, had no difficulty making up his own mind and replied immediately accepting the offer of Canterbury, though with typical frankness remarked that he had five more years of work left in him. In fact, he was to shoulder the workload of the post for another six years.

Two important matters demanded the new Archbishop's immediate attention after his enthronement in Canterbury Cathedral on Friday, 8 January 1897: first, a response to Pope Leo XIII's Bull of 1896, *Apostolicae Curae*, declaring Anglican orders to be 'absolutely null and void,' which Benson never lived to complete, and secondly, the arrangements for the Lambeth Conference.

As early as 1893, Benson had circulated the bishops of the Anglican Communion informing them of his decision to call the Conference one year earlier than expected—in 1897 instead of 1898—in order to mark the thirteen-hundredth anniversary of the landing of St Augustine's mission in Kent.

Benson had previously engaged all his administrative, as well as his somewhat theatrical skills, in preparing for and presiding over the previous Conference in 1888, and so, with that experience 'under his belt,' he had everything lined up for what would have been his second chairmanship of a Lambeth Conference. This time around he planned the Conference not so much 'for the decision of matters of debate, but for setting before the whole Anglican Communion the lesson of brotherly love, for realizing its unity and growth, for laying the foundation of a stronger life in the recognition of the power of the indwelling Spirit.'[4] In the light of those aspirations for the conference it was decided to gather the bishops together at the start for a Quiet Day. Although there had been no Quiet Day in 1888, from the outset of his time at Canterbury Benson had become increasingly concerned that the bishops of his Province should act as a body, and spend time together to confer on matters of mutual concern. To that end he held his first Quiet Day for the bishops of the Canterbury Province in April 1888, and that precedent may have encouraged him to include a Quiet Day at the start of the next Lambeth Conference and that his friend Bishop King should lead it.

Temple, who came from a quite different theological stable from King, was still regarded by many as too liberal after his controversial contribution to *Essays and Reviews* in 1860. Bishop Wilberforce, conspicuous and vociferous among the book's many critics, was particularly distressed that Temple should have agreed to have his contribution published alongside writers of what Wilberforce termed 'scarcely veiled Atheism' and 'open scepticism.'[5]

Temple was very ambivalent about the Tractarians. Writing to his sister, he openly admits that 'the Pusey party are the quietest and most unobtrusive set you can imagine ... They are exceedingly clever men, and decidedly they embody the chief part of the religious portion of Oxford.' However, 'in spite of the profound fascination the Movement exercised over him, he preserved still the attitude of a critic and a spectator, as of one watching with absorbing interest, yet from some standing ground of his own.'[6] We do not know what he thought of King personally, or what his impressions of King's addresses at the Quiet Day were, but from what we do know, it must be almost certain that King would not have been his preferred choice.

The Lambeth Conference 1897

At any event, come the summer of 1897, something like one-hundred-and-ninety-seven bishops, travelling from all over the Anglican Communion gathered for the fourth Lambeth Conference. There were plans for a little 'pilgrimage' to Ebb in Kent on 1 July to celebrate Augustine's landing at that spot in 597, while the inaugural service for the Conference in Canterbury Cathedral, at which the Archbishop was to preach, was scheduled for 2 July. But first the bishops met in the chapel at Lambeth Palace on 30 June for their Quiet Day, led by Bishop King.

KING'S OPENING EUCHARISTIC HOMILY

King's opening homily, delivered in the context of the Eucharist, and his three subsequent addresses later in the day, were given in a vastly different age to our own, and heard by an assembly radically different in complexion (at that time, all white) from that of similar gatherings at future Lambeth Conferences. They are, nevertheless, still remarkably relevant and would connect with the needs and aspirations of bishops and spiritual leaders in today's Church and world. From start to finish they are vintage King and as the fruits of his entire ministry, they also give us more than a hint as to the secret of his disciplined, inner life of the spirit through personal prayer, Word and Sacrament.

Admittedly, much of what he said in that opening homily would be said today, with variations, in any opening address for a Quiet Day, seeking simply to encourage those present to be quiet, still, and open to God's presence and the promptings of the Holy Spirit. King had conducted many retreats throughout his ministry, as well as Quiet Days, both of which had become increasingly part of the spiritual renewal which characterized the Catholic revival in the Church of England. Notably, King had introduced the practice of Quiet Days for his clergy at the outset of his ministry as bishop. Yet, there is no question that the three main addresses which followed after the Eucharist, and which were given from the pulpit of St Mary's Church, right next door to Lambeth Palace, offer an arresting and much more original personal account of King's theological and spiritual vision for himself, for the Church and for the wider Anglican Communion. At the same time, he was not afraid to tackle some of the questions and issues of the day, yet always with his innate ability to move on and to take hold of God and his promises, his grace and his power. All that would have spoken volumes to the assembled bishops, called by God not only to preach and teach the Gospel, but to embody that same Gospel of the Spirit in their lives and ministries, as King himself had consistently striven to do.

King's text for his opening homily was 'Behold, I am with thee, and will keep thee ... I will not leave thee, until I have done that which I have spoken to thee of' (Genesis 28:15).

He emphasized that the main purpose of a Quiet Day was simply 'to be with God' and to fulfil the injunction of the psalmist, 'Be still then, and know that I am God' (Psalm 46:19). He spoke tellingly, and again undoubtedly from his own experience, of how in a busy life there is 'very little time to realize the presence and guidance and love of God for ourselves.'[7]

To emphasize the importance of making time for reflection and stillness in busy lives, he spoke of how 'Eugenius, Bishop of Rome, pressed his old friend, Saint Bernard, to write something to help him in his own spiritual life,' and of how the saint had composed his little treatise, *De Consideratione*. Bernard was 'fearful lest his former companion should be so much occupied with the work of this great position that he would not get time to think, so he said to him, "*Vacare Considerationi*" [*Allow time for reflection*], and surely our only safeguard and ground of confidence, and hope of perseverance, is in the reality of the presence and guiding hand of God.' Clearly that had been King's own experience.

The Lambeth Conference 1897

> Our object then today is to be with God ... to try to lay down the burden of our work for a few hours; to lift up our hearts afresh to Him and say, 'Lord, what is it that Thou wouldest have me to do?' 'Show Thou me the way that I should walk in, for I lift up my soul unto Thee!'

King's opening homily, of which only an outline and bare bones can be represented by these extracts, contained nothing particularly special. Its power, as in all preaching, lay not so much in the words spoken, as in the person speaking them, and according to several present, even after that first short homily, something of King's magnetic power spoke directly and deeply into the hearts and the experience of his hearers. One witness records how 'many of the bishops remained long on their knees when the service had ended.' And then, 'in the interchange of loving greetings between long-parted men around the breakfast table in the 'Guard Room,' with its portraits of the Archbishops of Canterbury, from Warham to the lately loved and lost-for-a-time Benson, there was a solemn joy, fitting for such an occasion thus prefaced by Word and Sacrament.'

> In the spirit and fashion of the old days, one of the Chaplains read to the Bishops assembled around the table a sermon by the late Dean Church, preached on the occurrence of a consecration to the episcopal office. The meal over, the hundred and fifty bishops, after a turn in the gardens of Lambeth Palace, betook themselves to St Mary's Church, just outside the gatehouse of the Palace built by Archbishop Morton in 1490, and itself also dating from the fifteenth century. In this memorable church no less than seven former archbishops of Canterbury are buried.[8]

FIRST ADDRESS

After Matins had been said in St Mary's, King mounted the pulpit and took as his opening text: 'And the disciples gathered themselves together unto Jesus, and told Him all things, both what they had done and what they had taught' (Mark 6:30).

At the very opening, and almost by way of an apology, King admitted that much of what he wanted to say was based on his own experience and not primarily on book learning. It is worth recalling that the famous three-legged stool of Scripture, Tradition and Reason, commended by Hooker as the model for Anglican theology, had been modified to include a fourth leg—the leg of experience—by none other than John Wesley. It is noteworthy that King, who was familiar with Wesley's theology and spirituality, should, right at the outset, have laid such emphasis on the place of experience by extending reason to include the witness of the heart as well as the mind, in itself, all very much in accordance with the teaching of Sailer.

And it has a further significance. With Bishop Stubbs and several other learned and more academic bishops seated in front of him, it is as though King is still harping back to his perceived academic inadequacy which had daunted him, quite unnecessarily, from early life.

> One special difficulty besets me ... and that is that very much of the little that I know was learnt from books which you yourselves have written, or is the result of turns of mind which you yourselves have given me by your conversation, so that the only source of knowledge from which I can hope to draw anything that I do not know that you have already known, is the source of my own experience. This is indeed very simple and humble compared with your own, but to me, at least, it is real; and, if one speaks at all, one must speak with a sense of message. Forgive me, then, if I should speak with too much earnestness, or seeming presumption, about things which are to you simple and obvious; to me, at least, they have been, and are, real.

And then, turning to his opening text, he speaks of the two matters which the apostles reviewed when returning to

Jesus, telling him both what 'they had done' and 'what they had taught.'

> Let us look back over our lives and see how the account we shall have to render stands ... when arranged under the double column as the first Apostles arranged theirs ... all that they had *done*, and all that they had *taught*. The column of what we have done may stand pretty well. This is a busy age, and Bishops, thank God, are expected to work, and the danger perhaps is being over-busy, doing too much and forgetting the other column of what we have taught.

At this point, King pitches straight into what today we still continue to discuss—the relation of religion and science.

> Natural science, as it was often too exclusively called, was the star in the ascendancy, promising to lead us to results which were often most beautiful, most attractive, and full of real benefit to mankind—but some were over-fascinated by the new inquiries, and so accustomed themselves to the new methods of obtaining truth that they forgot, and even lost the capacity for using evidences which would lead them to the discovery and possession of truths of another kind.

In addressing this perennial issue, King pleads for the place of a different kind of knowledge, based not just on information and facts which inform only the mind by way of 'a mere intellectual conclusion,' but other facts also which are apprehended through the Spirit, by the whole personality, 'reason, affection and will.'

> Moral phenomena became our facts as sure as those of any other science: we learnt not to be ashamed to say we did not know all. Others were getting to know enough to see that they could not explain everything. There were found to be mysteries on both sides, and it was not thought unscientific to admit it.

Clearly, here there are words reminiscent of a letter he wrote in 1859: 'Always remember that knowledge and wisdom are two different things. Knowledge is proud that she knows so much: Wisdom is humble that she knows no more.'[9]

King had always contended, along with Sailer, that knowledge and learning are apprehended not through the mind and the intellect only, but also through the whole being—truth communicated through beauty and moral goodness, apprehended through 'experience.' So, he continues:

> We saw the exceeding excellence of moral beauty in others quite apart from wealth, or rank, or intellect; we saw it in the poor, we felt the thrill of it in ourselves. And from the vantage ground of the Divine pathway, we were led to look upward, and we received new assurances as to our belief in a personal God—not as a mere intellectual conclusion, but as the outcome of our entire personality acting as a whole—our reason, our affection, our will.
>
> We felt we could not afford, so to say, to let go our hold on God by any one part of our nature; God had so distributed the evidences of Himself to our whole being, that our duty towards God was evidently to believe in Him, to fear Him, and to love Him with all our *heart*, all our *mind*, all our *soul*, all our *strength*.

And then, as he moved on to speak specifically of ethics, he clearly felt himself more on home ground.

> Thus the study of ethics acquired for us a new reality, we saw more clearly its relation on the one side, to the despair of materialism, and on the other to the Divine pathway of duty leading up to the living God.

He goes on to assert the insufficiency of the ethics of the ancient world with its exemplary four cardinal virtues, much trumpeted in the public-school religion of Arnold, as well as by his successor at Rugby, Temple (who was present among the listeners):

> True and beautiful as the pre-Christian morality was—teaching us prudence, justice, courage, temperance—pitiably wonderful as the heights were to which their

greatest minds had attained, feeling after God, Who yet remained an unknown God, we saw the need of adding to the four cardinal virtues of the older code the three theological virtues of Christianity—faith, hope, and love—not merely adding them as something more of the same kind, but accepting them as newly manifested means of placing us in relation to new and richer truths, which brought new power into the moral forces we already possessed, and made them capable of attaining a higher perfection; not destroying the law but fulfilling it.

And how had that higher perfection been realized, and what was the nature of it?

> Our happiness, we saw, was not to be found in the mere exercise of our highest faculties, but in being brought into the presence of the true personal God. We saw that we must no longer be self-centred, but that we needed to go out of ourselves; and we saw how God was revealed in the face of Jesus Christ, and how through Him, in the power of the Spirit, we had real access to the Father.
>
> We realized that Christian morality meant a new standard, even the measure of the stature of Christ—that a true Christian should be a Christ-like man. We realized that Christianity meant not merely the manifestation of a new example, but the gift of new power, that the Incarnation was the moral force by which the Image of God in man was to be restored. And we saw that this line of thought could not stop here; it could not stop in the consideration of the individual.

He then expounded the role of the church both for the individual and for society at large.

> It was obvious that there is a society called the Church, claiming to be the covenanted sphere of the Divine love; not the *exclusive* sphere, not hindering God from working elsewhere, but having the promise that we shall find him *there*—'The place that he had chosen to put His Name there.'

'This led,' King continued, 'to a great interest in the study of Church history.' At this point surely, Bishop Stubbs (the great church historian), would have looked up to see where King was leading.

> The threat of our disestablishment helped it, but the observable point is not so much the increase in the knowledge of the *facts* of Church history as the higher point of view with which it is regarded. The Acts of the Apostles, as the starting point, has been called 'the Gospel of the Holy Ghost,' and it has been so called from the desire to trace the operation of the Holy Spirit in the Church, and to see its growth as the Body of Christ, deriving its life from him, the living, ever-present, ruling, guiding Head. This has been coming into view, thank God, with increasing reality. This has given a new interest, a new reverence, and a new value to the study of the history of the Church.

King had always made a habit, both in his own preaching and in teaching others the art of preaching, of leading the congregation on from information, to the challenge of transformation, often, as on this occasion, in the form of a question.

> We might ask ourselves what has been the effect of the events of the past fifty years on *my own teaching*? How far, since I was made a Bishop, has the pressure of the secular part of my work, the ceaseless letters, the routine of business, and much that is exhausting, and yet that has little in it that is spiritual or even of an elevating, intellectual, or moral character, taken my mind away from these higher things? ... How far, since we were made bishops, have we taken our due share in the intellectual and spiritual troubles of our people, and made them our own? ... And we, too, may humbly hope that He who knows all things will look mercifully on the confusion and lowness of our present lives. Yet shall we not do well to remember the double column of the Apostles' report, and pause to consider how far we are doing our best to prepare an account of what we have done and what we have *taught*?

Once again, after the conclusion of that first address, the same eye-witness reports that 'many of the bishops remained on their knees long afterwards ... Others walked apart in the beautiful grounds of the Palace. It was an hour for thought and prayer.'

SECOND ADDRESS

In his second address, King gets into his stride as he tackles on several fronts the dangers, spelt out in Paul's caution to Timothy, for a Church which holds 'the form of religion without the power of it' (2 Timothy 3:5). He does this on three fronts: The Bible and our reading of it: Ritual and our liturgical practice of it: and the Life of a Christian.

After the Litany in St Mary's which prefaced his second address, or noontide meditation, King took as his text: 'Ye search the scriptures, because ye think that in them ye have eternal life; and these are they which bear witness of Me; and ye will not come to Me, that ye may have life' (John 5:39–40).

The question of biblical criticism had been the subtext in all theological teaching since King's days in Oxford and would still be on the minds of the bishops attending this conference.

> I cannot speak to you, my most reverend and right reverend brethren, of the highest criticism; it is for you to speak to me of that, but I wish to venture to call your attention to this text, in which the Saviour finds fault with those who apparently did spend a good deal of time over the Scriptures, with a certain amount of belief, and yet stopped short of what the Saviour wanted them to learn. They were inclined to rest in the letter of the Old Testament instead of interpreting it by the help of the Living Word; they were inclined to *repose* where they should have been moved to *expectation*; they set up a theory of holy Scripture which was really opposed to

the Divine purpose of it: 'Ye search the scriptures, and ye will not come to Me, that ye might have life.'

King shows a 'yet more excellent way,' citing no less an authority than Charles Marriott.

> It was Charles Marriott who used to say, though as you know he was a true scholar, and quite willing that scholarship and honest criticism should have full freedom to do its own work—he used to say: 'The utmost that criticism can do is to prepare a correct text for the reading of the Spiritual Eye.'

There was the crunch, not stopping short and getting stuck in the letter of the text, albeit corrected as far as possible by the best literary criticism, but going further to read it with the spiritual eye which points beyond the literal words to the Word made flesh—the person of Christ. So again, King continues:

> My learned and saintly predecessor, Bishop Christopher Wordsworth, wrote, as you know, a Commentary on the whole Bible. It is obvious that any person undertaking such a task as that could not be expected to do full justice to each single word; but I would venture to submit that if anyone would read consecutively the Prolegomena to the different books of the Bible in Bishop Wordsworth's Commentary, he would get a most valuable insight into the spiritual connection and articulation and scope of the whole revelation of God's will, so as to feel that he was following the Saviour's own method of teaching the old Scriptures, when beginning from Moses, and from the prophets, He interpreted to His disciples in all the Scriptures the things concerning Himself. Christ is really the key to the Old Testament; there are things written in the Law of Moses, and in the prophets, and in the Psalms concerning *Him*—the Law is our schoolmaster to bring us to Christ …
>
> The danger against which the Saviour warns us in the text is the danger of not coming to Him as the source of our new life. We may stop short even in a wrong study of the Scriptures as well as in other ways.

King then goes on to explore the application of this same principle by not 'stopping short' in matters of ritual.

> It is obvious, for example, that we may stop short in the wrong use of ritual ... Bishop Butler in his charge to the clergy of Durham in 1751 [says] ... 'The form of religion may indeed be where there is little of the thing itself, but the thing itself cannot be preserved amongst mankind without the form.'
>
> Unless we bear this in mind, unless we make the externals of religion more and more subservient to promote the reality and power of it, we may be like the Jews who searched the Scriptures but would not come to Christ that they might have life; the mere external enjoyment of ritual is, in truth, only a modern form of Epicureanism, in fact materialism, and has no attraction for the really spiritually minded among our people, and no true power of spiritual edification.

What a word of warning that must have been concerning ritualism and all its controversies amongst the Anglo-Catholics and the second generation of the Tractarians, as well as to those who had branded King a ritualist only a few years previously.

King then continues to apply the same principle of outward conformity rather than by being led inwardly by the Spirit, by preserving, as he puts it, 'the form and phraseology of Christianity,' but losing the inner substance and power that alone comes from the Source.

> We have regained, I thankfully believe, a real position in morals ... But real and great as this moral progress has been, it is just here that with all humility, but with the most sincere earnestness, I am anxious to ask you to consider the application of my text ... The new forces in society, the newly extended political power among those who constitute the middle and lower classes of modern society, and the increased power of *pleasure* in *all* classes, are so strong that there is a danger that ... modern society may still preserve the form and

phraseology of Christianity, but lose, if not deny, the power of it.

Now what I am anxious to say is, that in the face of these new forces, and in order that we may direct them aright, some of us at least need to make our way of reading the Bible more *real*.

King is always insistent that the Bible, the Sacraments and even the institutional Church itself should be perceived as being 'means of grace,' divinely given to point beyond themselves to that end of which they are only the means—to the Person of Christ, as being both the author of our faith, as well as being the source of the power to practise it in daily life.

As the address builds to a climax, and as in his earlier address, King illustrates the theological principles he has outlined by applying a list of various New Testament texts and challenging the assembled bishops to apply them.

> Col. 3:10: 'The new man which is being renewed unto knowledge after the image of Him that created him.' Do I hope that something corresponding to this is going on in me? If so, do I find that my love is purer, less partial, less prejudiced, so as to be rightly independent of race or class, and that Christ is all and in all?

In conclusion comes that quasi 'altar call,' inviting the personal application of King's deliberately Christ-centred words:

> By these and other texts of Scripture, we might examine ourselves to see if we may hope that we are not giving way to a form of Christianity which is the outcome of the new forces in the world, nor are being tempted to repose on a morality that may free us from the inconveniences of sin, and satisfy society, but that we search the Scriptures with the earnest desire to surrender ourselves, and to come to Christ, knowing that 'where He is, there is safety and plenty'; for as Charles Marriott said, fifty four years ago, 'Meditation on Him, prayer to Him, learning of Him, conformity to Him, partaking of Him, are the chief business of the Christian life.' Oh! If we had only made it so, how much happier, how much

stronger, we might have been; how much stronger to help others, and to make them happy!

THIRD ADDRESS

After lunch at the Palace the bishops later returned to St Mary's for Evensong and for the closing words of the Quiet Day in King's third, final and by far the longest of his addresses.

For this he took a double text: 'Thy Gentleness hath made me great' (Psalm 18:35), and 'I Paul, beseech you by the meekness and gentleness of Christ' (2 Corinthians 10:1). At the start, King picks up on where he left off.

> I have ventured to speak of the danger of stopping short of that true union with God in Christ, which as Christians should be ours. I have suggested that such a warning may be needed now, when new forces are developing around us, and producing ways of life, and a conventional Christianity which in some ways it is difficult to reconcile with the natural interpretation of the Gospel and other parts of Revelation.
>
> 'Ye search the Scriptures ... and you will not come to me that you might have life.'
>
> The remedy suggested for this danger was a more *real* way of reading our Bibles, a prayerful and patient waiting for the unfolding of the meaning of the deeper texts, and this in order that we may first keep before ourselves, and our people, the true standard of Christian ethics.

And what is that true standard? Here, suggests King, comes the goal of all our theological strivings, indeed the whole point of religion in general and Christianity in particular.

> Our aim is nothing less than ... the restoration of the image of God in which we were originally created. Christ has come to show us what that image was. 'He

> that hath seen me hath seen the Father.' Our aim, then, is to be Christ-like Christians. This endeavour to set the life of Christ before ourselves as a practical guide of life, as a pattern for the formation of our own character, was first definitely brought home to me by the example of Charles Marriott. When Constantine Prichard wrote his little 'Commentary on the Epistle to the Romans' he dedicated it ... 'To the memory of Charles Marriott, whose noble life was a living commentary on the Four Gospels.' A Christ-like clergy would make it so much easier for the people to believe that we are what we are.

How are we to do that? King goes on to give the answer: by reclaiming the reality of the power and resources given to us by the Holy Spirit.

> We need to keep before ourselves this standard of personal Christian ethics, and to consider the *reality* of the new forces which have been given to us through the Spirit, by which the new standard may be attained—'For we are His workmanship, created in Christ Jesus for good works' (Eph. 2:10).

At this point King broadens his approach and moves from any possible accusation of individualism to apply the ethics of personal discipleship to society at large, living as responsible citizens and also as members of the Church. He is clearly drawing on the well-tried material of his lectures as Pastoral Professor.

> This concerns us as individual Christians ... Even the heathen moralists could see that the individual man could not realise his full perfection unless he entered into, and rightly used, his social relations. They saw that ethics should be regarded as the vestibule to politics, and we Christians know that we should train ourselves and our children, not merely as separate units, but to be 'citizens of the great communities of the civilized world and the Church,' and we know that these great communities, if rightly used, are of the utmost importance for perfecting the individual life.

He then moves on to present the true nature of the Christian Church. The consistent theme of the Tractarians from the outset, indeed from that Assize Sermon of 1833, was that the Church is not simply a human organization, but a living organism, nothing less than the mystical Body of Christ.

> The church is not merely a human society, and therefore morally helpful to the individual life; but, as Christians, we need to consider what being in Christ means. To be in Christ, Charles Marriott taught us, does not merely mean being placed in a system which Christ established, or which depends on Him, or which is formed on the basis of His acts and doctrine; but rather a baptized Christian implies a real union with a living body, the life of which is in Him—a real introduction into the midst of heavenly powers by virtue of union with Him, a real state in which we are related to Him as branches to a vine, although that relation may be forfeited by our unfruitfulness.

At this point, the climax of King's last address, we are compelled to see him pointing beyond that 'conventional Christianity' to which he had referred, to the ultimate claim that all Christians are called to live in God, as God lives in them, in that union and communion which Christ enjoys with His Father and which is ours in the communion of the Holy Spirit: in a word *theosis* or 'divinization' as the Eastern Orthodox Christians refer to this. Such is the point and goal of all discipleship, and to miss the point of our faith, is the ultimate tragedy of all religion. King clearly points out that all this is 'searching the deep things of God,' which always requires the 'aid of the Holy Spirit.'

> For as St Chrysostom says, 'there is need of spiritual wisdom that we may perceive things spiritual.' First, then, there is the great passage in that Holy of Holies of Holy Scripture, the 17th chapter of St John: 'That they may be one, even as we are one; *I* in them, and Thou in Me, that they may be perfected into one.'

> Here we have the great assurance that the desire of our hearts is *real*. Unity is the true goal to which we are pressing, and it shall *be*; *koinonia* is the natural end of *philia*, but it has been well pointed out here that if we take our Lord's words as a pledge of what one day shall be, we must be careful to follow our Lord's example. He speaks of unity, but He speaks of it in prayer. He prays for it: 'Neither for these only do I pray, but for them also that believe on Me through their word; that they all may be one.'

For King, the unity of the Church is related to the union with Christ in God of the individual disciple, and so has little or nothing to do with an organizational unity. Furthermore, in such a fellowship of the spirit, unity will not demand conformity, but rather will readily permit a diversity, reflecting differing cultures, all of which can enrich the whole body. As he develops this, King is clearly ahead of his day and, not least, ahead of many who would claim to be true followers of Pusey.

> The idea of the body ... should lead us not to be suspicious of, but to welcome, diversity of gifts; it should teach us not to require the outward expression of Christianity to be exactly the same, but to allow a liberty for difference of race and class.

And then, reaching a concluding climax, King really pushes the ecclesiological boat out, with a remarkable word at such a time, by pointing to the extension of the Anglican Communion as needing to work towards a fuller expression of what it is to be Church—a Church freed from the religious 'tribalism' of the past, to become truly Catholic and inclusive in the best sense—a word indeed for our own day just as much as then:

> India and Japan and China may well have their own contributions to offer for the perfecting of the Body of Christ ... The Anglican Communion is not confined to the limits of the British Empire. Not long ago we were

reminded by one who was competent to speak [Lord Acton], how 'the centre of gravity, moving from the Mediterranean nations to the Oceanic, from the Latin to the Teuton, has also passed from the Catholic to the Protestant.'[10] ... If the great lesson of the display of England's greatness was the excellence of moral power, it is for us to witness to the truth that the source of moral power is the Spirit ... Organization does not produce life, though life may produce organization—but the secret of the power, is the life.

'The people have seen, and appreciated, the beauty and the value of moral power; it is for us, as the stewards of the mysteries of God, to save them from disappointment by showing them the greater beauty and the higher value of the Spirit.'

And then, in conclusion:

It is this that I have been wanting to say. There are thank God, many members of the great Anglican Communion now who are looking to us to guide them and to lead them in the spiritual life ... and how is this to be done? 'Not by might, nor by power, but by my Spirit says the Lord of Hosts'; not by giving way to the temptation to introduce human authority in the sphere of things that are Divine; not by putting obedience in the place of truth; not by trying to make the truth stronger or more attractive, by additions of man's devising; but by handing on to the people in its purity, and therefore in its strength, the faith once delivered to the saints, as it has come down to us in the one Holy, Catholic and Apostolic Church, and as it may be proved, 'by the most certain warrant of Holy Scripture.'

It is for this guidance in their spiritual life that I believe many in the great Anglican Communion are looking to us today. God grant that we may not disappoint them.

'Thus, closed the Bishop's Day of Prayer,' commented that same episcopal eyewitness. Referring to King, he continued: 'The bowed form of the speaker, the sweet, sad voice weakened by age, the face lighting up with the anticipated glory of the life immortal, the stillness unbroken by a sound, the dim religious light and stern simplicity of the undecorated walls, made up a service and a scene which can never fade away from memory.'

REFLECTIONS ON KING'S LAMBETH ADDRESSES

A précis of King's words on that Quiet Day cannot do justice to the outstanding quality of the addresses. We have no record of Temple's reaction, either by way of a letter of thanks or from anything written that would indicate how the addresses were received by the assembled bishops, other than what Russell records from his anonymous witness. What can be in no doubt, however, is that King's addresses, more than fulfilled Benson's original aspirations for the Conference he never lived to chair. Inevitably, King touched on various topics of contemporary concern, not least on such matters as biblical criticism, the unity of the Church and its cultural diversity in the evolving life of the Anglican Communion. However, King's distinctive take on all such matters was to see them, as with so much else, in the context and from the perspective of prayer, enlightened and empowered by the Holy Spirit—'live the life and you will know of the doctrine.' Benson, in his earliest aspirations for the Conference had spoken so earnestly of the need for building up 'a fellowship of brotherly love.' This could only be achieved, as King insisted throughout his entire ministry, to the extent that Christians and the Church as a whole are drawn ever more deeply into the communion and fellowship of the Holy Spirit—in King's own frequently repeated words—more 'Christ-like Christians.'

Although disestablishment was being aired in certain quarters, along with other contentious issues of an ecclesiastical and divisive theological nature, King, throughout his addresses, appears not to have concerned himself directly with any of them. In many ways, the three addresses together with the introductory homily mark not merely the culmination of a lifetime of theological study, prayer and pastoral oversight, but above and beyond that—as he was at pains to point out—his words were essentially authenticated from experience.

His primary concern was to recall the assembled bishops to the interior life of the spirit, the very mainspring of the Church's life and witness, nurtured by prayer in the Spirit and leading not only to a knowledge *about* God, but also going on to explore the promise of Christ that, a way had been opened up so that all can come to know and 'dwell' *in* God in an intimate relationship with him.

Throughout, King is drawing on many resources, especially on those from whom he had learned so much not only from their writings and wise words, but also and more fundamentally from their example of holiness of life. Dante, as in all King's preaching and teaching, is drawn upon, as are the writings of Bishop Butler and Charles Marriott. Although the Church then, as now, was faced with contentious and divisive issues, King sought to raise the hearts and minds of the assembled bishops in order to recapture the vision of God's great promises to his Church as the mystical Body of Christ and the riches of God's grace and presence open to all those who come to place their trust in Him. In a word, the addresses throughout are essentially a call to the spiritual renewal of the Church, but in language and content which drew on the evolving tradition of the Oxford Movement, the Tractarians and the Anglo-Catholic witness, while also pointing beyond, to both the dangers and responsibilities, and to the great potential of the emerging and yet still very fragile Anglican Communion.

No person can be expected to transcend completely the cultural limitations of his or her own age, and like Benson, King does not question the triumphalist, imperialist mindset of his day, even perceiving the hand of Providence in both the emerging Anglican Communion and the expanding British Empire as being providential

On further reflection, however, it seems that his words on that Quiet Day mark the beginning of an 'enlarging of the tent' of King's theological comfort zone. He kept Charles Gore inside the tent of his theology and churchmanship as one of his examining chaplains, even after Gore had edited and contributed to the controversial publication *Lux Mundi* in 1889, which for many represented a serious departure from the patristic theology of the early Oxford Reformers.

For King, as for Benson, the new learning of science and philosophy was not a threat, nor was it ever for Gore.

> The Church of England has no fear. She need never be afraid of education, never afraid of research, or anything that science or philosophy may find out, because science and philosophy have their foundation in the Throne above.[11]

Then again, it is surely inconceivable that King would have been unaware that his generous remarks about the widening and diverse contribution which nations and cultures beyond the bounds of the British Empire could bring to the emerging Anglican Communion, might be perceived by some as coming dangerously close to similar claims made by the controversial Bishop Colenso of Natal. It had been the questionable biblical criticism of Colenso in his writings on *The Pentateuch* which had prompted Archbishop Longley to summon the first Lambeth Conference back in 1867.

Colenso, in his lecture to the Marylebone Literary Institute in May 1865, had stated that 'we cannot presume to assert that the human family will never be benefited by light reflected even from the thinkers of Zululand.' Similarly, and going even further, Colenso suggested that the question was not whether the Zulu nation would benefit from European civilization and the Christian religion, but whether Europe and Christianity might benefit from what the Zulus had to give them.¹² In an open letter to the Archbishop in 1862, Colenso maintained that God's forgiveness extended to everyone, Christian or non-Christian alike, and even to those whose marital customs like polygamy differed from the West's.¹³

While King would never have gone that far in welcoming the diverse contributions that peoples of different cultures and nations could make to the Anglican Communion, he must have been aware that he was approaching unresolved questions associated with a bishop whose views stoked up bitter controversy, and one of whose most vociferous opponents had been Samuel Wilberforce, King's own ordaining Bishop.

Indeed, the question of polygamy which Bishop Colenso had raised in his *Letter to the Archbishop of Canterbury upon the Proper Treatment of Polygamist Converts from Heathenism* was still a matter for lively debate and was not resolved until as late as the Lambeth Conference of 1988.

Then again, in those same addresses, King got to the heart of the matter over Church unity. Both he and Benson had a passion for the reunion of Christians. Writing in 1895 to Lord Halifax, that great protagonist of union with the Roman Catholics, Benson had expressed himself with even more fervour:

> With my whole soul I desire Union. Disunion with Nonconformists, Foreign Reformers, Rome, Easterns, is the main and most miserable cause of delay in the Christianisation of all men in Christian and Heathen countries alike. The love of Christ compels a burning desire for Unity.¹⁴

King would have shared that same 'burning desire,' but in his addresses he moves the whole question of ecumenism into a different dimension. Unity and the Communion of the Spirit are two sides of the same ecumenical coin. The unity for which Christ prayed is that we 'may all be one' in

Him, together with his Father and ours in the unity of the Holy Spirit. The unity of the living organism of the Body of Christ is a far cry from organizational joinery and is best forwarded only by a deepening intimate relationship with God in Christ on the part of every member of the Body. Put another way, the Church will only be One to the extent that it is a holy Church.

The only Church that can be 'one' in that sense is the Church which is re-centred in the One 'whose centre,' as Augustine said, 'is everywhere and whose circumference is nowhere.' Only such a Church will be truly 'Catholic' and inclusive, and when Christ is 'all in all.' King's contribution to this continuing and vastly important topic of unity and reunion is of lasting significance and value.

Notes

1. G. K. A. Bell, *Randall Davidson Archbishop of Canterbury*, p. 284.
2. Edward Carpenter, *Cantuar The Archbishops in their Office*, p. 389.
3. *Ibid*.
4. A. C. Benson, *The Life of Edward White Benson*, vol. II, p. 695.
5. Samuel Wilberforce, 'Essays and Reviews' in *Quarterly Review*, no. 109, January and April 1861, p. 251.
6. Henry Scott Holland, *A Bundle of Memories*, p. 164.
7. All quotations from the Addresses as reproduced in *The Love and Wisdom of God*, pp. 304ff.
8. George W. E. Russell, *Edward King Sixtieth Bishop of Lincoln*, p. 314.
9. *Spiritual Letters of Edward King, D.D.*, Letter II.
10. In his *Lecture on the Study of History, Delivered at Cambridge, 11 June, 1895*. London: Macmillan & Co., 1895, p. 24.
11. Benson, *op. cit.*, vol. II, p. 7.
12. John William Colenso, 'Pioneer in the Quest for Authentic African Christianity,' in *Scottish Journal of Theology*, 44, 1991, p. 223.
13. Rowan Strong (ed.), *The Oxford History of Anglicanism*, Oxford University Press, 2017, vol. III, p. 227.
14. Carpenter, *op. cit.*, p. 382.

✢ 15 ✢

The Golden Years

THE LAST DECADE

'It always seemed to me that the last ten years of life are the most important of all (and, for myself, I build my hopes entirely on what I can do in them).'[1] So said Benjamin Jowett in a letter to Dean Stanley.

From the evidence of King's many and mainly personal letters from the last decade of his life, as well as from the testimony of friends and close colleagues, it seems he followed both the letter and the spirit of Jowett's reflection. A quotation from Claudius Ptolemy, the mathematician and astronomer, translated into English by Matthew Arnold, further endorses such a sentiment: 'As you draw near to your latter end, redouble your efforts to do good.'

'Love for God and man wrought in Bishop King, a grand fulfilment of that precept,' comments Russell. 'His sympathies seemed to widen as years advanced, and his activities to expand.'

Scott Holland improvises further on this same appraisal of King's last years:

> You saw that he was alive with a spirit of good cheer which years could not damp, nor infirmities becloud. He thought better and better of the world every year that he lived. It was impossible to depress him ... he was still an undying optimist. He believed in everything being for the best. He saw goodness and wisdom everywhere manifest. He loved everybody and everything. He grew

happier and happier. His eyes twinkled with dauntless merriment: his presence brimmed over with joy. After all, the earth was a good place: and heaven would be better still. God be thanked.[2]

Such an assessment, however, should not be mistaken for a bland optimism or an indifference to the darkness and tragedy of life. The theological virtue of hope is the bud sprung from the seed of a deeply rooted faith which matures into the full flowering of love, joy and peace, which rightly perceived constitute the 'fruits of the Spirit' and are not merely the product of an optimistic nature. 'It is not so easy as I thought it would be to keep bright, and cheerful, and full of hope as one gets old,' wrote King to a friend. 'We must not mind, but rather be thankful for the disappointments and dissatisfactions which years bring to us. It is God's way of cutting the lesser strings that tie us to the life below,' and quoting from a sermon he had recently heard—'the natural evening is the spiritual morning.'[3]

Scott Holland goes on to fill out his glowing portrait of King in his last years:

> Those kindly grey eyes could, indeed, shine with a glint of steel: and the level brows, with their bushy eyebrows, could wear a look of sternness. For he was a soldier at heart: and knew the stress of battle: and had a sword that he could wield. This touch of severity was apt to come out in photographs.[4]

It was that touch of severity which caused some of King's friends to criticize the portrait presented to him to mark the turn of the century.

A PORTRAIT

A couple of years or so earlier, the High Sheriff of Lincolnshire, Thomas Cheney Garfit, began a collection for a formal portrait of the bishop. Six hundred guineas was raised, of

The Golden Years

which no small part was donated by Nonconformists and Evangelicals, which speaks volumes about King's ecumenical spirit. The commission was given to Walter William Ouless, RA., who completed the portrait in time for it to be presented to King by the Lord Lieutenant, Lord Brownlow, in the County Assembly Room in Lincoln on 8 January 1900.

King's response to Brownlow's speech portrays in words something of a new confidence and maturity which the artist had clearly sought to reflect and to capture in the portrait. King is seated, simply dressed in his cassock, with no pectoral cross or episcopal ring showing — in stark contrast to the many portraits of his contemporary episcopal colleagues in their lawn sleeves and Convocation attire. It is understated and even, as was said at the time, 'a little severe,' when compared with earlier pictures or photographs. King's friend F. E. Brightman, later dismissed both this portrait and the earlier Richmond portrait at Cuddesdon, in the terse phrase, 'neither of them like him.'[5] However, for many then and since, the Ouless portrait, which still hangs in the Old Palace, is reckoned as the finest of all the various representations of King.

In thanking Lord Brownlow for his 'far too kind words,' as well as the High Sheriff who presided, for what he had said, King's opening words were light-hearted, poking fun at himself in the light of the portrait:

> Very often, when we stand up to speak, we do not know very much about the subject we are supposed to speak about. My difficulty is that I know a good deal too much about him (pointing to the portrait) to say anything strongly favourable. (Laughter.)

He then went on to explain why he had been painted holding a little book in his hands.

> Some may ask what the book is I have in my hand in the portrait. I will tell you its history. One morning it was very foggy, and the good artist said, 'I really can't get on with your face today, I had better work at the body and hands.' I said, 'I will sit as you like.' And Mr

> Ouless put a book into my hands. When he had done, I was a little curious to know what I was going down to posterity with, and I found it was a nice little volume of Erasmus, the scholarly Reformer in the early days of the Reformation. (Laughter)

But then the tone changed: 'It is impossible to open one's lips on a day like this without letting what is in one's head and heart have expression.' Apparently, there were two matters in his head and on his heart that January day at the beginning of the new century and the beginning of what was (although he could not have known it) to be the last decade of his episcopate. First, he referred to the Boer War as being an example of what God can continue to do with times of adversity and gloom.

> It may be that God wants the war to knock off from England some of those habits which very naturally accrue, with all the energy which England shows, and which has brought England to the front in the world. It may be that we want a little quietening down in that way, so that we can put aside anything overbearing, if there is any, which comes from our greatness. There is good to come out of this, I believe, in the future. It may be even that we shall be brought to a condition of want of real help. Then it may be the way He has of joining our Colonies together, not in the manner of patronage from the Mother Country, but of holding out a hand to receive a hand, and to be thankful for real, substantial help, just as when people grow up they should hold out a hand to help their homes.

(Could he, without knowing it, have been prophetically pointing to the need for dependent Colonies in an Empire to mature into interdependent countries within a Commonwealth of nations?)

And then he reiterates his profound and lasting belief in that formula which he held true in every aspect of life — whether the life of the Church, the nation or his own personal life: 'There is sunshine through the gloom, if we only

The Golden Years

look for it.' He concludes by applying that same well-tested formula to the work of the previous fifteen years.

> My work has not been easy during the fifteen years you have borne with me here. But the troubles we have had are passing away, and this part of the Church as well as the rest will come out stronger, purer, and more united than ever. It is that which is in my heart. It is that which has enabled me to continue here in this work. I thank you more than I can say in words for your continued support, kindness, and confidence in very difficult times. I assure you I would not have remained among you in the high position God has put me, unless I felt unshaken in my belief in the Church of England as being a real true portion of the one Holy, Catholic and Apostolic Church, which I believe Christ founded here on this earth to be the means of bringing humanity back again to God, and in God to be at peace with itself.

Finally, as though by reassurance that he was not about to quit, either to Rome or to take up retirement, he concluded: 'If it please God, I shall be thankful and glad as long as I have any power left in me to continue my work in this way for the good of the Diocese and County of Lincoln.'[6]

In many ways, the last ten years or so of King's work at Lincoln proved to be, at least when viewed retrospectively, the years when the fruits of his labours were ripening and becoming visibly evident in the parishes of his diocese — amongst the clergy and people, with Nonconformists and Evangelicals, as well as in the countless lives he had touched and enriched with his genius for friendship and pastoral care.

FURTHER PROBLEMS OF RITUALISM

In September 1897, after the Lambeth Conference, King had decided to take a well-earned break and set out on his annual holiday to his beloved Italy via the Swiss Alps. On this occasion he took with him his nephew, Robert Stuart

King (who had succeeded his father as Rector of St Clement's, Leigh-on-Sea).

Bob, was a great athlete: 'four times he had played association football for Oxford University' during his days at Oriel, 'and also gained an English international cap.'[7] Possibly more importantly, from the bishop's point of view, Bob shared his uncle's love of nature and the glorious landscape of the Swiss Alps: 'Bob is nearly wild with delight at the colouring and the flowers and the trees.' Clearly the whole holiday was a great success—'I think' King reflects in a letter home from Stresa, 'it is quite one of the nicest times we have ever had.'[8]

However, while they were in Switzerland King heard some disturbing news which must have reminded him of his earlier experiences in the years leading up to the Lincoln Judgment: vocal and episcopal opposition to a resurgence of over-enthusiastic and zealous ritualist clergy. A letter written during that same holiday finds King with his usual more balanced approach on the whole vexed question of ritualism:

> Some men have been adopting all kinds of medieval and modern Roman ways for which there is really no sort of authority in the Church of England and in the Primitive Church. Now I hope we shall come back nearer to the true English position of Holy Scripture and the Primitive Church. We need not be surprised if the zeal of some young men carried them too far in the matter of Confession and Eucharistic Doctrine ... One loves the zeal and self-devotion of many of the men who have been led on too far; but some, I fear, were in danger of losing sight of the highest and most spiritual things and becoming humanly Ecclesiastical.[9]

Sadly, not everyone in authority took such a balanced approach. This time the points at issue, at least in the view of Archbishop Temple and his colleague at York, was the question of the use of incense and portable lights—candles carried in procession. The two Primates set up a 'tribunal'

The Golden Years

of sorts at Lambeth, faintly resembling Benson's court, for a 'hearing' on 10 May 1899. On 31 July they gave their 'Opinion,' as Temple subsequently termed it, condemning both the use of incense and portable lights.

Many members of the English Church Union, of which King himself was a member and whose President, Lord Halifax, was a close friend, expected King to openly disobey the 'Opinion' of the Primates on this matter. Yet, contrary to expectation, and not least of Halifax himself, who had urged members to disobey the two Primates, King recommended his clergy to submit.

An apprehensive correspondent wrote imploring him to resign from the English Church Union in the light of Halifax's letter. In his reply we see again the mature King who, as on previous occasions fraught with division and disagreements, never loses his head.

> The reasons which you are so good as to quote at length from my last letter still oblige me to remain in the E. C. U. Although, as you know, I do not agree with all that is said and done by the President, or members. I regret very much that Lord Halifax did not counsel loyal and hearty obedience to the Archbishops' decision. You will have seen in the Papers that I have done this myself to all our clergy who it may concern ... I am doing what I can to obtain obedience to the Archbishops.[10]

As so often, the counsel that 'time will tell,' was eventually justified. Three years later, on 6 March 1903, he was able to write to Temple's successor, Archbishop Davidson, informing him that there was only one priest in his whole diocese who did not obey 'his request' with regard to ritual.

King's wise and loving counsel, as well as his example with regard both to Benson's findings back in 1890 and these later more questionable 'opinions' of the two Primates, prompted him to write:

> In my own diocese, therefore, I have every reason to be thankful for the Peace which we enjoy and for the

> readiness of my Brethren to obey their Bishop. I need not say that I regret the excesses to which in some instances the Clergy have gone, and that I have no sympathy with what is really Romanizing. If, however, the control of the Clergy is taken out of the Bishop's hands, and severe measures of restriction are adopted on the one side while lax and negligent Clergy are left to do as they please, I feel a sense of injustice will be deeply felt, which may lead to untold confusion.

And then, with that same quiet interior confidence so characteristic of him in times of difficulty and turmoil:

> As matters are going on, I believe in a few years the strength and weakness of Ritual will be better understood and people better able to form a true judgement on the matter.[11]

ADMINISTRATION

There were two undercurrents of complaint against King during his time in Lincoln. One concerned his administration, which had always been weak. Even Scott Holland, his devoted disciple, comments on his lack of organization, but spins it as a bonus rather than as a deficiency: King 'did not attempt organization, beyond the actual diocesan necessities ... He left all the "business" side of his office alone.'[12]

On a different level he had the reputation of being an excellent chairman, not least when chairing the Diocesan Conferences. Admittedly there was a muddle over the office and stipend of Walter Hicks, Canon-Missioner in the diocese after 1895, but apparently the muddle occurred during the last year of King's life when many administrative matters would necessarily have been on hold.[13] As the years rolled by, the frailty of age became increasingly apparent, and there was the perennial charge that he was increasingly lax in replying to letters. By modern standards he wrote an enormous number (albeit many of them are somewhat scrappy little notes rather than formal letters), but that was the age when the writing of letters would have had comparable priority to the emails and texts of our own time. King was certainly no match for the 'driven' Bishop Wilberforce, who was reputed capable of producing forty hand-written letters in an afternoon. Not so King, whose handwriting, never particularly good at the best of times, deteriorated further in his declining years, to the point of being almost totally illegible.

CHURCHMANSHIP

A second, more serious and potentially corrosive, cause of complaint was one often made against those in positions of leadership and responsibility. As a self-declared and notable High Churchman, King had surrounded himself with men of a similar outlook, who were unquestioningly devoted to him as well as being from the same or similar 'High Church stable.' Though inevitable to some extent, this could be perceived by others of a different outlook as isolating the bishop from the healthy crossfire and dialogue with those holding differing yet equally valid opinions.

Two of his three domestic chaplains who lived with him — B. W. Randolph, and later his nephew, Fred Wilgress — were from the unquestioning High Church school, while his examining chaplains included leading High Churchmen like Charles Gore and William Bright. Gore, however, was no 'yes' man: on the contrary, both as priest and later bishop he was highly contentious and somewhat different from King theologically in his controversial contribution to *Lux Mundi* and even more, as the title might suggest, in his later work *Reconstruction of Belief*—a bold and radical response to the new learning and new biblical criticism.

Edward King

King had been forward-looking when in 1886 he started a *Diocesan Magazine*, the first diocesan bishop to do so, and throughout the years he kept a close interest in its proceedings, though, as some came to feel, perhaps too close an interest. He was accused of ensuring that the articles reflected his own views, upholding and promulgating theological views which were not necessarily those of his clergy.

King had grown used to being revered and loved from his earliest days—by the lads at Wheatley, by his devoted and adoring students at Cuddesdon, and by a large number of undergraduates at Oxford who fell under the spell of that 'genius' for friendship which had had such a lasting influence. A bachelor, now without his mother, and living together with his devoted chaplains, King could be accused of seeking to perpetuate those blissful years which had been without the challenges of responsibility for an enormous workforce demanding a huge amount of his time and energy.

However, it was in his later years that King, whether deliberately or unconsciously through his hands-on patronage, clearly came to favour and to appoint men of differing opinions from his own. From the outset, he had befriended the Low Church Missionary College, founded at Burgh le Marsh under his predecessor, Bishop Wordsworth. Since the death of Bishop Trollope in 1893, he had overseen the diocese without a suffragan to help him, relying on assistance from two retired colonial bishops, Adelbert Anson, formerly of Qu'Appelle (in Canada), and Charles Corfe of Korea. He had a little further help from Bishop William Tozer, who after serving as Bishop of Central Africa, and, until 1899, as Vicar of South Ferriby, undertook some of the many Confirmations in the diocese, particularly when King was ill or away.

However, when in 1905 a vacancy occurred in the benefice of Grantham, King took advantage of an Act of Henry VIII to appoint a suffragan. Who would he choose? Someone

The Golden Years

from his own school of churchmanship? No—to the astonishment of many, and possibly on the advice of Wilgress, he chose Welbore McCarthy, a well-known Low Churchman. Wilgress records how this surprising appointment, though coming late in King's episcopate, did much to allay fears that the bishop was a party man, favouring only those from the same stable of churchmanship as himself.

A closer study of King's life would suggest, and indeed is the consistent contention throughout this whole biography, that such an appointment would not have represented a U-turn for King, even less an act of expediency or ecclesiastical window-dressing. Throughout his life, while inwardly and remarkably secure in his own position, theologically, spiritually and socially, King was never captive to form, outward appearance or labelling. Rather, as in his warm relations with Methodists, he recognized the fruits of the Spirit in ministry and mission, in whatever outward form or packaging they were evident.

The German scholar, Dieter Voll, in his perceptive work *Catholic Evangelicalism*, and with perhaps the wider and deeper perspective of an outsider, contends that in the later nineteenth century some of the teachings and traditions fondly labelled as Evangelical were accepted by the followers of the Oxford Movement. As the historian Bernard Manning later contended, it is frequently the case that 'in piety ... extremes agree: Catholic and Evangelical meet ... at the Cross.'[14] Archbishop Michael Ramsey, in a typically profound sermon preached at the 'Faith and Order Conference' in Nottingham in 1964, spoke of how at the deepest levels in the life of faith and discipleship, in expressions of devotion and in a deeper contemplative spirituality, it is often the case that ecclesiastical traditions so often perceived superficially as being widely opposed and separated, nevertheless find themselves surprisingly close together:

> In a depth below doctrinal thought and structure, heart speaks to heart. May there not be, to give another

instance, a similar apartness in the realm of thought and nearness in the depth of religious meaning in the case of some of the cleavages about faith, justification and the sacraments?[15]

Two further instances during King's later years, clearly challenge the view that he was locked within narrow party loyalties and blind or indifferent to other traditions. In 1895 Lord Halifax was strongly promoting a reunion with the Roman Catholic Church in the aftermath of the reactionary claims of papal infallibility and the declaration that Anglican Orders were invalid. King, who had always strongly supported the English Church Union, was a good friend of Halifax but never a Romanizer, and contrary to the expectations of Halifax's ardent followers he came out strongly against any proposals or suggestions for a stitched-up reunion.

REMARRIAGE OF DIVORCEES

Even more radical and outspoken, and equally, if not more surprising, was King's refusal to go along with the entire High Church party on the question of remarriage after divorce. High Churchmen, almost to a man, and certainly the party-spirited Church Union under Halifax's leadership, held rigidly to the view that marriage was indissoluble and consequently that remarriage after divorce constituted nothing short of adultery, barring the divorcee from Communion.

However, only two years before his death we see in King and his outspoken utterances on this issue, the pastor who as a former Professor of Pastoral Theology, had sought always to hold together the claims of traditional ethics with a personal ministry of compassion.

The Lambeth Conference of 1888 had recommended 'that the Clergy should not be instructed to refuse the Sacraments or other privileges of the Church to those who under civil sanction are thus married,' that is, in the case of the 'inno-

The Golden Years

cent party' having contracted another union. To many, both Evangelicals and Anglo-Catholics alike, such a declaration appeared to fly directly in the face of the traditional teaching of the Church and the teaching of scripture, and consequently many assumed that King, a paid-up member of the English Church Union, would have been deeply opposed to such a provision. Yet here again we see King, not only as being his own man and sitting lightly to perceived party allegiances by taking an independent line on such a highly controversial matter, but also as one who had struggled to combine in his teaching and ministry both discipline and mercy.

After the resolution of the 1888 Lambeth Conference, King was beginning to undergo a change of heart. We see signs of this at the meeting of the East Anglia bishops in November 1894, when he raised the question: 'What should be our practice with regard to persons divorced?' Reading between the lines of the reply recorded in the minutes, it seems his fellow bishops had spotted that King was beginning to 'wobble' in favour of Lambeth's more 'liberal' attitude: 'That in the question of granting licences to the innocent persons, it is desirable that Bishops take common action,' is the recorded reply.

Those same minutes record King as wanting to know if the Eastern Church permitted divorce 'for certain causes' (as he had found it said), and went on to inquire 'Was it the general practice to urge divorced persons desiring to marry, to go to the Registrar's Office?' He thought that in the interests of public morality the innocent party, if desiring a fresh union, should be urged to remarry at the Registrar's Office, though, as he reminded his brethren, he could not legally refuse to publish the banns, 'even of the guilty party.'

The Bishop of Norwich, John Sheepshanks, spoke up to say that 'he would absolutely refuse marriage in Church to the guilty: he wouldn't if pressed, refuse to marry the innocent party in Church, but he would dissuade.'

At this point we see King's mind and heart moving in his characteristically pastoral direction, confessing that 'he himself was tending towards the view which would transfer the matter from the scriptural absolute ground to the disciplinary ground'[16]

He was always troubled to find himself at odds with others, especially close friends, over such serious matters, and the line he took cost him the loss of many friends who had looked to him to uphold, as they saw it, the teaching of scripture and the traditional position of the Church on this matter. Yet, as he pointed out in a letter written only a few months before his death, the more pastoral approach in the question of the remarriage of divorcees had always been the practice of the Eastern Churches. Both in his Charge to the Diocese of 1895, as well as in Convocation, he chose to uphold the resolution of the Lambeth Conference.

'I think such marriages should be treated by the Church under the head of Discipline, as extending mercy to those in trouble and perplexity.' He concluded: 'There is much, indeed, to be said for the stricter view, though, as I have said already, under the head of Discipline and Mercy, I am willing to accept the less strict view.'[17] 'He would *dread*,' said someone who was deeply opposed to King's less strict stand, 'taking a line which might, even conceivably, be harder than the line our Lord took.'[18]

By 1895 King had resolved the matter in his own heart and mind, refusing to play it by the book or follow unquestioningly party allegiances: his Charge to his Diocese in that year, and his speech in Convocation on 7 July 1898, in which he declared his controversial stand, 'were two of the most important and influential utterances of his life.'[19] Although it proved to be a costly position to take up, there was some gain. As a direct result of his stand on remarriage after divorce, the rift between King and Archdeacon Kaye was lessened, and during the last years of King's life closed altogether. Indeed, the close and growing friendship between the two men who held very different positions, became well known and after King's death was recorded publicly in the *Record Journal*.

It seems that the liberal Kaye could no longer lock King up in a neat and precisely labelled box, restricting the spirit which always pushes back any preconceived boundaries of exclusion and prejudice. Those who call themselves liberal-minded are frequently just as rigid as those whom they oppose and even condemn for being rigid and blindfolded. It is the radical, the person of the spirit, who pushes back the boundaries to be inclusive and comprehensive, and not simply for the sake of peace, but more importantly for the sake of truth, which necessarily always lies beyond the boundaries of our limited comprehension. It is King the radical contemplative whom Kaye personally came to see in this larger context, and so should those of us who seek to encounter his person retrospectively from the perspective of a later age which is still restricted by the particular cultural conditioning of today's world, possibly with less obvious and more elusive but equally rigid prejudices of its own: no age or culture, however enlightened is without its blind spots.

LAY READERS

The role of the laity in all the mainstream churches has always had a somewhat chequered history. Since the earliest times, rampant clericalism has squandered the diverse gifts of the Spirit, so freely and generously given to the whole people of God, clergy and laity alike. The Church of England throughout King's life was no exception, and was slow to concede any ministerial role to the laity in most aspects of church life.

It was not until the second half of the nineteenth century that the office of Lay Reader began to be recognized and authorized, and at first mainly in the larger towns, especially London, where the clergy began to turn to laymen (not women) for assistance at services, but only to read lessons. The clericalism of the Established Church held a firm grip on every aspect of parish life, symbolized by the giving of both the 'temporalities' and the 'spiritualities' of a living by the bishop. Anglicans were always suspicious of laymen taking services in churches: for many, laymen leading services of worship or preaching smacked of Nonconformity. Lay help as Sunday School teachers or in the conducting of Bible classes was generally acceptable, but for a long while laymen were not allowed to take services, let alone preach, in consecrated buildings. Bishop Wordsworth held out against it to the end of his days by firmly refusing permission for Lay Readers to take services or preach in the churches of his diocese.

There was a further difficulty. Although laymen as Sunday School teachers, or engaged in other forms of pastoral work, were becoming increasingly common, they were mainly drawn from the same class in society, not surprisingly since many people could not read. 'The Bishop of Salisbury asked one of his eminent churchmen, Earl Nelson, to become a Reader. Nelson replied that he would only do so, if some of every grade of society became readers.'[20]

It was Frederick Temple, at the time Bishop of London, who, as late as 1891, took what was considered the bold step of licensing Lay Readers to preach in consecrated buildings in his diocese. That concession was very slow to spread: by 1904 only three other dioceses had followed London's lead—Salisbury, Rochester and Hereford. In Lincoln, King continued to hold out against it.[21]

King's caution on the subject of Lay Readers is to a large measure understandable. Much of his life had been focused on the training of the clergy, which he believed from experience required the special discernment of any latent sense of vocation, followed by an extended period of professional

The Golden Years

training and residential priestly formation. But even King could not hold out indefinitely and in his final years he yielded, albeit it cautiously and with prescribed limits.

At a special meeting in 1908 of existing Lay Readers, convened, in King's words, as a 'result and outcome of much thought and prayer and work,' the bishop set out clearly the terms and conditions on which the ministry of Lay Readers would go forward in his diocese.[22]

He began by thanking all who had been 'taking part in this effort to organize and perfect the lay work of the Diocese,' and continued by spelling out the general features of the new scheme. In reorganizing the work of the Lay Readers, and securing a larger number of lay helpers in all parts of the diocese, King conceded the need to 'increase the usefulness of Lay Readers by giving some of them commissions to take services in consecrated buildings.' This he added, 'is a great step in advance and, it is hoped, will be of great value.'

Yet, even with that concession, King covers his tracks: 'The chief danger against which we must guard is allowing the idea that the Commissioned Reader can relieve the incumbent of either of his legal services on a Sunday [Morning and Evening Prayers]. A clergyman must not, for example, go away for his holiday and leave either of his legal services to be taken by the Commissioned Reader.'

King identified two classes of reader: 'Licensed Readers' and 'Commissioned Readers.' Licensed Readers would continue to 'help as heretofore,' but only 'in un-consecrated buildings,' while Commissioned Readers would 'help in consecrated buildings, by taking, where there are two churches, a service which the incumbent is not legally bound to take, or by preaching occasionally after Evensong, when the sermon is regarded as not a statuary obligation.'

All very cautious—overcautious, many would say, when viewed retrospectively and in a different context—and yet to some extent understandable in a diocese where Nonconformity was firmly entrenched, and where self-styled, unauthorized preachers tended to proliferate out in the fens and the Wolds. So, 'cautious,' yes, but for King the ultimate and overriding qualification for any ministry was a passion for the Word and for preaching the Gospel, and it was this disposition which finally led him to sit more loosely to the 'letter' in the Office of Readership, and to press forward to the authority of the Spirit and the Word: it is at this point that he continues by lifting the meeting to another level.

'Although you have not received the full gift of Holy Orders, yet you have come to receive a special licence or commission from the Church to enable you to take a share in her ministration, more especially in the ministry of the Word, in the reading and expounding of the Holy Scriptures.' And then he goes into overdrive, as if he had been back in Oxford as Professor lecturing to ordinands on 'homiletics':

> Preaching is different from mere teaching. You may teach mathematics or geography without being fully convinced. But in delivering the Gospel message, if it is to be a living life-giving message, there must be in the preacher a sense of message and the desire to deliver it.

Cultivating this sense of message is achieved in three ways: by reading, especially and above all, the Holy Scriptures; by observation of creation and the natural world, as Jesus did in parables, and careful observation of human nature. But thirdly and supremely, as always with King, by prayer.

> Let me urge you, my brethren, to constant, earnest prayer, that you may feel in yourselves the ineffable value of your message, and with all the mysterious power of personal conviction, deliver it to the people. This will mean earnest prayer to God to teach you your message, and then trusting to the presence and power of the Holy Spirit to do his will.

Even at this late stage, within two years of his death, the inner flame of his calling as a minister of the Word was still

The Golden Years

burning brightly so that others might catch the flame and hand it on to others.

THE ENGLISH HYMNAL

A further inconsistency, or so it seemed to many during that last decade, was King's response to *The English Hymnal* which came out in 1906. The test of time has clearly vindicated those who compiled the new hymnal, which, more than a century later, is still widely used, though admittedly in churches of a more Catholic persuasion. It might have been supposed that with its Eucharistic hymns, and many hymns from the Early Church (translated by John Mason Neale), or written by Keble and other Tractarians or post-Tractarians (including King's friend, Professor William Bright or his predecessor Bishop Wordsworth), the new hymnal would have commended itself to King. It appears, however, that there was one stumbling block, from King's theological standpoint, which prompted him to issue a letter of caution to the rural deans of his diocese on 23 November 1906.

> You will have seen, no doubt, some controversial letters in the newspapers regarding a new Hymn Book, called 'The English Hymnal.' It is difficult to determine the exact liberty which might be allowed to Poetry, and words of Holy Aspiration, beyond what would be allowed in prose, and definite instruction; but I cannot but regret the admission into this Book of Hymns containing words of Invocation, or direct requests to the Saints for their Prayers.
>
> This appears to me to be a very serious and dangerous departure, knowing, as we do, the vast system of Devotions with which it may be connected.
>
> I cannot express my own mind better than by quoting the words of Dr Pusey in his book, 'The Truth and Office of the English Church,' page 114, where he says, 'And, generally, for Members of the English Church who

desire the Prayers of the departed, it has to him ever seemed safest to pray for them to Him of Whom and through Whom are all things, our God and our all.'

I feel it therefore to be my duty to ask you to express to the clergy in your Rural Deanery my desire that this Hymnal should not be introduced into our Diocese.[23]

(An 'abridged' edition was subsequently published, though it was probably never seen by him.) Here again we see King, the Tractarian and the disciple of Pusey to the last, drawing red lines to distinguish Catholic practice from the excesses and practice of Romanizers and later Anglo-Catholics, for whom the direct invocation of the saints eventually proved to be no longer an issue. In many ways, there is something about this 'edict' of King which is untypical of him, even perhaps lacking in that 'generous orthodoxy' of which he would have wished to be a champion. Coming, as it does, in what were his declining years, it does not sit easily with that lightness of touch and *largesse du cœur* which characterized so many of his episcopal pronouncements.

GRIMSBY CHURCH EXTENSION FUND

Throughout King's episcopate, the only two towns of any appreciable size in the diocese were Grimsby and Lincoln itself. Grimsby, an increasingly important seaport with burgeoning fishing and timber-trade industries, had experienced a sudden growth in population and needed new churches and a commensurate increase in the number of clergy. King was doubtless aware of this when in October 1886 he chaired a meeting in Lincoln of the Grimsby Spiritual Aid Association, where the 'spiritual needs of Grimsby and the best way of compassing them' were debated. 'It was plain,' King said, 'that there was need to do what we could to help Grimsby at once,' and it was agreed to open a subscription list, the funds raised being administered by a committee 'under the presidency of the Lord Bishop.' Earlier, the meeting had been told that an attempt to raise money for the cause in the late 1870s had produced disappointing results, and the Member of Parliament who was present said that this was perhaps not the right time and intimated that the people of Grimsby did not take kindly to being portrayed as paupers.[24]

In the event, this latest push for funds seems to have brought in little money and King himself pitched in generously from his own pocket for a temporary iron church in the Weelsby district—All Saints'—which he opened in April 1891.[25] The priest in charge of the district had asked if the bishop's personal gift could be put towards a school or hall that might also be used for church services and other purposes, until a permanent church was built. King's reply is worthy of attention:

> The question is really part of a very large one.' I think there is a danger of turning our churches into club-rooms and concert-rooms, and trusting to such agencies instead of the real Gospel Message. Five years or so of solid spiritual work would be to my mind, more valuable for the future of the Church than the more popular kind of work which is increasingly prevailing in the present time. I am not against the use of these secondary agencies, but I think there is a danger of their becoming primary.[26]

The question King raises is still relevant for today's Church, faced as it is with shrinking congregations and too many large buildings in need of constant financial support.

In 1901, King again turned his attention to the 'problem' of Grimsby, setting up a Commission to inquire into the spiritual needs of the town, and following on from its recommendations, a Church Extension Fund for Grimsby was opened. The cause was very dear to King and, says Scott Holland, 'he threw himself with eagerness into the work of Church Extension in Grimsby.'[27] Not only did he contribute generously to the Fund (which he also remembered in his will) but in his 1904 visitation he opened it up to the whole diocese.

> It is the greatest responsibility in our diocese. There are over 80,000 souls in Grimsby [many more than in Lincoln at that time] and only church accommodation for 6,000. I hope every parish in the diocese will try to realize that the diocese is the true ecclesiastical unit, and not the parish, and send some contribution to our Grimsby Church Extension Fund.[28]

In that simple phrase, claiming the diocese rather than the parish as 'the true ecclesiastical unit,' King declared the objective of his whole ministry in Lincoln, an objective he had in many ways achieved by the end of his twenty-five years as bishop. Parochialism and Congregationalism had taken root in the eighteenth century largely as a consequence of neglect by the bishops. In this respect things began to change for the better in the nineteenth century, the arrival of the railways making it easier for bishops to attend to their responsibilities in London without neglecting their responsibilities back in the dioceses, some of which were many miles distant from the capital. Wilberforce, a keen equestrian had been conspicuous in seeking to achieve a balance between loyalty to the parish at local level, while promoting a sense of interdependence between parishes, realized centrally as a diocese, with the person of the bishop as the chief pastor. Wilberforce had remodelled episcopal ministry with mighty energy, by making himself visible, out-and-about in his diocese, unlike many bishops of the past who were rarely seen in their parishes, preferring instead to focus more on London and their place in the House of Lords.

Later in the nineteenth century, other bishops, like Denison of Salisbury and Lonsdale of Lichfield, along with Wilberforce, did much to raise the expectations of what a bishop should be and how he should be more visible in his local diocese. They would travel to 'the parish church

The Golden Years

to institute its incumbent, instead of instituting him at a brief ceremony' at the bishop's residence. They would be expected to take trouble to know the clergy and their work, at the parish level, more frequently conspicuous 'at public meetings and taking part in parochial endeavours.' The older clergy 'had not expected to know their bishops, but the younger clergy hoped to know a little of him and were not content with a bishop who was only a voice behind a legal secretary. They thought of him as a leader whom they would like to consult, and from whom they might receive not only admonition if they offended, but encouragement and stimulus.'[29]

King exemplified these, and other new and refreshing expectations of the episcopal office, as he came to know the needs of the parishes in his care, and not least in those towns where a rise in population required pastoral reorganization, more church buildings and more clergy to service them. Such was the case in the port of Grimsby, with its expanding fishing industry.

In many ways the success of the Grimsby Church Extension Fund represents a benchmark for the success of King's ministry at Lincoln which becomes increasingly apparent in those final years. His popularity throughout the diocese continued to grow and with it increasingly strong support on several fronts, not least financial. On 29 December 1908, his eightieth birthday, he received a letter which would have gladdened his heart in so many ways. A sizable cheque was enclosed, and a letter stating the purposes for which the cheque had been sent.

> It was suggested some time ago that many in your diocese would like to offer you an expression of their affection and good wishes upon your entering on your eightieth year, and, as it was known how deeply you have the interests of the Church at Grimsby in your heart, it was thought that nothing would be more acceptable to your Lordship than a sum of money towards the erection

of another Church at Grimsby, under the Scheme of the Grimsby Church Extension Society. We have great pleasure in enclosing a cheque for £1951 13s 10d., with the hope that God will grant you health and strength to continue your labour of love amongst us.[30]

Acknowledging receipt of the cheque, King wrote:

> I can assure you that this expression of your kindness has been a very great comfort to me, and it will, I hope, encourage me to persevere and try to do better during the time that I may yet be spared to live and work amongst you. I am especially pleased to hear that the great sum includes many small gifts. The real comfort of a gift is the love that it represents. The birthday gifts of children to their parents are precious according to the love which the parents have for their children, and the love of the children represented by their gifts.

King's perception of the relationship between a bishop and his clergy and people is clearly manifested in those concluding words. Many in today's more cynical climate, might be tempted to write this off as blatantly, even outrageously paternalistic, pleading that bishops and leaders in an age such as ours need to be made of sterner stuff. Nevertheless, bishops who made a permanent and enduring mark, are those who have shown love, and related intimately to their dioceses by their peripatetic presence. The person of the bishop must never be obscured by the *persona* of the office.

King's words, therefore should not be dismissed as unacceptably paternalistic:

> So it is, my dear children, with a father in God. But your great gift means something more than kindly feeling towards myself. You have given a real help to the extension of God's Holy Church in Grimsby. For this only God Himself can duly bless you. I pray to God to remember you concerning this, and to reward you according to His perfect wisdom and love.[31]

Subsequently, the Fund received several large legacies from

The Golden Years

Grimsby people, and the sum originally suggested was eventually raised. The proposed extensions and alterations in the parishes of Grimsby were duly carried out, resulting in the building of St Luke's Church, which was finally completed after King's death as a memorial to him. Over the years, Grimsby, the largest town in the diocese became the place where he was always assured of the warmest of welcomes, not least from the local and grateful clergy.

King's continuing interest in the project from start to finish was the primary reason for its evident success, and not just financially. All had been glad to give and work for a movement so clearly close to the bishop's heart. As an early biographer concludes: 'This great achievement will always remain as a monument to his lengthened and wise episcopate, and to the affection held for him by all, whether clergy or laymen.'[32]

THE BISHOP AND RELIGIOUS EDUCATION

As we have noted previously, King's energies were mainly directed to the care of his diocese, frequently at the expense of regular attendance at and contributions to debates, whether in Convocation or the House of Lords. Nevertheless, he never lost sight of the need to engage with issues of national interest and importance. One such issue, which was something of a passion for him, was the question of the availability and priority of religious education at all levels, from school to university. Of supreme importance in that educational 'package' was the perennial and contentious debate on the question of the place of Church Schools where children, as King always insisted, could receive a proper grounding in the faith of the Church.

The Double System of Schools—'Council Schools' and 'Voluntary Schools'—which had existed for some time was becoming unacceptable to many people, who were agitating for the introduction of some plan of what was termed 'Unification.' In response, Parliament proposed to meet the bishops half-way: in exchange for Voluntary Schools coming under the wing of the Local Authorities—a proposal not particularly palatable to the bishops—Parliament would be willing to concede that a certain amount of time should be ringfenced for specific Church teaching in the timetable of both Council Schools and Voluntary Schools.

The price for this arrangement was to be the teaching of a united 'syllabus' and, furthermore—and for King, very much against the grain—religious teaching was to be undertaken by a 'qualified teacher, or some other person representing the denomination to which the parent belongs.' There was no provision for the teaching of the Catechism by the local incumbent, and for King that was especially unacceptable, in his own words, 'I feel very deeply on the matter.'[33]

He was even more indignant with what proved to be an abortive Bill introduced in 1906 by Augustine Birrell, President of the Board of Education, which succeeded in rousing him 'to a wholesome indignation,' uncharacteristically and forcefully expressed in a circular letter to his clergy:

> I have been deeply pained at the ungenerous tone of the Education Bill towards the Church of England ... The Bill singles out, and gives State support to, the very form of religious teaching—Undenominationalism—which our schools were built to save us from. This can never be satisfactory to Church of England parents. While we are thankful for any real instruction in the Bible as far as it goes (for all 'Church teaching' is 'Bible Truth'), yet we are conscious that the commonly used phrases, 'Fundamental Christianity,' 'Simple Bible Teaching,' etc., cover but a limited knowledge of the Bible, which cannot be considered adequate, and is fraught with dangers of a 'down-grade' tendency.[34]

King went further and convened a meeting of the citizens of Lincoln in the New Central Hall on the evening of 8 May

The Golden Years

1906. There was an immense attendance. The proceedings opened with a short time of prayer, after which King rose to his feet to address the gathering. He thanked them for coming at the end of 'a hard day's work,' and expressed his pride in the 'public spirit' which such a large attendance demonstrated:

> This is the first meeting of this kind which I have ventured to call or preside at during the twenty-one years I have been amongst you. (Applause.) Let me say at once I have not called you here together that we may have the opportunity of saying hard things against the present Government. (Hear, hear.) I hope we shall all understand that this gathering is not for the furtherance of party politics. (Loud applause.) And if I have not called you together to say hard things against the present Government, still less have I called you to say anything hard against our fellow-citizens who differ from us in many points of religion. (Applause.) For twenty-one years I have lived amongst you in unbroken harmony, and I do not think that in all that time, though I preached and spoke under various circumstances, the Lincoln reporters can find in their note-books one sentence—nay, I hope not one single word—of unkindness against our Nonconformist brethren. (Prolonged applause) My aim and my wish has been the consideration, as far as God might help me to do it, to promote our Church, so that our Nonconformist friends might see that the principal reason that led many of them years ago to separate from us is gradually being removed. (Applause.) The nearer we can come to God, the nearer we can come together.
>
> Let me say, in a few simple words, why I have called you together. I thought it my duty, as your Bishop, to call you together in order that we might consider, and that I might warn you against what appears to me to be a vital danger to our families, and, through them, to our Church and our nation. (Applause.) I thought it my duty to warn you and to ask you, if you please, at the close of the meeting to join together to-night

in protesting against this danger, so that if it please God it may yet be averted, for the Education Bill, as it now stands, would, I believe, endanger the religious education of our children, and would leave you no security that the children would be brought up in the faith of their fathers in the Church of England. The Resolution which will be proposed runs in this way:

'That this meeting protests against any measure regarding Education which removes the security that—
(a) The religious teaching should be in accordance with the desires of the parents of the children attending the schools. (Applause.)
(b) The religious teaching should be given by competent teachers who believe what they teach. (Applause.)
(c) The religious teaching should be given in the recognized school-hours. (Applause.)
(d) The trust-deeds of our schools should be respected as regards religious as well as secular teaching.'

King then went on to deal in a little more detail with the four headings of the resolution:

'The religious teaching should be given by competent teachers, who believe in what they teach.' Is there any branch of teaching that goes on that does not require some test of competency? What could be more dangerous than for the Teachers to be teaching religious education which they did not themselves in the least believe? Surely, we are to try to get that altered, and have it that they should believe what they teach. (Applause.)[35]

He saw the importance of ensuring 'that the religious teaching should be given in school-hours'; in other words, as inextricably part-and-parcel of the whole required syllabus, and not as an optional extra after school hours when other priorities would take over.

Even from this summary of the proceedings on that Tuesday evening, it is abundantly clear where King was coming from on this matter. For him (and he was not alone among the bishops in this), religious education meant the full-blown teaching of the Catechism from the Prayer Book, and the teacher being the resident Anglican incumbent of the parish as the only competent person with the authority to undertake it.

At first sight it might appear that King, and others of the same persuasion, were concerned only for the Church to retain power in the field of education. This was undoubtedly part of their motivation, but the broader question of some form of religious education in society, raises profound questions which are still pertinent for today's world in which religion and faith in any form is an increasingly vexed issue. As the nineteenth century struggled to free itself from what was increasingly perceived as the strangle-hold of the Church, it sought to separate out morality, ethics and responsible behaviour as no longer requiring a religious foundation.

The Forster Act of 1870, under the famous Cowper-Temple Clause, allowed School Boards to order religious teaching provided it was not teaching the formulas of any particular denomination. Furthermore, it required that all religious teaching, even in denominational schools, should be either at the beginning or the end of the teaching timetable, so that any parent could easily withdraw the child on the grounds of conscience. The Act also provided that in cases where a School Board chose not to teach religion of any kind, then morality must be taught.

That, of course, raised, and still raises, the question of whether it is possible to teach a code of ethics and morality in any meaningful sense without any religious foundation. In fairness to Forster, he maintained in the parliamentary debate that 'the enormous majority of the country'—and, with a sweep of the hand, included 'all' the members of the House of Commons—was agreed 'that the standard of right and wrong is based on religion, and that when you go against religion you strike a blow against morality.'[36]

Matthew Arnold, eldest son of Thomas Arnold, held like his father that religion should be primarily concerned with conduct and not with religious speculation. In his capacity as a Schools' Inspector, he admitted that he had never found any successful teaching in morals which was not also teaching in religion, but he did add that some way might yet be discovered of 'teaching morals apart from religion.'[37]

For King ethics, religion and politics were a package deal, and not just religion in a general sense, but specifically the Christian faith, with the need to hold together the teachings of Christ with the person of Christ. He would have maintained that you cannot observe the teachings of the Sermon on the Mount without reference to the One who taught it—no fruits without roots; no fruits of the Spirit without being rooted and grounded in the Spirit and Faith of Christ and living in personal communion with Christ.

All along that had been King's objection to the public-school religion of Thomas Arnold's Rugby, in contrast to the Woodard Schools, which were founded precisely as 'Places of Religion and Learning' where religion and learning were regarded as equal partners, where even the architecture held together the lecture room, library and chapel under the same roof and all of a piece, encouraging the common lifestyle of a community in which belief begets behaviour.

For King, an education which separated religion from behaviour and morals was inadequate. In a sermon at Brasenose College in the summer of 1909, he specifically spells out the shortcomings of Arnold's public-school religion:

> This was the case ultimately with the teaching of the great Headmaster of Rugby, despite all his marvellous centrifugal moral influence, no English Churchman could deny. The Priesthood, Sacraments, Apostolic Succession, Tradition and the Church ... In our great Public Schools there seems to be a hiatus somewhere; they please our mental palate rather than our soul, and a deep sympathy and moral yearning at the bottom of our nature is left more or less untouched by them.[38]

The Golden Years

While many today would go along with much of what King and others sought to establish and defend, with the benefit of hindsight few would feel able to hold out for special treatment for an exclusively denominational school supported by the tax payer: all have had to make concessions, as the incoming tide of secularism submerges even the most established rocks of faith. Faith schools in our own day are still under attack and would appear to many to be anomalous in an age when not only is the Church of England no longer the principal denomination of the nation, but when Christianity itself is only one of several different faith communities, and when the majority of tax payers are no longer churchgoers and would therefore severely question state support for schools of any exclusive denomination or faith.

THE QUESTION OF RETIREMENT

From King's handling of that meeting on the Religious Education Bill it is evident that his natural powers of leadership were far from abating. Yet there were signs—largely manifested in bouts of ill-health and increasing deafness, which diminished his ability to participate in debates—that the time for his retirement was approaching. In 1907 he collapsed at the Eucharist which preceded the Diocesan Conference and could not continue, and it is now evident from letters and casual asides that the question of retirement had been on his mind for some years. In 1903, in a letter to a priest working overseas, he wrote, somewhat wistfully: 'I sometimes feel that what they want is a younger Bishop; but that will come when God sees fit.'[39]

Even earlier, when writing to his life-long friend, Canon Wood, he raises the issue of retirement: 'My chief fear now is staying on, when a younger Bishop would obviously in many ways be much better. It is very hard to know when *to go*. Please ask that I may be guided rightly.'[40]

Prayers for guidance on such matters in today's church are largely redundant since the introduction of compulsory retirement for all clergy at the age of seventy. Our age has decided that youth and its associated energy and vitality is preferable to the maturity, experience and wisdom which often accompanies the later years of life. Benson's successor, Frederick Temple began his work as Archbishop at seventy-five, and Archbishop Garbett of York did his greatest work in his seventies. Grandparents sometimes have just as much, if not more, to offer to the young than parents, and not least in their declining years when receding physical energy and vitality is often succeeded by a new quality of influence as they share the experience of success and failure throughout long lives. In an age of artificial intelligence aided by robots and technology, a robot could run an institution or organization if efficiency were the only benchmark. Yet it was the love for his clergy and people rather than efficiency which distinguished Bishop King, a love which only increased with age, and it was that love of which he often spoke which distinguished his ministry from start to finish—no less in the concluding years than in the springtime of youth.

King may have been further prompted to keep his retirement constantly under review by the example of Archbishop Maclagan, King's senior by three years, who in 1908 resigned the See of York. On 12 November King wrote to him: 'Your last brave act of resignation has set us a further example, which comes very near to myself. I pray God to give me grace to follow it when it is His Will.'[41]

KING'S LAST VISIT TO THE HOUSE OF LORDS: THE 'PEOPLE'S BUDGET'

As King approached his eightieth birthday it was becoming increasingly evident to many, if not to King himself, that

The Golden Years

his health was seriously failing. In 1903, he had written to a friend: 'I find I get old and deaf, but, thank God I have no pain, and am (undeservedly) happy.'[42] Though visibly fading and much weaker than before, there was, in what proved to be his last full year, an inner strength which enabled him to continue with his beloved Confirmations, and one final Ordination service (in Advent 1909). He had always tried to attend necessary meetings out of the diocese, such as Convocation in London, but his visits to the House of Lords became increasingly infrequent.

However, he felt that the epoch-making Budget of 1909 demanded his attendance. Earlier that year, on 29 April, Lloyd George, the Liberal Chancellor of the Exchequer, had presented a Budget which came to be known as 'the People's Budget.' It introduced a tax on land, and proposed super-taxation, higher death-duties, and taxes on licence holders, all of which would substantially increase revenue, supposedly ring-fenced to finance, among other things, the Old Age Pension Bill of the previous July.

In the Old Age Pension debate, Archbishop Davidson had taken the unpopular line of supporting the Government, urging that the time had come for action, and that the cost of this great measure of social reform was a question for the Commons rather than the Lords. The financial chickens came home to roost in the 'People's Budget,' which was strongly opposed by the Tory and Unionist parties.

Budgets are important government measures, but at the time the House of Lords had the power to bring a government down by voting against it. Which way would the Archbishop vote and recommend the Bench of Bishops to vote? 'From the first, the Archbishop's own inclination was to abstain if the issue could be kept within strictly financial limits. But from the outset, he also feared the possibility of a transformation into a constitutional crisis.'[43] After much lobbying Davidson decided to abstain and recommended his episcopal colleagues to do likewise.

His speech in that debate is of great historical and lasting interest. Davidson clearly differentiates between matters on which bishops have the responsibility and competence to speak and vote, and those which he perceived as being outside their brief. He believed that the bishops had what he called 'peculiar opportunities' for knowing about and handling the moral, religious, educational, and social questions with which the House had to deal. Such questions, he said,

> range from Poor Law Reform and Prison Reform to University or Ecclesiastical Reform, from sweating and overcrowding at home to the treatment of Aborigines in Australia or West Africa and elsewhere ... I am satisfied as to the usefulness of that function, but I believe that its usefulness is enhanced, and that the weight attached to what is said from these Benches is augmented by the fact that, speaking generally, the Bishops have, in recent years at least, held themselves free from the ties of what is ordinarily known as party allegiance.[44]

Following Davidson's lead, the majority of the bishops abstained. Two, however, supported the Government, Cosmo Gordon Lang, recently appointed to York, and Charles Gore. Reflecting afterwards on what had been his maiden speech in the Lord's, Lang commented:

> I think my brother Archbishop was doubtful of the wisdom of such an excursion into the purely political arena. Was it, I wonder a resurgence of my old political ambitions? I imagine it caused some perturbation among the very conservative laymen of the north.[45]

There was not much 'perturbation,' of course, when Gore, who was well known for his more liberal views, rose to his feet and, as expected, voted with the Government. He was well known to be politically passionate about the needs of the poor and would have had no hesitation about increasing taxation for the disproportionately wealthy in order to alleviate the scourge of poverty.

The Golden Years

What did cause some measure of perturbation among the growing number of more liberal and socially reformist bishops, and possibly even with Davidson, was when the aged Bishop King supported Lord Lansdowne's amendment, which indirectly, along with others, brought about the defeat of the Government.

Many since have speculated on this seemingly incongruous attitude by the great 'Bishop for the Poor.'[46] Was it because he was a Tory to the last? When Gladstone had nominated him for Lincoln, he did not hide the fact that he did not share Gladstone's political persuasion. Was it because the Liberal Government in the Educational Bills had been so 'ungenerous,' as King had said, to the Church, while Lansdowne had supported the Church's position on Voluntary Church Schools? (Both of these explanations seem to be out of character in the case of King.) Or was it, as Russell, who was 'standing on the steps of the throne' during the debate, claims, that the bishop, who was always his own man, voted as he did simply and solely because he felt that the epoch-making 'People's Budget' ought to be 'submitted to the judgement of the country?'[47]

Whatever King's motive, his vote against the Bill was construed by many as a political move, and 'to some Liberals in his diocese as being scarcely intelligible.'[48] After King's death, it was reported in the local newspaper that one member of the City Council had shown his feelings by declining an invitation to the Bishop's annual dinner for the Mayor and City Councillors.[49] It was held on 4 January 1910 and proved to be King's last.

Lloyd George's Bill represents the first move towards a radical redistribution of the wealth of the nation, and in many ways marks an historical and political landmark, so that many (including perhaps King) who voted against the Government did so not so much on political grounds, as because they believed on 'constitutional grounds that so revolutionary a budget should not be introduced unless the government first received a mandate from the country.'⁵⁰

After the Government was defeated by a large majority on 30 November 1909, King left both the House of Lords and London for the last time, homeward bound in more senses than one.

KING'S LAST ORDINATION CHARGE—ADVENT 1909

Just three weeks after returning to Lincoln, on the Fourth Sunday in Advent (19 December), King held his last Ordination in the Cathedral. The previous evening he gave his customary Ordination Address or Charge to those who had been in retreat and whom he would be ordaining the following morning. While the Lambeth Addresses of 1897 represent the mature reflections of his later years on the inner life of the Church, it is the content of this final address to his ordination candidates to which we should turn to capture something of the secret of King's own inner life and the resources of that spiritual power, love and wisdom which he had drawn on and which he urged those who are called to ministry to practise.

Taking as his text words from the Book of Revelation, 'These shall make war with the Lamb, and the Lamb shall overcome them' (Rev. 17:14), he began with two 'concise statements' to illustrate the contemporary state of the world. First, 'The seer sees the kings of the earth gathering for battle.' That, he said, 'is one certain fact: they will make war with the Lamb,' possibly anticipating the rise of Germany, of which he had spoken in the past, and the outrage of the First World War.

> The other certain fact is the victory of the Lamb. The Lamb shall conquer them. He will conquer the hostile coalitions of the future, as in the past He has overcome the solid resistance of a great Empire (Babylon)—and

the seer gives the reason for that—even that the Lamb is the 'Lord of Lords and King of Kings.'

To our eyes the conditions of this world will often seem to be what Bishop Butler called a 'mere scene of distraction' a wild scene which Mr Keble depicted with beautiful simplicity, comparing the great Empires of the world to the passing of the clouds:

> *In outline dim and vast*
> *Their fearful shadows cast*
> *The giant forms of Empires on their way*
> *To ruin: one by one*
> *They tower and they are gone.*

It would seem to be the great object of the Visions in the Apocalypse to proclaim the final triumph of right over wrong, of good over evil ... Babylon, to the surprise of the world, falls, and the New Jerusalem comes down from Heaven to stand as the city that hath foundations.

After developing this theme in Revelation, he then applies it to the world in which his ordinands will be ministering, and it is worth reflecting that within a little more than four years they would as, junior clergy, all witness the ravages of the First World War. King continued:

> It is into this restless world that you are to be commissioned to go forth tomorrow; but the terms of the final, great Commission assure you of strength and support. 'All power is given unto ME in Heaven and in earth: Go ye therefore and teach all nations ... and, lo, I am with you alway, even unto the end of the world.'

And so now to the foundation of faith and that inner confidence, to which King himself could witness as being the source of his power and inner strength throughout the trials and pressures of his life.

> Here is the all-sufficient, double promise: His power is sufficient, and you are to be commissioned by One Who has all Power in Heaven and in Earth. His presence will go with you. In his strength you may behold this

confusion of the world without being confused: very beautifully does Mr Keble express this for us—

> *The giddy waves so restless hurled,*
> *The vexed pulse of this feverish world,*
> *He views and counts with steady sight,*
> *Used to behold the Infinite.*

There, is the secret of your strength and peace. Imitate, as far as you can, the example of the Saviour; to Him the changes of dynasties and political upheavals looked but like the giddy waves or the feverish pulse, because He constantly beheld the Infinite ... You see, then, wherein your great strength lies: it is in Communion with GOD.

Then follows a passionate plea to his future priests to give priority to times alone with God in prayer, in solitude, silence and stillness, as all the great spiritual giants of the past have done, following the example of Christ himself.

> Remember what we were told yesterday of the Preparation of the Baptist in the wilderness alone with GOD; of St Paul, in Arabia; and of our Lord during the Forty Days, and at many other times of special retirement, in the night, and in the early mornings, in the Garden of Gethsemane, on the Mount of Olives—'Jesus oft-times resorted thither with His disciples.'
> Get times for special and deliberate communion with GOD; your prayers, your Bible, and the Blessed Sacrament will be the great normal occasions, and you will find it also to be a great help if you can attend a Retreat or Quiet Day every year: 'Be still then and know that I am GOD,' the psalmist says. 'Vacare Considerationi'—get time to try St Bernard's advice to his kind friend the Pope Eugenius.
> Mr Keble speaks of that 'deep silence in the heart, for thought to do her part.' All teach us the same truth, the value of retirement, silence in solitude, in order that we may realize more the Presence and the Power of GOD.
> It is this we want more of. In other words, we want more faith: we want to pray more for the help of the Holy Spirit, that we may see the richness and the preciousness

The Golden Years

and the power of the things that have been given us of God.

No doubt, tonight, waiting for your great Commission there must be some feeling of fear mixed with your joy. It should not be otherwise; it is quite right, if it is Holy Fear, *i.e.*, a fear that leads you to draw near to GOD in trustful love.

Tonight, though you may be tired, let there be an *extraordinary moment* of trustful, loving prayer ...

The right realisation of GOD, and His Power and Presence, naturally tends to humility, and humility enables GOD's Power to work in us, unchecked by the thought of self. If GOD could create the world out of nothing, then he may be able to do something through me.

That should be our way of thinking: mistrust of self and trust in GOD — that is the very essence of the spiritual life; that is indeed the Life of Faith; it is that which enabled Abraham to become the father of Isaac in his old age, and through Isaac to have a seed like the 'sand on the sea-shore for multitude.'

Try to set GOD always before yourself, and to know and to do His Will, and you will be astonished at the great things He will do in and through you; only always remember that the work is really His work, and so give Him the glory. This is set forth in the perfected Personality which enabled the Apostle St Paul to say, 'yet not I, but Christ in me.'

If you realise the Promise of Christ to be with you, you not only will not be afraid, but you will cease to be surprised at the wonderful things that He will do through you.

Lift up your hearts then, dear Brothers, lift them up unto the Lord; give yourselves wholly to Him tomorrow; put yourselves at His disposal; do not let yourselves be alarmed by the Enemy, under whatsoever form or in whatever numbers they may appear against you. 'They shall make war with the Lamb.' — that is one fact, AND 'the Lamb shall conquer them' — that is the concluding fact.

> Every life has a purpose and every life is different, and no human example perfectly satisfies your mind; it may help you, but not perfectly satisfy. The Presence of Christ alone can do that, and He will help you if you ask Him.[51]

The power of that address lay not only in the eloquence of the words; it encapsulated a lifetime's experience in which, when reading between the lines and the words, we catch, as in King's addresses at the Lambeth Conference, a great deal of his personal struggle on his inner journey of faith, foundationally sustained by a hidden and interior life of prayer.

KING'S EIGHTIETH BIRTHDAY

Immediately following what proved to be his last Christmas, King celebrated his eightieth birthday, on 29 December 1909. He appeared to be in remarkably good health throughout the modest celebration, evidently enjoying the many words and acts of kindness which marked the occasion.

One birthday gift which gave him particular pleasure was a new hat and pair of gloves from his servants, presented to him before he got up that morning. Then there was the particularly beautiful cake his cook had made which appeared at lunch. To show his appreciation he said he would eat a little of it, 'even if it should kill him.' And then he said, with his usual playfulness and thoughtfulness, that he would walk over to the Cathedral to take the left-overs himself to the choir boys. Despite the inclement weather, and having difficulty in walking, he did indeed stroll over to the Cathedral to present the cake in person.

From some of the letters written during his last months it is clear King was beginning to have concerns about the direction of the Church and the world in general. Writing to an old friend on the eve of that eightieth birthday:

The Golden Years

> We must keep quietly to the old ways, and trust. The great comfort is knowing that the Church and the world are both under the eye and control of our Blessed Lord. He is Head over all, and over the Church. Our only anxiety should be to know and do His will, then calmly, thankfully, lovingly, to trust.[52]

And then again, the day after his birthday, to a friend who had attended his lectures back in Oxford, he refers obliquely to 'much that is rough on the surface round about, just now,' and, rather as though he was trying to convince and reassure himself, he continues:

> The older one gets, the more, thank God, one feels that the world, and, still more, the Church, are under His eye and guidance. If we can watch His eye and guiding Hand, and only not hinder by our narrow views, all will be well.[53]

What are the 'narrow views' to which he is referring? Did he sense something of a departure from the original Tractarian vision into a 'narrowing' born of party strife?

As the New Year opened, we find words written on the first page of his diary for 1910: 'I will trust and will not be afraid' (Isaiah 12: 2). Some of his apprehension was more personal: he constantly alludes to the question of retirement, something perhaps even more in his mind having reached the age of eighty. During that first decade of the new century, he had been aware of declining energies and the 'rumblings' about inefficiency in administration which would not have receded, although it seems that the love and loyalty of the diocese, had markedly increased with the years in inverse proportion. The burden of diocesan work continued to increase, not least with the growing demands of the expanding number of organizations, many of his own making. He was well aware that in the world of politics radical changes were inevitable, stoking an underlying apprehension, despite protestations to the contrary. Yet at the outset of 1910, he seemed determined to 'put his shoulder to the burden of another year,'⁵⁴ if only to complete a full twenty-five years as Bishop of Lincoln.

The customary parties and hospitality of the Christmas and New Year season continued much as before. In addition to the annual dinner for the Mayor and Corporation on 4 January, there were several other dinner parties which he hosted.

INTO THE SUNSET

On 12 January two nieces came to stay. King was keen to walk down into the city with them that afternoon to have their advice when buying a wedding present for a young lady and near neighbour of whom he was very fond. For some time he had experienced difficulty in walking, but, despite the cold that cheerless January afternoon, he managed the steep walk down and back up again without evident fatigue, and in the evening hosted a dinner party at which he was apparently as bright and lively as ever.

But the next day something was clearly not right. In the morning he had, as usual, celebrated the Eucharist in his chapel at 8.15am, breakfasted afterwards and begun to carry out his daily routine. At 11.00am he went to his chapel, for what turned out to be the last time, to say the Office of Morning Prayer and it was during the recitation of that short daily Office that he appeared to be suffering some discomfort, although afterwards he spent some time with his secretary and did not complain of feeling especially unwell. At one o'clock, however, he was seized with an attack of sickness and was finally persuaded to go back to bed and to send for the doctor.

The doctor thought he was probably suffering from a chill and would soon be well again. However, during the next week he noticed 'a symptom which first gave rise to grave apprehension.'⁵⁵ At first the doctor's treatment

The Golden Years

seemed to help, nevertheless King spent a lot of time in bed during January.

Incidentally, on 31 January, the compiler of a 'Symposium' for *Sunday at Home*, wrote to him asking 'What are the Chief Difficulties [to Religious and Social Work] in your Diocese?' King replied succinctly: 'Myself and my old age.' (It was around the same time that *The Times* invited a response from readers to a similar question: 'What is wrong with the world?' and G. K. Chesterton replied on a postcard, even more briefly, 'I am!')

The period of the Spring Confirmations was rapidly approaching. Initially, he reluctantly sought some help from Bishop Farrar, formerly of Antigua—'reluctantly,' because Confirmations had become his chief delight of the whole year. Throughout January his whole daily routine had changed. 'He did not come down from his bedroom until 12 o'clock; he had all his meals by himself and saw very few people.'[56]

On 8 February, feeling a little better, he was determined to try to undertake some Confirmations. The first of these was at Great Hale, a village about twenty-four miles out of Lincoln. Usually, he would have travelled, as he had always loved to do, by train, but after much persuasion, he finally consented to go in a motor-car—a great luxury.

> It was most distressing to see him during the Confirmation Service. He could only walk with difficulty, his voice was very weak, and he sat all through his addresses. He returned to Lincoln immediately after the service, without waiting for tea, which he was unwilling to do, for he used to consider tea after the service as an essential part of the proceedings.

In that same week he took two more Confirmations, and did not seem to be too much the worse as a result.

During the middle weeks of February, he undertook a Confirmation in a distant part of the diocese which necessitated him sleeping a night away from home. As soon as he arrived at the priest's house, he went straight to his bedroom, remaining there until the hour of the service, only to return there immediately after the service was over, and did not appear again until it was time for him to return to Lincoln the following day. Clearly, by this stage he was extremely ill, and must have known that the end was not far off.

On Assize Sunday (24 February), he entertained the Judges to luncheon after the service, as had been his custom throughout his time at Lincoln. All present could see how ill he was, how lifeless he seemed, and how different from the vivacious and charming host of so many previous occasions

The following day he insisted on going to West Allington, near Grantham, in order to take what proved to be his last Confirmation. On returning to Lincoln, he was undoubtedly relieved to learn that arrangements had been made during his absence for Bishop Corfe to move in and to take the remaining Confirmations of that week. The same day, his doctor called to see him and was not at all happy with his condition, to the point of expressing a wish to call in further advice.

Unsurprisingly, King did not attend Convocation in London the previous week. Archdeacon John Kaye did attend, and on his return wrote a touching letter, expressing sentiments from which it is clear that, after the years of estrangement and opposition, he had finally come to appreciate King's outstanding spiritual qualities, very different though they were from those of his late father, the highly esteemed Bishop Kaye of Lincoln:

> I have been truly glad to learn that you had obtained the help which would enable you to confirm by Deputy, during this very inclement weather ... In the old days, my father always confirmed in the summer months; and Bishop Jackson [who followed Kaye at Lincoln] was the first to confirm in the Spring of the year. I think you may benefit greatly by the comparative rest which the present arrangement will secure to you, and which

The Golden Years

may the Lord abundantly bless to you, in answer to the prayers of your diocese, and of no member of it more earnestly than

Yours very sincerely,

W. F. John Kaye.

P.S.—I shall be afraid to write to you, if you deem it necessary, as I hope you will not, to acknowledge these very imperfect expressions of my feelings. Please, take me at my word.[57]

Even in what proved to be the last few weeks of his life, and on his death bed, King had finally stooped to conquer yet again one of his most formidable adversaries.

For the details of the last few days of February and the first week of March, we have the first-hand account of his devoted chaplain Canon Wilgress. As in so many Victorian (and later) biographies, the process of dying is never truncated in the narrative, in the way biographies of a later age tend to do. That is not incidental. King, as well as his friends and relatives, would have prayed for a holy death and peace at the last, upheld by the sacramental ministry of the Church, together with the cognitive and intimate support from loved ones continuously, by day and by night, as death approached.

And so, with King. As soon as Dr Clifford Allbutt had diagnosed his condition as terminal, Father Congreve of the Cowley Fathers came and stayed at the Old Palace, in order to hear King's Confession.

> In the evening King sent to the Dean with the petition that prayers might be asked in the Cathedral for him. He specially desired that the form used should be 'for our Bishop.' At the same time, he gave instructions that the prayers of the Diocese should be requested.
>
> He spent the Sunday quietly, but in the evening he told his Chaplain that he wished to talk over a few matters with him; he told him how he had arranged his will, and how he wished certain things to be disposed

of, including his vestments ... which he wished to be handed over to his successor.

Wilgress comments,

> This was a single example of the trustful spirit he showed all through his illness, for, although he had great apprehensions as to what might happen to the Diocese after his resignation, yet he determined to leave all in the hands of God, trusting that He would send to it a Bishop who would not make any great break in the teaching.

Just ten days before his death, King managed to write to Canon Porter, his great friend of sixty years who had been the first student to enter Cuddesdon. Canon Porter's brother, 'Willie,' who had also been a priest, had died in November the previous year. 'My dearest old friend,' wrote King in what proved to be the very last letter in his own hand:

> I hear you are like me, wondering and waiting if we are to be called ... May God support our faith. 'In THEE have I put my trust; deliver me in THY righteousness.' This is the only sure ground of peace. Thank you for so many years of affection. Willie will be waiting for us. I pray for you always, and, D.V., will continue to do so; and do you remember me. God bless you, and keep you to the end, which is really, D.V., the great beginning.[58]

Wilgress helpfully records how on 'Tuesday, March 1st, the Bishop's younger brother [William] came to see him, and talk over some business points which King wished to have settled.' Nearly ten years younger than his brother, William King, who lived on to 1920, does not appear to have figured prominently in King's life. There is no record of him in any of the biographies, nor is any correspondence between them known to have survived. But they must have kept in contact, and, as we have seen (p. 16), King took the funeral of William's young wife in 1880, and in 1902 he appointed William to be an executor of his will. It was doubtless that impending

The Golden Years

executorship as well, of course, as the very natural human desire to see his brother again before he died, which drew William to Lincoln from his home in Somerset, to talk over various matters. One thing King was most anxious to do was to see how his faithful housekeeper, Deborah Blunden, could be best provided for. Sussex-born and in her early sixties, she had been with him for nearly forty years.

KING'S WILL

King had made his will on 8 August 1902, naming his brother William and his nephew Walker Stuart King, 'retired Commander RN,' as executors and trustees. (Commander King's father was Edward's elder brother, Walker.) He subsequently added three codicils.

By the standards of the time, King was a relatively wealthy man, though probably no more or less so than a bishop of his lineage and position. Nineteenth-century bishops needed private resources to keep up their establishments—King himself had wondered if he could afford to live in the episcopal residence at Riseholme—and sometimes unfair accusations were levelled that their preferment might owe more to the depth of their pockets than to their suitability for the post.[59] In fact the value of King's estate at his death, £24,069, was substantially less than his father's, the Archdeacon, whose 'effects' in 1859 were valued at £45,000.

In drawing up his will, it is clear that his aim was to provide for his immediate family, which included many nephews and nieces, his many friends and for those who had served him faithfully over the years. William King was a prime beneficiary, an indication that although they lived very different lives, the bonds of family between the two brothers still held firm, and it was to William, in a codicil, that he left 'the gold inkstand which was given to me by my grandfather and which is now in the drawing room of the

Old Palace.' That grandfather must have been Dr Herberden, King's paternal grandfather, the Bishop, having died before he was born.

To each of his chaplains, including his nephew Wilgress, King bequeathed £1000, 'to be spent on books or applied in any manner which the legatees respectively may prefer.' And to the Grimsby Church Extension Fund, one of the projects most dear to King's heart, he bequeathed 'such a sum of money as with the amounts I shall have contributed in my life time, shall make up the sum of One Thousand pounds which I have promised to give to that fund.'

The few charitable bequests might seem a little strange in the will of a wealthy man whose compassion and concern for the poor and deprived runs like a *leitmotiv* throughout his life. In practice, of course, he was a regular and generous contributor to charity, as this following, rather touching, recollection, reminds us:

> Among the manuscript reminiscences collected by Canon Caulton from Lincolnshire is a letter ... which records, 'that on a day in April each year Mr. Tibbits, the butler, would present King with all the outstanding bills, and that after settling them, King would distribute the remainder of his income among charities and persons in need.'[60]

KING'S FINAL DAYS

On Wednesday morning, 2 March, King said goodbye to his secretary and to his domestic servants. It was a touching scene, as they left the bedside of their beloved master and friend, all sobbing. To his housekeeper, he said, 'Goodbye. God bless you. You have done well. My mother would be pleased to know you are with me.' In the evening he dictated his farewell letter to his Diocese, which undoubtedly deserves to be quoted in full.

The Golden Years

> My dear people, I fear I am not able to write the letter I should wish to write. I have for some time been praying God to tell me when I should give up my work. Now He has sent me, in his loving wisdom, a clear answer. It is a very great comfort to me to be relieved from the responsibility of leaving you. All I have to do is to ask you to forgive the many faults and immeasurable short-comings during the twenty-five years I have been with you, and to ask you to pray God to perfect my repentance and strengthen my faith to the end. All has been done in perfect love and wisdom.

And then the continuing antiphon throughout his whole ministry:

> My great wish has been to lead you to be Christ-like Christians. In Christ is the only hope of purity and peace. In Him we may be united to God and to one another.
>
> May God guide and bless you all, and refresh you with the increasing consciousness of His presence and His love. I am, to the end,
> Your friend and Bishop,
> E. Lincoln.[61]

The following morning, he asked for a celebration of the Holy Eucharist and received the Blessed Sacrament for the last time. The keynote of his mind throughout those days was the loving wisdom of God; this was the burden of the messages he sent to his friends from his death bed. Once again, Canon Wilgress takes up the narrative of the final days.

> From now onwards, he was more frequently unconscious; but he was just able to receive a visit from one of the cabmen who had driven him frequently to and from the station and elsewhere, and whom he was very anxious to get Confirmed. And to his comfort, the man promised that he would do as the Bishop wished.
>
> It is impossible to give an adequate description of his demeanour during the last days of his illness. He seemed to have been quite aware that it was fatal, and he seemed to anticipate very nearly the actual moment

when his end would come. Perhaps two things stand out more vividly than any others. His mind seemed lifted so entirely above the things of this world, it seemed already to be living in a higher sphere. 'It is all done by the perfect love and perfect wisdom of God.' 'Politics and controversy—what are they in themselves but things you may snap your fingers at? Only love in the fear and love of God, and conform your life to God's plan, and that must be a good one.' 'Trust that through it all God is ruling the world, and He will make his power to be known.' That was the tenor of his thoughts.

Yet it was extraordinary how constantly his mind was turned to little acts of kindness—e.g., he gave orders that a sum of money promised to a poor man suffering from cancer to buy milk for him, should be continued to be paid out of his estate, so long as the sufferer should live. He expressed a wish that the scarlet robe with an ermine hood, which he had worn in the House of Lords (when the Sovereign opened Parliament in person), should be given to one of his nieces, and proposed that she should make it into an opera cloak. He left orders that a Prayer Book should be given to the cabman who had come to see him on his death-bed, when he was confirmed; he gave instructions for a gold pencil-case to be bought for his doctor, and that upon it should be inscribed the words, 'With the gratitude and blessing of E. Lincoln,' and that a present should be made to his nurse.

Wilgress continues:

When the doctor came on the following Sunday, March 6th, he found a great diminution of strength, and in the course of the day there was a marked change in the breathing, and it was thought that the end might come before the next morning. However, the Bishop rallied a little. All Monday he lay seemingly unconscious, quite peaceful. Two or three of his relatives came and saw him, but it is doubtful whether he recognized them.

About 4 o'clock the next morning the nurse summoned those who were in the house to his bedside, and the Prayer of Commendation was said; after this he rallied

The Golden Years

again for a few hours, but about 8 o'clock this flicker of life began to die away, and at 9.45, just as the Cathedral Bells were summoning the worshippers to Matins, absolutely quietly and peacefully, his soul passed into the hands of his Fatherly Creator.

His body was robed in the white linen vestments in which he had so often celebrated the Holy Eucharist in his Chapel; a Bible lay on his breast, clasped by both hands; flowers were strewn beside him. Two candles were kept burning on a table at the foot of the bed; and between them stood a wooden Cross, which he had had in his study at Oxford.

Three days later, on 11 March 1910, King's body was laid to rest in the Cloister Garth at Lincoln, under the shadow of the Cathedral's great central tower. Holy Communion had been celebrated in the Choir at 7.30am.

It was singularly fitting that the Archbishop of Canterbury, Randall Davidson, chose to lead the funeral service in the afternoon before a vast congregation in the Cathedral. As we have seen, it was Davidson who had strongly supported King's nomination for Lincoln to the Queen, as well as to Benson and Gladstone. He was there at the beginning and now at the end of King's twenty-five years as the saintly Bishop of Lincoln.

'So,' concludes Russell in his biography, 'the earth closed over as true a saint as God ever fashioned for His own glory and the service of men.'[62]

Perhaps it is fitting that Scott Holland, King's beloved disciple, should have the last word, as from the cloister of King's great Cathedral:

> As we laid him to rest in that beautiful Garth, in a grave heaped high with flowers and carpeted with white lilies, the tears in the voice, as we sang our last hymn over his body, told of the deep passion of love which was following, with its longing prayers, into the quiet place, him who had shown us, as none other had ever done, what the tender Grace of the love of Jesus could mean.[63]

Edward King

Notes

1. John Witheridge, *Excellent Dr Stanley: The Life of Dean Stanley of Westminster*, Norwich: Michael Russell, 2013, p. 317.
2. Henry Scott Holland, *A Bundle of Memories*, pp. 50–1.
3. *Spiritual Letters of Edward King, D.D*, Letter LIX.
4. Scott Holland, *op. cit.*, p. 50.
5. F. E. Brightman, article on King in *A Dictionary of English Church History* (ed. S. L. Ollard and G. Crosse), 1912, p. 308.
6. George W. E. Russell, *Edward King Sixtieth Bishop of Lincoln*, pp. 252–4.
7. Bundock, *Old Leigh: A Pictorial History*.
8. Russell, *op. cit.*, p. 243.
9. *Ibid.*, pp. 244–5.
10. *Ibid.*, p. 250.
11. *Ibid.*, p. 251.
12. Scott Holland, *op. cit.*, p. 60.
13. Owen Chadwick, *Edward King: Bishop of Lincoln 1885–1910*, p. 23.
14. Bernard Lord Manning, *The Hymns of Wesley and Watts*. London: Epworth Press, 1942, p. 133.
15. John Newton, *Search for a Saint*, p. 109.
16. Bishop's House, Ely, Minutes of the Conferences of East Anglia Bishops, November 1904.
17. Russell, *op. cit.*, p. 279.
18. *Ibid.*, p. 280.
19. Chadwick, *op. cit.*, p. 24.
20. Owen Chadwick, *The Victorian Church*, part 2, p. 165.
21. *Ibid.*, p. 164.
22. King, *Sermons and Addresses*, pp. 132ff.
23. Russell, *op. cit.*, p. 272.
24. *The Lincolnshire Chronicle*, 22 October 1886, p. 6.
25. *The Sleaford Gazette*, 25 April 1891, p. 7.
26. Randolph and Townroe, *The Mind and Work of Bishop King*, p. 167.
27. Scott Holland, *op. cit.*, p. 60.
28. Randolph and Townroe, *op. cit.*, p. 168.
29. Chadwick, *The Victorian Church*, part 2, p. 342.
30. Russell, *op. cit.*, p. 286.
31. Randolph and Townroe, *op. cit.*, p. 169.
32. *Ibid.*, p. 170.
33. Russell, *op. cit.*, p. 260.
34. *Ibid.*
35. Russell, *op. cit.*, pp. 260–4.

The Golden Years

36 Hansard, *Parliamentary Debates*, 3rd series, HC, vol. CXCIX, col. 1938 (14 March 1870).
37 Parliamentary Papers, 1888, xxxv, 137, quoted in Owen Chadwick, *The Victorian Church*, part 2, p. 301.
38 King, *The Love and Wisdom of God*, p. 228.
39 Russell, *op. cit.*, p. 258.
40 *Ibid.*, p. 286.
41 *Ibid.*, pp. 285–6.
42 *Ibid.*, p. 281.
43 G. K. A. Bell, *Randall Davidson Archbishop of Canterbury*, p. 594.
44 *Ibid.*, pp. 596–7.
45 J. G. Lockhart, *Cosmo Gordon Lang*. London: Hodder and Stoughton, 1949, p. 236.
46 See Graham Neville's critical article, 'Bishop King: Right Heart, Wrong Head,' in *The Modern Churchman*, 28, 1986, pp. 15–19.
47 Russell, *op. cit.*, p. 290.
48 Chadwick, *op. cit.* (*Edward King*), p. 28.
49 *The Lincolnshire Chronicle*, 11 March 1910, p. 5: Russell, *op. cit.*, p. 298.
50 Chadwick, *op. cit.* (*Edward King*), p. 28.
51 Russell, *op. cit.*, pp. 290–5.
52 *Ibid.*, p. 296.
53 *Ibid.*, p. 297.
54 *Ibid.*, p. 298.
55 *Ibid.*, p. 299.
56 *Ibid.*
57 *Ibid.*, p. 301.
58 *Ibid.*, p. 303.
59 Nigel See Scotland, *Joseph Cotton Wigram, Bishop of Rochester*, 2021, p. 148.
60 Lord Elton, *Edward King and Our Times*, p. 115.
61 Russell, *op. cit.*, p. 304.
62 *Ibid.*, p. 307.
63 Scott Holland, *op. cit.*, p. 61.

✢ 16 ✢

Epilogue

'A POWER, NOT A FASHION'

Soon after King's interment, the Dean and Chapter began making plans for a memorial to him within the Cathedral similar to that of his immediate predecessor Bishop Wordsworth. Sir William Richmond (1842–1921), the artist and sculptor now best remembered for his mosaic decoration at St Paul's Cathedral, was commissioned to undertake the work. The memorial committee's choice of artist was singularly appropriate: in 1873 Sir William's father, George Richmond, had painted the portrait of King which now hangs at Cuddesdon, and in 1906 William designed the memorial in Hawarden church to the man who had nominated King for those two life-changing appointments—Professor of Pastoral Theology and Bishop of Lincoln—William Ewart Gladstone.

Initially the Dean and Chapter had in mind a traditional recumbent figure, like that of Wordsworth.[1] Fortunately, this early preference did not prevail, and far from portraying a recumbent King, Richmond's bronze statue shows him in action not in repose, a larger-than-life seated figure, his right hand raised 'as if about to be placed on the head of a kneeling candidate,'[2] as he would have done in Confirmation, that aspect of his episcopal ministry which delighted him the most. (An unsubstantiated oral tradition has it that the original intention was to portray King in the act of Confirming a young boy, but this gave rise to some unease and the design was changed, see p. 270.) The statue sits on a marble pedestal on which are inscribed the words 'Edward King, Bishop of Lincoln, 1885–1910,' and two texts from scripture: 'Beloved, let us love one another, for love is of God' (1 John 4:7), and 'Blessed are the meek, for they shall inherit the earth' (Matthew 5:5).

After a long delay, and further wrangling, the statue was erected in July 1915 and finally dedicated at a special service on 22 September, when the address was given by Canon Randolph, King's devoted disciple and friend, a last-minute replacement for the Archbishop, Randall Davidson, who had been taken ill. One passage in Randolph's address struck a particular chord with the *Lincolnshire Chronicle*:

> Bishop King believed in the power of gentleness to bring out the best in man. People in all walks of life — cabmen, railwaymen, servants, shop assistants, farm hands, ploughboys, laymen of all ranks — not to speak now of clergymen and ordination candidates — all these could testify to his gentleness and kindness.[3]

Memorials of a different sort, in the form of publications of his many sermons and addresses began appearing soon after King's death: *Spiritual Letters* and *The Love and Wisdom of God: Being A Collection of Sermons*, came out in 1910; *Sermons and Addresses* and *Duty and Conscience, Addresses Given in Parochial Retreats*, followed in 1911, and *Easter Sermons Preached in Lincoln Cathedral*, in 1914. They were all edited by Canon Randolph, whom King had appointed, along with the Revd Henry Thornhill Morgan, Vicar of St Peter's East Gate, Lincoln, as his literary executors, entrusting to them 'all the letters, manuscripts and private documents and papers of every description which shall be in my possession at the time of my decease to deal with and dispose of in such manner as they see fit.' Randolph was the joint author, with Canon Townroe of St Peter-at-Gowts, of much the best of the early biographies — *The Mind and Work of Bishop King*, published in 1918. G. W. E. Russell's more Victorian-style biography,

Epilogue

Edward King Sixtieth Bishop of Lincoln (1912), includes endless letters and extracts from diaries, but is less successful in giving a portrait of King or penetrating the inner man.

Fast forward now to Lincoln Cathedral on 24 May 1935, for a special service to mark the fiftieth anniversary of King's consecration as bishop in the Church of God. Archbishop Cosmo Gordon Lang, the last of the patrician and princely archbishops, celebrated a solemn Eucharist and addressed the huge congregation on 'Edward King, Bishop and Saint.' The Collect, Epistle and Gospel had been specially prepared for what is still observed as the 'Commemoration of Edward King,' and which have been used in the Lincoln Diocese and widely throughout the Church annually on 8 March to mark the anniversary of his death.

In his sermon, Lang spoke of an early personal encounter with King and the impact it had made on him at a turning point in his life when, as a young man, he was struggling to discern his vocation—should it be the Bar or ordination to the priesthood. The occasion of that decisive meeting was further reinforced early the following morning, when he was Confirmed by King in his private chapel at Lincoln. In a letter to his mother describing his Confirmation, the youthful Lang speaks of King as 'one of the most saintly and delightful of men,' and as having 'the Divine light in his eyes.'[4] Many years later, that same claim was further reiterated and articulated, but this time not from the pen of that young Fellow of All Souls College, Oxford, but now with the authority and from the lips of the Primate of all England in memorable words from the pulpit of King's own Cathedral: King, he proclaimed, 'was the most saintly of men, and the most human of saints.'

So, if we have to choose a particular point, it was on that day in 1935 that the English Church formally and with great joy recognized a modern saint by acclamation rather than by juridical scrutiny, as is the practice of the Roman Catholic Church, and placed him where he surely belongs in that updated trio of Lincoln episcopal saints—Hugh (*c.* 1140–1200), Robert Grosseteste (*c.* 1170–1253) and now King.

Until the formal process of canonization began to be more rigorously systematized and centralized under the authority of the papacy in the thirteenth century, the veneration of a saint would have arisen spontaneously within the local community: a cult of devotion, confirmed by popular acclamation, would spring up which, in the course of time, would be approved and regularized by the bishop of the diocese.

A special Commission appointed by the Archbishop of Canterbury to consider *The Commemoration of Saints and Heroes of the Faith in the Anglican Communion* took note of that event in Lincoln Cathedral in 1935 and claimed that it amounted to 'a direct "raising to the altar," as overt a case of "canonization" technically as may be.' Whether the Archbishop understood fully the implications of his bold claims from the pulpit that day is uncertain, and yet probable. The Bishop of Lincoln (Nugent Hicks), certainly did. He had prepared, and would subsequently issue, *Propers*[5] for the Commemoration of Bishop King for use in the diocese on 8 March each year 'at the will of incumbents.' At the same time, Hicks acknowledged, even at that early stage, that 'the commemoration of Bishop King now extends beyond the borders of the diocese.'[6]

Defining a saint is singularly difficult, not least in a celebrity-culture age like our own, which is often cynical and iconoclastic in its retrospective judgments of heroes; all too eager to tear down those whom an earlier age had revered and honoured. Yet, in honouring the saints, we are not claiming them to be specimens of flawless humanity or morally sanitized beyond reproach. 'A human being is holy not because he or she triumphs by will-power over chaos and guilt and leads a flawless life,' says Rowan Williams, 'but because that life shows the victory of God's faithfulness in the midst of disorder and imperfection.'[7] No one, however saintly, is totally free from the blind spots of their

Epilogue

contemporary cultural conditioning and the limitations of the age in which they have lived, and King was no exception.

In any consideration of saints, and not least that particular saint, Edward of Lincoln, we need to set aside the tired images and projections we have of what the world chooses to recognize as saintly, and recall the saints for what they are, neither more nor less, otherwise we will consign them to the archives of nostalgic sentimentality and total irrelevance, setting them in stone and thereby re-entombing them.

The voice of a true saint challenges as well as comforts: 'God is always calling us out of our well-established *status quo* and into the ever beyond.'[8]—to a stretch beyond our reach. The saint refuses to be classified as liberal, or conservative; the saint pushes back the boundaries of our limited expectations for humanity; the saint is a signpost pointing us beyond themselves to a goal and a fullness of life to which they themselves are still striving.

King never sought to draw people to himself, but rather, as the Collect for his day emphasizes, he drew them to Christ, the Light of the World, of which, like all saints, he was, even at best, only a dim reflection.

'Holiness, a message that convinces without the need for words, is the living reflection of the face of Christ.'[9] It was King's face, especially in his later years, which was so compellingly attractive. As Scott Holland so vividly recalls:

> Those eyes of his were an illumination ... Was there ever such a face, so gracious, so winning, so benignant, so tender? Its beauty was utterly natural and native. It made no effort to be striking, or marked, or peculiar, or special. It possessed just the typical beauty that should, of right, belong to the human countenance. It seemed to say, 'This is what a face is meant to be. This is the face that a man would have if he were, really, himself. This is the face that love would normally wear.'[10]

'We have buried our Saint,' wrote Bishop Winnington-Ingram after the funeral, 'and his beautiful face will never be seen by us on earth again, nor his winning playful smile; and to many of us who have loved him so much and so long this world will be much poorer.'[11]

Yet we must not bury him—nor indeed any of those whose lives have been lights in a dark world—either by casting him in stone or bronze as an effigy or statue, or even, as in more recent times, by honouring him in the architecturally striking new chapel at Cuddesdon which bears his name. Neither must we forget him or consign him to the dusty archives of church history. 'The world needs saints, just as a plague-stricken city needs doctors ... We are living in times that have no precedent ... Today, it is not nearly enough merely to be a saint, but we must have the saintliness demanded by the present moment, a new saintliness, itself also without precedent ... This new saintliness will require *genius*,' (that same word again, from Liddon's tribute to King from his earliest days), as being 'almost a new revelation of the universe and of human destiny.'[12]

So, the history of Christian holiness and the unfolding narrative of those who throughout the ages have come to be regarded as the Saints, will always have 'new, unique phases; hence it must always be discovered anew (even though always in the imitation of Christ who remains the inexhaustible model), and this by all Christians. Herein lies the special task which the Saints [however recognized, formally or less formally 'canonized'] have to fulfil ... They are the initiators and the creative models of the holiness which happens to be right for, and is the task of, their particular age. They create a new style; they prove that a certain form of life and activity is a really genuine possibility; they show experimentally that one can be a Christian even in *this* way; they make such a type of person believable as a Christian type.'[13] It is the claim of this biography that King did exactly that for his day, and in his way; and furthermore, that he did it as whatever 'type'—in terms of class, political persuasion or churchmanship—research 'typifies' him as having been.

Epilogue

The constant in all of this, for a vastly different Church and world to that of King, is the compelling, ongoing responsibility to recall and reclaim the very title deeds of the Church if, with any credibility, it is to be termed 'holy.' If the Church in any age is to be true to its calling as being *Lumen gentium*[14] (a 'Light for the Gentiles'—the 'outsiders' and the 'alienated'), it will need to tune in again to that same call to universal holiness which was the recurring theme in King's teaching and preaching, while also being supremely exemplified in his life—a theme which he reiterated with perhaps a more accessible vocabulary when he spoke and wrote repeatedly of the need for 'more Christ-like Christians.'

True holiness of life is authenticated not in some rarefied 'laboratory' of professionals, but rather in the workplace, the home, the family and communities, living out the 'trivial round, the common task.'[15] Neither is holiness of life the exclusive calling of some spiritual elite, or superhuman specimens of spirituality. We are all called to holiness, to personal conversion and transformation of life. For it is not the saints who are superhuman, so much as that the rest of us are less than human, constantly failing to realize, and falling short of our full, divinely human potential

So, in searching for such men and women—saints for today's Church and world—we are not looking for clones of King, to perpetuate the outward form of his nineteenth-century manners, mannerisms, words or attitudes to the issues of his day. Rather we need to transpose them into the 'key' which will ring true for a very different age, for it is the inner spirit and not the outward form of King, or indeed of all those we acclaim as saints, which is the same yesterday, today and forever. Often, we do not recognize such men and women in their day, but only retrospectively as we recall their message which they embodied, as this biography seeks to do, so that 'although dead,' yet by the power of the Spirit in which they lived, 'they are still speaking' (Hebrews 11:4) to encourage and comfort but also to challenge those who strive for that same measure of holiness in our own day.

'For ten years, [King] was the moving power of that Ritualistic centre whence his influence gradually made itself felt throughout the church ... He is a power, not a fashion' concludes the *Spy* cartoon at the time of his trial.[16] As we have seen with King, the powerful ripple-effect going out from one life lived with and in God, sacrificially and persistently for the sake of others, empowered with the Spirit of God's own unconditional love, seen once and for all in the face of Jesus the Christ of God—and such is the bold claim of this biography—resulted in far-reaching waves of transformed and redirected lives, which in turn transformed countless others for the work and challenge of the following generation: then, as always, and in that way, the many are influenced by the few as the few are influenced and transformed by the One. That is the road-map for renewal in every aspect of life, needed as much in today's Church, and always for the sake of the world, as it was in the days of Edward King, teacher, pastor, bishop and saint.

COLLECT FOR THE COMMEMORATION OF EDWARD KING ON 8 MARCH

God of peace, who gave such grace to your servant Edward King that whomever he met he drew to Christ: Fill us, we pray, with tender sympathy and joyful faith, that we also may win others to know the love that passes knowledge; through him who is the Shepherd and Guardian of our souls, Jesus Christ your Son our Lord, who is alive and reigns with you, in the unity of the Holy Spirit, one God, now and for ever. AMEN.[17]

Epilogue

Notes

1. Lincoln Cathedral Archives, Minutes of Dean and Chapter Meetings, 21 February 1911, pp. 191–3.
2. *The Lincolnshire Chronicle*, 17 July 1915, p. 3.
3. *Ibid.*, 25 September 1915, p. 6.
4. J. G. Lockhart, *Cosmo Gordon Lang*, p. 77.
5. *Propers*—the name for the series of Collect, Epistle and Gospel appointed for use on any specific Holy Day in the Church's Calendar.
6. *The Commemoration of Saints and Heroes of the Faith in the Anglican Communion*, p. 40.
7. Rowan Williams, *Open to Judgement: Sermons and Addresses*, London: Longman and Todd, 1994, p. 136.
8. Donna Orsuto, *Holiness*. Continuum, 2006, p. 4.
9. *Novo millennio ineunte*, John Paul II's Apostolic Letter to the Bishops, Clergy and Lay Faithful at the Close of the Great Jubilee Year, 2000. Vatican City: Case Editrice Vaticana, 2000, n. 7.
10. Henry Scott Holland, *A Bundle of Memories*, p. 48.
11. Quoted in *Pastoral Lectures of Bishop Edward King* (ed. Graham), p. xvi.
12. Simone Weil, *Waiting for God*, trans. Emma Craufurd. Harper Perennial Modern Classics, 2001, p. 51.
13. Karl Rahner, 'The Church of the Saints' in *Theological Investigations*, London: Darton, Longman & Todd, 1971, vol. III, pp. 99–100.
14. See Chapter 5 of *Dogmatic Constitution on the Church—Lumen Gentium*, promulgated by Pope Paul VI on 21 November 1964.
15. John Keble, 'Morning' (verse 14), first published in *The Christian Year*, 1827, pp. 13–15.
16. 'A Persecuted Bishop,' in *Vanity Fair*, 13 September 1890.
17. Collect appointed for King's Commemoration (8 March), EPISTLE, Hebrews 13:1–8, GOSPEL, Matthew 9:35–7.

Select Bibliography

WORKS OF EDWARD KING

Counsels to Nurses by Edward, Lord Bishop of Lincoln. Being his Addresses and Letters to the Guild of S. Barnabas for Nurses (ed. E. F. Russell). London: A. R. Mowbray & Co. Ltd, 1911.

Duty and Conscience, Addresses Given in Parochial Retreats at St Mary Magdalen's, Paddington (ed. B. W. Randolph). London: A. R. Mowbray 1911.

Easter Sermons Preached in Lincoln Cathedral (ed. B. W. Randolph). London: A. R. Mowbray, 1914.

The Love and Wisdom of God: Being A Collection of Sermons (ed. B. W. Randolph). London: Longmans, Green & Co., 1910.

Pastoral Lectures of Bishop Edward King (edited with an introduction by Eric Graham, MA, Principal of Cuddesdon Theological College). London and Oxford: A. R. Mowbray & Co. Ltd, 1932.

Meditations on the Last Seven Words of Our Lord Jesus Christ. London: A. R. Mowbray, 1910.

Sermons and Addresses (ed. B. W. Randolph). London: Longmans, Green & Co., 1911.

[Townroe, J. W.], *Some Maxims Gathered from the Writings of Edward King, Bishop of Lincoln.* Privately Published and dedicated to the Parish of St Peter-at-Gowts, Lincoln.

Spiritual Letters of Edward King, D.D. (ed. B. W. Randolph). London: A. R. Mowbray, 1910.

RESEARCH SOURCES

Lincolnshire Archives, St Rumbold Street, Lincoln, LN2 5AB for copies of the *Lincoln Diocesan Magazine* (1886–8; 1889–91; 1910–11): *A Notebook of King's Days at Oriel and Summaries of Sermons.* Also, *Visitation Records* and also a collection of letters from William Bright. In 1967, Geoffrey Larken deposited a valuable collection of King's papers, originally from H. R. Bramley and Canon Hubert Larken.

Edward King

Keble College, Oxford: Liddon Papers and Bright Papers.
Pusey House, Oxford: A selection of King's unpublished letters. Minute Book and records of The Brotherhood of the Holy Trinity. Heurtley Papers, a collection of letters and reflections of Miss Frances Heurtley. Liddon MSS., Liddon Diaries.
Bishop's House, Ely: Minutes of the Conferences of East Anglia Bishops, from 1889.
Church of St Mary, Stone, Kent: Personal Journal of Archdeacon King, known as 'The Dark Green Ledger.'

PUBLISHED STUDIES OF EDWARD KING

Chadwick, Owen, *Edward King, Bishop of Lincoln, 1885–1910*. Friends of Lincoln Cathedral, 1968. Lincoln Minster Pamphlets, Second Series, No. 4.
Cuddesdon College, *Cuddesdon College 1854–1929: A Record and Memorial*. Oxford University Press, 1930.
Elton, Lord, *Edward King and Our Times*. London: Geoffrey Bles Ltd, 1958.
Newton, John A., *Search for a Saint: Edward King*. London: Epworth Press, 1977.
Randolph, B. W., *Edward King Bishop of Lincoln*, Little Biographies No. 12. London: Wells, Gardner, Darton & Co., 1911.
Randolph, B. W., and J. W. Townroe, *The Mind and Work of Bishop King*. London: A. R. Mowbray, 1918.
Russell, George W. E., *Edward King, Sixtieth Bishop of Lincoln: A Memoir*. London: Smith, Elder & Co., 1912.
Wilgress, G. F., *Edward King, Bishop of Lincoln 1885–1910*. [Lincoln]: Bishop of Lincoln's Appeal Fund, [?1930].

OTHER WORKS CONSULTED

Ashwell, A. R., and R. G. Wilberforce, *The Life of the Right Reverend Samuel Wilberforce, D.D.*, 3 vols. London: John Murray, 1880–2.
Battiscombe, Georgina, *John Keble: A Study in Limitations*. London: Constable, 1963.
Beaken, Robert, *Cosmo Gordon Lang: Archbishop in War and Crisis*. London: I. B. Tauris & Co. Ltd, 2012.

Select Bibliography

Bell, G. K. A., *Randall Davidson Archbishop of Canterbury*. Oxford University Press, 1938.

Benson, Arthur Christopher, *The Life of Edward White Benson Sometime Archbishop of Canterbury*, 2 vols. London: Macmillan & Co. Ltd, 1899.

Bundock, John F., *Old Leigh: A Pictorial History*. Chichester: Phillimore & Co. Ltd, 1978.

Carpenter, Edward, *Cantuar: The Archbishops in Their Office*. London: Cassell, 1971.

Carpenter, James, *Gore. A Study in Liberal Catholic Thought*. London: The Faith Press, 1960.

Carpenter, S. C., *Church and People, 1789–1889*, 3 vols. London: SPCK, 1959.

—— *Winnington-Ingram: The Biography of Arthur Foley Winnington-Ingram, Bishop of London 1901–1939*. London: Hodder & Stoughton, 1949.

Chadwick, Owen, *The Founding of Cuddesdon*. Oxford University Press, 1954.

—— *The Victorian Church*, 2 parts. London: Adam & Charles Black, 1966, 1970.

—— *The Secularization of the European Mind in the Nineteenth Century*. Cambridge University Press, 1975.

—— *The Mind of the Oxford Movement*. London: Adam & Charles Black, 1960.

Chandler, Michael, *Queen Victoria's Archbishops of Canterbury*. Durham: Sacristy Press, 2019.

Church, R. W. (ed. Geoffrey Best), *The Oxford Movement: Twelve Years 1833–1845*. University of Chicago Press, 1970.

Clark, Revd Kenneth, *'The Lantern of Kent,' A Guide to the History of St Mary the Virgin, Stone*. London: Gavin Martin, Colournet Ltd, 2015.

Davidson, Randall Thomas, and William Benham, *Life of Archibald Campbell Tait: Archbishop of Canterbury*, 2 vols. London: Macmillan & Co., 1891.

Faber, Geoffrey, *Oxford Apostles: A Character Study of the Oxford Movement*. London: Faber & Faber, 1933.

Green, V. H. H., *Religion at Oxford and Cambridge*. London: SCM Press, 1964.

—— *The History of Oxford University*. London: B. T. Batsford Ltd, 1974.

Howe, Anthony, 'The Rule of SSC and the Brotherhood of the Holy Trinity,' in William Davage (ed.), *In This Sign Conquer*. London: Continuum UK, 2006.

Hutchinson, F. W., *Reminiscences of a Lincolnshire Parson*. Ely: W. Jefferson & Son, Ltd, 1950.

Johnson, Malcolm, *Bustling Intermeddler? The Life and Work of Charles James Blomfield*. Leominster: Gracewing, 2001.

Johnston, J. O., *The Life and Letters of Henry Parry Liddon*. London: Longmans, Green & Co., 1904.

Liddon, Henry Parry, *Life of Edward Bouverie Pusey*, 4 vols. London: Longmans, Green & Co., 1893–7.

Lockhart, J. G., *Cosmo Gordon Lang*. London: Hodder & Stoughton, 1949.

Lough, A. G., *The Influence of John Mason Neale*. London: SPCK, 1962.

Marsh, P. T., *The Victorian Church in Decline: Archbishop Tait and the Church of England, 1868–1882*. London: Routledge & Kegan Paul, 1969.

Matthew, H. C. G., *Gladstone 1809–1898*, Oxford University Press, 1997.

May, Trevor, *The Victorian Clergyman*. Shire Publications Ltd, 2006.

Newsome, David, *Godliness and Good Learning: Four Studies on a Victorian Ideal*. London: John Murray, 1961.

Ollard, S. L., *A Short History of the Oxford Movement*. London: A. R. Mowbray, 1915.

Overton, J. H., and Elizabeth Wordsworth, *Christopher Wordsworth, Bishop of Lincoln*. London: Rivingtons, 1888.

Prestige, G. L., *The Life of Charles Gore: A Great Englishman*. London: William Heinemann Ltd, 1935.

Rack, Henry D., *Reasonable Enthusiast: John Wesley and the Rise of Methodism*. London: Epworth Press, 1989.

Ramsey, Arthur Michael, *From Gore to Temple: the Development of Anglican Theology between Lux Mundi and the Second World War, 1889–1939* (Hale Lectures 1959). London: Longmans, Green, 1960.

Rowell, Geoffrey, *The Vision Glorious: Themes and Personalities of the Catholic Revival in Anglicanism*, Oxford University Press, 1983.

Rowell, Geoffrey (ed.), *Tradition Renewed: The Oxford Movement Conference Papers*. London: Darton, Longman & Todd, 1986.

Scott Holland, Henry, *A Bundle of Memories*. London: Wells Gardner, Darton & Co. Ltd, 1915.

Select Bibliography

Simpson, Jennifer and Ed (eds), *Letters from Leigh.* The Leigh Society, 2017.

Smith, B. A., *Dean Church: The Anglican Response to Newman.* Oxford University Press, 1958.

Strong, Rowan (ed.), *The Oxford History of Anglicanism: Partisan Anglicanism and its Global Expansion, 1829–c. 1914*, vol. III. Oxford University Press, 2017.

Symondson, Anthony (ed.), *The Victorian Crisis of Faith: Six Lectures.* London: SPCK, 1970.

Weintraub, Stanley, *Disraeli: A Biography.* London: Hamish Hamilton Ltd, 1993.

Wilson, A. N., *God's Funeral.* London: John Murray, 1999.

—— *The Victorians.* London: Hutchinson, 2002.

—— *Charles Darwin: Victorian Mythmaker.* London: John Murray, 2017.

Witheridge, John, *Excellent Dr Stanley: The Life of Dean Stanley of Westminster.* Norwich: Michael Russell Publishing Ltd, 2013.

Woodward, E. Llewellyn, *The Age of Reform, 1815–1870* (Oxford History of England, 13). Oxford University Press, 1962.

INDEX

Abbott, Eric 102, 147
Abraham, Charles, Bp of Wellington 31
Acland, Sir Henry 310
Adcock, Revd H. H. 440
Adderley, Fr J. G. 291
Addison, William 359
Aelred of Rievaulx 276, 277, 278
Albert, Prince Consort 37, 107
Alexander, Mrs Cecil Frances 429
Allbutt, Dr Clifford 521
Andrewes, Bp Lancelot 5 2, 109, 145, 177, 244, 315, 376
Andrews: Elizabeth Catherine (*née* King) 16; Revd Charles Gerrard 16
Anglican Communion, The 149, 293, 453–6 *passim*, 470–5 *passim*, 539
Anglo-Catholicism and Anglo-Catholics 45, 52, 60, 62, 82, 102, 135, 136, 334, 382, 393, 473, 489, 496
Anselm of Canterbury, St 170, 274, 276, 307, 446
Anson, Adelbert, Bp of Qu'Appelle 486
Apologia pro Vita Sua (Newman) 44–5, 48
Arch, Joseph 366
Aristotle (works of) 70, 71, 144, 177, 181, 360
Arnold, Matthew 45, 477, 505–6; on secularisation of Oxford 114
Arnold, Thomas 18, 20, 26, 33, 43–6, 47, 48, 203, 460, 505, 506; favours reuniting sects with the Church of England 44
Arthur, William 367
Asperne, James 5
Assize Sermon (Oxford, 1833) *see under* Keble

Atlay, James, Bp of Hereford 401, 408
Augustine of Canterbury, St 453, 455
Augustine of Hippo, St 144, 177, 238–40, 243, 273–5, 281, 356, 360, 421, 476

Bangor, Bp of [C. Bethell] 110
Barff, Albert 119, 123
Barth, Karl 235
Baxter, Richard 176, 178
Bell, Edward (farm hand) 442
Benson, Arthur Christopher (son of E. W.) 400
Benson, Edward White, Archbp (C) 169, 300, 301–2, 315, 317, 389–90, 418, 419, 433, 435, 473, 474; at EK's consecration 313, 315; visits to Lincoln (1887) 330, 391, (1890) 399; tries EK for alleged unlawful ritualistic practices (the 'Lincoln Judgement') 392–412; plans 4th Lambeth Conference 452, 453, 454, 472; death 452; successor 452–3; on the reunion of Christian churches 475
Benson, Revd J. P. 389
Benson, Maggie [Margaret] 404–5
Benson, [Mary Eleanor] 418
Benson, Mrs [Mary] 418, 452
Benson, Richard Meux 60, 64, 146, 359
Bereford Hope, Alexander 384
Bernard of Clairvaux, St 73, 177, 272, 276, 456, 514
'Bethel' *see under* Oxford, Christ Church
Betjeman, John 61
Bickersteth, Edward, Bp of Exeter 302, 304, 314, 315

547

Bickersteth, Robert, Bp of Ripon 300, 302
Birkenhead, St Aidan's Theological College 101
Birmingham: Queen's Theological College 101; *for* Bp of (1909) *see* Gore
Birrell, Augustine 502
Blakesley, Joseph Williams, Dean of Lincoln 311, 336–7, 338
Blomfield, C. J., Bp of London 110, 201
Blunden, Deborah (housekeeper) 523
Bodley, George Frederick (architect) 200, 330
Boer War 480
Bombay, Bp of (Mylne) 149
Bonn, Old Catholic Conferences at 210, 213
Book of Common Prayer 23, 30, 34 (presented to EK), 48, 52, 62, 66, 119, 177, 239, 288, 342, 358, 380, 388, 409
Bradley, A. C. 187
Bradley, George Granville, Dean 432
Bright, Canon (Professor) William 143, 167, 197, 202, 330, 336, 346, 397, 485, 495
Brightman, F. E. 87, 170, 286, 293
Brighton, St James's 380
British Empire 4, 207, 470, 474, 480
British Rheumatology Society 8
Brooks, Phillips 242
Brotherhood of the Holy Trinity (Oxford) 59–70
Brotherhood of St Mary (Oxford) 60–1
Browne, Harold, Bp of Winchester 307, 327, 395, 401
Brownlow, Countess (wife of 3rd Earl) 30
Brownlow, 3rd Earl 30, 479
Bryce, James 433
'Burford, Bp of' (Samuel Wilberforce) 105

Burgess, Thomas, Bp of St David's 100
Burgh le Marsh, Lincs (Missionary College) 486
Burgon, John William, Vicar of St Mary's, Oxford/Dean of Chichester 51, 52, 77, 82–3, 129, 130, 132–3, 138, 166; on EK 56, 68, 82–3, 132
Burke, Edmund 10–12, 172
Burn, [Revd] Andrew 54
Burnand, Francis C. 105, 120, 124
Burne-Jones, Edward 61
Butler, Bp Joseph 71, 144, 172, 174, 299, 465, 473, 513
Butler, William John, Dean of Lincoln 60, 252, 308, 338–43, 367–8
Buxton, Derbyshire 361

Cairns, Lord (1st Earl) 384
Calcutta 149
Cambridge: Holy Trinity Church 233; Magdalene College 134; Trinity College 116, 305; University 41, 100, 305 (Public Orator)
Cambridge Camden Society 379
Canterbury, Archbps of *see* Benson; Davidson; Fisher; Howley; Longley; Ramsey; Tait; Temple; Tenison; Tillotson
Canterbury Cathedral 452, 453, 455
Caroline Divines 40, 52, 150, 376
'Cathedral of Meres' *see under* Ellesmere
Catholic Emancipation (1829) 4, 11, 23, 44
Catholics *see* Roman Catholics
Cattle Plague 349
Caulton, Canon John 524
Charlie (from Wheatley) 88–90, 92, 147, 288, 355, 436, 438
Charlotte, Queen 8
Charlton, Oxon 338
Chartists and Chartism 4, 37

Index

Chase, D. P. 70
Chester, Bps of 100 (Law), 307 (Stubbs)
Chesterton, G. K. 519
Chichester: Bp of (Ashurst T. Gilbert) 110, 111; Dean of *see* Burgon; Theological College 57, 101, 108, 111, 115, 133
cholera 55, 93–4, 425
Chretien, C. P. 70
Christian, Ewan (architect) 329
Christian Socialist Movement 168
Christian Year (Keble, 1827) 86, 150, 160(n.36)
Church, Richard W., Dean of St Paul's 38, 51, 52, 55, 202, 261, 302, 307, 308, 377–8, 457; on Marriott 58, 59; on Newman 246; on Oxford life 46–7
Church Association ('Church Ass') 313, 315, 335, 343, 364, 388–90, 398, 401, 405, 411, 413
Church Lawford, Warwicks 54
Church Lecture Society 364
Church schools 104, 501, 511; *see also* Voluntary schools
Churchmanship, problems of 301–5
Churton, T. T. 125(n.31)
Clapham Sect 50
Clee-cum-Cleethorpes, Lincs 389
Clements, Jacob, Sub-Dean of Lincoln 317, 375, 396, 411, 417, Fig. 2
Clements, Joseph (commercial traveller) 406
Clergy Discipline Act 420
clergy training xix, 99–103 *passim*, 109, 115, 116, 140, 146, 154, 155, 219, 233, 292, 293, 341, 357, 422, 492–3; *see also* priestly formation *and* Theological Training Colleges
Clough, Arthur Hugh 39
Colenso, John William, Bp of Natal 474–5
Coleridge, H. J. 39

Coleridge, S. T. (poet) 151
Collect for the Commemoration of EK 538
Commissioned Readers *see* Lay Readers
Community of St Mary the Virgin (CSMV), Wantage 341
Compton, W. Berdmore 415(n.6)
Confession (Sacrament of) and use of the Confessional 62, 68, 120, 133, 136, 165, 195, 196, 248, 312, 379, 384, 482; EK's teaching on 263, 264–6, 359, 482
Confirmation (Sacrament of) *see under* King (Edward) *and* Wilberforce (Samuel)
Congreve, Fr George 521
Convocation 47, 107, 195, 290, 382, 384, 385, 393, 397, 490; on training for Holy Orders 155; Convocation dress 333, 396, 408, 479; Proctors of 321
Cook, A. M., Sub-Dean of Lincoln 241
Co-operative Association 399
Copeland, W. J. 377
Copleston, Edward, Provost of Oriel 42–3
Corfe, Charles, Bp of Korea 486, 520
Council schools 501, 502
Cowley Fathers (Society of St John the Evangelist) 60, 146, 359, 521
Cuddesdon, Oxfordshire: parish and church 88, 139, 146; episcopal palace 101, 106, 107, 108, 114; vicarage 142, 146, 198, 234
Cuddesdon Theological College 99, 101, 103, 105, 106, 107–124, 129–59, 162, 164, 191, 229, 234, 275, 280, 316, 422, 522 foundation stone ceremony 108–9; opening ceremony 109–11, Fig. 7; early criticism

549

of 116–17, 118, 119–21, 137–8; extra accommodation needed 157–8; new (20th-century) chapel 536
Chaplains: *see* Barff; King (Edward); Swallow
Principals and Vice-Principals: *see* Graham; Johnston; King (Edward); Liddon; Pott; Swinny; Willis
Culham, Teacher Training College 67, 88, 109, 142
Curry Rivill, Somerset 16

Dale, Pelham 388
Danbury, Essex, episcopal palace 332
Danckwerts, William 401
Daniel, Walter 278
Dante (Alighieri) 15, 71, 144, 145, 172, 181, 208, 228, 273, 473
'Dark Green Ledger' (Archdeacon King's journal) 21–2, 36(n.22),
Darwin, Charles 104, 169, 183
Datchet, Berks 9
Davey, Sir Horace 401
Davey, Revd W. H. 133, 134, 135
Davidson, Randall: as Dean of Windsor 303–4, 315, 394, 396, 407, 430; as Bp of Rochester 431–5, 452–3; as Archbp of Canterbury 483, 509–11, 527, 532
Davies, Llewelyn 365
Davison, John (of Oriel) 43
Dawson, James 334
Day, David Hermitage (banker) 24
Day, Revd John David, Vicar of Ellesmere 24–8, 32–3, 34, 35, 49, 54, 59, 66, 74, 82, 116, 437, Fig. 1
Deane, James Parker, Vicar-General 313, 397, 398, 408
Dearmer, Percy 378
Delitzsch, Professor Franz 218
Denison, Edward, Bp of Salisbury 498

Disestablishment 377, 413, 462, 472
Disraeli, Benjamin 4, 105, 194, 207, 249, 306, 384, 386, 430
Dissenters 11, 12, 99, 194, 234, 368; *see also* Methodists; Nonconformists; Wesleyans
Dixon, R. W. 114
Döllinger, Johann J. I. von 209–10
Doncaster, Vicar of (Vaughan) 116
Donne, John 244, 274
Dover, Revd T. B. 316
Dresden (EK spends Long Vac there) 211–12
Drew, Mary 307
Dru, Alexander 215, 216
Dupanloup, Félix, Bp of Orléans 209, 238
Durham: Bp of *see* Lightfoot; Theological College 108; University 44

Ebb, Kent 455
Ecclesiastical Commissioners 328, 351
Ecclesiastical Courts Commission 395
ecumenism 214, 215, 216, 228–9, 367, 369, 475–6,
education 26, 30–1, 33–4, 116, 219, 220–2, 505; *see also under* King, Edward
Education Bill (1906) 502–4, 511
Egerton, William Henry, Vicar of Ellesmere 25
Elgin, Lord (Geoffrey, 1st Baron) 22
Eliot, George 4, 103
Ellesmere, Shropshire: College (formerly St Oswald's) 28–34; St John's Hill 25; St Mary's Church ('Cathedral of the Meres') and parish 25–6, 27; Vicar of *see* Day, John *and* Peake, John
Ellis, Havelock 271
Elton, Edward, Vicar of Wheatley 83–7, 93–4, 96, 403–4

Index

Elton, Lord (1st Baron) 84–6, 267–9, 273
Ely, Bp of 420 (Compton); *see also* Woodford
Ely Theological College 43, 283, 293, 402
English Church Union 330, 335, 402, 411, 483, 488, 489
English Hymnal (1906) 495–6
English School of Spirituality 274–6, 282, 288
Enlightenment, The 183, 214, 216, 217, 228–9, 243
Enraght, Richard 388
Erastianism 44, 381
Essays and Reviews (1860) 43, 51, 185, 454
Evangelicalism and Evangelicals 44, 50, 77, 82, 102–3, 104, 120, 122, 136, 224, 302, 313, 332, 364, 369, 385, 388, 389, 403, 411, 479, 481, 487, 489
Exeter, Bp of: Bickersteth 302, 304, 314, 315; Temple 300, 356
Exeter, Diocese of 300, 302, 303, 314

Faber, Geoffrey 267
Farrar, Archdeacon Frederick 337
Farrar, Walter, Bp of Antigua 519
Farrer, Thomas Henry 169
Fénelon, François 144, 215, 218, 225
First World War 512, 513
Fisher, Geoffrey, Archbp (C) 333
flagellation *see* self-flagellation
Forster, W. E. 505
Forster Education Act (1870) 505
Francis de Sales, St 150, 215, 218, 307
Freeman, (Professor) Edward Augustus 60
French Revolution 3, 4, 6, 10, 17
Frewer, Canon George E. 175
Froude, Richard Hurrell 38, 43, 65, 267

Garbett, Cyril, Archbp (Y) 508
Garfit, Thomas Cheney 478
Geiselmann, J. R. 215, 216
George III, King 8
Germany: religion and culture 212, 217, 214, 219, 512; EK's visits to 207, 209–12, 218, 227
Gibbon, Edward 40–1
Gladstone, Stephen 162
Gladstone, William Ewart:
  episcopal and ecclesiastical appointments 299–300, 304, 337–9, 343; 'excess of consciousness' 304; chooses EK for See of Lincoln 299–307
  professorial appointments 161–2, 308; chooses EK for Chair of Pastoral Theology 155, 161–4; defends choice 166
  favourable opinion of EK 166, 301, 302; EK's correspondence with 162, 163, 304, 329, 339; opposes Public Worship Regulation Bill 194; pall-bearer at Pusey's funeral 197; relatives of 162, 210–11, 307, 338; monument in Hawarden church 531; other references 172, 190, 193, 200, 283, 328, 329, 346, 356, 380, 384–5, 452, 511
'Glyde, Mr D'Oyley' (H. P. Liddon) 120
Golightly, Charles Portales 120–2
Gore, Charles 185, 186, 189, 190, 257, 309, 336, 397, 430, 432, 435, 474, 485, Fig. 2; as Bp of Birmingham 510
Graham, Eric 175
Grantham, Suffragan See of 344, 485
Grantham Clerical Reading Society 252
Granville, Lord (2nd Earl) 168
Great Hale, Lincs (Confirmation at) 519
Green, Sidney 388

Green, Thomas Hill 186–90, 220
Griffiths, J. 125(n.31)
Grimsby 496–8; All Saints', Weelsby 497; population 498; Spiritual Aid Society 496; St Luke's 501; Suffragan See of 344
Grimsby Church Extension Fund 496–501, 524
Grosseteste, St Robert 329, 534
Guild of St Barnabas for Nurses 87, 225, 341

'H' (unidentified) 284
Halifax, 2nd Viscount 330, 396, 439, 475, 483, 488
Halle, Saxony, University of 218
Hamilton, W. K., Bp of Salisbury 299
Hanchard, J. 335
Harrow School 305
Harvey ('dear old') 338
Hastings, Warren 11
Hawarden, Cheshire: Castle 452; parish church 452, 531
Hawkins, Edward, Provost of Oriel 43, 65
Heberden, Anne *see under* King
Heberden, [George] (Anne's brother) 9
Heberden, Sir William, the elder 7, 8
Heberden, Sir William, the younger 7, 8
Heberden Society 8
Hegel, G. W. F. (and Hegelianism) 184, 186, 188
Henley Regatta (1847) 425
Herbert, George 150, 245, 274, 376
Hereford: Bp of (James Atlay) 401, 408; Diocese of 492 (lay readers)
Heurtley, Professor Charles Abel 92 (his butler), 197, 305, 325, 354
Hicks, Nugent, Bp of Lincoln 534
Hicks, Walter (Canon-Missioner) 484

Hindu religion 11
Holland, Canon Henry Scott 167–8, 185, 307, 432; influence on of T. H. Green 187, 189–90; friendship with EK and comments on his character 92, 186, 189, 278, 376, 418–19; describes EK's burial 527
Holy Club (of the Wesleys) 60, 64, 65
Holy Land (EK's visit) 74, 75, 76, 81 (Dead Sea)
Honington, Lincs (Confirmation at) 345
Hooker, Richard 105, 109, 144, 147, 176, 177, 180, 235, 292, 458
Hope, James (friend of Gladstone) 283
Hopkins, Gerard Manley 276, 290
Hort, F. J. A. 51, 52
Hough-on-the-Hill, Lincs (Confirmation at) 345
Hours of Prayer for Daily Use throughout the Year (College Office Book, 1856) 119, 120
House of Lords *see under* Parliament
Housman, A. E. 249–50
Howley, William, Archbp (C) 23
Hügel, Baron Friedrich von 57, 275
Hugh of Lincoln, St 314, 329, 330, 534
Hume, David 181, 187, 188
Hunt, R. W. Carew 94
Hutton, W. H. 172, 293
Huvelin, Abbé 181
Huxley, T. H. 104

Insole, Richard ('young fisherman') xx, 440, 442
Irish Church Temporalities Act (1833) 47–8

Jackson, John, Bp of Lincoln/London 300, 306, 327, 520
Jelf, William Edward 165

Index

Jeune, Francis, Q.C. 397, 401
Jews 44, 56, 194, 465
John of the Cross, St 150, 218
Johnston, J. O. 310
Jones, William Basil (Bp of St David's) 63
Jones, William West, Bp of Cape Town 199
Jowett, Benjamin 477
Julian of Norwich 274
Justin Martyr 101

Kaye, John, Archdeacon (son of Bp Kaye) 312, 327, 414, 490–1, 520–1
Kaye, John, Bp of Lincoln 306, 327, 328, 333, 349
Keble, John 38, 48, 52, 104, 119, 150, 177, 281, 292, 307, 376; *Christian Year* (1827) 86, 150, 160(n.36); Assize Sermon (1833) 24, 48–9, 377, 413; on dissenters 368; on secularisation of Oxford 114; works quoted 150, 495–6, 513–14, 537; funeral 377–8
Kempe, Alfred Bray 401
Kempe, Margery (of Lynn) 274
Ken, Bishop 376
King, Anne (sister) 15, 19, 152, 208
King (*née* Heberden), Anne (mother) 7–9, 16, 20, 22, 142, 157, 159, 197–200, 230(n.4), 269–70, 305, 524
King, Charles James (brother) 16
King, Edward, Bp of Lincoln:
  LIFE
  ancestry and family 7–16;
  birth and baptism 7–8;
  confirmation 21, 22–3
  education: at home 18, 20–1, 23; with John Day (at Ellesmere) 24, 25, 26, 27, 32, 116; at Oxford (Oriel College) 37–73 *passim*
  ordination 82–3
  appearance: 34–5, 66, 198, 249, 256, 269, 325–6, 335, 366, 418, 471, 478, Figs 1–4; well-developed chin 286, 326, 376; shabby dresser 356–7; portraits 159, 285–6, 478–9, 531; statue 270, 531–2
  character and personality: 14, 57, 68, 131, 164, 170, 201–2, 283, 286, 426, 446, 477–8; at ease in any level of society 348, 439; a gentleman 83, 348, 439; gentleness 13, 282, 285–6, 326, 439, 532; holiness 170, 279, 313, 315, 370; lightness of touch 139, 291, 427, 496; magnetic 242, 457; piety 59, 66, 82; refined and retiring 66; saintliness 267, 286, 307, 403, 404, 413–14, 527, 533; self-discipline and restraint 281–3; sympathetic and sensitive 162 ('a form of genius'), 263, 284, 308, 390, 423, 430,
  health 14, 20, 54, 70, 83, 113, 208, 304, 418, 425, 507, 509, 516, 518–19, 520, 521; deafness 507, 509; overwork 192–3; final illness 525–7
  celibacy and sexuality 267–9, 271, 282
  close to his mother 142, 157, 167, 197–200, 198, 269–70, 305, 524
  relations with his siblings 15, 16, 87, 328, 424–5, 522
  friendships and intimacy 87, 92, 266–72, 277, 281–2, 288, 363, 486; 'genius for friendship' 57
  handwriting 485
  retirement 507–8
  death and burial 527; memorial to 531–2
  will and bequests 92, 521, 522, 523–4, 526; literary executors 532; value of estate 523
  canonization (*de facto*) 3, 533–7

Edward King

APPOINTMENTS
 private tutor 81
 curate at Wheatley 83–9, 118
 chaplain at Cuddesdon 111–13
 Principal of Cuddesdon 139–40; legacy 154–9
 Professor of Pastoral Theology, Oxford 162–7
 Bishop of Lincoln 299–310; election 311–13; consecration 313–17; enthronement 317–22

MISCELLANEOUS
 academic limitations (perceived) 70, 71, 143, 165, 169–73, 250, 261, 458; intimidated by the intellectual challenges of Oxford 316–17
 administration 107, 142–3, 346–7, 462, 484–5, 517
 authority of the Church of England 49
 Biblical criticism and scholarship 52, 173, 186, 196, 240, 361–2, 463–4; favourite Psalm 13, 149
 'Bishopric of Love' 308
 chaplains 185, 328, 336, 346, 440, 441, 474, 485, 486, 524
 Charges and Visitations 349, 361–2, 363, 364, 368, 423, 427–9, 490, 512
 concern for and love of the poor 87, 92, 213, 214, 307, 317, 345, 352, 353–6, 361, 429, 436, 524; 'a Bishop of [God's] Poor' 354
 concern for the welfare of the clergy 329, 352–3, 356, 357, 359, 365, 418–21, 423–4
 Confession 165, 196, 248, 263, 264–6, 359, 482, 521
 Confirmations 253–4, 255, 345, 361, 418, 443, 447, 509, 519, 520
 Convocation, attendance at 290, 327, 419, 490, 498, 501, 509, 520

correspondence with Gladstone 162, 163, 304, 329, 339
education (generally) 26, 33–4, 72, 88, 252, 290, 506; religious education in schools 29, 501–5
ecumenism 228–9, 367, 369, 475–6, 479
ethics 180–90, 360, 460, 468, 488, 506; ethical outlook 181
foreign languages 15, 171, 208–12 *passim*, 230(n.4), 302, 447
High Churchman 165–7, 246, 301, 302, 303. 332–6, 349. 367, 376, 390, 485
holidays and foreign travels 73–6, 81, 82, 87, 155, 207–13, 218, 343, 446–8, 481–2
House of Lords, attendance at 327, 419, 501, 508–9, 512, 526
ideals for the priestly life 357
influence 170, 193, 201, 261–2, 286–94
intellectual resources 164, 165, 173–80, 261
interests: botany and natural history 15, 19, 86, 88, 90, 152, 347, 447; poetry 145, 188; Lambeth Addresses (1897) 53, 56, 185, 186, 451–76, 512, 516
Leeds speech (1872) 165
letter writing 346–7, 522
London Club (Athenaeum) 327
marriage 269; divorce and re-marriage 488–90
materialism 53, 186, 212, 357, 436, 445, 460, 465
mentors *see* Day (John); Burgon; Church (Richard); Marriott (Charles); Wilberforce (Samuel)
morality and religion 11, 188, 212, 466, 247, 506
Nonconformity: an admirer of Wesley 364; sympathy with Methodists and dissenters

554

Index

xix, 12, 49–50, 364–70, 481, 487, 503
nurses 87, 225–7
Oddfellows 437–8
Old Palace at Lincoln built for 327–31
pastoral theology xix, 174–9, 214, 233, 243–5, 357, 420
Pastoral (Pastoralia) Lectures 171, 175–9, 220–5, 281, 283–5
'People's Budget' (1909) 508–12
popularity 303, 313, 499; 'adored' in Lincoln 400
prayer 59, 62, 96, 144, 146, 177–8, 403, 494, 514, 516
preaching: teaching on 233–6, 237–8, 494; sermon construction 236–40; style and power of EK's preaching 143, 240–5, 249, 255–8, 261–2; University sermons 245–9; 'Bethel' addresses 179, 250; Occasional sermons 251–3; Confirmation sermons 253–5; other sermons 275, 290, 309, 320–1, 358, 404, 422, 443; *see also* Lambeth Addresses
prison ministry xx, 224, 440–2
Quiet Days 558, 362, 455, 514; at 1897 Lambeth Conference 448, 451, 454, 455, 456
railways 345, 443–4; empathy with railway workers 251, 252, 442–5, 532
reading: advice to students on 70, 71–2, 145, 181, 188, 239, 252; EK's own 70, 71, 72–3, 89, 143–7, 178, 181, 354; poetry 145, 188; favourite poets *see* Dante *and* Wordsworth (William)
repentance 265, 420–1
retreats 250, 264, 358–60, 362, 363, 455, 512, 514, 532
ritualism 51, 95, 193, 266, 334, 342–3, 375–7, 396, 401, 403–4, 412, 465, 482, 484, 538; tried for irregular ritual practice *see* Lincoln Judgment
Roman Catholics and Catholicism 12, 33–4, 77, 208, 229, 265–6, 335, 343, 447–8, 496
servants 198, 332, 516, 524; for named individuals *see* Blunden; Norton; Tibbetts; White
science and faith 362, 459, 474
sexual violence 281
teaching style 147, 175, 176, 183, 192, 202, 243, 289–90, 366
Tractarianism 52–4, 77, 195, 202, 299, 308, 321, 376, 496
vestments 318, 332, 335, 376, 522; mitre 332–3, 334, 335, 366, Fig. 2
visits to the sick 55, 94, 146, 147–8, 345, 425; advice on 223, 226
King, Elizabeth Catherine (Mrs Andrews, sister) 16
King, Captain Henry (brother) 14, 87
King, Isabella (sister-in-law) 16
King, James (grandson of Robert) 10
King, James, Dean of Raphoe 10
King, Mary (Mrs Wilgress, sister) 16, 328
King, Robert (of Kirby Malhamdale) 10
King, Robert (son of Thomas) 10
King, Robert ('Bob') Stuart (nephew) 425, 426, 482
King, Sarah Frances ('Fanny', sister, Mrs Nicholl) 16, 211
King, Thomas (of Kirby Malhamdale) 10
King, Thomas (great grandson of Thomas) 10
King, Walker, Archdeacon and Rector of Stone (father) 10, 13, 17–18, 20, 21–2, 198, 230(n.4), 523

King, Walker, Bp of Rochester (grandfather) 10, 11, 12, 13, 16, 21,
King, Walker Stuart, Commander RN (nephew) 523
King, Walker, Vicar of Leigh-on-Sea (brother) 13–14, 16, 20, 198, 269, 424–7, 429
King, William (brother) 16, 522–3
King family 9–10, 11,
Kirby Malhamdale, Yorks 10
Kirk, Professor Kenneth 178
Kranz, Gisbert 217
Kynnersley, Shropshire 54

Lacordaire, Henri 144, 209
Lambeth Addresses of 1897 *see under* King, Edward
Lambeth Conferences of Bishops: First (1867) 149, 474; Third (1888) 400, 453; Fourth (1897) 56, 240, 448, 451–76
Lambeth Palace *see under* London
Lampeter, St David's Theological College 100
Lancing College 33–4
Lang, Cosmo Gordon, Archbp 510 (Y), 533 (C)
Lang, Dr Marshall 432
Lansdowne, Lord (5th Marquess) 511
'lantern of Kent' *see under* Stone
Law, George Henry, Bp of Chester 100
Lay Readers/Commissioned Readers 424, 491–4
Lee, F. G. 120
Leeds: Church Congress at (1872) 165; EK's speech at 165; St John's 417; St Saviour's 133
Leigh-on-Sea, Essex: 425; St Clement's 13, 424, 425, 482
Leipzig (EK's visit) 218
Lewis, C. S. 271
Library of the Fathers series 56
Lichfield, Bp of: *see* Lonsdale *and* Selwyn

Liddell: Alice 309; Henry George, Dean of Christ Church 309
Liddon, Henry Parry 60, 63, 64, 133, 134, 137–8, 164, 167, 172, 177, 210, 290, 308, 313, 326, 346, 390, 397
character 57, 131, 132, 314; Vice-Principal of Cuddesdon College 64, 68, 118–23, 129, 130–2, 135, 136, 137; Vice-Principal of St Edmund's Hall 131; preaches at Cuddesdon (1873) 141, 153, 158–9; declines Wardenship of Keble College 161; Professor of Exegesis 161; opinions about 301, 303, 315; preaching style 131, 143, 241; wanted by Gladstone for the See of Lincoln 300–2; preaches at EK's consecration 313–15, 376; comments on EK's trial 390
Lightfoot, Bp J. B. (of Durham) 390
Lincoln, Abraham 363
Lincoln 390, 445–6, Fig. 12
Cathedral 270, 317, 318, 341 (rose windows), 342, 343, 531, Figs 12–13, 16; Chapter House 311, 343, Fig. 13; Cloister Garth 527
Old Palace (now Edward King House) 87, 95, 327–30, 331–2, 445, 479, 523–4, Figs 14, 16; private chapel (St Hugh's) 330, 342, 439, 533, Figs 14–16
Theological College (Bishop's Hostel/Chancellor's School) 102, 147, 155, 221, 293, 342, 422
Castle 440; County Assembly Room 479; Hannah Memorial Chapel 445; Hilton House, Union Road 331, 445; New Central Hall 502; Prison 440; St Peter-at-Gowts 330, 391, 401, 405, 436; St Peter, East Gate 532
Lincoln: Bps of *see* Hicks; Jackson;

Index

Kaye; King (Edward); Wordsworth; Diocese of 344–53
Lincoln, Deans and Sub-Deans of *see* Blakesley; Butler; Clements; Cook; Wickham
Lincoln, Mayor and Corporation (City Councillors) 318, 511, 518
Lincoln Church Railway Guild 251, 442–5 *passim*
Lincoln Diocesan Magazine 336, 342, 364, 486
Lincoln Judgment 313, 336, 375–415, 482
Lincolnshire, High Sherriff of 478 (T. C. Garfit), 479 (Sir George Whichcote)
Liturgical Movement 217
Liverpool and Manchester Railway 5
'living wage' conference (1893) 432–3
Llandaff: Archdeacon of (Williams) 69; Bp of (Ollivant) 300
Lloyd George, David 509, 511
London:
  Churches: St Agnes, Kennington 316; St Alban, Holborn 135, 388, 402; St Edmund, Lombard Street 352; St James, Hatcham 387; St James, Piccadilly 8; St Mary, Lambeth 456, 457, 463, 467; St Mary-le-Bow, Cheapside 309, 312; St Mary Magdalene, Munster Square 316; St Paul's Cathedral 280, 310, 313, 315, 316, 531; Westminster Abbey 306, 432 (Jerusalem Chamber)
  Athenaeum Club, Pall Mall 327, 337; Crystal Place (Carter's Nursery) 309; Kennington Park Road 431; Lambeth Palace 393, 396, 400, 407, 455, 456, 457, 463, 467; Marylebone Literary Institute 474; Oxford House, Bethnal Green 291; Palace of Westminster 93; Pall Mall 7, 8; Royal Courts of Justice 108; St George's Hospital 9; St James's Place 7; St James's Palace 7, 8; Scotland Yard 5; Wandsworth Prison 309; Southwark; University of 45; water companies 93
London, Bps of *see* Blomfield; Jackson; Tait; Temple; Winnington-Ingram
Longley, Charles, Archbp (C) 149, 380, 474
Lonsdale, John, Bp of Lichfield 498
Lothian, 8th Marquess of 81
Louis, Crown Prince (later King) of Bavaria 224
Lowder, Charles 60, 63, 378
Luthardt, Professor C. E. 212, 218
Lux Mundi (1889) 185–7, 474, 475
Lyons (EK stays there) 76

McCarthy, Welbore 344, 487
Mackay, H. F. B. 95
Mackay, Queensland 16
Mackonochie, Fr Alexander H. 388–9
Maclagan, William, Archbp (Y)/Bp of Lichfield 28, 482, 508
Magee, William C., Bp of Peterborough/Archbp (Y) 173, 313
Mallett, Sir Charles 41
Malta 14, 87
Manchester 6; Bp of [James Fraser] 356
Manning, Bernard 487
Manning, Henry xix, 104, 105, 123–5
Manual of Intercessions for Missions (Willis) 149
Marriott, Charles 38, 51, 53–9, 61, 65, 101, 307, 469, 473
  on Biblical criticism 239, 464;
  on the Christian life 466, 469;
  influence of on EK 57–9, 82,

557

142, 148, 173, 177, 468, 473; EK on CM 468
Marriott, John (brother of CM) 54, 55
Marriott, Revd John (father of CM) 54
Marylebone Literary Institute 474
Maude, J. A. 124
Maurice, F. D. 58, 190, 257, 430, 435
Mechanical Engineers, Institution of 251
Methodists and Methodism 50, 64, 102, 365, 366, 367, 368–9; strong presence in Lincolnshire 50, 366; EK's sympathetic to 12, 49–50, 364, 366, 368, 487; *see also* Wesleyans *and* Wesleyan Methodist Conference
Metropolitan Police 5
Meyrick, Frederick 61, 63
Mill, John Stuart 39, 181, 187, 188
Milman, Robert 143, 149
Mirfield Community 336
Missionaries, Missionary Colleges and Missionary Societies 148–9, 282, 429, 486
Moberly, George, Bp of Salisbury 299
Moberly, Dr R. C. 185, 186, 447
Moore, Revd W. 27
Moral Groundwork of Clerical Training (Liddon, 1873) 158–9
Morgan, Revd Henry Thornhill (literary executor) 532
Morris, William 61
Morton, Archbp (C) 457
Mozeley, J. B. 161, 182
Murray, Canon (Frederick) 21
Murray, Bp of Rochester (George) 21
Mylne, Louis, Bp of Bombay 149

National Agricultural Labourers' Union 350, 365
Natural History (pursuit of country parsons) 19
Neale, John Mason 177, 495

Nelson, 3rd Earl 492
Newcastle-upon-Tyne: 5; Bp of 175 (Graham), 316 (Wilberforce); Cathedral 402; Diocese of 300
Newman, John Henry xix, 24, 35, 38–9, 44–5, 48–9, 50, 52, 54, 55, 56, 57, 65, 104, 114, 120, 181, 183–4, 203, 241, 242, 246, 267, 283 (scourge), 292, 377; on Thomas Arnold 45; *Apologia pro Vita Sua* 44–5, 48
Nicholl: Sarah Frances ('Fanny', née King) 16, 211; Revd Stephen Henry Fox 16
Nightingale, Florence 87
Noetics (Noetic School) 42–3, 47
Nonconformists and Nonconformity 194, 303, 370, 377, 433, 445, 479, 481; EK and 364–70, 481, 503; *see also* Dissenters; Methodists; Wesleyans
Norman, Edward 375
Norton, William (butler) 92
Norwich: Bp of (Sheepshanks) 489; Diocese of 347, 353
Nottingham: Bp of 321; Diocese of 321; Faith and Order Conference at (1964) 487

Oddfellows Society 27–8, 473–4
Oden, Thomas C. 178
Ogilvie, Dr Charles 162
old-age pensions 433, 509 (Bill)
Ollivant, Alfred, Bp of Llandaff 300
Orthodox Church/Christians 87, 211, 287–8, 469, 489, 490
Ottley, Canon 366
Ouless, Walter William (artist) 479–80
Oxford: Cathedral 167, 199, 200, 240, 245, 309, 330, Figs 8–10; EK a Canon of 162, 167, 200, 245 ('elderly canon')

Index

churches: St Barnabas 197, 240, 310, 404; St Mary (University Church) 24, 48, 51, 240, 245, 246, 249, 377, Fig. 11; SS Philip and James 240

Christ Church 65, 92, Figs 8–10; EK resides in Tom Quad 159, 167, 179, 197, 291, 342; 'Bethel' (in EK's garden) 190–3, 250, 310, 311; EK's lectures at 179–80, 275, 291; EK's neighbours 167, 182, 197, 330; Dean of (Liddell) 309; graduates, undergraduates and Students of 31, 54, 63, 167, 196, 245; other references 65, 92, 162, 200, 275, 291

Oriel College 13, 16, 21, 35, 39, 42, 44, 66, 67, 104, 425, 482, Fig. 6; and the 'Noetics' 42–3, 47; and the Oxford Movement 35, 38, 45–9; Provosts of 42, 43, 65; EK's mentors and teachers at 50–9, 70

other colleges: Balliol 166, 186, 187; Brasenose 24, 252; Keble 161, 249, 252, 289, 290, 394; Lady Margaret Hall 200; Pembroke 114; 'for Poor Scholars' (proposed) 54; St Edmund's Hall 132; St John's 249; Somerville 190

University: in the 18th and early 19th centuries 39–42, 114–15; secularisation of 47, 114, 182, 187; R. W. Church on Oxford life 46–7; likened to Savonarola's Florence 47; male dominated 268; opposition to women in 200; Reform Act (1854) 100, 162–3; provision of training for the ministry deficient 99–100, 101–2, 108, 114–16, 163

other references: Mission House (Marston Street) 359; population (1831) 45; Radcliffe Infirmary 309; Pusey House 185; St Aldate's (street) 245; St Edward's School 33; St Stephen's House 155, 200, 310

see also Brotherhood of the Holy Trinity; Oxford Movement; Tractarianism

Oxford, Bp of 313 (Mackarnes); *see also* Paget; Stubbs; Wilberforce

Oxford Liberal Association 190

Oxford Movement 26, 35, 38, 45–9, 59, 61, 104, 182, 192, 267, 287, 288, 338, 376, 377, 381, 382, 473, 487

Oxford Plainsong Society 109

Paget, Francis 167–8, 185, 293, 308, 397; on EK's preaching 246–7

Palmer, Professor Edwin 338

Parkinson, Dr James 437

Parliament: and the regulation of the State Church and Public Worship xx, 11, 47–9, 195, 380; EK's view of 49, 195–6; *see also* Catholic Emancipation, Irish Church Temporalities Act *and* Public Worship Regulation Act; other references 17, 33, 42, 93, 99, 162, 502

Commons 11, 48, 116, 38, 385, 505, 509

Lords 48, 107, 117, 193, 306, 333, 498, 509, 510; EK's attendance 327, 419, 501, 508–9, 512, 526

Peake, Revd John, Vicar of Ellesmere 26, 27, 28, Fig. 1

Peel, Robert 4, 5, 6, 162

'People's Budget' (1909) 508–12

Perry, Canon George Gresley 397

Peterborough: Bp of (Magee) 173, 313; Diocese of 353

Peterloo Massacre 6

Pevsner, N. 84

559

Phillimore, Sir Walter 397, 401, 405–6
Plato (works of) 42, 71, 144
plough-boys 254, 349, 439
polygamy/polygamist converts 475
Ponsonby, Revd F. J. 316
Ponsonby, Sir Henry 303
Poor Benefices Association 424
Poor Clergy Relief Corporation 352
Poor Laws, Royal Commission on 433–4
Popes: Eugenius 456, 514; Francis 422; John XXIII 216; Leo XIII 453; Paul VI 539(n.14)
Porter, Canon C. F., and his brother, 'Willie' 522
Pott, Revd Alfred, First Principal and Vicar of Cuddesdon 112
poverty and deprivation *see under* rural
Powell, Baden, Professor 43
Prayer Books of Edward VI 380, 401
preaching *see under* King, Edward
Prichard, Constantine 468
Priest in Absolution, The 195
priestly formation 99, 101, 115, 116, 118, 155, 493; *see also* clergy training
Privy Council, Judicial Committee of 380–1, 394, 401, 409, 411
Prolegomena to Ethics (T. H. Green) 187–8; EK's copy 188
Ptolemy, Claudius 477
Public schools 18, 20, 26, 30, 118, 460; EK on 33, 506
Public Worship Regulation Act (1874) 194–5, 315, 382–9; imprisonment of clergy under 387, 388
Purchas, Revd John 380, 381
Pusey, Dr Edward 24, 38, 48, 52, 56, 77, 104, 165, 167, 172, 177, 185, 262, 283, 292, 307
    character 57, 65, 68; liturgical dress and practice 52, 333, 376; owned portable altar 331; disciples/pupils of 119, 121, 301; rules for the Brotherhood of the Holy Trinity 61–3; EK's confessor 264; warns EK against overworking 192–3, 262; death and funeral 196–7; memorial 417; quoted 182 (on challenges to Christian faith), 495–6 (on prayer)

Quiet Days 358, 362, 514; at 1897 Lambeth Conference 448, 451, 454, 455, 456

Radcliff, Timothy 266
Railton, William (architect) 328
railways 5, 105, 345, 443–4, 498; EK's empathy with railway workers 251, 252, 442–3, 444, 445, 532
Ramsey, Michael, Archbp (C) 333, 487
Randall, Archdeacon James 106
Randolph, Canon B. W. 257, 283, 293, 336, 396, 485, 532
Randolph, E. S. L. 353, 429
Read, Ernest de Lacy 389–90, 406
Real or Constitutional House that Jack Built, The (1819) 5
Reform Act (1832) 17, 47
Reform Bill (Second) 190
Reformed Pastor, The (Baxter) 176
Regensburg (Ratisbon): Bp of *see* Sailer; EK visits 227
Reisbach, Bavaria 220
Richard of Chichester, St 276
Richmond, George (artist) 159, 285–6, 479, 531
Richmond, Sir William (artist and sculptor) 531
Ripon, Bp of 300 (Bickersteth), 432 (Carpenter)
Riseholme, Lincs, episcopal residence at 327–9, 523
Ritual Commission (1867) 380

Index

Ritualism and Ritualists 193–6, 301, 375–81, 382, 383, 388, 404, 481–4; *see also under* King (Edward); anti-ritualist movement 381–2; *see also* Public Worship Regulation Act
Rochester: Archdeacon of *see* King (Walker); Bps of *see* Davidson; King (Walker); Murray; Thorold; Wigram
Rochester, Diocese of 431, 492 (lay readers)
Rohr, Richard 58, 421
Roman Catholics/Catholicism/ Church of Rome 44, 209–10, 213, 215, 219, 224, 475, 488, 533; validity of Anglican orders 453; Papal infallibility 209; Anglican converts 38, 39, 61, 65, 105, 122–3, 124, 183, 380; EK's relations with and attitude to 12, 33–4, 77, 208, 229, 265–6, 335, 343, 447–8; S. Wilberforce abhors 121; *see also* Catholic Emancipation; Popes
Romanizers and Romanizing 105, 119, 120, 167, 380, 388, 496; EK and 377, 402, 484, 488
Rousseau, J. J. 151
Rowsell, Canon T. J. 337
Rugby School 18, 20, 33, 43, 54, 401, 460, 506
Rumbell, Henry (fisherman) 441–2
Runcie, Robert, Archbp (C) 268, 271
Rural Deans 106; EK's letters to 412, 495–6
rural poverty and deprivation; among local communities 4, 349–54, 430; among the clergy 4, 351–3, 419; *see also* concern for *under* King, Edward
Russell, E. F. (chaplain to the nurses' guild) 225, 227
Russell, George W. E. 179, 263, 293, 326, 432, 472, 477, 527, 532–3
Russell, Lord John 37

Sailer, Johann Michael, Bp of Regensburg: life and character 176, 213, 215; influence on EK 146, 176, 178, 210, 213–18, 225, 226, 228, 229, 357, 419, 442, 458; portrait presented to EK 227–8
'St Bede's College' (Cuddesdon) 105
St Bees, Theological College 100
St David's, Bp of 63 (Jones), 100 (Burgess), 110 (Thirlwall), 395 (Watson)
St David's Theological College, Lampeter 100
St Edward's School, Oxford 33
St Oswald's College *see under* Ellesmere
sainthood and saintliness 57, 267, 273, 534–7
Salisbury: Bps of *see* Denison; Hamilton; Moberly; Wordsworth (John); Diocese of 492 (lay readers)
Salisbury, Lord (3rd Marquess) 384, 431
Schenk, Eduard von 219
School Boards 505
Schwäbl, Fr Franz Xaver von 220–1
Scott, George Gilbert (architect) 25
Scott Holland, Henry *see* Holland
Scriptural inerrancy 50, 51
Scutari, Turkey 87
Seddon, Philip 274
self-flagellation and the scourge ('discipline') 283
Selwyn, George, Bp of New Zealand/Lichfield 31, 110, 111, 148, 327
servants 198, 332, 516; for named individuals *see* Blunden; Norton; Tibbetts; White

Shaftesbury, Lord (7th Earl of) 195, 384, 385, 386
Sheepshanks, John, Bp of Norwich 489
Sheffield (EK lectures in) 364
Sheldrake, Philip 272
shepherd(s), on the Lincolnshire Wolds 289, 439
Sherrard, Philip 287
Simeon, Charles 50, 102, 233
Sketch of the Life of Bishop King, A 335
Smith, Thomas (photographer) 335
Snow, Dr John 93
'Soapy Sam' (Samuel Wilberforce) 105
Society of St John the Evangelist *see* Cowley Fathers
Sodor and Man, Diocese of 100
Song of Songs 272, 277
Southwark, Diocese of 431
Southwell, Diocese of 300, 321
Spencer, Arthur (pork butcher) 440–1
Spilsby, Lincs 241
Sprat, Bp Thomas (of Rochester) 21
Spurgeon, Charles 272
Stanley, Dr A. H., Dean of Westminster 249, 301, 306, 477
Stanton, Arthur 135, 136, 138, 139, 157
Stone, Kent: 17, 21, 23; St Mary's Church ('lantern of Kent') 17; Stone Park 18; Woodside (House) 18, 23 (ball at)
Street, George Edmund (architect) 84
Stresa, Italy 482
strikes and industrial unrest 109, 430, 431–2, 434
Stubbs, William, Bp of Chester/Oxford 307, 395, 401, 410, 462
Sturges, Edward (curate at Haseley) 118
Swallow, [Revd] James E. 144, 291

Swinny, Henry Hutchinson (Principal of Cuddesdon) 114, 134–140, 146; maintains cordial relations with Liddon 137
Swinny, Mrs 135
Switzerland: EK's visits 447; Evolena (Evolène) 447; Rieder Furca Hotel, Bel Alp 407

Tait, A. C., Archbp (C) 44, 125(n.31), 300, 301, 377, 382, 392, 452
  critical of EK's appointment as Pastoral Professor 165–6;
  on EK's influence 202–3;
  opposes ritual practices 193, 388, 389; pilots Public Worship Regulation Act through Parliament 194, 382–7, 410
Talbot, Edward Talbot, Warden of Keble College/Bp of Winchester 183, 185, 210, 215, 249, 289
  quoted on aspects of EK's life and career: as Pastoral Professor 171, 176–7, 191–2, 200–2, 248, 292–3; on the Richmond portrait of EK 286; on EK's mother 197–8, 199; on EK's looming trial 394
Temple, Frederick, Archbp (C), Bp of Exeter/London 43, 300, 302, 392, 401, 452–4, 460, 472, 492, 508; ruling on ritual practices 482–3
Temple, William, Archbp (C) 102, 435
Teresa of Avila, St 150, 218
Theological Training Colleges 100–1, 114, 116–17, 141, 147, 154, 155, 163, 290, 293; *see also* Birkenhead; Birmingham; Chichester; Cuddesdon; Durham; Ely; Lampeter; Lincoln; St Bees; Wells
Theophan, Bishop 146
Tholuck, Professor August 218

Index

Thomson, William, Archbp (Y) 154, 381, 383, 386, 387
Thorold, Anthony, Bp of Rochester 332, 401, 408
Thurneysen, Eduard 176
Tibbetts (Tibbits), William (butler) 91, 92, 524
Tillotson, John, Archbp (C) 175
Tooth, Revd Arthur 387, 388
Townroe, Canon James Weston 261, 391, 436–7, 532
Tozer, William, Bp of Central Africa 486
Tractarians and Tractarianism 24, 28, 30, 38, 43, 44, 45, 49–50, 51, 52, 54, 57, 60, 61, 65, 103, 114, 140, 157, 177, 185, 190, 217, 261, 283, 301, 425, 435, 454, 465, 473, 495; Church not a department of State 377; Church a living organism 469
  appointed professors 161
  appointed bishops 299, 308
  parishes and churches 25, 133, 391, 404, 426
  EK and 52, 77, 182, 195, 202, 318, 321, 333, 376, 496, 517
  S. Wilberforce and 104–5, 122, 299
Tracts for the Times ('Oxford Tracts') 45, 105, 262, 292, 376, 378
tramp (on road to High Wycombe) 94–5
Trevor, Revd George 12
'Trimmer, Dr' (Samuel Wilberforce) 105
Tristram, Dr Thomas H. 401
Trollope, Anthony (novelist) 103
Trollope, Edward, Bp of Nottingham 321, 486
Truro, Bp of: Benson 300, 393; Wilkinson 299

Unamuno, Miguel de 243
University Reform Acts (1854, 1878) 42

Vaughan, C. J. 116
Vaughan, Cardinal H. A. H. 432
Venables, Canon Edmund, writes to Gladstone about EK 328–9, 346, 356
Victoria, Queen 4, 37, 93, 107, 161, 162, 170, 207, 299, 301–4, 337, 383, 386, 452–3; views on the clergy 301, 452; petitioned by the Church Association 312
Voll, Dieter 487
Voluntary schools 501, 502, 511; *see also* Church schools

Wakeman, H. O. 396, 397
Wakeman, Sir Offley (3rd Bt) 31
Walker, Revd Gilbert 241
Walsh, Walter (journalist) 405–6
Wantage, Berks 284, 308, 338, 341, 343
Watson, Dr 83
Watson, Thomas, Bp of St David's 395
Webb, Alan, Bp of Bloemfontein 149
Wellesley, Dean (of Windsor) 170
Wellington, (1st) Duke of 37
Wells, Somerset 16; Theological College 101, 108, 111, 115
Wesley: Charles 224; John 50, 64, 65, 75, 145, 262, 364, 366, 458; Charles and John (the Wesleys) 50, 60, 64, 224
Wesleyan Methodist Conference (1909) 364, 367
Wesleyans 216, 364, 367, 368; *see also* Methodists
West, Canon J. R. 335
West Allington, Lincs (EK's last Confirmation at) 520
Westcott, Professor Brooke Foss 51, 52, 338, 434, 435
Whately, Richard 43, 237
Wheatley, Oxon 84–96, 338–9, 354, 438; carpenter from 95, 279; Vicar of *see* Elton, Edward; *see also* Charlie

White, James (butler) 90–2
White Cross League 200
Wickham, Edward Charles, Dean of Lincoln 338, 343, 521
Wigram, Joseph Cotton, Bp of Rochester 332
Wilberforce, Ernest, Bp of Newcastle 316
Wilberforce, Henry 122
Wilberforce, Robert 50, 65, 111, 122, 168
Wilberforce, Samuel, Bp of Oxford/Winchester:
career summarised 103–7; episcopal appointments 103, 299; drive and energy 448, 485; reforms episcopal ministry and diocesan care 105–7 *passim*, 117, 201, 345, 498; encourages diocesan church building and restoration 84, 106; founder of Culham Teacher Training College 67, 109; Confirmations 105–6, 109; Tractarianism 104–5, 122, 299; abhors Roman Catholicism 121; critical of *Essays and Reviews* 454; fatal riding accident 168–9
EK's relationship with 103, 168, 169; ordains EK 83; favourable opinion of 83; advises EK to accept the Pastoral Professorship 163
Cuddesdon Theological College (established by SW) 99, 106, 107–24; 129–38 *passim*; chooses EK as first chaplain 111–13; offers Principalship to EK 139–40
other references 43, 50, 82–3, 105, 193, 201, 193, 306, 345, 346, 475
Wilberforce, William 50, 104
Wilgress, George Frederick, Vicar of Cudmore 16, 328
Wilgress, Frederick ('Fred', EK's nephew and chaplain) 147, 328, 336, 347, 446, 485, 487, 521–2, 524–6
Wilgress (*née* King), Mary 16, 328
Wilkinson, George, Bp of Truro 299
Williams, Garnons 81
Williams, Richard Davies 69
Williams, Mrs (Mary, R.D.'s mother) 70
Willis, E. F. 149
Wilson, Henry 125(n.31)
Wilson, Thomas, Bp of Sodor and Man 100
Winchester: Bps of *see* Browne; Thorold; Wilberforce; Diocese of 431
Winnington-Ingram, A. F., Bp of London 293, 535
Wood, Canon 507
Woodard, Nathaniel 30–1, 33
Woodard Corporation 34
Woodard Schools 26–34 *passim*, 506
Woodford, James R., Bp of Ely 143, 299, 307
Woodside House, Stone, Kent 18, 23 (ball-supper)
Woollcombe, Revd E. C. 166
Worcester: Bp of (Henry Pepys) 110, 111; Diocese of 431
Wordsworth, Charles, Bp of St Andrews 306
Wordsworth, Christopher, Bp of Lincoln 210, 300, 302, 304, 305–6, 307, 314, 317, 318, 327, 329, 342, 367, 422, 464, 486, 492 (lay readers), 495, 531 (monument to); EK pays tribute to 321
Wordsworth, Revd Christopher (son of Bp Christopher) 337, 407
Wordsworth, John, Bp of Salisbury 306, 401, 492
Wordsworth, William (poet) 71, 86, 145, 151, 305,
Wrawby, Lincs 335
Wylde, Revd J. 417

Index

'Year of the Great Stink' (1858) 93
'Year of Revolutions' (1848) 37
York, Archbps of *see* Garbett; Lang; Maclagan; Thomson

Zanzibar 190, 429
Zululand/Zulus 474–5

www.ingramcontent.com/pod-product-compliance
Lightning Source LLC
Chambersburg PA
CBHW021713300426
44114CB00009B/125